CW00722974

THE COMMON LAW LIBRARY

NUMBERS 1 and 2

CHITTY
ON
CONTRACTS

Second Cumulative Supplement
to the
Twenty-Seventh Edition

Up-to-date until July 31, 1997

LONDON
SWEET & MAXWELL
1997

Published in 1997 by
Sweet & Maxwell Limited of
100 Avenue Road, London NW3 3PF
(http://www.smlawpub.co.uk)
Typeset by Mendip Communications Ltd, Frome, Somerset
Printed in Great Britain by The Bath Press, Bath, Somerset

No natural products were destroyed to make this product.
Only farmed timber was used and replanted.

A catalogue record for this book is available from the British Library

ISBN Main Work (full set)   0 421 48550 7
ISBN Supplement   0 421 60770 X

HOW TO USE THIS SUPPLEMENT

This is the Second Cumulative Supplement to the Twenty-Seventh Edition of *Chitty on Contracts*, and has been compiled according to the structure of the two main work volumes.

At the beginning of each chapter of this supplement the mini table of contents from the main volume has been included. Where a heading in this table of contents has been marked with the symbol ■, the material under that heading has been added to or amended in this second supplement, and should be referred to. Where a heading is marked with the symbol □, the material under that heading was added to or amended in the first supplement but has not been updated in this supplement.

Within each chapter, updating information is referenced to the relevant paragraph in the main volume.

[v]

[vi]

TABLE OF CONTENTS

VOLUME I

TABLE OF CASES

TABLE OF CASES

[xxiii]

TABLE OF CASES

TABLE OF CASES

TABLE OF CASES

[xlii]

TABLE OF CASES

[xliv]

TABLE OF STATUTES

TABLE OF STATUTORY INSTRUMENTS

TABLE OF EUROPEAN COMMUNITY CASES

TABLE OF NON-U.K. STATUTORY MATERIAL

CHAPTER 1

INTRODUCTORY

1. – THE NATURE OF CONTRACT

[*Add to note 66: page* [7]]   **1–005**
Oceangas (Gibraltar) Ltd v. Port of London Authority [1993] 2 Lloyd's
Rep. 292.

[*Add to text after note 66*]
In *Norweb plc v. Dixon*,[66a] the nature of the relationship between a public
supplier of electricity and a general tariff customer foreseen by the
Electricity Act 1989, section 16 arose for the purposes of determining
whether money claimed as allegedly owed by a customer in respect of such a
supply constituted "money claimed . . . as a debt due under a contract" so as
to attract the application of section 40 of the Administration of Justice Act
1970 concerning the harassment of debtors. In this respect, the Divisional
Court held that an agreement between the parties in these circumstances
was not contractual: "the legal compulsion as to both the creation of the
relationship and the fixing of its terms is inconsistent with the existence of a

[1]

contract".[66b] The Divisional Court held, therefore, that section 40's provisions regarding the harassment of debtors could not apply as the offence which it created required proof that the supplier had made demands for payment of a debt which he claimed was due under a contract which he claimed to exist: "the rights and liabilities as between tariff customers and their public electricity suppliers are governed by statute and not by contract".[66c]

[66a] [1995] 1 W.L.R. 637.

[66b] *ibid.* at p. 643, *per* Dyson J.

[66c] *ibid.* at p. 644.

1–009   [*Add to note 19: page* [12]]
The E.C. Directive on Unfair Terms in Consumer Contracts was implemented in English law by the Unfair Terms in Consumer Contracts Regulations (S.I. 1994 No. 3159, *post*, §§14–088). On the Directive, see Collins (1994) 14 O.J.L.S. 229.

Good faith

1–011   [*Add to text after first paragraph: page* [14]]
Where a contract on its terms provides that a particular act of one of its parties will result in a liability in the other, then the courts have on occasion held that this act must impliedly be made in good faith to have this effect. For example, in *Colbelfret NV v. Cyclades Shipping Co. Ltd (The "Linardos")*,[35a] a charterparty provided that the ship's master's "notice of readiness" to receive cargo would, after a delay, start "notice time" running so as to allow its owner to claim demurrage, even though a port marine surveyor later declared that it was unready (as insufficiently clean). However, Colman J. added that "a notice of readiness proved to be given by the master or chief officer with knowledge that it was untrue, that is to say in the knowledge that the vessel was not then ready would be ineffective to start time running. There must by implication be a requirement of good faith."[35b] Similarly, where a person enjoys a power of sale of another's property so as to satisfy a debt arising from a charge such as a mortgage, that party must exercise it in good faith, but otherwise may do so as it chooses: *Huish v. Ellis*,[35c] following *China & South Seas Bank v. Tan Soon Gin*[35d] and *Downsview Nominees Ltd v. First City Corp. Ltd.*[35e]
Malik v. Bank of Credit and Commerce International SA (in liq.)[35f] may serve as a clear example of English law's occasional use of implied terms to a give at least limited effect to a notion of contractual good faith. There, the House of Lords accepted that a term is to be implied in contracts of employment that the "employer would not, without reasonable and proper

cause, conduct itself in a manner likely to destroy or seriously damage the relationship of confidence and trust between employer and employee" (though the existence of such a term had been conceded).[35g]

Moreover, English courts have accepted that powers arising under certain types of contract must be exercised in good faith, this notion here including a reference to the propriety of the purpose for which the power is exercised. A notable example may be found in the Privy Council's recognition in *Downsview Ltd v. First City Corp. Ltd*[35h] that a mortgagee of property must exercise his powers in good faith and for the purpose of obtaining repayment of the debt, though given this purpose these powers may be exercised in such a way that disadvantageous consequences accrue to the borrower.[35i] This approach to a mortgagee's powers has recently been applied by the Court of Appeal in *Albany Home Loans Ltd v. Massey*.[35j] There a mortgagee applied to the court for an order for possession of the property against one of two joint mortgagors (who were husband and wife), despite not applying for such an order against the other one (the wife). For Schliemann L.J., where the ejection of one of two borrowers is of no benefit to the lender, it is not in general right for a court to make an order requiring him to leave within the period during which the other borrower was in possession and entitled to possession.

[35a] [1994] 1 Lloyd's Rep. 28.

[35b] *ibid.* at p. 32.

[35c] [1995] N.P.C. 3.

[35d] [1990] 1 A.C. 536.

[35e] [1993] A.C. 295, 315.

[35f] [1997] 3 All E.R. 1.

[35g] *ibid.* esp. at pp. 4, 5, 16.

[35h] [1993] A.C. 295.

[35i] *ibid.* at p. 312.

[35j] *The Times*, February 14, 1997.

2. – CLASSIFICATION OF CONTRACTS

(a) *Classification of Contracts according to their Subject-matter*

Classification for common law purposes

[*Add to text after note 64: page* [16]]   1–015
In *Spring v. Guardian Assurance plc*,[64a] Lord Woolf approved and applied Lord Bridge's approach to the implication of terms which he had taken in *Scally v. Southern Health and Social Services Board*.[64b] The question before the House of Lords in *Spring* was whether an employer owes a duty to his

employees or former employees to take care in the making of a reference for a potential new employer, a majority holding that such a duty should be found in the tort of negligence (on which see *post*, §1–060 at Note 8). While Lord Woolf did not dissent from this view, he also based such a duty on a finding of an implied term in the contract between the parties in the circumstances of the case. These circumstances were: "(i) The existence of the contract of employment or for services. (ii) The fact that the contract relates to an engagement of a class where it is the normal practice to require a reference from a previous employer before employment is offered. (iii) The fact that the employee cannot be expected to enter into that class of employment except on the basis that the employer will, on the request of another prospective employer made not later than a reasonable time after the termination of a former employment, provide a full and frank reference as to the employee".[64c]

[64a] [1995] 2 A.C. 296.

[64b] [1992] 1 A.C. 294, 307.

[64c] [1995] 2 A.C. 296, 353–54.

[*Add to note 67*]
The Pioneer Container [1994] 2 A.C. 324.

Commercial practice

1–016   [*Add to note 74: page* [17]]
And see the "Timeshare Directive", Dir. 94/47, *post*, §4–002.

(d) *Classification of Contracts according to their Effects*

Void contracts

1–023   [*Amend note 90a: page* [20]]
Boddington v. Lawton [1994] I.C.R. 478.

3. – Contracts Contained in Deeds

(a) *Form and delivery*

Deeds executed by companies incorporated under the Companies Acts

[*Add to note 27: page* [23]]
On possible reforms of the law relating to the execution of deeds by companies, see Law Commission Consultation Paper No. 143, *The Execution of Deeds and Documents by or on behalf of Bodies Corporate* (1996).

(c) *Other Aspects*

Period of limitation

[*Add to note 87: page* [28]]   **1–040**
See *Aiken v. Stewart Wrightson Members Agency Ltd* [1995] 1 W.L.R.
1281, 1292 applying this rule to a contract for the provision of services made
in a deed and upholding the "well established and universally accepted"
understanding of "specialties" as being contracts made under seal.

4. – THE RELATIONSHIP BETWEEN CONTRACT AND TORT

(b) *Differences of Substance between Contract and Tort*

General

[*Add to note 23: page* [32]]   **1–043**
For the impact of recent decisions on the significance of the doctrine of
"assumption of responsibility" for the purposes of *Hedley Byrne & Co. Ltd
v. Heller & Partners Ltd* [1964] A.C. 465, see *post*, §§1–048—1–071.

[*Add to note 27*]   **1–044**
For further discussion of the special protection of expectations in contract,
see Friedmann (1995) 111 L.Q.R. 628; Whittaker (1996) 16 O.J.L.S. 191, 207
et seq. Cf. Stapleton (1997) 113 L.Q.R. 257.

[*Add to text after note 33: page* [33]]
But see the discussions of the decisions of the House of Lords in
Henderson v. Merrett Syndicates Ltd,[33a] *post*, §§1048–1071 and *White v.
Jones,*[33b] *post*, §1–077A at note 25, both of which upheld the existence of a
duty of care in the tort of negligence in respect of pure economic loss other
than in the context of a mis-statement by the defendants.

[33a] [1995] 2 A.C. 145.

[33b] [1995] 2 A.C. 207.

Differences of regime between contract and tort: damages

[*Add to note 46: page* [34]]   **1–045**
Beoco Ltd v. Alfa Laval Co. Ltd [1995] Q.B. 137; *Galoo Ltd v. Bright
Grahame Murray* [1994] 1 W.L.R. 1360.

[*Add to note 47*]
Barclays Bank plc v. Fairclough Building Ltd [1995] Q.B. 21; *Barclays Bank plc v. Fairclough Building Ltd (No. 2)* [1995] I.R.L.R. 605.

[*Add to note 49*]
Malik v. Bank of Credit and Commerce International SA (in liq.) [1997] 3 All E.R. 1, 20.

[*Add to note 52*]
Watts v. Morrow [1991] 1 W.L.R. 1421; *Knott v. Bolton* [1995] E.G.C.S. 59; *Malik v. Bank of Credit and Commerce International SA (in liq.), ante.*

[*Replace sentence in text after Note 53 on page:* [35] *with following new paragraph*]
Traditionally, it was sometimes said that damages for loss of reputation are not available in contract in contrast to tort,[54] but there were conflicting decisions on this point[55] and some cases clearly recognised such recovery in contract in appropriate cases, such as injury to a trader whose business reputation is affected by the breach[56] and where the contract can be said to be for the maintenance or promotion of the plaintiff's reputation.[56a] In *Malik v. Bank of Credit and Commerce International SA (in liq.)*,[56b] the House of Lords accepted that these particular kinds of case where damages of this type were accepted should be seen as reflecting a general rule. In *Malik*, two employees of the defendant bank had been made redundant and then found that they could not obtain other suitable employment, as their former employer had conducted its business fraudulently and corruptly (it was assumed for the purposes of the issue before the House), even though the two employees had not acted in any way dishonestly. The employees sued the bank for damages for the damage to their employment prospects stemming, they argued, from breach of its obligation not, without reasonable and proper cause, to conduct itself in a manner likely to destroy or seriously damage the relationship of confidence and trust between employer and employee, an obligation which was broken by the fraudulent conduct of the banking business. The House of Lords in *Malik* interpreted its much earlier decision in *Addis v. Gramophone Co. Ltd* (1909)[56c] as being restricted (on the issue of recovery for damages for lost reputation[56d]) to the denial of recovery of damages for financial loss for harm to reputation caused by the *manner* in which a contract was breached, this leaving open the question whether damages for financial loss for harm to reputation could be recovered when caused by the breach of contract itself.[56e] As Lord Steyn observed, "[p]rovided that a relevant breach of contract can be established, and the requirements of causation, remoteness and mitigation be satisfied, there is no good reason why in the field of employment law recovery of financial loss in respect of damage to reputation caused by breach of contract is necessarily excluded."[56f]

[54] *Addis v. Gramophone Co. Ltd* [1909] A.C. 488; *Withers v. General Theatre Corp. Ltd* [1933] 2 K.B. 536.

[55] *cf. Withers v. General Theatre Corp. Ltd, ante,* with *Marbe v. George Edwardes (Daly's Theatre) Ltd* [1928] 1 K.B. 269.

[56] *Wilson v. United Counties Bank Ltd* [1920] A.C. 102.

[56a] *Rolin v. Steward* (1854) 14 C.B. 595; *Aerial Advertising Co. v. Batchelors Peas (Manchester) Ltd* [1938] 2 All E.R. 788.

[56b] [1997] 3 All E.R. 1.

[56c] *ante.*

[56d] Lord Nicholls noted that the House of Lords in *Malik* was not concerned with the observations in *Addis v. Gramophone Co. Ltd, ante,* on the question of recovery of damages for mental distress in an action for breach of contract: [1997] 3 All E.R. 1, 9.

[56e] See esp. at [1997] 3 All E.R. 1, 20–21, *per* Lord Steyn.

[56f] *ibid.* at p. 21.

Other differences

[*Add to note 66 after Bonython v. Commonwealth of Australia: page*   **1–047**
[36]]
Private International Law (Miscellaneous Provisions) Act 1995, ss.9–14.

(c) *Concurrence of Actions in Contract and Tort*

General

The discussion in these paragraphs must be read subject to the important **1–048—**
decision of the House of Lords in *Henderson v. Merrett Syndicates Ltd* **1–071**
("*Henderson*")[a] (the decision of the Court of Appeal *sub. nom. Arbuthnott v. Feltrim* is noted at §1–070). The following pages discuss this decision, together with the related decisions of the Court of Appeal in *Barclays Bank plc v. Fairclough Building Ltd (No. 2),*[b] *Holt v. Payne Skillington,*[c] and the decision of Potter J. in *Aiken v. Stewart Wrightson Members Agency Ltd.*[d] After this more general discussion, particular amendments will be noted under the numbers of their respective paragraphs.

In *Henderson* itself, it was held, *inter alia,* that a party to a contract may rely on a tort committed by the other party, as long as doing so is not inconsistent with its express or implied terms. In so deciding, the House of Lords made clear (with respect, correctly) that the much-quoted passage in Lord Scarman's speech in *Tai Hing Cotton Mill Ltd v. Liu Chong Hing Bank Ltd*[e] should not be interpreted as assigning to contract a domain exclusive of tort. However, in finding a duty of care on which to base the plaintiffs' claim in tort, Lord Goff of Chieveley in *Henderson* relied on *Hedley Byrne* as establishing a very broad principle of liability based on an "assumption of responsibility" and this principle suggests a very considerable overlap between the tort of negligence and liability in contract between parties to contracts.[f]

In *Henderson* the plaintiffs were all Lloyd's "Names" who had agreed to take unlimited liability in respect of certain proportions of risks to be underwritten in the insurance market, but who had done so through different forms of arrangement. In the case of "indirect Names", they had entered agreements with underwriting agents, known as "members' agents", who advised Names, *inter alia*, on their choice of syndicates and placed them on a syndicate once chosen, but who entrusted the placing of the insurance to others, "managing agents", for the syndicate which they had chosen. The claims of these indirect Names against their managing agents for negligence in the conduct of their underwriting business necessarily went beyond privity of contract and will be discussed *post*, §1–077A at Note 26a. However, in the case of "direct Names", those persons who acted as their members' agents also acted as their managing agents (being known sometimes as "combined agents", though being termed "managing agents" here) and therefore any claim for negligence in respect of their claims was within privity of contract. For present purposes, the important preliminary issue which came before the House of Lords was whether the direct Names could opt to sue their managing agents in the tort of negligence in respect of the management of the underwriting, the limitation period for their action for breach of contract having expired. In this respect, Lord Goff of Chieveley, who gave the leading speech and with whom Lords Keith of Kinkel, Browne-Wilkinson, Mustill and Nolan concurred, held that prima facie the managing agents did owe a duty of care in the tort of negligence to the Names. Such a duty was, according to Lord Goff, to be based on a broad principle found in *Hedley Byrne & Co. Ltd v. Heller & Partners Ltd*,[g] according to which a person possessed of special skill or knowledge may owe a duty of care in tort by assuming a responsibility to another person within a relationship (whether special or particular to a transaction and whether contractual or not): the principle was not, therefore, restricted to cases of statements.[h] The House of Lords further held that on the facts of the case there was no reason why the Names should not opt to sue on the breach of such a duty of care in the tort of negligence rather than for breach of an implied term in their contract with the managing agents. Lord Goff stated[i]:

> My own belief is that, in the present context, the common law is not antipathetic to concurrent liability, and that there is no sound basis for a rule which automatically restricts the claimant to either a tortious or a contractual remedy. The result may be untidy; but, given that the tortious duty is imposed by the general law, and the contractual duty is attributable to the will of the parties, I do not find it objectionable that the claimant may be entitled to take advantage of the remedy which is most advantageous to him, subject only to ascertaining whether the tortious duty is so inconsistent with the applicable contract that, in

[8]

accordance with ordinary principle, the parties must be taken to have agreed that the tortious remedy is to be limited or excluded.

On the facts, the contract between the parties imposed the same standard of reasonable care on the managing agent as is owed under a duty of care in the tort of negligence and there was, therefore, nothing inconsistent with their contract in allowing the direct Names to claim on the basis of this tort.[j] Lord Browne-Wilkinson, who gave the only other speech, agreed with Lord Goff's analysis, but added his own comments on the relationship between the liability in tort which had been found and that based on breach of fiduciary duty.[k]

This decision therefore expressly recognises the existence of an option to sue in either tort or contract where the constituent elements allow (as stated at §1–056, second paragraph, with support from earlier authorities at §1–058). Moreover, its qualification of this right of option for cases where the existence of liability in tort is inconsistent with the applicable contract gives support to the statement found in §1–056, second paragraph and explained in §§1–059—1–062 that such an option "will not be allowed to subvert the contract's express or implied terms nor any legal immunity attaching to the other party *qua* contractor". Although Lord Goff's discussion of the "inconsistency of the contract" did not go beyond reference to its express or implied terms, on the facts there was no reason for it do so and, it is respectfully submitted, the decision therefore does not cast doubt on the proposition that such an "inconsistency" *may* be found in the existence of a certain contractual *immunity* on the part of the defendant (on which see the discussion at §1–062, in particular in relation to the decision of the Court of Appeal in *Bank of Nova Scotia v. Hellenic Mutual War Risks Association (Bermuda) Ltd (The Good Luck)*.[l]

However, with respect, Lord Goff's approach in *Henderson* to the existence of a duty of care in tort on which a party to a contract may choose to rely is more problematic. As has been noted, this approach rested on a broad principle of assumption of responsibility drawn from *Hedley Byrne*. From this speech and from Lord Goff's speech in the earlier case of *Spring v. Guardian Assurance plc*,[m] see *post*, §1–060 at Note 8, and his and other speeches in the later case of *White v. Jones*,[n] which, however, concerned the liability in tort of a party to a contract *beyond* privity and in the absence of any reliance by the *plaintiff* on the defendant's skill and care (see *post*, §1–077A), it seems that the broad principle will apply where: (i) the defendant has *agreed* to perform a service or otherwise to do something for the plaintiff, whether under a contract or not (see esp. *White v. Jones*[o]; (ii) the defendant possessed or held himself out as possessing special skill or knowledge in relation to these services or this task: *Henderson*[p]; and (iii) some evidence of reliance by the plaintiff can be made out. As regards the last of these conditions, as regards cases of liability for misstatements towards their recipients, the plaintiff's reliance provides the causal link between the defendant's statement and the plaintiff's loss: *Henderson*.[q]

[9]

However, outside this type of case and as between parties to a contract the element of "reliance" by the plaintiff may be found in the plaintiff's entering the contract under which the services, etc., are agreed to be done by the defendant (see *Henderson*[r]). This basis of liability in tort is not merely "equivalent to contract"; it is likely in very many cases to be parasitic on it.

Moreover, according to Lord Goff, the broad principle of *Hedley Byrne* is not restricted to liability for actions, but may apply also to omissions (*Henderson*[s]), his example of *Midland Bank Trust Co. Ltd v. Hett, Stubbs & Kemp*[t] suggesting that omissions in the course of action rather than "pure omissions" were intended. Finally, according to Lord Goff, where an alleged duty of care is based on the doctrine of assumption of responsibility there is no need to enter the question of whether it is "fair, just and reasonable" to impose such a duty, even in cases where the plaintiff's loss is purely economic: "the concept [of assumption of responsibility] provides its own explanation why there is no problem in cases of this kind about liability for economic loss; for if a person assumes responsibility to another in respect of certain services, there is no reason why he should not be liable in damages for [*sic*: to] that other in respect of economic loss which flows from the negligent performance of those services".[u]

One effect of judicial acceptance of such a very broad principle of "assumption of responsibility" may be seen to be the creation of a very wide means of circumventing the doctrine of consideration: for as long as a defendant is possessed of special skill or knowledge, his agreement with the plaintiff to perform a service within that skill or pertaining to that knowledge will give rise to a cause of action in tort based on the negligent performance of those services, whether they were to be paid for or not. A second type of effect may be found in the decision of the Court of Appeal in *Barclays Bank plc v. Fairclough Building Ltd (No. 2)*,[v] since this illustrates how the broad principle may lead to the dis-application of other established rules of contract law as between the parties. In this case, building sub-contractors ("the roofing contractors") had been engaged by main building contractors to do certain works of repair and renovation on warehouses, and they in their turn engaged their own contractors ("the cleaners") to effect the industrial cleaning of asbestos cement roofs (and *cf. Barclays Bank plc v. Fairclough Building Ltd*[w] which concerned the claim by the owner of the buildings against the main building contractors). In *Fairclough Building Ltd (No. 2)* the roofing contractors claimed an indemnity against the cleaners in respect of monies paid to the main building contractor in settlement of their own liabilities to the latter, on the ground of breach of an implied term in their contract that the work should be done by the cleaners with the care and skill necessary to perform the task safely and without causing extensive contamination of the surrounding area. The Court of Appeal upheld the existence of such a term (thereby reversing the decision at first instance on this issue) and supported the judge's finding of the cleaners' negligence. However, the cleaners alleged that their contractual liability to indemnify the roofing contractors should be reduced by way of application of the defence of contributory negligence. In this respect, the Court of Appeal held that such a defence could apply to a claim in contract only where it is brought for breach of an obligation to take reasonable care concurrent with the existence of a liability in tort based on breach of a duty of reasonable care (thereby accepting the approach found in *Forsikringsaktieselskapet Vesta v. Butcher*[x]). The question therefore arose whether the cleaners owed any duty of care in the tort of negligence in respect of the admittedly pure economic loss which they had caused the roofing contractors. To this end, Beldam L.J., with whom Sir Tasker Watkins and Nourse L.J. agreed, noted the passages of Lord Goff of Chieveley's speech in *Henderson* where the possibility of concurrence of actions in contract and based on the broad principle of assumption of responsibility under *Hedley Byrne* was accepted[y] and concluded[z] that:

> A skilled contractor undertaking maintenance work to a building assumes a responsibility which invites reliance no less than the financial or other professional adviser does in undertaking his work. The nature of the responsibility is the same though it will differ in extent.

The Court of Appeal held, therefore, that the cleaners had owed the roofing contractors a duty to take reasonable care in tort and that this entitled them (the *cleaners*) to oppose against the roofing contractors the latter's negligence in failing to take steps to inform themselves of the problems involved in cleaning asbestos cement in the way intended. In the result, the Court of Appeal reduced the cleaners' liability by one half. Here, the cleaners' contractual undertaking to do a job which required special skill and which they held themselves out as capable of doing, coupled with the roofing contractors' reliance on this as evidenced by their entering into the same contract, was enough to support the existence of a duty of care in tort in respect of the cleaners' negligence in doing the job.

However, the existence of the *possibility* of the reduction of a plaintiff's claim on the basis of its contributory negligence will not necessarily lead to such a reduction. In *Henderson v. Merrett Syndicates Ltd (No. 2)*[aa] the question arose whether the defendant agents or sub-agents whose duties of care in the tort of negligence had been established by the House of Lords in *Henderson v. Merrett Syndicates Ltd*[ab] were in breach of those duties and if so whether their resulting liability should be reduced on the grounds of contributory negligence in the plaintiffs. Cresswell J. held that, having regard to the relevant agency and sub-agency agreements, the engagement of a third party to audit the syndicate, the regulatory regime and in particular to the role of the managing agents on the one hand and the role of the auditors on the other in relation to the business in question, the plaintiffs could not be said to have suffered damage "partly as a result of their own fault" within the meaning of the Law Reform (Contributory Negligence) Act 1945, s.1(1).[ac] In the alternative, the learned judge considered that it would not on the facts be just and equitable to reduce the plaintiffs' damages having regard to their share in the responsibility for the damage.[ad]

Clearly, then, while in some cases, notably those turning on issues of limitation of actions such as *Henderson* itself, judicial acceptance of such a wide basis for establishing a duty of care in tort will benefit *plaintiffs*, allowing them to avoid disadvantageous incidental rules applicable to actions in contract, paradoxically in others, such as *Fairclough Builders Ltd (No. 2)*, it will instead benefit *defendants*.

Two further questions relating to the imposition of liability in the tort of negligence between parties to a contract have arisen in cases subsequent to the decision of the House of Lords in *Henderson*: first, does a contractual obligation which imposes a *higher* standard of care on a defendant also control the standard of care owed by him in the tort of negligence to the other party? And, secondly, can a duty of care in tort based on an "assumption of responsibility" be found as between parties to a contract in the *absence* of any express or implied term in that contract relating to the facts which give rise to such a duty, *i.e.* where the contract is silent on the issue?

(i) *Higher contractual standards and the standard in tort*

As has been noted, *Henderson* established that any claim in tort by one party to a contract against the other should be allowed only or only to the extent that the express or implied terms of the contract are not inconsistent with it (*ante*, p. 6). However, in *Aiken v. Stewart Wrightson Members Agency Ltd* ("*Aiken*"),[ae] the question arose, *inter alia* (for further discussion, see *post*, §1–077A), whether the fact that the defendant owed a contractual duty *more onerous* than one of reasonable care could and should affect the standard of care owed in the tort of negligence. The question arose in the context of a claim by Lloyd's "indirect Names" against their "Members' agents", *i.e.* their agents who had contracted with them to advise them on their choice of syndicates and to place them on any syndicate once chosen, leaving the placing of the insurance to "managing agents". It was conceded by the members' agents that they owed the plaintiff Names a contractual duty that "the actual underwriting would be carried out with reasonable care and skill so that the members' agent remains directly responsible to its Names for any failure to exercise reasonable care and skill by the managing agent of any syndicate to whom such underwriting has been delegated".[af] The Names contended that the members' agents also owed them a duty of care in the tort of negligence of the same content, a "parallel and *co-extensive* duty of care in tort", arguing that it was inherent in Lord Goff's observations on the need for no inconsistency between contract and any liability in tort that its express and implied terms "ought in logic and in law to be definitive also of the nature and extent of their duty in tort".[ag] However, the members' agents disputed that they owed such a co-extensive duty of care in tort on the basis that breach of the contractual duty in question did not require proof of personal negligence on their part (and none had been alleged), whereas any liability in the tort of negligence must do so, unless the care concerned a "non-delegable duty".[ah] In this respect, Potter J. noted that the liability of the "pure" members' agents (*i.e.* those who were not also managing agents) had not been in issue in the House of Lords in *Henderson*, but that (as the members' agents before him had conceded) the authorities supported the existence of their owing a duty of care in tort to the Names based on their "assumption of responsibility".[ai] However, the learned judge rejected the plaintiffs' contention that this duty in tort was made *more extensive* by the "contractual context" of the more onerous contractual obligation, both as a matter of authority (notably, *Tai Hing Cotton Mill Ltd v. Liu Chong Hing Bank Ltd, ante*, p. 6) and principle. As regards the latter, the learned judge approved a *dictum* of Le Dain J. in *Central Trust Co. v. Refuse*,[aj] that "[a] claim cannot be said to be in tort if it depends for the nature and scope of the asserted duty of care on the manner in which an obligation or duty has been expressly and specifically defined by a contract" and concluded that on the facts before him the "common law duty of care ... falls short of the specific obligation or duty imposed by the express terms of the contract, *unless* that common law duty of care can be shown to be non-delegable in character for the purposes of the law of tort",[ak] a condition which was not satisfied on the facts before him.[al]

(ii) *Contractual silence*

In *Holt v. Payne Skillington*,[am] the Court of Appeal had to decide whether a party to a contract could rely on an "assumption of responsibility" made by the other party where the express and implied terms of the contract had been found to be *silent* as to the subject-matter of the claim in tort. In *Holt* the plaintiffs had indicated to the defendant estate agents that they wished to purchase a property in London with the view to letting it on "holiday lets", a use which they made clear they required so as to benefit from tax relief in respect of a capital gain they had already made (the plaintiffs also claimed against their solicitors, but no issue relating to the latters' liability arose before the Court of Appeal). One of the estate agents' employees had, at some time before any retainer, assured them that he knew about the local planning requirements which would need to be satisfied to allow the plaintiffs to use whatever property they bought for this purpose. In the result, however, the property which the estate agents put forward and which the plaintiffs bought could not be used for holiday lets as no "short-term use" had been established for it for the purposes of the planning rules applicable. At first instance, the judge held the estate agents liable in the tort of negligence, but *not* liable for breach of contract on the basis that there was no express term of the retainer agreement (nor of a second "valuation agreement") between the parties that the agents should investigate the

[13]

planning issue. The estate agents appealed against this decision as to their liability in tort, but no appeal was made by the plaintiffs on the decision made against them in contract. Before the Court of Appeal, therefore, the estate agents argued that any duty of care in tort which they might have owed to the plaintiffs could not be wider than the express and implied terms of the contract between them, citing the well-known passage in Lord Scarman's advice in *Tai Hing Cotton Mill Ltd*[an] and contending that the judge's decision on the terms of their contracts meant that they could not be liable in tort. Hirst L.J., however, rejected this argument, relying on a passage in Lord Goff of Chieveley's speech in *Henderson*[ao] and stating[ap] that:

> There is no reason in principle why a *Hedley Byrne* type of duty of care cannot arise in an overall set of circumstances where, by reference to certain limited aspects of those circumstances, the same parties enter into a contractual relationship involving more limited obligations than those imposed by the duty of care in tort. In such circumstances, the duty of care in tort and the duties imposed by the contract will be concurrent but not co-extensive.

The judge below was, therefore, entitled to rely on a factual context wider than the contractual agreements between the parties to establish a duty of care.

As a matter of general principle, and with respect, this approach is entirely to be supported. If the existence of a contractual duty relating to, but not inconsistent with, a duty of care in tort does not prevent a claim based on tort, then *a fortiori* nor should the *mere* existence of a contract between the parties silent as to the issues which are the subject-matter of the claim in tort (as is argued in the text at §1–064, especially the final paragraph). However, it is submitted that more difficult is the application of this principle to liability in tort based on an assumption of responsibility under *Hedley Byrne*. The decision of the Court of Appeal in *Holt* certainly based the estate agents' liability in tort on this ground, but, while Hirst L.J. relied on passages from Lord Goff's speech in *Henderson*[aq] he found (as he had been invited to by *both* parties) the "essential characteristics of a situation giving rise to a cause of action in negligence based on a duty of case of the *Hedley Byrne* type" in a passage in Lord Oliver's speech in *Caparo Industries plc v. Dickman*[ar] which looks rather to the defendant's giving of advice to a person who he knows is likely to rely on it.[as] This approach, moreover, was entirely understandable on the facts, since it was clearly the bad or inadequate advice which the plaintiffs were given by the estate agents' employee which formed the basis of any imposition of liability in tort. It is submitted that where liability under *Hedley Byrne* is put in terms of a negligent mis-statement given by a person who can foresee that it will be relied on, rather than in the broader terms of an "assumption of responsibility" in the sense of an agreement to perform a service for the other party, then there is certainly nothing inconsistent in finding a duty of care under *Hedley Byrne* but no express or implied duty of care in contract. By contrast, however, to the extent to which a defendant's having "assumed responsibility" for doing something is to mean that he "agreed to do it", then it is submitted that it is much more difficult to hold that a party "agreed to do it" for the purposes of the tort but did not "agree to do it" for the purposes of the contract (see Main Work, §§1–063—1–064). As Ralph Gibson L.J. observed in *Reid v. Rush & Tompkins Group plc*[at]:

> where there is a contract between the parties, and any "voluntary assumption of responsibility" occurred, if at all, at the time of making and by reason of the contract, it seems unreal to me to try to separate a duty of care arising from the relationship created by the contract from one "voluntarily assumed" but not specifically assumed by a term of the contract itself.

Indeed, where the parties' silence is to be taken as evidence of a choice *not* to impose liability in respect of a particular matter, a contract may be held "inconsistent with any assumption of responsibility beyond that which has been expressly undertaken": *Greater Nottingham Co-Operative Society Ltd v. Cementation Piling & Foundations Ltd.*[au]. Having said this, to the extent to which the *reasoning* in such cases as *Reid v. Rush & Tompkins Group plc, supra, Greater Nottingham Co-Operative Society Ltd v. Cementation Piling & Foundations Ltd* and *National Bank of Greece S.A. v. Pinios Shipping Co. No. 1 (The Maira)*[av] relied on Lord Scarman's observations in *Tai Hing Cotton Mill Ltd v. Liu Chong Hing Bank Ltd*[aw] as establishing that there should *never* be concurrent liability in tort and contract then this reasoning has been vitiated by the decision of the House of Lords in *Henderson* itself. In conclusion, this difficulty of reconciling an "assumption of responsibility" in tort with a finding of *no* contractual assumption of responsibility is caused not so much by any doubt as to the principle applicable to torts in general arising between parties to a contract, but rather by the apparent lack of independence from contract of liability in tort based on assumption of responsibility.

[a] [1995] 2 A.C. 145, and see further Whittaker (1997) 17 *Legal Studies* 169.

[b] [1995] IRLR 605.

[c] *The Times*, December 22, 1995.

[d] [1995] 1 W.L.R. 1281.

[e] [1986] A.C. 80, 107.

[f] See Burrows (1995) C.L.P. 103, 118 *et seq.*

[g] [1964] A.C 465.

[h] [1995] 2 A.C. 145, 180–181.

[i] *ibid.* at pp. 193–194.

[j] *ibid.* at p. 194.

[k] *ibid.* at pp. 204–206.

[l] [1990] 1 Q.B. 818, revd. on other grounds [1992] 1 A.C. 233.

[m] [1995] 2 A.C. 296, 315 *et seq.*

[n] [1995] 2 A.C. 207, 262, 268 (Lord Goff), 273–276 (Lord Browne-Wilkinson), 292–295 (Lord Nolan), 282–289 (Lord Mustill, dissenting on the application of the principle to the facts).

[o] *ibid.* at pp. 207, 273–274 (Lord Browne-Wilkinson, referring to "assumption of responsibility for the task not the assumption of legal liability"), 280 and 288 (Lord Mustill).

[p] [1995] 2 A.C. 145, 180, *per* Lord Goff of Chieveley.

[q] *ibid.*

[r] *ibid.* and p. 182.

[s] *ibid.* at p. 181.

[t] [1979] Ch. 384.

[u] [1995] 2 A.C. 145, 181.

[v] [1995] I.R.L.R. 605.

[w] [1995] Q.B. 214.

[x] [1989] A.C. 852; see §26–019.

[y] [1995] I.R.L.R. 605, 612 citing [1995] 2 A.C. 145, 180–181, 193–194.

[z] *ibid.*

[aa] [1996] 1 P.N.L.R. 32.

[ab] [1995] 2 A.C. 145.

[ac] [1996] 1 P.N.L.R. 32, 43.

[ad] *ibid.* at pp. 43–44.

[ae] [1995] 1 W.L.R. 1281.

[af] *ibid.* at p. 1290.

[ag] *ibid.* at p. 1294.

[ah] *ibid.* at p. 1295.

[ai] *ibid.* at pp. 1299–1300.

[aj] (1986) 31 D.L.R. (4th) 481, 521–522.

[ak] [1995] 1 W.L.R. 1281, 1301.

[al] *ibid.* at p. 1305.

[am] *The Times*, December 22, 1995 (Lexis transcript used).

[an] [1986] 1 A.C. 80, 107.

[ao] [1995] 2 A.C. 145, 193.

[ap] At pp. 15–16 of Lexis transcript.

[aq] Notably, [1995] 2 A.C. 145, 178 and 193–194.

[ar] [1990] 2 A.C. 605, 638.

[as] Transcript at p. 12.

[at] [1990] 1 W.L.R. 212, 229.

[au] [1989] Q.B. 71, 106, *per* Woolf L.J.

[av] [1990] 1 A.C. 637.

[aw] [1986] A.C. 80, 107.

(i) *Pre-contractual Liability*

Representations

[Add to note 7: page [40]]   1–051
Holt v. Payne Skillington, The Times, December 22, 1995, *ante*,
§§1–048—1–071.

Liability for non-disclosure

[Add to note 28: page [43]]   1–053
Henderson v. Merrett Syndicates Ltd [1995] 2 A.C. 145, 181, discussed *ante*,
§§1–048—1–071.

(ii) *Torts Committed in the Course of Performance of a Contract*

The recognition of an option

[Amend note 89: page [49]]   1–058
Arbuthnott v. Feltrim in the House of Lords reported as *Henderson v.*
Merrett Syndicates Ltd [1995] 2 A.C. 145, *ante*, §§1–048—1–071.

Contractual standards of care

[Text at note 92: page [49]]   1–059
The statement in the text appears at first to be contradicted by the decision
of the Court of Appeal in *Holt v. Payne Skillington, The Times*, December
22, 1995, as there it was accepted that the tort of negligence could impose a
greater liability than that undertaken by a contract between the parties.
However, this contradiction is only apparent, since *Holt* concerned the case
where the contract was found to impose *no duty* in relation to the facts which
were held to give rise to a duty of care in the tort of negligence, whereas the
statement in the text makes clear that only where "either the express or
implied terms of the contract or the law itself governs the standard of care" is
a party prevented from imposing on the other party a higher standard by
claiming in tort. See further on *Holt, ante*, §§1–048—1–071.

1–060   [*Text at note 8 et seq.: page* [51]]

The decision of the Court of Appeal in *Spring v. Guardian Assurance plc* was reversed by a majority of the House of Lords (Lord Keith of Kinkel dissenting).[a] Lord Goff of Chieveley founded his decision on the existence of a duty of care in tort on the basis of a broad principle of liability for assumption of responsibility which he found was the basis of the decision in *Hedley Byrne & Co. Ltd v. Heller & Partners Ltd*,[b] though he made it clear that this basis for liability had not been argued before him. Given this foundation, Lord Goff considered that there was "no good reason why the duty to exercise due skill and care which rests upon the employer should be negatived because, if the plaintiff were instead to bring an action for damage to his reputation, he would be met by the defence of qualified privilege which could only be defeated by proof of malice."[c] Indeed, justice required that liability in negligence in respect of references by employers be imposed. Lords Lowry, Slynn and Woolf also upheld the existence of a duty of care in the tort of negligence, relying for their decision on the fact that the parties in *Spring* were proximate, that an employer could reasonably foresee that the statements in its reference relating to an employee would be relied on and that the alleged policy reasons for denying the existence of such a duty based on the defence of fair comment in defamation were unconvincing.[d] As to the question of the existence of an implied *contractual* duty to take reasonable care in making the reference, Lord Goff did not pronounce on it as "in the present case this adds nothing to the duty of care which arises under the *Hedley Byrne* principle"[e]; Lord Slynn thought that such a term could be implied given the particular regulatory context in which both the employers and employees in *Spring* worked and which meant that the employee could get no job from another member of the employer's industry without a reference.[f] Lord Woolf specified the circumstances in which such a term could be implied as: "(i) The existence of the contract of employment or for services. (ii) The fact that the contract relates to an engagement of a class where it is the normal practice to require a reference from a previous employer before employment is offered. (iii) The fact that the employee cannot be expected to enter into that class of employment except on the basis that the employer will, on the request of another prospective employer made not later than a reasonable time after the termination of a former employment, provide a full and frank reference as to the employee".[g]

[a] [1995] 2 A.C. 296.

[b] [1964] A.C. 465.

[c] [1995] 2 A.C. 296, 324.

[d] *ibid.* at pp. 325–326, 336, 339, 345, and 351.

[e] *ibid.* at p. 320 and see *per* Lord Lowry at p. 327.

[f] *ibid.* at pp. 339–340.

[g] *ibid.* at pp. 353–354.

[Add to text after note 12: page [52]]
A further example of the imposition by means of an implied term in the contract of a stricter liability than would be imposed in tort may be found in the decision of the Privy Council in *Wong Mee Wan v. Kwan Kin Travel Services Ltd.*[12a] There, the plaintiff's daughter, a resident of Hong Kong, had bought a package tour of mainland China from the first defendant, a travel agent, but she drowned when the speed boat in which she was travelling, and which was driven by a person chosen by one of the travel agent's agents, hit a junk. The Privy Council accepted that her contract with the travel agent included all transportation as specified in the itinerary and held that it owed her an obligation that the services which it had been engaged to perform *would be* carried out with reasonable care.[12b] Therefore, the travel agent had been properly held liable in respect of its customer's death, for while no personal negligence had been shown in it (notably, in relation to the choice of its agents in China), negligence had clearly been found in its mainland China agents and this finding meant that it had breached its stricter contractual obligation. See also the discussion, *ante*, §§1–048—1–071 of *Aiken v. Stewart Wrightson Members Agency Ltd*,[12c] in which Potter J. rejected an argument that the existence of more onerous contractual obligation between the parties controlled the content of the duty of care in the tort.

[12a] [1996] 1 W.L.R. 38.

[12b] *ibid.* at 46.

[12c] [1995] 1 W.L.R. 1281.

[Text at note 76: page [59]]   **1–065**
The decision of the Court of Appeal in *White v. Jones* discussed in the text was upheld by a majority of the House of Lords, but on somewhat different reasoning[a]: see *post*, §1–077A.

[a] [1995] 2 A.C. 207.

Damages

[Amend note 15: page [63]]   **1–068**
See the decision of the House of Lords in *Banque Bruxelles Lambert SA v. Eagle Star Insurance Co. Ltd sub nom. South Australia Asset Management Corpn. v. York Montague Ltd* [1997] A.C. 191 esp. at pp. 216–217.

[Add to note 28: page [64]]
According to Sir Thomas Bingham M.R., "somewhat different language has been used to define the test [of remoteness] in contract and tort, but the

essence of the test is the same in each case": *Banque Bruxelles Lambert SA v. Eagle Star Insurance Co. Ltd* [1995] Q.B. 375, 405 (though the decision of the Court of Appeal was reversed on other grounds *sub nom. South Australia Asset Management Corp. v. York Montague Ltd* [1997] A.C. 191).

1–069   [*Amend note 32: page* [65]]
Galoo Ltd v. Bright Grahame Murray [1994] 1 W.L.R. 1360. Glidewell L.J.'s observation may be found at p. 1375, though it is to be noted that the point was agreed by opposing counsel (*ibid.* at p. 1369).

[*Amend note 40*]
Barclays Bank plc v. Fairclough Building Ltd [1995] Q.B. 214 and see also *Barclays Bank plc v. Fairclough Building Ltd (No. 2)* [1995] I.R.L.R. 605, discussed *ante*, §§1–048—1–071.

Limitation of actions

1–070   [*Text at note 50a: page* [67]]
The decision of the Court of Appeal reported as *Arbuthnott v. Feltrim* was affirmed by the House of Lords in *Henderson v. Merrett Syndicates Ltd*,[a] *ante*, §§1–048—1–071.

   [a] [1995] 2 A.C. 145.

The conflict of laws

[*Add to text after note 57: page* [68]]
This view of the position was taken by the Court of Appeal in *Source Ltd v. TUV Rheinland Holding AG*.[57aa] In that case, the plaintiffs claimed that the English courts had jurisdiction to hear their claim in tortious negligence against the defendants, a claim which arose out of and was concurrent with a claim against them for breach of their contractual obligation to exercise reasonable care and skill in presenting a report following the inspection of goods which they (the plaintiffs) had wished to import from China and Taiwan. The Court of Appeal noticed that the European Court of Justice in *Kalfelis v. Schröder*,[57ab] had held that the phrase "matters relating to tort" in article 5(3) of the Brussels Convention refers to "all actions which seek to establish the liability of a defendant and which are not related to a 'contract' within the meaning of article 5(1)".[57ac] For Staughton L.J., with whom Waite and Aldous L.JJ. agreed, this meant that a claim which may be brought under a contract, or independently of a contract on the same facts save that a contract did not need to be established, was excluded from article 5(3) by the European Court's words "which are not related to a 'contract' within the meaning of artile 5(1)". In the result, therefore, both the contractual and tortious claims of the plaintiffs "related to a contract" and they could not by relying on article 5(3) bring the tortious claim before the English courts.

[57aa] *The Times*, March 28, 1997.

[57ab] Case 189/87 [1987] E.C.R. 5565.

[57ac] *ibid.* at p. 5585.

[*Add to text after note 57a: page* [68]]   **1–071**
In *Kleinwort Benson Ltd v. City of Glasgow District Corp.*[57aaa] a majority of
the Court of Appeal held that a claim for restitution of money paid under a
contract which was a nullity because of the recipient's want of capacity to
enter into it was a matter "relating to a contract" within the meaning of
article 5(1) of the Brussels Convention. Leggatt L.J., dissenting, expressed
the view that the claim was neither a matter "relating to a contract" under
article 5(1) nor a matter "relating to tort, delict or quasi-delict" under article
5(3) of the same Convention.[57aab]

[57aaa] [1996] 2 All E.R. 257.

[57aab] On this decision see the critical comments of Riley, (1996) L.M.C.L.Q. 182.

(d) *The Influence of Contract on Tort beyond Privity*

Introduction

[*Advice on note 58*]   **1–072**
On the ability of a "(voluntary) assumption of responsibility" to found a
duty of care in the tort of negligence, see *ante*, §§1–048—1–071.

[*Text at note 62: page* [69]]
See for discussion of recent decisions on this point, including *White v.
Jones,*[a] *post*, §1–077A.

[a] [1995] 2 A.C. 207.

Interference with contractual relations

[*Amend note 67a: page* [70]]   **1–073**
Law Debenture Trust Corp. v. Ural Caspian Oil Corp. Ltd [1994] 3 W.L.R.
1221, esp. at pp. 1231–1232.

A contractor's liability beyond privity and independent torts

[*Amend note 76: page* [70], *replacing text from* "The Law Commission   **1–075**
... (1991)]
The Law Commission has recommended that the law of privity of contract
be reformed by statute so as to grant to a third party a right to enforce a
contract in circumstances where the contract contains an express term to this
effect or where it purports to confer a benefit on that third party, as long as
(in the latter case) on its proper construction it does not appear that the

parties did not intend the contract to be enforceable by the third party: Law Commission, *Privity of Contract: Contracts for the Benefit of Third Parties* (1996), Law Com. No. 242. See *post*, §18–011.

[*Note 88: page* [71]]
The decision of the Court of Appeal in *Spring v. Guardian Assurance plc* [1993] IRLR 122 was overturned by a majority of the House of Lords: [1995] 2 A.C. 296, on whose decision see *ante*, §1–060 at Note 8.

1–077   [*Note 10: page* [73]]
The decision of the Court of Appeal reported as *Arbuthnott v. Feltrim* was affirmed by the House of Lords in *Henderson v. Merrett Syndicates Ltd* [1995] 2 A.C. 145, *post*, §1–077A at Note 26a.

[*Text at second paragraph: page* [75]]
The decision of the Court of Appeal in *Marc Rich & Co. AG v. Bishop Rock Marine Co.* ("*Marc Rich*") (1994) was upheld by a majority of the House of Lords.[a] Lord Steyn, with whom Lords Keith of Kinkel, Jauncey of Tullichettle and Browne-Wilkinson agreed, Lord Lloyd of Berwick dissenting, considered that since *Dorset Yacht Co Ltd v. Home Office*[b] it had been settled law that considerations of fairness, justice and reasonableness as well as the elements of foreseeability and proximity are relevant to the imposition of a duty of care in the tort of negligence, whatever the nature of the harm sustained by the plaintiff and, therefore, including the situation where the plaintiff has sustained damage to property.[c] On the facts before the House in *Marc Rich*, Lord Steyn considered that the property damage suffered by the cargo owners was only indirect as it was the shipowners rather than the classification society which were primarily responsible for the vessel's sailing in a seaworthy condition nor was there any direct contact between the plaintiffs and the classification society and therefore no element of reliance so as to give rise to an assumption of responsibility in the sense explained by Lord Goff in *Henderson v. Merrett Syndicates Ltd*.[d] Even so, Lord Steyn was prepared to assume that there was sufficient proximity between the cargo owners and the classification society, but considered that it was not "fair, just and reasonable" to impose a duty of care.[e] First, such a duty would outflank the bargain between the shipowners and the cargo owners. He stated[f]:

> The dealings between shipowners and cargo owners are based on a contractual structure, the Hague Rules, and tonnage limitation on which the insurance of international trade depends ... Underlying it is the system of double or overlapping insurance of the cargo. Shipowners take out liability risks insurance in respect of breaches of their duties of care in respect of the cargo. The insurance system is structured on the

basis that the potential liability of shipowners to cargo owners is limited under the Hague Rules and by virtue of tonnage limitation provisions. And insurance premiums payable by owners obviously reflect such limitations on the shipowners' exposure.

Secondly, the classification society before them was an independent and non-profit-making entity, created and operating for the sole purpose of promoting the collective welfare, namely the safety of lives and ships at sea and Lord Steyn considered that there "must be some apprehension that the classification societies would [if held to owe a duty of care] adopt, to the detriment of their traditional role, a more defensive position".[g] Finally, Lord Steyn found various other policy factors against imposing a duty of care, including the scale of the classification society's potential liability and the added complication to the settlement of proceedings concerning lost or damaged cargo of such societies' involvement.[h]

[a] [1996] 1 A.C. 211.

[b] [1970] A.C. 1004.

[c] [1996] 1 A.C. 211, 235.

[d] *Henderson v. Merrett Syndicates Ltd* [1995] 2 A.C. 145; *Marc Rich* [1996] 1 A.C. 211 at pp. 237–238.

[e] [1996] 2 A.C. 211 at pp. 241–242.

[f] *ibid.* at p. 239.

[g] *ibid.* at p. 241.

[h] *ibid.*

[*Amend note 24: page* [76]]   1–077A
McCullagh v. Lane Fox and Partners Ltd [1994] E.G.C.S. 2. cf. *Tidman v. Reading Borough Council* [1994] 3 P.L.R. 72; *Goodwill v. British Pregnancy Advisory Service* [1996] 2 All E.R. 161.

[*Text at note 25 et seq.*]
The decision of the Court of Appeal in *White v. Jones* noted in the text was upheld by a majority of the House of Lords, though their lordships did so on somewhat different bases.[a] Lord Goff of Chieveley considered that "there is great difficulty in holding, on ordinary principles, that the solicitor has assumed any responsibility towards an intended beneficiary under a will which he has undertaken to prepare on behalf of his client",[b] but in the interests of practical justice the House of Lords should "in cases such as these extend to the intended beneficiary a remedy under the *Hedley Byrne* principle by holding that the assumption of responsibility should be held in law to extend to the intended beneficiary".[c] Lord Browne-Wilkinson considered that a duty of care should be imposed, by incremental analogy with existing categories of special relationship giving rise to a duty of care to

prevent pure economic loss: "the solicitor by accepting the instructions has entered upon, and therefore assumed responsibility for, the task of procuring the execution of a skilfully drawn will knowing that the beneficiary is wholly dependent upon his carefully carrying out his function".[d] Lord Nolan considered also that the solicitor could be held liable for his assumption of responsibility: "a professional man or an artisan who undertakes to exercise his skill in a manner which, to his knowledge, may cause loss to others if carelessly performed, may thereby implicitly assume a legal responsibility towards them".[e] Lord Keith of Kinkel dissented from this decision on the ground that "to admit the plaintiffs' claim in the present case would in substance ... be to give them the benefit of a contract to which they were not parties", finding "no decided case the grounds of decision in which are capable of being extended incrementally and by way of analogy so as to admit of a remedy in tort being made available to the plaintiffs".[f] In his much more extensive dissent, Lord Mustill took the view that the principle of assumption of responsibility could not be relied on to find a duty of care, as the task of drawing a will was undertaken for the testator, not for the beneficiaries and he did not consider that the facts before him were sufficiently special to distinguish them from "the general situation ... where A promises B for reward to perform a service for B, in circumstances where it is foreseeable that performance of the service with care will cause C to receive a benefit, and that failure to perform it may cause C not to receive that benefit".[g] For further discussion of and an alternative means of allowing the claim beyond privity in *White v. Jones* see Whittaker.[h]

In *Woodward v. Wolferstans (a Firm)*[i] Mr Michael Mann Q.C. applied the reasoning of the majority of the House of Lords in *White v. Jones* to the different facts before him. In *Woodward*, the plaintiff, then aged 22 years, had purchased a property by raising a 95 per cent mortgage, the mortgage being guaranteed by her father, who instructed the defendant solicitors to handle the conveyancing. The plaintiff was unaware of her obligations under the mortgage and believed that her father's guarantee meant that he was responsible for repayment. Mr Michael Mann Q.C. found that the defendants' contract of retainer was with the plaintiff's father, but relied on *White v. Jones* to establish that a solicitor could owe a duty of care to an individual who was not his client if a special relationship existed between them. On the facts, he held that the defendants had assumed responsibility for carrying out tasks which they knew or ought to have known would closely affect the plaintiff's economic well-being, thereby owing a duty of care. However, he further decided that it would not be fair, just and reasonable to hold that this duty of care extended beyond the exercising of reasonable care in securing a good and marketable title to the property, to a duty to give the plaintiff advice: the court could not rewrite the contract of retainer so as to bring the plaintiff within its ambit nor should it do so by the back door of tort.

On the other hand, in *R.F. Hill & Associates v. Van Erp*[j] the High Court of Australia followed the majority of the House of Lords in *White v. Jones* in imposing a duty of care in the tort of negligence in respect of a defendant solicitor's negligence in executing a person's will under which the plaintiff would have benefited, but in reaching this result it rejected Lord Goff of Chieveley's reasoning in that case which rested on an extension of the *Hedley Byrne* principle of assumption of responsibility.

[a] [1995] 2 A.C. 207.

[b] *ibid.* at p. 262.

[c] *ibid.* at p. 268.

[d] *ibid.* at p. 275.

[e] *ibid.* at p. 294.

[f] *ibid.* at p. 251.

[g] *ibid.* at pp. 290–291.

[h] (1996) 16 O.J.L.S. 191, esp. 218–219.

[i] *The Times*, April 8, 1997.

[j] (1997), transcript used (to appear in C.L.R.).

[*Text at note 26a et seq.*]
The decision of the Court of Appeal noted in the text *sub. nom. Arbuthnott v. Feltrim* was upheld by the House of Lords *sub. nom. Henderson v. Merrett Syndicates Ltd*[a] (for discussion of the claim in tort of the "direct Names" within privity see *ante*, §§1–048—1–071). Lord Goff of Chieveley, who gave the leading speech and with whom Lords Keith of Kinkel, Browne-Wilkinson, Mustill and Nolan concurred, based the decision on a finding of an assumption of responsibility by the managing agents (sub-agents) to the "indirect Names" so as to give rise to a duty of care in the tort of negligence *beyond* privity. However, Lord Goff added that he "strongly suspect[ed] that the situation ... [was] most unusual; and that in many cases in which a contractual chain comparable to that in the present case is constructed it may well prove to be inconsistent with an assumption of responsibility which has the effect of, so to speak, short circuiting the contractual structure so put in place by the parties"[b] and he gave as an example of where such an assumption of responsibility would be inconsistent with a contractual structure the case of a claim by a building owner against his sub-contractor in respect of a failure to conform to the required standard, in which "it will not ordinarily be open to the building owner to sue the sub-contractor ... direct under the *Hedley Byrne* principle".[c] Lord Browne-Wilkinson, who gave the only other speech, agreed with Lord Goff's analysis, but added his own comments on the relationship between the liability in tort which had been found and that based on breach of

fiduciary duty.[d] For further discussion of and an alternative means of allowing the claim beyond privity in *Henderson* see Whittaker.[e]

[a] [1995] 2 A.C. 145.

[b] *ibid.* at p. 195.

[c] *ibid.* at p. 196.

[d] *ibid.* at pp. 204–206.

[e] (1996) O.J.L.S. 191, esp. 219 *et seq.*

[*Add after final paragraph: page* [77]]
In *Aiken v. Stewart Wrightson Members Agency Ltd*,[26f] Potter J. felt able to impose a duty of care in the tort of negligence beyond privity and yet within a contractual structure. This case, like *Henderson v. Merrett Syndicates Ltd*,[26g] arose from the Lloyd's insurance market, but *Aiken* included claims by "indirect Names" *other than those actually identified or known* by the defendant managing agents at the time at which the latters' negligence was alleged to have been committed. Potter J. considered that in these circumstances, it was not appropriate to expound the problem of liability in terms of "assumption of responsibility" and "reliance" but instead in terms of foreseeability, proximity and "justice and reasonableness", relying, *inter alia*, in this respect on the approach of the Court of Appeal in *White v. Jones*.[26h] The learned judge found that the managing agents owed a duty of care even to those Names who had only become members of the syndicates which they managed after the time of their alleged negligence, this duty being "the logical and reasonable outcome of the workings of the Lloyd's market, whereby the market is the Syndicate, as the sum of its Names from time to time, it being the duty of [the defendant in question] as managing agents to manage and promote the interests of the Syndicate as a whole".[26i]

[26f] [1995] 1 W.L.R. 1281.

[26g] [1995] 2 A.C. 145.

[26h] *White v. Jones* [1993] 3 W.L.R. 730; see *Aiken* [1995] 1 W.L.R. 1281 at p. 1308—the House of Lords had not given judgment at the date of judgment in *Aiken*.

[26i] [1995] 1 W.L.R. 1281 at p. 1312.

The effect of contractual terms on established torts beyond privity

1–078   [*Add to note 29*]
White v. Jones [1995] 2 A.C. 207, 268.

[*Amend note 31*]
Owners of cargo lately laden on board K.H. Enterprise v. Owners of Pioneer Container now reported as *The Pioneer Container* [1994] 2 A.C. 324.

[*Add to note 36: page* [78]]

cf. the discussion *ante*, §1–077, of the decision of the House of Lords in
Marc Rich & Co. AG v. Bishop Rock Marine Co. [1996] 1 A.C. 211 and see
the decision of the Court of Session in *British Telecommunications plc v.
James Thomson & Sons (Engineers) Ltd, The Times*, January 28, 1997.

5. – CONTRACT AND OTHER LEGAL CATEGORIES

Contract and trust

[*Note 48: page* [80]]   **1–079**

The decision of the Court of Appeal in *Target Holdings Ltd v. Redferns*
noted here as an example of the existence of a trust relationship between
parties to a contract was reversed by the House of Lords: [1995] 3 W.L.R.
352. However, the issue which was in dispute in the House of Lords was not
the existence of the parallel trust duty or its breach but whether this breach
had caused the loss claimed by the plaintiffs for the purposes of the claim in
equity. It was held that where monies were held by a solicitor for the purpose
of completing a transaction (the mortgage) with a third party as agreed
between the trustee and beneficiary under a contract, the solicitor could not
be expected to reconstitute the trust fund *after* the transaction envisaged was
completed, even though the monies had been paid by him in breach of trust
(*ibid.* at p. 362). On the facts, it was the transaction with the third party which
had caused the beneficiary's loss, not the solicitor's breach of trust.

Part One

FORMATION OF CONTRACT

CHAPTER 2

THE AGREEMENT

1. – INTRODUCTION

Offer defined

2–002   *[Add to note 9: page* [90]*]*
First Energy (UK) Ltd v. Hungarian International Bank Ltd [1993] 2 Lloyd's Rep. 195, 201; *Bowerman v. Association of British Travel Agents Ltd* [1995] New L.J. 1815, *post*, §2–010.

[Add to note 12]
O.T. Africa Line Ltd v. Vickers plc [1996] 1 Lloyd's Rep. 700, 702. In this case, solicitors who had been instructed to settle a claim for $155,000 offered to settle it for £150,000 and it was held that acceptance of the offer by the plaintiffs (who neither knew nor ought reasonably to have known of the mistake) gave rise, on the objective test, to a binding contract.

[*Add to note 14: page* [91]]
O.T. Africa Line Ltd v. Vickers plc [1996] 1 Lloyd's Rep. 700, *supra*, n. 12.

2. – THE OFFER

Conduct as offer

[*Note 21: page* [92]]   2–003
The Arbitration Act 1950, s.13A has been repealed by the Arbitration Act
1996, s.107(1) and Sched. 3. The power to dismiss a claim on the ground of
"inordinate and inexcusable delay" is now conferred on arbitrators by
s.41(3) of the 1996 Act.

The principles which apply to the statutory power to dismiss arbitration
proceedings are (*mutatis mutandis*) the same as those which apply to
dismissing an action for want of prosecution: *James Lazenby & Co. v.
McNicholas Construction Co. Ltd* [1995] 1 W.L.R. 615.

Advertisements of unilateral contracts

[*Add after second paragraph: page* [97]]   2–010
Carlill v. Carbolic Smoke Ball Co. Ltd[65a] was followed in *Bowerman v.
Association of British Travel Agents Ltd*[65b] where a package holiday had
been cancelled owing to the insolvency of the tour operator, who was a
member of the defendant association (ABTA). A notice displayed on the
tour operator's premises contained (*inter alia*) the statement that, in the
event of the financial failure of an ABTA member before the commencement of the holiday, "ABTA arranges for you to be reimbursed the money
you have paid for your holiday". A majority of the Court of Appeal held that
these words constituted an offer as they would reasonably be regarded as
such and as capable of being accepted by doing business with an ABTA
member.

[65a] [1893] 1 Q.B. 256.

[65b] [1995] New L.J. 1815.

Timetables and passenger tickets

[*Add to note 74: page* [98]]   2–012
Dillon v. Baltic Shipping Co. (The Mikhail Lermontov) was reversed by
the High Court of Australia, but without reference to the point discussed in
§2–012 of the Main Work: (1993) 176 C.L.R. 344.

Tenders

[*Add to note 80: page* [99]]   2–013
cf. *Fairclough Building v. Port Talbot B.C.* (1992) 62 B.L.R. 82.

[*Add to note 81*]
See also *Reg. v. Portsmouth City Council, ex p. Coles, The Times*,
November 13, 1996.

Share offers

2–014   [*Add to note 84: page* [100]]
National Westminster Bank plc v. I.R.C. [1995] A.C. 119, 126.

3. – THE ACCEPTANCE

(a) *Definition*

Continuing negotiations

2–017   [*Add to note 97: page* [101]]
Ignazio Messina & Co. v. Polskie Linie Ozeaniczne [1995] 2 Lloyd's Rep.
566 (where there was held to be no contract); *Frota Oceanica Brasilieira S.A.
v. Steamship Mutual Underwriting Association (Bermuda) Ltd (The Frota-
norte)* [1996] 2 Lloyd's Rep. 461 (where no contract was concluded as
matters of substance remained unresolved in the negotiations).

[*Add to end of paragraph*]
A fortiori the binding force of an oral contract is not affected or altered
merely because one party, after its conclusion, sends to the other a form
containing terms significantly different from those which had been orally
agreed.[98a]

[98a] *Jayaar Impex Ltd v. Toaken Group Ltd* [1996] 2 Lloyd's Rep. 437.

Acceptance by conduct

2–018   [*Add after note 1 in text: page* [102]]
Similarly an offer taking the form of a request for services can be accepted
by the conduct of the person to whom the request is addressed in beginning
to render the services.[1a]

[1a] *Smit International Singapore Ltd v. Kurnia Dewi Shipping S.A. (The Kurnia
Dewi)* [1997] 1 Lloyd's Rep. 553, 559.

[*Add to note 2*]
cf. in another context, *Re Leyland Daf Ltd* [1995] 4 All E.R. 300, aff'd. *sub
nom. Powdrill v. Watson* [1995] 2 A.C. 394.

[*Add at end of paragraph*]
Brogden v. Metropolitan Ry[6a] was distinguished in *Jayaar Impex Ltd v.
Toaken Group Ltd*[6b] where, after an oral contract of sale had been made,[6c]

the sellers sent the buyers a written contract form which made "fundamental"[6d] changes to the sellers' obligations under the oral contract. Subsequent acceptance of delivery by the buyers was held not to amount to conduct accepting the varied terms contained in the written document: this conduct of the buyers was referable to their entitlement to delivery under the oral contract and not (as in *Brogden's* case) solely to the terms of the document.

[6a] (1877) 2 App. Cas. 666.

[6b] [1996] 2 Lloyd's Rep. 437.

[6c] See *post*, §2–082.

[6d] [1996] 2 Lloyd's Rep. at p. 445.

Acceptance in ignorance of offer

[*Add to note 47: page* [108]]   2–024
For conflicting decisions on the duty of care owed by the fire services in the absence of contract, see *John Munroe (Acrylics) Ltd v. London Fire & Civil Defence Authority* [1996] 4 All E.R. 318; *Capital & Counties plc v. Hampshire C.C.* [1996] 1 W.L.R. 1553 (both aff'd. [1997] 2 Lloyd's Rep. 161) and *Nelson Holdings Ltd v. British Gas plc, The Times*, March 7, 1997. No reference is made in any of these reports to *Upton R.D.C. v. Powell* [1942] 1 All E.R. 220 (discussed in the Main Work on p. 107), presumably because no such question arose in that case.

(b) *Communication of acceptance*

Exceptions

[*Add to note 65: page* [110]]   2–028
cf. Minories Finance Ltd v. Afribank Nigeria Ltd [1995] 1 Lloyd's Rep. 134, 140, where a contract was made "by inaction or silence" (p. 139), the normal rule to the contrary being displaced "by the custom and practice of banking [that] a contract can come into existence by doing nothing" (p. 140). The actual decision in *Vitol SA v. Norelf Ltd* was reversed by the Court of Appeal but restored by the House of Lords: see *post*, §2–047. *cf.* also *Smit International Singapore Pte Ltd v. Kurnia Dewi Shipping S.A.* [1997] 1 Lloyd's Rep. 553, 559: acceptance by conduct "or perhaps" when the fact of that conduct was communicated to the offeror.

[*Add to note 75*]
Schelde Delta Shipping B.V. v. Astarte Shipping Ltd (The Pamela) [1995] 2 Lloyd's Rep. 249, 252.

(c) *Posted acceptances*

Instantaneous communications

2–031　　[*Note 85: page* [112]]
　　　　cf. Schelde Delta Shipping B.V. v. Astarte Shipping Ltd (The Pamela)
[1995] 2 Lloyd's Rep. 249, 252 (telexed notice withdrawing ship from
charterparty).

(d) *Prescribed mode of acceptance*

Mode must generally be complied with

2–042　　[*Add at end of paragraph: page* [117]]
　　　　Similarly, in *Beta Computers (Europe) v. Adobe Systems Europe*[23a] a
supplier of computer software delivered it in a package on which was printed
the statement that the supply was made, subject to licence conditions and the
further provision that "opening the package indicates acceptance of these
terms and conditions." These terms were visible through the wrapping of the
package. It was held that the supplier was not entitled to the price where the
customer had sought to return the package *without* opening it.

　　[23a] 1996 S.L.T. 604. Even opening the package would not necessarily have
amounted to an acceptance of the seller's offer so as to incorporate the licence
conditions: see Tapper (ed. Rose) in *Consensus ad Idem, Essays in the Law of
Contract in Honour of Guenter Treitel*, pp. 287–288 (1996).

Other equally efficacious mode

2–044　　[*Note 26*]
　　　　cf. Edmond Murray v. BSP International Foundations (1992) 33 Con.L.R.
1.

(e) *Silence*

Offeree generally not bound

2–047　　[*Replace note 30: page* [118] *with the following*]
　　　　Arbitration Act 1996 s.41(3), *ante*, §2–003.

　　　　[*Replace note 31: page* [118] *with the following*]
　　　　Arbitration Act 1996 s.41(2), *ante*, §2–003, so provides.

　　　　[*Add to note 33: page* [119]]
　　　　For an illustration of the equivocal nature of "silence," see *Jayaar Impex
Ltd v. Toaken Group Ltd* [1996] 2 Lloyd's Rep. 437, esp. at p. 445.

[32]

[*Add to note 35: page* [119]]

In *Vitol SA v. Norelf Ltd (The Santa Clara)* a contract for the sale of propane was wrongfully repudiated by the buyers. After receipt of the repudiation, the sellers made no further attempt to perform the contract, nor did they take any other active steps to manifest their acceptance of the repudiation. The question was raised whether the sellers had by such inactivity accepted the buyers' repudiation (since, if they had not, the buyers could have withdrawn it before acceptance and so have escaped liability in damages). The arbitrators found that the repudiation had been accepted; and the question of law raised on appeal from their decision was, in the words of Phillips J., "whether, as a matter of law, mere failure to perform contractual obligations can ever constitute acceptance of an anticipatory repudiation by the other party": [1993] 2 Lloyd's Rep. 301, 304; the learned judge gave an affirmative answer to this question. This decision was reversed by the Court of Appeal: [1996] Q.B. 108, but restored by the House of Lords: [1996] A.C. 800. Some reliance was placed on the (admittedly imperfect) analogy of the rule that, while silence cannot generally amount to an acceptance in the formation of contracts, it can have this effect "in most exceptional circumstances", such as those described in §2–048 of the Main Work. The Court of Appeal had rejected this analogy on the ground that failure to perform a contractual obligation was necessarily equivocal, being just as consistent with a "misunderstanding by the innocent party of his rights, . . . indecision or even inadvertence" as with an intention to accept the repudiation ([1996] Q.B. 108, 116). But the House of Lords took the view that it was impossible to lay down an absolute rule on the point; that an innocent party's failure to perform its obligations under the repudiated contract was not *necessarily* equivocal; and that such inactivity was not, therefore, as a matter of law, incapable of constituting acceptance of the repudiation.

[*Add to note 39: page* [119]]

cf. *Minories Finance Ltd v. Afribank Nigeria Ltd* [1995] 1 Lloyd's Rep. 134, 139 (custom).

[*Note 40: page* [119]]

Replace "Arbitration Act 1950 s.13A" with Arbitration Act 1996 s.41(3), *ante*, §2–003.

[*Add to note 40*]

cf. *Re Selectmove* [1995] 1 W.L.R. 474, 478.

Can offeree exceptionally be bound?

2–048   [*Add to text at end of first paragraph: page* [119]]
Where the offeree is under a "duty to speak," his failure to perform that duty may enable the *offeror* to treat that failure as an acceptance by silence. But it is not open to the *offeree* in such cases to treat his own silence (in breach of his duty to speak) as an acceptance where the offeror had not indicated that he would treat silence as consent,[40a] so that there was no possibility of holding him liable on this basis in accordance with the suggestion made in §2–049 of the Main Work.

[40a] *Yona International Ltd v. La Réunion Française, etc.* [1996] 2 Lloyd's Rep. 84, 110.

[*Add to note 41: page* [120]]
This principle was held to be inapplicable in *Yona International Ltd v. La Réunion Française, etc.* [1996] 2 Lloyd's Rep. 84, 107 on the ground that A, the person alleged to be bound by virtue of it, had had no contact with B, the party to whom the alleged offer had been made by a third party, C, who had not been authorised by A to make it.

Silence and conduct

2–050   [*Note 53: page* [121]]
For "Arbitration Act 1950 s.13A, as inserted by Courts and Legal Services Act 1990 s.102; *ante* §2–003" substitute: Arbitration Act 1996 s.41(3); *ante* §2–003.

2–051   [*Add to end of paragraph: page* [122]]
Rust v. Abbey Life Ins. Co.[60a] was distinguished in *Yona International Ltd v. La Réunion Française*[60b] on the grounds (a) that in the latter case it was the *offeree* who was relying on his *own* silence as acceptance of the offeror's proposal of terms in the course of negotiations for insurance cover (see *ante*, §2–048); and (b) that in the former case the insured had been sent the policy and must be "taken to have examined it on receipt"[60c] (so that there could be no doubt as to its terms) while in the latter the proper inference to be drawn from the offeree's failure to respond to proposals made in the course of negotiation was that he was unwilling to proceed on those terms.

[60a] [1979] 2 Lloyd's Rep. 335.

[60b] [1996] 2 Lloyd's Rep. 84.

[60c] *ibid.*, p. 110.

(f) *Unilateral contracts*

In general

2–052   [*Add to note 62: page* [122]]
Bowerman v. Association of British Travel Agents [1995] N.L.J. 1815.

Unilateral contract becoming bilateral

[*Add to note 75, line 1, after "51–2": page* [124]]   **2–056**
*Smit International Singapore Pte Ltd v. Kurnia Dewi Shipping S.A. (The
Kurnia Dewi)* [1997] 1 Lloyd's Rep. 553, 559.

[*Add to note 75 at end*]
According to *Little v. Courage* (1995) 70 P. & C.R. 469, 474, it is
"impossible to imply terms … which impose legal obligations … into a
unilateral contract". The reason for this view appears to be that such an
implication would destroy the unilateral character of the contract. But it is
not obvious why this should preclude the implication of a term imposing an
obligation on the *promisor*, nor does it necessarily exclude the possibility
that an intention to undertake an obligation may be inferred from the
conduct of the promisee *after* the unilateral contract has come into existence.
This possibility is recognised in the dictum cited in §2–056, n. 74 of the Main
Work and, it is submitted, illustrated by the example there given in the text
to the present note.

4. – TERMINATION OF OFFER

(a) *Revocation*

Exception to the requirement of communication

[*Add to note 94: page* [127]]   **2–062**
Schelde Delta Shipping B.V. v. Astarte Shipping Ltd (The Pamela) [1995] 2
Lloyd's Rep. 249, 252.

(g) *Supervening corporate incapacity*

Company as offeror

[*Add to note 34: page* [133]]   **2–077**
Little v. Courage has been reversed by the Court of Appeal: (1995) 70 P. &
C.R. 469, where Millett L.J. (at p. 474) described an option as a unilateral
contract.

5. – SPECIAL CASES

Difficulty of offer and acceptance analysis in certain cases

[*Add to note 40: page* [134]]   **2–079**
cf. *Commissioner for the New Towns v. Cooper (Great Britain) Ltd* [1995]
Ch. 259.

6. – INCOMPLETE AGREEMENT

Agreement in principle only

2–080   [*Add to note 47: page* [135]]
cf. Southwark L.B.C. v. Logan [1996] 10 C.L. 292 (letter containing no term as to payment held not to give rise to a tenancy).

[*Add to note 48: page* [135]]
cf. Hillreed Land v. Beautridge [1994] E.G.C.S. 55; *Avinter v. Avill* 1995 S.C.L.R. 1002.

[*Add to note 51: page* [136]]
cf. Russell Brothers (Paddington) Ltd v. John Elliott Management Ltd (1995) 11 Const. L.J. 377.

Stipulation for the execution of a formal document

2–082   [*Add to note 63: page* [137]]
Ignazio Messina & Co. v. Polskie Linie Oceaniczne [1995] 2 Lloyd's Rep. 566, 579; *Drake & Scull Engineering Ltd v. Higgs & Hill (Northern) Ltd* (1995) 11 Constr. L.J. 214.

[*Add to note 64: page* [137]]
cf. Jayaar Impex Ltd v. Toaken Group Ltd [1996] 2 Lloyd's Rep. 437 (binding force of oral agreement not deferred until execution of seller's contract form even if that form had been referred to in the oral agreement).

Agreement "subject to contract"

2–084   [*Add to note 75: page* [138]]
Enfield L.B.C. v. Arajah [1995] E.G.C.S. 164.

General requirement of "exchange of contracts"

2–085   [*Note 77*]
cf. Commission for the New Towns v. Cooper (G.B.) Ltd [1995] Ch. 259, discussing the impact of the formal requirements imposed by Law of Property (Miscellaneous Provisions) Act 1989 s.2. In consequence of that section, the process of offer and acceptance cannot create a contract for the disposition of an interest in land where each document is signed only by the party from whom it emanates, since the section requires the document

recording all the expressly agreed terms of the contract to be signed by both parties; *Hooper v. Sherman* [1995] 3 C.L. 96 not followed. See *post*, §4–047A.

Letters of intent; letters of comfort

[*Note 2: page* [141]]   2–089
cf. Monk Construction v. Norwich Union Life Assurance Society (1992) 62 B.L.R. 107 (where it was made clear in such a letter that contract documents should be signed before building work started, and negotiations for this contract then broke down).

Terms to be agreed

[*Add to text after note 7: page* [142]]   2–090
Even where the points left outstanding are of relatively minor importance, there will be no contract if it appears from the words used or other circumstances that the parties did not intend to be bound until agreement on these points had been reached: *Metal Scrap Trade Corporation v. Kate Shipping Co. Ltd (The Gladys).*[7a]

[7a] [1994] 2 Lloyd's Rep. 402.

Options and rights of pre-emption

[*Add to note 10*]   2–091
For the purposes of the Landlord and Tenants (Covenants) Act 1995, " 'option' includes a right of first refusal": s.1(6).

Agreement not incomplete merely because further agreement is required

[*Add to note 16: page* [143]]   2–092
Granit S.A. v. Benship International Inc. [1994] 1 Lloyd's Rep. 526; *Mitsui Babcock Energy Ltd v. John Brown Engineering Ltd* (1996) 51 Const. L.R. 129.

Criteria or machinery laid down in the agreement

[*Add to note 31: page* [145]]   2–094
This position is preserved by Unfair Terms in Consumer Contracts Regulations 1994, S.I. 1994 No. 3159, Reg. 4(4) and Sched. 3, para. 2(b).

[*Add to note 39: page* [145]]
cf. Royal Bank of Scotland v. Jennings [1996] E.G.C.S. 168.

Contract to make a contract

[*Add to note 57: page* [147]]   2–097

Little v. Courage has been reversed on other grounds, (1995) 70 P. & C.R. 469; see further *ante*, §2–077.

7. – CERTAINTY OF TERMS

Qualifications of the requirements of certainty

2–100   [*Add to note 79: page* [150]]
Clement v. Gibbs [1996] 5 C.L. 124. *cf. Hanjin Shipping Co. Ltd v. Zenith Chartering Corp. (The Mercedes Envoy)* [1995] 2 Lloyd's Rep. 559, 564, concluding that there was a contract as "the parties clearly thought so over a long period".

Reasonableness

2–102   [*Add to note 85: page* [151]]
cf. Baynham v. Phillips Electronics (U.K.) Ltd, The Times, August 19, 1995, where uncertainty in a long-term health insurance agreement was resolved by reference to circumstances existing at the time of its formation.

8. – CONTRACTUAL INTENTION

Burden of proof

2–106   [*Add to note 94: page* [152]]
cf. Coastal (Bermuda) Petroleum Ltd v. VTT Vulcan Petroleum S.A. (The Marine Star) (No. 2) [1994] 2 Lloyd's Rep. 629, 632, where an agreement between two companies in the same group was found to be legally binding even though its terms "might not be strictly enforced between [the parties];" revsd. on other grounds [1996] 2 Lloyd's Rep. 383.

[*Note 96: page* [153]]
cf. Ignazio Messina & Co. v. Polskie Linie Oceaniczne [1995] 2 Lloyd's Rep. 566, 571 for a statement of the objective test in a case where, applying this test, the court found that there was no contractual intention; similar reasoning (*ibid.* p. 581) negatived a collateral contract in this case.

[*Add to note 98*]
Bowerman v. Association of British Travel Agents Ltd [1995] New L.J. 1815, *ante*, §2–010.

Intention expressly negatived

2–107   [*Add to note 8: page* [154]]
Ali v. Ahmed (1996) 71 P. & C.R. D39.

[38]

[*Add to note 9: page* [154]]
In Scotland, it has been argued that such honour clauses in football pool coupons may be unreasonable and hence ineffective: see *Ferguson v. Littlewoods Pools* 1997 S.L.T. 309.

[*Add to text after second paragraph: page* [154]]
Similarly, the statement made during charter negotiations that "we are fixed in good faith" has been held not to negative contractual intention: *Hanjin Shipping Co. Ltd v. Zenith Chartering Corp. (The Mercedes Envoy).*[12a] If the phrase had any effect, it was merely a "collateral understanding" that due account should be taken of damage to the vessel, of which both shipowner and charterer were aware.

[12a] [1995] 2 Lloyd's Rep. 559.

Social agreements

[*Add to note 21: page* [156]]   2–109
For another context in which sharing of expenses did not give rise to an inference of contractual intention, see *Monmouth C.C. v. Marlog, The Times*, May 4, 1994.

Agreements giving wide discretion to one party

[*Add to note 51 (after "Unfair Contract Terms Act 1977 s.3(2)(b)(i)"*:   2–113
page [159]]
and of Unfair Terms in Consumer Contracts Regulations 1994 (S.I. 1994 No. 3159), especially Sched. 3, para. 1(c).

Other cases

[*Add to note 62: page* [161]]   2–117
cf. Glatzer & Warrick Shipping Ltd v. Bradston Ltd [1997] 1 Lloyd's Rep. 449, 484 (no contract because the transaction was a sham, there being "no intention ... to create bona fide legal relations").

[*Add to note 63: page* [161]]
cf. County Ltd v. Girozentrale Securities [1996] 3 All E.R. 834, 837, discussed *post*, §3–129; *Burrows v. Brent London Borough Council* [1996] 1 W.L.R. 1448 where a landlord, having obtained an order for possession against a secure tenant who had fallen into arrears with her rent, agreed with the tenant not to enforce the order. The House of Lords held that this agreement did not give rise to a new secure tenancy as "the parties plainly did not intend to create a new tenancy or licence" (*per* Lord Browne-Wilkinson at 1454): its effect was merely to turn the tenant into a "tolerated trespasser" (*ibid.* at 1455).

[*Add to note 67: page* [161]]

Diocese of Southwark v. Coker, The Times, July 17, 1997 (assistant curate held not to be an employee of the Church of England since there was no intention to create legal relations and hence no contract between these parties).

2–118   [*Add after note 75: page* [162]]

Where a husband and wife had on the same day executed indentical wills, it was held that these were not "mutual wills" (for the purpose of the rule precluding the survivor from revoking or altering his will) in the absence of a legally binding contract that neither will would be revoked.[75a] For this purpose a mere "common understanding"[75b] was not enough. One possible explanation of the case is that it had not been shown that there was "some agreement or representation intended to have legal effect"[75c] and that the claim therefore failed for want of contractual intention. But it is at least equally plausible to argue that there was simply no agreement, express or implied, as the wife "regarded the arrangement as irrevocable, but ... [the husband] did not;"[75d] and if there was no agreement no further question of contractual intention could arise.

[75a] *Re Goodchild* [1997] 3 All E.R. 63.

[75b] *ibid.* p. 69.

[75c] *ibid.* p. 68, quoting from the decision at first instance [1996] 1 All E.R. 670, 684.

[75d] [1997] 3 All E.R. 63, 71.

CHAPTER 3

CONSIDERATION

2. – DEFINITIONS

Either sufficient

3–005

[Add to note 13: page [167]]
cf. *Gill & Duffus S.A. v. Rionda Futures Ltd* [1995] 2 Lloyd's Rep. 67, 82.

Other definitions

3–007   [*Note 26: page* [169]]
cf. *Colonia Versicherung A.G. v. Amoco Oil Co.* [1995] 1 Lloyd's Rep. 570, 577 (affd. without reference to this point [1997] 1 Lloyd's Rep. 261): where the words "(a) the reason for and (b) ample consideration for" a payment clearly treat these two concepts as distinct.

Consideration and condition

3–010   [*Note 42: page* [171]]
For a further illustration of the distinction between consideration and condition, see *Marshall v. N.M. Financial Management Ltd* [1995] 1 W.L.R. 1461. The defendant engaged the plaintiff as an exclusive agent for the sale of certain financial products, promising to pay the plaintiff a renewal commission, subject to a proviso containing a stipulation which was void for restraint of trade but severable. The plaintiff was held entitled to the commission in spite of the fact that the proviso was severed: "The consideration for the payment of the renewal commission [was] not the acceptance by [the plaintiff] of the proviso, but his services in procuring business ... ". The proviso was merely a condition, so that its deletion from the contract did not leave the defendant's promise unsupported by consideration. *Cf. Ellis v. Chief Adjudication Officer, The Times*, May 14, 1997 for an illustration of a conditional gift, which failed because the condition (that the donee of a flat should look after his mother there) was not performed by the donee.

Executed and executory consideration

3–011   [*Add to note 46: page* [171]]
Contrast *The Kaliningrad and Nadezhda Krupskaya* [1997] 2 Lloyd's Rep. 35, 39, where a "proposal not yet agreed," forming merely a step in a series of "counter-offers and proposals," was held not to be capable of constituting consideration.

3. – ADEQUACY OF CONSIDERATION

3–013   [*Add to note 60: page* [173]]
The principle that the court will not, in general, investigate the adequacy of consideration is correspondingly recognised and preserved by Unfair Terms in Consumer Contracts Regulations 1994, S.I. 1994 No. 3159, Reg. 3(2)(b), giving effect to the Directive cited in n. 60 on p. 172 of the Main Work.

[Amend note 61, replacing second sentence with new text]
The Regulations cited in the previous note would not apply in *Gaumont-British Pictures Corp. v. Alexander* [1936] 2 All E.R. 1686: see Reg. 3(1) and Sched. 1 para. (a).

Illustrations

[Add to note 67: page [174]]   **3–014**
Contrast *Re Goodchild* [1997] 3 All E.R. 63 (*ante* §2–118) where a mere common understanding (as opposed to a legally binding contract) that identical wills executed by a husband and wife on the same day would not be revoked was held to be insufficient to make them "mutual wills". But the understanding was held to impose on the surviving husband a moral obligation, to which effect was given by an order in favour of the intended beneficiary under the Inheritance (Provision for Dependants) Act 1975.

Nominal consideration

[Note 85: page [176]]   **3–016**
For protection of third parties under Insolvency Act 1986 s.423 against transactions at an undervalue, see *Barclays Bank plc v. Eustice* [1995] 1 W.L.R. 1238; *Agricultural Mortgage Corp. plc v. Woodward* [1995] B.C.L.C. 1.

4. – REALITY OF CONSIDERATION

Discretionary promise

[Add to note 12: page [179]]   **3–021**
For clauses which may be ineffective because they leave performance to the discretion of one party, see Unfair Terms in Consumer Contracts Regulations 1994, S.I. 1994 No. 3159, Sched. 3, paras. 1(c) and 1(f).

5. – PAST CONSIDERATION

Past act done at promisor's request

[Add to note 26: page [182]]   **3–025**
Contrast *Southwark L.B.C. v. Logan* [1996] 10 C.L. 292 (defendant's act in leaving council property no consideration as not due at plaintiff's request).

6. – CONSIDERATION MUST MOVE FROM THE PROMISEE

Consideration need not move to the promisor

3–034   *[Add to note 70: page* [187]]
cf. Pearl Carriers Inc. v. Japan Lines Ltd (The Chemical Venture) [1993] 1
Lloyd's Rep. 509, 522 (payments made by charterers of a ship to the crew
regarded as consideration for promise by shipowners to charterers).

7. – FORBEARANCE TO SUE

(c) *Invalid or doubtful claims*

Claims which are doubtful or not known to be invalid

3–042   *[Add to note 22: page* [192]]
Colonia Versicherung A.G. v. Amoco Oil Co. [1995] 1 Lloyd's Rep. 570,
577 (affd. without reference to this point [1997] 1 Lloyd's Rep. 261).

    [Add to note 24: page [193]]
Freedman v. Union Group plc [1997] E.G.C.S. 28.

3–043   *[In line 11, after mistake, add new reference: page* [193]]
NOTE 28a: *cf. Grains & Fourrages S.A. v. Huyton* [1997] 1 Lloyd's Rep. 628, where
parties agreed to correct quality certificates believed to contain one mistake but in
fact containing a fundamentally different one and the resulting agreement was held
to be void. It was not a true compromise since both parties were in agreement as to
the result which they wished to achieve; their mistake lay in the steps taken to achieve
it.

8. – EXISTING DUTIES AS CONSIDERATION

(b) *Duty Imposed by Contract with Promisor*

Factual benefit to promisor

3–053   *[Add note 67: page* [199]]
Hird and Blair [1996] J.B.L. 254.

Other consideration

3–054   *[Add to note 76: page* [200]]
For formal requirements for "crew agreements", see now Merchant
Shipping Act 1995, s.25.

(c) *Contractual Duty owed to a Third Party*

Performance of the duty

3–056   *[Add to note 99, end of line 5: page* [203]]
The Mahkutai [1996] A.C. 650, 664.

9. – DISCHARGE AND VARIATION OF CONTRACTUAL DUTIES

(b) *Variation*

Agreements to vary contracts

[*Add after note 24 in text: page* [207]]   3–062
In *Burrows v. Brent London Borough Council*[24a] it was held that a
landlord's promise not to enforce a possession order against a secure tenant
if the tenant paid off her arrears of rent did not give rise to a new tenancy as it
was not intended by the parties to have this effect.[24b] It was said that the
effect intended by the parties was "that upon the tenant complying with the
intended conditions, the landlords will forbear from enforcing the order."[24c]
In substance this would amount to a variation of the original contract by
allowing late payment, and such a variation would prima facie be unsupported by consideration as it could benefit only the tenant. But the question
of consideration was not discussed, presumably because the landlord made
no attempt to enforce the agreement and the tenant, having failed to
perform the "conditions," was not entitled to do so.

[24a] [1996] 1 W.L.R. 1448.

[24b] *ante*, §2–117.

[24c] [1996] 1 W.L.R. 1448, 1455.

Waiver or forebearance at common law

[*Add to note 34: page* [208]]   3–063
Similarly, "waiver" is used in *Royal Boskalis Westminster NV v. Mountain*
[1997] 2 All E.R. 929 to refer to a variation which would have been
contractually binding if it had not been vitiated by duress and illegality. Only
Phillips L.J. took the view that the agreement "was not a contract under
which meaningful consideration moved from both sides;" but "meaningful"
here seems to mean no more than "adequate." For the effects of duress in
the present context, *cf.* Main Work §§3–052, 3–073, 3–086.

Relationships within the doctrine

[*Add to note 48: page* [211]]   3–067
The Stolt Loyalty has been affirmed, but without reference to the point
under discussion in the text: [1995] 1 Lloyd's Rep. 599.

Promise or representation

[*Add to note 76: page* [214]]   3–069
The Stolt Loyalty has been affirmed, without reference to the point here
under discussion: [1995] 1 Lloyd's Rep. 599. See also the reference in

Petrotrade Inc. v. Stinnes Handel G.m.b.H. [1995] 1 Lloyd's Rep. 142, 151 to representations by "conduct (including silence)"—evidently referring to the exceptional situations referred to in the text.

Reliance

3–070   [*Add to note 78*]
The Nerano [1996] 1 Lloyd's Rep. 1, 6.

3–071   [*Note 87: page* [215]]
cf. Transatlantica de Commercio S.A. v. Incrobasa Industrial e Commercial Brazileira S.A. [1995] 1 Lloyd's Rep. 215, 219 (discussion of waiver both in the sense here under discussion and in the sense of election between remedies).

In *Southwark L.B.C. v. Logan* [1996] 10 C.L. 292, there was said to be no "detriment" to the alleged promisee and nothing "inequitable" in the alleged promisor's enforcement of its strict legal rights.

Suspensive effect of the doctrine

3–073   [*Add to text after paragraph: page* [216]]
The reason for the general rule that, in equity, the effect of the representation is only suspensive, is that the equitable doctrine gives the court a discretion to do what is equitable in all the circumstances: *Roebuck v. Mungovin.*[95a] In cases such as *Hughes v. Metropolitan Ry.*[95b] it would be neither equitable nor in accordance with the intention of the parties to treat the promisor's rights as having been wholly extinguished. The same is true of cases such as *Tool Metal Manufacturing Co. Ltd v. Tungsten Electric Co. Ltd*[95c] (Main Work, §3–099) and *Ajayi v. R.T. Briscoe (Nig.) Ltd*[95d] (*ibid.*, §3–098).

[95a] [1994] A.C. 224, 234.

[95b] (1877) 2 App.Cas. 439.

[95c] [1955] 1 W.L.R. 761.

[95d] [1964] 1 W.L.R. 1326.

Analogy with estoppel

3–077   [*Add to note 23 at line 1: page* [220]]
cf. Halliwell 5 L.S. 15.

[*Add to note 24 at line 10*]
Roebuck v. Mungovin [1994] 2 A.C. 224, 235.

[*Note 28*]
cf. the statement by Millett L.J. in *First National Bank plc v. Thompson* [1996] Ch. 231, 236 that the "attempt ... to demonstrate that all estoppels other than estoppel by record are now subsumed in the single and all-embracing estoppel by representation and that they are all governed by the same principle" has "never won general acceptance".

Analogy with waiver

[*Add to note 34, line 14, after "Ch. 232, 253": page* [222]]   **3–078**
Pearl Carriers Inc. v. Japan Line Ltd (The Chemical Venture) [1993] 1 Lloyd's Rep. 509, 521.

[*Add to note 34, at end*]
The reference in *Union Eagle Ltd v. Golden Achievement Ltd* [1997] 2 All E.R. 215, 218 to "waiver or estoppel" is likewise to election between remedies rather than to the relinquishing of rights under discussion in the present Chapter.

[*Note 36*]
For the view that "in this context ... waiver or estoppel are really the same thing" see also *The Nerano* [1996] 1 Lloyd's Rep. 1, 6.

Distinguished from estoppel by convention

[*Note 41: page* [223]]   **3–080**
cf. the dictum of Millett L.J. in *First National Bank plc v. Thompson* [1996] Ch. 231, 236, quoted in §3–077, note 28 *ante*.

[*Note 40*]
For the requirement that it must be unjust (or "unconscionable") for the party alleged to be estopped to rely on the true facts, see *Crédit Suisse v. Borough Council of Allerdale* [1995] 1 Lloyd's Rep. 315, 367–370 (where this requirement was not satisfied); affd. on other grounds [1996] 2 Lloyd's Rep. 241.

Requirements of estoppel by convention

[*Note 50: page* [224]]   **3–081**
See also *Crédit Suisse v. Borough Council of Allerdale* [1995] 1 Lloyd's Rep. 315, 367 (where the requirement that the conduct of the party alleged to be estopped must have "influenced the mind" of the other party was not satisfied); affd. on other grounds [1996] 2 Lloyd's Rep. 241.

[*Add after note 52 in text*]
Nor does estoppel by convention arise merely because one party to negotiations knows of a mistaken assumption made by the other. In

Republic of India v. Indian Steamship Co. (The Indian Endurance) (No. 2)[52a]
the Court of Appeal accordingly held that no estoppel by convention
operated against the defendants, even if they had such knowledge. There
was an additional requirement of conduct by both parties, or of agreement,
based on a common assumption;[52b] and this was not satisfied because the
Court could not "find that [the defendants] ever agreed to [the assumption
made by the plaintiffs] or that there was any mutually manifest conduct
which was based on a common assumption, *i.e.* one held by both parties."[52c]

[52a] [1996] 3 All E.R. 641.

[52b] *K. Lokumal & Sons (London) Ltd v. Lotte Shipping Co. Ltd (The August P.
Leonhardt)* [1985] 2 Lloyd's Rep. 28, 35.

[52c] *The Indian Endurance (No. 2)*, *supra*. n. 52a at p. 653.

Whether estoppel by convention creates new rights

3–083   *[Add to note 65: page* [226]*]*
In *Wilson Bowden Properties Ltd v. Milner and Bardon 22 Ltd* [1996] 4
C.L. 182 estoppel by convention precluded the vendor of land from denying
that a disputed strip of land was included in contract of sale. The purchaser
was held entitled to damages, but the cause of action arose out of the
contract (about the existence of which there was no dispute) rather than out
of the estoppel.

[Add to note 66]
cf. also *Mitsui Babcock Energy Ltd v. John Brown Energy Ltd* (1996) 51
Const. L.R. 129, 185–186 where the actual decision was that a contract *had*
been concluded, but the effect of estoppel (if no contract had been found to
exist) would have been to hold the plaintiff to the payment term of the
contract which he would have been precluded from denying, instead of
claiming a reasonable remuneration.

[Add to note 67: page [226]*]*
cf. Russell Brothers (Paddington) Ltd v. John Elliott Management Ltd
(1995) 11 Const. L.J. 377, rejecting the view that estoppel by convention
could be used as a sword.

Invalidity of assumed term

3–084   *[Add to note 71: page* [227]*]*
Godden v. Merthyr Tydfil Housing Association [1997] 4 C.L. 580 (where
the source of invalidity was Law of Property (Miscellaneous Provisions) Act
1989 s.2).

10. – Part Payment of a Debt

(a) *General Rule*

General rule at common law

[*Add to note 75: page* [227]]   **3–085**
The general rule is recognised in *Johnson v. Davies* [1997] 1 All E.R. 921,
926, where the actual decision was based on Insolvency Act 1986 s.260, *post*
§3–094 note 8.

Effects of the rule

[*Amend note 87a: page* [229]]   **3–086**
Re Selectmove is now reported in [1995] 1 W.L.R. 474.

(b) *Limitations at Common Law*

Disputed claims

[*Add at end: page* [229]]   **3–087**
In *Ferguson v. Davies*[90a] a defendant in legal proceedings, from whom
£486.50 had been claimed, admitted liability for £150 and paid this amount.
The plaintiff then amended his claim to an amount in excess of £486.50 and
the defendant argued that the claim was barred by the payment of the £150.
The argument was rejected by Evans L.J. on the ground that, on the true
construction of the documents, there had been no agreement that acceptance of the £150 should be regarded as full settlement of the plaintiff's claim;
and by Henry L.J. on the ground that there was "no consideration for the
accord suggested"[90b] since the case fell within the rule in *Foakes v. Beer*.[90c]
Aldous L.J. agreed with both the other judgments, so that the case supports
the view that, where a claim is partly disputed and partly undisputed,
payment of the undisputed part cannot constitute consideration for a
promise to accept that payment in full settlement of the whole claim.[90d]

[90a] [1997] 1 All E.R. 315.

[90b] *ibid.* p. 329.

[90c] (1884) 9 App. Cas. 605; see Main Work §3–085.

[90d] *cf.* Main Work §3–090.

Composition with creditors

[*Add to note 8, last line, after "meeting": page* [232]]   **3–094**
see *Re Cancol Ltd* [1996] 1 All E.R. 37.

[49]

[*Add to note 8: page* [232]]
The view that an individual voluntary agreement with creditors under
Insolvency Act 1986 s.260 operates merely by statute and not by way of
contract is supported by *Johnson v. Davies* [1997] 1 All E.R. 921. The legal
consequences of such an agreement are therefore governed by the statute
above; in particular, the agreement does not discharge the debt so that
co-debtors of the insolvent debtor are not released.

(c) *Limitations in Equity*

Inequitable

3–104   Another factor making it not "inequitable" for the promisor to go back on
his promise is the promisee's failure fully to perform his promise of part
payment.[a]

[a] *Re Selectmove* [1995] 1 W.L.R. 474.

11. – PROPRIETARY ESTOPPEL

(a) *Nature of the doctrine*

Introductory

3–105   [*Add to note 71: page* [239]]
cf. Midland Bank plc v. Cooke [1995] 4 All E.R. 564, 573 ("equities in the
nature of an estoppel").

[*Add to end of note 71*]
Smith in (ed. Rose) *Consensus ad Idem: Essays in the Law of Contract in
Honour of Guenter Treitel*, p. 235 (1996).

(b) *Bases of Liability*

Expenditure on another's land in reliance on a promise

3–107   [*Add to note 86: page* [240]]
Lloyds Bank v. Carrick [1996] 4 All E.R. 632, 640.

Alternative explanation: contract

3–109   [*Note 95: page* [242]]
There is no scope for proprietary estoppel where there is already a trust
arising out of an enforceable contract for the sale of the land in question: see
Lloyds Bank plc v. Carrick [1996] 4 All E.R. 630.

(c) *Conditions giving rise to liability*

Kinds of promise capable of giving rise to proprietary estoppel

[*Add to note 11: page* [244]]   **3–110**
In *Lloyds Bank v. Carrick* [1996] 4 All E.R. 632 the purchaser of a
leasehold maisonette sought to rely on proprietary estoppel against a bank
to which the vendor had (after the sale) charged the property. The contract
of sale was void for non-registration against the bank and the argument that
proprietary estoppel arose by virtue of the purchaser's expenditure on
outgoings was rejected on the ground (inter alia) that, by virtue of the
contract of sale, the purchaser had become owner of the property (the
vendor being in the position of a bare trustee after payment of the purchase
money) and so the purchaser had incurred expenditure only on her *own*
property.

(d) *Effects of the Doctrine*

Remedy

[*Add at end*]   **3–117**
Conversely, the Court may deny a remedy to the promisee where, on
balance, giving effect to the promise would produce greater injustice than
allowing the promisor to go back on it. This was the position in *Sledmore v.
Dalby*[51a] where the promisee had contributed to major improvements to the
promisor's premises but had already enjoyed 20 years' rent-free occupation
and was at the time of the proceedings gainfully employed, while the
promisor was a widow living on social security benefits. The promisee's
claim for a licence for life to live in the house was accordingly rejected and
the promisor was held to be entitled to possession.

[51a] (1996) 72 P. & C.R. 196.

(e) *Comparison with Other Doctrines*

Proprietary and promissory estoppels

[*Note 88: page* [252]]   **3–121**
cf. the dictum of Millett L.J. in *First National Bank plc v. Thompson* [1996]
Ch. 231, 236, quoted in §3–077 n. 28 *ante*.

12. – Special Cases

Exceptions

[*Add to note 39: page* [258]]   **3–129**
cf. *County Ltd v. Girozentrale Securities* [1996] 3 All E.R. 834, 837: an
"indicative commitment" to take up new shares in a company was described

as "an offer to subscribe" which was not legally binding but was regarded by City convention as binding in honour unless unforeseen exceptional circumstances intervened. It seems that the "commitment" was here given, not to the company, but by prospective investors to each other. Hence the case did not fall within the principles discussed in §2–014 of the Main Work.

Gratuitous services

3–134   *[Add to note 65: page* [261]]
Contrast *Henderson v. Merrett Syndicates Ltd* [1995] 2 A.C. 145, 181, suggesting that there may be no liability in respect of services rendered on "an informal occasion".

[Add to note 66]
White v. Jones has been affirmed by the House of Lords, where liability in tort for pure omissions was recognised in circumstances in which there was a "duty to act": [1995] 2 A.C. 207, 268, 295; *post* §18–017. But it is submitted that such a duty would not be imposed by a purely gratuitous promise.

FORM

1. – IN GENERAL

Types of formal requirement

[Add to text at end of paragraph: page [264]]   **4–002**

A further type of formal requirement may be found in the "Timeshare Directive" which requires that those offering timeshare rights in respect of immovable property inform their would-be customers in writing of various matters relating to the contract, such as the services to which the customer would have access and the exact period for which the customer's rights may be exercised (Directive 94/47 on the protection of purchasers in respect of certain aspects relating to the purchase of the right to use immovable properties on a timeshare basis, art. 4 and Annex). Failure to comply with these requirements leads to a right in any customer entering such a contract to cancel it within three months of its being made: *ibid.* art. 5.1. (This directive therefore goes considerably further than the Timeshare Act 1992.)

The form of a contract may also affect the regulation which it attracts, rather than going to its validity. Thus, for example, the scheme of rules governing "construction contracts" under Part II of the Housing Grants, Construction and Regeneration Act 1996 applies only "where the construction contract is in writing", any other agreement between the parties being "effective for the purposes of this Part only if in writing".[10a]

[10a] Housing Grants, Construction and Regeneration Act 1996, s.107 (which defines what is meant by agreement in writing for this purpose).

2. – CONTRACTS FOR THE SALE OR OTHER DISPOSITION OF AN INTEREST IN LAND

Legislative history

4–004   [*Add to text at end of paragraph: page* [265]]
However, the old law may not always be appropriate for use in interpreting the new. As Peter Gibson L.J. observed in *Firstpost Homes Ltd v. Johnson*[20a] "the Act of 1989 seems to me to have a new and different philosophy from that which the Statute of Frauds 1677 and section 40 of the Act of 1925 had. Oral contracts are no longer permitted. To my mind it is clear that Parliament intended that questions as to whether there was a contract, and what were the terms of the contract, should be readily ascertained by looking at the single document said to constitute the contract." Peter Gibson L.J., with whom Hutchison and Balcombe L.JJ. concurred, therefore rejected as inapplicable old authorities which gave to the term "signature" an artificial meaning.[20b]

[20a] [1995] 1 W.L.R. 1567 at p. 1576 and see *McCausland v. Duncan Lawrie Ltd* [1996] 4 All E.R. 1995, 1001.

[20b] [1995] 1 W.L.R. 1567 at 1575–1577.

(a) *The Old Law: Contracts made on or before September 26, 1989*

(i) *Contracts within section 40 of the Law of Property Act 1925*

4–007   [*Insert new paragraph: page* [268]]
4–007A   **Variation**. In *Morall v. Krause*[47c] the Court of Appeal held that any variation of a contract for the sale or other disposition of land must also satisfy the formal requirements of section 40 of the Law of Property Act 1925. In the absence of either a written memorandum or of part performance, any oral variation of such a contract can have no effect.

[47c] [1994] E.G.C.S. 177.

(iii) *The Effect of Failure to Comply with the Formal Requirements*

Acts by the person seeking to enforce the contract

4–033   [*Add to text at end of paragraph: page* [279]]
However, in *United Bank of Kuwait plc v. Sahib* [1995] 2 W.L.R. 94, 108, 110 the court accepted that, by way of exception to this rule, a deposit of deeds with the intention of creating an equitable mortgage avoids the need to satisfy the formal requirements of section 40, even though the deposit

(and therefore the act of part performance) is made by the mortgagor and therefore not by the person seeking to enforce the contract.

[*Add to note 90: page* [281]]   **4–035**
Lloyds Bank plc v. Carrick, The Times, March 13, 1996.

  (b) *The New Law: Contracts made on or after September 27, 1989*

Law of Property (Miscellaneous Provisions) Act 1989, s.2.

[*Add new reference at end of paragraph: page* [283]]   **4–039**

NOTE 18a: This paragraph of §4–039 on page [283] was quoted with approval by Simon Brown L.J. in *Godden v. Merthyr Tydfil Housing Association* [1997] 1 N.P.C. 1.

[*Insert new paragraph: page* [283]]
Agreements made "subject to contract". In *Enfield L.B.C. v. Arajah*[18a]   **4–039A**
the Court of Appeal held that, quite apart from the question whether the formal requirements contained in section 2 of the 1989 Act had been satisfied, a letter which was headed "subject to contract" and which was relied on by a tenant as creating a new tenancy, clearly envisaged that a new lease would be completed before the parties were bound, with the result that, while this qualification was in force, the relationship did not become binding on either party unless and until there was an exchange of lease and counterpart.

[18a] [1995] E.G.C.S. 164.

  (i) *Contracts within section 2 of the Law of Property (Miscellaneous)
Provisions) Act 1989*

General

[*Add to note 22: page* [283]]   **4–040**
cf. Simmons v. Simmons, FAFMF 95/0485/F, [1996] 5 C.L. 225, in which the Court of Appeal held that an agreement which compromised an action arising out of claims for land by Mrs Simmons, the cohabitant of the other party, Mr Simmons, was not a contract for the disposition of land, but rather related to accounting for the proceeds of sale of the properties.

[*Add to text at end of paragraph*]
In *Singh v. Beggs*[23a] it was held that section 2 of the Law of Property (Miscellaneous Provisions) Act 1989 applies equally to an executory agreement, that is in this context, an agreement which was made at a time when neither of its parties possessed any proprietary interest in the property in question.

[23a] (1996) 71 P. & C.R. 120.

[*Insert new paragraph: page* [283]]

4–040A　　**Variation.** In *Morall v. Krause*,[23b] which was decided under the old law, the Court of Appeal held that any variation of a contract for the sale or other disposition of land must also satisfy the formal requirements of section 40 of the Law of Property Act 1925.

In *McCausland v. Duncan Lawrie Ltd*[23c] the Court of Appeal had to decide whether and if so how section 2 of the Law of Property (Miscellaneous Provisions) Act 1989 applied to variations of contracts within its purview. In that case, the defendant bank contracted with the plaintiff in signed writing to sell a particular property, but on discovering that the date which they had set for completion was a Sunday, the parties agreed by letter to advance the completion date to the previous Friday. On the plaintiff purchaser's failure to place the full purchase price in the vendor's hands on this date as varied, the vendor first gave notice to complete and later gave notice to rescind the contract, purportedly acting under the terms of the contract and based on the purchaser's failure to pay over the price. Later, however, the purchaser sued for specific performance of the original contract of sale, alleging that there had been no effective variation and therefore no valid rescission of the sale. The vendor bank failed to have this claim struck out as the Court of Appeal held that variations of contracts of sale, etc. of an interest in land also have to fulfill the formal requirements contained in section 2 of the 1989 Act. This means that the contract as varied has to be in writing and incorporated in one document, or each document if contracts were exchanged, and signed by or on behalf of each party to the contract.[23d] Morritt L.J. stated:

> the formalities prescribed by s.2 [of the 1989 Act] must be observed in order to effect a variation of a term material to the contract for the sale or other disposition of an interest in land but are not required for a variation which is immaterial in that respect.[23e]

On the facts of *McCausland*, the variation was held to be material as it attempted to advance the contractual date for completion and therefore the time when either party might make time of the essence by service of a notice to complete.

[23b] [1994] E.G.C.S. 177.

[23c] [1996] 4 All E.R. 995.

[23d] The Court of Appeal thereby followed the approach of the House of Lords in *Morris v. Baron & Co* [1918] A.C. 1, 31 and 39 and Willes J. in *Noble v. Ward* (1867) L.R. 2 Ex. 135, 137, though in relation to different formal requirements.

[23e] [1996] 4 All E.R. 995, 1006.

Equitable Mortgages

[*Delete first sentence and note 28 and substitute: page* [284]] **4–042**
In *United Bank of Kuwait plc v. Sahib*,[28] the Court of Appeal, affirming the
decision of Chadwick J.,[28a] held that equitable mortgages or charges arising
out of a deposit of documents of title found their basis in an implied contract
and that such a contract could only exist if the rigorous formal requirements
of section 2 of the Law of Property (Miscellaneous Provisions) Act 1989 are
satisfied.

[28] [1996] 3 All E.R. 215.

[28a] reported at [1995] 2 W.L.R. 94.

[*Delete the last sentence and Note 35*]

[*Insert new paragraph: page* [285]] **4–044**
Compromises. In *Payne v. Zafiropoyloy*[42a] the Eastbourne County Court **4–044A**
held that a compromise of a dispute over the parties' respective interests in a
property which were the subject of legal proceedings did not constitute a
contract for the sale or other disposition of an interest in land for the
purposes of section 2 of the Law of Property (Miscellaneous Provisions) Act
1989.

[42a] [1994] C.L.Y. 3513.

Composite agreements

[*Add to note 43: page* [285]] **4–045**
See also *Simmons v. Simmons*, FAFMF 95/0485/F, [1996] 5 C.L. 225.

[*Add text after note 44: page* [285]]
On the other hand, in *Godden v. Merthyr Tydfil Housing Association*[44a]
the Court of Appeal rejected counsel's argument that the parties' agreement
could be divided in this type of way. According to Simon Brown L.J.,

> The reality here is that ... there was in this case but one single unified
> agreement—an agreement under which the defendants undertook to
> purchase from the plaintiff land which in the first place he was to
> acquire, prepare and develop to their order. It seems to me entirely
> unreal to attempt to separate that out into two discrete, or even distinct,
> agreements—one involving the disposition of land, the other not.
> Rather, all the obligations between the parties were integral to each
> other, part and parcel of a single scheme.[44b]

Given that it was central to the entire scheme that the plaintiff transfer land to the defendants and given that no part of the parties' agreement was in writing, the agreement certainly failed to comply with the formalities imposed by section 2 of the 1989 Act.

[44a] [1997] 1 N.P.C. 1 (Lexis transcript used).

[44b] Lexis transcript, p. 7.

Excluded contracts

4–046   [*Insert at end of paragraph: page* [286]]
A further type of contract which has subsequently been excluded from the requirements of form imposed by section 2 of the Law of Property (Miscellaneous Provisions) Act 1989 are *variations* of "development agreements" within the meaning of the Channel Tunnel Rail Link Act 1996, *i.e.* agreements "to which the Secretary of State is a party and under which another party has responsibilities in relation to the design, construction, financing or maintenance of the rail link" with which the 1996 Act is concerned.[47a]

[47a] Channel Tunnel Rail Link Act 1996, ss.41(1) and 56(1).

(ii) *Formal Requirements*

"Made in writing"

4–047   [*Insert new heading to second paragraph beginning "At first sight": page* [286]]

"All the terms which the parties have expressly agreed in one document" and rectification

4–047A   [*Insert new text at end of second paragraph*]
In *Firstpost Homes Ltd v. Johnson*[50a] an owner of certain farm property had agreed orally with a director of the plaintiff company to sell the property to the company at a cost of £1,000 per acre. The director had then had typed a letter purporting to come from the owner agreeing to sell the land at this price, with a place for her signature and with an enclosed plan, which showed the land in question outlined in colour and which was signed by the director. The Court of Appeal affirmed the judgment below striking out the plaintiff's claim for specific performance of a contract to sell the land brought against the deceased owner's personal representatives on the basis that the requirements of section 2 of the Law of Property (Miscellaneous Provisions) Act 1989 had not been fulfilled. The court held, first, that the letter and the plan constituted *two* documents, the former referring to the latter as being enclosed with it, but the letter (which allegedly contained the contract) had

not been signed by the director on the behalf of the plaintiffs as was required by section 2 (and see *post*, §4–048). It also held that, quite apart from the lack of the plaintiffs' agent's signature, the letter did not contain a contract at all: "[a] contract must contain mutual obligations and a commitment by each party",[50b] whereas the letter contained no commitment by the plaintiffs to purchase the property. In this respect, however, Peter Gibson and Balcombe L.JJ. noted that there would have been the possibility of the plaintiffs' applying to the court to rectify the letter so as to reflect the oral agreement under which they had agreed to buy the property in question,[50c] a power which section 2(4) of the 1989 Act expressly recognises.

In *Robert Leonard (Developments) Ltd v. Wright*,[50d] this question of the relationship of the requirement in section 2(1) of the 1989 Act that all the terms of a contract for the sale or other disposition of an interest in land and the Act's recognition in section 2(4) of the court's power of rectification came squarely before the Court of Appeal. The court below had held that the plaintiff had made an oral agreement with the defendant under which the latter agreed to convey to her a leasehold interest in a flat owned by it and to sell to her various chattels then furnishing the flat, an arrangement which it considered to be one single agreement. However, the terms of the contract contained in the documents which the parties' solicitors exchanged by telephone made no reference to the sale of the chattels and the defendant later removed them from the flat before completion and the plaintiff entering possession. Prima facie, therefore, the formal requirements of section 2 of the 1989 Act had not been met by the exchange of documents: they did not contain *all* the terms of the previous oral contract as the terms relating to the chattels were not included. The trial judge avoided this difficulty, which would have rendered the whole contract (including any obligation to sell the chattels) a nullity, by treating the disposition of the interest in land as one contract (contained in a signed writing) and the agreement as to the chattels as another, collateral contract which, not being for the sale of an interest in land, could stand even though orally made (and see §4–045 of the Main Work). However, the Court of Appeal disagreed, holding that the parties' single oral agreement could not be split in this way. Instead, it considered that it was (on the plaintiff's application) entitled to order the rectification of the formal contract so as to include all the terms of the oral agreement and thereby satisfy the requirement of section 2(1) of the 1989 Act. In this respect, the Court of Appeal recognised that allowing rectification is contrary to the legislative purpose of section 2 which was to prevent disputes either as to whether the parties had entered into a binding agreement or as to what terms they had agreed; but it noted that section 2(4) plainly recognised the availability of rectification and considered that it would be unjust if this remedy were unavailable.[50e] As Henry L.J. observed, having looked at the relevant passages in the Law Commission's report,[50f] "it was clearly the intention of the Act that the all terms requirement should not be so inflexible as to cause hardship or unfairness where there has been a mistake resulting in a venial non-compliance with the Act".[50g] The Court of Appeal therefore ordered that the formal contract be rectified so as to include reference to the sale of the chattels and further held, in exercise of its power under subsection (4) of section 2 of the 1989 Act, that this rectified contract should be deemed to have come into being from the date of the exchange of documents. By contrast, in the later case of *Enfield L.B.C. v. Arajah*,[50h] the Court of Appeal held that an agreement by a landlord to enter a new lease had failed to satisfy section 2's formal requirements as it did not contain all, but only the main terms which had been agreed. From the brief report, it would appear, however, that the possibility of rectification was not raised before the court.

4–047B **"Exchange of contracts."** In *Commission for the New Towns v. Cooper (Great Britain) Ltd*,[50i] the Court of Appeal explained the significance of the alternative formal requirement in section 2 of the Law of Property (Miscellaneous Provisions) Act 1989 that all the terms of the contract which the parties have expressly agreed be incorporated "where contracts are exchanged, in each [document]". According to Stuart-Smith L.J.[50j] the expression "exchange of contracts", even if not a term of art, possesses the following features.

1. Each party draws up or is given a document which incorporates all the terms which they have agreed, and which is intended to record their proposed contract. The terms that have been agreed may have been agreed either orally or in writing or partly orally or [*sic*: and] partly in writing.
2. The documents are referred to as "contracts" or "parts of contract", although they need not be so entitled. They are intended to take effect as formal documents of title and must be capable on their face of being fairly described as contracts having that effect.
3. Each party signs his part in the expectation that the other party has also executed or will execute a corresponding part incorporating the same terms.
4. At the time of execution neither party is bound by the terms of the document which he has executed, it being their mutual intention that neither will be bound until the executed parts are exchanged.
5. The act of exchange is a formal delivery by each party of its part into the actual or constructive possession of the other with the intention that the parties will become actually bound when exchange occurs, but not before.
6. The manner of exchange may be agreed and determined by the parties. . . .

As a result, the Court of Appeal held (though strictly *obiter*) that this requirement was not satisfied by the mere exchange of a signed letter of offer and a signed letter of acceptance, even if each had contained the (same) express terms of the contract as alleged. In this respect, it rejected the position accepted by a majority of the same court in the earlier unreported decision in *Hooper v. Sherman*,[50k] the court in *Commission for the New Towns v. Cooper (Great Britain) Ltd* finding that the earlier decision could be distinguished on the facts but had anyway been based on a wrong concession by counsel and by reference to a paragraph in the Law Commission report, *Transfer of Land: Formalities for Contracts for Sale, etc. of Land*[50l] which had referred to the draft bill, even though the latter differed significantly from the terms of section 2 as enacted.[50m]

[50a] [1995] 1 W.L.R. 1567.

[50b] *ibid.* at p. 1573, *per* Peter Gibson L.J.

[50c] *ibid.* at pp. 1576, 1577 respectively.

[50d] [1994] N.P.C. 49.

[50e] Lexis transcript, p. 8, *per* Dillon L.J.

[50f] No. 164, *op.cit.*, §5.6.

[50g] Lexis transcript, p. 10.

[50h] [1995] EGCS 164.

[50i] [1995] Ch. 259.

[50j] *ibid.* at p. 285.

[50k] November 30, 1994.

[50l] Law Com. No. 164, §4.15.

[50m] See [1995] Ch. 259, 289, 295.

Signature

[*Add to text at end of paragraph*]   **4–048**
In *Firstpost Homes Ltd v. Johnson*,[52a] the Court of Appeal held that "signature" in section 2 of the Law of Property (Miscellaneous Provisions) Act 1989 should be given its ordinary linguistic meaning, with the result that the section requires that the parties must write their names with their own hands upon the document (adopting a dictum of Denning L.J. in *Goodman v. J. Eban Ltd*[52b]). The court thereby rejected the applicability of earlier authorities on the meaning of "signature" for the purposes of the Statute of Frauds 1677 and section 40 of the Law of Property Act 1925 (notably, *Evans v. Hoare*[52c] which accepted that their requirements might be satisfied in circumstances where a party who is only named as the addressee of a letter prepared by him may be said to have signed it, as long as evidence is adduced that that name is shown to have been written with the intention that the document should be the contract and that it is not apparent from the document that the parties are actually to sign in the conventional sense).[52d] As Balcombe L.J. observed, "the clear policy of [section 2] is to avoid the possibility that one or other party may be able to go behind the document

and introduce extrinsic evidence to establish a contract, which was undoubtedly a problem under the old law".[52e]

On the other hand, in the same case, Peter Gibson L.J. accepted that the principle laid down by the House of Lords in *Caton v. Caton*[52f] in relation to the Statute of Frauds 1677 to the effect that the party's signature must be inserted in such a way as to authenticate the whole instrument (on which see §4–023 of the Main Work) applies equally to the requirement of signature made by section 2 of the 1989 Act. Thus, where a letter in which A agrees to sell a piece of land to B refers to a plan of the land in question and the court considers that the letter and the plans constitute a single document, B's signature of the plan may well not constitute authentication of the whole.[52g]

[52a] [1995] 1 W.L.R. 1567.

[52b] [1954] 1 Q.B. 550, 561.

[52c] [1892] 1 Q.B. 593.

[52d] [1995] 1 W.L.R. 1567, 1574–1577.

[52e] *ibid.* at p. 1577.

[52f] (1867) L.R. 2 H.L. 127.

[52g] [1995] 1 W.L.R. 1567, 1573, though on the facts, the Court of Appeal held that the letter and plan before them constituted *two* documents: see *ante*, §4–047B.

(iii) *The Effect of Failure to Comply with the Formal Requirements*

Effect of non-compliance

4–049　[*Add to text after note 57a: page* [287]]

In *Singh v. Beggs*[57b] Neill L.J. doubted the view of the judge below that section 2 of the Law of Property (Miscellaneous Provisions) Act 1989 had "abolished" the doctrine of part performance. Neill L.J. observed that

> It is true that it is provided by section 2(8) of the 1989 Act, that section 40 of the Law of Property Act 1925 will cease to have effect, the doctrine [of part performance] is an equitable doctrine, and it may be that in certain circumstances the doctrine could be relied on.[57c]

However, on the facts before the Court of Appeal, the doctrine of part performance would not have assisted the party seeking to uphold the contract.

[57b] (1996) 71 P. & C.R. 120.

[57c] *ibid.* at p. 122.

Proprietary estoppel

[*Add to note 70: page* [288]]   4–051
And see *Godden v. Merthyr Tydfil Housing Association*, Lexis transcript, pp. 8–9, *per* Simon Brown L.J. (decision also reported in [1997] 1 N.P.C. 1.)

[*Add to text at end of paragraph: page* [288]]
An example of the application of proprietary estoppel in this context may be found in *Wayling v. Jones*.[71a] In that case, A had promised his companion of some ten years, B, that he would bequeathe B the business in which he worked at very low wages, but died without having done so. The Court of Appeal held that B was entitled to rely on a proprietory estoppel against A's executors and therefore ordered them to pay the proceeds of sale of the business to B. If, by contrast, B had alleged that he had *contracted* with A that the latter would bequeath him the business in return for working for low wages, his claim would have failed for lack of fulfilling the formal requirements in section 2, Law of Property (Miscellaneous Provisions) Act 1989.

[71a] [1995] 2 F.L.R. 1029.

[*Insert new paragraph: page* [288]]   4–051A
Other types of estoppel. In *McCausland v. Duncan Lawrie Ltd*[71b] the question arose whether a seller of property could rely on the "doctrine of estoppel" to give some effect to the agreement underlying a *variation* of a contract for the sale, etc. of an interest in land, the variation itself being void for failing to comply with the formal requirements imposed by section 2 of the Law of Property (Miscellaneous Provisions) Act 1989.[71c] It does not appear from the report of the case which particular doctrine of estoppel was intended, whether promissory estoppel (forbearance in equity) or estoppel by convention, though, as has been noted, no claim for proprietary estoppel could have been relied on by a seller of land as the latter would not be claiming for some right to land.[71d] Neill L.J. considered estoppel to be "plainly arguable" as a defence, but incapable of resolution without evidence and therefore in an application for the plaintiff's claim to be struck out.[71e] Morritt L.J. took the view that the estoppel was not so plain as to warrant a striking out, but added that

> Section 2 does not give rise to any illegality if its terms are not observed and the need for an estoppel arises in just those circumstances where there is no enforceable contract. For my part I would not place weight on the contention that an estoppel such as the vendor would advance is impossible as a matter of law but it still has to be made out as a matter of fact.[71f]

Tucker L.J. agreed.
A very different approach to the application of estoppel (and specifically,

estoppel by convention) in the context of section 2 of the Law of Property (Miscellaneous Provisions) 1989 Act was taken by a differently constituted Court of Appeal in the important decision *Godden v. Merthyr Tydfil Housing Association*[71g]. This case concerned a claim for damages by a building contractor for breach of an oral agreement with the defendant Housing Association, under which he had agreed to purchase a particular site, obtain planning permission for the building of seven houses and prepare the site for development, the defendants agreeing to reimburse him for the costs of this acquisition and work and that they would enter a contract with him for the construction of the houses. It was made clear that it was part of the plaintiff's case that the agreement assumed that he would convey the freehold of the property to the defendants. The defendants applied for the action to be struck out as the agreement between the parties fell foul of the formal requirements of section 2 of 1989 Act and it was this claim which came before the Court of Appeal.

Simon Brown L.J., with whom Thorpe L.J. and Sir John Balcombe agreed, considered that the plaintiff's argument that he could rely on the doctrine of estoppel by convention was "superficially more promising" than his argument based on the composite nature of the parties' agreement (on which see *ante*, pp. 57–58). As to this type of estoppel, the plaintiff argued that both parties contracted in ignorance of the provisions of the Act, and therefore that the defendants were precluded from relying on those provisions so as to deny that there was indeed an agreement reached between the parties.[71h] According to Simon Brown L.J.

> This is a clear enough submission, but it necessarily involves saying that, although Parliament has dictated that a contract involving the disposition of land made otherwise than in compliance with s.2 is void, the defendants are not allowed to say so. That, to my mind, is an impossible argument. ... [I]f it were soundly made, it is difficult to see why it should not operate to escape the intended constraints of s.2 in virtually all cases.[71i]

Having found no special features in the case as presented by the plaintiff, he found "the central objection to this whole line of argument" in a short passage in *Halsbury's Laws of England*, according to which

> The doctrine of estoppel may not be invoked to render valid a transaction which the legislature has, on grounds of general public policy, enacted is to be invalid.[71j]

For Simon Brown L.J., the cases which applied the doctrine of estoppel by convention did not break this "cardinal rule" being concerned rather with situations where the

> parties have, in certain circumstances where the justice of the case requires, been precluded from relying upon this, that or the other

technicality of a quite different character; not, as here, a specific statutory requirement for writing which is, of course, designed to avoid just such a factual dispute as the plaintiff's pleaded case would, if allowed, provoke.[71k]

As Sir John Balcombe added, if the plaintiff's argument from estoppel by convention were accepted, it "would drive a coach and horses through a recent Act of Parliament enacted for very specific reasons of public policy."[71l]

The contrast in approach to the possible application of estoppel in the decisions of the Court of Appeal in *McCausland v. Duncan Lawrie Ltd* and *Godden v. Merthyr Tydfil Housing Association* is striking. According to Morrison J. in *McCausland* section 2 of the 1989 Act does not concern "illegality" and therefore estoppel may (on suitable facts) apply; whereas for the court in *Godden*, the nullifying effect of section 2 is very much a matter of public policy. It is to be recalled, however, that the views of the court in *McCausland* were tentatively expressed and in the context of a striking-out claim in *support* of which the estoppel was raised (and which the court was clear could not be made out before trial). Certainly, and with the greatest respect for the views expressed by the members of the Court of Appeal in *McCausland*, even if the constituent elements of estoppel *by convention* had been made out on the facts, the force of the position taken by the Court of Appeal in *Godden* remains.

The position of the Court of Appeal in *Godden* leaves, of course, the possibility of reliance by the *purchaser*, etc. of an interest in land on the doctrine of proprietary estoppel.[71m] Less clear is the position of an argument based on promissory estoppel (or "forbearance in equity").[71n] If the facts of *Godden* had been somewhat different, for example, if the defendant Housing Association had specifically represented to the plaintiff either that no formalities were required for the type of contract which they entered or that they (the Association) would not in the future rely on the absence of formal requirements which were required, then the case for promissory estoppel would be that much stronger. However, even if the effect of such a promissory estoppel was thought prima facie to preclude the defendants from going back on these statements, it would not surmount the problem for the plaintiff that he would need to sue on a void contract in order to succeed. This last point does not give rise to concern as regards proprietary estoppel, of course, for here a successful claimant of an estoppel may expressly sue on it.[71o]

[71b] [1996] 4 All E.R. 995. On the application of s.2 of the Law of Property (Miscellaneous Provisions) Act 1989 to contractual variations, see *ante*, p. 56.

[71c] See *ante*, p. 56.

[71d] See §4–051, Main Work as amended, *ante*, p. 56.

[71e] [1996] 4 All E.R. 995 at 1005.

[71f] *ibid.* at p. 1007.

[71g] Lexis transcript used, though reported in [1997] 1 N.P.C. 1.

[71h] On estoppel by convention more generally, see §3–080 ff. of the Main Work.

[71i] Lexis transcript, p. 10.

[71j] Vol. 16 (4th ed.), §962.

[71k] Lexis transcript, p. 12.

[71l] Lexis transcript, p. 16.

[71m] As the court itself accepted: Lexis transcript, pp. 8–9.

[71n] See generally, §3–065 Main Work.

[71o] See generally, §3–105 ff. Main Work.

CHAPTER 5

MISTAKE

2. – MISTAKE AT COMMON LAW

Generally

[*Note 8: page* [294]]   **5–002**
Update reference to Cheshire, Fifoot and Furmston (12th ed.), pp. 229–230 to (13th ed.), pp. 235–236.

(a) *Mutual Mistake*

Varying interpretations

[*Note 29: page* [297]]   **5–007**
Update reference to Cheshire, Fifoot and Furmston (12th ed.), p. 240 to (13th ed.), p. 246.

Risk

[*Add to note 32*]   **5–008**
Grains & Fourriers SA v. Huyton [1997] 1 Lloyd's Rep. 628.

Existence of the subject-matter of the contract

[*Note 54: page* [300]]   **5–011**
Update reference to Cheshire, Fifoot and Furmston (12th ed.), p. 232 to (13th ed.), pp. 238–239.

Implied condition that exists

5–012   [*Amend note 59: page* [301]]
The reference should now be to Treitel, *the Law of Contract* (9th ed., 1995), pp. 263–264.

[*Amend note 63: page* [302]]
Update the reference to Treitel to (9th ed., 1995), p. 273; and to Atiyah, *Sale of Goods* (9th ed., 1995), pp. 70–71.

Mistake as to quality of subject-matter

5–015   [*Amend note 72: page* [303]]
Update the reference to Treitel to (9th ed., 1995), pp. 268–269.

False and fundamental assumption

5–018   [*Add to note 92: page* [305]]
In *Grains & Fourriers SA v. Huyton* [1997] 1 Lloyd's Rep. 628 the parties believed the results in two certificates of analysis to have been transposed. An agreement to rectify them was void when it was discovered that there had been no transposition, so the rectification would produce the very result it was supposed to avoid.

(b) *Unilateral Mistake*

Mistake known to the other party

5–022   [*Note 11: page* [308]]
Part of the majority judgment in *Taylor v. Johnson* (1983) 45 A.L.R. 265 was adopted by the Court of Appeal in *Commission for New Towns v. Cooper (Great Britain) Ltd* [1995] 2 Ch. 259, a case of rectification, without discussion of the majority's view that a unilateral mistake renders a contract voidable rather than void. See *post*, §5–049.

In *Mannai Investment Co. Ltd v. Eagle Star Life Assurance Co. Ltd* [1997] 2 W.L.R. 945 the House of Lords, reversing the Court of Appeal [1995] 1 W.L.R. 1508, held that a contractual notice to determine a lease was effective although it did not comply exactly with the break clause in the contract, provided that the notice given would convey the lesee's intention to exercise its rights under the clause unambiguously to a reasonable recipient. Under the clause the notice should have expired on the third anniversary of the commencement date of the lease, which would have been

[68]

June 13; the notice purported to determine from June 12. The majority held that the relevant test was whether the intention of the party giving the notice was, in its context, obvious to a reasonable recipient; if it was, it was immaterial that it contained a minor error. To require literal compliance with the clause in all cases would be to confuse the meaning of words with the question of what meaning in the particular setting the use of words was intended to convey, and the notice would be effective if, as here, the reasonable recipient was left in no doubt that the tenant intended to determine the lease and to do so from the date permitted by the clause. The principle was stated (at pp. 962 and 973) to be applicable to contractual notices generally, though a more restricted approach is to be applied to documents such as bankers' commercial credits where the same document might "have different meanings to different people according to their knowledge of the background".

[*Add to note 14: page* [309]]
See also *OT Africa Line Ltd v. Vickers Plc* [1996] 1 Lloyd's Rep. 700, in which Mance J. said that the objective principle would be displaced if a party knew or ought to have known of the mistake. The latter situation would include cases in which the party refrained from making enquiries or failed to make enquiries when these were reasonably called for (see, *post*, §5–049), but first there must be a real reason to suspect a mistake.

Mistake as to the terms of the contract

[*Note 16: page* [309]]   **5–023**
In *G & S Fashions v. B & Q* [1995] 1 W.L.R. 1088 it was held that, if a landlord purports to forfeit a lease in the mistaken belief that the tenant is in breach of covenant, the fact that the tenant knows of the landlord's mistake does not prevent it accepting the forfeiture.

Effect of mistake as to terms

[*Amend note 21: page* [310]]   **5–024**
Update the reference to Treitel to (9th ed., 1995), pp. 285–286.

[*Add at end of paragraph*]
If one party knows the other has made a mistake and fails to point it out when the reasonable person would expect him to do so were he acting honestly and reasonably, an estoppel by silence or acquiescence may arise and result in liability where there would otherwise be none.[22a]

[22a] *Pacol Ltd v. Trade Lines Ltd, The Henryk Sif* [1982] 1 Lloyd's Rep. 456, 465; *The*

Stolt Loyalty [1993] 2 Lloyd's Rep. 281, 290; *Republic of India v. Indian Steamship Co., The Indian Grace (No. 2)* [1994] 2 Lloyd's Rep. 331, 344). See, *ante*, §2–048.

Mistake must be as to identity

5–026   [*Amend note 34: page* [312]]
Update the reference to Treitel to (9th ed., 1995), p. 278.

(c) *Non est Factum*

Distinction between nature and contents of document

5–034   [*Add to note 63: page* [316]]
cf. *Hambros Bank Ltd v. British Historic Buildings Trust and Din* [1995] N.P.C. 179.

Negligence

5–036   [*Add to note 71: page* [317]]
Negligence was one ground for failure of the plea in *Hambros Bank Ltd v. British Historic Building Trust and Din* [1995] N.P.C. 179.

3. – MISTAKE IN EQUITY

(b) *Rectification of Written Agreements*

Common mistake

5–041   [*Replace last sentence of note 94: page* [320]]
Provided that there is an issue capable of being contested by the parties it is no bar to rectification that both sides wish the document to be rectified so as to reduce ones party's tax liability; *Lake v. Lake* [1989] S.T.C. 895; *Racal Group Services v. Ashmore* [1995] S.T.C. 1151.

Parol Evidence

5–043   [*Add to note 1: page* [320]]
In *J.J. Huber (Investments) Ltd v. Private DIY Co. Ltd* [1995] N.P.C. 102, (ChD) it was held that the presence on an "entire agreement" clause in the contract does not prevent rectification.

Concluded agreement

[*Add to note 11: page* [322]]   **5–044**
No prior agreement was shown in *Mangistaumunaigaz Oil Production
Association v. United World Trading Inc.* [1995] 1 Lloyd's Rep. 617 and
rectification was refused.

Unilateral mistake

The full report of *Commission for New Towns v. Cooper (Great Britain)* **5–049**
Ltd[a] shows, first, that the court will be prepared to find that a party had actual
knowledge of a mistake when it wilfully shuts its eyes to the obvious, or
wilfully and recklessly fails to make such inquiries as an honest and
reasonable man would make. It applied the analysis of various forms of
knowledge made by Peter Gibson J. in *Baden v. Société Générale pour
Favouriser le Développement du Commerce et de l'Industrie en France SA*[b]
and adopted by Millett J. in *Agip (Africa) Ltd v. Jackson.*[c] According to this
analysis, those types of knowledge would count as actual, whereas "knowledge of circumstances which would indicate the facts to an honest and
reasonable man" or "knowledge of facts which would put an honest man on
inquiry" would constitute constructive notice only—though Millett J.[d]
warned against "a too ready assumption that [these last cases] are
necessarily cases of constructive notice only. The true distinction is between
honesty and dishonesty."
Secondly, the report shows that the Court of Appeal was prepared if
necessary to hold that actual knowledge by party A of party B's mistake is
not always a prerequisite of B being granted rectification on the ground of a
unilateral mistake. If A intends B to be mistaken as to the terms of the
agreement, so conducts himself that he diverts B's attention from discovering the mistake and B in fact makes the very mistake that A intends,
rectification to bring the document into accordance with B's understanding
may be granted without proof of actual knowledge on A's part or of
misrepresentation by A. In the Australian case of *Taylor v. Johnson*[e] the
High Court had held that this sort of unconscionable conduct on A's part
would suffice for the contract to be rescinded on the ground of mistake (see
ante, §5–022). The same principle does not necessarily apply to cases of
rectification, since the court is not simply undoing the bargain but also
imposing a different bargain on A. However, it is not unjust to insist that the
contract be performed according to B's understanding where that was the
very meaning that A intended B to put on it, and rectification may be
granted.

[a] [1995] 2 Ch. 259.

[b] [1993] 1 W.L.R. 509.

^c [1990] Ch. 265.

^d at p. 293.

^e (1983) 45 A.L.R. 265.

(c) *Rescission*

Unilateral mistake

5–065   In the Australian case of *Taylor v. Johnson*^a the High Court adopted the view that a unilateral mistake by one party as to the terms of a contract will, if the mistake was known to the other, make the contract voidable rather than void. Whether this represents English law is doubtful, though there is something to be said for this approach. See §§5–022 and 5–024 of the main work and, in this Supplement, §5–022, *ante*.

^a (1983) 45 A.L.R. 265.

Scope of equitable jurisdiction

5–068   [*Note 5: page* [331]]
Update reference to Atiyah (4th ed.), p. 242 to (5th ed.), p. 226.

MISREPRESENTATION

2. – WHAT CONSTITUTES EFFECTIVE MISREPRESENTATION

Statements of opinion and intention

The third and fourth sentences, beginning "However, in certain ... " (page **6–004**
[335]) were cited with approval in *Economides v. Commercial Union
Assurance Co. plc* [1997] 3 All E.R. 636, 645, 655. In that case it was held that
a statement by an insured, private person with no specialist knowledge, of
the value of the contents of a flat which contained his parents' belongings as
well as his own, did not carry an implication that he had an objectively
reasonable basis for the value stated. Thus a statement of the value which the
insured made honestly was not a misrepresentation even though it was
inaccurate. *Brown v. Raphael* [1958] Ch. 636 was distinguished on the
grounds that the statement in that case the vendors could be expected to
know the facts; *Credit Lyonnais Bank Nederland v. Export Credit Guarantee
Department* [1996] 1 Lloyd's Rep. 200, in which the bank's statement that a
management was "respectable and trustworthy" was held to be a misrepresentation, was distinguished on the ground that this was contrary to the
bank's actual experience of the management. Simon Brown and Peter
Gibson L.JJ. expressed the view that under Marine Insurance Act 1906,
s.20(5), which states that a representation as to a matter of expectation or
belief is true if it be made in good faith, there is no room for such an

implication, doubting a dictum to the contrary by Steyn J. in *Highlands Insurance Co. v. Continental Insurance Co.* [1987] 1 Lloyd's Rep. 109, 112–113. Sir Iain Glidewell preferred to leave the matter open. See further *post*, §§6–006 and 39–028.

[*Add to note 9: page* [335]]
Crédit Lyonnais Bank Nederland v. E.C.G.D. [1996] 1 Lloyd's Rep. 200.

Non-disclosure

6–009   [*Add new reference at end of first paragraph: page* [339]]

NOTE 50a: In certain situations failing to disclose information may be a criminal offence, *e.g.* Timeshare Act 1992, s.1A (inserted by Timeshare Regulations 1997 (S.I. 1997 No. 1081).

Partial non-disclosure

6–012   [*Note 60: page* [341]]
See however *Taittinger v. Allbev* (1993) 12 Tr.L.R. 165, a passing-off case in which it was held that the labelling and "get-up" of a bottle constituted a false representation.

[*Add to note 62*]
It has been said that if a person who has made a representation of fact which, before the contract is made, he discovers to be untrue, he is not fraudulent in failing to correct the representation, as he will not be dishonest: *Thomas Witter Ltd v. T.B.P. Industries Ltd* [1996] 2 All E.R. 573. It is submitted that there may still be fraud if the person knows that he should tell the other party but fails to do so; see (1995) 111 L.Q.R. 385.

The representor

6–014   [*Add to note 80: page* [343]]
For a recent example, see *Williams v. Natural Life Health Foods Ltd*, *The Times*, January 9, 1997.

Constructive notice

6–016   Under the doctrine of *Barclays Bank plc v. O'Brien* [1994] 1 A.C. 180, the creditor is put on enquiry when (a) the transaction is not on its face to the advantage of the wife and (b) there is a substantial risk that the husband has committed a legal or equitable wrong that entitles the wife to set aside the transaction.

(i) *Is the creditor put on enquiry?*

In relation to the first question, the fact that the loan appears to be a joint one to husband and wife may, as in *CIBC Mortgages Ltd v. Pitt*,[a] mean that the creditor is not put on enquiry; but the mere fact that the loan is joint will not have this effect. Thus in *Allied Irish Bank plc v. Byrne*[b] the Bank knew that the loan was primarily for the benefit of the husband and it was made as a joint loan to husband and wife at the Bank's suggestion; the Bank was put on notice. The creditor must look at the substance of the matter so far as it is apparent to the creditor. In *Goode Durant Administration v. Biddulph*[c] a loan was made to a property company, the husband and the wife jointly. The creditor knew that the company was a new vehicle for the business schemes of the husband and that the wife owned only 2.5 per cent of the shares. Again the creditor was put on enquiry. See also *Hill Samuel Bank v. Medway*.[d]

If the loan is on the face of it for the joint benefit of husband and wife, the fact that a solicitor who is acting for both the borrowers and the lender knows that the loan is actually to be used to pay the husband's business debts does not fix the lender with notice of that purpose. The solicitor is under a duty to the borrower not to disclose the relevant facts and, when a conflict of interest emerged he should notify the lender that he can no longer act for it, rather than revealing the information that has come to him as solicitor for the borrower, so his knowledge will not be imputed to the lender: *Halifax Mortgage Services Ltd v. Stepsky*.[e]

(ii) *Reasonable steps*

If the creditor has been put on enquiry, Lord Browne-Wilkinson said in *O'Brien*'s case that the steps which should be taken by in order to avoid being fixed with constructive notice of any wrong by the husband should normally include a private meeting with the wife (in the absence of the husband) at which the wife is told of the extent of her liability as surety, is warned of the risk she is running and is urged to take independent advice. In a number of subsequent cases (the facts of many of which occurred before the House of Lords' decision in *O'Brien*), the creditor had relied on a certificate from a third party, typically a solicitor employed by the husband, that the wife had been given some explanation. It has been held that a creditor is not justified in relying on a certificate that advice *would be* given by an unnamed solicitor (*Bank Melli Iron v. Samadi-Rad*[f]; though see an apparently contrary suggestion by Nourse L.J. in *TSB Bank plc v. Camfield*,[g] in which the point was not argued). Nor can the creditor rely on the mere fact that the wife has seen a solicitor where the solicitor was only retained by the creditor to prepare the charge and had not been given the relevant information (*Allied Irish Bank plc v. Byrne*[h]). However, if the creditor requires the wife to be advised independently and then learns that a solicitor has seen the wife and explained the charge to her, the creditor may rely on this as satisfying the requirements, even though the solicitor is acting for the husband and gave the explanation of the charge in the husband's presence:

Massey v. Midland Bank plc.[i] In that case the C.A. said that it was not for the Bank to stipulate the nature and extent of the advice; it was entitled to assume that the solicitor had given the proper advice. The *O'Brien* guidelines were not exhaustive and the substance of the matter was that the wife had received independent advice.

It is the appearance to the creditor which is important: *Banco Exterior Internacional v. Mann.*[j] In that case the bank had received a certificate from the solicitor to the husband's company to the effect that he had explained the nature of the transaction to the wife. The trial judge held that the bank had not taken reasonable steps, as the solicitor might consider that an explanation in the husband's presence (the husband was in fact present for part of the time) would suffice; the wife did not view the solicitor as independent; and ensuring that the wife understood the transaction was of little help in a case such as this where the wife had actually said to the solicitor when they were alone that she felt she had no choice. But this decision was reversed by the Court of Appeal. The husband's presence and the wife's views were not apparent to the bank. The majority held that the bank was entitled to rely on the solicitor to know why the advice was needed and to advise the wife that she did not have to sign. It could be assumed that if the solicitor felt there was a conflict of interest, he would bring in another solicitor to advise the wife. (See also *Bank of Baroda v. Rayarel.*[k])

What if the creditor itself arranges for a solicitor to advise the wife but the solicitor does not do so adequately? There have been cases in the Court of Appeal which are not easy to reconcile. In *Barclays Bank plc v. Thomson*[l] the bank wrote to the solicitors who acted for the husband's business, requesting them to explain the content of the charge to the wife; the solicitors wrote to the bank that they had done so. The wife argued that the explanation was insufficient and that, as the solicitor's were acting as agents of the bank, knowledge of any deficiency would therefore be imputed to the bank. This argument was rejected; there was no reason why a creditor which specifically instructs a solicitor to advise the wife should be disabled from relying on the solicitor's certificate that the advice has been given. As Sir Thomas Bingham M.R. has said in *Mann's* case,[m] the creditor may assume that the solicitor will do his professional duty regardless of who is paying his fee. But in *Royal Bank of Scotland v. Etridge,*[n] a differently constituted Court of Appeal distinguished *Massey v. Midland Bank plc* and *Banco Exterior Internacional v. Mann.* In *Etridge's* case the solicitor who had certified that he had explained the charge to the wife, but who, she alleged, had failed to do so, had been instructed by the bank to "act on our behalf in completion of the security". It was held that the bank had delegated its task to its own solicitor and thus it would be responsible for the solicitor discharging that duty, so the wife had an arguable defence. It is not wholly clear that the solicitor was in reality being asked to do more than his counterpart in *Thomson's* case.

Where a certificate is given by a solicitor who is not acting for the creditor in other respects and thus is not the creditor's agent, it appears from *Mann's* case that the creditor may normally rely on the wife having been advised. However, with respect it may be questioned whether the decision in *Mann's* case, in requiring the certificate neither to state more than that the nature and effects of the transaction have been explained, nor that the wife was seen on her own, is wholly consistent with the approach of the House of Lords in *O'Brien*. In that case Lord Browne-Wilkinson said that, to avoid being fixed wih constructive notice, the creditor should insist that "the wife attend a private meeting (in the absence of the husband) with a representative of the creditor at which she is told of the extent of her liability as surety, warned of the risk she is running and urged to take independent legal advice."[o] It is submitted that the kind of certificate accepted in *Mann's* case may fall short in two ways.

Firstly, as Hobhouse L.J. pointed out in his dissenting judgment, in cases of undue influence the critical point is not that the weaker party does not understand the transaction, but that she has no independence. Therefore a certificate that the transaction has been explained to her does not end the matter; the bank should take reasonable steps to ensure she is advised to take independent advice, and, in his view, the bank had not done this.

Other judges have also expressed the view that an explanation of the transaction may not suffice. In *Credit Lyonnais Bank Nederland NV v. Burch*,[p] a case of undue influence, Millet L.J. thought that the solicitor should satisfy himself that the transaction is one which the client could sensibly enter if free from improper influence, and, if he was not so satisfied, to advise her not to enter it and to refuse to act further for her if she persists. The creditor is normally entitled to assume that the solicitor has discharged his duty and that the complainant has followed his advice, but he cannot make any assumption if he knows or ought to know that this is not the case.[q] It is hard to see that the creditor can safely assume that the solicitor has advised on the wisdom of the transaction if the solicitor certifies only that the effect of the transaction has been explained. In contrast, in *Mann's* case Sir Thomas Bingham said[r] that it was no part of the solicitor's duty to advise the wife not to sign and this seems to represent the majority view.[s]

The argument of the majority in *Mann's* case that a solicitor can be trusted to give the wife independent advice, or to warn her to get it, does not wholly meet Hobhouse L.J.'s point. If the solicitor gives advice himself, even to the bank there must surely appear to be a risk that a wife who is under pressure from her husband may *feel* that solicitor whom she knows to be acting for him is not really independent, and thus be reluctant to confide in him. This means that the facts which might lead the solicitor to give strong advice or to bring in a colleague to advise may never emerge. Even if she does confide her misgivings, the refusal to sign may have such connotations of disloyalty that she may be very slow to take advice. It seems much more likely that she would make an independent decision were she to see a solicitor or other adviser who she felt to be really independent of the husband. Equally there may be a problem when the husband has made misrepresentations to the wife about the prospect for the business and matters not apparent from the documents (*cf. Massey's* case). When dealing with her husband's adviser, the wife may feel very loath to check the veracity of what her husband has told her. Therefore it seems more consistent with *O'Brien* that, if it is the husband's solicitor who advises the wife, the solicitor should have to advise the wife to get independent advice elsewhere.

Secondly, there is the problem that the husband may be present. Even if the solicitor advises the wife to get independent advice elsewhere, but does so in her husband's presence, the husband is surely very likely to persuade the wife that this is not necessary. Although it was said by Hoffmann L.J. in *Bank of Baroda v. Rayarel*[t] that it would be a professional discourtesy for the bank to tell a solicitor acting for the husband and wife to advise the wife separately, it is hard to see why it is so discourteous to request a certificate that this has been done, given that it is clear that this is not universal practice. Indeed, the solicitor might welcome the need for a certificate to this effect as a reason for insisting on seeing the wife alone despite the wishes of a possibly uncooperative husband.

A creditor which itself advises the wife to get independent advice, as in *Massey's* case, must in the normal case have complied with the *O'Brien* requirements. The same must be true of a creditor which receives a certificate (1) that a solicitor not acting for either bank or husband (or one employed specifically to give that advice or only for some other, limited purpose[u]) has given her advice, or (2) that she has been advised by a solicitor, *in the absence of the husband*, to get such independent advice. What is contestable is whether a creditor is really justified, as the majority held in *Mann's* case, in relying on a certificate from the husband's or husband's company's solicitor which does not state either of these two things, but only that the wife has been seen and the nature of the transaction explained to her. At the very least, it is suggested, the certificate should have to state that the solicitor saw the wife on her own.

It should also be remembered that in *O'Brien's* case Lord Browne-Wilkinson said that these were guidelines for the "normal" case. If the bank knew facts suggesting actual undue influence or misrepresentation, rather than the mere possibility of it, it would come under a duty to insist that the wife take independent advice. In *Credit Lyonnais Bank Nederland NV v. Burch*[v] the transaction was so obviously disadvantageous to the defendant that the bank should have ensured that she actually received advice; it was not enough to rely on a letter from her, but which was clearly written at the debtor's instigation, stating that she was fully aware of the implications of what she was doing. In that case it was suggested by Nourse and Millett L.JJ. that the defendant might have had a direct right against the bank to avoid the transaction on the grounds of unconscionability.[x]

The creditor need not give the wife all details of the husband's situation, *e.g.* the amount of the borrowing, if it advises her to get independent advice.[y]

But if there is some unusual feature of the transaction, for example that there is a second security to another lender which is to be given priority to the creditor's charge, the creditor cannot rely on the fact that a solicitor has advised the wife if this fact had not been disclosed to the wife or to the solicitor.[z]

(iii) *Effect of constructive notice*

After *O'Brien*'s case there was some uncertainty as to the position when, as in that case, the husband had misrepresented the extent of the charge and the bank had constructive notice of the misrepresentation. Is the charge completely unenforceable against the wife or enforceable to the extent she was given to believe? (It seems that £60,000, which was the sum the wife had been led to believe was the limit of her liability, had been paid before the final decision, which did not discuss its fate.) In *TSB Bank plc v. Camfield*[aa] the C.A. held on similar facts that the charge was completely unenforceable. As against the husband the wife would have the right to set aside the whole charge; this is implicit in the Misrepresentation Act 1967, s.2(2), which implies that the court had no discretion save under that subsection. The bank took subject to the equity in favour of the wife and could not be in a better position. Section 2(2) does not apply as between a misrepresentee and a third party. However, in *Midland Bank v. Greene*[bb] it was held that, if the charge secures a loan which, though disadvantageous to her as a whole, was in part of direct benefit to the wife, the court should strive to do what is practically just; and if the wife exercises her right to rescind she must make an allowance for the benefit she has in fact received, just as when a contract is rescinded on the ground of undue influence the weaker party may have to account for profits received (see *O'Sullivan v. Management Agency Ltd*,[cc] and Main Work §7–041).

(iv) *Need the party who made the misrepresentation be a party to the transaction?*

In *TSB v. Camfield* (above) the Court of Appeal treated the bank as having constructive notice of the wife's right to set aside the charge as against the husband. What would be the position if the husband were not a party to the charge? As a matter of principle it seems that a party to a contract who has actual notice that the other party has entered the contract as the result of a misrepresentation by a third party should be unable to enforce it, and it is submitted that the same should apply in cases of constructive notice. In *Banco Exterior Internacional SA v. Thomas*[dd] (a case of alleged undue influence) Sir Richard Scott V-C expressed the view that it could not have made a difference if in *O'Brien's* case the wife had been sole owner of the home, but the case was decided on other grounds, Roch L.J. reserving this question.

[79]

(v) *Pleading*

A party who wishes to rely on the defence against the creditor of constructive notice of wrongdoing by the debtor need only plead the relevant facts and need not plead constructive notice in so many words.[ee]

[a] [1994] 1 A.C. 200. For post *O'Brien* cases see Fehlberg (1996) 59 M.L.R. 675.

[b] [1995] 2 F.L.R. 325. Compare *Barclays Bank plc v. Sumner* [1996] E.G.C.S. 65; *Britannia Building Society v. Pugh* [1997] 2 F.L.R. 7.

[c] [1995] 1 F.L.R. 196.

[d] November 10, 1994, unreported.

[e] [1996] Ch. 207.

[f] [1995] 1 F.L.R. 465.

[g] [1995] 1 W.L.R. 430.

[h] [1995] 2 F.L.R. 325.

[i] [1995] 1 All E.R. 929.

[j] [1995] 1 All E.R. 936, 944.

[k] [1995] 2 F.L.R. 376.

[l] [1997] 1 F.C.R. 541.

[m] at p. 950.

[n] [1997] 3 All E.R. 628.

[o] [1994] 1 A.C. 180 at 196.

[p] [1997] 1 All E.R. 144.

[q] [1997] 1 All E.R. 144, 156.

[r] [1995] 1 All E.R. 936, 950. See also *Akins v. National Australia Bank* (1994) 34 N.S.W.L.R. 155.

[s] See also *Banco Exterior Internacional SA v. Thomas* [1997] 1 W.L.R. 221; and Main Work §7–036.

[t] [1995] 2 F.L.R. 376.

[u] *Midland Bank plc v. Serter* [1995] 1 F.L.R. 1034.

[v] [1997] 1 All E.R. 144.

[x] See further below, §7–044.

[y] *Midland Bank plc v. Kidwai* [1995] N.P.C. 81.

[z] *Bank of Scotland v. Bennett* [1997] 1 Fam.L.R. 801.

[aa] [1995] 1 W.L.R. 430. Compare recent Australian authority, below §6–067.

[bb] (1995) 27 H.L.R. 350. See also *Dunbar Bank plc v. Nadeem* [1997] 2 All E.R. 253.

[cc] [1985] Q.B. 428.

[dd] [1997] 1 W.L.R. 221.

[ee] *Barclays Bank plc v. Boulter*, *The Independent*, 25 April 1997.

[Note 89: page [344]]
A Third Edition of the Code of Banking Practice was issued in 1997.

The representee

[Add to note 99: page [346]]   **6–018**
Standard Chartered Bank v. Pakistan National Shipping Corp. [1995] 2
Lloyd's Rep. 365.

Inducement

[Note 5: page [347]]   **6–019**
In *Pan Atlantic Insurance Co. Ltd v. Pine Top Insurance Co. Ltd* [1995] 1
A.C. 501 the House of Lords held that, for both marine insurance under
Marine Insurance Act 1906, s.18(2) and non-marine insurance, a misrep-
resentation or non-disclosure must actually have induced the making of the
policy for the policy to be voidable.

[Note 10]
In *Pan Atlantic Insurance Co. Ltd v. Pine Top Insurance Co. Ltd* [1995] 1
A.C. 501, 542, Lord Mustill refers to the "presumption of inducement" in the
case of fraud, but he does not deny that there may be a similar presumption
in other cases of positive misrepresentation.

[Add to note 13: page [348]]
However, in a case in which it was argued that an insurance company, by
accepting premiums waived its right to avoid a policy for non-disclosure, it
was held that the company did not have sufficient knowledge to found a
waiver unless the information was received by a person authorised and able
to appreciate its significance. On the facts, the fact that there had been
disclosure in an earlier application and declaration of health did not suffice:
Malhi v. Abbey Life Assurance Co. Ltd, The Times, June 26, 1994.

Treitel, *The Law of Contract* (9th ed., 1995), p. 316, points out indications **6–020**
in the House of Lords in *Smith v. Eric S. Bush*[a] to the effect that buyers of
expensive or commercial properties would be expected to have their own
survey done, and thus would fail in a claim for negligent misrepresentation
against a surveyor employed by the lender. He suggests that in the light of
this, the rule in *Redgrave v. Hurd*[b] that a misrepresentee's failure to take
advantage of an opportunity to discover the truth is no bar to rescission may
require re-consideration. The rule should be limited to cases in which it was
reasonable not to take the opportunity. It is not clear, however, that the
same approach should apply as between contracting parties as is taken when
a party relies on a negligent misstatement by a person with whom he is not in

a contractual relationship, as in *Smith v. Eric S. Bush*. When the misstatement leads to a contract with the misrepresentor, there is at least the possibility that the misrepresentor will have benefited from his misstatement, for example by obtaining a better price for the property he is selling. The fact that he was innocent, and the other party careless of his own interests, does not necessarily justify allowing him to retain the advantage gained.

[a] [1990] 1 A.C. 831, 854, 872.

[b] (1881) 20 Ch.D. 1.

Materiality

[*Amend note 30: page* [349]]
The reference should now read: Treitel, *The Law of Contract* (9th ed., 1995), p. 313. The cross-reference should be to §6–020.

Intention

6-024   [*Add to note 38: page* [350]]
In *McCullagh v. Lane Fox and Partners Ltd, The Times*, December 22, 1995 it was held that an estate agent who had misstated the area of a property, but whose particulars contained a disclaimer, was not liable to the purchaser. The majority took the view that no duty arose quite apart from the disclaimer.

[*Add to note 39: page* [351]]
Compare *Morgan Crucible Co. plc v. Hill Samuel Bank Ltd* [1991] Ch. 295. In *Galoo Ltd (in liquidation) v. Bright Grahame Murray* [1994] 1 W.L.R. 1360, it was held that an auditor of a company's accounts may owe a duty of care to a take-over bidder if he has expressly been informed that the bidder will rely on the accounts for the purpose of deciding whether to make an increased bid and intends that the bidder should so rely.

3. – DAMAGES FOR MISREPRESENTATION

(a) *Fraudulent misrepresentation*

6-027   See §6–012, note 62, *ante*.

Defendant's knowledge of falsity of statement

6-029   [*Add to note 55: page* [353]]
Standard Chartered Bank v. Pakistan National Shipping Corp. [1995] 2 Lloyd's Rep. 365.

[Add to note 65: page [354]]
Hughes v. Clewley, The Siben (No. 2) [1996] 1 Lloyd's Rep. 35.

Measure of damages for fraudulent misrepresentation

In *Smith New Court Securities Ltd v. Scrimgeour Vickers (Asset Manage-* **6–032**
ment) Ltd [1997] A.C. 254, 263, Lord Browne-Wilkinson described *Doyle v. Olby (Ironmongers) Ltd* as re-stating the law correctly. He stated (at p. 267) the principles applicable in assessing damages where a party has been induced by a fraudulent misrepresentation to buy property as follows:

"(1) The defendant is bound to make reparation for all the damage directly flowing from the transaction.
(2) Although such damage need not have been foreseeable, it must have been directly caused by the transaction.
(3) In assessing such damage, the plaintiff is entitled to recover by way of damages the full price paid by him, but he must give credit for any benefits which he has received as a result of the transaction.
(4) As a general rule, the benefits received by him include the market value of the property acquired at the date of the transaction; but such general rule is not to be inflexibly applied where to do so would prevent him obtaining full compensation for the wrong suffered;
(5) Although the circumstances in which the general rule should not apply cannot be comprehensively stated, it will normally not apply where either (a) the misrepresentation has continued to operate after the date of the acquisition of the asset so as to induce the plaintiff to retain the asset or (b) the circumstances of the case are such that the plaintiff is, by reason of the fraud, locked into the property.
(6) In addition, the plaintiff is entitled to recover consequential losses caused by the transaction.
(7) The plaintiff must take all reasonable steps to mitigate his loss once he has discovered the fraud."

Lord Mustill said (at p. 269) that the judgment of Lord Denning in *Doyle v. Olby (Ironmongers) Ltd* was in some respects too broad-brush; the case had not been fully argued. He considered that in future courts would do well to be guided by Lord Browne-Wilkinson's seven propositions.
As Lord Browne-Wilkinson's sixth proposition states, damages for fraud may include compensation for consequential loss. A party who has been induced to enter a contract by a fraudulent or negligent misrepresentation and who seeks damages need not show that, but for the misrepresentation, he would not have entered the transaction. He need only show that he was

induced to enter the contract by a material misrepresentation and the loss that followed from entering it: *Downs v. Chappell* [1997] 1 W.L.R. 426.

[Add to note 68: page [354]]
The award in *East v. Maurer* based on a hypothetical profitable business in which the plaintiff would have engaged but for the deceit has been described by Lord Steyn as "classic consequential loss": *Smith New Court Securities Ltd v. Scrimgeour Vickers (Asset Management) Ltd* [1997] A.C. 254, 282.

[add new reference at end of paragraph: page [355]]

NOTE 68a: The rule that damages for fraud are not assessed in accordance with the contractual measure was confirmed in *Smith New Court Securities Ltd v. Scrimgeour Vickers (Asset Management) Ltd* [1997] A.C. 254, 281–282, *per* Lord Steyn, who emphasised the point made by Treitel (1969) 32 M.L.R. 558–559 that the plaintiff who has made a bad bargain will do better under the tortious measure than the contractual one.

6–033   *[Add to text after note 71: page [355]]*
The plaintiff may also recover the difference between the contract price and the value of the property at a later date even if the reduction of value is not the result of the fraud. One case is if the result of the fraud was that the plaintiff has bought a "already flawed asset", the value of which falls when the flaw is discovered. In *Smith New Court Securities Ltd v. Scrimgeour Vickers (Asset Management) Ltd*,[71a] SNC had bought shares in Ferranti as the result of fraudulent misrepresentations by the defendants. SNC intended to keep the shares for a period of time. Their value fell drastically when it was discovered that Ferranti had been the victim of a fraud by a third party. The House of Lords, reversing the Court of Appeal,[71b] held that SNC were not limited to recovering the difference between the contract price and the market value of the shares at the date of the transaction; they could recover the difference between the contract price and the value of the shares after the discovery of the fraud. As stated in the fourth and fifth propositions of Lord Browne-Wilkinson quoted above (see §6–032), the date of transaction rule will not be applied if it would prevent the plaintiff obtaining full compensation, for example, if the plaintiff is locked into the transaction. As Lord Steyn put it,[71c] the date of transaction rule is simply a second-order rule applicable only if the valuation method is followed, and the court is entitled to assess the loss flowing directly from the fraud without any reference to the date of the transaction or indeed any particular date. In this case, as SNC had intended to keep the shares and it was not commercially feasible to re-sell them immediately, it was locked into the property.
Secondly, in an appropriate case the damages may include losses which result from a subsequent fall in the general values of property of the kind in

question. The House of Lords held in *Banque Bruxelles Lambert SA v. Eagle Star Insurance Co. Ltd*[71d] that such losses are not normally recoverable in a case of negligence at common law, but the House left open the possibility in cases of fraud.[71e] In *Downs v. Chappell*[71f] the plaintiffs had bought a business as the result of the defendant's fraudulent statements; they recovered the difference between the price paid and the value of the business when the fraud was discovered even though that may have been increased by a general fall in property prices.

In that case, Hobhouse L.J. said that only losses flowing from the tort would be recoverable, and as a means of testing whether the loss was caused by the tort and preventing over-compensation, proposed comparing "the loss to consequent upon entering the transaction that which what would have been the position had the represented, or supposed, state of affairs actually existed.". This last aspect of the case was disapproved by the House of Lords in *Smith New Court Securities Ltd v. Scrimgeour Vickers (Asset Management) Ltd.*[71g] Thus it appears that in a fraud case the plaintiff can recover the full fall in value of the property, at least up to the date of discovery of the fraud. Lord Steyn justified a special rule for cases of deceit by considerations of morality and deterrence.[71h]

[71a] [1997] A.C. 254.

[71b] [1994] 1 W.L.R. 1271.

[71c] [1997] A.C. 254, 284.

[71d] [1997] A.C. 191.

[71e] See at p. 215.

[71f] [1997] 1 W.L.R. 426.

[71g] [1997] A.C. 254.

[71h] at p. 280.

[*Note 82: page* [357]]
In *Hughes v. Clewley, The Siben (No. 2)* [1996] 1 Lloyd's Rep. 35 the **6–034** misrepresentee was permitted to claim damages for fraud although part of the business transferred to him was used for immoral purposes, as it was said that he did not have to rely on the illegal contract. Moreover, in calculating the value of what he had received for the purposes of damages, the value of this part of the business was disregarded.

(b) *Negligent Misrepresentation*

Effect of section 2(1)

[*Add to note 94: page* [359]] **6–037**
Presumably it would follow from the decision that damages under s.2(1) can include compensation for loss of value caused by a fall in the market, *cf.*

Downs v. Chappell [1997] 1 W.L.R. 426 (above, §6–033). In *Smith New Court Securities Ltd v. Scrimgeour Vickers (Asset Management) Ltd* [1997] A.C. 254 both Lords Browne-Wilkinson and Steyn declined to comment on the correctness of the *Royscot* case.

Hedley Byrne & Co. Ltd v. Heller and Partners Ltd

6–045   For a full discussion see now *Clerk and Lindsell on Torts* (17th ed., 1995), §§7–61—7–77. On the role played by an "assumption of responsibility", see also Main Work, §1–077A and *ante*, §§1–048—1–071 (especially pp. 10–14) and §1–077A. On the measure of damages see *ante*, §6–033 n. 71.

The decision in *Downs v. Chappell* [1997] 1 W.L.R. 426 as far as the vendor's accountants were concerned may have been interpreted in *Bristol and West Building Society v. Mothew* [1997] 2 W.L.R. 43 as applying the fraud measure in cases of negligence, but Hobhouse L.J., who delivered the only full judgment in *Downs*, has said that this is not an accurate account of the decision: *Swindle v. Harrison, The Times*, April 17, 1997.

Statement in connection with a particular transaction

6–046   [*Add to note 33: page* [364]]
In contrast see *Morgan Crucible Co. plc v. Hill Samuel Bank Ltd* [1991] Ch. 295. In *Galoo Ltd (in liquidation) v. Bright Grahame Murray* [1994] 1 W.L.R. 1360, it was held that an auditor of a company's accounts may owe a duty of care to a take-over bidder if he has expressly been informed that the bidder will rely on the accounts for the purpose of deciding whether to make an increased bid and intends that the bidder should so rely. See also *Possfund Custodian Trustee Ltd v. Diamond* [1996] 1 W.L.R. 1351.

Other statutory provisions creating liability for negligent misrepresentation

6–054   [*Note 67: page* [369]]
Update reference to Boyle & Birds to (3rd ed., 1995), para. 5.19.

(c) *Innocent Misrepresentation*

Misrepresentation Act, s.2(2)

6–058   In *Thomas Witter Ltd v. T.B.P. Industries Ltd*[a] Jacob J. expressed the view that damages could have been awarded under s.2(2) even though the misrepresentee had lost the right to rescind. He considered the section to be ambiguous and referred to a statement of the Solicitor-General during a debate on the Misrepresentation Bill. The statement itself lends some support to this view but further investigation of the legislative history throws some doubt on it.[b]

[a] [1996] 2 All E.R. 573.

[b] see (1995) 111 L.Q.R. 385.

Exercise of court's discretion

A court is unlikely to exercise its power to declare the contract subsisting 6–060
under s.2(2) when an award of damages against the misrepresentor will be an empty remedy: *TSB Bank plc v. Camfield.*[a]

[a] [1995] 1 W.L.R. 430, 439.

4. – RESCISSION FOR MISREPRESENTATION

(a) *General*

Preliminary

[*Note 4: page* [375]]   6–061
The conferral of a discretion on the court by s.2(2) has been said to imply that, apart from that section, there is no power to declare the contract subsisting; the right to rescind is that of the representee, not that of the court, which merely has to decide whether the rescission was lawful: *TSB Bank plc v. Camfield* [1995] 1 W.L.R. 430, 439. However, in *Hughes v. Clewley, The Siben (No. 2)* [1996] 1 Lloyd's Rep. 35 it was held that rescission will not be ordered [*sic*] if the effect would be to transfer any business being used for unlawful purposes from one party to the other. This was a case of fraud, so there was no power to declare the contract subsisting under s.2(2).

Misrepresentation as defence to proceedings

[*Amend note 18: page* [378]]   6–066
The reference should now read: Treitel, *The Law of Contract* (9th ed., 1995), pp. 344–345.

Mode of rescission

[*Add to note 23*]   6–067
See also *TSB Bank plc v. Camfield* [1995] 1 W.L.R. 430, 439. In Australia the High Court has taken a different approach, holding that even in a case of fraud, equity does more than recognise rescission effected by the action of

the innocent party. It may impose terms to achieve observance of the requirements of good conscience and practical justice and this enables it to grant partial rescission. Thus it could set aside the part of a contract of guarantee to which the fraud related (previous supplies) but leave the rest (as to future supplies) intact: *Vadasz v. Pioneer Concrete (S.A.) Pty Ltd* (1995) 184 C.L.R. 102, noted (1997) 113 L.Q.R. 16.

(c) *Bars to Remedy of Rescission*

Restrictions on the right to rescind

6–076   In *Hughes v. Clewley, The Siben (No. 2)*[a] it was held that rescission will not be ordered [*sic*: see §6–061 *ante*] if the effect would be to transfer any business being used for unlawful purposes from one party to the other. (This was a case of fraud, so there was no power to declare the contract subsisting under s.2(2).) This seems to constitute a new bar to rescission.

[a] [1996] 1 Lloyd's Rep. 35.

5. – EXCLUSION OF LIABILITY FOR MISREPRESENTATION

Misrepresentation Act, s.3

6–083   [*Note 89: page* [387]]
A properly worded clause which excludes a right of avoidance will be effective notwithstanding a purported rescission of the contract as a whole by the misrepresentee: *Toomey v. Eagle Star Insurance Co. Ltd (No. 2)* [1995] 2 Lloyd's Rep. 88.

[*Note 90*]
Thus a clause stating that a contract of re-insurance was "neither cancellable nor voidable by either party" was held to apply only to cases of innocent misrepresentation or non-disclosure, and not to alleged negligence, nor to exclude the right to damages under the Misrepresentation Act 1967, s.2(1): *Toomey v. Eagle Star Insurance Co. Ltd (No. 2)* [1995] 2 Lloyd's Rep. 88. A disclaimer "without responsibility" does not prevent rescission on the ground of misrepresentation: *Crédit Lyonnais Bank Nederland v. E.C.G.D.* [1996] 1 Lloyd's Rep. 1.

Effect of a contractual term that representee not to rely on statements

6–085   [*Add to note 97: page* [389]]
Thus a clause which purports to exclude liability for misrepresentation of any kind will be unreasonable, since it is not reasonable to exclude liability for fraud, and the clause as a whole will be invalid: *Thomas Witter Ltd v. T.B.P. Industries Ltd* [1996] 2 All E.R. 573. *Cf.* §14–076 of the Main Work.

Other statutory provisions affecting disclaimers

The Unfair Terms in Consumer Contracts Directive has now been **6–086** implemented by Unfair Terms in Consumer Contracts Regulations 1994[a]; see *post*, §§14–088 *et seq*. It seems clear that any clause excluding or limiting liability for misrepresentation, however it is worded, will be within the Regulations provided that it is "in a contract concluded between a seller or supplier and a consumer" and "has not been individually negotiated".[b]

[a] S.I. 1994 No. 3159.

[b] Reg. 3(1).

6. – CONTRACTS UBERRIMAE FIDEI

Contracts of insurance

In *Pan Atlantic Insurance Co. Ltd v. Pine Top Insurance Co. Ltd*[a] the **6–088** House of Lords held that, for both marine insurance under Marine Insurance Act 1906, s.18(2) and non-marine insurance, the test of materiality is not whether the matter would have had a decisive effect on the prudent insurer's decision whether to accept the risk or at what premium, but whether it would have an effect on the mind of the prudent insurer in weighing up the risk.[b] In *St Paul Fire and Marine Insurance Co. Ltd v. McConnell Dowell Constructors Ltd*[c] it was held that a matter did not necessarily have to lead to an increase in the risk in order to be material; it was sufficient that the risk was different.[d]

But in the *Pan Atlantic* case the House of Lords held that, in addition to being material, a misrepresentation or non-disclosure must have induced the making of the policy.[e] In this respect the law on insurance contracts is parallel to the general law on positive misrepresentation.[f] Lord Mustill[g] refers to "a presumption in favour of causative effect", as there is in the case of a positive misrepresentation.[h] See also *St Paul Fire and Marine Insurance Co. Ltd v. McConnell Dowell Constructors Ltd.*[i]

[a] [1995] 1 A.C. 501.

[b] See further *post*, §39–025.

[c] [1996] 1 All E.R. 96.

[d] *ibid.* at p. 107.

[e] [1995] 1 A.C. 501, 549–550.

[f] See §6–019 *ante*.

[g] [1995] 1 A.C. 501, at p. 542.

[h] See *ante*, §6–109, note 10.

[i] [1996] 1 All E.R. 96, 112.

6–090   On the scope of the duty of disclosure see *post*, §39–026.

[*Add to note 29: page* [392]]
On the interpretation of this section see *PCW Syndicates v. PCW Reinsurers* [1996] 1 W.L.R. 1136.

[*Add to note 30, after reference to Joel v. Law Union and Crown Insurance Co.*]
In *Economides v. Commercial Union Assurance Co. plc* [1997] 3 All E.R. 636 it was held that an insured who is not acting in the course of business has only to disclose material facts actually known to him; provided that he did not wilfully shut his eyes to the truth (so-called "Nelsonian blindness") he is not under a duty to inquire further, for example, by checking that his honest belief in the value of the property is in fact accurate.

Suretyship

6–096   In *Levett v. Barclays Bank plc*[a] it was held that there is a duty to disclose to the surety any unusual feature of the contract between the principal debtor and the creditor which makes it materially different in a potentially disadvantageous respect from what the surety might naturally expect. In *Crédit Lyonnais Bank Nederland v. E.C.G.D.*[b] it was held that any duty to disclose unusual features only applied to unusual features of the transaction itself, not too unusual features of the risk; and it did not extend to matters of which the Bank had no knowledge, even if what it knew might have led it to make further enquiries.[c]

[a] [1995] 1 W.L.R. 1260.

[b] [1996] 1 Lloyd's Rep. 200.

[c] See further *post*, §42–020.

CHAPTER 7

DURESS AND UNDUE INFLUENCE

1. – DURESS

(e) *Nature of Threats Amounting to Duress*

Threat to commit an unlawful act

In *Dimskal Shipping Co. SA v. ITWF, The Evia Luck* [1992] 2 A.C. 152 the **7–011**
House of Lords held that the question of whether economic pressure
amounted to duress was prima facie a matter for the proper law of the
contract, so that whether the conduct was lawful or not fell to be determined
by the proper law of the contract rather than by that of the place where the
threat was made. In *Royal Boskalis Westminster Nv v. Mountain* [1997] 2 All
E.R. 929, 944, 980 it was said that, nonetheless, counsel had been correct to
concede, in the light of *Kaufman v. Gerson* [1904] 1 K.B. 591, that some
forms of duress are so shocking that English law would not enforce a
contract made under such duress irrespective of whether the threat would be
acceptable and the contract valid under the governing law. See Main Work,
§30–110.

Threat to commit otherwise lawful act

In *CTN Cash and Carry Ltd v. Gallagher Ltd*[a] the plaintiffs had ordered **7–012**
goods from the defendants, who delivered them by mistake to the wrong
warehouse, from which they were stolen. The defendants, honestly but

wrongly believing that the goods were at the plaintiffs' risk, invoiced them. The plaintiffs refused to pay until the defendants threatened to withdraw the plaintiffs' credit facilities, which, it was said, would seriously jeopardise the plaintiffs' business. The defendants had the right to withdraw credit facilities at any time. The plaintiffs later sought repayment. The Court of Appeal upheld the trial judge's decision that no case of economic duress had been made out. Steyn L.J., with whom the other members of the Court agreed, said that the combination of the facts that (i) the defendants were entitled to refuse to enter into any future contracts with the plaintiffs for any reason and (ii), critically, that the defendants bona fide thought that the plaintiffs owed the sum in question, was sufficient to distinguish cases in which a plea of economic duress had succeeded. The fact that the defendants were in a sense in a monopoly position was irrelevant, the control of monopolies being a matter for Parliament. Although there are cases in which the courts have accepted that a threat of a lawful action coupled with a demand for payment may be illegitimate (*e.g. Thorne v. Motor Trade Association*),[b] it would be a relatively rare case in which "lawful act duress" could be established in a commercial context.

[a] [1994] 4 All E.R. 714.

[b] [1937] A.C. 797.

Threat not to contract

7-013   See §7–012 *ante*. The Merchant Shipping Act 1995, s.224, provides for the Salvage Convention 1989 (contained in Schedule 11 to the Act) to have the force of law. The Convention provides in Article 7:

Annulment and modification of contracts

A contract or any terms thereof may be annulled or modified if—

(a) the contract has been entered into under undue influence or the influence of danger and its terms are inequitable; or

(b) the payment under the contract is in an excessive degree too large or too small for the services actually rendered.

Article 13 sets out criteria for fixing the proper reward.

(g) *General effect of duress*

Contract under duress is voidable

7-022   In *Royal Boskalis Westminster NV v. Mountain* [1997] 2 All E.R. 929, 981, Phillips L.J. expressed some difficulty in saying that a contract has been avoided on the grounds of duress if it is governed by a foreign law which would afford no right of avoidance but where the duress was so unconscionable that English law would override the proper law of the contract (see above, §7–011). However, he considered that English law would not recognise the effects of the contract (p. 982).

2. – UNDUE INFLUENCE

Express influence

An example of actual coercion might be a salvage case: see *ante*, §7–013. **7–028**

[Insert new paragraph: page [426]]
Equitable compensation. If a transaction which has been entered into as **7–039A**
the result of actual or presumed undue influence cannot be rescinded because *restitutio in integrum* is no longer possible, and the defendant does not retain any profits for which he may be made to account, the plaintiff may still be given compensation in equity. In *Mahoney v. Purnell*[14a] May J. held that equitable compensation under *Nocton v. Lord Ashburton*[14b] is also available in such circumstances and the plaintiff could recover the value of what he had transferred, giving credit for what he had received. The judge described this as the practical equivalent of awarding damages, though it should be noted that equitable compensation will not include compensation for consequential losses.[14c] There may be some doubt whether equitable compensation is available in every case of undue influence, or only those in which there is a fiduciary relationship of a narrower sort, such as between solicitor and client or beneficiary and trustee.[14d] In *Bank of Credit and Commerce International SA v. Aboody*[14e] Slade L.J. treated such cases as different to normal cases of undue influence[14f] and said that cases such as *Tate v. Williamson*[14g] did not draw a sufficiently clear distinction between the two types of case; but there is no sign that May J. saw the case before him to be anything other than one of Class 2B undue influence.

[14a] [1996] 3 All E.R. 61.

[14b] [1914] A.C. 932 (a case of a mortgagee suing his solicitor, see Main Work, §6–044).

[14c] See Main Work §6–045, note 25.

[14d] See Heydon (1997) 113 L.Q.R. 8, 9 and §6–045 of the Main Work.

[14e] [1990] 1 Q.B. 923, 943.

[14f] See Main Work, §6–045 at notes 35 and 36.

[14g] (1866) L.R. 2 Ch. App. 55.

Undue influence by third parties

7–040   The decisions following *Barclays Bank plc v. O'Brien*[a] and *CIBC Mortgages plc v. Pitt*[b] are discussed above, see *ante*, §6–016. Note that it seems that in an extreme case, despite having been given independent advice, the plaintiff may be able to set aside the transaction on the basis of unconscionability. See below, §7–044.

[a] [1994] 1 A.C. 180.

[b] [1994] 1 A.C. 200.

3. – UNCONSCIONABLE BARGAINS AND INEQUALITY OF BARGAINING POWER

Salvage cases

7–043   See now the Salvage Convention 1989, §7–013 *ante*.

7–044   In *Barclays Bank plc v. Schwartz*,[a] Millett L.J. observed that a person whose illiteracy or inability to speak English is taken advantage of may, in an appropriate case, be able to have the contract set aside on the grounds of unconscionability.[b]

The jurisdiction to set aside contracts on the ground of unconscionability has been said not to extend to gifts, as this would mean that in the case of all gifts by poor and ignorant persons without independent advice, an onus would be placed on the recipient to show that the gift was fair, just and reasonable: *Langton v. Langton*.[c]

[a] *The Times*, August 2, 1995.

[b] See *post*, §8–001.

[c] *The Times*, February 24, 1995.

[*Note 36*]
Unconscionability was not found on the facts in *Pye v. Ambrose* [1994] N.P.C. 53.

Unconscionable bargains with poor and ignorant persons

7–044   [*Add at end of paragraph: page* [429]]
In *Credit Lyonnais Bank Nederland NV v. Burch*[36a] the defendant had given a guarantee and charged her flat to secure the borrowings of her employer's company, in circumstances in which the transaction was manifestly disadvantageous to her. The case was decided on the ground that the bank had constructive notice of undue influence by the employer, but both Nourse and Millett L.JJ. suggested that it might have been argued that

she had a direct right, as against the bank, to set aside the transaction on the grounds of unconscionability. Millett L.J. pointed out that it would be necessary to show that the bank had imposed the objectionable terms in a morally objectionable manner, but said that impropriety might be inferred from the terms of the transaction itself in the absence of an innocent explanation.[36b]

[36a] [1997] 1 All E.R. 144, noted (1997) 113 L.Q.R. 10.

[36b] at p. 153, referring to *Multiservice Bookbinding Ltd v. Marden* [1979] Ch. 84, 110 and *Alec Lobb (Garages) Ltd v. Total Oil G.B. Ltd* [1983] 1 W.L.R. 87, 95. See *post*, §7–045.

Unconscionable conduct

In *Boustany v. Piggott*,[a] Lord Templeman, delivering the judgment of the **7–045** Privy Council, agreed in general terms with the submissions of counsel for the appellant: (1) there must be unconscionability in the sense that objectionable terms have been imposed on the weaker party in a reprehensible manner; (2) "unconscionability" refers not only to the unreasonable terms but to the behaviour of the stronger party, which must be morally culpable or reprehensible; (3) unequal bargaining power or objectively unreasonable terms are no basis for interference in equity in the absence of unconscionable or extortionate abuse where, exceptionally and as a matter of common fairness, "it is unfair that the strong should be allowed to push the weak to the wall", (4) a contract will not be set aside as unconscionable in the absence of actual or constructive fraud or other unconscionable conduct; and (5) the weaker party must show unconscionable conduct, in that the stronger party took unconscientious advantage of the weaker party's disabling condition or circumstances.

[a] (1995) 69 P. & C.R. 298, 303.

[*Add to note 42: page* [430]]
Credit Lyonnais Bank Nederland NV v. Burch [1997] 1 All E.R. 144, noted (1997) 113 L.Q.R. 10.

Part Two

CAPACITY OF PARTIES

CHAPTER 8

PERSONAL INCAPACITY

1. – IN GENERAL

Contractual incapacity

8–001   [*Add to text after note 4: page* [435]]

On the other hand, illiteracy and unfamiliarity with the English language are not to be equated with disabilities like mental incapacity or drunkenness. According to Millett L.J. in *Barclays Bank plc v. Schwartz*,[4a] although all four conditions are disabilities which may prevent the sufferer from possessing a full understanding of a transaction into which he enters, "mental incapacity and drunkenness [may] not only deprive the sufferer of understanding the transaction, but also deprive him of the awareness that he [does] not understand it", which is not the case as regards an illiterate or a person unfamiliar with English. However, as Millett L.J. observed, such a person may in an appropriate case claim that the transaction be set aside as a harsh and unconscionable bargain, on which see §7–042 of the Main Work.

[4a] *The Times*, August 2, 1995.

4. – MENTALLY DISORDERED PERSONS

Nature of Understanding required

[Add to text end of paragraph: page [464]]   8–066
Thus, where a gift or gifts *inter vivos* are of trivial value in relation to the
donor's other assets, then a low degree of understanding will suffice; but
where they have the effect of substantially reducing the donor's estate,
thereby trenching upon the reasonable expectations of his relatives, a much
higher standard of capacity should be required, one which involves an
appreciation of the competing claims upon the donor's bounty: *Clarke v.
Prus,*[89a] approving the dictum of Martin Nourse Q.C. in *Re Beaney.*[89b]

[89a] [1995] N.P.C. 41.

[89b] [1978] 1 W.L.R. 770, 774.

5. – DRUNKEN PERSONS

Effect of drunkenness

[Add to text at end of paragraph: page [467]]   8–074
In *Barclays Bank plc v. Schwartz,*[18a] Millett L.J. accepted that the reason
for drunkenness of a party to a contract affecting its validity is that like
mental incapacity it deprives a person not only of a full understanding of a
transaction, but also of the awareness that he does not understand it.

[18a] *The Times*, August 2, 1995.

CHAPTER 9

CORPORATIONS AND UNINCORPORATED ASSOCIATIONS

1. – CORPORATIONS

(b) *Corporations in General*

Corporation created by statute

9–004   [*Add to text at end of second paragraph: page* [471]]
It is trite law that a company must act through the instrumentality of individuals in order to enter into binding contracts. The company will be bound where contractual acts of individuals can be attributed to the company and the rules by which such attribution is affected were analysed by the House of Lords in *Meridian Global Funds Management Asia Ltd v. Securities Commission.*[20a] The company's "primary rules of attribution" will normally be found in its constitution, that is, its articles of association or implied by company law, for example, the principle that the unanimous agreement of all of the shareholders, even though given informally, constitutes a valid act of the company.[20b] These primary rules of attribution are not sufficient to determine when the acts of an individual will be attributed to a company and need to be supplemented by general rules of attribution which are equally applicable to natural persons, namely, the principles of the law of agency: "It [*i.e.* the company] will appoint servants

and agents whose acts, by a combination of the general principles of agency and the company's primary rules of attribution, count as the acts of the company".[20c]

[20a] [1995] 2 A.C. 500.

[20b] *ibid.* at 506.

[20c] *ibid.*

Deeds

[*Add to note 38: page* [473]]   **9–008**
See also *The Execution Of Deeds And Documents By Or On Behalf Of Bodies Corporate*, Law Commission, Consultation Paper, No. 143.

(c) *Registered Companies*

(i) *Contracts between Companies and Third Parties*

Appointment of a receiver or manager

[*Add to text after note 50: page* [498]]   **9–049**
In *Powdrill v. Watson*[50a] the House of Lords upheld the decision of the Court of Appeal but held that the administrative receiver's liability (and also an administrator's) was restricted to liabilities arising under contracts during the period when the receiver was in office.

[50a] [1995] 2 A.C. 394.

Administrators and existing contracts

[*Add to note 75: page* [500]]   **9–053**
For contracts of employment see §9–049 of the Main Work.

(ii) *Contracts between Companies and Promoters or Directors*

Directors

[*Add to note 93: page* [501]]   **9–055**
Neptune (Vehicle Washing Equipment) Ltd v. Fitzgerald [1995] 1 B.C.L.C. 352; *Neptune (Vehicle Washing Equipment) Ltd v. Fitzgerald (No. 2)* [1995] B.C.C. 1000.

Managing directors

[*Add to note 7: page* [503]]   **9–057**
See also *Buchan v. Secretary of State for Employment* [1997] I.R.L.R. 80 as to whether or not a controlling shareholder can be an employee.

2. – Unincorporated Associations

(b) *Clubs*

(i) *Members' Clubs*

Expulsion of members

9–071   [*Note 96: page* [512]]
Update reference to de Smith (4th ed.), pp. 160–161 to *De Smith, Woolf and Jowell, Judicial Review of Administrative Action*, (5th ed., 1995), pp. 382, 476–477.

CHAPTER 10

THE CROWN, PUBLIC AUTHORITIES AND THE EUROPEAN COMMUNITY

1. – THE CROWN

See now Arrowsmith, *The Law of Public and Utilities Procurement* (1996). **10–001**

Incidence of Crown privilege

[*Add to note 22: page* [519]] **10–003**
See also Deregulation and Contracting Out Act 1994, ss.69–70 for the extension of the principle in *Carltona Ltd v. Commissioners of Works* [1943] 2 All E.R. 560 to non-departmental bodies. Part II of the Housing Grants, Construction and Regeneration Act 1996 applies to the Crown: s.117.

Types of remedy available against the Crown

[*Add to note 26: page* [529]] **10–017**
R. v. H.M. Treasury, ex p. British Telecommunications plc [1995] C.O.D. 56 (C.A.); *R. v. Secretary of State for Health, ex p. Macrae Seafoods* [1995] C.O.D. 369.

2. – PUBLIC AUTHORITIES

Ultra vires rule

[*Add to notes 45 and 46: page* [531]] **10–021**
Crédit Suisse v. Allerdale D.C. [1996] 3 W.L.R. 894; *Crédit Suisse v. Waltham Forest B.C.* [1996] 4 All E.R. 176. *cf. R. v. Yorkshire Purchasing Organisation, ex p. B.E.S.* [1997] C.O.D. 211. Note that the Local Government Contracts Bill 1997 (296 H.C. Deb. 623, Second Reading) seeks to remove private sector concerns about entering partnership deals with local

authorities. It clarifies local authorities' powers to enter contracts and introduces a certification scheme. The effect of which is to preclude any parties to the contract arguing in private law proceedings that a certified contract is unenforceable because the local authority did not have the power to enter it.

Local authorities

10–022   [*Add to note 55: page* [532]]
Local Government (Wales) Act 1994.

Statutory control: UK Legislation
10–024—   See Arrowsmith, *The Law of Public and Utilities Procurement* (1996). On
10–026 the tendering requirements of the Environmental Protection Act 1990, s.51, see *R. v. Cardiff C.C., ex p. Gooding Investments Ltd* [1996] C.O.D. 129.

Statutory control: European Community Law

10–025   [*Add to note 73: page* [534]]
Utilities Contracts Regulations 1996 (S.I. 1996 No. 2911).

[*Add to note 79: page* [535]]
See *R. v. Portsmouth C.C., ex p. Coles, The Times,* November 13, 1996 (effect of breach of Reg. 20).

10–028   [*Add to note 93: page* [536]]
The exercise of contractual powers by a public authority is in principle reviewable but probably only for fraud, corruption or bad faith: *Mercury Ltd v. Electricity Corp.* [1994] 1 W.L.R. 521 (termination of contractual arrangements).

Legitimate expectation

10–033   [*Add to note 19: page* [539]]
R. v. Secretary of State for the Home Department, ex p. Hargreaves [1997] 1 All E.R. 397.

Local authority injunctions

10–034   [*Add to note 23: page* [539]]
R. v. Inspectorate of Pollution, ex p. Greenpeace Ltd [1994] 1 W.L.R. 570, 573–574, 576–577.

[*Add to note 24: page* [539]]
R. v. Secretary of State for Environment, ex p. R.S.P.B. (1995) 5 Admin. L.R. 434, 443; *R. v. Secretary of State for Health, ex p. Generics (U.K.) Ltd, The Times,* February 25, 1997.

CHAPTER 11

POLITICAL AND PROFESSIONAL IMMUNITY AND INCAPACITY

1. – FOREIGN STATES, SOVEREIGNS, AMBASSADORS AND INTERNATIONAL ORGANISATIONS

Foreign states and sovereigns: the common law rule

[*Amend note 7: page* [541]]   **11–001**
Littrell v. Government of the United States is now reported at [1995] 1 W.L.R. 82, C.A.

State Immunity Act 1978

[*Note 15: page* [542]]   **11–002**
See now *Kuwait Airways Corp. v. Iraqi Airways Corp.* [1995] 1 W.L.R. 1147, H.L.

[*Notes 29 and 30*]   **11–003**
See *ante*, §11–002.

Acts of sovereign states

[*Note 39*]   **11–004**
See now *Kuwait Airways Corp. v. Iraqi Airways Corp.* [1995] 1 W.L.R. 1147, H.L.

Foreign heads of state, ambassadors and their staffs

11–005   [*Note 41*]
On heads of state, see *Bank of Credit and Commerce International (Overseas) Ltd v. Price Waterhouse* [1997] 4 All E.R. 108; Watts (1994) 224 *Recueil des Cours*, III, 9.

3. – PROFESSIONAL PERSONS

Solicitors

11–020   [*Note 87: page* [556]]
See now *White v. Jones* [1995] 2 A.C. 207 (C.A. and H.L.); *Woodward v. Wolferstans, The Times*, April 8, 1997. See *ante*, §1–077A.

Part Three

THE TERMS OF THE CONTRACT

CHAPTER 12

EXPRESS TERMS

1. – PROOF OF TERMS

(a) *Contractual Undertakings and Representations*

Collateral contracts

[*Add to note 22: page* [561]]   **12–004**
Wake v. Renault (U.K.) Ltd, *The Times*, August 1, 1996.

A collateral contract may also have the effect of varying the main contract: **12–005**
Wake v. Renault (U.K.) Ltd.[a]

[a] *The Times*, August 1, 1996.

Third parties

12–006 [*Amend note 35: page* [563]]
Law Debenture Trust Corp. v. Ural Caspian Oil Corp. Ltd (C.A.) is
reported in [1995] Ch. 152.

(b) *Standard Form Contracts*

Contracts in standard form

12–007 [*Add to text after note 37*]
But the document signed must be one which purports to be a contract or to
have contractual effect: *Grogan v. Robin Meredith Plant Hire*,[37a] (signature
of plant driver's time sheet did not vary the contract of hire so as to
incorporate the standard conditions of the Contractors Plant Association).

[37a] *The Times*, January 20, 1996 (C.A.) (noted [1996] C.L.J. 427).

Contractual document

12–008 See also *Grogan v. Robin Meredith Plant Hire*,[a] (plant hire time sheet not
contractual document).

[a] *The Times*, January 20, 1996 (C.A.).

Course of dealing

12–010 [*Add to note 52: page* [565]]
Contrast *Grogan v. Robin Meredith Plant Hire, supra*.

Reasonable sufficiency of notice

12–012 Reasonably sufficient notice was held not to have been given in *Poseidon
Freight Forwarding Co. Ltd v. Davies Turner Southern Ltd*[a] where, on
documents sent by fax, reference was made to terms stated on the back,
which were, however, not stated or otherwise communicated, since what was
described as being on the back was never sent.

[a] [1996] 2 Lloyd's Rep. 388.

[*Add to note 59: page* [566]]
Crédit Suisse Financial Products v. Societe Generale d'Enterprises [1996] 5
Bank L.R. 220 (C.A.).

2. – CLASSIFICATION OF TERMS

(a) *Conditions*

Conditions and other contract terms

[*Add to note 97: page* [571]]   **12–024**
To the reference to *Torvald Klaveness A/S v. Arni Maritime Corp.* add
[1994] 1 W.L.R. 1465 (H.L.).

(c) *Intermediate Terms*

[*First sentence of text*]   **12–034**
As amended by the Sale and Supply of Goods Act 1994, Sched. 2, paras 4
and 5.

A stipulation as to the place of delivery in an f.o.b. contract[a] and a
stipulation "linerterms Rotterdam" in a.c. & f. contract[b] is not an intermediate term, but a condition.

[a] *Petrotrade Inc. v. Stinnes Handel GmbH* [1995] 1 Lloyd's Rep. 142.

[b] *Soon Hua Seng Co. Ltd v. Glencore Grain Co. Ltd* [1996] 1 Lloyd's Rep. 398.

[*Add to note 47: page* [576]]
See also *Total International Ltd v. Addax BV* [1996] 2 Lloyd's Rep. 333
("usual Dakar refinery quality" in fuel oil contract held to be intermediate
term).

[*Add to note 74: page* [578]]   **12–035**
To the reference to *Torvald Klaveness A/S v. Arni Maritime Corpn.* add
[1994] 1 W.L.R. 1465 (H.L.).

3. – CONSTRUCTION OF TERMS

(a) *General Rules of Construction*

Intention of the parties

[*Add to note 92: page* [580]]   **12–040**
See also *Guardian Ocean Cargoes Ltd v. Banco do Brasil S.A.* [1994] 2
Lloyd's Rep. 152 (objective ascertainment of the contract, not subjective
thoughts).

(b) *Ordinary Meaning to be Adopted*

Absurdity, inconsistency etc.

12–046   In *Wickman Machine Tools Sales Ltd v. L. G. Schuler A.G.*[a] Lord Reid said: "The fact that a particular construction leads to a very unreasonable result must be a relevant consideration. The more unreasonable the result, the more unlikely it is that the parties can have intended it, and if they do intend it the more necessary it is that they shall make their intention abundantly clear." This was cited with approval in *Niobe Maritime Corpn. v. Tradax Ocean Transportation S.A.*[b], *International Fina Services A.G. v. Katrina Shipping Ltd*[c], and *Charter Reinsurance Co. Ltd v. Fagan.*[d]

[a] [1974] A.C. 235, 251.

[b] [1995] Lloyd's Rep. 579 (H.L.).

[c] [1995] 2 Lloyd's Rep. 344, 350.

[d] [1997] A.C. 313, 355 (C.A.).

[*Add to note 16: page* [583]]
*Investors Compensation Scheme Ltd v. West Bromwich Building Society,
The Times*, June 24, 1997 (H.L.).

Mercantile contracts

12–048   [*Add to note 24: page* [584]]
International Fina Services A.G. v. Katrina Shipping Ltd [1995] 2 Lloyd's
Rep. 344, 350.

[*Add to note 25*]
International Fina Services A.G. v. Katrina Shipping Ltd [1995] 2 Lloyd's
Rep. 344, 350; *Charter Reinsurance Co. Ltd v. Fagan* [1997] A.C. 313, 355
(C.A.).

(c) *Whole Contract to be Considered*

The whole contract is to be considered

12–053   [*Add to note 44: page* [586]]
Cementation Piling and Foundations Ltd v. Aegon Insurance Co. Ltd
[1995] 1 Lloyd's Rep. 97, 101; *International Fina Services A.G. v. Katrina
Shipping Ltd* [1995] 2 Lloyd's Rep. 344, 350.

Alterations and deletions

12–058   Where a one-off contract has been drafted by reference to a standard form
contract which formed the basis of its drafting, the court can take into
account the omission from the one-off contract of words that appear in the

standard form contract in order to resolve an ambiguity in the former document: *Team Services v. Kier Management and Design.*[a]

[a] (1994) 63 Build.L.R. 76 (C.A.).

[*Add to note 68: page* [589]]
Trasimex Holding SA v. Addax BV [1997] 1 Lloyd's Rep. 610, 614.

Printed and written clauses

[*Add to note 69: page* [589]]   **12–059**
See also *Barry D. Trentham v. McNeil* 1996 S.L.T. 202 (O.H.); *Evergos Naftiki Eteria v. Cargill plc* [1997] 1 Lloyd's Rep. 35, 38.

(d) *Effecting the Intention of the Parties*

Modifying

[*Add to note 80: page* [591]]   **12–063**
Coral (U.K.) Ltd v. Rechtman [1996] 1 Lloyd's Rep. 235.

Rejecting

[*Add to note 90: page* [592]]   **12–065**
Mangistaumunaigaz Oil Production Association v. United World Trade Inc. [1995] 1 Lloyd's Rep. 617 (in an arbitration clause "arbitration, if any, by ICC rules in London", the words "if any" might be rejected as surplusage).

Clauses incorporated by reference

See also the cases cited in §15–011, note 79, *post*.   **12–067**

(e) *Construction against Grantor*

Construction against grantor

In *Tam Wing Chuen v. Bank of Credit and Commerce Hong Kong Ltd*[a] **12–071**
Lord Mustill said[b] " ... the basis of the contra proferentem principle is that a person who puts forward the wording of a proposed agreement may be

assumed to have looked after his own interests, so that if words leave room for doubt about whether he is intended to have a particular benefit there is reason to suppose that he is not."

[a] [1996] 2 B.C.L.C. 69, P.C.

[b] At p. 77.

Crown contracts

12–073   The rule has no application to commercial contracts, let alone those where the contract is in standard form: *Lonrho Exports Ltd v. Export Credit Guarantee Department.*[a]

[a] [1996] 2 Lloyd's Rep. 649, 663.

(f) *Ejusdem Generis Rule*

Ejusdem generis rule

12–074   In *Andre & Cie. S.A. v. Orient Shipping (Rotterdam) B.V.*[a] the rule was applied to an off-hire clause in a charterparty which referred to a number of specified causes followed by "or by any other cause preventing the full working of the vessel". It was held that these words did not cover a port authority's refusal to allow the vessel to work or leave since that was not a cause of the same kind as those specified in the clause.

See also *Barking and Dagenham I.B.C. v. Stamford Asphalt Co. Ltd*[b] (clause in JCT standard form of building contract requiring the employer to insure against "fire" and certain other risks did not extend to fire caused by the negligence of a sub-contractor as the other risks referred to were for the most part natural phenomena or "Act of God" risks).

[a] [1977] 1 Lloyd's Rep. 138.

[b] *The Times*, April 10, 1997, C.A.

(h) *Stipulations as to Time*

Time in contracts

12–079   [*Add to note 59: page* [599]]
Bevan Ashford v. Malin [1995] I.R.L.R. 360.

4. – ADMISSIBILITY OF EXTRINSIC EVIDENCE

(a) *The Parol Evidence Rule*

"Entire agreement" clauses

12–089   In *Thomas Witter Ltd v. T.B.P. Industries Ltd*[a] it was held that a clause in the form "Purchaser acknowledges that it has not been induced to enter into this agreement by any representation or warranty other than the statements contained in Schedule 6" did not prevent a party showing that in fact he had relied on a representation not mentioned in the Schedule.

ᵃ [1996] 2 All E.R. 573 (noted (1995) 111 L.Q.R. 385; [1995] L.M.C.L.Q. 466).

(b) Evidence as to the Validity or Effectiveness of the Written Instrument

Documents that are not contracts

[Add to note 26: page [607]]   **12–092**
[1992] 2 Lloyd's Rep. 193, [1994] 2 Lloyd's Rep. 152.

(c) Evidence as to the True Nature of the Agreement

Evidence of agency

[Note 58: page [609]]   **12–099**
In *Siu Yin Kwan v. Eastern Insurance Co. Ltd* [1994] 2 A.C. 199 (noted [1994] C.L.J. 223) the Judicial Committee of the Privy Council found it unnecessary to decide whether *Humble v. Hunter* and *Formby Bros. v. Formby* were still good law.

[Note 61]
A contract of indemnity insurance is not a personal contract: *Siu Yin Kwan v. Eastern Insurance Co. Ltd (supra).*

(d) Evidence to Interpret or Explain the Written Instrument

Meaning of words and phrases

[Add to note 69: page [611]]   **12–104**
Adams v. British Airways plc [1995] I.R.L.R. 577.

[Add to note 71]
Levett v. Barclays Bank [1995] 1 W.L.R. 1260; *International Fina Services A.G. v. Katrina Shipping Ltd* [1995] 2 Lloyd's Rep. 344, 350; *Cresspark Ltd v. Wymering Mansions Ltd* [1996] E.G.C.S. 63; *Investors Compensation Scheme Ltd v. West Bromwich Building Society, The Times,* June 24, 1997 (H.L.).

Subsequent acts

[Add to note 9: page [615]]   **12–111**
Haydon v. Lo & Lo [1997] 1 W.L.R. 198, 205 (P.C.).

(e) *Evidence of Custom or Mercantile Usage*

Conflict with written instrument

12–113   [*Add to note 15: page* [616]]
Danowski v. Henry Moore Foundation, The Times, March 19, 1996 (C.A.).

Requirements

12–114   [*Amend note 22a: page* [616]]
Sucre Export S.A. v. Northern Shipping Ltd is now reported in [1994] 2 Lloyd's Rep. 266.

CHAPTER 13

IMPLIED TERMS

Intention of the parties

[*Add to note 8: page* [620]] **13–004**
Aspden v. Webbs Poultry & Meat Group (Holdings) Ltd [1996] I.R.L.R.
521.

Efficacy to contract

In *Triad Shipping Co. v. Stellar Chartering & Brokerage Inc.*[a] a term was **13–005**
implied into a charterparty that, if the shipowners incurred loss in complying
with the charterers' orders, they were entitled to be indemnified by the
charterers against such loss.

In *J. & J. Lee v. Express Lift Co.*,[b] where a building contractor sub-contracted the installation of a lift to sub-contractors, a term was implied that the contractor would inform the sub-contractors as to the general progress of the works so as to enable them to complete the sub-contract on time.

In *Wong Mee Wan v. Kwan Kin Travel Services*,[c] the Judicial Committee of the Privy Council held that, in a contract to provide a package tour holiday, a term would be implied, not that the customer would be reasonably safe while on the tour, but that reasonable care and skill would be used in rendering the services which the tour organiser had contracted to provide, whether these were carried out by the tour organiser or by others.

In *Cargill International SA v. Bangladesh Sugar Food Industries Corpn*[d] a term was implied in a contract of sale of goods, under which the seller was to procure a performance bond, that the buyer would account to the seller for the proceeds of the bond, retaining only the amount of any loss suffered by the seller's breach of contract.

In *Royal Bank of Scotland v. Jennings*[e] terms were implied in a rent review clause in a lease, where the market rent had fallen, that the landlord would secure the nomination of a valuer to establish the market rent and repay to the tenant the amount of any interim payments in excess of the market rent so established.

In *St Alban's City and District Council v. International Computers Ltd*[f] a term was implied into a contract for the supply of a computer program that the program would be reasonably fit for, *i.e.* reasonably capable of achieving, the intended purpose.

[a] [1994] 2 Lloyd's Rep. 227 (noted [1996] L.M.C.L.Q. 15).

[b] (1994) 10 Const.L.J. 151.

[c] [1996] 1 W.L.R. 38.

[d] [1996] 2 Lloyd's Rep. 524.

[e] (1995) 70 P. & C.R. 459.

[f] [1996] 4 All E.R. 481, C.A. (noted [1997] C.L.J. 21).

Obvious inference from agreement

13–006   [*Add to note 20: page* [621]]
K/S Stamar v. Seabow Shipping Ltd [1994] 2 Lloyd's Rep. 183; *Fletamentos Maritimos S.A. v. Effjohn International BV* [1995] 1 Lloyd's Rep. 311; *Cargill International S.A. v. Bangladesh Sugar & Food Industries Corp.* [1996] 2 Lloyd's Rep. 524, 531.

[*Add to note 22*]
Ductform Ventilation (Fife) v. Andrews-Weatherfoil 1995 S.L.T. 88 (O.H.).

[*Add to note 26: page* [622]]
Aspden v. Webbs Poultry & Meat Group (Holdings) Ltd [1996] I.R.L.R. 521.

Incomplete contract

See also *Aspden v. Webbs Poultry & Meat Group (Holdings) Ltd*[a] (implied **13–007** term that employee's employment would not be terminated when he was incapacitated for work). Contrast *Ali v. Christian Salvesen Food Services Ltd*[b] (no implied term that employee entitled to be paid overtime for excess hours worked).

[a] [1996] I.R.L.R. 521.

[b] [1997] 1 All E.R. 721.

Where term not implied

In a contract of insurance, the fact that the insured is under an obligation **13–008** to make reasonable efforts to prevent or minimise a loss which may fall to the insurer does not of itself raise any implication that the insured is entitled to be indemnified in respect of expenditure incurred in performance of that obligation: *Yorkshire Water Services Ltd v. Sun Alliance & London Insurance plc.*[a]

[a] [1997] 2 Lloyd's Rep. 21.

[*Add to note 37: page* [623]]
Thomson v. Thomas Muir (Waste Management) 1995 S.L.T. 403, O.H.

[*Add to note 38*]
John Mowlem & Co. v. Eagle Star Insurance Co. (1994) 62 Build.L.R. 126; *Ductform Ventilation (Fife) v. Andrews-Weatherfoil* 1995 S.L.T. 88, O.H.; *Thomson v. Thomas Muir (Waste Management)* 1995 S.L.T. 403, O.H.

When implied from usage or custom

[*Add to note 91: page* [628]]   **13–014**
Danowski v. Henry Moore Foundation, The Times, March 19, 1996 (C.A.).

[*Amend note 92: page* [628]]
Sucre Export S.A. v. Northern Shipping Ltd is now reported in [1994] 2 Lloyd's Rep. 266.

Sale of Goods, hire-purchase and hire

13–021   [*Text at note 26: page* [632]]
As amended by the Sale and Supply of Goods Act 1994, s.1 (see *post*, §41–070) and Sched. 2, para. 5.

[*Text at note 27*]
As amended by the Sale and Supply of Goods Act 1994, Sched. 2, para. 4.

[*Text at note 28*]
As amended by the Sale and Supply of Goods Act 1994, Sched. 2, para. 6.

Supply of goods

13–022   [*Text at note 29: page* [633]]
As amended by the Sale and Supply of Goods Act 1994, Sched. 2, para. 6.

Trading stamps

13–023   [*Note 38*]
See the amendments to the Trading Stamps Act 1964 effected by the Sale and Supply of Goods Act 1994, Sched. 2, para. 1.

[*Add new paragraph*]
13–023A   **Disposition of property.** Part I of the Law of Property (Miscellaneous Provisions) Act 1994 sets out the covenants for title that are implied on a disposition of property. "Property" is defined in s.1(4) in the same terms as s.205(1)(xx) of the Law of Property Act 1925 to include "a thing in action, and any interest in real or personal property".

Supply of services

13–024   [*Note 42*]
See *John Lelliott (Contracts) v. Byrne Bros. (Formwork)* (1994) 31 Con.L.R. 89.

[*Note 45: page* [634]]
See also *John Lelliott (Contracts) v. Byrne Bros. (Formwork)* (1994) 31 Con.L.R. 89 (hire); *St Alban's City and District Council v. International Computers Ltd* [1996] 4 All E.R. 481 (C.A.) (supply of computer program).

Package travel etc.

13–025   For the position at common law, see *Wong Mee Wan v. Kwan Kin Travel Services.*[a]

[a] [1996] 1 W.L.R. 38; *supra*, §13–005.

CHAPTER 14

EXEMPTION CLAUSES

2. – RULES OF CONSTRUCTION

General principles

In *Bovis Construction (Scotland) v. Whatlings Construction*[a] contractors **14–005** agreed with sub-contractors under a construction contract that damages "in respect of time related costs" should be limited to £100,000. The contractors determined the contract on the ground of the sub-contractors' alleged failure to proceed diligently with the contract and claimed damages from the sub-contractors in excess of £2 million. The House of Lords held that the limitation clause did not cover damages flowing from a repudiatory breach leading to termination and non-performance of the contract.

[a] 1995 S.L.T. 1339, H.L.

Extent of clause

A disclaimer "without responsibility" on the part of a bank does not **14–006** prevent the rescission or avoidance of a contract of guarantee on the ground of misrepresentation: *Crédit Lyonnais Bank Nederland v. Export Credit Guarantee Department.*[a]

ᵃ [1996] 1 Lloyd's Rep. 1.

14-007   [*Add to note 30: page* [638]]
British Sugar Plc v. NEI Power Projects Ltd, *The Times*, February 21, 1997.

Liability for negligence

14-011   A clause in a contract for the carriage of goods by road: "The Owners shall indemnify the Company against all claims and demands whatever by whoever made. ... ." is not one where there is a specific reference to negligence or a synonym for it, but these words are wide enough (subject to Lord Morton's third test) to cover negligence: *Shell Chemicals Ltd v. P. & O. Roadtanks Ltd.*ᵃ

ᵃ [1995] 1 Lloyd's Rep. 297.

[*Amend note 86: page* [644]]
Caledonia Ltd v. Orbit Value Co. Europe is reported in [1994] 1 W.L.R. 1515 (C.A.).

14-012   In *Shell Chemicals Ltd v. P. & O. Roadtanks Ltd*ᵃ it was held in relation to the exemption clause referred to in §14–011 *ante*, that there were "other grounds" not fanciful or remote, for example, a claim by a non-contracting owner in conversion, with the result that the clause failed under Lord Morton's third test.
    Also in *Toomey v. Eagle Star Insurance Co. Ltd*ᵇ it was held that a clause in a contract of reinsurance "this contract is neither cancellable nor voidable by either party" on its true construction only excluded the right to rescind for innocent misrepresentation or innocent non-disclosure and not for negligent misrepresentation or negligent non-disclosure, and it did not exclude the right to claim damages under section 2(1) of the Misrepresentation Act 1967.

ᵃ [1995] 1 Lloyd's Rep. 297.

ᵇ [1995] 2 Lloyd's Rep. 88.

[*Amend note 92: page* [645]]
Caledonia Ltd v. Orbit Valve Co. Europe is reported in [1994] 1 W.L.R. 1515, C.A.

Indemnity clauses

14-014   [*Add to note 1: page* [646]]
Shell Chemicals Ltd v. P. & O. Roadtanks Ltd [1995] 1 Lloyd's Rep. 297.

[*Amend note 3*]
Caledonia Ltd v. Orbit Valve Co. Europe is reported in [1994] 1 W.L.R.
1515 (C.A.). And add: *Shell Chemicals Ltd v. P. & O. Roadtanks Ltd* [1995] 1
Lloyd's Rep. 297.

[*Add to note 4 (in the list of cases on effective indemnities)*]
Nelson v. Atlantic Power and Gas 1995 S.L.T. 46.
Caledonia Ltd v. Orbit Valve Co. Europe is reported in [1994] 1 W.L.R.
1515 (C.A.).
And add at end: *Shell Chemicals Ltd v. P. & O. Roadtanks Ltd* [1995] 1
Lloyd's Rep. 297.

Deliberate breaches

[*Add to note 13: page* [647]]
See also *National Semiconductors (UK) Ltd v. Ups Ltd* [1996] 2 Lloyd's
Rep. 212 (wilful misconduct), *cf.*, *Bovis International Inc. v. Circle Ltd
Partnerships* [1995] N.P.C. 128 (C.A.) ("default or wilful neglect"); *Lacey's
Footwear Ltd v. Bowler International Freight Ltd*, *The Times*, May 12, 1997
(C.A.) (wilful misconduct).

14–015

4. – APPLICATION OF RULES OF CONSTRUCTION TO PARTICULAR CONTRACTS

Carriage of Goods

[*Amend note 92: page* [657]]
Sucre Export S.A. v. Northern Shipping Ltd is reported in [1994] 2 Lloyd's
Rep. 266. And add at end: *Pyramid Sound N.V. v. Briese Schiffahrts GmbH
& Co.* [1995] 2 Lloyd's Rep. 144.

14–028

5. – EXEMPTION CLAUSES AND THIRD PARTIES

The general rule: benefit

[*Add to note 15: page* [661]]
See also *The Mahkutai* [1996] A.C. 650.

14–033

Vicarious immunity

[*Add to note 19: page* [661]]
See also *The Mahkutai* [1996] A.C. 650 (bailment on terms).

14–034

Bailment

[*Amend notes 47 and 52: page* [665]]
Owners of Cargo lately laden on board K.H. Enterprise v. Owners of

14–041

Pioneer Container is reported *sub nom. The Pioneer Container* [1994] 2 A.C. 324 (noted [1994] C.L.J. 440).

[*Add to notes 47 and 52*]
Spectra International Plc v. Hayesoak Ltd [1997] 1 Lloyd's Rep. 153. See also *Devonshire,* [1996] J.B.L. 329.

[*Add to note 49*]
The Mahkutai [1996] A.C. 650.

[*Add to note 52*]
Sonicare International Ltd v. East Anglia Freight Terminal Ltd [1997] 2 Lloyd's Rep. 48.

14–042   [*Add to note 55: page* [666]]
The Mahkutai [1996] A.C. 650.

[*Add to note 60: page* [667]]
Sonicare International Ltd v. East Anglia Freight Terminal Ltd [1997] 2 Lloyd's Rep. 48.

Building and construction contracts

14–043   [*Add to note 64: page* [667]]
Contrast *National Trust v. Haden Young Ltd* (1995) 72 Build.L.R. 1 (C.A.).

[*Add to note 65*]
cf. National Trust v. Haden Young Ltd (1995) 72 Build.L.R. 1 (C.A.).

6. – STATUTORY CONTROL OF EXEMPTION CLAUSES

(a) *Unfair Contract Terms Act 1977*

Varieties of exemption clause

14–048   [*Add to note 97: page* [671]]
Fastframe Ltd v. Lochinski, unreported, Court of Appeal, March 3, 1993 (noted [1994] 57 M.L.R. 960).

[*Amend note 1*]
Delete the reference to the Consumer Arbitration Agreements Act 1988, and substitute "Arbitration Act 1996, ss.89–92."

[*Add to note 8 before "('entire agreement' clause)": page* [672]] **14–049**
Thomas Witter Ltd v. T.B.P. Industries Ltd [1996] 2 All E.R. 573 (noted (1995) 111 L.Q.R. 385; [1995] L.M.C.L.Q. 466).

Dealing as consumer

[*Add to note 21: page* [673]] **14–052**
Contrast *St Alban's City and District Council v. International Computers Ltd* [1996] 4 All E.R. 481, 490 (C.A.).

Negligence liability

[*Note 35: page* [674]] **14–055**
See *Salvage Association v. Cap Financial Services* [1995] F.S.R. 654 (limitation of liability in computer accounting contract to £25,000 held unreasonable).

Liability arising in contract

The question whether one party has dealt "on the other's written standard **14–056**
terms of business" is one of fact. In *St Alban's City and District Council v. International Computers Ltd*[a] it was held that one party may be dealing on the other's standard terms of business even though he negotiates over those terms before he enters into the contract if in fact he enters into the contract on those terms. But in *Salvage Association v. Cap Financial Services*[b] this condition was not satisfied where the defendant's standard terms were a starting point for negotiation, the plaintiff sought legal advice and the defendant largely agreed amendments sought by the plaintiff, the parties were of equal bargaining power and the negotiations continued for some time.

[a] [1996] 4 All E.R. 481, 490–491 (C.A.).

[b] [1995] F.S.R. 654.

[*Add to note 43: page* [675]] **14–057**
St. Alban's City and District Council v. International Computers Ltd [1996] 4 All E.R. 481 (C.A.).

[*Add to note 44*]
See also *Timeload Ltd v. British Telecommunications Plc* [1995] E.M.L.R. 459 (C.A.).

14-058   But in *Timeload Ltd v. British Telecommunications Plc*[a] the Court of
Appeal held unreasonable a term in BT's standard terms and conditions
which permitted BT to terminate the contract on one month's notice since
the term was not limited to cases where there was good reason for the
termination.

[a] [1995] E.M.L.R. 459.

Test of reasonableness

14-068   [*Add to note 90: page* [680]]
Contrasts s.11(3) (notices) and see *First National Bank Plc v. Loxley*
[1996] E.G.C.S. 174 (C.A.).

Guidelines

14-069   [*Notes 96 and 97: pages* [680] *and* [681]]
See *St Alban's City and District Council v. International Computers Ltd*
[1995] F.S.R. 686; [1996] 4 All E.R. 481 (C.A.).

[*Add to note 99*]
AEG (UK) Ltd v. Logic Resource Ltd [1996] C.L.C. 265 (noted [1996]
L.M.C.L.Q. 334).

[*Add to note 1*]
Sargant v. CIT (England) (t/a Citalia) [1994] C.L.Y. 566; *Knight Machinery (Holdings) v. Rennie* 1995 S.L.T. 166.

Limits on amount

14-070   [*Note 4: page* [682]]
See *St Alban's City and District Council v. International Computers Ltd*
[1995] F.S.R. 686, affd. [1996] 4 All E.R. 481 (C.A.); *Salvage Association v.
Cap Financial Services* [1995] F.S.R. 654.

Burden of proof

14-071   It is unnecessary for a plaintiff to indicate in his pleadings that he intends
to challenge the reasonableness of a term in a contract relied upon by the
defendant: *Sheffield v. Pickfords Ltd.*[a]

[a] *The Times*, March 17, 1997 (C.A.).

Judicial application of the reasonableness test

14-074   In *Fastframe Ltd v. Lochinski*,[a] a "no set-off or deduction" clause in a
business format franchise agreement was held to be unreasonable.

In *Edmund Murray Ltd v. BSP International Foundations Ltd*[b] a term in a contract for the sale of a drilling rig with detailed requirements for performance, which purported to exclude liability on the part of the seller for breach of both express and implied obligations, did not satisfy the requirement of reasonableness.

In *St Alban's City and District Council v. International Computers Ltd*[c] a term in a computer software contract made with a local authority limited the liability of the supplier to £100,000. It was held that this limitation was unreasonable, having regard to the fact that the supplier had ample resources to meet any liability and was insured for £50 million worldwide, that very few companies could meet the authority's requirements and all of those companies dealt on similar standard terms, that the supplier was in a strong bargaining position and that no evidence was adduced to show why the limit of £100,000 was justified.

In *Salvage Association v. Cap Financial Services*[d] a term in computer accounting contracts limited the liability of the supplier to £25,000. It was held that this limitation was unreasonable, having regard to the fact that it would be prohibitively expensive for the purchaser to insure and the supplier had insurance up to £5 million.

In *AEG (UK) Ltd v. Logic Resource Ltd*[e] a term in a contract for the sale of radar equipment provided that all warranties and conditions implied by the Sale of Goods Act 1979 were excluded, save for a warranty that the equipment was free of defects caused by faulty materials or bad workmanship. This was held in the circumstances to be unreasonable.

See also *Timeload Ltd v. British Telecommunications Plc*,[f] *ante* §14–058.

[a] Unreported, Court of Appeal, March 3, 1993 (noted in (1994) 57 M.L.R. 960).

[b] (1994) 33 Con.L.R. 1 (C.A.).

[c] [1995] F.S.R. 686, affd. [1996] 4 All E.R. 481 (C.A.), noted.
(noted in [1997] C.L.J. 21).

[d] [1995] F.S.R. 654.

[e] [1996] C.L.C. 265 (noted [1996] L.M.C.L.Q. 334).

[f] [1995] E.M.L.R. 459.

In *McCullagh v. Lane Fox Partners Ltd*,[a] an action for negligent **14–075** mis-statement was brought against estate agents with respect to a misrepresentation as to the size of a neighbouring plot of land. It was held that no duty of care arose due to a disclaimer in the sale particulars and that the disclaimer was reasonable.

In *Sargant v. CIT (England) (t/a Citalia)*,[b] a term in a package tour holiday contract which required complaints to be made within 28 days of returning home was held to pass the test of reasonableness.

In *Sonicare International Ltd v. East Anglia Freight Terminal Ltd*[c] a clause in the conditions of contract of the National Association of Warehouse Keepers limiting liability to £100 per tonne was held to be reasonable.

[a] *The Times*, December 22, 1995 (C.A.).

[b] [1994] C.L.Y. 566.

[c] [1997] 2 Lloyd's Rep. 48.

Appeals

14–077   [*Note 41: page* [686]]
See also *Edmund Murray Ltd v. BSP International Foundations Ltd* (1994) 33 Con.L.R. 1 (C.A.); *St. Alban's City and District Council v. International Computers Ltd* [1996] 4 All E.R. 481, 491 (C.A.).

Schedule 1

14–079   Para. 1(c) of Sched. 1 only applies to those provisions in a contract which deal with the creation or termination of a right or interest in the relevant intellectual property, and does not necessarily extend to the whole contract: *Salvage Association v. Cap Financial Services.*[a]

[a] [1995] F.S.R. 654.

[*Note 43*]
Para. 1(b) of Sched. 1 is not limited to that part of an agreement which creates or transfers an interest in land but extends to those parts of a mortgage agreement (the terms for repayment of money secured by a mortgage) which relate to the creation of such an interest: *Cheltenham and Gloucester Building Society v. Ebbage* [1994] C.L.Y. 3292 (Cty.Ct.).

Contractual provisions approved by a competent authority

14–085   In *Timeload Ltd v. British Telecommunications Plc.*[a] the Court of Appeal held that s.29(2) was inapplicable to BT's standard terms and conditions which had been seen and not objected to by the Director General of Fair Trading. Although the Director General was a public authority within s.29(3), he could not be said to have approved them in the exercise of a statutory function.

[a] [1995] E.M.L.R. 459.

(b) *Misrepresentation Act 1967*

Liability for misrepresentation

14–087   In *Toomey v. Eagle Star Insurance Co. Ltd*[a] it was held that it was possible to write a clause into a contract which excluded the right to rescind the contract for misrepresentation or material non-disclosure, although the clause in question[b] did not achieve this result. Section 3 of the Misrepresentation Act 1967 was not referred to.

[a] [1995] 2 Lloyd's Rep. 88.

[b] See *supra*, §14–012.

[*Note 62: page* [689]]
See also *Thomas Witter Ltd v. T.B.P. Industries Ltd* [1996] 2 All E.R. 573 (noted (1995) 111 L.Q.R. 385; [1995] L.M.C.L.Q. 466).

(c) *Council Directive 93/13/EEC on Unfair Terms in Consumer Contracts*

The Directive

Council Directive 93/13 has been implemented in the United Kingdom by **14–088** the Unfair Terms in Consumer Contracts Regulations 1994,[a] made under the European Communities Act 1972. The Regulations came into force on 1st July 1995 and so apply to all relevant contracts made after that date.

The wording of the Regulations follows closely the wording of the Directive (the Preamble being omitted).

[a] S.I. 1994 No. 3159 (noted [1995] C.L.J. 235).

Scope of the Directive

The definitions of "consumer", "seller" and "supplier" are contained in **14–089** Regulation 2(1). "Business" is defined to include a trade or profession and the activities of any government department or local or public authority.

The Regulations do not, any more than the Directive, expressly state to **14–090** which types of contract they apply, apart from those expressly excluded in Schedule 1 (contracts relating to employment, succession rights, rights under family law, and contracts relating to the incorporation and organisation of companies or partnerships).

[*Text at note 72: page* [691]]
Contrast [1995] Conveyancer 10 and Bright and Bright, "Unfair Terms in Land Contracts: Copy Out or Cop Out?".[a]

The statement in the text should not be taken to infer that all aspects of land transactions fall outside the scope of the Directive and of the Regulations. For example, the lending of money secured by a mortgage or charge will constitute the supply of financial services and be within the Regulations. It may also be that certain aspects of leases will involve the supply of goods or services.

[a] (1995) 111 L.Q.R. 385.

[125]

14–091   Schedule 1, para. (e), of the Regulations provides that the Regulations do not apply to—

"any term incorporated in order to comply with or which reflects—
(i) statutory or regulatory provisions of the United Kingdom; or
(ii) the provisions or principles of international conventions to which the member States or the Community are party".

14–092   [*Note 85: page* [692]]
See Schedule 3 to the Regulations.

14–093   [*Note 86*]
See Schedule 3, para. 1(q), to the Regulations.

Unfair terms

14–094   The test for "unfairness" in Regulation 4(1) follows the wording of the Directive.

"Not individually negotiated"

14–095   See Regulation 3(1)(3)–(5).

Unfairness of term

14–096   The concept "contrary to the requirement of good faith" is retained in Regulation 4(1) of the Regulations. In determining whether a term satisfies the requirement of good faith, regard is to be had in particular to the matters specified in Schedule 2 to the Regulations. See Harrison, *Good Faith in Sales* (1996).

14–097   Article 4(1) of the Directive is reproduced in Regulation 4(2).

14–098   See Regulation 3(2).

Annex to Directive

14–099   The Annex to the Directive is reproduced in Schedule 3 to the Regulations. The "indicative and non-exhaustive list of the terms which may be regarded as unfair" should be regarded as a "grey list", since such a listed term will not necessarily be unfair, nor will a term which is expressly excluded from the list necessarily be fair. The overriding test is still that contained in Regulation 4(1).

Plain and intelligible language

14–100   See Regulation 6.

Construction contra proferentem

See Regulation 6.   **14-101**

Effect of unfairness

See Regulation 5.   **14-102**

Conflict of laws

Regulation 7 provides—   **14-103**

> "These Regulations shall apply notwithstanding any contract term
> which applies or purports to apply the law of a non-member State if the
> contract has a close connection with the territory of the member States"

and "member State" is defined in Regulation 2(1) to mean a State which is a
party to the EEA Agreement (*i.e.* the Agreement on the European
Economic Area signed at Oporto on May 2, 1992 as adjusted by the protocol
signed at Brussels on March 17, 1993) but until the EEA Agreement comes
into force in relation to Liechtenstein does not include the State of
Liechtenstein.

Further measures

Regulation 8 imposes a duty on the Director General of Fair Trading to **14-104**
consider any complaint made to him that a contract term drawn up for
general use is unfair, unless the complaint appears to him to be frivolous or
vexatious. If he considers the term unfair he may bring proceedings for an
injunction against any person appearing to him to be using or recommending
the use of such a term in contracts concluded with consumers. He must give
reasons for his decision to apply or not to apply, as the case may be, for an
injunction.

The court on an application of the Director may grant an injunction on
such terms as it thinks fit. An injunction may relate not only to use of a
particular contract term drawn up for general use but to any similar term, or
term having a like effect, used or recommended for use by any party to the
proceedings.

The High Court has referred to the European Court of Justice a case
which raises the issue whether the U.K. Government has, in Regulation 8,
adequately implemented Article 7(2) of the Directive: see the Department
of Trade and Industry's press release entitled "The Unfair Terms in
Consumer Contracts Regulations 1994" (Press notice P/96/160 dated
February 28, 1996).

On rulings by the Director General of Fair Trading, see OFT News Release 22/96, dated May 22, 1996; OFT News Release 40/96, dated October 1, 1996; and the *Unfair Contract Terms Bulletin* published by the OFT.

(d) *Other Statutes*

Carriage

14–106　[*Note 14: page* [699]]
The Athens Convention relating to the Carriage of Passengers and their Luggage by Sea is now contained in Sched. 6 to the Merchant Shipping Act 1995.

Fair Trading Act 1973

14–115　See also the powers of the Director under the Unfair Terms in Consumer Contracts Regulations 1994,[a] reg. 8, §14–104, *ante*.

[a] S.I. 1994 No. 3159.

7. – COMMON LAW QUALIFICATIONS

Acknowledgements

14–117　See also *Thomas Witter Ltd v. T.B.P. Industries Ltd.*[a]

[a] [1996] 2 All E.R. 573 (noted (1995) 111 L.Q.R. 385).

Fraud

14–120　*cf. Armitage v. Nurse* [1997] 2 All E.R. 705 (clause in settlement deed absolving trustee from liability unless loss or damage caused "by his own actual fraud" upheld).

8. – FORCE MAJEURE CLAUSES

Force majeure clauses

14–121　[*Delete note 57 and substitute: page* [704]]
See Treitel, *Frustration and Force Majeure* (1994); McKendrick (ed.), *Force Majeure and Frustration of Contract* (2nd ed., 1995).

Burden of proof

14–124　[*Add to notes 70 and 71: page* [705]]
Hoecheong Products Co. Ltd v. Cargill Hong Kong Ltd [1995] 1 W.L.R. 404 (P.C.).

Force majeure

[*Add to note 28 at end : page* [711]]   **14–131**
Coastal (Bermuda) Petroleum Ltd v. VTT Vulcan Petroleum SA (No. 2)
[1996] 2 Lloyd's Rep. 383 (C.A.).

Conditions precedent

In *Hoecheong Products Co. Ltd v. Cargill Hong Kong Ltd*[a] it was held that **14–133**
a clause in a contract of sale requiring the sellers to furnish a certificate
attesting to a *force majeure* event did not require them to state in the
certificate the effect on the sellers' individual position and inability to buy
elsewhere.

[a] [1995] 1 W.L.R. 404 (P.C.).

Council Directive 93/13

This Directive has been implemented in the Unfair Terms in Consumer **14–136**
Contracts Regulations 1994,[a] §14–088, *ante*.

[a] S.I. 1994 No. 3159.

CHAPTER 15

ARBITRATION CLAUSES

Introductory

The draft Arbitration Bill referred to in this paragraph was withdrawn in **15–001** favour of new proposals put forward by a Departmental Advisory Committee on International Commercial Arbitration Law chaired by Saville L.J. These proposals were embodied in a new Bill, which became, with very few changes, the Arbitration Act 1996. The Committee published a detailed report on the Bill, which will no doubt be referred to in construing the Act's provisions.

To some extent the Act restates existing legislation on arbitration, as set out in the Arbitration Acts 1950, 1975 and 1979, whilst at the same time codifying principles established by recent case law. But it also introduces certain important changes designed to improve arbitration and reflects as far as possible the provisions of the United Nations Commission on International Trade Law (UNCITRAL) Model Law on International Commercial Arbitration.

The Act reflects the view that the decision of the parties to choose a private tribunal rather than the courts to resolve their dispute must be respected. It strengthens the powers of arbitrators and the role of the court is limited to those occasions when it is obvious that either the arbitral process needs assistance or that there has been or is likely to be a clear denial of justice. General principles applicable to Part I (sections 1–84) are set out in section 1 of the Act.

For the scope of application of the provisions of Part I of the Act, see sections 2 and 3.

Certain provisions of Part I are mandatory (section 4 and Schedule 1), the other provisions of that Part being non-mandatory.

The Act was brought into force on January 31, 1997 by the Arbitration Act 1996 (Commencement No. 1) Order 1996 (S.I.1996 No.3146) (C.96), except for ss.85–87 relating to domestic arbitration agreements. It is unlikely that ss.85–87 will be brought into force since it is arguable that to draw a distinction between domestic and non-domestic agreements is contrary to Article 6 of the Treaty of Rome: see *Philip Alexander Securities & Futures Ltd v. Bamberger, The Times*, July 22, 1996 (C.A.).

The provisions of Part I of the Act apply to arbitral proceedings commenced on or after January 31, 1997 under an arbitration agreement whenever made. They do not apply to arbitral proceedings commenced before that date (s.84(1) and article 4 and Schedule 2(2)(a) to the Commencement No. 1 Order). But, for transitional provisions in respect of applications relating to arbitration made by or in legal proceedings (whether or not arbitral proceedings have commenced), see article 4 and Schedule 2 to the Commencement No.1 Order.

In order to give effect to the Act, an entirely new R.S.C., Ord.73, came into effect on the same day: see (S.I.1996 No.3219 (L.18) rule 6, and *Practice Note (Arbitration: New Procedure)* [1997] 1 W.L.R.391.

Arbitration Act 1950

15–002   Part I and s.42(3) of the 1950 Act have been repealed by the Arbitration Act 1996.

Administration of Justice Act 1970

15–003   Section 4 and Sched. 3 of this Act have been repealed by the Arbitration Act 1996 and replaced by section 93(6) and Sched. 2 of the 1996 Act.

Arbitration Act 1975

15–004   The 1975 Act has been wholly repealed by the Arbitration Act 1996.

Arbitration Act 1979

15–005   The 1979 Act has been wholly repealed by the Arbitration Act 1996.

Consumer Arbitration Agreements Act 1988

15–006   This Act has been wholly repealed by the Arbitration Act 1996. Consumers are now protected by section 89 of the 1996 Act, which extends to a term which constitutes an arbitration agreement the application of the Unfair Terms in Consumer Contracts Regulations 1994.[a] The Regulations, however, are stated (s.90) to apply where the consumer is a legal person, *e.g.* a company as they apply where the consumer is a natural person. Further such a term is to be unfair for the purposes of the Regulations—and so not binding on the consumer—so far as it relates to a claim for a pecuniary remedy which does not exceed the amount specified by order for the purposes of section 91. The amount of £3,000 has been so specified by S.I.1996 No.3211 and S.R.1996 No.598 (Northern Ireland).

[a] S.I. 1994 No. 3159 (implementing Council Directive 93/13); see *ante*, §14–088).

Definition of "arbitration agreement"

15–007   Where an arbitration clause provided for "arbitration, if any, by ICC rules in London", the words "if any" were to be interpreted as meaning "if any dispute arises" or were to be rejected as surplusage: *Mangistaumunaigaz Oil Production Association v. United World Trade Inc.*[a]

Part I of the 1996 Act applies only where the arbitration agreement is in writing, but the concept of an agreement in writing is widely defined (section 5). This does not affect any rule of law as to the effect of an oral arbitration agreement (s.81(1)(b)).

[a] [1995] 1 Lloyd's Rep. 617.

Separability of the arbitration agreement

Section 7 of the 1996 Act establishes the separability of the arbitration agreement. **15–008**

[*Add to note 64 at end: page* [721]] **15–009**
Dalhuisen (1995) 11 *Arbitration International* 151.

Scope of the arbitration agreement

[*Note 68: page* [722]] **15–010**
See also *Cruden Construction Ltd v. Commission for New Towns* [1995] 2 Lloyd's Rep. 254 ("dispute or difference" to be given its ordinary everyday meaning).

[*Note 70*]
See also *Chimimport plc v. G D'Alesio SAS* [1994] 2 Lloyd's Rep. 366.

[*Add to note 73 at end*]
Chimimport plc v. G D'Alesio SAS [1994] 2 Lloyd's Rep. 366.

[*Note 76: page* [723]]
But see sections 30, 31 and 32 of the 1996 Act.

Incorporation by reference

See section 6(2) of the 1996 Act. **15–011**

[*Add to end of paragraph: page* [723]]
Where the parties enter into an agreement subsequent to an agreement which contains an arbitration clause, the clause may be incorporated in the subsequent agreement only if that agreement is not a separate and independent contract.[79a]

[79a] *Taylor v. Warden Insurance Co. Ltd* (1933) 45 Ll.L.R.218, *Kianta Osakeytio v. Bretain & Overseas Trading Co. Ltd* [1954] 1 Lloyd's Rep. 247; *Union of India v. E.B. Aaby's Rederi A/S* [1975] A.C. 797; *Faghirzadceh v. Rudolf Wolff (S.A.) Pty Ltd* [1977] 1 Lloyd's Rep. 630; *Fletamentos Maritimos S.A. v. Effjohn International B.V.* [1996] 2 Lloyd's Rep. 304

[*Add to note 79*]

Partenreederei m/s Heidberge and Vega Reederei Friedrich Dauber v. Grosvenor Grain and Feed Co. [1994] 2 Lloyd's Rep. 50; *Daval Aciers d'Usinor et de Sacilor v. Armare SRL* [1996] 1 Lloyd's Rep. 1. See also *Co-operative Wholesale Society v. Saunders and Taylor* [1995] 11 Const.L.J. 118; *Excess Insurance Co. v. Mander (C.J.)* [1995] C.L.Y. 2921; *OK Petroleum A.B. v. Vitol Energy S.A.* [1995] 2 Lloyd's Rep. 160; *Ceval Alimentos v. Agrumpex Trading Co. Ltd* [1996] 2 Lloyd's Rep. 319; *Extrudakerb (Maltby Engineering) Ltd v. Whitemountain Quarries Ltd, The Times*, July 10, 1996.

Pre-conditions

15–012   Where parties agreed that arbitration would be held in London before two arbitrators and an umpire in accordance with ICC rules, the fact that the ICC declined jurisdiction did not frustrate the reference: *Sumimoto Heavy Industries v. Oil and Natural Gas Commission.*[a]

[a] [1994] 1 Lloyd's Rep. 45.

[*Text at note 81*]
But see sections 30, 31 and 32 of the 1996 Act.

Challenge to the jurisdiction of the arbitrator

15–013   Section 30 of the 1996 Act provides that the arbitral tribunal may (subject to challenge in the court) rule on its own substantive jurisdiction. Sections 31, 32 and 73 contain new and important provisions (derived from the UNCITRAL Model Law) as to the timing of an objection to that jurisdiction and how the tribunal may respond, and as to the determination by the court of a preliminary point of jurisdiction.

Section 67 of the 1996 Act enables a party to apply to the court challenging an award as to the substantive jurisdiction of the arbitral tribunal or for an order declaring the award to be of no effect on the ground of want of substantive jurisdiction, and states how the court may respond to such an application. But a party may lose his right to object if the objection is not made timeously (section 73).

Section 72 of the 1996 Act further provides that a person alleged to be a party to arbitral proceedings but who takes no part in the proceedings may question whether there is a valid arbitration agreement, whether the tribunal is properly constituted, or what matters have been properly submitted to arbitration in accordance with the arbitration agreement, by proceedings in the court for a declaration or injunction or other appropriate relief. He also has the same right as a party to the arbitral proceedings to apply to the court under section 67.

Parties bound by arbitration agreement

[*Text at note 98: page* [725]]   **15–014**
See section 8 of the 1996 Act (whether agreement discharged on death of party).

[*Text at note 1*]
Part I of the 1996 Act is expressed to bind the Crown (section 106).

Resort to court proceedings

An injunction may be granted to restrain the continuance of proceedings **15–015**
in a foreign court even though a challenge to the jurisdiction of the foreign court has not been resolved. An English court should not be "too diffident" in granting this remedy: *Aggeliki Charis Compania Maritima S.A. v. Pagnan SpA.*[a]

[a] [1995] 1 Lloyd's Rep. 87 (C.A.).

[*Add to note 11: page* [727]]
cf., *University of Reading v. Miller Construction Ltd* (1995) 11 Const. L.J. 388

[*Add to note 13*]
Aggeliki Charis Compania Maritima S.A. v. Pagnan SpA was reversed by the Court of Appeal: [1995] 1 Lloyd's Rep. 87. See also *Sokana Industries Inc. v. Freyre & Co. Inc.* [1994] 2 Lloyd's Rep. 57; *Shiffahrtsgesellschaft Detlev von Appen GmbH v. Voest Alpine Intertrading GmbH* [1997] 1 Lloyd's Rep. 179.

[*And add at end*]
Partenreederei m/s "Heidberg" v. Grosvenor Grain and Feed Ltd [1994] 2 Lloyd's Rep. 287; *Arab Business Consortium International Finance and Investment Co. v. Banque Franco-Tunisienne* [1996] 1 Lloyd's Rep. 485, aff'd. [1997] 1 Lloyd's Rep. 531 (C.A.); *Lexmar Corp. and Steamship Mutual Underwriting Association (Bermuda) Ltd v. Nordisk Skibsrederforening* [1997] 1 Lloyd's Rep. 288 (Lugano Convention); *Union de Remorquage et de Sauvetage SA v. Lake Avery Inc.* [1997] 1 Lloyd's Rep. 540. cf. *Toepfer International GmbH v. Molino Boschi Srl* [1966] 1 Lloyd's Rep. 510.

[*Add to note 15*]
But see the observations on this case in *Aggeliki Charis Compania Maritima S.A. v. Pagnan SpA* [1995] 1 Lloyd's Rep. 87 (C.A.).

Staying proceedings: discretionary stay

15–016   A guarantor of a party to a contract containing an arbitration clause has, in general, no right to make an application for a stay under section 4 of the 1950 Act as he is not a person "claiming through or under" the contracting party; but if the words of the guarantee provide expressly that the guarantor is to be liable for the amount awarded in the arbitration (*i.e.* that he agrees to be bound by the arbitrator's award), then there is a strong case for a stay: *Alfred McAlpine Construction v. Unex Corporation.*[a]

Section 86 of the 1996 Act provides that, in the case of a domestic agreement (as defined in section 85(2)), the court is to grant a stay unless satisfied—

  (a) that the arbitration agreement is null and void, inoperative, or incapable of being performed, or
  (b) that there are other sufficient grounds for not requiring the parties to abide by the arbitration agreement.

The latter condition is similar to the requirement in section 4 of the 1950 Act, but the burden of proof is reversed. Sections 85 and 86 are not, however, in force (see *ante* §15–001.).

  [a] [1994] NPC 16 (C.A.).

Exercise of court's discretion to stay

[*Add to note 34: page* [729]]
15–018   *Trustee of the Property of Andrews v. Brock Builders (Kessingland) Ltd* [1997] 3 W.L.R. 124.

Staying proceedings: mandatory stay

15–020   A cross-claim by way of legal set-off which is subject to a mandatory stay under section 1 of the Arbitration Act 1975 cannot be set-off against a claim in court for summary judgment: *Acctra Refining and Manufacturing Inc v. Exmar NV.*[a]

Section 9 of the 1996 Act reproduces section 1 of the 1975 Act, with changes, and provides for a mandatory stay of legal proceedings unless the arbitration agreement is null and void, inoperative, or incapable of being performed. The further ground in the 1975 Act "that there is not in fact any dispute between the parties with regard to the matter agreed to be referred" has been omitted. But see section 86 (domestic arbitration agreements), *ante,* §15–016.

  [a] [1994] 1 W.L.R. 1634.

Claims indisputably due

Because section 9 of the 1996 Act no longer empowers the court to refuse 15–021
a stay on the ground "that there is not in fact any dispute between the parties
with regard to the matter agreed to be referred" (see *ante*, §15–020) it is no
longer open to the court to give summary judgment on an indisputable, but
nevertheless disputed, claim. Accordingly a party will only be entitled to
summary judgment where the claim is admitted.

However, in the case of a domestic, agreement (as defined in section 85(2)
of the 1996 Act) the powers of the court under section 86 to refuse a stay are
more widely formulated (see *ante*, §15–016). It is arguable that the fact that a
claim is indisputably due would be a sufficient ground for not requiring the
parties to abide by the arbitration agreement (s.86(2)(b)). But sections 85–87 of the Act are not yet in force and may not be brought into force:
see *ante*, §15–001.

Admiralty proceedings

Section 11 of the 1996 Act reproduces section 26 of the Civil Jurisdiction 15–022
and Judgments Act 1982, but omits subsection (2) of that section.

Interpleader issues

Section 10 of the 1996 Act contains provisions similar to those in section 5 15–023
of the 1950 Act.

[*Add to note 84: page* [743]]
cf., Hickie v. Alternative Software Ltd [1996] 6 C.L. 40 (C.A.).

Award a condition precedent to action

See sections 13(2), (3) and 71(4) of the 1996 Act. 15–024

Conditions as to time

[*Note 4: page* [735]] 15–025
See also *Crown Estate Commissioners v. John Mowlem & Co.* [1994] 10
Const.L.J. 311 (C.A.) (clause in construction contract under which the final
certificate issued by the architects was to be conclusive evidence of quality of
materials and standard of workmanship barred the claim and left no room
for the application of section 27 of the 1950 Act after the prescribed period
of 28 days for commencing legal or arbitral proceedings had elapsed).

[*Note 8: page* [736]]

15–026   See also *Fordgate (Bingley) Ltd v. National Westminster Bank Plc* [1995] E.G.C.S.97 (time extended) and *Evergos Naftiki Elteria v. Cargill Plc* [1997] 1 Lloyd's Rep. 35; *Mauritius Oil Refineries Ltd v. Stolt-Nielsen Nederlands BV* [1997] 1 Lloyd's Rep. 273 (time not extended).

Section 12 of the 1996 Act confers upon the court the power to extend a time limit imposed by an arbitration agreement for the commencement of an arbitration, but the circumstances in which an extension may be granted differ from those set out in section 27 of the 1950 Act and the case-law on that section. It also empowers the court to extend the time to begin other dispute resolution procedures (*e.g.* conciliation) which are required as a pre-condition of arbitration.

Appointment of arbitrators

15–028   Where an arbitration clause provided for "arbitration in London", it was held that the parties must have intended that two arbitrators be appointed and, if they disagreed, an umpire. There was no presumption that three arbitrators were to be appointed. The appointment of a person as a third arbitrator was therefore invalid: *Fletamentos Maritimos S.A. v. Effjohn International BV.*[a]

Under section 15 of the 1996 Act the parties are free to agree on the number of arbitrators to form the tribunal and whether there is to be a chairman or umpire. Unless otherwise agreed by the parties, an agreement that the number of arbitrators is to be two or any other even number is to be understood as requiring the appointment of an additional arbitrator as chairman of the tribunal. And if there is no agreement as to the number of arbitrators, the tribunal is to consist of a sole arbitrator. For the power in case of default to appoint a sole arbitrator, see section 17 of the Act.

[a] [1995] 1 Lloyd's Rep. 311.

15–029   If two arbitrators appoint an umpire, there is an implied term that the umpire should be entitled to attend the hearing before the arbitrators if the arbitrators so request: *Fletamentos Maritimos S.A. v. Effjohn International BV;*[a] *Fletamentos Maritimos S.A. v. Effjohn International BV (No. 2).*[b]

The power of the court to appoint an arbitrator under section 10 of the 1950 Act is discretionary: *Petredec Ltd v. Tokumaru Kaiun Co. Ltd*[c] and *Frota Oceanica Brasiliera S.A. v. Steamship Mutual Underwriting Association (Bermuda) Ltd* (*infra*) (no appointments made).

Where an application is made to the court to appoint an arbitrator under s.10 of the 1950 Act and the respondent resists the application on the ground of undue delay in prosecuting the arbitration, he does not have to satisfy the court that the arbitration has been prejudiced by the delay, as in the cases on striking out for want of prosecution. He can merely say that in all the circumstances the claimant has not shown that justice requires the appointment of an arbitrator: *Frota Oceanica Brasiliera S.A. v. Steamship Mutual Underwriting Association (Bermuda) Ltd.*[d]

For the procedure for appointment of arbitrators in the 1996 Act, see section 16. For the powers in case of failure of the procedure for the appointment of the arbitral tribunal, see sections 18 and 19 of the Act. For the position of the Chairman, and for awards by a majority of the arbitrators, see sections 20 and 22 of the Act. For the position of an umpire, see section 21 of the Act.

[a] [1995] 1 Lloyd's Rep. 311.

[b] [1997] 1 Lloyd's Rep. 295, 644.

[c] [1994] 1 Lloyd's Rep. 162.

[d] [1996] 2 Lloyd's Rep. 461.

15–030

Revocation of arbitrator's authority

Section 23 of the 1996 Act deals with the circumstances in which the authority of an arbitrator can be revoked. The revocation must normally be consensual—the power of the court being confined to revocation of an appointment (section 18) or removal of the arbitrator (section 24). 15–031

Removal of arbitrator

In *Turner v. Stevenage B.C.*,[a] before the commencement of the arbitration the arbitrator made a request to both parties for an interim fee. Party A paid but party B did not. Three months later the arbitrator returned the fee paid by A. B sought removal of the arbitrator under s.23(1) of the 1950 Act, but this was refused. The arbitrator had done nothing improper in requesting an interim fee. An arbitrator could not accept a fee from one party only and it was better for him to return it immediately. But there was no deliberate wrongdoing in this case to justify removal. 15–032

Section 24 of the 1996 Act deals with the power of the court to remove an arbitrator and the grounds for removal.

[a] [1997] 3 W.L.R. 309 (C.A.).

[Note 51: page [741]]
Section 13(2) of the 1950 Act is superseded by section 50 of the 1996 Act (power of the court to extend the time for making an award) and section 19 of the 1950 Act by section 56 (power to withhold award in case of non-payment).

Power of court where authority revoked or arbitrator removed

15–033   Section 25 of the 1996 Act provides for the consequences of the resignation of an arbitrator; section 26 deals with the death of an arbitrator or the person appointing him; and section 27 provides rules for the filling of vacancies in the tribunal and for the standing of previous proceedings.

Conduct of reference

15–034   An application may be made under section 5 of the 1979 Act if default is made in compliance with an order made by the arbitrator, even though a past default has been remedied: *Waverley SF Ltd v. Carnaud Metalbox Engineering plc*.[a] And an order can be made under section 5 where the curial law of the arbitration is English law notwithstanding that the law applicable to the contract and the arbitration agreement is a foreign law: *Sumimoto Heavy Industries v. Oil and Natural Gas Commission*.[b] See also Rhidian Thomas, *Default Powers of Arbitrators* (1996).

For the provisions of the 1996 Act dealing with the conduct of the arbitral proceedings, see sections 33 (general duty of the tribunal), 34 (procedural and evidential matters), 35 (consolidation of proceedings and concurrent proceedings with agreement of the parties), 36 (legal or other representation), 37 (power to appoint experts, legal advisers or assessors), 38 (general powers exercisable by tribunal), and 39 (provisional awards). These considerably expand the powers ot the tribunal and introduce a welcome flexibility into its procedures.

For the general duties of the parties contained in the Act, see section 40.

Section 41 of the 1996 Act sets out the powers of the arbitral tribunal in the event that a party refuses to co-operate in the arbitral process or fails to comply with a peremptory order of the tribunal.

[a] [1994] 1 Lloyd's Rep. 38.

[b] [1994] 1 Lloyd's Rep. 45.

[*Note 60: page* [742]]
But section 38(3) of the 1996 Act gives to the arbitral tribunal the power to order a party to provide security for costs.

[*Note 63: page* [743]]
See also *Waveriey SF Ltd v. Carnaud Metalbox Engineering plc* [1994] 1 Lloyd's Rep. 38 on the interpretation of this section.

Powers of the High Court

15–035   In the 1996 Act, the court is empowered to assist the arbitral process by sections 42 (enforcement of peremptory orders made by the tribunal that have not been complied with) and 43 (power to secure the attendance of witnesses). Section 44 confers the same powers on the court in respect of certain specified matters as it has for the purposes of court proceedings, but these may only be exercised if the arbitral tribunal or institution has no power or is unable for the time being to act effectively.

[*Add to note 60 at beginning*]
Regia Autonoma de Electricitate Renal v. Gulf Petroleum International Ltd [1996] 1 Lloyd's Rep. 67, 72.

[*Add to note 70*]
Regia Autonoma de Electricitate Renal v. Gulf Petroleum International Ltd [1996] 1 Lloyd's Rep. 67.

[*Note 73: page* [744]]
See also *Gidrxslme Shipping Co. Ltd v. Tantomar Transportes Maritimos Lda.* [1994] 1 W.L.R. 299, *post*, §15–060.

Delay in prosecuting arbitration

It is an error of law for an arbitrator, in the exercise of his power under **15–036** section 13A of the 1950 Act, to dismiss a claim which is not time-barred save in exceptional circumstances: *James Lazenby & Co. v. McNicholas Construction Co. Ltd.*[a]
Section 41(3) of the 1996 Act confers upon the arbitral tribunal the power to make an award dismissing the claim in the event of delay in prosecuting the arbitration.

[a] [1995] 1 W.L.R. 615.

[*Amend note 91: page* [745]]
L'Office Cherifien des Phosphates v. Yamashita-Shinnihon Steamship Co. Ltd is reported in [1994] 1 A.C. 486.

Determination of preliminary point of law by court

Section 45 of the 1996 Act confers a power on the court to determine a **15–037** preliminary point of law arising in the arbitral proceedings. It is in terms similar to, but not identical with, section 2 of the 1979 Act. But the court must be satisfied that the point of law substantially affects the rights of one or more of the parties.

Arbitrator's award

The parties may agree to the arbitrator taking counsel's opinion on the **15–038** legal questions surrounding the arbitration, in which case such opinion, and the award based on it, will not be lightly overturned: *Gladesmere Investment v. Canada Heating*.[a]

Section 46 of the 1996 Act provides that the arbitral tribunal shall decide the dispute—

(a) in accordance with the law chosen by the parties as applicable to the substance of the dispute, or
(b) if the parties so agree, in accordance with such other considerations as are agreed by them or determined by the tribunal.

This latter provision enables the arbitral tribunal to decide *ex aequo et bono* or as *amiable compositeur* if the parties so agree (but see S.I. 1996 No. 3146 (C.96), Art. 4 and Sched. 2(4) for transitional provision).

If there is no such choice or agreement the tribunal is to apply the law determined by the conflict of laws rules which it considers applicable.

Section 48 of the Act enables the parties to agree the powers exercisable by the tribunal in relation to remedies. The section provides a list of powers to order remedies if the parties do not otherwise agree. These include the power to make a declaration, the power to order the payment of a sum of money in any currency, and the same powers as the court to give injunctive relief, to order specific performance of a contract (other than a contract relating to land), and to order the rectification, setting aside or cancellation of a deed or other document.

Section 49 of the Act enables the parties to agree the powers of the tribunal as regards the award of interest. The section sets out the provisions that apply if the parties do not otherwise agree. Those provisions contain new powers to award compound interest and to award interest at a rate different from that of a judgment debt.

[a] (1994) 15 E.G. 159.

[Note 14: page [747]*]*

Section 34 of the Limitation Act 1980 is repealed and replaced by section 13 of the 1996 Act.

[Note 20: page [748]*]*

But s.19A of the 1950 Act differs from the Supreme Court Act 1981, s.35A: *B.P. Chemicals Ltd v. Kingdom Engineering (Fife) Ltd* [1994] 2 Lloyd's Rep. 373.

[Notes 21 and 22]

Section 3 of the Private International Law (Miscellaneous Provisions) Act 1995 substituted a new section for s.20 of the 1950 Act, but this was repealed by the 1996 Act. Section 49 of the 1996 Act now provides that, subject to contrary agreement of the parties, the arbitral tribunal may award simple or compound interest, in respect of periods before and after the award, at such rates and with such rests as it considers meets the justice of the case.

Section 58 of the 1996 Act provides that, unless otherwise agreed by the **15–039** parties, an award is final and binding between the parties and on any persons claiming through or under them. But this does not affect the right of a person to challenge the award by any available arbitral process of appeal or review or in accordance with the provisions of Part I of the Act.

Section 39 of the Act empowers the parties to authorise the arbitral tribunal to make provisional awards (but the tribunal cannot so act without the agreement of the parties). And Section 47 empowers the tribunal to make more than one award at different times on different aspects of the matters to be determined, and to make interim awards.

The 1996 Act also contains a number of further provisions relating to awards: Sections 50 (power of the court to extend the time for making an award), 51 (settlement in the form of an agreed award), 52 (form of award), 53 (place where award treated as made), 54 (date of award), 55 (notification of award), 56 (power to withhold award in the event of non-payment of the fees and expenses of the arbitrators), 57 (power to correct award or make an additional award).

Remitting or setting aside award

Section 68 of the 1996 Act empowers the court to remit an award to the **15–040** arbitral tribunal, in whole or in part, for reconsideration upon the application of a party challenging the award on the ground of "serious irregularity" affecting the tribunal, the proceedings or the award. The irregularities referred to are listed in the section, but they must also be of a kind which the court considers has caused or will cause substantial injustice to the applicant. The right of a party to apply for an order remitting the award is subject to the restrictions in section 70—in particular the duty to exhaust arbitral procedures, and a party may lose the right to object to an irregularity regarding the tribunal or the proceedings (section 73).

Where the award is remitted, the arbitral tribunal is to make a fresh award in respect of the matters remitted within three months of the date of the order for remission or such longer or shorter period as the court may direct (section 71(3)).

A person alleged to be a party to arbitral proceedings but who takes no part in the proceedings may also challenge an award by an application under section 68 (s.72(2)).

[*Add to note 38: page* [749]]
cf. Albany Marine Inc. v. South Loyal Shipping Inc. [1994] 1 Lloyd's Rep. 741.

[Add to note 46: page [750]]
Glencore International A.G. v. Beogradska Plovidba [1996] 2 Lloyd's
Rep. 310.

15–041   Section 68 of the 1996 Act empowers the court to set an award aside in
whole or in part for "serious irregularity" (see §15–040, *supra*).

Section 67 of the 1996 Act also empowers the court to set an award aside
upon the application of a party challenging the award as to the substantive
jurisdiction of the arbitral tribunal or to make an order declaring the award
to be of no effect on the ground of want of substantive jurisdiction.

The right to apply to the court under sections 67 and 68 is subject to the
restrictions in section 70—in particular the duty to exhaust arbitral
procedures.

The right to object to an irregularity regarding the tribunal or the
proceedings, and the right to object to the jurisdiction of the tribunal, may be
lost in the circumstances set out in section 73.

A person alleged to be a party to arbitral proceedings but who takes no
part in the proceedings may also challenge an award by an application under
sections 67 or 68 (section 72(2)). See also section 72(1).

[Note 54: page [751]]
Section 34(5) of the Limitation Act 1980 is repealed and replaced by
section 13(2) of the 1996 Act.

Misconduct

15–042   It is misconduct for an arbitrator to ignore unchallenged evidence before
him: *Amego Litho v. Scanway*.[a]

The concept of "misconduct" as such has disappeared with the enactment
of the 1996 Act. The grounds for remitting or setting aside an award on the
ground of "serious irregularity"[b] are now set out in section 68.

[a] (1994) 2 E.G. 110.

[b] See §15–040, *ante*.

Time limit for application to remit or set aside

15–044   Under section 70(3) of the 1996 Act, an application to remit or set aside an
award must be brought within 28 days of the date of the award or, if there has
been any arbitral process of appeal or review, of the date when the applicant
was notified of the result of that process.

[Add to note 77 at end: page [753]]
Mount Charlotte Investments v. Prudential Assurance [1994] N.P.C. 110.

Judicial review of award

See Rhidian Thomas, *The Law and Practice relating to Appeals from* **15–045**
Arbitration Awards (1994).

Section 69 of the 1996 Act provides that, unless otherwise agreed by the parties, a party may appeal to the court on a question of law arising out of an award made in the proceedings. An appeal may not be brought except with the agreement of all the other parties to the proceedings or with the leave of the court. Leave of the court will be given only if the court is satisfied that the circumstances set out in the section exist. These are—

(a) that the determination of the question will substantially affect the rights of one or more of the parties,

(b) that the question is one which the arbitral tribunal was asked to determine,

(c) that, on the basis of the findings of fact in the award—
   (i) the decision of the tribunal on the question is obviously wrong, or
   (ii) the question is one of general public importance and the decision of the tribunal is at least open to serious doubt, and

(d) that, despite the agreement of the parties to resolve the matter by arbitration, it is just and proper in all the circumstances for the court to determine the question.

The application for leave to appeal must, under section 69(4) of the Act, identify the question of law to be determined and state the grounds on which it is alleged that leave to appeal should be granted.

The application is subject to the restraints set out in section 70—in particular the duty to exhaust arbitral procedures.

By section 69(5) the court is to determine an application for leave to appeal without a hearing unless it appears to the court that a hearing is required.

The orders that the court may make are set out in section 69(7).

In *Secretary of State for the Environment v. Euston Centre Investments* **15–048**
Ltd[a] an application for leave to appeal under section 1(3)(b) of the 1979 Act was lodged in time, but there was delay in the hearing of the application for leave. It was held that the court had an inherent jurisdiction to strike out the appeal. This jurisdiction was not limited to cases where the delay occasioned by one party was such as to cause serious prejudice to the other, but was exercisable whenever there had been a failure to conduct and prosecute the appeal with proper despatch. On the facts, however, the Court of Appeal held[b] that the appeal should not have been struck out.

Under section 70(3) of the 1996 Act an appeal must be brought within 28 days of the date of the award or, if there has been any arbitral process of appeal or review, of the date when the applicant was notified of the result of that process.

[a] [1995] Ch. 200 (C.A.).

[b] reversing [1994] 1 W.L.R. 563.

[Add to note 94: page [755]]
Euripides v. Gascoyne Holdings Ltd [1995] E.G.C.S. 199 (C.A.).

Reasons for award

15–049   Section 70(4) of the 1996 Act provides that, if on an application or appeal under sections 67, 68 or 69 it appears to the court that the award—

(a) does not contain the tribunal's reasons, or
(b) does not set out the tribunal's reasons in sufficient detail to enable the court properly to consider the application or appeal

the court may order the tribunal to state the reasons for its award in sufficient detail for that purpose.

15–050   The proper time for an application under section 1(5) of the 1979 Act to remit the case to the arbitrator to state further reasons for the award is before any application is made for leave to appeal and no later than the hearing of the application for leave: *Cefetra BV v. Alfred C. Toepfer International GmbH.*[a]

[a] [1994] 1 Lloyd's Rep. 93.

[Add to note 22: page [758]]
cf. B.P. Chemicals Ltd v. Kingdom Engineering (Fife) Ltd [1994] 2 Lloyd's Rep. 373 (reasons contained in a separate document formed part of the award).

Appeals to the Court of Appeal

15–051   In *Vitol SA v. Norelf Ltd*[a] the Court of Appeal ruled that the only proper role of the Court of Appeal under section 1(7) of the 1979 Act was to consider and resolve certified questions of law on which leave to appeal had been granted. A respondent who wished to raise on such an appeal issues of loss other than those certified should apply to the High Court for such a certificate and would be entitled to pursue the point only if he obtained such a certificate and leave of either court. The House of Lords[b] held that this ruling was wrong: a respondent requires no leave to appeal in such a case.

The 1996 Act provides that leave of the court is required for any appeal from a decision of the court under section 69 (appeal on point of law) to grant or refuse leave to appeal. The decision of the court under that section is to be treated as a judgment of the court for the purposes of a further appeal. But no such appeal lies without the leave of the court which is not to be given unless the court considers that the question is one of general importance or is one which for some other special reason should be considered by the Court of Appeal (section 69(6), (8)).

ᵃ [1996] Q.B. 108.

ᵇ [1996] 1 A.C. 600.

Exclusion agreements

Under the 1996 Act, the parties are free to agree that the right to have a **15–053** preliminary point of law determined by the court (section 45) or the right of appeal to the court on a question of law arising out of the award (section 69) are to be excluded. But in the case of a domestic arbitration agreement (as defined in section 85(2)) any agreement to exclude the jurisdiction of the court under section 45 or 69 is not to be effective unless entered into after the commencement of the arbitral proceedings in which the question arises or the award is made (section 87). Sections 85–87 are not, however, in force: see *ante*, §15–001.

Costs

Sections 59 to 65 of the 1996 Act deal with the costs of the arbitration. **15–054** Section 65 contains a new provision enabling the tribunal to limit the recoverable costs of the arbitration.

[*Add to note 57: page* [761]]
Metro-Cammell Hong Kong Ltd v. FKI Engineering Plc (1996) 77 Build.L.R. 84.

[*Add to note 59: page* [761]]
Cohen v. Baram [1994] 2 Lloyd's Rep. 138.

Taxation of costs

Section 28 of the 1996 Act provides for the remuneration of arbitrators **15–056** and sets out the obligations of the parties in this regard. A party may apply to the court for an order that the amount of the arbitrator's fees and expenses shall be considered and adjusted. Section 56 provides for an application to the court in the event that the tribunal refuses to deliver an award to the parties except upon full payment of the fees and expenses of the arbitrators. And section 64 provides that, unless otherwise agreed by the parties, the recoverable costs of the arbitration shall include in respect of the fees and expenses of the arbitrators only such reasonable fees and expenses as are appropriate in the circumstances, and that a party may apply to the court for the determination of this matter.

Enforcement of awards

15–057   Section 66 of the 1996 Act contains a provision similar to that of s.26 of the 1950 Act for the enforcement of an award in the same manner as a judgment but sets out expressly the circumstances in which the court may decline to enforce an award. This provision does not affect any rule of law as to the enforcement of an arbitral award by an action on the award (Section 66(4)).

Foreign awards

15–058   Once a foreign award has been converted into an English judgment, the judgment is subject to the same procedural rules and conditions as generally apply to such judgment. So, in principle, a court can grant a stay of execution of the judgment. However, it would rarely, if ever, be appropriate to order a stay in respect of a foreign award enforceable under the New York Convention when, by definition under the Convention, the time for enforcement had arrived; *Far Eastern Shipping Co. v. AKP Sovcomflot.*[a]

Section 66 of the 1996 Act,[b] does not affect the recognition or enforcement of an award under the statutes referred to in this paragraph. Part III of the Act deals with recognition and enforcement of New York Convention Awards and awards enforceable under Part II of the Arbitration Act 1950 (which is not repealed).

[a] [1995] 1 Lloyd's Rep. 520.

[b] *ante*, §15–057.

Civil Jurisdiction and Judgments Act 1982

15–059   An arbitration award which has been registered as a judgment in a foreign state party to the Brussels Convention cannot be registered as a judgment in England under the 1982 Act, since such a judgment falls within the exception in art. 1(4) of that Convention relating to arbitration: *Arab Business Consortium International Finance and Investment Co. v. Banque Franco-Tunisienne*. Section 66 of the 1996 Act,[b] does not affect the recognition or enforcement of an award under the 1982 Act.

[a] [1996] 1 Lloyd's Rep. 485, *affd.* [1997] 1 Lloyd's Rep. 531 (C.A.).

[b] *ante*, §15–057.

Injunction in aid of execution

A *Mareva* injunction in support of an arbitration award may be granted **15–060** under section 12(6)(f) of the 1950 Act even before judgment is entered in terms of the award under section 26 of the Act: *Gidrxslme Shipping Co. Ltd v. Tantomar Transportes Maritimos Lda.*[a]

[a] [1994] 1 W.L.R. 299.

Limitation

In *International Bulk Shipping and Services Ltd v. Minerals and Metals* **15–061** *Trading Corpn of India,*[a] the Court of Appeal held that the limitation period for enforcement of an arbitral award accrued when the claimant was entitled to enforce the award. Alternatively, if the claim was for damages for breach of an implied promise to pay the award, then it accrued when a reasonable time to pay the award (in this case three months) had elapsed.

[a] [1996] 1 All E.R. 1017.

Arbitration and exemption clauses compared

[*Add to text after note 32: page* [767]]
The Consumer Arbitration Agreements Act 1988 has been repealed and replaced by sections 89–92 of the Arbitration Act 1996.

[*Add to note 32*]   **15–064**
Implemented in the Unfair Terms in Consumer Contracts Regulations 1994 (S.I. 1994 No. 3159).

Valuers, experts etc.

In *West of England Ship Owners Mutual Insurance Association (Luxem-* **15–065** *bourg) v. Cristal*[a] a "sole judge" clause was upheld: a decision by the person designated as sole judge was binding on matters of fact and was not reviewable, provided that he acted fairly and not perversely in making any determination.

[a] [1996] 1 Lloyd's Rep. 370 (C.A.).

[*Add to note 40: page* [768]]
cf., John Barker Construction Ltd v. London Portman Hotel Ltd (1996) 12 Const.L.J. 277 (extension of time granted by architect).

[*Add to note 41*]
Contrast *Cape Durasteel Ltd v. Rosser & Russell Building Services Ltd* (1996) 46 Const.L.J. 75 (JCT Works Contract Conditions (Works Contract/2)).

[*Note 43*]

Section 29 of the 1996 Act confers immunity from liability upon an arbitrator for acts or omissions in the discharge or purported discharge of his functions as arbitrator unless the act or omission is shown to have been in bad faith, and this immunity extends to his employees and agents. However, this section does not affect any liability incurred by an arbitrator by reason of his resigning (but see section 25 as to relief by the court). See also section 74 (immunity of arbitral institutions).

Part Four

ILLEGALITY AND PUBLIC POLICY

CHAPTER 16

ILLEGALITY AND PUBLIC POLICY

2. – THE POSITION AT COMMON LAW

(a) *Generally*

Scope of public policy

[*Note 19: page* [774]]   **16–005**
Update reference to Hartley to (3rd ed., 1994)

[151]

(c) *Objects Injurious to good government*

(i) *Domestic affairs*

Other civil wrongs

16–018   [*Add to note 93: page* [783]]
cf. *Lancashire County Council v. Municipal Insurance Ltd [1996] T.L.R.*
22.

(d) *Objects Injurious to the Proper Working of Justice*

(ii) *Other Contracts affecting the Course of Justice*

Interference with course of justice

16–033   [*Add to text at end of paragraph: page* [793]]
However, there are many circumstances in which parties can agree as to
the future course of legal proceedings. Thus, for example, in a commercial
agreement relating to the sale of land, it has been held not to be against
public policy for one of the parties to agree to support the other party's
application for planning permission: *Fulham Football Club Ltd v. Cabra
Estates Plc.*[90a]

[90a] [1994] 1 BCLC 363.

(iii) *Ouster of Jurisdiction*

Questions of fact and expert valuation

16–040   [*Add to note 24: page* [796]]
West of England Shipowners Mutual Insurance Association v. Cristal Ltd
[1996] 1 Lloyd's Rep. 370. Such a decision, however, is open to challenge on
the grounds of fraud or perversity: *West of England Shipowners etc., ibid.* at
248–249.

(iv) *Maintenance and Champerty*

Examples of justification

16–045   [*Add to note 56: page* [799]]
There is authority for the proposition that a party who has a legitimate
interest in litigation will nevertheless be held liable as a maintainer where he
fails to undertake to pay the costs of the other party if successful: *McFarlane
v. E.E. Caledonia Ltd (No. 2)* [1995] 1 W.L.R. 366. Why this should be so is
far from clear. The preferable position is that where the maintainer has a

legitimate interest in the litigation, there is no superadded requirement that he should be willing to pay the costs of the other party so as not to be treated as a maintainer: *cf. Tharros Shipping Co. Ltd and Den Norske Bank plc v. Bias Shipping Ltd* [1997] 1 Lloyd's Rep. 246 (C.A.). See also, *Murphy v. Young & Co.'s Brewery Plc* [1997] 1 Lloyd's Rep. 236.

[*Add to note 64: page* [800]]
It has been held that despite the decision of the Court of Appeal in *Prudential Assurance Co. Ltd v. Newman Industries Ltd* [1982] Ch. 204, a major shareholder in a company possesses a sufficient interest so that the assignment to him of a cause of action by the company was not against public policy: *Circuit Systems Ltd and Basten v. Zuken-Redac (U.K.) Ltd* 11 Const.L.J. 201, 209 (at first instance). On appeal ([1996] 3 All E.R. 748) the Court of Appeal held that this issue did not arise as the liquidator had power to assign the cause of action and it was not necessary for the assignee to prove any interest for the assignment to be valid.

Effect of maintenance

[*Add to note 66*]   16–046
In *Grovewood Holdings plc v. James Capel & Co. Ltd* [1995] Ch. 80 the court held that in appropriate circumstances the court could grant a stay where an assignment of a cause of action was invalid on the grounds of champerty.

Champertous agreements between solicitor and client

[*Add to text at end of paragraph: page* [801]]   16–048
It is also champertous for a solicitor to enter into an agreement whereby he agrees to accept a reduction in his normal costs with respect to cases that are lost.[83a]

[83a] *Aratra Potato Co. Ltd v. Taylor Joynson Garrett* [1995] 4 All E.R. 695.

Non-champertous agreements between solicitor and client

[*Add to note 85: page* [802]]   16–049
Conditional Fee Order 1995 (S.I. 1995 No. 1674); Conditional Fee Agreement Regulations 1995 (S.I. 1995 No. 1675).

[*Add to text at end of paragraph*]
Provided there is no prior agreement that they will do so, solicitors can, when the outcome of litigation is known, unilaterally waive their entitlement to fees: *British Waterways Board v. Norman.*[90a]

[90a] (1993) 26 H.L.R. 232.

Assignment incidental to transfer of property

16–053   [*Add to text at end of paragraph: page* [806]]

In *Candex International Ltd v. Bank of Zambia*,[19a] the court held that the assignment of a debt in accordance with section 136 of the Law of Property Act 1925, in circumstances where it was contemplated that an action would be necessary in order to obtain payment, did not constitute maintenance. Also, such an assignment would not be contrary to public policy even if the assignor maintained some interest in the debt.

[19a] [1996] 3 W.L.R. 759.

Assignment by trustee in bankruptcy and liquidator

16–055   [*Add to text at end of paragraph*]

It is not possible for a company to obtain legal aid.[24a] In addition, it is possible for a security for costs order to be made against a company if it appears to the court on the evidence presented to it that the company will be unable to pay the costs of the defendant should it be unsuccessful.[24b] The combined effect of these rules has serious consequences for a company that goes into liquidation since it will often find it difficult to fund litigation unless the creditors are willing to put it in funds. To circumvent these rules, the question arises as to whether it is possible for the liquidator to assign a cause of action of the company to an individual with an interest in the litigation, for example, a director or the majority shareholder. The reason for such assignment is that the individual, unlike the company, is entitled to legal aid and not subject to a security for costs order. *Norglen Ltd (in liq.) v. Reeds Rams Prudential Ltd*[24c] involved such an assignment which, *inter alia*, provided that the fruits of the action would be first used to pay the company's creditors and any balance divided equally between the company and the assignee. The assignment was made under the liquidator's powers to sell the company's property which includes choses in action.[24d] The court held that the assignment was valid and on established principles was not subject to the rules relating to maintenance or champerty. A number of points need to be made with respect to such an assignment: (a) an assignment to an administrative receiver would also be valid and not subject to objections on the ground of public policy[24e]; (b) the assignment must not be a sham[24f]; (c) the cause of action must be the property of the company so that it can be assigned either by the liquidator or the administrative receiver[24g]; (d) the legal aid board in deciding whether or not to grant legal aid should carefully scrutinise such applications to determine whether it was appropriate to fund them out of public funds[24h]; (e) it may not be possible for the liquidator to surrender his fiduciary power to control proceedings commenced on behalf of the company[24i]; (f) it has been held that the rules relating to maintenance and champerty apply to the assignment of the fruits of an action (but not the cause of action itself) where the assignee agrees to fund the action[24j]. This decision, without expressing any definite view, has been doubted.[24k] It is submitted that these doubts are justified. There are no compelling reasons for placing such a gloss on the power of the liquidator to assign a cause of action vested in the company. If an assignment of the fruits of an action where the assignee does not undertake to provide funding for the action is valid,[24l] it is difficult to see why an undertaking to provide such funding should make a difference; and (g) similar principles apply to an assignment of a bankrupt's cause of action by the trustee in bankruptcy.[24m]

[24a] Legal Aid Act 1988, s.2(11); *Wallersteiner v. Moir (No. 2)* [1975] Q.B. 373.

[24b] Companies Act 1985, s.726.

[24c] [1996] 1 All E.R. 945 (and cases cited therein); *Eastglen Ltd v. Grafton* [1996] 2 B.C.L.C. 279.

[24d] Insolvency Act 1986, s.436, Sched. 4, para. 6.

[24e] *Norglen Ltd (in liq.) v. Reeds Pains Prudential Ltd* [1996] 1 All E.R. 945 at 966 (the assignment was to a creditor who has an interest in the assignment).

[24f] *ibid.* at 962.

[24g] *Re Oasis Merchandising Services Ltd* [1995] 2 BCLC 493; *Re Ayala Holdings Ltd (No. 2)* [1996] 1 BCLC 467.

[24h] *Circuit Systems Ltd v. Zuken-Redac (U.K.) Ltd* [1996] 3 All E.R. 748.

[24i] *Grovewood Holdings plc v. James Capel & Co. Ltd* [1995] Ch. 80 at 89; *Re Oasis Merchandising Services Ltd* [1995] 2 B.C.L.C. 493.

[24j] *Grovewood Holdings plc v. James Capel & Co. Ltd* [1995] Ch. 80. This case was not followed in *Re Movitor Pty Ltd* (1996) 19 A.C.S.R. 440.

[24k] *Re Oasis Merchandising Services Ltd* [1996] 1 All E.R. 1009.

[24l] *Glegg v. Bromley* [1912] 3 K.B. 474.

[24m] *Stein v. Blake* [1996] 1 A.C. 243.

Effect of champerty

[Add to text after note 35: page [807]]   **16–058**
Where a champertous agreement is entered into, a solicitor who provides services under it cannot recover on the grounds of *quantum meruit* or any other basis for the services that he has rendered. However, where payment has been made to a solicitor under a champertous agreement and he has not behaved unconscionably towards the payer or has not been unjustly enriched, the payee is not entitled to recover the price of those services while retaining the benefit of them: the champertous agreement in this situation is simply unenforceable.[35a]

[35a] *Aratra Potato Co. Ltd v. Taylor Joynson Garret* [1995] 4 All E.R. 695.

(e) *Objects Injurious to Morality and Marriage*

(ii) *Interference with Marriage*

Marriage brokage contract

16–062   *[Note 69: page* [811]]
Update reference to Atiyah to (5th ed., 1995), p. 323.

(f) *Contracts in Restraint of Trade*

(i) *Scope of the Doctrine*

General rule

16–066   *[Amend note 90a: page* [813]]
Boddington v. Lawton is now reported in [1994] I.C.R. 478.

Legitimate interests of the parties

16–075   *[Add to note 57: page* [820]]
Dawnay Day & Co. Ltd v. D'Alphen [1997] T.L.R. 334.

(ii) *Employer and Employee*

Employee's activities after determination of employment

16–083   *[Add to text after note 27 as new paragraph: page* [829]]
In a number of recent cases the courts have held that a restraint in an
employment contract, which applied no matter how the contract was
terminated, was unreasonable in that it could apply even where the
employer unlawfully terminated the contract.[27a] The Court of Appeal
recently held that these cases were misconceived. In *Rock Refrigeration Ltd
v. Jones*[27b] it held, applying the reasoning in *General Billposting Co. Ltd v.
Atkinson*,[27c] that the effect of the acceptance by an employee of the
repudiatory breach by the employer was to terminate the contract and with it
the restraint clause. There therefore could be no question of construing the
restraint to determine its reasonableness since it ceased to be binding on the
employee. Phillips L.J. doubted whether the *General Billposting* case now
reflected the law on the effect of repudiatory breach in the light of
developments since that date. It is clear that certain clauses may survive the
acceptance of a repudiatory breach and regulate the rights of the parties and

he considered that in certain circumstances this could cover a restraint of trade clause. Whether this is indeed the case will need to be decided in the future. What is clear, however, contrary to what Phillips L.J. considered,[27d] the survival of such restraints are not necessary to protect the proprietary interest of the employer as these will be protected by normal common law doctrines.[27e]

[27a] See *e.g.*, D. v. M. [1996] I.R.L.R. 192.

[27b] [1997] 1 All E.R. 1, (noted (1997) 113 L.Q.R. 377).

[27c] [1909] A.C. 118.

[27d] [1997] 1 All E.R. 1 at 20.

[27e] [1997] 1 All E.R. 1 at 14, *per* Morritt L.J.

Trade secrets and connections with customers

[*Add to note 49: page* [831]]   **16–086**
Poly Lina Ltd v. Finch [1996] F.L.R. 751.

Limits on scope of restraint

[*Add to note 69: page* [833]]   **16–088**
Austin Knight (U.K.) v. Heinz [1994] F.S.R. 52; *Aramark Plc v. Sommerville* [1995] S.L.T. 749.

(iv) *Partners*

Covenants on dissolution of partnership

[*Notes 36; page* [840] *and page* [841]]   **16–096**
Update references to Lindley & Banks on Partnership (17th ed., pp. 254–265, pp. 262–264 and pp. 248–309.

[*Insert new paragraph: page* [841]].

Miscellaneous agreements

It is well established that the categories involving the restraint of trade **16–096A**
doctrine are neither rigid nor exclusive.[43a] The traditional categories for applying the restraint of trade principles are vendor and purchaser and employment contracts. This obviously is a small sub-set of commercial relationships. In *Kall-Kwik (U.K.) Ltd v. Frank Clarence Rush*[43b] the court had to deal with the application of the restraint of trade doctrine to a franchise agreement whereby on the termination of the franchise, the franchisee was restrained from competing with the franchisor. The court

held that such a restraint was more akin to a restraint in a vendor and purchaser situation. The franchisee had an obligation to transfer the "goodwill" attached to the franchise at the end of the franchise period and this was analogous to the situation where the vendor of property enters into a restraint in order to protect the goodwill which has been transferred to the purchaser. Where a majority shareholder sells his shares and enters into a contract of service with the company which contains a covenant in restraint of trade, this could be categorised as a vendor and purchaser covenant and not one relating to employment.[43c]

[43a] *Dawnay Day & Co. v. D'Alphen* [1997] T.L.R. 334 (a joint venturer had a sufficient interest to enforce an anti-competition covenant).

[43b] [1996] F.S.R. 114.

[43c] *Alliance Paper Group plc v. Prestwich* [1996] I.R.L.R. 25.

(vi) *Restraints on the Use of Land or Chattels*

Restraint on use of chattels

16–106   [*Note 84: page* [846]]
Update reference to Cornish to (3rd ed.), pp. 250–251.

3. – CONTRACTS UNENFORCEABLE BY STATUTE

(a) *General Principles*

Express voidness by statute

16–124   [*Add to text at end of paragraph: page* [854]]
The effect of illegality is "to avoid the contract *ab initio* ... if the making of the contract is expressly or impliedly prohibited by statute ... ".[40a]

[40a] *per* Devlin J., *Archbolds (Freightage) Ltd v. Spanglett Ltd* [1961] 1 Q.B. 374, 388. See also *D.R. Insurance Co. v. Central National Insurance Co. of Omaha* [1996] C.L.C. 64, 68. On the consequences of an illegal contract see Main Work, §16–160 *et seq.*

Aids to statutory interpretation

16–127   [*Add to note 46: page* [855]]
Hughes v. Asset Managers plc [1995] 3 All E.R. 669.

[*Add to note 51*]
Deutsche Ruckversicherung AG v. Walbrook Insurance Co. Ltd [1996] 1 All E.R. 791; [1996] 1 W.L.R. 1152. Section 132 has been held to be retrospective: see *Bates v. Robert Barrow Ltd* [1995] C.L.C. 207. It is submitted that this is to be preferred to the opposite conclusion in *D.R.*

Insurance Co. v. Seguros America Banamex [1993] 1 Lloyd's Rep. 120 which was not followed in the *Bates* decision.

[*Add to note 61 at end: page* [857]]   16–128
See the very helpful guidance for determining whether breach of the statute renders a contract illegal and unenforceable: *Nelson v. Nelson* (1995) 132 A.L.R. 133, 192–193.

4. – ENFORCEMENT OF COLLATERAL AND PROPRIETARY RIGHTS

(a) *The Maxim Ex Turpi Causa Non Oritur actio and Related Rules*

Ex turpi causa non oritur actio

[*Add to note 96 at end of first sentence: page* [862]]   16–139
at 217.

[*And add after second sentence*]
Where the *ex turpi* maxim is applicable, it applies to assignees: see *D.R. Insurance Co. v. Central National Insurance Co. of Omaha* [1996] C.L.C. 64, 73; [1996] 1 Lloyd's Rep. 74, 82.

Benefits resulting from crime

[*Add to note 9 at end: page* [863]]   16–142
See also *Thorne v. Silverleaf* [1994] 1 B.C.L.C. 637, 643–645.

[*Add to note 12: page* [864]]
See also *Thorne v. Silverleaf* [1994] 1 B.C.L.C. 637, 645.

The Forfeiture Act 1982

[*Add to note 23 at end: page* [865]]   16–144
Re S., decd [1996] 1 W.L.R. 235.

Indemnity against liability resulting from commission of tort

[*Add to note 50: page* [868]]   16–148
K. v. P. [1993] Ch. 140 (in an action against the defendant for conspiracy to

defraud, the *ex turpi causa* maxim did not preclude the defendant from serving a contribution notice on a third party).

(b) *Collateral Transactions*

Alternative course of action

16–149   [*Add to note 56 page* [869]]
Hughes v. Clewley (The "Siben") (No. 2) [1996] 1 Lloyd's Rep. 35.

[*Add to text at end of paragraph*]
Also, where services are rendered under a contract which is intended to be performed in an illegal manner, or which is illegal at its inception, a *quantum meruit* claim will not lie: *Taylor v. Bhail*.[60a] Such a claim would circumvent the public policy underlying the making of a contract illegal.

[60a] [1996] C.L.C. 377 (cost of repairs inflated to defraud insurers).

(c) *Recovery of money paid or property transferred under illegal transactions*

Determination of limited interests created by illegal transactions

16–154   [*Add to text at the end of paragraph: page* [873]]
In *Tinsley v. Milligan*[86a] the House of Lords considered that its reasoning would not apply to a situation where there was a presumption of advancement between the plaintiff and the defendant[86b] (in that the presumption would negative the resulting trust). This was the issue that was before the court in *Tribe v. Tribe*.[86c] In that case, a father transferred to his son shares in a company in order to protect them against the possible claims of his creditors, the shares to be held by his son on trust for him until he had settled the claims. Eventually he settled with his creditors and sought to recover the shares from his son who refused to re-transfer them. The court held that the father could recover his shares. The court reasoned that provided the "illegal purpose has not been carried into effect in any way",[86d] the father could recover his shares on the grounds that he did not intend to confer the beneficial interest on the son and therefore the presumption of advancement would be successfully rebutted. On the facts of the case the court held that, as the illegal purpose had not been carried into effect since no deception had been practised on the father's creditors, the father could recover the shares. This decision extends, in a way that is unacceptable, the principles on the right of withdrawal with respect to illegal contracts, in that it enables the transferor of property to recover it where the illegal purpose for which it was transferred in the first place is no longer needed to protect the transferor's interests.[86e] Millett L.J. considered that the policy underlying the *locus poenitentiae* was the discouragement of fraud and therefore it

necessarily also encouraged "withdrawal from a proposed fraud before it is implemented".[86f] However, Millett L.J. recognised that in *Tribe v. Tribe* recovery by the father would not be necessary to encourage withdrawal since the reason for the withdrawal was not a change of mind but simply that it was no longer needed.[86g] This, rather than discouraging illegal contracts, produces the opposite effect since the transferor of property has nothing to lose and everything to gain by entering into the illegal transaction. On these grounds, *Tribe v. Tribe* should be viewed as an extreme, if not wrong, application of the *locus poenitentiae* rule.

The approach in *Tinsley v. Milligan*, depending as it does on proprietary concepts, was not followed in the important decision of the High Court of Australia, *Nelson v. Nelson*.[86h] It is not possible to do justice to the subtlety and scholarship of this judgment. *Nelson v. Nelson* involved a contract designed to acquire for the transferor of property under the contract a statutory benefit to which she would not have been entitled had the transfer not been effected. Thus it was a situation on all fours with *Tinsley v. Milligan*. Rather than adopt the proprietary based reasoning of *Tinsley v. Milligan*, the approach of the High Court was to determine whether the statutory rule which rendered the contract illegal precluded relief and the court held that it did not. The court cited with approval the views of an American author to the effect: "if illegality consists of the violation of a statute, courts will give or refuse relief depending upon the fundamental purpose of the statute".[86i] The majority also held that in granting relief the court could do it on terms; such a power enables the harshness of the illegality doctrine to be tempered in appropriate circumstances.

The *Bowmakers* principle can, as with the illegality doctrine in general, operate in a capricious way. The capriciousness of its operation was trenchantly criticised in the Australian Higher Court decision, *Nelson v. Nelson*[86j]:

> "The *Bowmakers* rule has no regard to the legal and equitable rights of the parties, the merits of the case, the effect of the transaction in undermining the policy of the relevant legislation or the question whether the sanctions imposed by the legislation sufficiently protect the purpose of the legislation. Regard is had only to the procedural issue; and it is that issue and not the policy of the legislation or the merits of the parties which determines the outcome. Basing the grant of legal remedies on an essentially procedural criterion which has nothing to do with the equitable positions of the parties or the policy of the legislation is unsatisfactory, particularly when implementing a doctrine that is founded on public policy."

[86a] [1994] 1 A.C. 340.

[86b] *ibid.* at 372.

[86c] [1996] Ch. 107.

[86d] *ibid.* at 121, *per* Nourse L.J.; see also Millett L.J. at 135.

[86e] See Rose (1996) 112 L.Q.R. 386.

[86f] [1996] Ch. 107, 134.

[86g] *ibid.* at 135.

[86h] (1995) 132 A.L.R. 133.

[86i] *ibid.* at 149.

[86j] *ibid.* at 190.

5. – SEVERANCE

Scope of agreement to be left unchanged

16–168   [*Add to note 54: page* [881]]
See also *Silverstone Records Ltd v. Mountfield* [1993] E.M.L.R. 152.

[*Add to text after note 54*]
Many covenants will be in conditional form and provide that X will receive
£Y provided he refrains from doing a particular act. The question inevitably
arises as to whether the severance of the condition as being in restraint of
trade is at all possible in that it will transform a conditional obligation on the
part of the covenantor into an absolute one; that is, payment of the £Y will be
due even though X does not perform part of the bargain. This was the issue
before the court in *Marshall v. N.M. Financial Management Ltd.*[54a] The case
involved a provision in a contract for the payment of commission to a
self-employed sales agent after the contract's termination. Payment of the
commission was conditional on the ex-employee not competing with the
defendant for a period of one year. The court held that the anti-competition
covenant was in restraint of trade, citing *Wyatt v. Kreglinger and Fernau,*[54b]
and the question therefore arose as to whether it could be severed. The court
considered that there were certain covenants (in conditional form) where
the only consideration for covenantor's promise was the restraint itself. Such
a condition could not be severed without changing the character of the
contract and accordingly the contract was unenforceable. *Wyatt v. Kreglinger* was cited as an example of this. There were other types of conditional
restraints, for example, an employment contract which provides for payment
of a pension subject to a proviso which constituted an unreasonable restraint
of trade, where the restraint could be severed. *Bull v. Pitney-Bowes Ltd*[54c]
was cited as an example of this. The court considered that the basis on which
these different types of covenant were to be distinguished is to ask "what
benefit is conditional on the recipient not competing and what, irrespective

of the form of the agreement, is the *substance of the consideration for that benefit?*" (emphasis added).[54d] In *Marshall*, the court held that the consideration provided by the covenantor was not the acceptance by him of the restraint but rather the procuring of the business before his resignation. On this analysis, it was possible to sever the proviso without altering the character of the contract, the character of the contract being the provision of services which gave rise to the commission.

[54a] [1995] 1 W.L.R. 1461.

[54b] [1933] 1 K.B. 793.

[54c] [1967] 1 W.L.R. 273.

[54d] *Marshall v. N.M. Financial Management Ltd* [1995] 1 W.L.R. 1461, 1467.

Part Five

JOINT OBLIGATIONS, PRIVITY AND ASSIGNMENT

CHAPTER 17

JOINT OBLIGATIONS

[*Add to note 1: page* [889]]
The Department of Trade and Industry in 1996 published a Consultation Document, *Feasibility Investigation of Joint and Several Liability, by the Common Law Team of the Law Commission*, HMSO.

Judgment against one joint debtor

17–007   [*Delete the words "or debt", line 8 of first paragraph: page* [893]]

Release, accord and satisfaction and covenant not to sue

17–008 A voluntary arrangement with creditors entered by one of co-debtors does not discharge the other co-debtors: see *R.A. Securities Ltd v. Mercantile Credit Co. Ltd* [1995] 3 All E.R. 581 and *Johnson v. Davies* [1997] 1 All E.R. 921.

[*Add to note 54: page* [894]]
In contrast, where two persons are concurrently liable for the same damage, settlement with one does not operate to release the other if the settlement does not amount to full satisfaction of the plaintiff's claim:

Jameson v. Central Electricity Generating Board [1997] 2 W.L.R. 151 (concurrent tortfeasors).

Bankruptcy

See above, §17–008.   **17–012**

Contribution between persons liable in respect of the same damage

In Civil Liability (Contribution) Act 1978, s.1, "same damage" means **17–015** damage suffered by the same person: *Birse Construction Ltd v. Haiste Ltd.*[a] However, "damage" refers to the wrong causing the injury rather than the loss suffered as a result, so that a concurrent tortfeasor which had been made liable to the victim's widow for loss of dependency under Fatal Accidents Act 1976 could recover contribution from another concurrent tortfeasor from whom the victim, before his death, had accepted partial satisfaction.[b]

[a] [1996] 1 W.L.R. 675, C.A. See also *Guinness Plc v. CMD Property Developments Ltd (Formerly Central Merchant Developments Ltd)* (1996) 46 Con. L.R. 48.

[b] *Jameson v. Central Electricity Generating Board* [1997] 2 W.L.R. 151.

CHAPTER 18

PRIVITY

1. – INTRODUCTION

(a) *Parties to the agreement*

Collateral contracts

18–003   [*Add to note 6: page* [902]]
National Trust v. Haden Young Ltd (1994) 72 Build.L.R. 1; nor was there in that case a collateral contract between employer and subcontractor.

Consideration in collateral contracts

18–004   [*Add to note 13: page* [903]] *Penn v. Bristol & West Building Society* [1997] 3 All E.R. 470, 477.

Contractual intention in collateral contracts

18–005   [*Amend note 23: page* [904]]
The decision of the Court of Appeal in *Law Debenture Trust v. Ural Caspian Oil Corp. Ltd* is now reported in [1995] Ch. 152.

Agency

[*Add to note 33: page* [906]]   **18–007**
Henderson v. Merrett Syndicates Ltd [1995] 2 A.C. 145; *cf. Bowerman v. British Association of Travel Agents Ltd* [1995] New L.J. 1815, *ante* §2–010, where the booking for the first plaintiff's holiday had been made for her by her teacher, the second plaintiff.

(c) *Development of the doctrine*

The doctrine established

[*Add to note 48: page* [908]]   **18–011**
Palmer, *The Paths to Privity: The History of Third Party Beneficiary Contracts at English Law* (1992); Andrews, 69 Tulane L. Rev. 69 (1995).

[*Add to note 56: page* [909]]
The Law Commission's most recent proposals for reform are contained in its Report on *Privity of Contract: Contracts for the Benefit of Third Parties*, Law Com. No. 242 (1996). This Report proposes a detailed legislative reform, but not a complete abolition, of the doctrine of privity: in the words of the Report (para. 5.16) the "proposed statute carves out a wide-ranging exception to the third party rule but it leaves that rule intact for cases not covered by the statute." In particular, the reform is to be without prejudice to any right or remedy of a third party which exists apart from the proposed Act, so that the existing exceptions to the doctrine will be retained (para. 12.2); and the proposed Act will not affect the present rule whereby parties to a contract cannot impose liabilities on a third party (para. 10.32). The central proposal of the Report is that a third party may in his own right enforce a contract if the contract either (a) contains an express term to that effect or (b) purports to confer a benefit on the third party (unless in case (b) it appears on the true construction of the contract that the contracting parties did not intend the contract to be enforceable by the third party). For the purposes of this proposal "enforcement" by a third party includes his availing himself of exclusion or limitation clauses in it (paras 7.6 and 3.32). Where a contract is thus to be made enforceable by a third party, it may not (unless it otherwise provides) be varied or cancelled by the contracting parties once the third party has communicated his assent to the contract to the promisor or the promisor is aware that the third party has relied on the contract or should reasonably have foreseen such reliance (and it has taken place) (paras 9.26, 9.30, 9.40, 9.42). Defences and set-offs available to the promisor against the promisee are (unless the contract otherwise provides) to be available equally against the third party (paras 10.12 and 10.16). So as

to avoid double liability, it is to be provided that, where the promisee has recovered damages in respect of the third party's loss, any award in favour of the third party is to be reduced to such an extent as the court thinks appropriate (para. 11.21). In certain contracts for the carriage of goods by sea and for the international carriage of goods by road, rail or air, the rights of third parties (such as lawful holders of bills of lading or consignees) are already the subject of detailed legislative regulation. Such third parties are therefore not to acquire rights under the Law Commission's proposals except to the extent that they are to be entitled to enforce exclusion or limitation of liability clauses in the contract by virtue of these proposals (paras 12.11, 12.15); any right which they may have to rely on such clauses at common law remains unaffected (para. 12.12). Contracts contained in bills of exchange, promisory notes and other negotiable instruments are to be excluded from the scope of the proposed reforms for similar reasons (para. 12.17); and arbitration and jurisdiction agreements are also to be excluded (para. 14.19). See Burrows [1996] L.M.C.L.Q. 467.

[*Add to note 60*]
White v. Jones [1995] 2 A.C. 207, 252, 266; *Amsprop Trading Ltd v. Harris Distribution Ltd* [1997] 2 All E.R. 991, 994; *The Mahkutai* [1996] A.C. 650, 658.

Beswick v. Beswick

18–013   [*Note 70: page* [911]]
Judicial reform of the doctrine of privity of contract is favoured by Steyn L.J. in *Darlington B.C. v. Wiltshier Northern Ltd* [1995] 1 W.L.R. 68, 77; the case is discussed in §18–036 *post*. For proposals for legislative reform, see *ante*, §18–012. See also Beale, 9 J.C.L. 103 (1995).

(d) *Scope of the Doctrine*

General

18–014   [*Add to note 73: page* [911]]
cf. The Mahkutai [1996] A.C. 650, where the actual decision is based, not on the doctrine of privity, but on the fact that an exclusive jurisdiction clause was not, as a matter of construction, one of the "exceptions, limitations, provisions, conditions and liberties" of the contract on which the third party sought to rely. Hence it was not necessary to decide whether the English courts should, in cases of this kind, adopt the Canadian view taken in the *London Drugs* case [1992] 3 S.C.R. 299, but Lord Goff at 665 in *The Mahkutai* left the point open.

[*Add to note 75*]
Herd v. Clyde Helicopters Ltd [1997] 1 All E.R. 775.

(i) *Liability in Negligence to Third Parties*

Duty of care may be owed to third party

[*Add to note 78, line 6* after §14–041: page [912]]   **18–015**
Contrast *The Mahkutai* [1996] A.C. 650, where it was held that the
principle of *The Pioneer Container* [1994] 2 A.C. 324 did not enable the
sub-bailee to take advantage of a term in the contract between the bailor and
the head bailee: it merely enabled the sub-bailee to rely on the terms of his
own contract with the head bailee as against the bailor where the latter had
authorised the relevant terms of the sub-bailment.
For application of the principles laid down in *The Pioneer Container,
supra*, see *Spectra International plc v. Hayesoack Ltd* [1997] 1 Lloyd's Rep.
153; *Sonicare International Ltd v. East Anglia Freight Terminals Ltd* [1997] 2
Lloyd's Rep. 48.

[*Add to note 80*]
Henderson v. Merrett Syndicates Ltd [1995] 2 A.C. 145; *Aitken v. Stewart
Wrightson Members Agency Ltd* [1995] 1 W.L.R. 1281.

[*Note 81*]
Marc Rich & Co. A.G. v. Bishop Rock Marine Co. Ltd (*The Nicholas H*)
has been affirmed by the House of Lords: [1996] A.C, 211, *post* §18–019.

[*Add to note 83*]
Baker v. Kaye, The Times, December 13, 1996 (doctor retained by
company held to owe duty of care to job applicant); *Barings plc v. Coopers &
Lybrand, The Times*, December 6, 1996 (auditor of subsidiary company
arguably owed duty to parent holding company).

[*Note 84*]
White v. Jones has been affirmed by the House of Lords: [1995] 2 A.C. 207,
post §18–017, §18–024.

[*Add to note 88: page [913]*]
Peach Publishing Ltd v. Slater & Co. [1997] 5 C.L. 1 (no duty owed to
purchasers of all the shares in a company by accountants who had prepared
the company's management accounts, the purchaser being advised by its
own solicitors and accountants); *Bank of Credit and Commerce Overseas
Ltd v. Price Waterhouse, The Times*, February 10, 1997.

The *Junior Books* case

18–016   [*Add to note 90, last line, after "332"*]
Henderson v. Merrett Syndicates Ltd [1995] 2 A.C. 145; *Sumomito Bank Ltd v. Banque Bruxelles Lambert S.A.* [1997] 1 Lloyd's Rep. 487, 512–514.

Tort and contract liability distinguished

18–017   [*Add to text after note 91: page* [914]]
In one group of cases, A has indeed been held liable in tort to C for simple failure to take steps in the performance of his contract with B. These are cases, such as *White v. Jones*,[91a] which hold that where a solicitor (A) negligently fails to carry out his client's (B's) instructions to make a will in favour of C, then A can, after B's death, be held liable in tort to C for the value of the benefit lost by C as a result of A's failure to act. But one reason for this conclusion was that A's omission made him liable in tort, as well as for breach of contract, even to his own client B. This would not have been the position if, in the *Junior Books* case,[91b] A had wrongfully repudiated his contract with B or had simply failed to do any work under it: such a repudiation or omission would have made A liable to B only for breach of contract. The "disappointed beneficiary" cases are also distinguishable from the building contract cases for other reasons to be discussed in §18–024, *post*; and they therefore do not support any general proposition that A's omission to perform his contract with B can give a cause of action in tort to C merely because, as a result of the omission, C suffers loss. Indeed, in *White v. Jones* itself Lord Goff [91c] recognised the general principle that in tort there was no liability for pure omissions; but he subjected[91d] it to an exception where, as in that case, there had been an "assumption of responsibility" by A towards C. The basis of that assumption seems to have been that A undertook a duty of care in relation to the provision of professional services, making him liable even to B in contract and tort for failure to act with due diligence and care. This reasoning would not apply to cases of A's simple failure to take any steps in the performance of his building contract with B, causing loss to C.

[91a] [1995] 2 A.C. 207 (*post*, §18–024).

[91b] [1983] 1 A.C. 520.

[91c] at p. 258.

[91d] *ibid.* p. 268.

Restrictions on scope of the duty of care

18–018   [*Note 5: page* [915]]
For the different position in New Zealand, as recognised by the Privy Council, see *Invercargill City Council v. Hamlin* [1996] A.C. 624.

[Add to note 7]
Losinjska Plovidba v. Transco Overseas Ltd (The Orjula) [1995] 2 Lloyd's
Rep. 395, 401.

[Add to note 8]
cf., in Scotland, *British Telecommunications plc v. James Thomson & Sons
(Engineers) Ltd, The Times,* January 28, 1997.

[Add to text after note 8]
   The duty owed by A to C in tort may also be less extensive than that owed
by A to the other contracting party, B. It has, for example, been held[8a] that,
though A, a solicitor employed by B, who was guarantor of C's mortgage,
might owe a duty to C, that duty did not extend to requiring A to explain the
implications of the mortgage to C, since the imposition of such an extensive
duty might give rise to a conflict between A's duty to his own client (B) and
the alleged duty to C.

   [8a] *Woodward v. Wolfertrans, The Times,* April 8, 1997.

Economic loss and physical harm

[Add to text at line 3, after "Chapter 6"]   **18–019**
(another type of situation in which "special relationship" may arise is that in
which A agrees to render professional services to B. Such an agreement may
give rise to such a relationship between A and C by virtue of A's assumption
of responsibility towards C: see *Henderson v. Merrett Syndicates Ltd*[8b];
White v. Jones[8c])

   [8b] [1995] 2 A.C. 145.

   [8c] [1995] 2 A.C. 207, *post* §18–024.

[Add to note 12: page [916]]
   The soundness of the decisions discussed in this paragraph is not
questioned in *Henderson v. Merrett Syndicates Ltd* [1995] 2 A.C. 145, where
the liability in tort of a subagent to a principal with whom he was in no
contractual relationship was said at p. 195 to be based on the "most unusual"
situation in that case.

[Add to note 12a]
X (Minors) v. Bedfordshire C.C. [1995] 2 A.C. 633, 739.

[Add to note 12b]
ibid. p. 749. *Mark Rich & Co. A.G. v. Bishop Rock Marine Co. Ltd (The*

Nicholas H) has been affirmed by the House of Lords: [1996] A.C. 211, approving the reasoning of Saville L.J. in the Court of Appeal and rejecting the argument that there had been an "assumption of responsibility" by the classification society towards the cargo owners so as to give rise to liability in tort; *cf. Reeman v. Department of Transport* [1997] 6 C.L. 429.

Defects in the very thing supplied insufficient

18–020   [*Delete "not" from existing heading. Add to text at end of paragraph*]
A defendant may be liable in tort in respect of defects in the very thing supplied if those defects constitute a danger giving rise to possible liability on the part of the plaintiff and the plaintiff has to incur expense in removing this source of danger: see *Losinjska Plovidba v. Transco Overseas Ltd (The Orjula)*,[16a] where it was also arguable that the defective things supplied by the defendant had caused physical harm to *other* property in which the plaintiffs had a prior interest as lessees.

[16a] [1995] 2 Lloyd's Rep. 395.

Plaintiff having no title to thing damaged

18–021   [*Add to note 22: page* [918]]
See also *Sidhu v. British Airways plc* [1997] 1 All E.R. 193, 210 suggesting that, in a case governed by the Conventions regulating international carriage by air, those Conventions should be regarded as "providing a uniform rule about who can sue for goods which are lost or damaged during carriage by air, with the result that the owner who is not a party do the contract has no right to sue in his own name" (and apparently casting some doubt on the contrary view supported by *Gatewhite Ltd v. Iberia Lineas Aerenas de Espanea Sociedad* [1990] 1 Q.B. 326). The actual decision in *Sidhu's* case was that a passenger who *was* a party to the contract of carriage had no common law claim where none was available under the relevant Convention.

Tort and contract damages contrasted

18–024   [*Add to text after "effectively." on line 4 of page* [921]]
In *White v. Jones*[39a] A had instructed his solicitor B to draw up a will containing bequests in favour of his daughters C and D, but B negligently and in breach of his contract with A had done nothing by the time of A's death to carry out these instructions. The House of Lords by a majority (Lords Keith and Mustill dissenting) held that B was liable in tort to C and D and that the damages to which they were entitled consisted of the amounts

which they would have obtained under A's will, if B had duly carried out A's instructions. The case presented certain special features, namely that C had discussed A's testamentary instructions with B, and that the letter setting out A's wishes had been drafted by D's husband. The majority do not seem to restrict the principle of liability to such special circumstances,[39b] though they do accept that "there had to be boundaries to the availability of the remedy" which "would have to be worked out as practical problems came to light".[39c] It is, for example, an open question whether such a remedy would be available to a prospective beneficiary who had no previous connection with the testator or knowledge of his intentions. Where the principle (whatever its precise scope may be) does apply, its effect is to put the third party, C, into the position in which he would have been if the contract between A and B had been performed, and to compensate C for loss of his expectation of inheriting under A's will. For the reasons given in the text of §18–024, however, *White v. Jones* and similar "disappointed beneficiary" cases are distinguishable from the building contract cases discussed in §18–023 at n.37; and the "expectations" in respect of which damages are awarded are distinct from the expectations created by a contract, for which damages are recoverable only in a contractual action. The "disappointed beneficiary" cases are further distinguishable from the building cases in that no more than nominal damages could (in the former group of cases) be recovered from the solicitor by the client's estate, since it would have suffered no loss in consequence of the solicitor's breach of duty. The negligent solicitor would thus escape all substantial liability if he were not held liable to the disappointed beneficiary for the value of the lost benefit. In the building contract cases, on the other hand, the employer will usually have a substantial remedy against the defaulting builder; and such a remedy may be available to the employer, not only in respect of his own loss, but also (in appropriate circumstances: see *post* §18–036) in respect of loss suffered by the third party.

White v. Jones was distinguished on similar grounds in *Carr-Glynn v. Frearsons*[39d] where A instructed her solicitor B to leave her share in a house to C. B drew up a will giving effect these instructions, but the house had, some 20 years before, been conveyed to A and her nephew P as joint tenants, so that on A's death her undivided share in it passed to P by right of survivorship and C took nothing. It was held that C had no remedy against B even on the assumption that B had been negligent (which was found not to have been the case) in not advising B to sever the joint tenancy. Such negligence would have caused loss to A's estate, so that the case differed from *White v. Jones* in that it was not one in which, if no duty were owed by B to C, the person who had a cause of action against B (A or the estate) would have suffered no loss while the person who had suffered loss (C) would have no claim.[39e] To give C a claim against B would, moreover, have been open to the objection of making B liable twice over, to A (or the estate) and to C "when recovery by one would not bar recovery by the other."[39f]

[39a] [1995] 2 A.C. 207. *Cf.* in Australia, *Hill v. Van Erp* (1997) 142 A.L.R. 687 (a case of actual misfeasance by the solicitor).

[39b] see [1995] 2 A.C. at p. 295, *per* Lord Nolan.

[39c] at p.269, *per* Lord Goff.

[39d] [1997] 2 All E.R. 614.

[39e] *ibid.* pp. 623–624.

[39f] *ibid.* p. 628.

[*Make the remaining text of §18–024 into a new paragraph, delete "In such cases it has been held[40] that B can be held liable in negligence to C, and" and substitute:*]

Where a disappointed beneficiary (C) has a claim against a negligent solicitor (B), it has been held.[40]

[40] [Take in note 40 on page [921]].

[*Add at end of new paragraph: page* [921]]

The view that a "disappointed beneficiary" cases are (as suggested at §18–024 of the Main Work) *sui generis* derives some support from their description as "an unusual class of cases"[42a] in *Goodwill v. Pregnancy Advisory Service*[42b]. In that case, the defendant arranged for one M to have a vasectomy and, after the operation had been carried out, informed him that it had been successful and that he no longer needed to use any other method of contraception. Some three years later, M formed a sexual relationship with the plaintiff, to whom he communicated the information given to him by the defendant relating to the vasectomy; she ceased to use any method of contraception after having consulted her own general practitioner who told her that there was only a minute chance of her becoming pregnant. The vasectomy having undergone a spontaneous reversal, the plaintiff became pregnant by M and claimed damages from the defendant. One ground given for rejecting the claim was that a doctor performing a vasectomy could not realistically be described as having been employed to confer a benefit on his patient's future sexual partner.[42c] The case was also said to be unlike the "disappointed beneficiary" cases in that dismissal of the plaintiff's claim would not produce the "rank injustice"[42d] that would arise in those cases if the only person with a claim against the negligent solicitor were the testator's estate, which would have suffered no loss. In a sterilisation case a substantial remedy for negligence (if established) would normally be available to the patient him (or her) self.

[42a] *Goodwill v. Pregnancy Advisory Service* [1996] 2 All E.R. 161, 167.

[42b] *supra.*

[42c] For dismissal on other grounds in Scotland of a similar claim by the patient's wife, see *McFarlane v. Tayside Health Board, The Times*, November 11, 1996.

[42d] [1996] 2 All E.R. 161, 167.

(iii) Liability to Third Party in Restitution?

Restitution

[*Add at end: page* [923]]   **18–026**

In *Brennan v. Brighton Borough Council*[51a] the defendant broke its contract to grant a 31-year lease to a company which had been incorporated by the plaintiff for the purpose of developing land owned by the defendant as a tennis centre. The plaintiff had incurred considerable expenditure for the purpose of the development; the company was wound up; and the defendant took possession of the site which had been increased in value by considerably more than the defendant's contribution to the scheme. It was admitted that the plaintiff had no claim in contract against the defendant. Dicta in the Court of Appeal support the view that the plaintiff's claim in restitution was not so clearly unarguable as to justify the "draconian" remedy of striking out the claim; but the claim failed on the ground that leave to amend a claim originally based on misrepresentation could not be granted after expiry of the period of limitation.

[51a] *The Times*, May 15, 1997.

2. – ATTEMPTS TO CONFER BENEFITS UPON STRANGERS

(a) *Effects of a Contract for the Benefit of a Third Party*

(i) *Promisee's Remedies*

Further exceptions

[*Note 6: page* [929]]   **18–036**

The decision of the Court of Appeal in *Ruxley Electronics and Construction Ltd v. Forsyth* has been reversed by the House of Lords: [1996] A.C. 344.

[*Add to text as new paragraph after* "18–033 *above*"]

The principle applied in the *Linden Gardens* case was significantly extended in *Darlington B.C. v. Wiltshier Northern Ltd*.[6a] The plaintiff, a local authority, wished to develop land which it already owned as a leisure centre; the building work was to be done by the defendant (a construction company). Finance was to be provided by a bank, but this could not be done in the most obvious way, by a loan from the bank to the plaintiff, as such a course of action would have violated government restrictions on local authority borrowing. The transaction was therefore cast in the form of a tripartite agreement consisting of two contracts: (1) a building contract in which the bank was the employer and the defendant the building contractor, and (2) a contract between the bank and the plaintiff, by which the bank undertook to procure the erection of the buildings on the site, to pay to the defendant all sums due under the building contract and to assign to the plaintiff the benefit of any rights against the defendant to which the bank might be entitled at the time of the assignment. Clause 4(5) of this second contract also provided that the bank was not to be liable to the plaintiff "for any incompleteness or defect in the building work"; and it was this provision which was the principal source of the legal difficulties which arose in the case. The bank duly assigned its rights against the defendant to the plaintiff which as such assignee claimed damages from the defendant in respect of defects in the work. At first instance, it was held that the plaintiff was not entitled to more than nominal damages since an assignee cannot recover more than the assignor could have done, and since here the assignor (the bank) could have recovered no more than nominal damages in respect of the builder's breach as it had no interest in the land on which the work had been done and as it was, by virtue of clause 4(5) of its contract with the plaintiff, not liable to the plaintiff and hence had no remedy over against the defendant. The Court of Appeal reversed this decision, holding that the bank could have recovered substantial damages from the defendant in respect of the plaintiff's loss and that it was this right which had been assigned to the plaintiff. Dillon L.J.[6b] described this result as a "direct application" of the carriage by sea exception stated in §18–034 of the Main Work as extended to building contracts in the *Linden Gardens* case.[6c] But one factor regarded as crucial in the carriage by sea cases, and also stressed in the *Linden Gardens* case, was that the parties to the contracts in question envisaged the *transfer* of the property in respect of which the services were to be performed; and another factor stressed in the *Linden Gardens* case was that the building contract prohibited assignment without the consent of the contractor, who could therefore foresee that a later owner of the site would not acquire rights against him.[6d] Neither of these factors was present in the *Darlington* case, so that Steyn L.J. was, with respect, right in saying[6e] that Lord Browne-Wilkinson's formulation in the *Linden Gardens* case did not "precisely fit the material facts of the present case". But he added that "only a very limited and conservative extension" of the principle was required "to apply it by analogy to the present case". He appears to have been impelled to make this extension by the fear that, if it were not made, a prima facie meritorious claim would have "disappeared down a legal black hole".[6f] The source of that "black hole", however, appears to have been clause 4(5) of the contract between the plaintiff and the bank, rather than any defect in the law. But for clause 4(5), the bank would have been liable to the plaintiff in respect of the defect, and so it would have had a claim over against the bank. Waite L.J. expressed his agreement with both the other judgments but his own reasoning (based on the sea carriage cases as extended by Lord

Browne-Wilkinson in the *Linden Gardens* case) appears to be closer to that of Dillon L.J. than to that of Steyn L.J.

The *Darlington* case no doubt goes further than the *Linden Gardens* case in recognising the right of a promisee to recover damages in respect of a third party's loss. The difficulty to which the case gives rise is that it provides very little guidance as to the scope of the exception (to the general rule that a promisee cannot recover such damages) which it applies. One possibility is that the exception is restricted to cases in which the contract involves services in relation to property which is in, or comes into, the hands of the third party. Another, much broader, possibility is that the exception applies whenever loss to the third party is within the contemplation of the parties and refusal to award such damages would enable the promisor to escape all substantial liability. The difficulty with this suggestion, however, is that it would seem to be in direct conflict with the recognition of the general rule in the *Woodar* case[6g] and with the view of the majority of the House of Lords in *Beswick v. Beswick*[6h] that, at common law, the promisee in that case could have recovered no more than nominal damages.[6i]

The above difficulties are not resolved, nor even reduced, by an alternative ground for the decision given by Dillon L.J. This was that the bank was constructive trustee for the plaintiff of its contractual rights against the defendant since, if the bank had before assigning its rights under the contract to the plaintiff, sued the defendant, it would have held any damages recovered in such an action on a constructive trust for the plaintiff. This reasoning appears, however, to lead back to the question, what damages could the bank have recovered in such an action; and if, by reason of the contractual structure, it had suffered no loss, then it would have been entitled to no more than nominal damages, so that there would have been no substance to the constructive trust. Trust reasoning would only have affected the outcome if it had given the plaintiff a direct right of action against the defendant under the trust exception to the doctrine of privity[6j]; but (in spite of the reference at p. 75 to *Lloyd's v. Harper*[6k]) the supposition in this part of the judgment is that the action is being brought by the bank, i.e. not by the third party but by the promisee.

[6a] [1995] 1 W.L.R. 68.

[6b] At p. 75.

[6c] Main Work, §§18–035 to 18–036.

[6d] *ibid.* §18–036, nn. 2 and 3.

[6e] At p. 79.

[6f] *ibid.*

[6g] [1980] 1 W.L.R. 277 (Main Work, §18–033).

[6h] [1968] A.C. 58.

[6i] Main Work, §18–031.

[6j] *ibid.* §18–045 to 18–054.

[6k] (1880) 16 Ch.D. 290.

(b) *Exceptions to the Doctrine*

In general

18–044   For further statutory exceptions to the doctrine of privity in the law relating to leases of land, see Landlord and Tenant (Covenants) Act 1995. Detailed discussion of exceptions to the doctrine relating to land are, as stated in the text, beyond the scope of this book.

(i) *Equitable exceptions*

Trusts of promises

18–045   [*Note 34: page* [934]]
For a recent recognition of the trust device, see *Atlas Shipping Agency (U.K.) Ltd v. Suisse Atlantique Société d'Armement Maritime S.A.* [1995] 2 Lloyd's Rep. 188.

Effects of the trust

18–050   [*Note 65: page* [937]]
The principle here stated does not apply where a trustee makes a claim against a professional adviser engaged for the purpose of administering the trust in respect of that adviser's alleged professional negligence: see *Bradstock Trustee Services Ltd v. Nabarro Nathanson* [1995] 1 W.L.R. 1405 where, after pension scheme trustees had discontinued an action for negligence against solicitors engaged to give advice in relation to the scheme, it was held that the beneficiaries of the trust were not entitled to be substituted as plaintiffs in the action against the solicitors.

[*And add at end of note*]
Atlas Shipping Agency (U.K.) Ltd v. Suisse Atlantique Société d'Armement Maritime S.A. [1995] 2 Lloyd's Rep. 188.

(ii) *Statutory exceptions*

Law of Property Act 1925, s. 56(1)

18–057   [*Add to note 10: page* [941]]
Amsprop Trading Ltd v. Harris Distribution Ltd [1997] 2 All E.R. 991 gives further support to the view that s.56(1) does not enable a person who is not named as a party to a covenant to enforce it merely because it is for his

benefit: he can do so only if the covenant purports to be made with him. Accordingly it was held that a covenant in a sub-lease by the sub-tenant with his lessor to repair could not be enforced by the superior landlord against the sub-tenant, there being neither privity of contract nor privity of estate between these parties. The case thus supports what in §18–057 of the Main Work is described as the third limitation on the scope of s.56(1).

Insurance by persons with limited interests

[*Add to note 18, line 5 after " ... re-insurance)": page* [942]]   **18–060**
Sumomito Bank Ltd v. Banque Bruxelles Lambert S.A. [1997] 1 Lloyd's Rep. 487, 495 (holding that the third party, not being a party to the contract of insurance, does not in cases of this kind owe any duty of disclosure to the insurer).

[*Add to note 18, line 8, after "subcontractors"*]
For similar reasoning, see *Colonia Versicherung A.G. v. Amoco Oil Co.* [1997] 1 Lloyd's Rep. 261, 270–272.

[*And add at end of note*]
Glengate Properties Ltd v. Norwich Union Fire Insurance Society [1996] 2 All E.R. 487, 497; *cf. National Oilwell (U.K.) Ltd v. Davy Offshore Ltd* [1993] 2 Lloyd's Rep. 582.

Third parties' rights against insurers

[*Add to note 25, line 8: page* [943]]   **18–063**
Cox v. Bankside [1995] 2 Lloyd's Rep. 437, 457, 466–467; *Schiffahrts-gesellschaft Detlev von Appen G.m.b.H. v. Voest Alpine Intertrading G.m.b.H.* [1997] 1 Lloyd's Rep. 179, 187; *Total Graphics Ltd v. A.G.F. Insurance Ltd* [1997] 1 Lloyd's Rep. 599.

[*Add to note 31: page* [944]]
See also *Cambridge v. Callaghan, The Times*, March 21, 1997 for the requirement of serving notice on the Bureau of proceedings against the negligent driver.

3. – ATTEMPTS TO IMPOSE LIABILITIES ON STRANGERS

Strangers generally not bound by contract

[*Add to note 37: page* [945]]   **18–065**
cf. Herd v. Clyde Helicopters Ltd [1997] 1 All E.R. 775, where legislation limiting the liability of a party to the contract was held to be effective as against a third party.

Scope of the rule

18–067   [*Add to note 42: pages* [945–46]]
There is no tortious liability for inducing *unfair* dismissal (which is not a breach of contract): *Wilson v. Housing Corporation, The Times*, December 18, 1996.

Remedy

18–071   [*Amend note 64: page* [948]]
Law Debenture Trust Corp. v. Ural Caspian Oil Corp. Ltd is now reported in [1995] Ch. 152.

Third party's liability in tort

18–072   [*Notes 69 and 77: pages* [949], [950]]
See §18–071, note 64.

CHAPTER 19

ASSIGNMENT

1. – ASSIGNMENT

(a) *Statutory Assignments*

Law of Property Act 1925, s.136

[Add to note 26, line 7, before "Another example": page [955]]   **19–003**
Note also that some aspects of the reasoning in *Warner Bros. Records Inc v. Rollgreen Investments Ltd* [1976] Q.B. 430 were disapproved by the majority of the Court of Appeal (Peter Gibson L.J., with whom Waite L.J. agreed) in *Three Rivers D.C. v. Bank of England* [1995] 4 All E.R. 312.

"Debt or other legal thing in action"

[Add to text after note 32]   **19–004**
In *Investors Compensation Scheme Ltd v. West Bromwich Building Society, The Times,* June 24, 1997, the House of Lords clarified that a right to rescind a mortgage is not a chose in action or part of a chose in action and an owner cannot therefore assign a right to rescission separately from his property. On the other hand, a right to damages is a chose in action which can be assigned. It followed that there was no objection to a clause in the Investors Compensation Scheme claim form by which investors assigned a

right to damages against a building society to the Investors Compensation Scheme Ltd but which did not assign (because legally impossible) a right to rescission of the investors' mortgages with the building society.

[Delete the second sentence with note 33 and substitute]

In *Stein v. Blake*[33] it was held by the House of Lords that, if A and B have mutual claims against each other and A becomes bankrupt, the effect of section 323 of the Insolvency Act 1986 is that the debt due to A ceases, on A's bankruptcy, to exist as a chose in action and is replaced by a new chose in action, namely the claim to the net balance owing. (The reasoning on this in *Farley v. Housing and Commercial Developments Ltd*[33a] was approved). The House of Lords went on to decide that, like any other chose in action, that right to the net balance (if any) can be assigned by the trustee in bankruptcy before it has been ascertained by the taking of an account between the trustee and B.

[33] [1996] A.C. 243.

[33a] [1984] BCLC 442.

(b) *Equitable Assignments*

Formalities for equitable assignments

19–013   *[Add to note 96, line 10, before "On the": page [963]]*

A covenant by a mortgagor to insure the mortgaged property, combined with notice given by the second mortgagee to the insurer of its interest in the insurance policy, operated by way of equitable assignment to create a charge in favour of the second mortgagee (subject to the first mortgage) over the proceeds of the policy: *Colonial Mutual General Insurance Co. Ltd v. A.N.Z. Banking Group (New Zealand) Ltd* [1995] 1 W.L.R. 1140 (P.C.).

[Add to note 98: Page [963]]

In *Neville v. Wilson* [1996] 3 W.L.R. 460, the Court of Appeal held that an oral agreement to assign an equitable interest in shares constituted the promisor an implied or constructive trustee for the promisee, so that the requirement for writing contained in s.53(1)(c) of the Law of Property Act 1925 was dispensed with by s.53(2).

Enforcement of legal chose in action equitably assigned

19–022   In *Three Rivers D.C. v. Bank of England*[a] the Court of Appeal (Staughton L.J. dissenting in part) decided that, where there has been an equitable assignment of a legal chose in action, the assignee is entitled to sue in his own name although as a matter of practice he would normally be required to join the assignor. An assignor will not be allowed to sue in his own name for himself and if he attempts to recover for himself he would be required to join the assignee. Most of the authorities cited in §19–022, n.42 were considered and applied by the Court of Appeal.

ᵃ [1996] Q.B. 292.

(c) *Principles Applicable to Statutory and Equitable Assignments*

(i) *What Rights are Assignable*

Rights declared by contract to be incapable of assignment

In *Oakdale (Richmond) Ltd v. National Westminster Bank Plc* [1997] 1 BCLC 63, a bank, under loan arrangements, had a specific charge over the book and other debts of a company. The company was prohibited from factoring, discounting, charging or assigning its book or other debts without the bank's prior written consent. The company sought a declaration that the loan arrangements were void as being contrary to Article 85 (and Article 86) of the E.C. Treaty. Chadwick J. rejected that argument. Such a prohibition clause was necessary if banks were to lend on the security of book debts and, far from being anti-competitive under Article 85, it promoted competition because it enabled a company to obtain additional finance from its bank under an all monies debenture.

[*Note 55: page* [971]]
The reference to "*Heston v. Hertfordshire C.C.*" should be deleted and replaced by "*Helstan Securities Ltd v. Hertfordshire C.C.*"

[*Add to note 55*]   **19–025**
Linden Gardens Trust Ltd v. Lenesta Sludge Disposal Ltd [1994] 1 A.C. 85 was followed on its "prohibition on assignment" point in *Circuit Systems Ltd v. Zuken-Redac (U.K.) Ltd* [1996] 3 All E.R. 748 (C.A.). In *Orion Finance Ltd v. Crown Financial Management Ltd* [1994] 2 B.C.L.C. 607, Vinelott J. had to consider a clause prohibiting assignment without the defendant's consent, consent not to be unreasonably withheld. Although the defendant had not given its consent, the assignment was held valid because in the circumstances the defendant was estopped from denying that the assignment was valid. In *British Gas Trading Ltd v. Eastern Electricity Plc*, unrep., December 18, 1996 (C.A.), there was a clause prohibiting assignment, without Eastern's written consent, consent not to be unreasonably withheld. The Court of Appeal, upholding Colman J., *The Times*, November 29, 1996, held that Eastern as unreasonably withholding consent to an assignment (or, on a strict analysis, withholding its approval of a novation) where the reason for Eastern's refusal of consent was not any objection to the suitability of the assignee was supplier but rather that Eastern wished to hold British Gas Trading Ltd to the contract so as to exercise a right, that had not yet accrued, to terminate the contract. In *Flood v. Shand Construction Ltd*, *The Times*,

January 8, 1997, a clause prohibited assignment, without consent, of a building sub-contract but permitted the assignment of "any sum which is or may become due and payable under this sub-contract." The Court of Appeal construed this as not allowing the assignment of the right to claim damages or other sums that were not yet due or payable but needed to be established as due and payable by litigation or arbitration or contractual machinery. Rather it only permitted assignment of the right to recover sums which were already due (*i.e.* essentially debts, including judgment debts).

Assignment prohibited by statute or public policy

19–026   *[Add to note 59, line 2, after "1972, s.5(1)"]*
Pensions Act 1995, s.91 (the right to a pension under an occupational pension scheme cannot be assigned other than in favour of one's widow, widower or dependant).

[Add to text at end of paragraph: page [972]]
The assignment of a right of action by a party not entitled to legal aid (for example, because a corporate plaintiff) to a party so entitled (for example, the directors and shareholders of a company), where the object and effect of the assignment was to enable the assignee to obtain legal aid that would not have been available to the assignor, was not contrary to public policy or unlawful; and this was so even though the assignor continued to be substantially interested in the fruits of the assigned rights of action. The same applied where the object in effect of the assignment was to enable the action to be brought by an assignee who, unlike the assignor, did not have to provide security for costs.[61a]

[61a] *Norglen Ltd v. Reed Rains Provincial Ltd* [1996] 1 W.L.R. 864; *Circuit Systems Ltd v. Zuken-Redac (U.K.) Ltd* [1996] 3 All E.R. 748 (in which Simon Brown L.J. indicated that, where the assignment has been designed to avoid the usual consequences of voluntary incorporation, the Legal Aid Board might think that it is only if the merits appear compellingly to favour the applicant that he should be granted legal aid.) See *ante*, §16–055.

Assignment savouring of maintenance

19–027   In *Camdex International Ltd v. Bank of Zambia* [1996] 3 All E.R. 431 it was held that an assignment of a debt is not invalid as champertous even if it is contemplated at the time of the assignment that it will be necessary to take legal action to recover the debt. The last two sentences of the second paragraph of 19–027 were cited with approval by the Court of Appeal.

[Add to note 64 at end]
Grovewood Holdings plc. v. James Capel & Co. Ltd [1995] Ch. 80 (no exemption for assignment by liquidator of the fruits of litigation—as

opposed to assignment of the bare cause of action—which included provision for the assignee to finance the litigation); *Norglen Ltd v. Reed Rains Prudential Ltd* [1996] 1 W.L.R. 864, 875–878, C.A.; *Circuit Systems Ltd v. Zuken-Redac (U.K.) Ltd* [1996] 3 All E.R. 748.

In *Re Oasis Merchandising Services Ltd* [1997] 2 W.L.R. 764, a liquidator wished to bring proceedings against directors for wrongful trading under s.214 of the Insolvency Act 1986. In order to found that action, the liquidator assigned the fruits of the s.214 action to a litigation support company. The liquidator argued that the assignment was not champertous because he was empowered "to sell any of the company's property" under Schedule 4 to the 1986 Act. But the Court of Appeal held that "the company's property" did not include the fruits of proceedings brought by the liquidator under s.214. A distinction was to be drawn between assets which are the property of the company at the time of the commencement of the liquidation, including the rights of action which arise and might have been pursued by the company itself prior to the liquidation, and assets which only arise after the liquidation of the company and are recoverable only by the liquidator pursuant to statutory powers conferred on him. The former constituted "the company's property" under Schedule 4, whereas the latter did not. The purported assignment was therefore void for champerty.

[*Add to text at end of final paragraph: page* [973]]
A creditor of an insolvent company has, absent some additional factor, a substantial and genuine commercial interest in proceedings to recover the assets of the company (here the claim was for delivery of a consignment of scaffolding): *Norglen Ltd v. Reed Rains Provincial Ltd.*[75a]

[75a] [1996] 1 W.L.R. 864, 888 (C.A.).

Personal contracts

[*Amend note 89: page* [975]]   **19–029**
Replace "Merchant Shipping Act 1970, s.11(1)(b)" by "Merchant Shipping Act 1995, s.34(1)(c)".

(ii) *Validity of Assignments against Assignor's Creditors and Successors in Title*

Company liquidator or creditors

[*Add to note 15: page* [978]]   **19–035**
For an illustration of an assignment constituting a charge and being void for non-registration against a liquidator, under s.395 of The Companies Act 1985, see *Orion Finance Ltd v. Crown Financial Management Ltd (No. 2)* [1996] 2 BCLC 382, C.A.

(v) *No Assignment of Liabilities*

Benefit and burden

19–045   In *Rhone v. Stephens*,[a] the House of Lords cast doubt on Megarry V.C.'s views in *Tito v. Waddell (No. 2)*[b] to the extent that he was recognising a "pure principle" that any party deriving any benefit from a conveyance must accept any burden in the same conveyance. Lord Templeman instead expressed the view that "the condition must be relevant to the exercise of the right".[c]

[a] [1994] 2 A.C. 310.

[b] [1977] Ch. 106.

[c] [1994] 2 A.C. 310, at p. 322.

CHAPTER 20

DEATH AND BANKRUPTCY

2. – BANKRUPTCY

(a) *Contracts made prior to Bankruptcy*

Effect of presenting a bankruptcy petition

[*Note 82: page* [1001]]   **20–016**
Amend reference to Bowstead (15th ed., 1985) to §§8–204—8–213.

(b) *Vesting of property in Trustee*

Choses in action

[*Add to note 7: page* [1003]]   **20–019**
Re Landau (A Bankrupt) [1997] 3 W.L.R. 225.

Transactions defrauding creditors

[*Add to note 27: page* [1006]]   **20–024**
Agricultural Mortgage Corporation plc v. Woodward [1995] 1 B.C.L.C. 1;
Barclays Bank plc v. Eustice [1995] 2 B.C.L.C. 630.

(c) *Trustee takes "Subject to Equities"*

Set-off and mutual dealings

[*Note 79: page* [1010] *and 81: page* [1011]]   **20–032**
Update references to Derham (1987), p. 71 to (2nd. ed., 1996), p. 171.

Part Six

PERFORMANCE AND DISCHARGE

CHAPTER 21

PERFORMANCE

1. – IN GENERAL

When notice to perform is required

21–008   [*Add to note 47 after "(1933) 102 L.J.K.B. 257": page* [1028]]
British Telecommunications plc v. Sun Life Assurance Society plc [1996]
Ch. 69 (although the court refrained from expressing a concluded view on
the case where the defect is caused by an occurrence which is wholly outside
the landlord's control).

2. – TIME OF PERFORMANCE

Time "of the essence of the contract"

21–010   [*Amend note 57: page* [1029]]
Update reference to Treitel to (9th ed., 1995), pp. 739–745.

21–011   [*Add to note 67: page* [1030]]
Hammond v. Allen [1994] 1 All E.R. 307, 311.

Time made expressly or implicitly "of the essence"

21–012   [*Add to note 80: page* [1031]]
Grant v. Cigman [1996] 2 B.C.L.C. 24, 31 (although Judge Weeks Q.C.
stated that the dicta in *Re Schwabacher* and *Hare v. Nicoll* "may be too wide"

[188]

and that "a property company may be different from a trading company, and a company in one line of business may be different from a company trading in another less dynamic market.").

[*Note 81*]
Schelde Delta Shipping B.V. v. Astarte Shipping Ltd (The Pamela) [1995] 2 Lloyd's Rep. 249 (an anti-technicality clause must state that the hire has not been punctually paid and that charterers have a given period of time in which to pay up or risk losing the ship).

[*Add to note 82*]
Torvald Klaveness A/S v. Arni Maritime Corporation [1994] 1 W.L.R. 1465 (obligation to make timely redelivery in time charterparty held not to be a condition).

[*Add to note 83*]
Hyundai Merchant Marine Co. Ltd v. Karander Maritime Inc. (The Niizuru [1996] 2 Lloyd's Rep. 66, 71.

Notice making time "of the essence"

[*Add to note 89: page* [1032]]   **21–013**
Bidaisee v. Sampath (1995) 46 W.I.R. 461, P.C.

[*Add to text at the end of paragraph: page* [1033]]
The notice procedure laid down in the contract may be held to be exhaustive of the rights of the parties so that it will not be open to them to serve a notice (for example, of shorter duration) under the general law rather than the contract.[95a]

[95a] *Rightside Properties Ltd v. Gray* [1975] Ch. 72; *Country and Metropolitan Homes Ltd v. Topclaim Ltd* [1996] Ch. 307, 314–315. The position is, of course, otherwise where the parties expressly reserve "any other right or remedy" available; *Dimsdale Developments (South East) Ltd v. De Haan* (1983) 47 P. & C.R. 1.

Consequences of time being "of the essence"

[*Add to text after note 98 as new paragraph*]   **21–014**
The right to terminate may, of course, be lost where the innocent party affirms the contract[98a] or is held to have waived (or to be estopped from exercising) the right to terminate.[98b] Additionally, equity may intervene to grant relief in cases of late payment of money due under a mortgage or rent due under a lease.[98c] But equity will not intervene at the request of a purchaser who has failed to comply with an essential time stipulation in a contract for the sale of land.[98d] The need for certainty in such cases is paramount and the very existence of a jurisdiction to grant relief from termination in cases where it would be unconscionable[98e] for the vendor to

exercise his right to terminate would detract from that need for a certain rule. The harshness of this general rule may, however, be tempered by the prospect of relief being granted in extreme cases. Where, for example, the vendor has been unjustly enriched by improvements made at the purchaser's expense, then the court may either relax the principle that specific performance will not be granted to a purchaser who has broken an essential condition as to time[98f] or, preferably, recognise that the purchaser has a personal restitutionary claim against the vendor.[98g]

[98a] See, *post*, §24–002—24–003

[98b] See, *post*, §24–005—24–007

[98c] *G. and C. Kreglinger v. New Patagonia Meat and Cold Storage Co. Ltd* [1914] A.C. 25, 35; *Shiloh Spinners Ltd v. Harding* [1973] A.C. 691, 722; see, *post*, §26–070.

[98d] *Union Eagle Ltd v. Golden Achievement Ltd* [1997] A.C. 514.

[98e] Such a jurisdiction has been developed in Australia: see, for example, *Legione v. Hateley* (1983) 152 C.L.R. 406 and *Stern v. McArthur* (1988) 165 C.L.R. 489. These developments generate too much uncertainty for English tastes.

[98f] As has been done in Australia (see note 98e). The occasional English example can also be found (see *Re Dagenham (Thames) Dock Co. ex p. Hulse* (1873) L.R. 8 Ch. App. 1022) but the authorities are generally hostile to such an approach (see *Steedman v. Drinkle* [1916] 1 A.C. 275). The English courts may "on some future occasion" have to consider whether to "relax" the principle in *Steedman v. Drinkle* (see *Union Eagle Ltd v. Golden Achievement Ltd* [1997] A.C. 514, 523B).

[98g] It seems clear that Lord Hoffmann's preference in *Union Eagle Ltd v. Golden Achievement Ltd* [1997] A.C. 514, 523 was for the development of an appropriate restitutionary remedy. There is much to be said for this view. It avoids the land being sterilised while the courts sort out whether or not the vendor is entitled to terminate, but at the same time it gives to the court a jurisdiction to remove any unjust enrichment which a vendor has obtained as a result of the termination. A further approach would be to develop the law of estoppel to deal with the case of the vendor who leads the purchaser to believe that the contractual time-scale will not be enforced.

Meaning of "day"

21–019   [*Add to note 33: page* [1036]]
    Schelde Delta Shipping B.V. v. Astarte Shipping Ltd (The Pamela) [1995] 2 Lloyd's Rep. 249.

3. – PARTIAL PERFORMANCE OF ENTIRE OBLIGATION

Entire and divisible obligations

21–022   [*Amend note 56: page* [1039]]
    Update reference to Treitel to (9th ed., 1995), pp. 697–703.

Partial performance of entire obligations

[*Amend note 67: page* [1040]]   **21–023**
Delete "Merchant Shipping Act 1970, s.15 (as amended)" and replace
with "Merchant Shipping Act 1995, s.38".

[*Add new reference 69a on the last line after "from day to day" and insert
note: page* [1040]]

NOTE 69a: A "day" means a calendar day and not a working day: *Re BCCI SA*
[1994] I.R.L.R. 282 and *Thames Water Utilities v. Reynolds* [1996] I.R.L.R. 186.

Substantial performance

[*Amend note 79: page* [1042]]   **21–025**
Update reference to Treitel to (9th ed., 1995), p. 703.

4. – PAYMENT

(a) *In General*

Distinction between claims for payment of a debt and claims for damages

[*Add to note 26 after "§26–064": page* [1046]]   **21–031**
Jervis v. Harris [1996] Ch. 195, 206–207.

[*Add to note 36 after "Pacific Associates Inc. v. Baxter* [1990] 1 Q.B. 993,
1033–1034": *page* [1047]]
Pacific and General Insurance Co. Ltd v Hazell [1997] L.R.L.R. 65, 79–80

5. – TENDER

Time of tender

[*Add to note 67 at end: page* [1070]]   **21–075**
and Apps [1994] L.M.C.L.Q. 525

DISCHARGE BY AGREEMENT

3. – ACCORD AND SATISFACTION

Compromise

22–012   [*Amend note 38: page* [1076]]
Update reference to Foskett (3rd ed.) to (4th ed., 1996)

Executory Satisfaction

22–014   [*Add to note 51: page* [1077]]
Jameson v. Central Electricity Generating Board [1997] 2 W.L.R. 151, 160–161.

Payment of part of a debt

22–015   [*Amend note 59: page* [1078]]
Re Selectmove is now reported in [1995] 1 W.L.R. 474.

[*Add to note 59 before* "see ante, §3–085": *page* [1078]]
Ferguson v. Davies [1997] 1 All E.R. 315, although Evans L.J. (at 326) expressed no view on this issue.

Evidence of Accord

22–019   [*Add to note 74: page* [1079]]
cf. Pereira v. Inspirations East Ltd (1992) C.A.T. 1048, discussed in more detail by Foskett, *The Law and Practice of Compromise* (4th ed.), pp. 28–29.

[*Add to note 75 after "Stour Valley Builders v. Stuart, supra"*]
Ferguson v. Davies [1997] 1 All E.R. 315.

[*Add to note 77*]
Ferguson v. Davies [1997] 1 All E.R. 315, 325.

5. – Variation

Effect of extra works

[*Amend note 42: page* [1086]]   **22–034**
Update reference to Keating to (6th ed., 1995), pp. 250–251.

6. – Waiver

Waiver of breach

[*Amend note 77: page* [1090]]   **22–042**
Update reference to Treitel to (9th ed., 1995), p. 726.

[*Amend note 79*]
Update reference to Treitel to (9th ed., 1995), pp. 725–729.

7. – Provision for Discharge in the Contract Itself

Express provision

[*Add to note 83 after "B.I.C.C. plc v. Burndy Corporation [1985] Ch. 232":* **22–043**
page [1091]]
Transag Haulage Ltd v. Leyland DAF Finance plc [1994] B.C.C. 356.

[*Add to note 83*]
Union Eagle Ltd v. Golden Achievement Ltd [1997] A.C. 514.

[*Add to note 84*]
Housing Act 1996, ss.81 and 82.

[*Add new reference 88a, line 6, after "the contractual right", and insert note:* **22–044**
page [1091]]

Note 88a: *Lockland Builders Ltd v. Rickwood*, (1996) 46 Con.L.R. 92 (contractually agreed procedure for dealing with the consequences of a particular breach held

impliedly to have excluded the common law right to terminate the contract in respect of a breach which fell within the scope of the clause).

Requirements as to notice

22–046　　[*Add to note 95: page* [1092]]
Schelde Delta Shipping B.V. v. Astarte Shipping Ltd (The Pamela) [1995] 2 Lloyd's Rep. 249.

[*Add to note 96*]
Schelde Delta Shipping B.V. v. Astarte Shipping Ltd (The Pamela) [1995] 2 Lloyd's Rep. 249 (held that notice of withdrawal of vessel sent by telex at 23.41 was not received by the charterer at that time but was received when the charterer's office opened shortly after 9 a.m. on the next working day).

CHAPTER 23

DISCHARGE BY FRUSTRATION

1. – INTRODUCTION

Introduction

[Amend note 1: page [1095]]   **23–001**
Update reference to McKendrick (ed.) to (2nd ed. 1995) and add: Treitel,
Frustration and Force Majeure (1994).

[Amend note 5: page [1096]]
Update reference to McKendrick (ed.) to (2nd ed., 1995).

2. – THE TEST FOR FRUSTRATION

Introduction

[Amend note 21: page [1098]]   **23–005**
Update reference to Treitel to (9th ed., 1995), pp. 832–836.

[195]

Test of a radical change in the obligation

23–008   [*Add to note 35: page* [1101]]
It has also been cited with approval in the Court of Appeal (*William Sindall plc v. Cambridgeshire County Council* [1994] 1 W.L.R. 1016, 1039).

Practical differences between the tests

23–013   [*Amend note 60: page* [1105]]
Update reference to Treitel to (9th ed., 1995), pp. 832–836.

3. – ILLUSTRATIONS OF THE DOCTRINE

(b) *Common Types of Frustrating Event*

(i) *Subsequent Legal Changes and Supervening Illegality*

Supervening illegality under foreign law

23–020   [*Add to note 96: after "[1920] 2 K.B. 287": page* [1109]]
Bangladesh Export Import Co. Ltd. v. Sucden Kerry S.A. [1995] 2 Lloyd's Rep. 1, 5–6 (where a contract is governed by English law, the mere fact that its performance has become illegal under the law of a foreign country does not of itself amount to frustration of the contract unless the contract expressly or impliedly requires performance in that country).

(ii) *Cancellation of an Expected Event*

The "coronation" cases

23–023   [*Amend note 21: page* [1112]]
Update reference to Treitel to (9th ed., 1995), pp. 797–799.

Delay

23–024   [*Amend note 25*]

Update reference to McKendrick (ed.) to (1995) pp. 129–138.

(c) *Application of the Doctrine to Common Types of Contract*

(ii) *Charterparties*

Other frustrating events

23–033   [*Amend note 86: page* [1119]]
Update reference to McKendrick (ed.) to (1995) pp. 129–138.

[*Amend note 93: page* [1120]]
Update reference to McKendrick (ed.) to (1995) 129–138.

(iii) *Sale and Carriage of Goods*

Sale and carriage of goods

[*Amend note 99: page* [1121]]   **23–035**
Update reference to Atiyah to (9th ed.), pp. 306–311.

(iv) *Building Contracts*

Building contracts

[*Amend note 10: page* [1123]]   **23–037**
Update reference to Hudson to (11th ed., 1995), 4.233–4.264; replace the
reference to McKendrick (ed.), Chap. 9 with "Chap. 10". Update reference
to Keating to (6th ed., 1995), pp. 143–150.

(vi) *Contracts for the Sale of Land*

Contracts for the sale of land

[*Add to note 49 after "Hillingdon Estates Co. v. Stoneyfield Estates Ltd":* **23–044**
page [1127]]
E. Johnson & Co. (Barbados) Ltd v. N.S.R. Ltd [1996] 3 W.L.R. 583,
587–588.

[*Add to note 51: page* [1128]]
It should, however, be noted that the Singapore Court of Appeal has
recently concluded that, in an appropriate case, a contract for the sale of land
can be frustrated; see *Lim Kim Som v. Sheriffa Taibah bte Abdul Rahman*
[1994] 1 S.L.R. 393, discussed by Phang (1995) 44 I.C.L.Q. 443. A similar
conclusion had earlier been reached by the Ontario Court of Appeal in
Capital Quality Homes Ltd v. Colwyn Construction Ltd (1975) 61 D.L.R.
(3d) 385.

4. – THE LIMITS OF FRUSTRATION

Express provision

[*Add to note 53: page* [1128]]   **23–045**
Bangladesh Export Import Co. Ltd v. Sucden Kerry S.A. [1995] 2 Lloyd's
Rep. 1.

Significance of a foreseen event

23–046   [*Amend note 63: page* [1129]]
Update reference to Treitel to (9th ed., 1995), pp. 813–817.

[*Add to note 64*]
Bangladesh Export Import Co. Ltd v. Sucden Kerry S.A. [1995] 2 Lloyd's
Rep. 1, 6 and update reference to Treitel to (9th ed., 1995) pp. 813–816.

[*Amend note 69: page* [1130]]
Update reference to Treitel to (9th ed., 1995), p. 814.

Allocation of available supplies

23–048   [*Amend note 83: page* [1131]]
Update reference to Treitel to (9th ed., 1995), pp. 819–820.

Partial "frustration"

23–052   [*Amend note 9: page* [1135]]
Update reference to Treitel to (9th ed., 1995), pp. 749 and 802.

[*Amend note 14*]
Update reference to Treitel to (9th ed., 1995), pp. 819–820.

5. – THE LEGAL CONSEQUENCES OF FRUSTRATION

Common law

23–053   [*Amend note 16: page* [1136]]
Update reference to McKendrick (ed.) to (1995), Chap. 11 and add:
Treitel *Frustration and Force Majeure* (1994) Chap. 15.

[*Amend note 21: page* [1137]]
Update reference to McKendrick (ed.) to (1995), pp. 123–129.

Law Reform (Frustrated Contracts) Act 1943

23–055   [*Amend note 26*]
Update reference to McKendrick (ed.) to (1995), Chap. 11 and add:
Treitel *Frustration and Force Majeure* (1994) 15–044—15–075.

[*Amend note 31: page* [1138]]
Update reference to McKendrick (ed.) to pp. 291–297.

The time of discharge

[*Amend note 45: page* [1140]]   **23–059**
Update reference to Treitel to (9th ed., 1995), p. 828.

[*Amend note 49*]
Update reference to McKendrick (ed.) to (1995), p. 230.

The basis of the proviso

[*Add to text at end of first paragraph: page* [1141]]   **23–060**
In *Gamerco S.A. v. I.C.M./Fair Warning (Agency) Ltd*[54a] these three views
were considered by Garland J., who concluded that he could see "no
indication in the Act, the authorities or the relevant literature that the court
is obliged to incline towards either total retention or equal division. Its task is
to do justice in a situation which the parties had neither contemplated nor
provided for, and to mitigate the possible harshness of allowing all loss to lie
where it has fallen".[54b] The emphasis is thus placed on the "broad nature" of
the discretion which the court enjoys and the imperative to do justice on the
facts of the case.

[54a] [1995] 1 W.L.R. 1226.

[54b] *ibid.* at p. 1235.

[*Delete from line 2 of second paragraph "There is no English case in
point but in" and substitute*]
It is now clear that the onus of proof lies on the defendant.[54c] A useful
illustration of the importance of the location of the onus of proof is provided
by

[54c] *Gamerco S.A. v. I.C.M./Fair Warning (Agency) Ltd* [1995] 1 W.L.R. 1226, 1235.

Identification of the benefit

[*Amend note 66: page* [1143]]   **23–063**
Update reference to McKendrick (ed.) to (1995), pp. 236–237.

[*Amend note 67*]
Update reference to Treitel to p. 827.

Contracts excluded from the Act

23–069   [*Amend note 88: page* [1147]]
Update reference to Treitel to pp. 830–832 and update reference to Atiyah to (9th ed.), pp. 311–315.

Arbitration

23–070   [*Add to note 90*]
Kuwait Supply Co. v. Oyster Marine Management (The Safeer) [1994] 1 Lloyd's Rep. 637.

CHAPTER 24

DISCHARGE BY BREACH

1. – IN GENERAL

Discharge by breach

[*Add to note 2: page* [1149]]   **24–001**
See further Pawlowski [1995] Conv. 379.

[*Add to note 7: page* [1150]]
Vitol S.A. v. Norelf [1996] A.C. 800.

Affirmation

[*Add to note 10: page* [1150]]   **24–002**
Yukong Line Ltd of Korea v. Rendsberg Investments Corporation of Liberia [1996] 2 Lloyd's Rep. 604, 607.

[*Add to note 11*]
Yukong Line Ltd of Korea v. Rendsberg Investments Corporation of Liberia [1996] 2 Lloyd's Rep. 604, 607.

[*Add to text at end of paragraph: page* [1151]]
The mere fact that the innocent party has called on the party in breach to change his mind, accept his obligations and perform the contract will not generally, of itself, amount to an affirmation: "the law does not require an injured party to snatch at a repudiation and he does not automatically lose his right to treat the contract as discharged merely by calling on the other to reconsider his position and recognise his obligation."[17a]

[17a] *Yukong Line Ltd of Korea v. Rendsberg Investments Corporation of Liberia,*

[1996] 2 Lloyd's Rep. 604, 608. Moore-Bick J. added that, in his view, the courts should generally be "slow" to accept that the innocent party has committed itself irrevocably to going on with the contract and leave it to "the doctrine of estoppel" to remedy any potential injustice which may arise in the case where the party in breach has relied upon a representation by the innocent party which suggests that the contract has been affirmed.

24-003   [*Add to note 18: page* [1151]]
Yukong Line Ltd of Korea v. Rendsberg Investments Corporation of Liberia [1996] 2 Lloyd's Rep. 604, 607.

[*Add to note 19*]
Yukong Line Ltd of Korea v. Rendsberg Investments Corporation of Liberia [1996] 2 Lloyd's Rep. 604, 607.

[*Add to note 21*]
Safehaven Investments Inc. v. Springbok Ltd (1996) 71 P. & C.R. 59, 68 ("the correct analysis ... is not that the innocent party is terminating on account of the original repudiation and going back on his election to affirm. It is that he is treating the contract as being at an end on account of the continuing repudiation reflected in the other party's behaviour after the affirmation," *per* Jonathan Sumption Q.C., sitting as a Deputy High Court Judge).

[*Add to note 22*]
Yukong Line Ltd of Korea v. Rendsberg Investments Corporation of Liberia [1996] 2 Lloyd's Rep. 604, 607.

Waiver and estoppel

24-005   [*Add to note 32: page* [1153]]
Yukong Line Ltd of Korea v. Rendsberg Investments Corporation of Liberia [1996] 2 Lloyd's Rep. 604, 607.

[*Add to note 38 after* "[1987] 2 Lloyd's Rep. 46": *page* [1154]]
Yukong Line Ltd of Korea v. Rendsberg Investments Corporation of Liberia [1996] 2 Lloyd's Rep. 604, 607.

[*Add to note 47*]
Yukong Line Ltd of Korea v. Rendsberg Investments Corporation of Liberia [1996] 2 Lloyd's Rep. 604, 607.

Effect of affirmation

24-008   [*Amend note 53: page* [1155]]
Update reference to Treitel to (9th ed., 1995), pp. 915–918.

[*Add to note 54*]
Stocznia Gdanska S.A. v. Latvian Shipping Co. [1995] 2 Lloyd's Rep. 592;
[1996] 2 Lloyd's Rep. 132 (C.A.).

[*Add to note 56 after "supra": page* [1156]]
Boyo v. Lambeth London Borough Council [1994] I.C.R. 727 (in the
absence of special circumstances the liability of an employer in damages for
wrongful dismissal does not extend beyond the notice period which the
employer could lawfully have given under the contract. Unconstrained by
authority, the majority (Ralph Gibson L.J. (pp. 742–744) and Staughton L.J.
(p. 747)) inclined to the view that the wrongfully dismissed employee should
be able to sue for his wages.)

Acceptance of repudiation

[*Add to text after note 71: page* [1158]]   **24–011**
An act of acceptance of a repudiation requires no particular form.[71a]

[71a] *Vitol S.A. v. Norelf Ltd* [1996] A.C. 800, 810–811.

[*Add to note 72*]
The innocent party need not personally, or by an agent, notify the
repudiating party of his election to treat the contract as at an end. It is
sufficient that the fact of the election is brought to the attention of the
repudiating party, for example, notification by an unauthorised broker or by
another intermediary may be sufficient: *Vitol S.A. v. Norelf Ltd* [1996] A.C.
800, 811

[*Add to note 74*]
Boyo v. Lambeth London Borough Council [1994] I.C.R. 727 (although it
should be noted that the court was rather reluctant to follow *Gunton*; see in
particular the judgment of Staughton L.J. at p. 747).

[*Add to note 75*]
Boyo v. Lambeth London Borough Council [1994] I.C.R. 727; *Vitol S.A. v.
Norelf Ltd* [1996] A.C. 800.

[*Delete from text, line 14*: ": for example, "where the parties are bound to
perform specific acts in relation to one another a failure to perform an act
which a party is obliged to perform of the contract remains alive may be very
significant" *and substitute: page* [1158]]
It all depends on "the particular contractual relationship and the
particular circumstances of the case"[77] whether a mere failure to perform
will suffice. An example of a failure to perform which has been suggested
would suffice to constitute an acceptance is the following:

"Postulate the case where an employer at the end of the day tells a contractor that he, the employer, is repudiating the contract and that the contractor need not return the next day. The contractor does not return the next day or at all. It seems to me that the contractor's failure to return may, in the absence of any other explanation, convey a decision to treat the contract as at an end."[77a]

While the flexibility which has been introduced into the law through the rejection of the proposition that a mere failure to perform can never amount to an acceptance is to be welcomed, it does not alter the fact that a contractor who wishes to make sure that he has accepted a repudiation would be well advised to draw that acceptance expressly to the attention of the repudiating party.

[77] *Vitol S.A. v. Norelf Ltd* [1996] A.C. 800, 811.

[77a] *Vitol S.A. v. Norelf Ltd* [1996] A.C. 800, 811.

Both parties in breach

24-014   [*Amend note 89: page* [1160]]
Update reference to Treitel to (9th ed., 1995), pp. 736–737.

2. – RENUNCIATION

Renunciation

24-016   [*Add to note 94 after* "[1993] B.C.C. 159, 168": *page* [1161]]
Nottingham Building Society v. Eurodynamics plc [1995] F.S.R. 605, 611–612.

[*Add to note 2: page* [1162]]
Torvald Klaveness A/S v. Arni Maritime Corporation [1994] 1 W.L.R. 1465, 1476 (charterers' persistence with last voyage order after it had become invalid showed that they did not intend to perform their obligations under the contract).

[*Add to note 4*]
Weeks v. Bradshaw [1993] E.G.C.S. 65.

24-017   [*Add to note 6*]
Nottingham Building Society v. Eurodynamics plc [1995] F.S.R. 605; *Safehaven Investments Inc. v. Springbok Ltd* (1996) 71 P. & C.R. 59, 69 (this applies to words and conduct said to demonstrate that a party is persisting in an earlier repudiation as well as to the earlier repudiation itself).

[*Add to note 7*]
Vaswani v. Italian Motors (Sales and Services) Ltd [1996] 1 W.L.R. 270

(not a repudiation of the contract for a party to assert a genuinely held but erroneous view of the effect of the contract where the conduct of that party was not inconsistent with the continuance of the contract); *Mitsubishi Heavy Industries Ltd v. Gulf Bank K.S.C.* [1997] 1 Lloyd's Rep. 343, 354; *Orion Finance Ltd v. Heritable Finance Ltd* Unrep. (C.A.). March 10, 1997.

Anticipatory breach

[*Add to note 12: page* [1163]]   **24–019**
Greenaway Harrison Ltd v. Wiles [1994] I.R.L.R. 380.

3. – IMPOSSIBILITY CREATED BY ONE PARTY

Anticipatory breach

[*Amend note 46: page* [1168]]   **24–026**
Update reference to Treitel to (9th ed., 1995), p. 775.

4. – FAILURE OF PERFORMANCE

Dependent promises

[*Add to note 65 after* "United Scientific Holdings Ltd v. Burnley B.C.   **24–032**
[1978] A.C. 904, 927": *page* [1170]]

Failure of performance: other situations

[*Add to note 84: page* [1172]]   **24–035**
Gunatunga v. DeAlwis (1996) 72 P. & C.R. 161, 171.

5. – CONSEQUENCES OF DISCHARGE

Effect on contract

[*Add to note 28: page* [1177]]   **24–042**
However, a restrictive covenant in a contract of employment will not generally survive where it is the employer who has repudiated the contract: *General Billposting Co. Ltd v. Atkinson* [1909] A.C. 118, *ante* §16–080, although the correctness of this proposition has recently been questioned by Phillips L.J. in *Rock Refrigeration Ltd v. Jones* [1997] 1 All E.R. 1, 18–20 on the basis that "the law in relation to the discharge of contractual obligations by acceptance of a repudiation has been developed and clarified" since *General Billposting* was decided. The employer may, however, be able to protect his property and trade secrets on the basis that his rights of property

will survive the termination of the contract as a result of the employee's acceptance of his repudiatory breach (*Rock Refrigeration Ltd v. Jones* [1997] 1 All E.R. 1, 14 and (on rather wider grounds) 20).

24–042   [*Delete the full point before note 28 in text and add after note 28: page* [1177]]

as may other clauses having a contractual function which is ancillary or collateral to the subject-matter of the contract.[28a]

[28a] *Yasuda Fire & Marine Insurance Co. of Europe Ltd v. Orion Marine Insurance Underwriting Agency Ltd* [1995] Q.B. 174: principal's contractual right to inspect documents and computer databases relating to transactions entered into by agents held to have survived the termination of the agency agreement.

[*Add to text at the end of the paragraph: page* [1177]]

Thus, while both parties are discharged from further performance of their primary obligations under the contract, "rights are not divested or discharged which have been unconditionally acquired."[30a] The party in breach can therefore enforce against the innocent party such rights as it has "unconditionally acquired" by the date of termination. However, in the case of the termination of a partnership agreement as a result of the acceptance by one partner of the repudiatory breach of the other partners, the innocent partner's liability to contribute to the liabilities of the partnership may extend beyond those rights to contribution which the partners in breach had "unconditionally acquired" before the date of dissolution of the partnership.[30b]

[30a] *McDonald v. Dennys Lascelles Ltd* (1933) 48 C.L.R. 457, 476–477; *Bank of Boston Connecticut v. European Grain and Shipping Ltd* [1989] A.C. 1056, 1098–1099.

[30b] *Hurst v. Bryk* [1997] 2 All E.R. 283. The exact basis of this more extensive obligation to contribute is unclear. Peter Gibson L.J. held that the innocent partner could not escape from his share of the expenses of the winding up of the affairs of the partnership (p. 293) and he held that the innocent partner was also liable to contribute to the rent payable under the lease of the partnership premises on the ground that he had an equitable interest in the lease which was not determined by the dissolution of the partnership. The termination of the contract did not thereby divest an "accrued property right and its concomitant obligation to indemnify the trustees" (p. 294). Simon Brown L.J. took a broader approach and concluded (p. 310) that the innocent partner's obligation to contribute to the various liabilities of the partnership was simply not one of those primary obligations from which a repudiatory breach discharged him. Hobhouse L.J. dissented on the basis that there was no justification for departing from the orthodox rules laid down in cases such as *Heymans v. Darwin Ltd* (above).

CHAPTER 25

OTHER MODES OF DISCHARGE

1. – MERGER

Merger of contract in conveyance

[Add to note 12: page [1182]]   **25–003**
Gunatunga v. DeAlwis (1996) 72 P. & C.R. 161, 180 (term of contract that vacant possession shall be given on completion did not merge in the conveyance).

Estoppel by judgment

[Add to note 53 after "[1982] A.C. 529, 540–541": page [1186]]   **25–011**
C (a minor) v. Hackney London B.C. [1996] 1 All E.R. 973.

[Add to text: footnote reference 57a to the word "decided", line 2 of second paragraph: page [1187]]

NOTE 57a: The issue should have been decided as well as raised in the earlier proceedings: *Barrow v. Bankside Agency Ltd* [1996] 1 W.L.R. 257 (plaintiff's claim not barred because it would not have been decided by the court in the earlier proceedings).

[Add to note 58: page [1187]]
Barrow v. Bankside Agency Ltd [1996] 1 W.L.R. 257; *Republic of India v. India Steamship Co. Ltd* [1997] 2 W.L.R. 538, 554–555.

[Add to note 60]
Barrow v. Bankside Agency Ltd [1996] 1 W.L.R. 257.

[Add to note 61]
Cf. Barrow v. Bankside Agency Ltd [1996] 1 W.L.R. 257, 260.

Ineffective judgments

25–013   [*Add to note 70: page* [1188]]
In the case of an English judgment, it is impeachable in an English court
on the ground that it was obtained by fraud but only by the production and
establishment of evidence newly discovered since the trial and not reasonably discoverable before the trial (*Boswell v. Coaks (No. 2)* (1894) 86 L.T.
365n). But in the case of a foreign judgment fresh evidence is not required
before it can be attacked on the ground of fraud in an English court
(*Abouloff v. Oppenheimer & Co.* (1882) 10 Q.B.D. 295). In *Owens Bank Ltd
v. Etoile Commerciale S.A.* [1995] 1 W.L.R. 44 the Privy Council noted this
disparity of treatment in disapproving terms and, while they indicated a
preference for the general application of the rule which presently governs
English judgments, they stopped short of overruling *Abouloff*. However the
Privy Council went on to hold that the court does have an inherent power to
prevent misuse of its process and that that power can be exercised to strike
out a defence based on an allegation that a foreign judgment has been
obtained by fraud where full particulars of the fraud have not been given.

Foreign judgments

25–015   [*Add to text after note 82: page* [1189]]
In deciding whether or not the proceedings are between the same parties,
or their privies, the court will consider whether or not the reality is that the
claim is between the same parties.[82a]

[82a] *Republic of India v. India Steamship Co. Ltd* [1997] 2 W.L.R. 538, 554 where it
was held that, where the owners of the vessel served in an Admiralty action *in rem*
were the same person as would be liable in an action *in personam*, the later claim was
barred by s.34. This was so notwithstanding the fact that English law has long held
that a judgment *in personam* is no bar to an action *in rem* and vice versa. The Court of
Appeal found it unnecessary to consider the effect of s.34 where an action *in rem* is
brought against a ship in new ownership, or where for any other reason some other
person acknowledges service in such an action.

[*Add to note 87: page* [1190]]
Owens Bank Ltd v. Etoile Commerciale S.A. [1995] 1 W.L.R. 44.

[*Add to note 97: page* [1191]]
Desert Sun Loan Corporation v. Hill [1996] 2 All E.R. 847 (no issue
estoppel arose because not sufficiently clear that the specific issue which
arose before the court had been identified and decided against the defendant
in the foreign court).

3. – MISCELLANEOUS MODES OF DISCHARGE

Set-off and counterclaim

[*Add to text at end of paragraph: page* [1194]]   **25–026**
Where a defendant claims a set-off but does not make a counterclaim when sued by a plaintiff, he can later issue fresh proceedings against the plaintiff even though the plaintiff has accepted a payment into court made by the defendant in settlement of the plaintiff's claim against the defendant and the allegations made by the defendant are essentially the same as those pleaded in his defence to the plaintiff's action: *Hoppe v. Titman*.[31a]

[31a] *The Times*, February 21, 1996.

Part Seven

REMEDIES FOR BREACH OF CONTRACT

CHAPTER 26

DAMAGES

1. – NATURE AND KINDS OF DAMAGES

(a) *In General*

Introduction

26–001   [*Add to text after note 15: page* [1199]]
A special category of wasted expenditure arises where the plaintiff can claim damages on the "no transaction" basis.[15a]

> [15a] See §26–038A, *post.*

[Insert new paragraph after footnote 16: page [1199]]
Concurrent liability. If the plaintiff is able to sue in tort (concurrent **26–001A**
liability[16a]) he will be able to take advantage of the more favourable rules on
damages in tort, *e.g.* on remoteness of damage.[16b] But concurrent liability in
tort may benefit the defendant, *e.g.* in regard to contributory negligence.[16c]

[16a] See *ante* §§1–048 to 1–071.

[16b] §§26–021 *et seq.*, *post.*

[16c] §26–019, *post.*

Difficulty of assessment: contingencies

[Add to notes 25 and 31: pages [1200]–[1201]]   **26–003**
See §26–046A, *post.*

[Text at notes 27 to 30: pages [1200]–[1201]]
See §26–017A, *post.*

(c) *Claims for an Agreed Sum*

Distinction between claims for payment of an agreed sum and claims for damages

[Add to note 37: page [1202]]   **26–005**
Jervis v. Harris [1996] Ch. 195.

(e) *Prospective Loss and Continuing Breaches*

Prospective loss

[Add to text after note 61: page [1204]]   **26–008**
The court may, however, defer the assessment of damages for future
losses which are very uncertain: *Deeny v. Gooda Walker Ltd (No. 3)* [1995] 4
All E.R. 289 (the plaintiff's liabilities to policyholders could not be predicted
with reasonable confidence; there was also the risk that, having received a
substantial sum for future losses, the plaintiff might allow the damages to be
dissipated before the policyholders' claims were made).

(f) *Substitute Performance (Cost of Completion or Repairs)*

Damages for the cost of completion, reinstatement or repairs

26–010   [*Add to note 67 at end: page* [1205]]
The House of Lords has recently accepted an award of damages for "loss
of amenity" which is between these two measures (cost of completion or
diminution in market value): see §26–041A *post.*

[*Add to note 68 at beginning*]
Ruxley Electronics and Construction Ltd v. Forsyth [1996] A.C. 344 (which
reversed the decision of the C.A. cited in this Note).
Add at end: *Channel Island Ferries Ltd v. Cenargo Navigation Ltd (The
"Rozel")* [1994] 2 Lloyd's Rep. 161.

[*Note 70*]
In the *Ruxley Electronics* case, *supra*, it was held that the plaintiff's
undertaking to spend the damages on reinstatement will not, on its own,
make it reasonable to do so (p. 373).

[*Note 71*]
In the *Ruxley Electronics* case, *supra*, it was held that the plaintiff's
subjective intention to reinstate could be relevant to the issue of reasonableness, *e.g.* if he did not intend to reinstate it would not be reasonable to do so
in the particular case.

[*Add to text after note 71*]
In *Ruxley Electronics and Construction Ltd v. Forsyth*,[71a] *supra*, the House
of Lords emphasised the role of reasonableness and held that where the cost
of reinstatement was out of all proportion to the advantage to be gained
from reinstatement, it would be unreasonable for the plaintiff to insist on
reinstatement. In this case, a swimming pool was not built to the depth
specified in the contract (7 feet 6 inches) but was only 6 feet deep, which was
sufficiently deep for diving according to normal standards so that the market
value of the property was not reduced. It was held that it was unreasonable
for the plaintiff to claim the cost of rebuilding the pool to the contractual
specification.[71b]

[71a] [1996] A.C. 344.

[71b] On the award of damages in this case, see *infra*, §26–041A; on the question
whether the "cost of cure" is disproportionate to the benefit, see *Channel Island
Ferries Ltd v. Cenargo Navigation Ltd (The "Rozel")* [1994] 2 Lloyd's Rep. 161.

[*Add to text after note 72*]
But the *Ruxley Electronics* case, *supra*, now enables damages to be
awarded for "loss of amenity" to reflect a personal, subjective value in
performance.[72a]

[72a] See §26–041A, *post.*

[*Add to note 72*]
(This article was cited by Lord Mustill in the *Ruxley Electronics* case, *supra*, at p. 360.)

(g) *Exemplary Damages and depriving the defendant of his Profit*

Exemplary damages

[*Add to text after note 83: page* [1206]]   **26–011**
The general statements in *Addis'* case have recently been qualified by the House of Lords in *Malik*'s case, which is discussed, *post* in §26–041 and §26–042.

Depriving the defendant of profit made through his breach

[*Add to note 89 at end: page* [1207]]   **26–012**
; or where a landlord wrongly ejects his tenant, damages for trespass are assessed as a reasonable rent for the entire trespass period, whether or not the landlord has derived any actual benefit from using the property: *Inverugie Investments Ltd v. Hackett* [1995] 1 W.L.R. 713, P.C.

[*Add to note 1 after the* Wrotham Park Estate *case*]
(approved by the C.A. in *Jaggard v. Sawyer* [1995] 1 W.L.R. 269 (the damages could be the amount which the plaintiff "could reasonably have demanded as the price of waiving [his] rights": at p. 289)).

[*Add to note 5: page* [1208]]
See now *Jaggard v. Sawyer, supra.*

(i) *Third party beneficiaries*

Breach of promises intended to benefit third persons

[*Add to note 28 at end: page* [1210]]   **26–014**
But in *Darlington B.C. v. Wiltshier Northern Ltd* [1995] 1 W.L.R. 68 (C.A.; leave to appeal has been granted by the H.L.: p. 81) the property was not transferred by A to C because it was already owned by C at the time the building contract was made between A and B. See *ante*, §18–036.

[*Add to note 30* [1210]]
See also the report of the Law Commission on *Privity of Contract: Contracts for the Benefit of Third Parties*: (1996) Law Com. No. 242.

[*Add to text after note 30*]
A consequential question is whether in this situation A holds the substantial damages recovered from B in trust for C, the third party

beneficiary. In the *Darlington* case, *supra*, it was held that A would hold the damages as constructive trustee for C.[30a] This is in line with another analogous situation: *Hunt v. Severs*.[30b]

[30a] [1995] 1 W.L.R. 68 at pp. 75, 81.

[30b] [1994] 2 A.C. 350.

2. – CAUSATION AND CONTRIBUTORY NEGLIGENCE

Requirement of a causal connection

26–015   *[Add to text after note 38: page* [1211]]
The plaintiff may recover damages for a loss only where the breach of contract was the "effective" or "dominant" cause of that loss: *Galoo Ltd v. Bright Grahame Murray*.[38a] The answer to whether the breach was the cause of the loss or merely the occasion for the loss must "in the end" depend on "the court's commonsense" in interpreting the facts.[38b] (The Court of Appeal quoted with approval the sentence in the text of §26–015 at Note 39). So where a company continued to trade after a negligent audit by the defendant failed to reveal the true financial position of the company, the Court of Appeal held that the auditor's breach of contract gave the company "the *opportunity* ... to incur ... trading losses: it did not *cause* those trading losses".[38c] The trading losses flowed from trading, not from auditing.

[38a] [1994] 1 W.L.R. 1360, at pp. 1374–1375, C.A.

[38b] *ibid. Racing Drivers' Club Ltd v. Hextall Erskine & Co.* [1996] 3 All E.R. 667, 671–672, 681–682.

[38c] The *Galoo* case, *supra*, at p. 1375.

Intervening act of the plaintiff

26–017   *[Add to text after note 51: page* [1213]]
In *Beoco Ltd v. Alfa Laval Co. Ltd*[51a] the defendant supplied a machine which, in breach of contract, was defective. When the plaintiff discovered the defect, he arranged repairs but he failed to inspect the repair before using the machine; an inspection would have shown that the repair was inadequate. The defect led to an explosion which damaged the plaintiff's plant and caused loss of production. It was held that the cause of the explosion was the plaintiff's negligence in using the machine without testing whether the repair was successful. Although the defendant was liable for the cost of repairing the original defect, and for the loss of the plaintiff's profit while the original repairs were made, the defendant was not liable for the cost of repairing the explosion damage, nor for the further loss of production after the explosion. The need for further repairs to remedy the original defect had been overtaken by the need for more extensive repairs due to the explosion, and the plaintiff could not recover damages for the loss of

production during the notional period which would have been necessary for further repairs even if there had been no explosion. (It is submitted that mitigation would be a more appropriate principle for the decision. The explosion was caused by the original defect, but the plaintiff had failed, after discovery of the defect, to take reasonable steps to avoid further loss: instead of saying the plaintiff *caused* the further loss it would be better to say that he failed to avoid it when he unreasonably decided to use the machine without testing it after the repairs.)

[51a] [1995] Q.B. 137, C.A.

[Add to note 51 at beginning]
Young v. Purdy [1997] P.N.L.R. 130.

[Insert as new paragraph after note 55]
Failure to act: the hypothetical consequences if the defendant had fulfilled 26–017A
his duty to act. Where the breach of contract is a failure to act, it is a hypothetical question what the consequences would have been if the defendant had fulfilled his contractual obligation. Where the plaintiff claims that he himself would have acted in a particular way, he must prove it on the balance of probabilities. For example, if his solicitor failed to give him proper advice, he must prove that he would, with proper advice, have been more likely than not to have taken a particular course of action: *Allied Maples Group Ltd v. Simmons and Simmons*[55a]; see also *Brown v. K.M.R. Services Ltd.*[55b] But where the plaintiff claims that, if the defendant had fulfilled his obligation, an independent third party would have acted in a particular way, he need not prove that hypothetical action on the balance of probabilities. Provided that the plaintiff can prove that there was a "real" or "substantial" (not a speculative) chance of the third party's action, the court must assess the chance of that action resulting (usually as a percentage), and then discount the plaintiff's damages for his loss by reference to that chance: *Allied Maples Group Ltd v. Simmons and Simmons, supra* (a solicitor's failure to advise, leading to the loss of the client's chance to negotiate better terms in a commercial deal with an independent third party) (followed in *Stovold v. Barlows*[55c]). So where a solicitor allowed his client's claim to become statute-barred, the damages against the solicitor were assessed at two-thirds of the amount which the original court would have awarded, thus reflecting the finding that he had a two-thirds chance of success in that claim: *Kitchen v. R.A.F. Association.*[55d]

[55a] [1995] 1 W.L.R. 1602, C.A.

[55b] [1995] 4 All E.R. 598, 617, 638.

[55c] *The Times*, October 30, 1995, C.A.

[55d] [1958] 1 W.L.R. 563, C.A.

Contributory negligence

26-019   [*Text at notes 66 and 67: page* [1215]]
The widening of concurrent liability in contract and tort[a] will have the effect of widening the scope of category 3.

An illustration of category 1 (a strict contractual duty not dependent on reasonable care) is *Barclays Bank Plc v. Fairclough Building Ltd*[b] where, in a building contract, the defendant undertook that the workmanship should be the best of its kind, and that the roofing work should be executed only by a specialist firm of roofing contractors: both undertakings were held to require a specified standard to be achieved, irrespective of reasonable care. Contributory negligence could not be pleaded against claims based on these strict undertakings.

[a] See *ante*, §§1–048 to 1–071.

[b] [1995] Q.B. 214, C.A.

3. – REMOTENESS OF DAMAGE

(a) *General rules*

Modern statement of the rule

26-023   [*Text at note 86: page* [1218]]
This sentence was quoted with approval by Stuart-Smith L.J. in *Brown v. K.M.R. Services Ltd.*[a]

[a] [1995] 4 All E.R. 598, at 621; see also *ibid.*, at pp. 642–643; and *Kpohraror v. Woolwich Building Society* [1996] 4 All E.R. 119.

The type or kind of loss

26-024   This paragraph was quoted with approval by Stuart-Smith L.J. in *Brown v. K.M.R. Services Ltd, supra*, at p. 621.

[*Add to note 97 after "at p. 1524.": page* [1219]]
Brown v. K.M.R. Services Ltd, supra, at p. 621; *Kpohraror v. Woolwich Building Society, supra.*

[*Add to note 99 after reference to Parsons v. Uttley: page* [1220]].
Brown v. K.M.R. Services Ltd, supra, at pp. 621, 642–643.

[*Add to note 99*]
Cf. also the limitation on the extent of a valuer's liability for a negligent overvaluation made for a lender: *South Australia Asset Management Corporation v. York Montague Ltd* [1997] A.C. 191 (*post*, §26–046).

[*Add to text at end of paragraph*]
The categorisation of loss into "types" or "kinds" is illustrated by a Scots appeal to the House of Lords, *Balfour Beatty Construction (Scotland) Ltd v. Scottish Power plc.*[2a] The plaintiff was building an aqueduct and the defendant was temporarily supplying electricity to the plaintiff's concrete batching plant. Through the defendant's breach of contract, the fuses were ruptured and caused the electricity to fail, so that the supply of concrete was interrupted. For the method of construction being followed by the plaintiff, a continuous pour of concrete was necessary: the interruption meant that the work already done on the aqueduct had to be demolished and rebuilt. The defendant was held not liable for the cost of the demolition and rebuilding, because it did not have technical knowledge of the details of concrete construction and did not know of the need to preserve a continuous pour of concrete: the type of loss in question was not in its reasonable contemplation at the time of contracting.[2b]

[2a] 1994 S.L.T. 807.

[2b] See also *Kpohraror v. Woolwich Building Society* [1996] 4 All E.R. 119 (C.A.); not contemplated that one day's delay by a bank in meeting a cheque might cause the plaintiff to lose the transaction in question or a trading loss in future.

(b) *Timing of the Assessment of Damages*

The relevant date for the assessment of damages

[*Add to note 37 after* Johnson v. Agnew: *page* [1224]]   26–029
See *Kennedy v. K.B. Van Emden & Co., The Times*, April 5, 1996 (C.A.).

(c) *Loss of Profits*

Seller's liability for loss of profits

[*Add to note 52: page* [1225]]   26–030
See *Brown v. K.M.R. Services Ltd* [1995] 4 All E.R. 598, 621.

(d) *Expenditure Wasted or Incurred as a Result of the Breach*

[*Insert new paragraph after note 15: page* [1232]]   26–038
Damages assessed on a "no transaction" basis. In a limited number of   26–038A
situations, where the plaintiff claims that he would not have entered into a particular transaction but for the defendant's negligent advice (or failure to

advise), his damages have been assessed at the amount needed to restore him to the position he would have been in if he had never entered the transaction. So in *Hayes v. Dodd*[15a] a solicitor negligently advised the plaintiff that he had a right of way to give access to the leasehold property he proposed to acquire as a site for his business. There was no right of way and the business failed through the lack of adequate access. Damages were assessed on the "no transaction" basis, *viz.*, all the wasted expenditure incurred by the plaintiff (the initial cost of the lease and goodwill, rent, rates, insurance, bank interest and other expenses wasted until the time he reasonably gave up the business) *less* the amounts recovered by the plaintiff through selling the lease and his plant (the mitigation rules applied). An analogous case is where negligent advice from a solicitor led the client to take a disadvantageous underlease: the damages were the sum paid by the client over five years later to secure its surrender: *County Personnel (Employment Agency) Ltd v. Alan R. Pulver and Co.*[15b] In the *South Australia* case[15c] the House of Lords said that the distinction between "no transaction" and "successful transaction" cases should be abandoned; but the House approved the two cases just mentioned on the basis of the mitigation or "extrication" principle ("a reasonable attempt to cope with the consequences of the defendant's breach of duty"). However, in *Hayes v. Dodd* the damages went beyond "extrication".

[15a] [1990] 2 All E.R. 815 (C.A.).

[15b] [1987] 1 W.L.R. 916.

[15c] [1997] A.C. 191 (*post*, §26–046).

(e) *Non-pecuniary losses*

Mental distress and disappointment: nervous shock

26–041   [*Note 33: page* [1234] *Delete reference to the* Malik *case*]

[*Add to text after note 35*]
In *Malik v. Bank of Credit and Commerce International S.A.*[35a] the House of Lords held that in principle (and subject to the principles of causation, remoteness and mitigation) damages may be awarded in respect of financial loss arising from the plaintiff's loss of reputation caused by breach of contract.[35b] The breach in question was of the implied term in a contract of employment whereby the employer is obliged not, without reasonable and proper cause, to conduct his business in a manner likely to destroy or seriously damage the relationship of confidence and trust between himself and his employee (see §37–105, *post*). So where, in breach of this obligation, the employer conducted a dishonest and corrupt business, with the result that his former employees found that their future employment prospects were prejudiced by the stigma of their former employment, they were

entitled to recover damages for their financial losses caused by that prejudice. The decision in *Malik* has narrowed the effect of *Addis v. Gramophone Co. Ltd* (cited in note 34 to this paragraph); but the *Addis* principle still excludes damages for the plaintiff's injured feelings and anxiety caused by the breach of contract, or (in an employment case) for loss caused by the mere fact that he was wrongfully dismissed, or for the manner in which he was dismissed. The *Malik* decision allows damages in the narrow situation "where the manner of dismissal involved a breach of the trust and confidence term and this caused financial loss"[35c] through the plaintiff suffering handicap in the labour market.[35d]

[35a] [1997] 3 W.L.R. 95.

[35b] At p. 115, Lord Steyn spoke of this principle "in the field of employment law" but there appears to be no justifiable reason for limiting the principle to this area of law.

[35c] *ibid.* at p. 103.

[35d] On the damages recoverable generally for wrongful dismissal or for unfair dismissal, see *post* §§37–141 *et seq.*, 37–168 *et seq.*

[*Add to text after note 36*]
The "loss of enjoyment" concept in the holiday cases has been extended to a personal, subjective "loss of amenity" expected from the performance of a building contract.[36a]

[36a] See §26–041, *post.*

[*Add to note 40: page* [1235]]
See also *Knott v. Bolton* [1995] E.G.C.S. 59 (C.A.: no damages for distress caused by breach of architect's contract to design a house).

[*Insert new paragraph after note 45*]
Loss of amenity (consumer surplus). In *Ruxley Electronics and Construc-* **26–041A**
tion Ltd v. Forsyth[45a] the House of Lords accepted that damages may be awarded for the "loss of amenity" suffered by the plaintiff where the purpose of the contract was to give him a subjective, even idiosyncratic pleasure or amenity. The defendant, in breach of contract, built a swimming pool whose depth was only six feet in the diving area, instead of the specified seven feet six inches. Despite evidence that a depth of six feet was perfectly safe for diving, and that the market value of the property was not adversely affected by the breach, the Court of Appeal[45b] had allowed the full cost of re-building the pool. Their Lordships reversed this decision[45c] and appeared to support the trial judge's award (not appealed) of £2,500 as substantial damages for "loss of amenity" because the purpose of the contract was "the provision of a pleasurable amenity" (as in the holiday cases cited in Main Work, §26–041, Note 36). Two Lords agreed with Lord Mustill's speech: citing the *Law Quarterly Review* article by Harris *et al*,[45d] he upheld the award as

representing the loss of the "consumer surplus", the personal, subjective gain which the plaintiff expected to receive from full performance—an advantage not measured by any increase in the market value of his property.

[45a] [1996] A.C. 344.

[45b] [1994] 1 W.L.R. 650.

[45c] *ante*, §26–010.

[45d] (1979) 95 L.Q.R. 581.

Loss of reputation

26–042   [*Add to text after line 3, "defamation": page* [1235]]
This general statement has recently been qualified by the House of Lords in *Malik's* case, which is discussed *ante* in §26–041.

[*Add to note 48*].
Wither's case has been overruled: see note [48b] to §26–042, *post*.

[*Add to text after note 48*]
In *Malik's* case, *supra*, the House of Lords preferred the view expressed in *Marbe's* case[48a] that when assessing damages for loss flowing from a failure to provide promised publicity the loss may include loss to existing reputation.[48b] Subject to remoteness, damages are recoverable where the breach of contract causes loss of commercial reputation involving loss of trade.[48c]

[48a] Cited in note 47.

[48b] On this point, *Wither's* case (cited in note 47) was overruled.

[48c] *Malik's* case, *supra*, at p. 115; *Cointax v. Myham & Son* [1913] 2 K.B. 220 (*post*, §41–312); *G.K.N. Centrax Gears Ltd v. Matbro Ltd* [1976] 2 Lloyd's Rep. 555 (*post*, §41–315).

4. – ILLUSTRATION OF THE REMOTENESS OF DAMAGE AND THE ASSESSMENT OF DAMAGES

(b) *Carriage of Goods*

Carriage of goods

26–044   [*Add to note 57 after the reference to* Slater's case: *page* [1236]]
(But see now *Bence Graphics International Ltd v. Fasson U.K. Ltd* [1997] 3 W.L.R. 205). (See §§41–305 and 41–307, *post*).

(c) *Contracts Concerning Land*

Surveyor's failure to report defects

In the *South Australia* case (also known as the *B.B.L.* case)[a] the House of 26–046
Lords imposed a limit on the extent of the damages payable by a valuer who
negligently over-values the intended security. The lender's "ultimate loss"
(*viz.* the difference between (i) the capital of the actual loan and (ii) the net
proceeds of realising the security, plus any repayments by the borrower) is
caused by, and is not too remote a consequence of, the negligence; but the
lender's damages may not exceed the extent of the initial shortfall in the
supposed value of the security, *viz.* the difference between the amount of the
negligent over-valuation and what would have been a proper valuation at
the time of the loan. Within this limit, however, the lender may recover his
ultimate loss of capital even though it is due to a fall in the value of the
security since the loan was made.[b]

[a] [1997] A.C. 191.

[b] See also *ante*, §26–038A.

[*Add to note 80 after* Perry v. Sidney Phillips & Son: *page* [1239]]
See also *Gardner v. Marsh & Parsons* [1997] 1 W.L.R. 489 (the fact that
five years after the purchase the landlord remedied the defect at his expense
was held to be too remote to be taken into account in assessing the
purchaser's damages).

[*After* §26–046, *add the following new paragraph*]

Assessing the "proper" valuation of property

Where the court must fix the "proper" valuation of a property there is 26–046A
normally a range of valuations which might have been made by reasonably
careful valuers; the court must choose the figure which it considers to be the
most likely outcome of careful assessment: the defendant is not given the
benefit of damages being assessed by reference to the highest figure which
might have been given without negligence.[86a]

[86a] The *South Australia* case [1997] A.C. 191 (following the P.C. in *Lion Nathan Ltd
v. C-C. Bottlers Ltd* [1996] 1 W.L.R. 1438 (a contractual duty to take reasonable care
in making a forecast of likely profits)).

5. – MITIGATION OF DAMAGE

Benefits independent of mitigation

[*Add to note 53: page* [1247]]
; and *Gardner v. Marsh & Parsons* [1997] 1 W.L.R. 489 (see note 80 to
§26–046, *ante*).

26–056   [*Add to note 56: page* [1248]]
cf. *Brown v. KMR Services Ltd* [1995] 4 All E.R. 598, 640–641.

[*Add to note 57*]
But see *Bence Graphics International Ltd v. Fasson U.K. Ltd* [1997] 3
W.L.R. 205 (see §§41–305 and 41–307, *post*).

[*Add to text at end of paragraph*]
Even where a benefit to the plaintiff arises in the course of his mitigating
action, there may not be a sufficient causal connection between the
defendant's breach and that benefit to justify taking it into account in
assessing the plaintiff's damages: *Famosa Shipping Co. Ltd v. Armada Bulk
Carriers Ltd (The "Fanis").*[57a]

[57a] [1994] 1 Lloyd's Rep. 633.

Recovery of loss or expense suffered while attempting to mitigate

26–058   [*Add to note 65: page* [1249]]
The principle stated in the text covers legal costs incurred by the plaintiff
in reasonable attempts to mitigate: *British Racing Drivers' Club Ltd v.
Hextall Erskine & Co.* [1996] 3 All E.R. 667. If the amount of the legal costs is
disputed, they should be taxed on the standard basis: *ibid.*

[*Add to note 66*]
The "extrication" principle was accepted by the House of Lords in the
South Australia case [1997] A.C. 191, 218–219.

6. – Penalty or Liquidated Damages

Damages fixed by the parties

26–061   [*Add to note 5 at end: page* [1253]]
In a loan agreement, a modest increase in the rate of interest, which
operates only from the date of default by the borrower, is not a penalty:
Lordsvale Finance plc v. Bank of Zambia [1996] Q.B. 752 (one per cent
increase: if the increase operated retrospectively, it might be a penalty).

The scope of the law on penalties

26–064   [*Add to note 34: page* [1257]]
See also *Jervis v. Harris* [1996] Ch. 195, 206–207.

[*Add to text at the end of third paragraph*]
In *Nutting v. Baldwin,*[37a] there was a pooling arrangement by a group of

Lloyd's Names to finance litigation and to share its proceeds; the Committee had power, when members of the group failed to pay a contribution levied on them for expenses, to exclude them from any share in the proceeds of the litigation, but this was held not to be a penalty.

[37a] [1995] 1 W.L.R. 201.

Other cases outside the law on penalties

[*Add to note 51: page* [1259]]   **26–065**
cf. *Lordsvale Finance plc v. Bank of Zambia* [1996] Q.B. 752 (see *supra*, §26–061, note 5).

Limitation of liability for damages

[*Add to note 61 at end: page* [1260]]   **26–067**
Cf. also the *South Australia* case [1997] A.C. 191 (*ante*, §26–046).

[*Add to note 62 at end*]
The 1977 Act has been applied to a clause placing a monetary ceiling of £100,000 on liability for breach of contract: *St. Albans City Council v. International Computers Ltd* [1996] 4 All E.R. 481.

Forfeiture: purchase by instalments and pre-payment of price

[*Add to note 86: page* [1263]]   **26–070**
In *Union Eagle Ltd v. Golden Achievement Ltd* [1997] A.C. 514, the Privy Council refused to extend the principle set out in the text at note 86.

[*Add to note 89 after the reference to* The Scaptrade: *page* [1264]]
(followed in *Union Eagle Ltd v. Golden Achievement Ltd*, *supra* (P.C., failure by ten minutes to pay balance of purchase price on time, when time was "of the essence")).

[*Insert new paragraph after note 18: page* [1267]]   **26–072**
The Unfair Terms in Consumer Contracts Regulations 1994.[18a] These **26–072A**
regulations came into force on July 1, 1995, and provide that in a contract between a business and a consumer an "unfair term" will not be binding on the consumer.[18b] The Regulations give illustrations of terms which will *prima facie* be regarded as unfair: relevant to clauses fixing damages is "(e) requiring any consumer who fails to fulfil his obligation to pay a dispro-portionately high sum in compensation". So a consumer will be able to appeal to this standard, as well as to the common law on penalties.

[18a] S.I. 1994 No. 3159.

[18b] See §§14–088 *et seq.*, *ante*.

7. – THE TAX ELEMENT IN DAMAGES

Instances where the Gourley principle is irrelevant

26–076   [*Add to note 51: page* [1270]]
See *Deeny v. Gooda Walker Ltd (No. 2)* [1996] 1 W.L.R. 426 (H.L.) ("...
payments in compensation for what would have been revenue items in the
trade": at p. 437).

[*Add to note 56 at end: page* [1271]]
The dictum of Diplock L.J. in this case was discussed by the H.L. in *Deeny
v. Gooda Walker Ltd (No. 2), supra.*

[*Add to text after Note 56*]
Damages received by a Lloyd's Name in an action against his agent are
receipts of his underwriting business and as such are chargeable to income
tax under Schedule D: *Deeny v. Gooda Walker Ltd (No.2).*[56a]

[56a] [1996] 1 W.L.R. 426 (H.L.).

8. – INTEREST AND RATE OF EXCHANGE

Statutory power to award interest

26–080   [*Add to note 92 at end: page* [1274]]
In *Westdeutsche Landesbank Girozentrale v. Islington London B.C.*
[1996] A.C. 669, the House of Lords held that in equity compound interest
may be awarded only in cases of fraud or against a trustee (or other person in
a fiduciary position) in respect of profits improperly made by him. In the
same case the majority of their Lordships rejected the view that equity, in aid
of a common law claim, could award compound interest more generally. See
also *Mathew v. T.M. Sutton Ltd* [1994] 1 W.L.R. 1455, 1463.

[*Add to note 4 at end*]
cf. *Mathew v. T.M. Sutton Ltd, supra.*

Arbitration awards

26–084   [*Add to text after note 42 and new paragraph: page* [1278]]
The statutory power enabling an arbitrator to award interest is now found
in section 49 of the Arbitration Act 1996 (in force January 1, 1997) which
provides that (unless the parties agree otherwise) the arbitral tribunal may
award simple or compound interest from such date at such rates and with
such rests as it considers meets the justice of the case. Such interest may be
awarded on the whole or any part of (a) the amount awarded in respect of
any period up to the award; and (b) any amount which was claimed in the

arbitration and outstanding at the commencement of the arbitral proceedings, but was paid before the award was made in respect of any period up to the date of payment (section 49(3)). This power is similar to that granted to courts but wider in that compound interest may be awarded. By section 49(6) the provisions in section 49(3) do not affect any other power of the tribunal to award interest. (On interest from the date of the arbitration award, see §26–085, *post*.)

Interest on judgment debts and arbitration awards

[Add to text after note 50: page [1278]]   **26–085**
By section 49(4) of the Arbitration Act 1996 (in force from January 1, 1997) an arbitral tribunal may award simple or compound interest from the date of the award (or any later date) until payment; it has discretion to fix the rates of interest and the rests (if any).

CHAPTER 27

SPECIFIC PERFORMANCE AND INJUNCTION

1. – INTRODUCTION

Generally

27–001   [*Add to note 3: page* [1281]]
Co-operative Insurance Society Ltd v. Argyll Stores (Holdings) Ltd [1997] 3 All E.R. 297, 302, where Lord Hoffmann refers to the "heavy-handed nature of the enforcement mechanism."

[*Note 8: page* [1282]]
On facts such as those of *Re Wait* [1927] 1 Ch. 606, the buyer could now acquire ownership in common of the goods (which formed an undifferentiated part of a bulk shipment) under Sale of Goods Act 1979, s.20A(2), as inserted by Sale of Goods (Amendment) Act 1995, s.1(3); but such ownership would not necessarily give the buyer priority over competing interests such as the pledge which had been created in that case in favour of a bank by "hypothecation" of the bill of lading. The priorities between such interests would be governed by the principle that *nemo dat quod non habet* and by the exceptions to that principle. See further *post*, §27–011.

For an application of the rule that property in unascertained goods cannot pass, see *Re Goldcorp Exchange Ltd* [1995] 1 A.C. 74; contrast *Re Stapylton Fletcher Ltd* [1994] 1 W.L.R. 1181, where goods were segregated from the seller's own stock after sale and stored in bulk together with goods bought by other buyers.

[*Add to note 11*]
Co-operative Insurance Society Ltd v. Argyll Stores (Holdings) Ltd [1997] 3 All E.R. 297 may, however, foreshadow a return to the more traditional view, though with modern justifications: see *post*, §20–016.

2. – The "Adequacy" of Damages

General

[*Add to note 13: page* [1283]]   27–003
Co-operative Insurance Society Ltd v. Argyll Stores (Holdings) Ltd [1997] 3 All E.R. 297, 302.

Land

[*Add to note 25, page* [1284]]   27–004
The mere warning that the land was likely to be required for Crown purposes does not frustrate a contract for its sale; but after title to the land had vested in the Crown by virtue of compulsory purchase the vendor's remedy was in damages and not by way of specific performance: *E. Johnson & Co. (Barbados) v. NSR Ltd*, *The Times*, July 29, 1996.

Difficulty of quantifying damages

[*Note 27: page* [1285]]   27–005
The last case in this note is now reported *sub nom. Napier and Ettrick v. Hunter* [1993] 1 A.C. 713.

[*Note 34*]
For similar reasoning see *Temehelp Ltd v. West* [1996] Q.B. 84, where an injunction was granted to restrain the defendant from making a claim on a performance guarantee provided by the plaintiff (who disputed liability) since the plaintiff would (if the claim were made) become liable to reimburse the guarantor and there was an appreciable risk of the plaintiff's not being able to recover the amount in question from the defendant if the dispute were resolved in the plaintiff's favour.

Cases where damages are regarded as adequate

[*Add to note 43, page* [1286]]   27–008
Grant v. Cigman [1996] B.C.L.C. 24, where specific performance was

ordered, appears to have been a case in which the shares were not available in the market.

Sale of goods

27–011   [*Note 57: page* [1288]]

After the passing of the Sale of Goods (Amendment) Act 1995 ("the 1995 Act") sales of undifferentiated parts of a larger bulk must be divided into two categories. The first consists of cases in which the part sold is expressed as a fraction or percentage of the bulk: *e.g.* half the cargo of the *Peerless*. Such a contract is one for the sale of specific goods (Sale of Goods Act 1979, s.61, definition of "specific goods" as amended by s.2(d) of the 1995 Act) so long as the bulk was identified and agreed upon when the contract was made; and it therefore falls within section 52 of the 1979 Act. The second consists of cases in which the part sold is expressed as a specified quantity to be taken from an identified bulk: *e.g.* 5000 out of the 10,000 bales of cotton forming the cargo of the Peerless; *Re Wait* [1927] 1 Ch. 606 was a case of this kind. Under s.20A(2) of the 1979 Act as inserted by the 1995 Act s.2(3), the buyer can in such a case become an owner in common of the bulk; but he can do so, not because the goods are regarded as ascertained, but in spite of the fact that they remain unascertained. This appears from s.20A(1), which refers to such goods as "a specified quantity of *unascertained* goods". Cases of this second kind therefore remain outside the scope of the court's discretion under s.52 of the 1979 Act to order specific performance of a contract for the sale of "specific or ascertained" goods.

[*Add to note 64, page* [1289]]

Wake v. Renault (U.K.) Ltd, The Times, August 1, 1996 could be explained on the same ground; for the difficulties to which this case gives rise, see *post*, §§27–016, 27–045.

3. – CONTRACTS NOT SPECIFICALLY ENFORCEABLE

Contracts involving personal service

27–013   [*Line 4 onwards: page* [1290]]

The text on page [1290] and note 69 (see below) refer to provisions as to "unfair" dismissal formerly contained in the Employment Protection (Consolidation) Act 1978, as amended. These have been replaced by Part X of the Employment Rights Act 1996; for further details, see addition to note 69.

[*Add to note 69: page* [1290]].

The provisions governing the *remedies* for "unfair" dismissal formerly contained in ss.69–71 of the Employment Protection (Consolidation) Act 1978 (as amended) are now contained in Employment Rights Act 1996, ss.113–117.

See also Disability Discrimination Act 1995, s.8(5) and Sched. 3, para. 2(1).

For the statutory "right to return to work," after maternity leave, which was formerly dealt with in Part III of the Employment Protection (Consolidation) Act 1978 (as amended), see now Employment Rights Act 1996, ss.79–85.

Constant supervision

[*Add to text after note 99: page* [1293]]   **27–016**

Similarly, in *Co-operative Insurance Society Ltd v. Argyll Stores (Holdings) Ltd*[99a] the 31 year lease of premises for use as a food supermarket in a shopping centre contained a covenant by the tenant to keep the premises open for retail trade during the usual hours of business. Some six years after the commencement of the lease, the supermarket was running at a loss and the tenant decided to cease trading there. The House of Lords held that specific performance of the covenant should not be ordered; and the principal reason for the decision was the difficulty of supervising the enforcement of the order because (a) this might require frequent reference to the court to determine whether the order was in fact being complied with; and (b) the covenant was not sufficiently precise to be specifically enforced (*cf.* Main Work §27–027). Lord Hoffmann also emphasised the "heavy-handed nature of the enforcement mechanism"[99b] by proceedings for contempt; the injustice of compelling the defendant to carry on business at a loss which might exceed the loss which the plaintiff would be likely to suffer if the covenant were broken; and the fact that it was not "in the public interest for the courts to require someone to carry on business at a loss if there is any plausible alternative by which the other party can be given compensation"[99c] (*i.e.* by way of damages). He also distinguished between orders which required a defendant "to carry on an activity" and those which required him "to achieve a result." In the latter case, compliance could be judged *ex post facto*: "the court . . . only has to examine the finished work;"[99d] and it was on this ground that the cases in which building contracts had been specifically enforced[99e] were to be explained.

[99a] [1997] 3 All E.R. 297.

[99b] *ibid*. p. 302.

[99c] *ibid*. p. 305.

[99d] *ibid*. p. 303.

[99e] See Main Work §27–017.

[Note 5: page [1294]]
Insolvency Act 1986, s.44 has been amended by Insolvency Act 1994 s.2.

[Add to note 8]
In *Co-operative Insurance Society Ltd v. Argyll Stones (Holdings) Ltd*
[1997] 3 All E.R. 297, 304 Lord Hoffmann likewise interpreted Lord
Wilberforce's remarks in *Shiloh Spinners Ltd* v. *Harding* [1973] A.C. 691,
724 as relating to relief against forfeiture rather than to the availability of
specific performance. He also referred at p. 305 to the "cumulative effect" of
the various reasons for refusing specific performance in the former case,
adding that "none of [these] would necessarily be sufficient on its own," thus
giving some support to the view that difficulty of supervision is not, of itself,
necessarily a justification for refusing specific performance.

[Add to text: after note 9: p. [1299]]
In *Wake v. Renault (U.K.) Ltd*[9a] an injunction was granted to restrain the
breach of an undertaking not to terminate a car dealership agreement
between a motor manufacturer and a dealer to whom the manufacturer had
granted a franchise. To the extent that the decision is based on that of the
Court of Appeal in *Co-operative Insurance Society Ltd v. Argyll Stores
Holdings Ltd*,[9b] its authority is undermined by the reversal of the latter
decision by the House of Lords.[9c]

[9a] *The Times* August 1, 1996.
[9b] [1996] 3 All E.R. 934.
[9c] [1997] 3 All E.R. 297, *supra.*

4. – Other Grounds for Refusing Specific Performance

General

27–018 *[Add new reference in line 4 at "remedy": page* [1295]]

NOTE 15A: *cf. Co-operative Insurance Society Ltd v. Argyll Stores (Holdings) Ltd*
[1997] 3 All E.R. 297, 302 ("may justify a refusal of specific performance even when
damages are not an adequate remedy").

[Add to note 16: page [1295]]
Co-operative Insurance Society Ltd v. Argyll Stores (Holdings) Ltd [1997]
3 All E.R. 297, 299, 305 [2, 9] ("There are no binding rules, but this does not
mean that there cannot be settled principles . . . which the courts will apply in
all but exceptional circumstances").

Severe hardship to defendant

[*Add to note 18*]]
Jaggard v. Sawyer [1995] 1 W.L.R. 269 (injunction); *Insurance Co. v. Lloyd's Syndicate* [1995] 1 Lloyd's Rep. 273, 276 (injunction).

27–019

Inutility

[*Add at end: page* [1299]]
On a similar principle, specific performance will not be ordered of a conditional contract until the condition has been satisfied (though where a contract for the sale of land is subject to the condition of the vendor's obtaining planning permission, the purchaser may nevertheless obtain a lien for the return of his deposit): *Chattey v. Farndale Holdings Ltd, The Times,* October 17, 1996.

27–025

Vagueness

[*Add to note 64: page* [1300]]
Co-operative Insurance Society Ltd v. Argyll Stores (Holdings) Ltd [1997] 3 All E.R. 297, 306 (covenant to keep premises "open for the retail trade" not sufficiently precise to be specifically enforced).

27–027

7. – INJUNCTION

Negative contracts

[*Note 63: page* [1310]]
The principle that an injunction is available for breach of a contract which is negative in substance was applied in *Insurance Co. v. Lloyd's Syndicate* [1995] 1 Lloyd's Rep. 273, 275, where it was said (at p. 276) to be subject only to the restriction (discussed below) that an injunction will not be granted if it would be oppressive in the sense of causing "severe hardship" to the defendant.

27–040

[*Add to note 67: page* [1311]]
Channel Tunnel Group Ltd v. Balfour Beatty Construction Ltd [1993] A.C. 334; *Tate & Lyle Industries v. Cia. Usina Bulhoes* [1997] 1 Lloyd's Rep. 355, where an interim injunction was refused against a third party as its effect, if granted, would have been to prevent the second defendant from performing its contractual obligations under foreign law to the first defendant; *Series 5 Software v. Clarke* [1996] 1 All E.R. 853..

[*Add to text as new paragraph after note 69*]
By statute, the court has power to award damages in lieu of specific performance or injunction.[69a] This power is likely to be exercised if the injury

to the plaintiff is small, if it can readily be estimated in money, if compensation in money would adequately compensate the plaintiff, and if the grant of an injunction would be oppressive to the defendant (see the tort case of *Shelfer v. City of London Electric Light Co.*[69b]). These conditions were satisfied, and an injunction was accordingly refused, in *Jaggard v. Sawyer*,[69c] where the defendants had built a house on land which could be reached only by committing a breach of covenant and a trespass against neighbouring house-owners, including the plaintiff. An injunction restraining such access would have rendered the new house "landlocked and incapable of beneficial ownership"[69d]; and this would have been oppressive as the defendants had acted "openly and in good faith"[69e] and not "in blatant disregard of the plaintiff's rights"[69f] when they built the house. The test is one of *oppression*, rather than one of *balance of convenience*: if the plaintiff had sought interlocutory relief *before* the house had been built, she "would almost certainly have obtained it".[69g]

An injunction will not be ordered to restrain breach of a restrictive covenant against a body which has acquired land under statutory powers where the legislation has provided for an exclusive remedy by way of statutory compensation: *Brown v Heathlands Mental Health, etc, Trust.*[69h]

[69a] See Main Work, §27–048.

[69b] [1895] 1 Ch. 287, 322–333.

[69c] [1995] 1 W.L.R. 269.

[69d] *ibid.* at p. 288.

[69e] *ibid.* at p. 289.

[69f] *ibid.* at p. 283.

[69g] *ibid.* at p. 289, *cf.* p. 283.

[69h] [1996] 1 All E.R. 133.

Restraint of trade

27–043   [*Add to text at end of paragraph: page* [1314]]
In such a case, the grant of an injunction might well be regarded as oppressive and refused on that ground.[88a]

[88a] See *ante*, §27–040.

Implied negative promises

27–045   [*Add to note 97: page* [1315]]
Wake v. Renault (U.K.) Ltd, The Times, August 1, 1996 could be regarded as analogous to the cases cited in note 97, in which injunctions were granted against breaches of exclusive dealing agreements. But the case goes beyond these authorities in granting an injunction against breach of an express

undertaking "not to terminate" such an agreement for some years. In this respect, it is open to the objection that it amounts to indirect specific performance of a contract that would not normally be specifically enforced (see Main Work §27–045 at notes 1 and 2) on the ground that specific performance would require "constant supervision:" see *ante*, §27–016.

No completed cause of action at law

[*Note 13: page* [1317]]   **27–049**
An injunction may be granted where the plaintiff, though having no right to damages, has a right to a declaration: *Newport Association Football Club v. Football Association of Wales* [1995] 2 All E.R. 87.

[*Note 14*]
See also *Mercantile Group (Europe) A.G. v. Aiyela* [1994] Q.B. 366, 375 (injunction against third party "incidental and dependent on the enforcement of a substantive right").

Assessment of damages

[*Add to note 26: page* [1318]]   **27–050**
Jaggard v. Sawyer [1995] 1 W.L.R. 269.

[*Add to text at end of paragraph*]
The general principle that there is no difference between the assessment of damages at common law and that of damages in lieu of specific performance or injunction is based on the assumption that the damages are claimed in respect of the same breach of contract or other cause of action. The principle obviously cannot apply where there is no cause of action at common law, *e.g.* where specific relief is sought in equity in respect of threatened or future breaches.[28a]

[28a] See *Jaggard v. Sawyer* [1995] 1 W.L.R. 269, 291–292.

8. – Damages and Specific Performance or Injunction

Limit of the court's power

[*Add to note 38: page* [1320]]   **27–053**
Jaggard v. Sawyer [1995] 1 W.L.R. 269, where specific relief was refused on the ground stated in §27–040, *ante*.

CHAPTER 28

LIMITATION OF ACTIONS

1. – PERIODS OF LIMITATION

Simple contracts

28–002   [*Amend note 8: page* [1324]]
Kleinwort Benson Ltd v. South Tyneside Metropolitan B.C. is reported in [1994] 4 All E.R. 972.

[*Add to note 12*]
Nelson v. Rye [1996] 1 W.L.R. 1378.

Specialties

28–003   Contracts of service are capable of being specialties. The words "action upon a specialty" in section 8 of the 1980 Act are not confined to an action for specific performance or to recover a debt but extend to an action for damages: *Aiken v. Stewart Wrightson Members' Agency Ltd.*[a]

[a] [1995] 1 W.L.R. 1281.

[234]

[*Note 16*]
The operation of s.19 is not limited to the recovery of arrears of rent from lessees but extends to the guarantors of lessees: *Romain v. Scuba TV Ltd* [1996] 3 W.L.R. 117 (C.A.).

[*Add to note 17*]
But where the mortgagor is seeking to redeem or the mortgagee is accounting to the mortgagor for the surplus, more than six years' interest may be retained by the mortgagee: *Edmunds v. Waugh* (1866) L.R. 1 Eq. 418; *Holmes v. Cowcher* [1970] 1 W.L.R. 834; *Ezekiel v. Orakpo* [1997] 1 W.L.R. 340 (C.A.).

Action on a judgment or award

[*Add to note 44: page* [1327]]   **28–009**
Lowsley v. Forbes, The Times, April 5, 1996 (C.A.); *Ezekiel v. Orakpo* [1997] 1 W.L.R. 340 (C.A.). Contrast *Re a Debtor (No. 50A–5D–1995)* [1997] 2 W.L.R. 57 (bankruptcy proceedings based on a statutory demand for moneys due under a previous judgment constitute an action upon a judgment within s.24(1)). See also *E.D. & F.Man (Sugar) v. Haryanto, The Times*, November 24, 1995.

[*Note 51*]
See also *International Bulk Shipping and Services Ltd v. Minerals and Metals Trading Corpn. of India* [1996] 1 All E.R. 1017.

Shipping

Article 23 of the International Convention on Salvage, contained in **28–013** Sched. 11 to the Merchant Shipping Act 1995, now prescribes that any action relating to payment under the Convention is to be time-barred if judicial or arbitral proceedings are not instituted within a period of two years from the day on which the salvage operations are terminated (although the period may be extended by a declaration to the claimant). Actions for an indemnity may be instituted within the time allowed by the *forum* where the proceedings are instituted.

Carriage by sea

The Athens Convention relating to the Carriage of Passengers and their **28–014** Luggage by Sea is now contained in Sched. 6 to the Merchant Shipping Act 1995.
The two year limitation period for personal injury claims in the Athens

Convention is not subject to the court's discretion to override the time limit for such claims contained in s.33 of the 1980 Act.[a]

[a] *Higham v. Stena Sealink Ltd* [1996] 1 W.L.R. 1107.

[*Add at end of note 71: page* [1329]]
Mauritius Oil Refineries Ltd v. Stolt-Nielson Nederlands B.V. [1997] 1 Lloyds Rep. 273.

2. – ACCRUAL OF THE CAUSE OF ACTION

General rule in contract

28–021   [*Add to Note 27: page* [1335]]
See, on concurrent actions in tort and contract, *Henderson v. Merrett Syndicates Ltd* [1995] 2 A.C. 145; *ante*, §§1–048–1–071.

[*Add to Note 29*]
See also *Henderson v. Merrett Syndicates Ltd* [1995] 2 A.C. 145; *ante*, §§1–048–1–071.

[*Add to note 30*]
Wessex Regional Health Authority v. HLM Design (1994) 10 Const.L.J. 165.

[*Add to note 31*]
Wessex Regional Health Authority v. HLM Design (1994) 10 Const.L.J. 165.

Successive and continuing breaches

28–022   [*Note 39: page* [1336]]
See also *Hopkins v. Mackenzie, The Times*, November 3, 1994 (C.A.) (solicitors allow medical negligence claim to be struck out for want of prosecution: limitation period begins when action struck out, but not before).

Principal and surety

28–028   [*Add to note 81: page* [1340]]
Bank of Baroda v. Patel [1996] 1 Lloyd's Rep. 390.

Insurance

28–030   [*Add to note 1: page* [1341]]
Bank of America National Trust and Savings Association v. Christmas [1994] 1 All E.R. 401.

Work and services

[*Add to note 28: page* [1343]]
See also *Sullivan v. Layton Lougher & Co.* (1995) 49 E.G. 127 (C.A.);
Tabarrock v. EDC Lord & Co., The Times, February 14, 1997.

[*Add to note 29*]]   **28–034**
But contrast *First National Commercial Bank v. Humberts* [1995] 2 All
E.R. 673 (C.A.) where a valuer negligently valued the future worth of a lease
so that a lender advanced money secured on the land leased, and the lender
would not have entered into the transaction had the valuation been properly
carried out; the limitation period accrued, not on the date when the advance
was made, but at the time at which the lender suffered loss when the security
became inadequate.

[*Add to note 31*]
See also *Henderson v. Merrett Syndicates Ltd* [1995] 2 A.C. 145; *ante*,
§§1–048–1–071.

Building contracts

In *Invercargill City Council v. Hamlin*[a] the Privy Council held that a claim   **28–035**
in respect of physical defects in a building caused by negligent supervision of
the works by a local authority was in reality a claim for economic loss for
depreciation in the value of the building and that loss did not occur until a
reasonably prudent owner would have discovered the defects (*Pirelli
General Cable Works Ltd v. Oscar Faber and Partners* not followed).

[a] [1996] 1 All E.R. 756.

Fiduciary relationships

In *Nelson v. Rye*[a] it was held by Laddie J. that—(i) an action for breach of   **28–036**
fiduciary duty simpliciter is outside the provisions of the Limitation Act 1980
and therefore is not subject to a period of limitation; (ii) where breach of
fiduciary duty gives rise to a constructive trust, the provisions of section 21 of
the 1980 Act determine whether there is a limitation period and its duration;
(iii) an action for breach of an express trust is, in like manner, subject to the
limitation provisions of section 21; (iv) in neither case (ii) nor (iii) is it
possible to avoid any limitation period imposed by the Act by treating the
case as one of breach of fiduciary duty.

But if no limitation period applies a plaintiff may be met by the equitable defences set out in §§28–101—28–109 of the Main Work: *ibid.*

[a] [1996] 1 W.L.R. 1378.

Restitution

28–037   [*Amend Note 54: page* [1346]]
Kleinwort Benson Ltd v. South Tyneside Metropolitan B.C. is reported in [1994] 4 All E.R. 972.

Arbitration and award

28–038   In *International Bulk Shipping and Services Ltd v. Minerals and Metals Trading Corpn of India,*[a] the Court of Appeal held that the limitation period for enforcement of an arbitral award accrued when the claimant was entitled to enforce the award. Alternatively, if the claim was for damages for breach of an implied promise to pay the award, then it accrued when a reasonable time to pay the award (in this case three months) had elapsed.
See section 13 of the Arbitration Act 1996.[b]

[a] [1996] 1 All E.R. 1017.

[b] See *ante,* §15–001.

Burden of proof

28–039   [*Add to note 69: page* [1347]]
Arab Monetary Fund v. Hashim [1996] 1 Lloyd's Rep. 589, 607–608 (C.A.).

[*Add to note 73*]
Arab Monetary Fund v. Hashim, supra.

4. – THE RUNNING OF TIME

Abrogation of arbitration award or agreement

28–044   Section 34(5)(7) of the Limitation Act 1980 has been repealed and replaced by section 13(2) of the Arbitration Act 1996.[a]

[a] See *ante,* §15–001.

Bankruptcy and winding-up

[*Add to note 2: page* [1350]]   **28–047**
See also *Re a Debtor (No. 50A–5D–1995)* [1997] 2 W.L.R. 57

5. – EXTENSION OF THE PERIOD

(b) *Fraud, Concealment or Mistake*

The decision of Saville J. in *Sheldon v. R.H.M. Outhwaite (Underwriting* **28–057**
Agencies) Ltd was reversed by the Court of Appeal,[a] but on appeal to the
House of Lords his interpretation of section 32(1) of the 1980 Act was, by a
majority, confirmed.[b]

[a] [1994] 1 W.L.R. 754.

[b] [1996] A.C. 102 (noted (1995) 111 L.Q.R. 580).

(c) *Latent Damage*

Extension of the period

A plaintiff is required to have knowledge of those facts which are causally **28–067**
relevant for the purposes of an action in negligence before the limitation
period starts to run.[a]
Knowledge by a person that any acts or omissions did, or did not, as a
matter of law, involve negligence is irrelevant.[b]
The court has jurisdiction to order a question of fact concerning whether
the plaintiff had the requisite knowledge for the purposes of section
14A(4)(*b*) to be tried as a preliminary issue.[c]
See also *Higgins v. Hatch & Fielding.*[d]

[a] *Hallam-Eames v. Merrett Syndicates, The Times,* January 25, 1995, (C.A.).

[b] *Bradstock Trustee Services Ltd v. Nabarro Nathanson* [1995] 1 W.L.R. 1405.

[c] *Busby v. Cooper, The Times,* April 15, 1996 (C.A.).

[d] [1995] EGCS 105 (C.A.)

[*Add to note 98: page* [1359]]
Wilson v. Lefevre Wood & Royle [1995] C.L.Y. 3165 (C.A.); *Spencer-
Ward v. Humberts* [1994] N.P.C. 105 (C.A.); *Finance for Mortgages Ltd v.
Farley & Co.* [1996] E.G.C.S. 35; *Hamlin v. Edwin Evans, TheTimes,* July 15,
1996 (C.A.).

[*Add to note 1*]
See *Campbell v. Meacocks* [1995] N.P.C. 141 (C.A.); *Coban v. Allen, The Times*, October 14, 1996 (C.A.).

(d) *Acknowledgement and Part Payment*

What constitutes part payment

28–073   [*Amend note 34: page* [1362]]
Kleinwort Benson Ltd v. South Tyneside Metropolitan B.C. is reported in [1994] 4 All E.R. 972.

6. – ABRIDGEMENT OF THE PERIOD

Exemption and other restrictive clauses

28–085   [*Add to note 93 at end: page* [1367]]
implemented in the Unfair Terms in Consumer Contracts Regulations 1994, S.I. 1994 No. 3159.

7. – COMMENCEMENT OF PROCEEDINGS

Legal proceedings

28–088   A writ issued within the limitation period but without the authority of the nominal plaintiff is not a nullity. The nominal plaintiff could subsequently ratify and adopt the writ notwithstanding the expiration of the limitation period: *Presentaciones Musicales SA v. Secunda.*[a]

[a] [1994] Ch. 271 (C.A.) (noted (1994) 110 L.Q.R. 448). A petition for leave to appeal to the House of Lords was dismissed.

[*Note 3: page* [1368]]
See also *Saris v. Westminster Transports SA* [1994] 1 Lloyd's Rep. 115.

[*Add to note 5 after* The Vita]
De Pina v. M.S. "Birka" Beutler Schiffahrts KG [1996] 1 Lloyd's Rep. 31.

[*Note 6*]
Ward-Lee v. Lineham was distinguished, and *Caribbean Gold Ltd v. Alga Shipping Co. Ltd* was disapproved, in *Singh v. Duport Harper Foundries Ltd*, now reported in [1994] 1 W.L.R. 769 (C.A.)

New claims in pending proceedings

28–089   [*Note 18: page* [1370]]
R.S.C. Ord. 20, r. 5(3), cannot be used to correct a mistake as to the

identity of the person intended to sue, but is confined to correcting mistakes as to the name of the plaintiff: *International Bulk Shipping and Services Ltd v. Minerals and Metals Trading Corp. of India* [1996] 1 All E.R. 1017 (C.A.).

[*Amend note 21*]
Arab Monetary Fund v. Hashim was reversed in part on other grounds by the Court of Appeal [1996] 1 Lloyd's Rep. 589.

[*Add to note 21*]
Sion v. Hampstead Health Authority, The Times, June 10, 1994 (C.A.). But where the new cause of action was statute-barred before the writ was issued, the court has no jurisdiction to allow an amendment to introduce it: *Clarke (E.) & Sons (Coaches) v. Axtell Yates Hallett* (1994) 30 Con.L.R. 123; *cf., Lloyd's Bank Plc v. Rogers, The Times,* March 24, 1997.

[*Add to note 24*]
Bank of America National Trust and Savings Association v. Christmas [1994] 1 All E.R. 401; *Bradstock Trustee Services Ltd v. Nabarro Nathanson* [1995] 1 W.L.R. 1405.

[*Amend note 28: page* [1371]]
Welsh Development Agency v. Redpath Dorman Long Ltd is reported in [1994] 1 W.L.R. 1409.

In *Toprak Enerji Sanayi A.S. v. Sale Tilney Technology plc* [1994] 1 W.L.R. 840 it was stated (*obiter*) that there was an apparent *lacuna* in that an order for the substitution of a party as plaintiff under R.S.C. Ord. 15, r. 7, could not be made after the limitation period had expired having regard to the provisions of s.35. But in *Yorkshire Regional Health Authority v. Fairclough* [1996] 1 W.L.R. 210, the Court of Appeal held that this was not so (substitution of trust for health authority as plaintiff after relevant period of limitation expired). See also *Industrie Chimiche Italia Centrale v. Alexander G. Tsavliris & Sons Maritime Co.* [1996] 1 W.L.R. 774; *cf. International Bulk Shipping and Services Ltd v. Minerals and Metals Trading Corpn. of India* [1996] 1 All E.R. 1017 (C.A.).

Arbitral proceedings

See sections 13 and 14 of the Arbitration Act 1996.[a] Section 14 corre- **28–092**
sponds to Article 21 of the UNCITRAL Model Law. S.34 of the 1980 Act has been repealed by the 1996 Act.

[a] *Ante,* §15–001.

[*Note 52*]
See also *Petredec Ltd v. Tokumaru Kaiun Co. Ltd* [1994] 1 Lloyd's Rep. 162.

9. – LIMITATION IN EQUITY

Statements of the doctrine

28–105   [*Add to note 5: page* [1378]]
Nelson v. Rye [1996] 1 W.L.R. 1378, 1392.

Awareness of facts

28–107   [*Add to note 8: page* [1379]]
cf., *Nelson v. Rye* [1996] 1 W.L.R. 1378.

Prejudice to defendant

28–108   In *Nelson v. Rye*,[a] Laddie J. left open the question whether a defendant must prove a causal link between the delay and the prejudice of which he complains.

   [a] [1996] 1 W.L.R. 1378, 1396

[*Add to note 15*]
See also *Nelson v. Rye, supra*, at pp. 1395, 1396.

10. – CONFLICT OF LAWS

Foreign Limitation Periods Act 1984

28–115   [*Notes 49, 53, 55, 56: page* [1383]]
Arab Monetary Fund v. Hashim was reversed in part on other grounds by the Court of Appeal: [1996] 1 Lloyd's Rep. 589. Saville L.J. stated (at p. 600) that the effect of disapplication of the foreign limitation period under s.2 of the 1984 Act would be to impose the relevant English limitation period as part of the procedural law of the forum.

Part Eight

RESTITUTION

CHAPTER 29

RESTITUTION

Note:

Westdeutsche Landesbank Girozentrale v. Islington L.B.C.: in paragraphs 29–002, 29–007, 29–018A, 29–021, 29–025, 29–031, 29–034, 29–037, 29–039, 29–043, 29–067, 29–125, references are made to the judgment of Hobhouse J. (1993) 91 L.G.R. 323. Hobhouse J.'s decision on the liability to make restitution and to pay compound interest was affirmed by the Court of Appeal [1994] 1 W.L.R. 938, but reversed as to the date from which interest was payable. The House of Lords [1996] A.C. 669, by a majority, held that there was no jurisdiction to award compound interest in this case and that *Sinclair v. Brougham* [1914] A.C. 398, should be overruled. Accordingly, no resulting trust arises when payment is made under a contract void on the ground of *ultra vires*. These issues do not affect the points for which the judgment of Hobhouse J. is cited in the above-mentioned paragraphs.

[*Add to note 1: page* [1387]]
Mason and Carter, *Restitution Law in Australia* (1995)

1. – INTRODUCTION

(a) *Nature of the Subject*

Equity

29–002   [*Add to note 12: page* [1389]]
Tribe v. Tribe [1996] Ch. 107.

(c) *The Principle of Restitution*

The principle of unjust enrichment

29–009   See also Pensions Act 1995, s.14 (power to make restitution order if there has been a contravention of the statutory provisions governing payments of surplus to the employer, the restrictions on employer related investments, or on the winding up of a scheme).

29–010 **The implied contract theory**

[*Delete the last sentence of the last paragraph beginning with* ("It is submitted that the House of Lords ...") *and substitute: page* [1396]]
Significantly in *Westdeutsche Landesbank Girozentrale v. Islington L.B.C.*[71] Lord Browne-Wilkinson stated[71a] that "the common law restitutionary claim is based not on an implied contract but on unjust enrichment ... In my judgment, your Lordships should now unequivocally and finally reject the concept that the claim for moneys had and received is based on an implied contract. I would overrule *Sinclair v. Brougham* on this point". Lord Slynn of Hadley[71b] and Lord Lloyd of Berwick[71c] agreed with

Lord Browne-Wilkinson's speech in its entirety. Lord Woolf agreed with this part of Lord Browne-Wilkinson's speech.[71d] Lord Goff of Chieveley[71e] was clearly in favour of rejecting the implied contract theory, but did not favour overruling *Sinclair v. Brougham*.

[71] [1996] A.C. 669.

[71a] *ibid.* at p. 710.

[71b] *ibid.* at p. 718.

[71c] *ibid.* at p. 738.

[71d] *ibid.* at p. 720.

[71e] *ibid.* at p. 688.

(d) *The content of the principle of unjust enrichment*

[*Add to notes 80 and 81 after reference to* Pan Ocean Shipping Ltd v. **29–011**
Creditcorp Ltd]
(Burrows [1994] Restitution L.R. 52).

The nature of the enrichment

[*Add to note 95: page* [1399]] **29–012**
See also *Bookmakers Afternoon Greyhound Services Ltd v. Wilfred Gilbert Staffordshire Ltd* [1994] F.S.R. 723, 742–4 (no restitution where a party received services which in the circumstances were clearly not rendered gratuitously but where the receiver always refused to pay for them).

[*Add to note 98*]
Such a right to restitution will not arise if the parties have contractually allocated the risk in a different manner; see *Regalian Properties Plc v. London Dockland Development Corp.* [1995] 1 W.L.R. 212. See also McKendrick [1995] Restitution L.R. 100. *Cf. Independent Grocers Co-operative Ltd v. Noble Lowndes Superannuation Consultants Ltd* (1993) 60 S.A.S.R. 525.

Enrichment at the plaintiff's expense

[*Add to note 8: page* [1400]] **29–014**
See also *Halifax Building Society v. Thomas* [1996] Ch. 217, 227.

[*Add to note 14*]
See also *Jaggard v. Sawyer* [1995] 1 W.L.R. 269.

2. – RESTITUTION

(a) *Payment under a mistake*

29–018A   [*Add to note 41 after the reference to* Chase Manhattan Bank N.A. v. Israel-British Bank (London) Ltd. [1981] Ch. 105, 119: *page* [1405]]
(note that in *Westdeutsche Landesbank Girozentrale v. Islington L.B.C.* [1996] A.C. 669, Lord Browne-Wilkinson, at p. 714–715, doubted the reasoning in *Chase Manhattan Bank* though not the result. He suggested that a trust could not arise on the mere receipt of the moneys because at that stage the recipient had no knowledge of the mistake, however, "the retention of the moneys after the recipient bank learned of the mistake may well have given rise to a constructive trust").

[*Add to note 41 after the reference to* Thavron v. B.C.C.I. S.A.: *page* [1405]]
See also *Re Goldcorp Exchange Ltd (in receivership)* [1995] 1 A.C. 74, 103 and *Friends' Provident Life Office v. Hillier Parker May & Rowden (a firm)* [1997] Q.B. 85, 105–106;

[*And add after the reference to* Westdeutsche Landesbank Girozentrale v. Islington L.B.C.]
See also *Bank Tejarat v. Hong Kong & Shanghai Banking Corporation (CI) Ltd* [1995] 1 Lloyd's Rep. 239, at 245–246 (an example of the importance of tracing in this area even when only a personal claim is being made, because it was stated that it must at least be possible to identify the defendant as receiving the money). On personal remedies and tracing see also *Boscawen v. Bajwa* [1996] 1 W.L.R. 328, 334.

Negligence: payer with means of knowledge

29–021   [*Add to notes 65 and 66: page* [1407]]
R.B.C. Dominion Securities Inc. v. Dawson (1994) 111 D.L.R. (4th) 230.

Mistake of law

29–025   [*Text at note 91*]
The mistake of law rule has also been held not to be part of the law of Scotland: *Morgan Guaranty Trust Co. of N.Y. v. Lothian Regional Council.*[a]

[a] [1995] S.L.T. 299.

[*Note 92*]
The Law Commission has confirmed the provisional view it expressed in Consultation Paper No. 120 that the mistake of law rule be abolished. The

Commission was of the view that the rule could be abolished judicially in England, as it has in the other jurisdictions mentioned in §29–025, if the matter came before the House of Lords. But it recommended legislation for a number of reasons, in particular the need to address the important and difficult question of changes of the law made by judicial decision.[a]

[a] *Mistakes of Law and Ultra Vires Public Authority Receipt and Payments*, Law Com. No. 227 (Cm. 2731). The Government has accepted this part of the Report: H.C. Deb. March 19, 1997 (written answer).

Exceptions to rule regarding mistake of law 29–027

[*Delete from note 24 the following sentence: page* [1414]]
"An equitable tracing order may be available despite a mistake of law: *Sinclair v. Brougham* [1914] A.C. 398, 452 (*post* §29–072)"

Change of position

[*Add to note 60: page* [1418]] 29–030
Bank Tejarat v. Hong Kong & Shanghai Banking Corporation (CI) Ltd [1995] 1 Lloyd's Rep. 239; Swadling in Birks (ed.), *Laundering and Tracing* (1995) Ch. 9.

Illustrations of change of position

[*Add to note 63: page* [1419]] 29–031
It has been held that acts done in reliance on a void contract where no payments had yet been received were not sufficient to raise a defence of change of position; see *South Tyneside M.B.C. v. Svenska International Plc* [1995] 1 All E.R. 545. See also *State Bank of N.S.W. Ltd v. Swiss Bank Corp.* (New South Wales Court of Appeal, September 8, 1995); Nolan in Birks (ed.), *Laundering and Tracing* (1995) Chap. 6. See also *Barber v. N.W.S. Bank* [1996] 1 W.L.R. 641.

[*Add to note 64*]
See also *R.B.C. Dominion Securities Inc. v. Dawson* (1994) 111 D.L.R. (4th) 230 (change of position not available in respect of expenses which would have been incurred even if the defendant had never received the payment in question, such as the payment of an existing debt, or in respect of expenses incurred once the defendant is aware of the plaintiff's claim); *Sullivan v. Lee* (1995) 95 B.C.L.R. (2d) 195 (British Columbia S.C.).

[*Add to note 67*]
See also *Sullivan v. Lee* (1995) 95 B.C.L.R. (2d) 195 (British Columbia S.C.).

[*Add to note 70: page* [1420]]
See now Law. Com. No. 227, *Mistakes of Law and Ultra Vires Public Authority Receipts and Payments* (Cm 2731) (1994), para. 2.21.

Relation between change of position and estoppel

29–033   [*Add to note 77: page* [1420]]
R.B.C. *Dominion Securities Inc. v. Dawson* (1994) 111 D.L.R. (4th) 230 (Canadian decision that since the recognition of change of position which operates *pro tanto* the defence of estoppel should no longer be available in actions for the recovery of money paid under a mistake of fact); *Boscawen v.* *Bajwa* [1996] 1 W.L.R. 328 (introduction of change of position defence allows re-examination of decisions in which judges may have distorted basic principles in order to avoid injustice to the defendant).

(b) *Failure of consideration*

29–034 **General principles**

[*Add to note 81: page* [1421]]
See also *Goss v. Chilcott* [1996] A.C. 788.

[*Add to note 81*]
cf. Goss v. Chilcott [1996] A.C. 788 and see *post*, §§29–039 and 29–040.

[*Add to note 85: page* [1422]]
See further, *Barber v. N.W.S. Bank* [1996] 1 W.L.R. 641.

Comparison with damages

29–035   [*Add to note 97: page* [1423]]
See also Goodhart, [1995] Restitution L.Rev. 3; Beale, (1996) 112 L.Q.R. 205, 208, and on the availability of restitutionary damages for breach of contract see generally Main Work, §26–012.

Total failure of consideration and detrimental reliance

29–036   [*Add to note 10: page* [1424]]
See also *Stocznia Gdanska S.A. v. Latvian Shipping Co., Latreefers Inc.* [1996] 2 Lloyd's Rep. 132 (on appeal to the House of Lords) and *The Salvage Association v. C.A.P. Financial Services Ltd* [1995] F.S.R. 654.

Partial failure of consideration

29–038   [*Add to note 24: page* [1426]]
See also *The Salvage Association v. C.A.P. Financial Services Ltd* [1995]

F.S.R. 654 (contract for the sale and development of software—the software being incomplete only amounted to a partial failure of consideration).

[*Add to note 34 after the reference to* DO Ferguson & Associates v. Sohl]   **29–039**
(1992) 62 BLR 92.

[*And add after the reference to* Pan Ocean Shipping Co. Ltd v. Creditcorp Ltd]
White Arrow Express Ltd v. Lamey's Distribution Ltd, The Times, July 21, 1995 (C.A.), noted Beale, (1996) 112 L.Q.R. 205.

[*Add to text after note 34: page* [1427]]
The Privy Council recently has shown support for one of these methods of relaxing the requirement for total failure of consideration, namely apportionment. In *Goss v. Chilcott,*[34a] it was suggested that apportionment is not always dependent on the parties' intentions. In that case it was acknowledged that a loan could be apportioned between principal and interest. This is not controversial, but Lord Goff delivering the judgment of the Court suggested that, if required, he would also apportion the principal so that any repayments made of the principal would not prevent there being a restitutionary claim based on failure of consideration but merely reduce the restitutionary claim to the balance of the loan. Moreover, in *Westdeutsche Landesbank Girozentrale v. Islington L.B.C.,*[34b] Lord Goff expressed support for the reformulation of the total failure of consideration rule.

[34a] [1996] A.C. 788. See *post*, §29–040.

[34b] [1996] A.C. 669, 682–683.

Partial failure of consideration in a divisible contract   **29–040**

[*Add to text after note 37*]
Whether a contract is divisible and whether apportionment can take place has traditionally been an issue of construction based on the presumed intention of the parties. However, in *Goss v. Chilcott* the Privy Council suggested that apportionment is not limited to the intention of the parties and may also occur as a matter of law in those cases in which it can be carried out without difficulty, for instance, where the benefit received by the payer was, as in that case, a monetary one.[37a]

[37a] [1996] A.C. 788, 798. See *ante* §29–039.

29–041 Recovery of Deposits

[*Add to note 46: page* [1428]]
See *County and Metropolitan Homes Surrey Ltd v. Topclaim Ltd* [1997] 1
All E.R. 254 (effect of exclusion of Law of Property Act 1925, s.49(2)).

Part payments not intended to be deposits

29–042   [*Add to note 52: page* [1429]]
See also *Guardian Ocean Cargoes Ltd v. Banco do Brasil SA. (Nos. 1 and
3)* [1994] 2 Lloyd's Rep. 152.

[*Add to note 53: page* [1429]]
See also *Stocznia Gdanska S.A. v. Latvian Shipping Co., Latreefers Inc.*
[1996] 2 Lloyd's Rep. 132, on appeal to the House of Lords.

(c) *Benefits conferred under a Void, Illegal or Unenforceable Contract*

Benefits conferred under a void contract

29–043   [*Add to note 61 after the reference to* Westdeutsche Landesbank Girozentrale v. Islington London Borough Council]
[1994] 1 W.L.R. 938 (C.A.). There has been an appeal to the H.L.: [1996] 2
A.C. 669.

[*And add to end of note*]
The idea of "no consideration" was also discussed in *Friends' Provident
Life Office v. Hillier Parker May & Rowden (a firm)* [1997] Q.B. 85, 98. *Cf.
Commissioner of State Revenue (Vic) v. Royal Insurance Australia Ltd*
(1994) 182 C.L.R. 51, 67.

[*Add to note 62 at end*]
See also *Kleinwort Benson Ltd v. South Tyneside Metropolitan Borough
Council* [1994] 4 All E.R. 972, 987–990 (one of the claims failed because the
parties could not be returned to their original positions—the contract being
void).

[*Delete note 63 and substitute: page* [1430]]
On restitution of money transferred under an *ultra vires* contract see
Westdeutsche Landesbank Girozentrale v. Islington L.B.C. [1996] A.C. 669,
ante §§29–001, 29–010. See also Companies Act 1989, s.108.

Illegal contracts

29–044   In *Aratra Potato Co. Ltd v. Taylor Joynson Garrett (a firm)*[a] monies paid
under an agreement that was champertous were not recoverable because the

contract was not void but unenforceable and there had been no total failure of consideration.

ᵃ [1995] 4 All E.R. 695.

(d) *Waiver of tort*

Which torts may be waived

[*Add to note 5 at end: page* [1434]]   29–049
See also Cooke (1994) 110 L.Q.R. 420. See also *Invergugie Investments Ltd v. Hackett* [1995] 1 W.L.R. 713.

The nature of the benefit

[*Add to note 22: page* [1436]]   29–050
Jaggard v. Sawyer [1995] 1 W.L.R. 269. See also Goodhart, [1995] Restitution L.Rev. 3.

Election of remedy

[*Add to note 31: page* [1437]]   29–052
See also *Halifax Building Society v. Thomas* [1996] Ch. 217; where it was held that an election to affirm a mortgage prevented any action being brought for the tort of deceit which in turn prevented that tort being waived.

[*Add to note 32*]
See also *Island Records Ltd v. Tring International Plc* [1995] 3 All E.R. 444 (time when an election between remedies for breach of copyright and account must be made); *The Personal Representatives of Tang Man Sit v. Capacious Investments Ltd* [1996] A.C. 514 (election between damages for breach of trust and account).

[*Add to note 38*]
See also the comments in *Halifax Building Society v. Thomas* [1996] Ch. 217, 227–228.

Limits on the right to rescind for fraud

[*Add to note 49: page* [1439]]
See also *Vadasz v Pioneer Concrete (S.A.) Pty Ltd* [1995] 185 C.L.R. 102, noted Carter & Tolhurst, [1996] J.C.L. 167.

[*Add to note 51: page* [1439]]   29–054
In *Halifax Building Society v. Thomas* [1996] Ch. 217 a mortgagee who was induced to enter into the mortgage due to fraudulent misrepresentations, lost any right it may have had to moneys recovered on the sale of the property in excess of the debt owed because in exercising its power of sale it had affirmed the contract.

(e) *Compulsory payments to the defendant*

Compulsory payments to the defendant

29–056   [*Add to note 64: page* [1440]]
CTN *Cash and Carry Ltd v. Gallagher Ltd* [1994] 4 All E.R. 714.

(f) Ultra vires *receipts by the Revenue and public authorities*

Ultra vires demands

29–066   [*Add to note 23: page* [1446]]
See also *British Steel plc v. Customs and Excise Commissioners* [1997] 2
All E.R. 366.

Defences

29–069   [*Add to note 40: page* [1448]]
See *South Tyneside M.B.C. v. Svenska International Plc.* [1995] 1 All E.R.
545, supplement to §29–031, note 63 *ante*).

[*Add to note 45 the following reference to* Kleinwort Benson Ltd v.
South Tyneside Metropolitan Borough Council: *page* [1449]]
[1994] 4 All E.R. 972

[*And add*]
See also *Commissioner of State Revenue (Vic) v. Royal Insurance
Australia Ltd* (1994) 182 C.L.R. 51 and *Mutual Pools & Staff Pty Ltd v.
Commonwealth* (1994) 179 C.L.R. 155. For example outside the field of tax
see *Kleinwort Benson Ltd v. Birmingham C.C.* [1997] Q.B. 380.

(g) *Proprietary remedies for tracing property*

Tracing orders

29–070   [*Add to note 46: page* [1449] *after* Lawson, (2nd ed.) Chap. 6;] Smith, *The
Law of Tracing*, (1997).

[*Add to note 47 after* Lipkin Gorman v. Karpnale Ltd
Trustee of the Property of F. C. Jones & Sons v. Jones [1996] 3 W.L.R. 703,
pet dismissed, [1997] 1 W.L.R. 51, noted Andrews & Beatson, (1996) 113
L.Q.R. 21.

See *El Ajou v. Dollar Land Holdings plc (No. 1)*[a] and *El Ajou v. Dollar
Land Holdings plc (No. 2)*[b] where the question of whether the possibility of a

claim by a third party could be a defence to a tracing claim was discussed and, although not ruled out, doubted. On the facts in that case no other claimant was seeking to claim and there was no realistic possibility of such a claim.[c]

[a] [1993] 3 All E.R. 717 at 747.

[b] [1995] 2 All E.R. 213 at 223.

[c] See also *Bank Tejarat v. Hong Kong & Shanghai Banking Corporation (CI) Ltd* [1995] 1 Lloyd's Rep. 239, at 245–246; *Boscawen v. Bajwa* [1996] 1 W.L.R. 328, 334, *ante*, §29–018A, note 41

Tracing at common law

[*Add to note 60: page* [1450]]   **29–071**
See also *Trustee of the Property of F. C. Jones & Sons v. Jones* [1996] 3 W.L.R. 703, pet. dismissed [1997] 1 W.L.R. 51, where tracing was allowed to extend not only to the exchanged product but also to profits made.

[*Add to note 63*]
See also *Trustee of the Property of F. C. Jones & Sons v. Jones* [1996] 3 W.L.R. 703, pet. dismissed [1997] 1 W.L.R. 51.

[*Add to note 65*]
See also *Trustee of the Property of F. C. Jones & Sons v. Jones* [1996] 3 W.L.R. 703, 710 *per* Millett L.J.

Tracing in equity

Note that although the decision in *Sinclair v. Brougham*[a] was overruled by **29–072** the House of Lords in *Westdeutsche Landesbank Girozentrale v. Islington L.B.C.*,[b] in relation to the issue of resulting trusts arising from the payment of money under *ultra vires* contracts, the particular doctrinal points made in the case in respect to tracing for which it is cited in these paragraphs are still good law. Lord Browne-Wilkinson stated[c] that no doubt was being cast on the principles of tracing as established in *Re Diplock's Estate*,[d] which suggests that the requirement of a fiduciary relationship remains necessary, but also stated[e] that stolen moneys are traceable in equity and that an equitable proprietary interest under a resulting trust or a constructive trust will suffice, which suggests that the courts will continue to manipulate this requirement where they think this is appropriate.[f] On the nature of tracing in equity see *Boscawen v. Bajwa*,[g] and see *Foskett v. McKeown*[h] in which it was held that the beneficiaries of a trust could not trace into the proceeds of an insurance policy in respect of which trust moneys had fraudulently been used to pay premiums.

[a] [1914] A.C. 398.

[b] [1996] A.C. 669.

[c] *ibid.* at p. 714.

[d] [1948] Ch. 465, affd [1951] A.C. 251.

[e] [1996] A.C. 669, 716.

[f] See, *e.g. Bristol & West B.S. v. Mothew* [1997] 2 W.L.R. 436, 454, *per* Millett L.J.

[g] [1996] 1 W.L.R. 328.

[h] [1997] 3 All E.R. 392, C.A.

[*Add to note 71: page* [1451]]
See also *Westdeutsche Landesbank Girozentrale v. Islington L.B.C.* [1996]
A.C. 669, 716.

[*Add to note 72: page* [1451]]
See also *Re Goldcorp Exchange Ltd (in receivership)* [1995] 1 A.C. 74.

[*Add to note 74*]
R. v. Preddy [1996] 3 W.L.R. 255, 264.

[*Add to note 77: page* [1452]]
See also *Style Financial Services Ltd v. Bank of Scotland* [1995] B.C.C. 785.

[*Add to note 79*]
See also *Re Goldcorp Exchange Ltd (in receivership)* [1995] 1 A.C. 74.

Withdrawals from a mixed fund in a bank account

29–075   [*Add to note 11: page* [1455]]
See also *Bishopsgate Investment Management Ltd v. Homan* [1995] Ch.
211 and *Goldcorp Exchange Ltd (in receivership)* [1995] 1 A.C. 74, 107.

(h) *Other equitable remedies and constructive trusts*

29–076 Constructive trusts

[*Add to note 15: page* [1455]]
In *Westdeutsche Landesbank Girozentrale v. Islington L.B.C.* [1996] A.C.
669, 716, Lord Browne-Wilkinson expressed support for the development of
the remedial constructive trust in English law.

[*Add to note 19: page* [1456]]
See also *Royal Brunei Airlines S.D.N. B.H.D. v. Phillip Tan Kok Ming*
[1995] 2 A.C. 378; *Deutsche Ruckversicherung A.G. v. Walbrook Insurance
Co. Ltd* [1994] 4 All E.R. 181, 201–2 and *Halifax Building Society v. Thomas*
[1996] Ch. 217. See further *Target Holdings Ltd v. Redferns (a firm)* [1996]
A.C. 421; *Re A.M.F. International Ltd* [1996] 1 W.L.R. 77, 83 (a trustee need
not compensate a beneficiary for loss arising from a breach of trust if it was
inevitable that the beneficiary would suffer that loss anyway).

3. – REIMBURSEMENT

(a) *Compulsory payments to a third person*

Assignees of a lease

The original lessee's right of indemnity from a subsequent assignee will be **29–085**
of less importance in practice since the liability of both the original parties to
a lease and of their assignees has been limited in respect of agreements for
leases made or leases granted after January 1, 1996 by the Landlord and
Tenant (Covenants) Act 1995.[a]

[a] See S.I. 1995 No. 2963 (commencement order).

Voluntary payments

[*Add to note 64: page* [1462]]   **29–088**
See also *Kleinwort Benson Ltd v. Vaughan* [1996] C.L.C. 620, C.A. (the
payment of a third party's debt in order to release a security and perfect an
independent right of reimbursement is not simply a voluntary payment).

(e) *Contribution*

The right to contribution

[*Delete first sentence of final paragraph and substitute: page* [1471]]   **29–101**
The Act therefore covers liability arising out of breaches of different
contractual obligations,[39] situations in which one person's liability is in
contract but the other's is in tort,[40] situations where one person's liability is in
either contract or tort and the other's is in restitution,[40a] as well as the case,
previously governed by an earlier statute,[41] where the liability of both
persons is in tort.

[40a] *Friends' Provident Life Office v. Hillier Parker May and Rowden (a firm)* [1997]
Q.B. 85.

Tortfeasors

29–110   [*Add to note 66: page* [1474]]
See now Merchant Shipping Act 1995, ss.187–189.

(f) *Agency of necessity*

Agency of Necessity

29–111   [*Add to note 68*]
See also Merchant Shipping Act 1995, s.40 (claims against seamen's wages
for maintenance of dependants).

(g) *Benefits conferred in an emergency*

Necessitous intervention on behalf of the defendant

29–112   [*Add to note 71*]
See also Merchant Shipping Act 1995, s.73(2) (obligation to repay
expenses in bringing shipwrecked seamen ashore and burial expenses).

4. – LIABILITY TO ACCOUNT TO THE PLAINTIFF

(c) *Agent or Employee Receiving a Bribe or Secret Profit*

Agent of employee receiving a bribe or secret profit

29–118   [*Add to note 23: page* [1480]]
cf. A.G. v. Blake [1997] Ch. 84.

[*Add to note 26: page* [1481] *after* Att.-Gen (Hong Kong) v. Reid]
See also *A.G. v. Blake* [1997] Ch. 84, 96.

(f) *Subrogation*

Subrogation

29–121   [*Add to note 34: page* [1482]]
Mitchell, *The Law of Subrogation* (Oxford University Press 1994);
Boscawen v. Bajwa [1996] 1 W.L.R. 328 (subrogation discussed under a
restitutionary analysis); Mitchell [1995] L.M.C.L.Q. 451. See also *Kleinwort
Benson Ltd v. Vaughan* [1996] C.L.C. 620 (C.A.).

[*Add to note 36*]
See *The "Surf City"* [1995] 2 Lloyd's Rep. 242 (waiver of subrogation
rights).

5. – RECOMPENSE

(a) Quantum meruit *Claims*

Quantum meruit to fix a price or remuneration

[*Add to note 86 after* Brewer Street Investments Ltd v. Barclays Wool- **29–127**
len Co. Ltd: *page* [1489]]
  Regalian Properties Plc v. London Dockland Development Corp. [1995] 1
W.L.R. 212, noted *ante*, §29–012 Note 98.

[*Add to note 99: page* [1490]]
  *Bookmakers Afternoon Greyhound Services Ltd v. Wilfred Gilbert
Staffordshire Ltd* [1994] F.S.R. 723, noted *ante*, §29–012 note 95.

Part Nine

CONFLICT OF LAWS

CHAPTER 30

CONFLICT OF LAWS

2. – COMMON LAW: THE DOCTRINE OF THE PROPER LAW OF A CONTRACT

Limitations on the power to choose

30–006   [*Note 35: page* [1502]]
Council Directive 93/13 of April 5, 1993, on Unfair Terms in Consumer Contracts ([1993] O.J. L95/29) is implemented in the Unfair Terms in Consumer Contracts Regulations 1994 (S.I. 1994 No. 3159), in force from July 1, 1995. The Regulations apply notwithstanding any contract term which applies or purports to apply the law of a non-Member State, if the contract has a close connection with the territories of the Member States (Reg. 7). See also *Akai Pty Ltd v. The People's Insurance Co. Ltd* (1996) 71 A.L.J.R. 156, noted by Reynolds [1997] L.M.C.L.Q. 177.

[*Add to note 36*]
DR Insurance Co. v. Central National Insurance Co. [1996] 1 Lloyd's Rep. 74 (Insurance Companies Act 1982 applies to reinsurance contracts whatever their proper law).

Incorporation by reference

[*Add to note 38*]   **30–007**
DR Insurance Co. v. Central Insurance Co. [1996] 1 Lloyd's Rep. 74, 81;
The Stolt Sydness (1997) 1 Lloyd's Rep. 273.

Implied choice of law

[*Add to note 51: page* [1504]]   **30–008**
Trade Indemnity plc v. Forsakringsaktiebolaget Njord [1995] 1 All E.R.
796 (strong presumption that reinsurance contract written on the London
market is written on the basis of an implied or imputed English proper law).

[*Add to note 55*]
Wahda Bank v. Arab Bank plc [1996] 1 Lloyd's Rep. 470 (C.A.) (in the
absence of an express choice of law to a different effect, parties intended a
counter-guarantee to be governed by the same law as the guarantee).

No choice of proper law

[*Add to note 72 at line 3: page* [1506]]   **30–009**
Minories Finance Ltd v. Afribank Nigeria Ltd [1995] 1 Lloyd's Rep. 134;
Bank of Credit and Commerce Hong Kong Ltd v. Sonali Bank [1995] 1
Lloyd's Rep. 227; *Batstone & Firminger Ltd v. Nasima Enterprises (Nigeria)
Ltd* [1996] C.L.C. 1902, 1910. See also *Bank of Baroda v. Vysya Bank Ltd*
[1994] 2 Lloyd's Rep. 87 (a case on the Rome Convention, *post*, §30–048,
note 52).

[*And add at end:*]
Wahda Bank v. Arab Bank plc [1996] 1 Lloyd's Rep. 470 (C.A.).

Renvoi

[*Note 92 and text thereto*]   **30–012**
In *Macmillan Inc. v. Bishopsgate Investment Trust plc (No. 3)*,[a] Millett J.
refused to apply the doctrine of renvoi in a case involving a dispute as to
priority of title to shares, and added that the doctrine "has not been applied
in contract or other commercial situations. It has often been criticised, and it
is probably right to describe it as largely discredited." Millett J.'s decision
was affirmed on other grounds,[b] Staughton L.J., who alone dealt with this
point, observing that renvoi did not apply to questions concerning title to
shares in a company.

^a [1995] 1 W.L.R. 987, 1008.

^b [1996] 1 W.L.R. 387 (C.A.).

3. – THE ROME CONVENTION

(a) *In General*

History and purpose

30–013   [*Note 97 and text thereto*]
An Accession Convention providing for the accession of Spain and
Portugal to the Rome Convention was signed at Funchal on May 18, 1992. It
was ratified by the Netherlands and Spain and entered into force on
September 1, 1993. The Funchal Convention is now scheduled to the
Contracts (Applicable Law) Act 1990 as Schedule 3A.^a It has now been
ratified by France, Germany, Italy, the Netherlands, Portugual and Spain.
An Accession Convention for Austria, Finland and Sweden was signed on
November 29, 1996 but has not yet entered into force.

^a See S.I. 1994 No. 1900.

(b) *Exclusions*

Meaning of "contractual obligations"

30–020   [*Note 46: page* [1515]]
See also *Atlas Shipping Agency (UK) Ltd v. Suisse Atlantique Société
D'Armement Maritime S.A.* [1995] 2 Lloyd's Rep. 188 (where A contracts
with B to pay a sum of money to C, an action brought to enforce the
obligation by C involves "matters relating to a contract" for the purposes of
Art. 5(1) of the Lugano Convention on Jurisdiction and the Enforcement of
Judgments in Civil and Commercial Matters 1988 (Civil Jurisdiction and
Judgments Act 1982, Sched. 3A)); *Agnew v. Lansforsakringsbolagens AB*
[1996] 4 All E.R. 978 (whether the making of a contract was induced by a
misrepresentation involves "matters relating to a contract" for the purposes
of the same provision, the obligation to avoid pre-contractual misrepresentation also to be construed to be capable of being an "obligation" for the
purposes of the provision, not following on this latter point the contrary view
expressed in *Trade Indemnity plc v. Forsakringsaktiebolaget Njord* [1995] 1
All E.R. 796).

[*Note 52 and text thereto*]
For the choice of law rules applicable to torts, see Private International
Law (Miscellaneous Provisions) Act 1995, Part III (in force from May 1,
1996^a). There is nothing in Part III of the Act which precludes an employee
from relying on an alternative claim in contract if it is more advantageous to

[260]

him to do so. See also *Henderson v. Merrett Syndicates Ltd* [1995] 2 A.C. 145, a case not involving the conflict of laws, in which it was confirmed that concurrent duties in contract and tort could co-exist (see *ante*, §§1–048— 1–071). See also *post*, §30–069, notes 79–83.

ᵃ S.I. 1996 No. 995

[*Notes 53–56 and text thereto*]
In *Kleinwort Benson Ltd v. Glasgow City Council* [1996] Q.B. 678, a majority of the Court of Appeal held that a claim for money paid under a void contract was a matter "relating to a contract" for the purposes of Article 5(1) of the modified version of the Brussels Convention on Jurisdiction and the Enforcement of Judgments in Civil and Commercial Matters 1968 (Civil Jurisdiction and Judgments Act 1982, Sched. 4) which is applicable as between the component parts of the United Kingdom. The European Court of Justice had earlier declined jurisdiction to interpret this version of the Brussels Convention: see Case C–346/93 *Kleinwort Benson Ltd v. Glasgow City Council* [1995] I E.C.R. 5615, [1996] Q.B. 57. See also *post*, §30–093, text after note 97.

Arbitration agreements and agreements on the choice of court

[*Note 80: page* [1517]]   30–025
Arbitration Act 1975, s.5(2)(b) is replaced by Arbitration Act 1996, s.103(2)(b), in force from January 31, 1997.

Power of agent to bind principal, etc.

[*Add to note 96: page* [1519]]   30–027
And see *Presentaciones Musicales S.A. v. Secunda* [1994] Ch. 271 (C.A.).

[*Note 97*]
See the EEC Directive on Self-employed Commercial Agents ([1986] O.J. L382/17) implemented in England and Wales and Scotland in the Commercial Agents (Council Directive) Regulations 1993 (S.I. 1993 No. 3053, as amended by S.I. 1993 No. 3173) in force from January 1, 1994. The Regulations govern the relations between commercial agents and their principals and apply in respect of the activities of commercial agents in Great Britain (Reg. 1(2)). It is specifically provided that Regulations 3–22 which deal with the mutual rights and obligations of agent and principal, remuneration of the agent, the conclusion and termination of the agency contract and miscellaneous matters such as service of notices, do not apply where the parties have agreed that the agency contract is to be governed by the law of another Member State (Reg. 1(3)). See Main Work §31–006.

Insurance

30–030 [*Notes 12 and 13: page* [1520]]
See now Third Council Directive of June 18, 1992 on the co-ordination of laws, regulations and administrative provisions relating to direct insurance other than life insurance ([1992] O.J. L228/1) (the Third Non-Life Directive), implemented in the United Kingdom by the Insurance Companies (Third Insurance Directives) Regulations 1994 (S.I. 1994 No. 1696), in force from July 1, 1994. Reg. 49 amends Insurance Companies Act 1982, Sched. 3A, Part I, para. 1. These Regulations also give effect in the United Kingdom to the Third Council Directive of November 10, 1992 on the co-ordination of laws regulations and administrative provisions relating to direct life assurance ([1992] O.J. L360/1) (the Third Life Directive), but this aspect of the Regulations has no substantial impact on the rules of the conflict of laws. For discussion, see Dicey and Morris, *The Conflict of Laws* (12th ed., 1993), *Fourth Cumulative Supplement* (1997), pp. 197–202; MacNeill (1995) 44 I.C.L.Q. 19.
For a case applying the conflict of laws' provisions contained in Insurance Companies Act 1982, Sched. 3A, Part 1, see *Credit Lyonnais v. New Hampshire Insurance Co.* [1997] 2 Lloyd's Rep. 1, C.A.

[*Add to note 19, line 11, after second sentence*]
For minor amendments, see Insurance Companies Act 1982, s.96(1)(1), inserted by S.I. 1994 No. 1696, Reg. 50.

(c) *Choice of Law by the Parties*

The general principle

30–031 [*Add to note 27: page* [1522]]
Hartley (1996) 45 I.C.L.Q. 271.

Meaning of a "choice of law"

30–032 [*Add to note 41: page* [1523]]
See also *DR Insurance Co. v. Central National Insurance Co.* [1996] 1 Lloyd's Rep. 74.

[*Add to note 45: page* [1524]]
See *Wahda Bank v. Arab Bank plc* [1996] 1 Lloyd's Rep. 470 (C.A.). *Cf. Minories Finance Ltd v. Afribank Nigeria Ltd* [1995] 1 Lloyd's Rep. 134; *Bank of Credit and Commerce Hong Kong Ltd v. Sonali Bank* [1995] 1

Lloyd's Rep. 227; *Batstone & Firminger Ltd v. Nasima Enterprises (Nigeria) Ltd* [1996] C.L.C. 1902, 1910.

[*Note 46 and text thereto*]
In *Egon Oldendorff v. Libera Corp.* [1995] 2 Lloyd's Rep. 64, an arbitration clause provided for arbitration in London by arbitrators "conversant with shipping matters". Mance J. held that this constituted a choice of English law for the purposes of Article 3(1) of the Rome Convention, in the context of an application for leave to serve the writ out of the jurisdiction under R.S.C. Ord. 11, r. 1(1)(d)(iii). In *Egon Oldendorff v. Libera Corp. (No. 2)* [1996] 1 Lloyd's Rep. 380, Clarke J. held that since the parties had agreed to arbitration in England in a well known English form of charterparty containing well known meanings in English law, the inference was to be drawn that they intended English law to be the applicable law for the purposes of Article 3(1) of the Rome Convention.

Mandatory rules

[*Add to note 99: page* [1530]]   **30–041**
Unfair Terms in Consumer Contracts Regulations 1994, Reg. 7, *ante*, §30–006, note 35. See also *Akai Pty Ltd v. The People's Insurance Co. Ltd* (1996) 71 A.L.J.R. 156, noted by Reynolds [1997] L.M.C.L.Q. 177.

[*Note 6*]
See previous entry.

Mandatory rules of the law of the forum

[*Note 8: page* [1530]]   **30–042**
Employment Protection (Consolidation) Act 1978, s.153(5) is repealed and replaced by Employment Rights Act 1996, s.204, in force from August 22, 1996.

[*Amend note 12: page* [1531]]
See Note 8 above.

[*And add*]
Unfair Terms in Consumer Contracts Regulations 1994, Reg. 7, *ante*, §30–006, note 35.

[*Add to note 13*]
DR Insurance Co. v. Central National Insurance Co. [1996] 1 Lloyd's Rep. 74. See also *Akai Pty Ltd v. The People's Insurance Co. Ltd* (1996) 71 A.L.J.R. 156.

(d) *Applicable Law in the Absence of a Choice by the Parties*

Specific applications

30–048   [*Note 48: page* [1534]]
The Dutch Hoge Raad has held that the characteristic performance of a contract of sale is that of the seller: see *Société Nouvelle des Papéteries de l'Aa S.A. v. B.V. Machinefabriek B.O.A.*, 1992 N.J. 750, discussed by Struycken [1996] L.M.C.L.Q. 18.

[*Note 50: page* [1535]]
In *HIB Ltd v. Guardian Insurance Co. Ltd* [1997] 1 Lloyd's Rep. 412 it was held that the characteristic performance of a contract between an English broker and an insurance company seeking reinsurance on the English market was that of the broker. Accordingly, the contract was governed by English law as the law of the country in which the principal place of business of the broker was situated.

[*Note 52 and text thereto*]
In *Bank of Baroda v. Vysya Bank Ltd* [1994] 2 Lloyd's Rep. 87, 92, it was accepted that for the purposes of Article 4(2) of the Rome Convention, the characteristic performance in respect of a contract between banker and customer was that of the bank. Accordingly, the applicable law was the law of the country in which the branch through which performance is effected was situated. More generally, this case presented the opportunity of considering the application of Article 4(2) of the Rome Convention to a letter of credit transaction. Indian buyers had instructed the defendant, an Indian bank, to issue a letter of credit in favour of Irish sellers who had an office in London. The credit provided that it was to be advised to the seller through the plaintiff, another Indian bank, at that bank's branch in London. The plaintiff bank confirmed the credit and paid the sellers under it. The defendant bank then withdrew its authorisation to the plaintiff to claim reimbursement before the due date at which point the plaintiff sought leave to serve the writ on the defendant out of the jurisdiction, pursuant to R.S.C. Ord. 11, r. 1(1)(d)(iii), claiming that the contract between the two banks was governed by English law for the purposes of that provision. There was no choice of law within the terms of Article 3(1) of the Convention, so the issue was governed by Article 4. Applying this provision, it was held that the contract between the plaintiff (the confirming bank) and the defendant (the issuing bank) was governed by English law. For the purposes of Article 4(2), the characteristic performance of the contract (which was treated as a contract of agency) was that of the confirming bank and consisted of that bank adding its confirmation to the credit and its honouring of the

obligations to the beneficiary, the sellers, which that confirmation entailed. The performance of the confirming bank's obligations was to be effected through a "place of business other than [that party's] principal place of business" (Art. 4(2), second sentence), namely through its London branch. Application of the presumption thus led to the conclusion that English law was the applicable law.

Mance J. also considered what the position would have been in relation to any contract which might exist between the confirming bank and the seller, and concluded that on the facts of this case such contract would also have been governed by English law. This is because the characteristic performance is still that of the bank, either because the bank is providing a banking service, or, alternatively, because it is of the essence of a confirmed letter of credit that the confirming bank undertakes to pay the beneficiary on presentation of the appropriate documents. The presumption in Article 4(2) thus leads once more to English law. Mance J., however, also proferred the view that this conclusion could also be reached by application of Article 4(5) of the Convention (see Main Work, §30–057). This view cannot be accepted. Article 4(5) is concerned with the circumstances in which the presumptions in Article 4 may be inapplicable or may be disregarded. It does not provide an initial route to the determination of the applicable law.

The learned judge also paid attention to the law which would have applied to the contract between the issuing bank and the beneficiary, although that question did not arise in the case itself. He concluded that the characteristic performance would be that of the issuing bank. On the facts, that would have meant that Indian law would have been the governing law, as the law of the issuing bank's principal place of business. This conclusion would give rise to considerable commercial inconvenience (see *Offshore International S.A. v. Banco Central S.A.* [1977] 1 W.L.R. 399). Mance J. therefore resorted to Article 4(5), and stated that the contract was more closely connected with English law than it was with Indian law, principally because England was the place of performance of the issuing bank's obligations to the beneficiary under the credit. Accordingly, the presumption in Article 4(2) could be disregarded and English law applied.

The outstanding question, which was not dealt with in this case, is as to the law applicable to the contract between the issuing bank and the buyer. It can be confidently asserted, however, that the characteristic performance is that of the bank, because the bank is providing banking services to the buyer. Accordingly, the applicable law will be the law of the issuing bank's principal place of business or place of business, as the case may be, subject to any circumstances which may bring Article 4(5) into play. For more detailed analysis of this case, see Morse [1994] L.M.C.L.Q. 560. See also *Bank of Credit & Commerce Hong Kong Ltd v. Sonali Bank* [1995] 1 Lloyd's Rep. 227, where Mance J.'s views were approved by Cresswell J. although the Rome Convention did not apply on the facts of the case. For similar approval, see *Batstone & Firminger Ltd v. Nasima Enterprises (Nigeria) Ltd*

[1996] C.L.C. 1902, 1910 (Rix J.). On the general question of the law applicable to letters of credit, see Davenport and Smith [1994] 9 Butterworths Journal of International Banking and Financial Law 3.

Immovables

30-053   [*Add to note 79: page* [1538]]
Case C–294/92 *Webb v. Webb* [1994] I E.C.R. 1717, [1994] Q.B. 696.

[*Note 80*]
Timeshare Act 1992 is amended by Timeshare Regulations 1997 (S.I. 1997 No. 1081) which implement in the United Kingdom Directive 94/47 [1994] O.J. L280 on the protection of purchasers in respect of certain aspects of contracts relating to the purchase of the right to use immovable properties on a timeshare basis, in force from April 29, 1997.

In *Jarrett v. Barclays Bank* [1997] 3 W.L.R. 654, English plaintiffs had entered into timeshare agreements in relation to property in Spain and Portugal, financing these transactions with money lent by British banks. The plaintiffs alleged that the owners of the timeshare properties they had acquired were guilty of misrepresentation or breach of contract and brought proceedings against the banks under sections 56(2) and 75 of the Consumer Credit Act 1974. According to section 56(2) a person conducting negotiations antecedent to an agreement falling within the section is deemed to act as agent for the creditor (the banks) while section 75 provides that if the debtor (timeshare purchaser) has a claim for misrepresentation or breach of contract against the supplier (timeshare owner) he will have a like claim against the creditor. It was held that the claim against the banks was not a claim the object of which was a tenancy of immovable property for the purposes of Article 16(1) of the Brussels Convention on Jurisdiction and the Enforcement of Judgments in Civil and Commercial Matters which gives exclusive jurisdiction to the courts of the *situs* of the immovable property. For although a timeshare was a tenancy within the meaning of Article 16(1), the claim against the banks arose out of the debtor—creditor—supplier agreement and not out of any tenancy. Consequently the English court had jurisdiction over the claim under Article 2 of the Convention. *Cf. Lynch v. Halifax Building Society and Royal Bank of Scotland plc* [1995] C.C.L.R. 42 which must now be taken to have been overruled.

Rebutting the presumptions

30-057   [*Notes 98–10 and text thereto: pages* [1540]–[1541]]
See generally, *Bank of Baroda v. Vysya Bank Ltd* [1994] 2 Lloyd's Rep. 87, *ante*, §30–048, note 52.

[*Note 5*]
In *Société Nouvelle des Papéteries de l'Aa v. B.V. Machinefabriek B.O.A.*, 1992 N.J. 750 the Dutch Hoge Raad decided that Article 4(5) of the Rome Convention should be applied restrictively. The presumption in Article 4(2) was the "main rule", which rule should only be disregarded if in the special circumstances of the case the place of business of the party who is to effect the characteristic performance has "no real significance as a connecting factor." See Struycken [1986] L.M.C.L.Q. 18.

(e) *Certain Consumer Contracts and Individual Employment Contracts*

"Certain consumer contracts"

[*Add to note 15*]   **30–059**
See also Case C–89/91 *Shearson Lehman Hutton Inc. v. TVB Treuhandge-sellschaft for Vermogensverwaltung und Beteiligungen mbH* [1993] 1 E.C.R. 1–139; Case C–318/93 *Brenner v. Dean Witter Reynolds Inc.* [1994] 1 E.C.R. 1–4725; Case C–269/95 *Benincasa v. Dentalkit Srl, The Times*, October 13, 1997.

Mandatory rules

[*Note 35: page* [1543]]   **30–061**
Council Directive 93/13 of April 5, 1993 is implemented in the United Kingdom by the Unfair Terms in Consumer Contracts Regulations 1994 (S.I. 1994 No. 3159), *ante*, §30–006, note 35. Timeshare Act 1992 is amended by Timeshare Regulations 1997 (S.I. 1997 No. 1081) which implement in the United Kingdom Directive 94/47 [1994] O.J. L280 on the protection of purchasers in respect of certain aspects of contracts relating to the purchase of the right to use immovable properties on a timeshare basis, in force from April 29, 1997.

Choice of law by the parties

[*Note 63: page* [1547]]   **30–066**
Employment Protection (Consolidation) Act 1978, ss.140, 141(2) and 153(5) are repealed and replaced respectively by Employment Rights Act 1996, ss.203, 196(2), (3) and 204(1), (2), in force from August 22, 1996.

[*Note 64*]
Part II of the Wages Act 1986, which provided for statutory minimum remuneration for certain workers in accordance with orders made by wages

councils, was repealed by the Trade Union Reform and Employment Rights Act 1993, s.35. The remaining relevant provisions of the Wages Act 1986 have been repealed and replaced by Employment Rights Act 1996, ss.13–27 which are concerned with the protection of wages. These provisions apply whatever the law which is applicable to the contract of employment (1996 Act, s.204), but do not apply where, under the employee's contract the employee ordinarily works outside Great Britain (1996 Act, s.196(3)(b)).

Contract and tort

30–069   [*Notes 79–83 and text thereto: pages* [1549] *to* [1550]]
There is nothing in Part III of the Private International Law (Miscellaneous Provisions) Act 1995 (in force from May 1, 1996[a]) which indicates that an employee is not free to plead and pursue a claim in tort if the case falls within Part III of the Act. The requirement imposed by the common law that the defendant's conduct be actionable as a tort by English law and civilly actionable by the law of the place where the tort is committed, at least as a general rule, is abolished by the 1995 Act (s.10(a)). The new general rule introduced by the 1995 Act requires application of the law of the country in which the events constituting the tort in question occur (s.11(1) and see the amplifications in s.11(2)) and is subject to a rule of displacement (s.12). These new rules may lead to a more favourable result for an employee than would the rules applicable at common law. For comment on Part III of the 1995 Act, see *Dicey and Morris on the Conflict of Laws* (12th ed., 1993), *Fourth Cumulative Supplement* (1997), Chap 35; Morse (1996) 45 I.C.L.Q. 888; Rodger [1996] Scottish Law and Practice Quarterly 397; Briggs [1995] L.M.C.L.Q. 519.

[a] S.I. 1996 No. 995.

4. – SCOPE OF THE APPLICABLE LAW

(a) *Material Validity of the Contract*

Identification of "putative applicable law"

30–078   [*Add to note 14: page* [1553]]
Egon Oldendorff v. Libera Corp. [1995] 2 Lloyd's Rep. 64.

[*Add to note 15*]
The Heidberg [1994] 2 Lloyd's Rep. 287; *The Lake Avery* [1997] 1 Lloyd's Rep. 540.

Formation of the contract

[*Notes 20–23 and text thereto: page* [1554]]

30–079

In *Egon Oldendorff v. Libera Corp., supra*, Mance J. held that English law should apply to determine whether a contract had been concluded and whether a clause providing for arbitration in London was incorporated into that contract because the contract was governed by English law (see *ante*, §30–032, note 46). The defendants sought, pursuant to Article 8(2) of the Rome Convention, to rely on Japanese law as the law of their habitual residence, claiming that it would not be reasonable to determine the effects of their conduct in accordance with English law. Mance J. rejected this argument. It was unreasonable *not* to apply English law and to apply Japanese law because this would ignore the arbitration clause, a result which would be contrary to normal commercial expectations.

(c) *Capacity*

Corporations

[*Add to note 75 at end: page* [1559]]

30–092

Companies Act 1985, ss.36, 36A and s.36C, as substituted and inserted by Companies Act 1989, s.130, as adapted and modified by Foreign Companies (Execution of Documents) Regulations 1994 (S.I. 1994 No. 950), as amended by S.I. 1995 No. 1729, made under Companies Act 1989, s.130(6).

(d) *Particular Issues: Article 10*

Introduction

[*Text after note 97: page* [1561]]

30–093

In *Kleinwort Benson Ltd v. Glasgow City Council* [1996] Q.B. 678, a majority of the Court of Appeal held that despite the United Kingdom's reservation to Article 10(1)(e) of the Rome Convention (Contracts (Applicable Law) Act 1990, s.2(2)), a claim for restitution of money paid under a contract which was a nullity was a matter "relating to a contract" within the meaning of Article 5(1) of the modified version of the Brussels Convention on Jurisdiction and the Enforcement of Judgments in Civil and Commercial Matters which is applicable within the United Kingdom as Schedule 4 to the Civil Jurisdiction and Judgments Act 1982. See also *Baring Bros & Co. Ltd v. Cunninghame District Council, The Times*, September 30, 1996 (Outer House of Court of Session), noted by Stevens (1997) 113 L.Q.R. 249; Bird [1997] L.M.C.L.Q. 182. On restitution in the conflict of laws, see generally Rose (ed.) *Restitution and the Conflict of Laws* (1995); Dickinson [1996] L.M.C.L.Q. 556. And see, *ante*, §30–020, notes 53–56.

Damages

30–098   [*Note 32: page* [1565]]
   The Indian Grace [1992] 1 Lloyd's Rep. 124 has been reversed on other grounds, *sub nom. Republic of India v. India Steamship Co. Ltd* [1993] A.C. 410.

Consequences of nullity of contract

30–103   [*Text at notes 61–62*]
   See *ante*, §30–020, notes 53–56 and §30–093, text after note 97.

Other unspecified issues

30–104   [*Add to note 63: page* [1568]]
   Cf. Meridien Biao Bank G.m.b.H. v. Bank of New York [1997] 1 Lloyd's Rep. 437 (whether there is a defence to a contractual claim governed by English law depends upon English law including its rules of private international law).

(f) *Illegality and Public Policy*

Illegality

30–108   [*Add to note 94: page* [1572]]
   Bangladesh Export Import Co. Ltd v. Sucden Kerry S.A. [1995] 2 Lloyd's Rep. 1, 5.

Public policy

30–110   [*Add to note 14: page* [1574]]
   See too *Fraser v. Buckle* [1996] 2 I.L.R.M. 34.

   [*Add to note 18*]
   Royal Boskalis Westminster NV v. Mountain [1997] 2 All E.R. 929.

   [*Add to note 20*]
   Royal Boskalis Westminster NV v. Mountain, supra.

(g) *Foreign Currency Obligations*

Money of Account

[*Note 41: page* [1577]]   **30–113**
The House of Lords unanimously dismissed an appeal from the decision
of the Court of Appeal ([1993] 1 Lloyd's Rep. 471) in *The Texaco Melbourne*
[1994] 1 Lloyd's Rep. 473 (H.L.).

Judgments in foreign currency

[*Note 69: page* [1580]]   **30–115**
A judgment in foreign currency carries interest at the rate fixed by statute
(Judgments Act 1838, ss.17, 18, as amended by Administration of Justice Act
1970, s.44, Main Work, §26–085): see *Practice Direction (Judgments: Foreign
Currency)* [1976] 1 W.L.R. 83, para. 10. The Law Commission had
recommended changes in this practice: see Law Com. No. 124 (1983), paras.
4.1–4.15. These recommendations have been implemented in Part I of the
Private International Law (Miscellaneous Provisions) Act 1995, in force
from September 26, 1996 (S.I. 1996 No. 2515). A new section 44A is inserted
into the Administration of Justice Act 1970 (1995 Act, s.1(1)), the new
section to apply to judgments pronounced after the commencement of the
provision (1995 Act, s.1(2)). According to section 44A(1), where a judgment
is given for a sum expressed in a currency other than sterling and the
judgment debt is one to which section 17 of the Judgments Act 1838 applies,
the court may order that the rate of interest applicable to the debt shall be
such rate as the court thinks fit. Where the court makes such an order,
section 17 of the 1838 Act shall have effect in relation to the judgment debt as
if the rate specified in the order were substituted for the rate specified in
section 17(s.44A(2)).
Section 2 of the 1995 Act inserts a new section 74(5A) into the County
Courts Act 1984. By virtue of section 74(1) of the 1984 Act, the Lord
Chancellor is empowered to provide by Order that county court orders shall
carry interest at the prescribed rate. Section 74(5A) extends that power to
enable the Lord Chancellor to make provision to allow a county court to
order that the rate of interest applicable to a sum expressed in a currency
other than sterling shall be such rate as the court thinks fit instead of the rate
that would otherwise be applicable. As to the powers of an arbitral tribunal
to award interest, see Arbitration Act 1996, s.49, in force from January 31,
1997. See *ante*, §15–038.

CHAPTER 31

AGENCY

1. – AGENCY IN GENERAL

Foreign Law

[*Amend note 13: page* [3]]   **31–004**
The reference to *Bowstead on Agency* should now be to *Bowstead and Reynolds on Agency* (16th ed.), §§1–018–1–019.

Commercial agents

The regulations are discussed in *Bowstead and Reynolds on Agency* (16th **31–005** ed.), Chap. 11.

Use of the terms "agent", "agency"

[*Add to note 33: page* [5]]   **31–007**
As another example of this problem, the question whether a tour operator acted as agent or as principal is discussed in *Wong Mee Wan v. Kwan Kin Travel Services Ltd* [1996] 1 W.L.R. 38 (firm was held principal supplying tour, and so liable for negligence of sub-contractor); *Sheppard v. Crystal Holidays Ltd* [1997] C.L. 500 (holiday company agent to make contract with skiing instructor).

General and special agents   **31–010**

The question whether a company was the general agent of its wholly owned subsidiary is however discussed (in connection with the validity of a tenant's break notice) in *Dun & Bradstreet Software Services (England) Ltd v. Provident Mutual Life Assurance*, C.A., June 9, 1997. The conclusion was that it was not; but it may be that in this sort of context the notion will acquire a new significance.

2. – EXAMPLES OF TYPES OF AGENT

Credit transactions

[*Add to note 1: page* [12]]   **31–018**
See also *Powell v. Lloyd's Bowmaker Ltd* 1996 S.L.T.(Sh.Ct.) 117 (trade-in: agency only as regards car principally sold].

3. – Creation of Agency

(c) *Ratification*

Proof of ratification

31–025   [*Amend note 35: page* [16]]
The reference to *Bowstead on Agency* should now be to *Bowstead and Reynolds on Agency* (16th ed.), §21–072. This view was accepted by Moore-Bick J. in *Yona International Ltd v. La Réunion Française S.A. d'Assurances et de Reassurances* [1996] 2 Lloyd's Rep. 84, noting however that "silence or inaction may simply reflect an unwillingness or inability on the part of the principal to commit himself"; and that ratification may be by an agent.

Who can ratify

31–026   [*Amend note 45: page* [17]]
The reference to *Bowstead on Agency* should now be to *Bowstead and Reynolds on Agency* (16th ed.), §2–063.

Limits on ratification

31–030   *Presentaciones Musicales S.A. v. Secunda* is further discussed in *Bowstead and Reynolds on Agency* (16th ed.), §2–087.

[*Add to note 68*]
It is said by the High Court of Australia that the explanation of such cases (specifically, notice to quit cases) is that the act is required to be valid and effective when it is done: *Re Construction Forestry Mining and Energy Union* (1994) 181 C.L.R. 539, 545.

(d) *Agency of Necessity*

First type of case

31–032   [*Delete the words "owner (or demise charterer)" from text, line 4, and substitute "cargo owner": page* [21]]

[*Add to note 90*]
The master is given authority to sign a salvage agreement by Merchant

Shipping Act 1995, s.224(1) and Sched. 11, Art. 6 (implementing the International Convention on Salvage of 1989 and effective January 1, 1996).

(f) *Delegation*

Effect of delegation

[*Add to note 34: page* [25]]   **31–037**
The contract duty may go further than this, but the tort duty is not likely to do so: see *Aiken v. Stewart Wrightson Members' Agency Ltd* [1995] 2 Lloyd's Rep. 618. See *ante*, §§1–048—1–071.

[*Amend notes 37, 38*]
The references to *Bowstead on Agency* should now be to *Bowstead and Reynolds on Agency* (16th ed.), §5–011 and Article 70 respectively.

[*Amend note 40*]
Arbuthnott v. Fagan and Feltrim Underwriting Agencies Ltd is now reported *sub nom. Henderson v. Merrett Syndicates Ltd* [1995] 2 A.C. 145.

4. – AUTHORITY

(a) *General Principles*

Usual authority

[*Amend note 57: page* [27]]   **31–042**
The reference to *Bowstead on Agency* should now be to *Bowstead and Reynolds on Agency* (16th ed.), §3–006.

5. – PRINCIPAL'S RELATIONS WITH THIRD PARTIES

(b) *Apparent Authority*

Apparent Authority

[*Amend note 34: page* [35]]   **31–055**
The reference to *Bowstead on Agency* should now be to *Bowstead and Reynolds on Agency* (16th ed.), Article 75.

Agents of companies

[*Add to note 41: page* [36]]   **31–056**
The rather different question of when the acts of an officer of a company rank as the acts of the company itself, as opposed to acts of the company's

agents, is considered by Hoffmann L.J. in *El Ajou v. Dollar Land Holdings plc* [1994] 2 All E.R. 685 and by Lord Hoffmann in *Meridian Global Funds Management Asia Ltd v. Securities Commission* [1995] 2 A.C. 500.

(c) *Undisclosed Principal*

Undisclosed principal

31–058   [*Amend note 64: page* [39]]
The reference to *Bowstead on Agency* should now be to *Bowstead and Reynolds on Agency* (16th ed.), §9–012.

[*Add to note 70*]
The doctrine was applied to a breach of section 14(5) of the Sale of Goods Act 1979 (*post*, §41–072) in *Boyter v. Thomson* [1995] 2 A.C. 628: see Brown, (1996) 112 L.Q.R. 49.

(d) *Further Rules*

Settlement with and set-off against agent

31–064   [*Amend note 20: page* [44]]
The reference to *Bowstead on Agency* should now be to *Bowstead and Reynolds on Agency* (16th ed.), Article 83.

31–065 **Effect of judgment against agent**

[*Add to note 37: page* [45]]
The matter was raised before the Privy Council in connection with an action against the principal on the contract and against the agent for breach of warranty of authority in *Bonus Garment Co. v. Karl Rieker GmbH*, June 19, 1997; but the Board did not pronounce on the issue.

Election

31–066   [*Amend note 40: page* [45]]
The reference to *Bowstead on Agency* should now be to *Bowstead and Reynolds on Agency* (16th ed.), Article 84.

Where principal is discharged by settling with agent

31–067   [*Amend note 59: page* [47]]
The reference to *Bowstead on Agency* should now be to *Bowstead and Reynolds on Agency* (16th ed.), Article 82.

Effect of bribery of agent

[*Add to note 67: page* [48]]   **31–068**
Arab Monetary Fund v. Hashim was affirmed by the Court of Appeal
[1996] 1 Lloyd's Rep. 589.

[*Add to note 69*]
The primary remedy against the agent is proprietary: see *post*, §31–107.

(e) *Agent's Torts*

Agent's torts

[*Add to note 71*]   **31–069**
Standard Chartered Bank v. Pakistan National Shipping Corp. [1995] 2
Lloyd's Rep. 367, 375–377 (fraudulent signature of bill of lading).

(f) *Dispositions of Property through agent*

Cases where the agent has some authority

[*Amend note 85: page* [50]]   **31–072**
The reference to *Bowstead on Agency* should now be to *Bowstead and
Reynolds on Agency* (16th ed.), Article 87.

[*And add*]
The supposed principle is considered in *Macmillan Inc. v. Bishopsgate
Investment Trust Plc (No. 2)* [1995] 1 W.L.R. 978, where counsel described it
as "the arming principle" and Millett J. said that it was a rule of priorities not
of agency.

Dispositions to agent

[*Amend note 14: page* [52]]   **31–076**
The reference to *Bowstead on Agency* should now be to *Bowstead and
Reynolds on Agency* (16th ed.), Article 91.

6. – AGENTS' RELATIONS WITH THIRD PARTIES

(a) *On the main contract*

When agent liable and entitled

[*Add to note 26: page* [53]]   **31–078**
Belleli SpA v. A.I.G. Europe (U.K.) Ltd, Rix J., Q.B.D., May 22, 1996.

Written documents

31–079   [*Add to note 32: page* [54]]
General principles are restated in *Messini & Co. v. Polskie Linie Oceanicze* [1995] 2 Lloyd's Rep. 566, 571–572; see also *Belleli SpA v. A.I.G. Europe (U.K.) Ltd,* 85 Q.B.D. Rix J., May 22, 1996 (agent able to sue, and (*obiter*) to recover damages on the basis of *Linden Gardens Trust Ltd. v. Lenesta Sludge Disposal Ltd* [1994] 1 A.C. 85, or as trustee.

[*Add to note 36*]
Seatrade Groningen B.V. v. Geest Industries Ltd (The Frost Express) [1996] 2 Lloyd's Rep. 375 ("Seatrade Groningen B.V. Groningen Holland as agents to owners or as Disponent Owners" in box in charterparty marked "Owners/Place of Business": signers liable though acting as agent, *semble*, as well as their principal).

Custom and usage of trade

31–080   [*Add to note 43 before* "(forwarding agents)": *page* [55]]
Cory Brothers Shipping Ltd v. Baldan Ltd [1997] 2 Lloyd's Rep. 58.

Agent for foreign principal

31–081   [*Amend note 47: page* [56]]
The reference to *Bowstead on Agency* should now be to *Bowstead and Reynolds on Agency* (16th ed.), §9–018.

Unnamed principal

31–083   [*Add to note 54: page* [57]]
Cory Brothers Shipping Ltd v. Baldan Ltd [1997] 2 Lloyd's Rep. 58.

[*Add to note 56 after reference to* Salsi v. Jetspeed Air Services Ltd]
Cory Brothers Shipping Ltd v. Baldan Ltd [1997] 2 Lloyd's Rep. 58.

Where "agent" is in fact principal: his liabilities

31–089   [*Amend note 73: page* [59]]
The reference to *Bowstead on Agency* should now be to *Bowstead and Reynolds on Agency* (16th ed.), Article 110.

[*Amend note 77*]
The reference to *Bowstead on Agency* should now be to *Bowstead and Reynolds on Agency* (16th ed.), §9–062.

Where "agent" is in fact principal: his rights

[*Amend note 80*]   **31–090**
The reference to *Bowstead on Agency* should now be to *Bowstead and Reynolds on Agency* (16th ed.), §9–088.

Where principal is company not yet in existence

[*Add to note 82: page* [60]]   **31–091**
An agent was held not personally liable in *Coral (U.K.) Ltd v. Rechtman* [1996] 1 Lloyd's Rep. 235; but it would seem that the contract was not with a non-existent company but with an entity more vaguely identified.

[*Add to note 89*]
See *Coral (U.K.) Ltd v. Rechtman, supra,* n.82.

(c) *Breach of Warranty of Authority*

Liability of agent acting without authority

[*Add to text after note 7: page* [62]]   **31–093**
In *Penn v. Bristol & West Building Society*, [1997] 3 All E.R. 470, the Court of Appeal held a solicitor who had (without his fault) acted without authority in a sale of land liable to the building society which had advanced money to one joint tenant on the faith of the transactions being duly authorised by the other. All of this paragraph except the first sentence can be taken to imply that the warranty is only given to a person who deals with the agent's principal. Such was undoubtedly the ordinary situation of warranty of authority and is still the principal situation for it: but the wording above should now be read subject to the broadened version of the doctrine recognised in the above case.

[*Amend note 6*]
The reference to *Bowstead on Agency* should now be to *Bowstead and Reynolds on Agency* (16th ed.), §9–062.

[*Add to note 7*]
But compare *Nelson v. Nelson* [1997] 1 W.L.R. 233, C.A., where a solicitor who had without negligence commenced an action for an injunction on behalf of person who unknown to him was bankrupt, in respect of property that had vested in the trustee in bankruptcy, was held not liable to pay the costs under the jurisdiction of the court over solicitors. A bankrupt can

authorise the bringing of certain actions. The solicitor warrants that he has a retainer, and that the principal is a person against whom a costs order can be made, both of which were true. He does not warrant that the principal's cause of action is a good one.

Damages

31–098   [*Amend note 12: page* [63]]
The reference to *Bowstead on Agency* should now be to *Bowstead and Reynolds on Agency* (16th ed.), §9–063.

(d) *Restitution*

[*Insert new note to this heading: page* [65]]
NOTE 29a: Certain sorts of agent may be liable to a third party in equity for knowing receipt or accessory liability in respect of breach of trust or fiduciary obligation. This liability, on which there is an important recent decision, *Royal Brunei Airlines Sdn Bhd v. Tan* [1995] 2 A.C. 378, is discussed in connection with banking, *post*, §§33–241A.

(e) *Tort*

Agent's liability in tort

31–102   [*Add to note 43: page* [66]]
The decision in *McCullagh v. Lane Fox & Partners Ltd* was affirmed by the Court of Appeal, but on different grounds: [1996] 1 E.G.L.R. 35.

[*Add to note 44*]
In *McCullagh v. Lane Fox & Partners Ltd* [1996] 1 E.G.L.R. 35, the headnote of which is misleading, it was held by the Court of Appeal that an estate agent could in principle be liable for a representation to a buyer as to the size of property. On the facts however no duty of care was owed; and there was also a disclaimer.

[*Add to note 45*]
In *McCullagh v. Lane Fox & Partners Ltd, supra*, Hobhouse L. J. was of the opinion that the immunity of a solicitor as held in *Gran Gelato, supra*, n. 44, was "based upon the special role of a solicitor and grounds of policy relating to that role": at p. 44H. See also *Henderson v. Merrett Syndicates Ltd* [1995] 2 A.C. 145; *Woodward v. Wolferstans*, Ch.D., March 20, 1997 [1997] T.L.R. 189 (solicitor of mortgage guarantor owes duty to purchaser/mortgagee).

[*Add to note 46 after reference to* Trevor Ivory Ltd v. Anderson]
Standard Chartered Bank v. Pakistan National Shipping Corp. [1995] 2 Lloyd's Rep. 365 (liability of signer of bill of lading); *Williams v. Natural Life*

Health Foods Ltd [1996] 1 B.C.L.C. 288 (personal liability of director); *Holding Oil Finance Inc. v. March Rich & Co. AG*, C.A., February 27, 1996 [1996] C.L. 125 (on inducement of breach of contract).

[*Add to note 46 at end*]
See also in this context *The Leon* [1991] 2 Lloyd's Rep. 611.

7. – OBLIGATIONS OF PRINCIPAL AND AGENT INTER SE

(a) *Duties of Agents*

(i) *Obedience*

Carrying out instructions

[*Add to note 59: page* [68]]   **31–104**
The notion of assuming responsibility has become more acceptable since *Henderson v. Merrett Syndicates Ltd* [1995] 2 A.C. 141: see *ante*, §§1–048—1–071.

(ii) *Exercise of care and skill*

Exercise of care and skill

[*Add to note 60*]   **31–105**
Henderson v. Merrett Syndicates Ltd, supra, n. 59, also decides that there can be concurrent liability in tort: but as to the extent of this see *Aiken v. Stewart Wrightson Members' Agency Ltd* [1995] 2 Lloyd's Rep. 618, *ante*, §31–037, n. 34.

[*Add to note 61*]
As to the liability of members' agents and managing agents at Lloyd's see *Brown v. K.M.R. Services Ltd* [1995] 2 Lloyd's Rep. 513.

(iii) *Honesty*

Bribes

[*Amend note 73: page* [69]]   **31–107**
The reference to *Bowstead on Agency* should now be to *Bowstead and Reynolds on Agency* (16th ed.), Articles 45–50.

(iv) *Conflicting Interests*

Duty not to have conflicting interest

31–109   [*Amend note 10: page* [72]]
The reference to *Bowstead on Agency* should now be to *Bowstead and Reynolds on Agency* (16th ed.), Article 47.

The nature of fiduciary duty is the subject of a valuable discussion (in the context of a solicitor acting for both purchaser and building society) in *Bristol & West B.S. v. Mothew* [1997] 2 W.L.R. 436. See also a more general discussion in the High Court of Australia in *Breen v. Williams* (1996) 186 C.L.R. 71, noted (1997) 113 L.Q.R. 220.

[*Add to note 13*]
Rescission may be ordered on terms: see *Maguire v. Makaronis* (1997) 71 A.L.J.R. 781.

Exclusion clauses

31–111   [*Add to note 26: page* [73]]
They are also subject to the E.C. Directive on Unfair Terms in Consumer Contracts, implemented in the United Kingdom by the Unfair Terms in Consumer Contracts Regulations 1994 (S.I. 1994 No. 3159), effective July 1, 1995. See *ante*, 14–088 *et seq.*; Treitel, *Law of Contract* (9th ed.), pp. 245–259. The impact of the regulations on the financial market is considered in Law Com. No. 236, *infra*, n. 28.

[*Add to note 27*]
See further *Bowstead and Reynolds on Agency* (16th ed.), §§6–046 *et seq.*

[*Add to note 28: page* [74]]
See further the Commission's report under the same title, Law Com. No. 236 (Cm 3049) (1995).

(vi) *Remedies*

Damages: contract and tort

31–113   [*Amend note 34*]
Arbuthnott v. Fagan and Feltrim Underwriting Agencies Ltd is now reported *sub nom. Henderson v. Merrett Syndicates Ltd* [1995] 2 A.C. 145.

[*And add*]
As to damages for breach of fiduciary duty (against an accountant) see *Hodgkinson v. Simms* [1994] 3 S.C.R. 377.

Equity

[*Note 50: page* [76]]   **31–115**
The decision in *Target Holdings Ltd v. Redferns* was varied by the House
of Lords [1996] A.C. 421: the speech of Lord Browne-Wilkinson contains
important discussion of the principles applicable to the assessment of
damages in cases of this sort.

[*Add to note 53*]
Re Fleet Disposal Services Ltd [1995] 1 B.C.L.C. 345.

Other remedies

[*Add to note 54: page* [76]]   **31–116**
As to rescission on terms see *Maguire v. Makaronis* (1997) 71 A.L.J.R.
781.

[*Add to note 60: page* [77]]
Warman International Ltd v. Dwyer (1995) 182 C.L.R. 544; *Tang Man Sit
v. Capacious Investments Ltd* [1996] A.C. 514 (distinguishing damages and
account); *Island Records Ltd v. Tring International Plc* [1995] 1 W.L.R. 1256.

(b) *Rights of Agents*

(i) *Remuneration*

Commission upon the introduction of a person "ready willing and able to purchase"

[*Amend note 4: page* [82]]   **31–124**
The reference to *Bowstead on Agency* should now be to *Bowstead and
Reynolds on Agency* (16th ed.), §7–019.

Agent must be effective cause of transaction

[*Add to note 23: page* [83]]   **31–128**
For examples where commission was due though the agent was not the
effective cause see further *Freedman v. Union Group Plc*, C.A., March 4,
1997; *Raja v. Rollerby Ltd*, C.A., May 15, 1997.

Commercial agents

[*Add to note 39: page* [85]]   **31–130**
Reg. 12 also provides for rights of the agents to inspect books, etc. For a
way in which this might be enforced at common law see *Yasuda Fire &*

Marine Insurance Co. Ltd v. Orion Marine Insurance Underwriting Agency Ltd [1995] Q.B. 174 (where it was held that a contractual right to inspect books persisted after the termination of the agency).

Opportunity to earn commission

31–131   [*Amend note 41: page* [86]]
The reference to *Bowstead on Agency* should now be to *Bowstead and Reynolds on Agency* (16th ed.), Articles 60, 125.

Termination of agency

31–132   [*Add to note 53: page* [87]]
See also *Hurst v. Bryk* [1997] 2 All E.R. 283, C.A. (wrongful termination of partnership releases partner from subsequent liabilities).

Where Commercial Agents Regulations applicable

31–133   [*Add to note 55*]
See also *Bowstead and Reynolds on Agency* (16th ed.), Chap 11.

[*Add to note 56: page* [88]]
See *King v. Tunnock* 1996 S.C.L.R. 742, Sh.Ct.; [1996] C.L. 617 (three months notice).

[*Add to note 61*]
See two cases on compensation, *Graham Page v. Combined Shipping & Transport*, [1997] 3 All E.R. 636 (though little is to be derived from the judgments); *Kingsley v. KJC Carpets*, November 9, 1995, Bristol County Court, unreported. Both cases are noted in [1996] J.B.L. 77.

[*Add to note 64*]
But this reasoning is on general comparative grounds almost certainly wrong: see *Bowstead and Reynolds on Agency* (16th ed.), §11–045.

(iii) *Lien*

Lien

31–142   [*Amend note 21: page* [93]]
The reference to *Bowstead on Agency* should now be to *Bowstead and Reynolds on Agency* (16th ed.), Article 67.

[*Add to note 24*]
Bentley v. Gaisford [1997] Q.B. 627.

[*Amend note 26*]
The reference to *Bowstead, op. cit.* should now be to Article 70.

(iv) *Right of Stoppage in Transit*

Right of stoppage in transit

[*Amend note 30: page* [94]]   **31–143**
The reference to *Bowstead, op. cit.* should now be to §1–019 and Article 71.

8. – TERMINATION OF AUTHORITY

How authority terminated

[*Add to note 35*]   **31–144**
See also *Hurst v. Bryk* [1997] 2 All E.R. 283, C.A. (repudiatory breach of partnership).

[*Add to note 37*]
But in *Nelson v. Nelson* [1997] 1 W.L.R. 233, the generality of such a proposition was doubted: a bankrupt can bring certain actions, and the authority of a solicitor is not therefore terminated in all respects by the bankruptcy of the principal. See *ante*, §31–093. In *Pacific & General Insurance Co. Ltd v. Hazell* [1997] L.R.L.R. 65, Moore-Bick J. held that the appointment of a provisional liquidator revokes the authority of agents appointed to act for or on behalf of the company by or under the authority of the directors.

Irrevocable authority

[*Add to note 48: page* [95]]   **31–145**
The problems of irrevocable authority are discussed in Reynolds, "When is an agent's authority irrevocable?", *Making Commercial Law: Essays in Honour of Roy Goode* (1997), Chap. 10. In *Society of Lloyd's v. Leighs*, Q.B.D., February 20, 1997, Colman J. was of the view that situations of irrevocable authority cannot be confined to those where the purpose of the authority is to secure the agent's money interest, and held that the authority of managing agents and run-off agents at Lloyd's to enter, on behalf of names, into transactions with Equitas was irrevocable. The decision was affirmed by the Court of Appeal on July 31, 1997 on slightly different reasoning.

CHAPTER 32

BAILMENT

1. – IN GENERAL

Bailment compared with trust, contract and tort

32–002 [*Add to note 13: page* [100]]
cf. Mathew v. T.M. Sutton Ltd [1994] 1 W.L.R. 1455 (*post*, §§32–090, 32–108).

[*Add to note 16 after* Bryant v. Herbert (1878) 3 C.P.D. 389: *page* [101]]
Yasuda Fire & Marine Insurance Co. of Europe Ltd v Orion Marine Insurance Underwriting Agency Ltd [1995] Q.B. 174, 186.

Failure of the bailee to return the chattel

[*Add to note 28: page* [102]]   **32–003**
The possession of a bailee may change to possession as donee under an
immediate gift or as donee under a *donatio mortis causa*: *Woodard v.
Woodard* [1995] 3 All E.R. 980.

The bailee and third party claimants

[*Add to note 52 at end: page* [104]]   **32–006**
Arguments which would have extended the scope of the bailee's estoppel
were rejected by the Privy Council in *Re Goldcorp Exchange* [1995] 1 A.C.
74.

Sub-bailment

[*Add to note 16: page* [111]]   **32–014**
Different principles apply when the sub-bailee seeks to take advantage of
the terms of the head bailment. In such a case the ability of the sub-bailee to
invoke the terms depends upon the scope of the agreement between the
bailor and the sub-bailee, entered into by the bailee as agent for the
sub-bailee: see *The Mahkutai* [1996] A.C. 650.

[*Add to note 20 after* The Pioneer Container]
(see the comments of Palmer and Merkin, 1994 All E.R. Annual Review
28–35; and Phang, (1995) 58 M.L.R. 422).

[*Add to note 20 after* [1993] 1 Lloyd's Rep. 311, 327–328]
Spectra International plc v. Hayesoak Ltd [1997] 1 Lloyd's Rep. 153, 155.

Attornment

[*Add to note 23*]   **32–015**
See also Palmer and Merkin, 1994 All E.R. Annual Review 23–25.
Arguments which would have extended the scope of attornment were
rejected by the Privy Council in *Re Goldcorp Exchange* [1995] 1 A.C. 74.

2. – GRATUITOUS BAILMENT

(b) *Involuntary Bailees*

Finding

[*Add to note 74 after* Parker v. British Airways Board [1982] Q.B. 1004: **32–022**
page [117]]
Waverley Borough Council v. Fletcher [1996] Q.B. 334.

3. – BAILMENTS FOR VALUABLE CONSIDERATION

(a) *The Supply of Services: Statutory Provisions*

The Supply of Goods and Services Act 1982

32–028   The Sale and Supply of Goods Act 1994 amends the 1982 Act mentioned in this paragraph.

(c) *Hire*

(i) *Hire (Unregulated by the Consumer Credit Act)*

Terms implied into a contract of hire

32–046   Section 10A of the 1993 Bill which is set out in the text of this paragraph has been enacted into law by para. 6(9) of Schedule 2 to the Sale and Supply of Goods Act 1994. (The wording of s.10A is identical with that of s.10A in the Bill.)

Implied terms as to description and sample

32–048   [*Text and notes 39 and 40: page* [133]]
By para. 6(8) of Schedule 2 to the Sale and Supply of Goods Act 1994, the words "rendering them unmerchantable" in section 10(2)(c) of the 1982 Act (which is quoted in the text of §32–048) have been replaced by the words "making their quality unsatisfactory". For the new definition of "quality" in the 1994 Act, see *post*, §32–049, note 43.

Implied terms as to quality and fitness

32–049   [*Note 43*]
By para. 6(10) of Schedule 2 to the Sale and Supply of Goods Act 1994 the definition of "quality" in s.18(1) of the 1982 Act is omitted, and a new subsection introduced into s.18 as follows:

"(3) For the purposes of this Act, the quality of goods includes their state and condition and the following (among others) are in appropriate cases aspects of the quality of goods—
(a) fitness for all the purposes for which goods of the kind in question are commonly supplied,

(b) appearance and finish,

(c) freedom from minor defects,

(d) safety, and

(e) durability."

[Text and notes 46 and 47]

By para. 6(7) of Schedule 2 to the 1994 Act, *supra*, a new s.9(2) is substituted for the old s.9(2) in the 1982 Act and new subsections added to s.9 as follows:

"(2) Where, under such a contract, the bailor bails goods in the course of a business, there is an implied condition that the goods supplied under the contract are of satisfactory quality.

(2A) For the purposes of this section and section 10 below, goods are of satisfactory quality if they meet the standard that a reasonable person would regard as satisfactory, taking account of any description of the goods, the consideration for the bailment (if relevant) and all the other relevant circumstances.

(3) The condition implied by subsection (2) above does not extend to any matter making the quality of goods unsatisfactory—

(a) which is specifically drawn to the bailee's attention before the contract is made,

(b) where the bailee examines the goods before the contract is made, which that examination ought to reveal, or

(c) where the goods are bailed by reference to a sample, which would have been apparent on a reasonable examination of the sample."

and section 9(9) in the 1982 Act is omitted.

Contributory negligence

[Add to note 49: page [157]]   **32–022**
Corporacion Nacional del Cobre de Chile v. Sogemin Metals Ltd [1997] 2
All E.R. 917, 921–923

(f) *Pledge*

(i) *Pledge at Common Law*

Definition of pledge

[Add to note 10 at end: page [161]]   **32–090**
Attenborough & Son v. Solomon [1913] A.C. 76, 84. The pledgee may be under some fiduciary obligations towards the pledgor: see *Mathew v. T.M. Sutton Ltd* [1994] 1 W.L.R. 1455 (*infra*, §32–108; commented on by Palmer and Merkin, 1994 All E.R. Annual Review 26–28).

(ii) *Statutory Control of Pledges*

Realisation of pawn

32–108   [*Amend note 49: page* [172]]
Mathew v. T.M. Sutton Ltd is now reported in [1994] 1 W.L.R. 1455.

BILLS OF EXCHANGE AND BANKING

1. – NEGOTIABLE INSTRUMENTS

(b) *Bills of Exchange*

(i) *Definitions and Requirements*

Unconditional order in writing

33–010   A withdrawal form was held not to constitute a bill of exchange; see *Weir v. National Westminster Bank.*[a]

   [a] 1994 S.L.T. 1251.

Delivery

33–025   [*Note 41 at end: page* [191]]
As to the application of s.21(2) to a holder taking from a holder in due course, see *Insurance Corporation of Ireland v. Dunluce Meats* [1991] N.I. 286.

(ii) *Capacity and Authority of Parties*

Personal liability of company's director

33–031   [*Add to note 65 at end: page* [195]]
See also *Jenice Ltd v. Dan* [1994] B.C.C. 43, in which the error arose in consequence of the misspelling of the company's name in the forms contained in the cheque provided by the bank.

(iii) *The Consideration for a Bill*

Need to move from promisee

33–047   The view taken in cases decided in Australia and New Zealand is that past consideration furnished by a third party constitutes good consideration under section 27(1)(*a*) provided there is a close link between the issuing of the bill and the consideration provided in the underlying transaction: *Electrical Technologies Ltd v. Auckland Electrical Services Ltd.*[a]

^a [1995] 3 N.Z.L.R. 726 and case there cited including *Walsh, Spriggs, Nolan and Finney v. Hoag & Bosh Pty Ltd* (1976) 12 A.L.R. 411 (Aust.); *Bonior v. Asiery Ltd* [1968] N.Z.L.R. 254; *Finch Motors Ltd v. Quin* [1980] 2 N.Z.L.R. 513; *International Ore and Fertilizer Corp. v. East Coast Fertilizer Co. Ltd* [1987] 1 N.Z.L.R. 9.

Holder in due course

[*Add to note 30 at end: page* [209]]   **33–058**
See also *Insurance Corporation of Ireland v. Dunluce Meats* [1991] N.I. 286.

(iv) *Transfer of Bills*

Negotiation to party already liable

[*Add to note 99: page* [218]]   **33–075**
Applied in *Insurance Corporation of Ireland v. Dunluce Meats* [1991] N.I. 286.

Rights of holder: generally

[*Add to note 1*]   **33–076**
As regards the effect of fraud and illegality on the position of immediate parties, see also *Universal Import Export v. Bank of Scotland (O.H.)* 1994 S.C.L.R. 944.

(vii) *Discharge of Bill*

Tracing orders

[*Add to note 38: page* [241]]   **33–118**
See also *Style Financial Services Ltd v. Bank of Scotland* [1986] 5 Bank L.R. 15 (I.H.), considering also the effect, in the context of tracing, of payment into an overdrawn bank account.

(c) *Cheques*

(i) *General Provisions*

Place of presentment: cheque truncation

[*Insert new paragraph: page* [246]]
Under the traditional arrangement, as endorsed by the Clearing House **33–131A**
Rules, cheques have to be presented through the clearing house at the branch on which they are drawn. The ensuing cumbersome clearing cycle involved is to be abrogated under a system santioning cheques truncation, to

be introduced in the wake of the promulgation of the Deregulation (Bills of Exchange) Order 1996.[80a] According to section 74A of the BEA, inserted by this Order, a bank may by a notice published in the London, Edinburgh and Belfast Gazettes specify an address at which cheques drawn on it may be presented for payment. A cheque presented at such an address is, then, deemed to have been presented at the "proper address". In addition, section 74B of the BEA, likewise inserted by the 1996 Order, sanctions the presentation of a cheque by means of an electronic or similar message which sets out the "fundamental features" of the instrument.[80b] These features are defined to comprise the serial number of the cheque, the code which identifies the drawee bank (namely, that bank's "sort code"), the number of the account on which the cheque is drawn and its amounts. However, even where such truncation is sanctioned, section 74B(3) confers on the drawee bank the right to demand that the cheque be presented physically. Under subsection (4) such a demand does not constitute a dishonour of the cheque by non-payment.

[80a] S.I. 1996 No. 2993.

[80b] And see consequential amendment, made by article 4(1) of the Order, to s.54(2) of the BEA.

2. – ASPECTS OF BANKING LAW

(a) *The Relationship of Banker and Customer*

Who is a banker: common law definition

33–188   [*Add to note 10: page* [271]]
As regards the weight given to a bank's promotional materials, see also *James v. Barclays Bank plc* (1995) 4 Bank. L.R. 131.

Criteria for authorisation

33–193   [*Add to note 25: page* [275]]
See also the Accountants (Banking Act 1987) Regulations 1994 (S.I. 1994 No. 524 (made under s.47(5) of the Act)) which impose on auditors of banks the duty to report any matter in which a bank falls outside the criteria for authorisation set out in Sched. 3 of the Act.

The deposit protection fund

33–200   [*Delete from note 42 reference following* Depositors Protection Fund v. Dalia *and substitute: page* [278]]
[1994] 2 A.C. 367; as regards the onus borne by an appellant who contests

a decision of the Banking Appeal Tribunal, see *Shah v. Bank of England* [1994] 3 Bank. L.R. 205. And see, generally, the Credit Institutions (Protection of Depositors) Regulations 1995 (S.I. No. 1442).

As regards the validity of the Bank of England's prohibition of the debiting of Serbian accounts maintained with banks in the United Kingdom with amounts accrued in respect of certain exports, see *R. v. The Treasury and the Bank of England, ex p. Centro-Com SRL, The Independent*, June 3, 1994.

Board of Banking Supervision

As regards the depositor's right to sue the Bank of England for loss 33–201 resulting from its alleged failure to exercise due care in its supervision, see *Three Rivers District Council v. Bank of England.*[a]

[a] [1995] 3 W.L.R. 650.

The 2BCD Regulations

[*Add to note 47 after "S.I. 1992 No. 3218"*]   33–202
as amended by the Banking Coordination (Second Council Directive) (Amendment) Regulations 1993 (S.I. 1993 No. 3225); and the Banking Coordination (Second Council Directive) (Amendment) Regulations 1995 (S.I. 1995 No. 1217).

O'Brien's Case

For the authorities applying the *O'Brien* doctrine, see §6–016, *ante*.   33–213

Other remedies: compound interest

[*Add to end of note 88: page* [290]]   33–222
But see, as regards other types of agreement, *Mitsubishi Heavy Industries Ltd v. Gulf Bank KSC* [1996] 1 Lloyd's Rep. 499 at p. 507 (case involving a guarantee and counter indemnity).

Every day transactions

As regards a bank's duty to advise the borrower about problems 33–224 respecting the security furnished, see *Levett v. Barclays Bank*[a]; as regards situations in which the bank's advice is sought about the business transaction financed by it, see *Verity v. Lloyds Bank.*[b]

As to whether a bank may owe a duty of care, such as the duty to draw attention to forgeries, not only to the customer but also to a sole agent in charge of his account, see *Weir v. National Westminster Bank.*[c]

[a] [1995] 2 All E.R. 615, *ante*, §6–096.

^b *The Independent*, September 9, 1995.

^c 1994 S.L.T. 1251.

[*And add to end of second paragraph: page* [292]]
As regards liability owed to third parties, arising in the context of an ordinary banking transaction, see: *T.E. Potterton Ltd v. Northern Bank Ltd.*[96a]

[96a] [1993] 1 I.R. 413.

33–241 [*Insert new paragraph at end: page* [300]]
33–241A ***Royal Brunei Airlines* case.** The "knowledge" issue has been re-examined in the Privy Council's decision in *Royal Brunei Airlines v. Tan.*[a] The airline appointed a firm called BLT to act as its general travel agent for the sale of passenger and cargo transportation. It was agreed that all sums collected by BLT for transportation and ancillary services were to be held in trust for the airline until "satisfactorily accounted for to the [airline] and settlement made". It was further agreed that the amounts so received by BLT on behalf of the airline would be paid over within 30 days. In breach of this agreement, BLT paid the amounts due to the airline to the credit of its own current account with its bankers and failed to remit them to the airline within the appointed time. When BLT became insolvent, the airline instituted proceedings to recover the amounts due to it from BLT's managing director and major shareholder, one T, seeking to hold him liable as an "accessory".

Reversing the Brunei Court of Appeal's decision and restoring Roberts C.J.'s judgment in favour of the airline, Lord Nicholls of Birkenhead pointed out that the express trustee's liability to the beneficiary was, by its nature, strict. It arose whenever the trustee failed to observe the terms of the trust deed; whether his departure was fraudulent or innocent was immaterial. By contrast, the liability of an "accessory" arose only when he had acted dishonestly or improperly so that it was possible to regard him a party to the express trustee's breach. Lord Nicholls illustrated this principle by referring to a hypothetical case, in which a trustee instructs a solicitor to pay a certain amount out of the trust moneys to a particular person in the belief that the payment is authorised by the trust deed. The solicitor knows that the payment involves a breach of trust and, further, is aware of the trustee's mistaken belief. Nevertheless he leaves the trustee under his misapprehension and prepares the necessary documentation. Lord Nicholls concluded that "if the accessory principle is not to be artificially constructed, it ought to be applicable in such a case".

This illustration, and a review of earlier authorities, led Lord Nicholls to the conclusion that the accessory could be held liable only where he had been guilty of some want of probity or dishonesty. Except in most unusual cases, his liability could not be based on negligence alone. He was, further, not subject to some general test of unconscionable conduct, except to the extent that such a test was understood to apply a duty to act honestly.

Lord Nicholls then considered the exact meaning of "dishonesty" or "lack of probity". His Lordship stressed that, basically, "honesty is an objective standard. The individual is expected to attain the standard which would be observed by an honest person placed in those circumstances." Adopting the words of Knox J. in *Cowan de Groot Properties Ltd v. Eagle Trust Plc*,[b] Lord Nicholls concluded that a person was "dishonest" when he was "guilty of commercially unacceptable conduct in the particular context involved". One specific instance of dishonesty was where a person acted in reckless disregard of the rights of others as, for instance, where he took unreasonable risks or where he carried out a patently dubious instruction without seeking advice.

Lord Nicholls went on to express his doubts about the attempts to classify the accessory's knowledge into different categories. The meaningful question, in each case, was whether the accessory had acted dishonestly when he assisted in what had subsequently turned out to be a breach of trust. Speculations about the required degree of "knowledge" would not necessarily lead to the correct solution. Lord Nicholls further emphasised that, when deciding such issues, it was wrong to treat Lord Selborne's dictum in *Barnes v. Addy*[c] as if it were a statutory provision. Whether or not an accessory was liable depended, in each case, on the issue of honesty.

Applying the test in question to the case before the Board, Lord Nicholls held that T was liable as an accessory. T was the very person who took all the decisions on BLT's behalf and was, of course, familiar with the terms of the trust deed. In acting as he had done, he had not met the standard expected of a person in his position. The fact that BLT's breach was technical rather than one involving dishonesty did not exonerate T.

[a] [1995] 3 W.L.R. 64.

[b] [1992] 4 All E.R. 700.

[c] (1874) L.R. 9 Ch.App. 244.

Duty of secrecy

[*Add to note 23 at end: page* [301]]   **33–242**
A bank is likewise not in breach of its duty of confidentiality where it produces documents as ordered in a *subpoena duces tecum*: *Robertson v. Canadian Imperial Bank of Commerce* [1994] 1 W.L.R. 824, P.C.

(b) *The Current Account*

(i) *Rights and Duties of the Banker*

Combining accounts

33–248   [*Add to text at end of final paragraph: page* [306]]
As regards the bank's right to set off an amount due to it under a loan
extended to a customer as against a claim due from the bank to a third party
in respect of a sum deposited to secure the loan involved, see *Re Bank of
Credit and Commerce International SA (No. 8).*[58a] The position differs where
the depositor has executed a guarantee in the Bank's favour in respect of an
amount due from a third party: *MS Fashions Ltd v. Bank of Credit and
Commerce International SA (in Liq.).*[58b]

[58a] [1994] 3 W.L.R. 911, and see, in the same spirit, *Tam Wing Chuen v. Bank of
Credit and Commerce Hong Kong Ltd (in liq.)* [1996] 2 B.C.L.C. 69, P.C.

[58b] [1993] Ch. 425.

Effect of agreement

33–249   [*Add to note 60*]
And see *Coca-Cola Financial Corporation v. Finsat International Ltd*
[1996] 3 W.L.R. 849, C.A. For a case involving a bank's refusal without
notice to sanction further advances under a facility agreement, see: *Socomex
Ltd v. Banque Bruxelles Lambert SA* [1996] 1 Lloyd's Rep. 156 (Mance J).

Customer's remedies for dishonour

33–250   [*Add to text at end of final paragraph: page* [307]]
As regards liability incurred by the drawee bank to third parties in
consequence of answers written on a dishonoured cheque, see: *T.E.
Potterton Ltd v. Northern Bank Ltd.*[69a]

[69a] [1993] 1 I.R. 413.

Damages for breach of contract

33–251   [*Add to note 70: page* [308]]
Kpoharor v. Woolwich Building Society, The Times, December 8, 1995,
C.A.

[*Add to note 71*]
Recently, though, the Court of Appeal has indicated that damage to
creditworthiness may be presumed even where the drawer of the wrongfully
dishonoured cheque is not a trader: *Kpoharor v. Woolwich Building Society,
supra.*

(ii) *Termination of Duty to Pay*

Garnishee orders

[*Add to note 28 at end: page* [311]]   33–258
As regards the issuing of a garnishee order against the United Kingdom
branch of a bank in respect of a debt situated overseas, see: *Zoenheath
Associates v. China Tianjin International Economic and Technical Cooperative Corp.*, *The Times*, April 8, 1994. As regards the garnishing of sums paid
by the European Commission to a foreign State, see: *Philipp Bros v.
Republic of Sierra Leone*, *The Times*, November 28, 1994, C.A.

(iii) *Protection of Paying Banker in Cases of Unauthorised Payment*

Irregularity in or absence of indorsement

[*Add to note 36: page* [320]]   33–275
As regards such a cheque's effect as a receipt, see the Cheques Act 1957,
s.3 as amended by art. 5 of the Deregulation (Bills of Exchange) Order 1996
(S.I. 1996 No. 2993).

(c) *Discount and Collection*

Causes of action

[*Add to note 68: page* [326]]   33–286
As regards the recovery of money paid under voidable swap currency
agreements, see *Westdeutsche Landesbank Girozentrale v. Islington L.B.C.*
[1996] 2 W.L.R. 802 (H.L.) (concerning mainly the issue of interest
claimable) and *Kleinwort Benson Ltd v. Birmingham City Council* [1996] 4
All E.R. 733 (question of recovery of a loss passed by the plaintiff to a third
party).

Protection in cases of forgery

[*Add to note 98: page* [332]]   33–295
For special problems arising in Canada under s.48(4) of the Canadian Bills
of Exchange Act (RSC 1985, c B–4), see *Enoch Band of Stony Plain Indian
Reserve No. 135 v. Morin* [1966] 5 Bank L.R. 396.

(d) *The Bank Giro*

In direct debits

[*Add to text at end of paragraph: page* [338]]   33–307
The legal nature of such a transaction was considered by the Court of

Appeal in *Esso Petroleum Co. Ltd v. Milton*.[20a] The majority of the Court held that in modern commercial practice a giro payment by way of direct debiting was to be treated as payment by cheque and, as such, as the equivalent of cash. In general, therefore, payment by direct debiting for goods or services received should preclude a defence of set-off.

[20a] [1997] 2 All E.R. 597 applying *Nova (Jersey) Knit Ltd v. Kammgarn Spinnerei GmbH* [1977] 1 W.L.R. 713.

Giro not an assignment

33–316   [*Add to text after note 37: page* [344]]
That a direct debit does not constitute an assignment to the payee of funds standing to the credit of the payor's account with the remitting bank is supported by Lord Penrose's decision in the Court of Session (O.H) in *Mercedes-Benz Finance Ltd v. Clydesdale Bank plc*.[37a]

[37a] *The Times*, September 16, 1996.

(e) *The Deposit Account*

Its nature

33–318   The bank's right to fix its interest rate remains intact even if the bank is being wound up: *Bank of Credit and Commerce International v. Malik*.[a]

[a] *The Independent*, March 13, 1995.

(f) *Giving Information on Financial Investments*

Advising on investments

33–322   As regards the weight given to a bank's promotional materials, see also *James v. Barclays Bank plc*.[a]

[a] (1995) 4 Bank. L.R. 131.

Banking references

33–323   [*Add to text after note 54: page* [347]]
A bank that provides a reference by telephone on a given customer does not warrant to the enquirer that the person who made reference to the bank is the real customer rather than an impostor. The bank, in other words, does not assume a duty of care to the enquirer as to the true identity of the customer.[54a]

[54a] *Gold Coin Joilliers SA v. United Bank of Kuwait, The Times*, November 4, 1996.

(h) *Bankers' Commercial Credits*

[*Amend note 64: page* [349]]
Jack R., *Documentary Creditors* (2nd ed., 1993).

(ii) *Types of Documentary Credits*

Standby credits

[*Add to note 6: page* [360]]   **33–350**
For the use of such letters of credit instead of cash deposits, see *Ludgate Insurance Co. Ltd v. Citibank* [1996] 2 Lloyd's Rep. 247.

(v) *The Relationship of Banker and Seller*

Ambit of rule

[*Add to note 89 at end: page* [376]]   **33–373**
And note that mere suspicions of a fraud do not justify the rejection of a regular set of documents: *Society of Lloyds v. Canadian Imperial Bank of Commerce* [1993] 2 Lloyd's Rep. 579.

Tender by third party

[*Add to text at end of paragraph: page* [377]]   **33–374**
This principle applies even if the injunction is sought only as against the beneficiary. In *Deutsche Rückversicherung AG v. Walbrook Insurance Co. Ltd*[95a] Phillips J. held that an injunction restraining the beneficiary from making a call under the credit would be granted only to extent that it was also to be available as an order precluding the bank from making payment. But *cf.*, in respect of a performance guarantee, *Themehelp Ltd v. West*[95b] (in which, however, there was evidence of fraud).

[95a] [1994] 4 All E.R. 181.

[95b] (1994) 3 Bank. L.R. 215, C.A.

(vi) *The Relationship of Issuing and Correspondent Bankers*

[*Insert text as new paragraph at end*]   **33–384**
Need to make enquiries about instructions where fraud might reasonably be suspected. In *Standard Bank London Ltd v. Bank of Tokyo Ltd*,[24a] one X asked the S Bank in London to finance certain transactions on the security of standby credits to be issued by the Kuala Lumpur office of BOT, a Japanese bank. Over a period of some eighteen months, X delivered to the S Bank three letters of credit which, on their face, appeared to have been issued by BOT. In reality, all three were skillfully perpetrated forgeries. Any

suspicions which the S Bank may have had were, however, allayed when it received in respect of each letter of credit a tested telex in which BOT confirmed the authenticity of the facility. But these tested telexes were also issued by the fraudsters, who got access to BOT's terminal and code. When called upon to pay, BOT denied liability. Its main argument was that the circumstances of each transaction were such as to put the S Bank on enquiry. In failing to investigate, the S Bank had committed a breach of a duty of care owed to BOT and, in consequence, was not entitled to enforce the letters of credit.

Waller J. gave judgment for the S Bank. Having cited the evidence of an expert witness, who described a "tested telex" as "the electronic signature of the bank sending the message", his Lordship emphasised that it was unchallenged that banks all over the world relied with complete confidence on tested telexes. "The tested telex system," he added, "is meant to avoid arguments in relation to authority". Rejecting an argument to the effect that, in the instant case, the S Bank was put on enquiry, his Lordship said that "the duty to inquire will depend on the circumstances of each and every case, and what should, or may, put someone on enquiry, will also depend on the circumstances of any individual case. Thus, the more usual the circumstances and the clearer a representation appears to be, the less the duty to inquire should be, and the less likely there will be circumstances which will put anyone on enquiry."

[24a] [1995] 2 Lloyd's Rep. 169.

(vii) *The Tender of Documents*

Construction of terms of credit

33–386   [Add to text at end of paragraph: page [383]]
It has, further, been held that courts will imply terms into a banker's irrevocable undertaking only in rare and exceptional circumstances. Although the case in point—*Cauxell Ltd v. Lloyds Bank*[32a]—concerned the construction of a performance guarantee, the principle ought to be equally applicable to the construction of documentary credits.

[32a] *The Times*, December 26, 1995.

Regularity of documents

33–388   As regards the meaning of "original" and the need to sign or initial a document produced by a computerised process, see: *Glencore International AG v. Bank of China.*[a]

[a] [1996] 1 Lloyd's Rep. 135, C.A.

Compliance with time

[Add new reference at end of paragraph: page [384]]   **33–389**

NOTE 40a. For the construction of art. 44 of the UCP, see *Bayerische Vereinsbank AG v. National Bank of Pakistan* [1997] 1 Lloyd's Rep. 59 (Mance J.).

The bill of lading

As regards the title conferred by the possession of the bill of lading on the   **33–393**
consignee where there was no intention that title should pass to him, see
"*The Future Express*".[a]

[a] [1994] 2 Lloyd's Rep. 542, C.A.

CHAPTER 34

CARRIAGE BY AIR

1. – INTRODUCTION

Amendments to the Warsaw Convention which are not yet in force

34–002   The Legal Committee of the ICAO has prepared a new draft Convention for consideration by a Diplomatic Conference, perhaps in 1998, which attempts to modernise the Warsaw system. It incorporates the Hague Protocol, Montreal Additional Protocols Nos. 3 and 4, the Guatemala City Protocol and the Guadalajara Convention. Many of the more important provisions, including those dealing with liability to passengers, were presented in the form of options, no consensus being reached within the Committee.

Scope of the Convention

34–005   The Convention applies to "carriage", and issues may present themselves as to whether the contract is one of carriage or for the provision of some other type of service. It has sometimes been argued that the notion of carriage implies that a flight is undertaken for the primary purpose of moving an individual or goods from Point A to Point B. This argument was not accepted by the Court of Session in *Herd v. Clyde Helicopters Ltd.*[a] The Strathclyde Police Force entered into a contract under which the defenders were to supply a "fully comprehensive air support service" including the carriage of personnel and equipment as required by the Chief Constable. The majority (the Lord Justice Clerk and Lord Morison) held that, even if the contract had wider purposes, it contained a contract of carriage. The same view prevailed in the House of Lords where it was held that in the absence of any relationship between the carrier and the person carried other than that of carrier and carried (for example, a relationship of employer and employee, or of instructor and student) the person carried was a passenger for the purposes of the Convention.[b]

[a] 1996 S.L.T. 976, I.H.

[b] *Herd v. Clyde Helicopters Ltd* [1997] 1 All E.R. 775, H.L.

[*Note 28: page* [396]]
Air Navigation Order 1989 is revoked. See now Air Navigation (No. 2) Order 1995 (S.I. 1995 No. 1970), art. 118(1). In *Herd v. Clyde Helicopters Ltd* (at first instance, Outer House, March 24, 1994, unreported), it was accepted that the requirement of "reward" did not necessitate any identifiable fare being paid in the case of each individual passenger; it was sufficient if, as in that case, the carrier was paid a lump sum covering a number of flights. The point was not taken on appeal.

Interpretation of the Convention

While giving due weight to the need for uniformity of interpretation, an **34–006** English court should "approach the Convention in an objective spirit in order to try to discover what its true intent is".[a] The terms of the carrier's conditions of contract or of carriage or of the documents of carriage (the passenger ticket or air waybill) cannot be relevant where the issue is one of interpretation of the Carriage by Air Act 1961 and the Warsaw Convention to which it gives effect: *Antwerp United Diamond B.V.B.A. v. Air Europe.*[b]

[a] *Swiss Bank Corp. v. Brink's-MAT Ltd* [1986] 2 All E.R. 188, 189; *Antwerp United Diamonds B.V.B.A. v. Air Europe* [1995] 3 All E.R. 424, C.A.

[b] *ibid.*

[*Note 36: page* [398]]
For the weight to be given to decisions of foreign courts, see Lord Hope of Craighead in *Abnett v. British Airways plc* [1997] 2 W.L.R. 26.

2. – International Carriage

(a) *General*

Definition

Although much discussion in the cases refers to places of departure and **34–007** destination and that is a part of the Convention's definition of "international carriage", the notion of "carriage" itself extends to circumstances in which the routes to be followed are undefined at the outset.[a]

[a] *Herd v. Clyde Helicopters Ltd* [1997] 1 All E.R. 775, H.L., *per* Lord Hope at 790–92.

No contracting out

34–008   In *Abnett v. British Airways plc*[a] the House of Lords regarded the matter as governed not by an exact analysis of the particular words used but by a consideration of the whole purpose of Article 17. In its context the purpose seemed to be to prescribe the circumstances—the only circumstances— in which a carrier would be liable in damages to the passenger for claims arising out of his international carriage by air. The Convention did not purport to deal with all matters relating to contracts of international carriage by air, but in those areas with which it dealt—and the liability of the carrier was one of them— the code was intended to be uniform and to be exclusive also of any resort to the rules of domestic law.[b] The same view was adopted in a later House of Lords decision, one involving domestic carriage.[c] A different conclusion was reached in cases decided at much the same time by the United States Court of Appeals for the Second Circuit[d] and (on the same facts as in *Abnett*) by the cour d'appel of Paris.[e]

It was held in *Abnett v. British Airways plc*[f] that the purpose of Article 23 was to protect the passenger or other person dealing with the carrier against provisions of the kind which it describes. When the Warsaw Convention was being negotiated, carriers engaged in international carriage by air were otherwise free to contract on whatever terms they cared to select, controlled only by the demands of the marketplace in which they were operating.

[a] [1997] 1 All E.R. 193, H.L.

[b] [1997] 1 All E.R. 193. The House heard together appeals raising the same issue from decisions of the Court of Appeal and the Court of Session.

[c] *Herd v. Clyde Helicopters Ltd* [1997] 1 All E.R. 775.

[d] *Tseng v. El Al Israel Airlines Ltd* (2nd Cir., 1997).

[e] *Sté British Airways v. Mohamed* (November 12, 1996).

[f] [1997] 1 All E.R. 193, H.L.

Jurisdiction

34–009   Article 28 gives the plaintiff the choice of forum. It is not open to the defendant to raise the plea of forum non conveniens: *Milor S.R.L. v. British Airways p.l.c.*[a]

In December 1995, the European Commission proposed a new Regulation on air carrier liability to passengers in case of air accidents.[b] Under its terms, persons entitled to compensation in the case of air accidents which take place within the Community could bring action for liability, in addition to the courts specified in Article 28 of the Convention, in the courts of the Member State where the passenger has its domicile or permanent residence.

It is very doubtful whether the exercise of jurisdiction under such a Regulation would be recognised in non-Member States party to the Convention.

[a] [1996] 3 All E.R. 537, C.A.

[b] See *post*, §34–018 for later developments, in which this proposal was not pressed.

[*Note 54: page* [401]]
See the Scottish decision to this effect: *Abnett v. British Airways p.l.c.* [1994] 1 A.S.L.R. 1 (Outer House).

[*Add to note 55*]
Milor S.R.L. v. British Airways p.l.c. [1996] 3 All E.R. 537, C.A.

Limitation of actions

[*Add to note 64: page* [402]]   **34–010**
Mediterranean Freight Services Ltd v. B.P. Oil International Ltd, The Fiona [1994] 2 Lloyd's Rep. 506, C.A. (*obiter*).

(b) *Passengers*

Who is a passenger

See entry to §34–005, above.   **34–011**

Liability for death and bodily injury

The meaning of "damage" in this context was examined by the United **34–015** States Supreme Court in *Zicherman v. Korean Air Lines Ltd.*[a] The Court held that it meant "legally cognizable harm", but that Article 17 leaves it to adjudicating courts to specify what harm is cognizable.

[a] 116 S.Ct. 629 (1996).

[*Add to note 88: page* [405]]
Galvin v. Aer Rianta (unreported, October 13, 1993, Irish High Ct).

The scope of Article 17

See *Chaudhari v. British Airways plc*,[a] where a passenger who suffered from paralysis on the left side of his body could not claim that a fall on board the aircraft occurring as he tried to stand was an "accident" for convention purposes.

^a *The Times*, May 7, 1997, C.A.

34–016   [*Note 95: page* [406]]
The position stated in the text was accepted by counsel for both parties in *Sidhu v. British Airways Plc* [1995] P.I.Q.R. P427, C.A. See, to the contrary, *Georgopoulos v. American Airlines Inc.* [1994] 1 A.S.L.R. 38 (N.S.W. Sup. Ct).

Upper financial limit of liability

34–018   The limit of liability is now £15,855.58: Carriage by Air (Sterling Equivalents) Order 1996 (S.I. 1996 No. 244).
The whole issue of liability limits has been addressed by the European Civil Aviation Conference, the Commission of the European Union, and the International Air Transport Association; major changes in aviation practice are likely to follow, but the position (as at April 1996) remains very confused.
The discussions within the European Civil Aviation Conference led to the acceptance by the triennial meeting of the Conference in June 1994 of the idea of a new agreement between air carriers, operating to, from, and within Europe adopting a limit of 250,000 SDRs and providing for the prompt payment of a fraction of this sum within days of the event causing loss and of the whole, so far as liability was uncontested, within three months.
The European Commission, however, decided that formal action by the European institutions was necessary. In April 1997, the Council published[a] a common position on a proposed Council Regulation. Article 3(1)(a) of the draft Regulation provides that the liability of a Community air carrier for damages sustained in the event of death, wounding or any other bodily injury by a passenger in the event of an accident must not be subject to any financial limit, be it defined by law, convention or contract. For any damages up to the sum of the equivalent in ecus of 100,000 S.D.R.s the Community air carrier must not exclude or limit his liability by proving that he and his agents have taken all necessary measures to avoid the damage or that it was impossible for him or them to take such measures (*i.e.* the defence under Article 20 of the Warsaw Convention).[b] However the defence of contributory negligence would remain available.[c] A Community air carrier would be required under Article 5 of the draft Regulation, without delay and in any event not later than 15 days after the identity of the natural person entitled to compensation has been established, to make such advance payments (which would not constitute recognition of liability) as may be required to meet

immediate economic needs on a basis proportional to the hardship suffered. Such an advance payment would be not less than the equivalent in ecus of 15,000 S.D.R.s per passenger in the event of death.

Meanwhile, work proceeding under the auspices of I.A.T.A. culminated in a major Airline Liability Conference held in Washington D.C. in June 1995. The Conference recommended a general liability limit of 250,000 SDRs with local provision for interim payments and "where circumstances so required" a waiver up to 250,000 SDRs of the defences under Article 20(1) of the Warsaw Convention texts. However the eventual outcome was an Intercarrier Agreement on Passenger Liability which was adopted at the I.A.T.A. Annual General Meeting in October 1995, which departed from the conclusions of the Conference. It was supplemented (and in effect amended) by an Intercarrier Implementation Agreement reached in Miami in February 1996. Signatory carriers agreed to include in their conditions of carriage and tariffs, so far as government requirements permitted by November 1, 1996:

(a) a waiver of the limitation of liability on recoverable compensatory damages in Article 22(1) of the Warsaw Convention as to claims for death, wounding or other bodily injury of a passenger within the meaning of Article 17 of the Convention; and
(b) a waiver of the defence under Article 20(1) of the Convention with respect to that portion of a claim which does not exceed 100,000 SDRs (though a more limited waiver could be applied to particular routes);

but, subject to the above, to reserve all available defences pursuant to the provisions of the Convention and their rights of recourse against any other person, including rights of contribution or indemnity, with respect to any sums paid by a carrier.

It was also agreed that carriers might, at their option, provide that recoverable compensatory damages may be determined by reference to the law of the domicile or permanent residence of the passenger; and to disapply any waiver as against a public social security or similar body.

The consistency of this Agreement with the terms of the Convention is by no means clear.

In November 1996, the U.S. Department of Transportation, which has a decisive influence in aviation practice, issued an order[d] approving the I.A.T.A. Agreements, subject to four conditions: (1) that the application, optional in the I.A.T.A. text, of the law of the domicile provision would be required for operations to, from, or with a connection or stopping place in the United States; (2) that the optional provision for less than 100,000 S.D.R.s strict liability on particular routes could not apply for any operations to, from, or with a connection or stopping place in the United States; (3) that the inapplicability for social agencies of that Agreement's waivers of the limit and Article 20(1) carrier defence of proof of non-negligence should have no application to U.S. agencies; and (4) that the provisions of an

[309]

agreement between U.S. carriers for withdrawal from the 1996 Montreal Interim Agreement would not take effect. However in January 1997, the Department modified its Order in the face of strong criticism from the airlines.[e] The modifications removed, but only *pendente lite*, conditions (1) and (4).

[a] [1997] O.J. C123/89.

[b] Art. 3(1)(b); see para. 34–017.

[c] Art. 3(2).

[d] Order 96–11–06.

[e] Order 97–1–2.

Loss of the carrier's protection: Article 25

34–019   The criteria in Article 25 have been described as "very strict": *Antwerp United Diamond B.V.B.A. v. Air Europe.*[a]

[a] [1995] 3 All E.R. 424, C.A.

Delay

34–024   In *Abnett v. British Airways p.l.c.*,[a] a claim based on delay within article 19 by a passenger detained in Kuwait by the invading Iraqi troops was dismissed, as there was nothing in the facts which could properly be regarded as "delay".

[a] [1994] 1 A.S.L.R. 1 (Outer House).

(c) *Baggage*

Upper limit of liability

34–035   The limit liability is now £15.89 per kilogramme: Carriage by Air (Sterling Equivalents) Order 1996 (S.I. 1996 No. 244).

[*Add to note 86, page* [1419]]
The limit of liability for hand baggage is now £317.71 per passenger: Carriage by Air (Sterling Equivalents) Order 1996 (S.I. 1996 No. 244).

(d) *Cargo*

Acceptability of goods for carriage

34–041   [*Note 15: page* [421]]
The statutory instruments cited are revoked. See now Air Navigation (Dangerous Goods) Regulations 1994 (S.I. 1994 No. 3187) as amended by S.I. 1996 No. 3100.

Upper financial limit of liability

The limit of liability is now £15.89 per kilogramme: Carriage by Air **34–043**
(Sterling Equivalents) Order 1996 (S.I. 1996 No. 244).
See *Antwerp United Diamonds B.V.B.A. v. Air Europe.*[a]

[a] [1995] 3 All E.R. 424, C.A.

Who can sue the carrier

[*Note 77: page* [428]] **34–052**
See dicta of Lord Hope of Craighead in *Abnett v. British Airways plc*
[1997] 1 All E.R. 193, H.L. casting some doubt as to the authority of
Gatewhite Ltd v. Iberia Lineas Aereas de Espana S.A. Lord Hope thought it
more consistent with the purpose of the Convention to regard it as providing
a uniform rule about who can sue for goods which are lost or damaged
during carriage by air, with the result that the owner who is not a party to the
contract has no right to sue in his own name; but the point was not fully
argued.

Airworthiness

[*Note 91: page* [429]] **34–055**
Air Navigation Order 1989 and Air Navigation (General) Regulations
1981 are revoked. See now Air Navigation (No. 2) Order 1995 (S.I. 1995 No.
1970) and Air Navigation (General) Regulations 1993 (S.I. 1993 No. 1622 (as
amended by S.I. 1995 No. 1093).

CHAPTER 35

CARRIAGE BY LAND

1. – INTRODUCTION

35–004   *[Insert text as new paragraphs at end: page* [435]*]*

35–004A   **The identification of a carrier.** The common law has recognised a variety of carriers—those who accept custody of or responsibility for persons or goods for the purpose of transporting them to a destination agreed between the carrier and the customer. The classification of a carrier depends on how his business of carriage is conducted. There are common carriers, private carriers and other "special" carriers. The status of the last category is dependent on Parliament's intervention (by virtue of domestic legislation or the incorporation of international conventions) or unusual exceptions etched by the common law. Whilst these distinctions potentially have relevance in the realm of international carriage, more often they arise for consideration in connection with the internal carriage of goods and persons, and even then the distinctions have less importance than of old. For this reason, the categorisation of carriers will be discussed as part of the section on internal carriage. It should not, however, be forgotten that the distinction unexpectedly may be resuscitated when an international carriage falls under the judicial microscope.

Before the law relating to carriers and carriage by land is considered in depth below, a moment's thought should be dedicated to the issue whether in a given case a person should be described as a "carrier" at all. **35–004B**

A "carrier" is a person who transports goods or passengers or both from any place to any place in the manner agreed with the passenger or the owner of the goods to be carried. The carrier need not be paid in any sense for this service. The test is whether the person said to be the carrier is in fact accepting the responsibility of the carriage.[12a] Although a person's business involves, whether necessarily or by choice, the conveyance of goods, that does not necessarily mean that that person is a carrier. If a person undertakes to carry a passenger or goods only for reasons associated with his own personal or commercial expedience, then technically that person is not a carrier. The carriage is not the *raison d'être* of that person. If the carriage is wholly incidental to that person's business, then he will not be a carrier. For example, a warehouseman,[12b] a stevedore[12c] and a wharfinger[12d] have all been held not to be carriers. The "carrier's" business should be examined to determine the purpose of the carriage.[12e] Such questions generally are more difficult to answer in the case of goods, as opposed to passengers. In the case of passengers, whether a person is acting as an agent or a carrier generally is clear. **35–004C**

Carrier or freight forwarder. A forwarding agent, or freight forwarder, is a person who contracts with the owner of goods to arrange for the transportation of those goods, rather than to carry the goods himself.[12f] A freight forwarder, therefore, usually is not classified as a carrier,[12g] so long as he remains true to his calling. Unlike the warehouseman, the stevedore, and the wharfinger, the freight forwarder often never acquires possession (that is, custody) of the goods to be carried.[12h] As the functions of a carrier and a freight forwarder are necessarily linked, uncertainty may arise as to whether a person describing himself as a freight forwarder is in fact a carrier.[12i] A freight forwarder, or any goods-handler, may also contract or act as a carrier as an adjunct to their principal business.[12j] It is a question of fact in every case whether a person is a carrier.[12k] **35–004D**

[12a] *Aqualon (U.K.) Ltd v. Vallana Shipping Corporation* [1994] 1 Lloyd's Rep. 669, 676. Cf. *M Bardiger Ltd v. Halberg Spedition APS*, unreported, October 26, 1990.

[12b] *Consolidated Tea and Lands Co v. Oliver's Wharf* [1910] 2 K.B. 395; *contra Maving v. Todd* (1815) 1 Stark 72; *Armour & Co. Ltd v. Tarbard Ltd* (1920) 37 T.L.R. 208.

[12c] *Scruttons Ltd v. Midland Silicones Ltd* [1962] A.C. 446.

[12d] *Chattock & Co. v. Bellamy & Co.* (1895) 64 L.J.Q.B. 250.

[12e] *Lacey's Footwear (Wholesale) Ltd v. Bowler International Freight Ltd,*

unreported, March 17, 1995 (aff'd on other grounds: *The Times*, May 12, 1997), where the Court examined the circumstances of the making of the contract of carriage.

[12f] As to the distinction between a forwarder (that is, a person who contracts with the carrier as a principal, so that the owner of the goods is not a party to the contract) and a forwarding agent (who contracts on behalf of the owner of the goods with the carrier), see *M Bardiger Ltd v. Halberg Spedition APS*, unreported, October 26, 1990; *Aqualon (U.K.) Ltd v. Vallana Shipping Corporation* [1994] 1 Lloyd's Rep. 669, 673.

[12g] *Moto Vespa SA v. MAT (Britannia Express) Ltd* [1979] 1 Lloyd's Rep. 175, 179; *Elektronska Industrija Oour TVA v. Transped Oour Kintinentalna Spedicna* [1986] 1 Lloyd's Rep. 49, 52; *cf. Swiss Bank Corporation v. Brink's-MAT Ltd* [1986] 2 Lloyd's Rep. 79.

[12h] In *Kala Limited v. International Freight Services (U.K.) Ltd*, unreported, June 7, 1988, the freight forwarder was held to have exercised legitimately a contractual lien and right of detention over goods, the right to the control of which the owners had given to the freight forwarder. The Court distinguished the freight forwarder's right to possession of the goods from mere custody, which was held by the actual carrier.

[12i] The fact that a freight forwarder describes himself as such is not a decisive answer to the question, although assistance is gained from any written contract: *Lacey's Footwear (Wholesale) Ltd v. Bowler International Freight Ltd*, unreported, March 17, 1995 (aff'd on other grounds: *The Times*, May 12, 1997); see also *Kala Limited v. International Freight Services (U.K.) Ltd*, unreported, June 7, 1988; *M Bardiger Ltd v. Halberg Spedition APS*, unreported, October 26, 1990; and *Aqualon (UK) Ltd v. Vallana Shipping Corporation* [1994] 1 Lloyd's Rep. 669, 676. *Cf. Texas Instruments Ltd v. Nason (Europe) Ltd* [1991] 1 Lloyd's Rep. 146.

[12j] *Hellaby v. Weaver* (1851) 17 L.T.OS 271; *Langley Beldon & Gaunt Ltd v. Morley* [1965] 1 Lloyd's Rep. 297, 306; *Lee Cooper Ltd v. C H Jeakins & Sons Ltd* [1967] 2 Q.B. 1; *Elektronska Industrija Oour TVA v. Transped Oour Kintinentalna Spedicna* [1986] 1 Lloyd's Rep. 49, 52; *M Bardiger Ltd v. Halberg Spedition Aps*, unreported, October 26, 1990.

[12k] Taking into account matters such as how the carrier or forwarder describes himself, how he charges, how he arranges the carriage, and what documents he issues: *M Bardiger Ltd v. Halberg Spedition Aps*, unreported, October 26, 1990.

2. – INTERNAL CARRIAGE

(a) *Goods*

(i) *Common and Private Carriers*

The common carrier

35–005   [*Delete first paragraph of text with footnotes 13–16 and substitute: page* [435]]

At common law, the rights and obligations of a carrier are defined by contract and the status of the carrier. As regards status, the classification of the carrier as a common or private carrier[13] will identify certain of the carrier's duties and liabilities. A common carrier is a person who publicly professes, orally or by conduct, to undertake for reward[14] to all such persons, indiscriminately,[15] who desire to employ him, the transportation of goods provided that he has room.[16] It is a question of fact in each case whether a person is a common carrier.[16a]

NOTE 13: It has been mooted that there is another class of carrier, namely a carrier, whilst not a common carrier, who has assumed the responsibilities of a common carrier, by virtue of their public employment. Such was the decision concerning lightermen in *Liver Alkali Co. v. Johnson* (1872) L.R. 7 Exch. 267, (1874) L.R. 9 Exch. 338. However, this view has been rejected, at least so far as carriage by road is concerned: *Nugent v. Smith* (1876) 1 C.P.D. 423, 433; *Watkins v. Cottell* [1916] 1 K.B. 10; *Belfast Ropework Co. Ltd v. Bushell* [1918] 1 K.B. 210; *cf. Aslan v. Imperial Airways Ltd* (1933) 149 L.T. 276, 278.

NOTE 14: That is, at a reasonable price: *Belfast Ropework Co. Ltd v. Bushell* [1918] 1 K.B. 210. If the carrier gives an estimate and seeks to negotiate the price with his customer, thus reserving a discretion to himself to refuse to carry the goods, he is not a common carrier: *Electric Supply Stores v. Gaywood* (1909) 100 L.T. 855. A gratuitous carrier is not a common carrier: *Tyly v. Morrice* (1699) Carth. 485.

NOTE 15: Discrimination against a person on the grounds of race or sex is prohibited in any event: Race Relations Act, 1976 and Sex Discrimination Act, 1975.

NOTE 16: *Bennett v. Peninsular & Oriental Steam-Boat Co.* (1848) 6 C.B. 775, 787; *Watkins v. Cottell* [1916] 1 K.B. 10, 14; *Belfast Ropework Co. Ltd v. Bushell* [1918] 1 K.B. 210, 212; *G N Ry v. LEP Transport* [1922] 2 K.B. 742, 765.

[16a] *Tamvaco v. Timothy* (1882) 1 Cab. & El. 1; *Belfast Ropework Co. Ltd v. Bushell* [1918] 1 K.B. 210, 212; *Eastman Chemical International AG v. NMT Trading Ltd* [1972] 2 Lloyd's Rep. 25; *A Siohn & Co. Ltd v. R H Hagland & Son (Transport) Ltd* [1976] 2 Lloyd's Rep. 428.

[*Delete last sentence of second paragraph with note 22 and substitute*]
The common carrier may hold this status for a particular type of goods only. The common carrier may voluntarily abdicate this status by giving notice that he will not accept custom from the public. Alternatively, the common carrier may shed this status as regards particular types of goods only.[22] A carrier therefore may choose to be a common carrier for such times, places, and goods as he considers it appropriate, provided that he offers carriage in accordance with the calling of the common carrier and is thereby prepared to accept the burden of that calling.

NOTE 22: *Johnson v. Midland Railway Co.* (1849) 4 Exch. 367; *Sutcliffe v. Great Western Railway Co.* [1910] 1 K.B. 478.

The identification of a common carrier

[*Add to text after note 27*]   35–006
A carrier will not be a common carrier if he reserves to himself the right of refusal of the goods which a customer asks him to carry.[27a] The question is always one of fact to be determined objectively, not dependent entirely upon

the subjective intention of the carrier,[27b] nor his appearance to a particular customer. In answering this question, regard may be had to the carrier's stated or published conditions of carriage[27c] and advertisements,[27d] policies adopted by the carrier to his customers, the nature of the goods carried and the routes taken by the carrier. All aspects of the carrier's business may be considered in identifying the carrier's status.[27e] The test whether a person is a common carrier generally will not turn upon whether passengers or goods are carried.[27f]

[27a] *Ingate v. Christie* (1850) 3 Car. & Kir. 61; *Belfast Ropework Co. Ltd v. Bushell* [1918] 1 K.B. 210, 215; *A Siohn & Co. Ltd v. R H Hagland & Son (Transport) Ltd* [1976] 2 Lloyd's Rep. 428, 429–430, although in the last case, the Court held that the carrier's decision not to carry goods for a particular customer who was unsatisfactory did not affect that carrier's status as a common carrier.

[27b] *A Siohn & Co. Ltd v. R H Hagland & Son (Transport) Ltd* [1976] 2 Lloyd's Rep. 428.

[27c] *Cf. Lacey's Footwear (Wholesale) Ltd v. Bowler International Freight Ltd*, unreported, March 17, 1995 (aff'd: *The Times*, May 12, 1997).

[27d] *A Siohn & Co. Ltd v. R H Hagland & Son (Transport) Ltd* [1976] 2 Lloyd's Rep. 428, 430.

[27e] *Upston v. Stark* (1827) 2 C. & P. 598; *Chattock & Co. v. Bellamy & Co* (1895) 64 L.J.Q.B. 250.

[27f] *Clarke v. West Ham Corporation* [1909] 2 K.B. 858, 879; *A Siohn & Co. Ltd v. R H Hagland & Son (Transport) Ltd* [1976] 2 Lloyd's Rep. 428.

35–007 [*Delete first two sentences of paragraph with footnotes 30–31 and substitute*]

Before 1963 the railway companies, and their successor the British Transport Commission, were undoubtedly common carriers of most kinds of goods.[30] But now by statute neither the British Railways Board nor the newly franchised and privatised railway undertakings are common carriers by rail.[31] Similarly, London Regional Transport[31a] and the operators of the Channel Tunnel[31b] have been declared by Parliament not to be common carriers. Given the diversification in the railways industry,[31c] it is perhaps not surprising that the common carrier by rail is now extinct.

NOTE 30: *G. N. Ry. v. L. E. P. Transport Co.*, *supra*, at p. 769.

NOTE 31: Transport Act 1962, s.43(6); Railways Act 1993, s.123.

[31a] London Regional Transport Act 1984, Schedule 2, para. 7; s.2(6).

[31b] Channel Tunnel Act 1987, s.19(2).

[31c] This diversification has been propelled by the E.C. Council Directive of July 29, 1991 (91/440) and the E.U. Council Directives of June 19, 1995 (95/18 and 95/19),

which require the separation and allocation of the management of railway infrastructure and railway services. The United Kingdom has sought to achieve this by privatising the railway undertakings by a system of franchising pursuant to the Railways Act 1993.

[*And add new reference to "common law liability", line 3: page* [437]]

NOTE 35a: See, for example, *Lacey's Footwear (Wholesale) Ltd v. Bowler International Freight Ltd*, unreported, March 17, 1995 (aff'd: *The Times*, May 12, 1997).

[*Insert as new paragraph at end*]   **35–008**
The consequences of the distinction between common and private **35–008A**
carriers. The importance of the classification of a carrier as a common or private carrier lies in the liabilities of and remedies available to the carrier. The key differences in the position of the two types of carrier are as follows. It is the duty of the common carrier to carry the goods entrusted to him by a customer, provided he can accommodate those goods on his conveyance.[39a] A common carrier effectively undertakes, save in circumstances recognised by the common law as providing an exception, to indemnify the owner of the goods he carries for any loss or damage sustained by the goods[39b]; whereas a private carrier is liable, as a consequence of the bailment of the goods to him, only as a result of conduct which at the least constitutes negligence.[39c] The common carrier has the right to demand advance payment of freight[39d] and has a common law right to exercise a particular lien over the goods in his charge for freight which is due.[39e] The rights of limitation of the liability of the carrier differ depending upon status.[39f] These rights and liabilities, and others, will be discussed below.

[39a] *Jackson v. Rogers* (1683) 2 Show 327; *Boson v. Sandford* (1690) 1 Show 101, 104; *Lane v. Cotton* (1701) 12 Mod.Rep. 472, 484; *Macklin v. Waterhouse* (1828) 5 Bing 212; *Johnson v. Midland Railway Co.* (1849) 4 Exch. 367; *Carr v. Lancashire and Yorkshire Railway Co.* (1852) 7 Exch. 707; *Oxlade v. North Eastern Railway Co.* (1864) 15 C.B.N.S. 680; *Clarke v. West Ham Corporation* [1909] 2 K.B. 858, 877. Main Work, §35–010.

[39b] *Coggs v. Bernard* (1703) 2 Ld.Raym. 909; *Dale v. Hall* (1750) 1 Wils. 281; *Forward v. Pittard* (1785) 1 Term Rep. 27; *Trent and Mersey Navigation v. Wood* (1785) 3 Esp. 127; *Covington v. Willan* (1819) Gow. 115; *Brooke v. Pickwick* (1827) 4 Bing. 218; *Riley v. Horne* (1828) 5 Bing. 217; *Brind v. Dale* (1837) 8 C. & P. 207. Main Work, §35–012.

[39c] *Coggs v. Bernard* (1703) 2 Ld.Raym. 909; *Hayman v. Hewitt* (1798) Peake Add.Cas. 170; *Richardson v. North Eastern Railway Co.* (1872) L.R. 7 C.P. 75; *John Carter (Fine Worsteds) Ltd v. Hanson Haulage (Leeds) Ltd* [1965] 2 Q.B. 495; *Morris v. CW Martin & Sons Ltd* [1966] 1 Q.B. 716. Main Work, §35–012.

[39d] *Batson v. Donovan* (1820) 4 B. & Ald. 21; *Wyld v. Pickford* (1841) 8 M. & W. 443. Main Work, §35–061.

[39e] *Skinner v. Upshaw* (1702) 2 Ld.Raym. 752. Main Work, §35–063.

[39f] *infra*, §§35–032—35–035.

(ii) *Carrier's Liabilities*

Liability for loss and damage

35–012   [*Add to text at end of the first paragraph: page* [438]]
A claim for loss of or damage to the goods carried cannot be enforced by a
set-off against or a deduction from the freight which is due to the carrier.[57a]

> [57a] *United Carriers Ltd v. Heritage Food Group (U.K.) Ltd* [1995] 2 Lloyd's Rep.
> 269. Indeed, a judgment obtained by a carrier for freight should not be stayed
> pending the obtaining and execution of a judgment against the carrier for loss or
> damage (at page 273).

[*Add to note 58*]
Including goods entrusted to a fraudulent sub-contractor with whom the
carrier has contracted (as opposed to a person falsely holding himself out to
the customer as the carrier): *John Rigby (Haulage) Ltd v. Reliance Marine
Insurance Co. Ltd* [1956] 2 Q.B. 468; *Harrisons and Crossfield Ltd v. London
and North Western Railway Co.* [1917] 2 K.B. 755. *Cf.* the definition of
"bogus sub-contractor" in a carriers' transit insurance policy in *London
Tobacco Co. (Overseas) Ltd v. DFDS Transport Ltd* [1994] 1 Lloyd's Rep.
394.

Incorporation of terms

35–019   [*Insert new reference, line 1, at "ticket": page* [441]]
NOTE 82a: *post,* §35–075.

[*Add to note 83*]
*Lacey's Footwear (Wholesale) Ltd v. Bowler International Freight Ltd,
The Times,* May 12, 1997. See also *Cory Brothers Shipping Ltd v. Baldan Ltd,*
unreported, March 17, 1995; aff'd [1997] 2 Lloyd's Rep. 58, 61–62.

[*Add to note 84*]
Lacey's Footwear (Wholesale) Ltd v. Bowler International Freight Ltd,
unreported, March 17, 1995, aff'd May 12, 1997, where it was held that a
carrier's mailshots to a customer before their first contract did not amount to
a prior course of dealing. In *Lacey's Footwear (Wholesale) Ltd v. Bowler
International Freight Ltd, The Times,* May 12, 1997, the majority of the Court
of Appeal concluded that a party's standard terms were incorporated
because the other party was aware that carriers and forwarding agents
tended to contract on the basis of limitation provisions, even though he had
not turned his mind to the content of those provisions; whether the party
who relied on such provisions had taken adequate steps to draw these
provisions to the attention of the other was irrelevant. In such cases, it is
legitimate to take into account the nature of the transaction and the position

and character of the parties: see also *Poseidon Freight Forwarding Co. Ltd v. Davies Turner Southern Ltd* [1996] 2 Lloyd's Rep. 388.

[*Add to note 85*]
cf. *Lacey's Footwear (Wholesale) Ltd v. Bowler International Freight Ltd*, *supra*.

[*Add to note 86*]
The party who relies on standard form conditions has to plead and bear the onus of proof that such terms are reasonable: *Sheffield v. Pickfords Ltd* [1997] T.L.R. 140. See also §§14–088—14–104 as to Council Directive 93/13 on Unfair Terms in Consumer Contracts.

Construction of contracts

[*Delete text between note 88 and "However", line 11 and substitute: page* **35–020**
[441]]
Such clauses of exemption or limitation will be construed strictly and narrowly[88a] and, therefore, will operate to exclude liability for the negligence of the carrier if the clause expressly (or necessarily by implication) so provides.[88b] If the clause makes no specific reference to negligence, liability for negligence will be excepted only if the carrier's only liability would lie in negligence.[88c] There may be an important difference between the positions of common and private carriers in respect of exemption clauses which do not specifically refer to negligence. The potential liability of a common carrier includes and extends beyond negligence. Such a clause therefore would not protect the common carrier from his own negligence.[89] On the other hand, the private carrier may be liable in tort or contract if he fails to take reasonable care. It is probable that such a clause would protect the private carrier from liability for negligence,[90] but it is arguable that the clause would operate to except liability in contract, but not in tort.[90a] Nevertheless,

[88a] *Alexander v. Railway Executive* [1951] 2 K.B. 882, 893.

[88b] *Page v. London, Midland & Scottish Railway* [1943] 1 All E.R. 455; *Buckmaster v. Great Eastern Railway Co.* (1870) 23 L.T. 471.

[88c] *Alderslade v. Hendon Laundry Ltd* [1945] K.B. 189; *Hollier v. Rambler Motors (AMC) Ltd* [1972] 2 Q.B. 71; *Shell Chemicals UK Ltd v. P & O Roadtanks Ltd* [1995] 1 Lloyd's Rep. 297, 301.

[89] [See Main Work].

[90] [See Main Work].

[90a] *White v. John Warwick & Co. Ltd* [1953] 2 All E.R. 1021.

British Railways Board's Conditions of Carriage

[*Add to text after note 11: page* [443]] **35–023**
However, the importance of these clauses will diminish as the newly

privatised railway companies commence and continue to operate and employ their own standard form contracts. Nevertheless, it is useful to examine the standard form contracts adopted by the British Railways Board. Reference will be made to such contracts below.

[*And substitute new item (d): page* [444]]
(d) Red Star Conditions of Carriage, operative from March 1, 1996. These provide comprehensive conditions for the carriage of Red Star parcels, *i.e.* express parcels.

35–024   [*Delete from note 20 "Red Star Conditions, para. 7a" and substitute*]
Red Star Conditions, para. 12(a).

Liability for loss or damage under British Railways Board's special interest Conditions of Carriage at Board's risk

35–026   [*Delete from note 32 "Red Star Conditions, para. 10.2" and substitute: page* [445]]
Red Star Conditions, para. 17(c).

Liability for loss or damage under British Railways Board's Conditions of Carriage at owner's risk

35–027   [*Delete from note 43 "Red Star Conditions, para. 11" and substitute: page* [446]]
Red Star Conditions, para. 18.

Upper financial limits of liability under standard form contracts

35–036   [*Add after the first sentence in note 83: page* [451]]
As to the construction of these two provisions, see *Spectra International plc v. Hayesoak Ltd* [1997] 1 Lloyd's 153; revd. unreported, April 30, 1997.

Upper financial limits of liability under standard form contracts

35–037   [*Delete from note 84 "Red Star Conditions, para. 12(a)(iii)" and substitute: page* [452]]
Red Star Conditions, para. 19(c).

[*Delete final two sentences of paragraph with note 87 and substitute*]
Where goods (other than livestock) are carried by the Red Star Parcels Service, the Conditions of Carriage provide for a limitation of their liability for loss of the whole consignment of £15,000 per 1,000 kilos of weight[87] and for a proportion of that sum in the event of loss of or damage to a part of the consignment.[87a]

NOTE 87: Red Star Conditions, para. 17(a).

[87a] Red Star Conditions, para. 17(b).

Dangerous and unusual goods

[*Add to note 88: page* [452]]   **35–038**
See *Giannis NK* [1994] 2 Lloyd's Rep. 171 as to the meaning of dangerous
goods.

[*Delete from note 90 "Red Star Conditions, para. 1g" and substitute*]
Red Star Conditions, para. 1f.

[*Delete from note 91 "Red Star Conditions, para. 23b(iii)" and substitute*]
Red Star Conditions, para. 30(b).

[*Delete from note 92 "Red Star Conditions para. 23c" and substitute*]
Red Star Conditions, para. 30(c).

[*Delete from note 93 "Red Star Conditions para. 23b(iv)" and substitute*]
Red Star Conditions, para. 30(b).

[*Insert as new paragraph at end: page* [453]]   **35–039**
The carriage of dangerous and radio-active goods in the United Kingdom **35–039A**
is governed by regulations[98a] made to implement European Council
Directives 94/55 of November 21, 1994 and 96/49 of July 23, 1996 on the
approximation of the laws of the Members States concerning the transport
of dangerous goods by road and rail respectively.

[98a] See, for example, Radioactive Material (Road Transport) (Great Britain)
Regulations 1996 (S.I. 1996 No. 1350), Carriage of Dangerous Goods by Rail
Regulations 1996 (S.I. 1996 No. 2089), Packaging Labelling and Carriage of
Radioactive Material by Rail Regulations 1996 (S.I. 1996 No. 2090), Carriage of
Dangerous Goods (Classification Packaging and Labelling) and Use of Transport-
able Pressure Receptacles Regulations 1996 (S.I. 1996 No. 2092), Carriage of
Explosives by Road Regulations 1996 (S.I. 1996 No. 2093), and Carriage of
Dangerous Goods by Road Regulations 1996 (S.I. 1996 No. 2095). See also
European Commission Directives 96/86 and 96/87.

Liability for deviation, delay and detention under standard form contracts

[*Delete from note 12 "Red Star Conditions, para. 10.1b" and substitute:* **35–043**
page [454]]
Under Red Star Conditions, para. 15, in the event of delay, the carrier is

liable only to refund the carriage charges. If the delay was caused by factors beyond the control of the carrier, the carrier will not be liable.

[*Delete from note 13 "Red Star Conditions, para. 10.2(i)" and substitute*]
Red Star Conditions, para. 17(c) and (d).

[*Delete from note 15 "Red Star Conditions, para. 11" and substitute*]
Red Star Conditions, para. 18.

Misdelivery

35–046   [*Delete from note 31 "Red Star Conditions, para. 11" and substitute:
page* [456]]
Red Star Conditions, para. 18.

Beginning and end of transit

35–048   [*Delete from note 36 "Red Star Conditions, para. 5(c)" and substitute:
page* [457]]
Red Star Conditions, para. 10(c).

[*Delete from note 37 "Red Star Conditions, para. 18" and substitute*]
Red Star Conditions, para. 14.

[*Delete from note 40 "Red Star Conditions, para. 15" and substitute*]
Red Star Conditions, para. 22.

Time for making claims

35–051   [*Delete from note 53 "Red Star Conditions, para. 13" and substitute:
page* [459]]
Red Star Conditions, para. 20.

[*Delete from note 55 "Red Star Conditions, para. 13" and substitute*]
Red Star Conditions, para. 20.

[*Delete from note 56 "Red Star Conditions, para. 13(b)" and substitute*]
Red Star Conditions, para. 20.

[*Delete from note 57 "Red Star Conditions, para. 13" and substitute*]
Red Star Conditions, para. 20.

Liability in tort

[*Insert new reference at "or for tort", line 3: page* [460]]   **35–054**

NOTE 66a: Although set-off against freight cannot be relied upon: *United Carriers Ltd v. Heritage Food Group (UK) Ltd* [1995] 2 Lloyd's Rep. 269.

[*Add to note 76: page* [462]]   **35–055**
See also *Spectra International plc v. Hayesoak Ltd* [1997] 1 Lloyd's 153; rev'd. on other grounds, unreported, April 30, 1997.

Exemption clauses in standard form contracts

[*Delete from note 84 "Red Star Conditions, para. 6(a)" and substitute:*   **35–057**
page [463]]
Red Star Conditions, para. 11(a).

[*Delete from note 85 "Red Star Conditions, para. 6(b)" and substitute*]
Red Star Conditions, para. 11(b).

(iii) *Carrier's Rights*

Consignor's warranty of fitness

[*Delete from note 99 "Red Star Conditions, para. 3(a)(c)" and substitute:* **35–060**
page [464]]
Red Star Conditions, para. 3(c).

Carrier's right to freight

[*Delete from note 8 "Red Star Conditions, para. 4(b)" and substitute:*   **35–061**
page [465]]
Red Star Conditions, para. 9(a).

[*And add to text at end of paragraph*]
Even without such protection in the carriage contract, the carrier (whether common or private) is entitled to the payment of freight on the due date without any deduction or set-off being made to allow for any claim which the consignor may have under the contract of carriage.[8a] This right to freight without set-off exists notwithstanding that the contract is for a series of carriages as opposed to one carriage and that the carrier may have obligations under the contract ancillary to that of carriage, although his claim must be for freight and not a charge unrelated to the carriage.[8b]

[8a] *United Carriers Ltd v. Heritage Food Group (U.K.) Ltd* [1995] 2 Lloyd's Rep. 269, 273; also see *A S Jones Ltd v. Burton Gold Medal Biscuits*, April 11, 1984, unreported.

[8b] *United Carriers Ltd v. Heritage Food Group (U.K.) Ltd, supra.*

Carrier's lien

35–063   *[Delete from note 21 "Red Star Conditions, para. 27" and substitute: page* [466]]
Red Star Conditions, para. 34.

Carrier's right to sell the goods

35–066   *[Delete from note 32 "Red Star Conditions, para. 9" and substitute: page* [468]]
Red Star Conditions, para. 14.

(b) *Passengers*

Common carriers

35–067   *[Delete from text between notes 39 and 41 and substitute]*
As we have seen,[40] the British Railways Board and the privatised railway companies are not regarded as common carriers; whether common carrier or not, they are not obliged to carry any person who is in an unfit condition.[41]

NOTE 40: *Ante*, §35–007.

NOTE 41: *Garton v. Bristol and Exeter Ry Co.* (1861) 1 B. & S. 112, at p. 162. See also the British Railways National Conditions of Carriage (published January 7, 1996), cl. 38, which allows a railway company, including the British Railways Board, to refuse carriage to any person who is believed to be acting in a riotous, disorderly or offensive manner.

Liability for death or personal injuries

35–068   *[Insert new reference at "fit for its purpose", line 10: page* [469]]

NOTE 43a: *John Carter (Fine Worsteds) Ltd v. Hanson Haulage (Leeds) Ltd* [1965] 2 Q.B. 495. The common law liability of the carrier probably is unchanged by the Occupiers' Liability Act 1957, whether the passenger has paid for the carriage or not.

Liability in tort

35–069   *[Delete from note 48 first two sentences, and substitute]*
Clerk and Lindsell on Torts (17th ed., 1995), §10–73. *Videan v. BTC* [1963]

[324]

2 Q.B. 650; *Commissioner for Rys v. Quinlan* [1964] A.C. 1054; *Herrington v. British Railways Board* [1972] A.C. 877. *Cf.* the liability of the carrier to a trespasser concerning the condition of his vehicle provided for by the Occupiers' Liability Act 1984, s.1.

Liability for negligence of independent contractors

[*Delete note 57 and substitute: page* [470]] **35–071**
s.2(4)(b). See *Clerk and Lindsell on Torts* (17th ed., 1995), §§10–59—10–60.

Special contract

[*Delete note 63 and substitute: page* [471]] **35–075**
Clerk and Lindsell on Torts (17th ed., 1995), §§2–18—23, 3–09—32 and 3–33—3–37.

Limitations on carriers' contracting out of liability for death and personal injury

[*Insert new reference at "public service vehicle", line 2 of second paragraph: page* [472]] **35–076**

NOTE 69a: s.1 of the 1981 Act defines a "public service vehicle" as a motor vehicle used for carrying passengers for hire or reward. This definition does not require a plaintiff to demonstrate that there was a legally enforceable agreement or right to be carried or that payment had been made: *Rout v. Swallow Hotels* [1993] R.T.R. 80 (where a hotel minibus provided for the benefit of hotel guests was held to be a public service vehicle); *D.P.P. v. Sikondar* [1993] R.T.R. 90 (where a vehicle used for the systematic carrying of girls to and from school, whose driver received the occasional contribution to the cost of petrol, was held to be a public service vehicle).

[*And add to text at end of second paragraph*]
Section 149 of the Road Traffic Act 1988 renders of no effect any agreement between the user[69a] of a vehicle on the road and a passenger whereby the liability of the user for death or personal injury is excluded or limited or whereby conditions are imposed on the enforcement of such liability.

[69a] That is, one who controls, manages or operates the vehicle: *Brown v. Roberts* [1965] 1 Q.B. 1. See also *Stinton v. Stinton* [1995] R.T.R. 157; *Hatton v. Hall, The Times*, May 2, 1996.

Exceptions to the general limitations on carriers' contracting out of liability

[*Add to note 75: page* [473]] **35–078**
s.16 of the 1979 Act has been repealed by the Merchant Shipping Act

1995. However, the 1987 Order continues to have force by virtue of the Interpretation Act 1978, s.17(2)(b), as if made under s.184 of the 1995 Act. Under s.184(5), the meaning of "contracts of carriage" exclude contracts which are not for reward.

[Delete note 77 and substitute]
The substantive provisions of the Convention are set out in the Merchant Shipping Act 1995, Sched. 6, Part I.

[Delete note 78 and substitute: page [474]]
Athens Convention, Art. 3: the Convention was implemented under the Merchant Shipping Act 1979, s.14. With the repeal of s.14, the Convention is now given the force of law in the United Kingdom by virtue of the Merchant Shipping Act 1995, s.183.

[Delete note 81 and substitute]
British Railways Board's National Conditions of Carriage, clause 5, published January 7, 1996.

Standard forms of contract

35–079   *[Second sentence of text, line 4.]*
The British Railways Board's current conditions are now the National Conditions of Carriage, which came into operation on January 7, 1996.

[Delete final sentence with note 84 and substitute]
There are no generally accepted Conditions of Carriage of passengers by road: The British Railways Board's National Conditions of Carriage do, however, apply "where relevant" to the carriage of passengers in road vehicles owned or operated by the British Railways Board or any other "Train Company" on whose behalf it has contracted.[84]

NOTE 84: National Conditions of Carriage, clause 60.

Liability for delay

35–081   *[Delete both paragraphs and substitute: page [475]]*
The British Railways Board and Train Companies on whose behalf it contracts have provided that they do not accept liability for loss (including consequential loss) caused by the delay or cancellation of any train, by a missed connection or by the closure of the railway,[89] other than delay caused by circumstances within the control of the Train Company, as a result of which the passenger arrives at his destination more than one hour late.[90] The passenger is entitled to compensation in accordance with the Passenger's Charter,[90a] published by the British Railways Board or other Train Company, and the National Conditions of Carriage, provided a claim is

lodged within two working days of the completion of the journey. Compensation takes the form of vouchers which entitle the passenger to discounts off the price of his next railway journey.[90b]

NOTE 89: National Conditions of Carriage, clause 45.

NOTE 90: *ibid.* clause 42.

[90a] *ibid.* clause 41.

[90b] *ibid.* clause 42.

[*Delete note 91 and substitute*]   35–082
National Conditions of Carriage, clause 44.

Scope of exemption clauses

[*Delete second sentence from text: page* [476]]   35–083

Carrier's right to receive the proper fare

[*Delete second sentence from text and substitute*]   35–084
This principle may be illustrated by reference to the British Railways Board National Conditions of Carriage[95a] and decided cases.

[95a] For example, clauses 7, 8, 12, 13 and 15.

[*Delete note 96 and substitute*]
British Railways Board National Conditions of Carriage, clause 2.

[*Delete note 98 and substitute*]
ibid. clause 11.

[*Delete note 99 and substitute*]
ibid. clause 7.

[*Delete note 1 and substitute*]   35–085
ibid. clauses 10 and 13.

[*Delete note 2 and substitute*]
ibid. clause 15. See *G. N. Ry v. Winder* [1892] 2 Q.B. 595; *G. N. Ry v. Palmer* [1895] 1 Q.B. 862.

[*Delete final sentence from text with note 4 and substitute*]
Of course, the contract of carriage may provide otherwise.[4]

NOTE 4: See, for example, National Conditions of Carriage, clause 15.

(c) *Passengers' Luggage*

Common carriers

35–086   [*Delete fourth sentence from text with note 7 and substitute: page* [477]]
No person, such as the British Railways Board, London Regional Transport or the newly franchised railway companies, shall be regarded as common carriers by rail.[7]

NOTE 7: Transport Act 1962, s.43(6); Transport (London) Act 1969, s.6(2)(g); Railways Act 1993, s.123.

[*Delete note 9 and substitute*]
National Conditions of Carriage, clause 60.

Permitted luggage

35–087   [*Delete second paragraph from text with notes 10, 11 and substitute*]
The British Railways Board's National Conditions of Carriage provide that the Board (and any other "Train Company") will accept luggage (including animals) accompanying a passenger, subject to specified exceptions, free of charge.[10] Although there is no precise limitation upon the size, quantity or weight of the luggage which accompanies the passenger, the Board may refuse to carry the luggage if there is no room for it, in which case it may choose to carry it in a luggage van at a charge.[11] The Board may refuse to accept luggage additionally where the luggage might cause injury, inconvenience or property damage, its loading or unloading might cause delay or it is not carried or packed in a suitable manner, notwithstanding that such luggage has been accepted previously or is accepted normally.[11a]

NOTE 10: National Conditions of Carriage, clause 46.

NOTE 11: *ibid.* clauses 46 and 47.

[11a] *ibid.* clause 46.

The requirement of personal use

35–089   [*Delete note 18 and substitute: page* [478]]
National Conditions of Carriage, clause 46. *cf.* the definition of passengers' luggage in the context of the international carriage by rail under CIV; *post*, §35–131.

[*Delete the final sentence of second paragraph, with note 22: page* [479]]   **35–090**

Liability for loss or damage in carriage by rail

[*Delete note 44 and substitute: page* [481]]   **35–095**
National Conditions of Carriage, clause 49. Hence some of the cases on liability for loss or damage at common law, particularly *Vosper v. G. W. Ry* [1928] 1 K.B. 340, would now be decided differently.

[*Delete note 45 and substitute*]
ibid. clause 49.

[*Delete note 46 and substitute*]
ibid. clauses 52 and 55.

Other articles

[*Delete whole paragraph*]   **35–098**

3. – International Carriage

(a) *Introduction*

International Convention on Carriage by Rail

[*Insert a new paragraph at end: page* [484]]   **35–100**
The CIM Uniform Rules have annexed to them 4 sets of regulations,   **35–100A**
concerning the international carriage by rail of dangerous goods (RID),[62a]
containers (RICO)[62b] and express parcels (RIEx)[62c] and the international
haulage by rail of private owners' wagons (RIP).[62d]

[62a] CIM, Annex I; CIM, Art. 4(D) and 5(1)(a). See also European Council
Directive 96/49, July 23, 1996 on the approximation of laws within Member States
concerning carriage of dangerous goods by rail.

[62b] CIM, Annex III; CIM, Art. 8(2).

[62c] CIM, Annex IV; CIM, Art. 8(3).

[62d] CIM, Annex II; CIM, Art. 8(1).

(b) *Goods by Rail*

Application of the Uniform Rules (CIM) under Appendix B to COTIF

[*Add to text after note 86: page* [486]]   **35–104**
CIM will not apply if the carriage of the consignment originates and ends
in the same State, but passes in transit through the territory of another State,

provided that the lines over which the transit occurs are operated exclusively by the railway of the State of departure or if the relevant States or railways have agreed not to treat the carriage as international.[86a]

[86a] Art. 2(1).

35–104A *[And insert new paragraph at end]*
The CIM Uniform Rules were drafted by reference to the concepts of "the railway" and "railway lines". Until recently, and when the CIM Uniform Rules were first implemented, it was invariably the case that the operator of the railway service (the service provider) and the owner or administrator of the railway infrastructure (that is, tracks, tunnels, stations) were the same enterprise. However, recently, these two roles of service provider and infrastructure operator now are in the process of separation both at the national and supra-national level.[86b] The CIM Uniform Rules therefore require revision to take account of this fundamental change in the nature of the international carriage of goods by rail. To attempt to adjust the application of the CIM Uniform Rules to the changing environment on an *ad hoc* basis will lead to innumerable inconsistencies in the regime governing international rail carriage. Further such difficulties may be found as a result of the fact that it is now permissible for one rail carrier to provide carriage services over the lines of more than one State.

[86b] See, for example, EU Council Directives 91/440, 95/18 and 95/19.

Obligation of the railway

35–107 *[Delete paragraph with notes 90–92 and substitute: page [486]]*
There is a general obligation laid on the rail carrier under the Convention[90] to carry any goods in complete wagon-loads, provided that the railway can undertake the loading, carriage and unloading of the goods by the normal resources and facilities available to it,[91] the carriage can be conducted without delay[92] and the goods do not fall within specified categories of unacceptable articles.[92a] Certain specified goods (such as dangerous goods, livestock, funeral consignments and the like) are acceptable for carriage provided they comply with the conditions imposed by or agreements reached between two or more Contracting States or railways.[92b]

NOTE 90: Art. 3(1).

NOTE 91: Arts. 3(1)(b) and 3(2).

NOTE 92: Art. 3(3).

[92a] Such as goods which are too large or too heavy for the rolling stock: Art. 4.

[92b] Arts. 5(1), 5(2) and 9.

[And insert as new paragraph at end]
Carriage Charges. The rail carrier is entitled to payment[92c] of charges[92d] **35–107A**
calculated in accordance with tariffs which are legally in force and which, if
required by the relevant State,[92e] are duly published, and surcharges[92f] and
disbursements, but no more.[92g] The tariffs must be applied to all users of the
railway on the same basis and without discrimination,[92h] although reductions
in the charges may be agreed privately for public or charitable purposes,
provided that the concessions are extended to all customers in comparable
circumstances.[92i]

[92c] See Art. 15.

[92d] Art. 6(1).

[92e] Art. 6(8).

[92f] Calculated in accordance with Art. 24.

[92g] Art. 6(9).

[92h] Art. 6(3).

[92i] Art. 6(4).

Consignment note

[Add to text at beginning of paragraph: page [487]]   **35–108**
The CIM Uniform Rules will apply only if a consignment note has been
made out.[92j] The consignment note evidences the making and content of the
contract of carriage,[92k] constitutes an important part of the carriage and
delivery of the goods,[92l] and should be produced in the event of a claim
against the railway.[92m]

[92j] Art. 1(1).

[92k] Arts. 11(1) and (3).

[92l] Art. 28.

[92m] Art. 53.

[Add to note 93 after "12 and 13."]
Also see Arts. 14(1), 16(1), 17(6), 19(1), 20(5), 22(1), 25(1) and 26(3).

[Add to note 95]
Each railway which takes over the goods and the consignment note, from
the railway which accepts the goods, will become a party to the contract of
carriage: Art. 35.

[Insert as new paragraph at end: page [488]]   **35–109**
Loading, Carriage and Delivery. The consignor must present his goods,[4a] **35–109A**
together with the consignment note, to the railway for carriage. When the
goods and the note are accepted, there is a contract.[4b] If required, the

consignor will be responsible for the packing and marking of the goods consigned.[4c] Either the consignor or the railway will be responsible for the loading of the goods, depending on the provisions in force at the forwarding station.[4d] Where the consignor is responsible for the packing, marking and loading of the goods, he will be liable for any defects in his performance in this regard.[4e] The particulars of the goods as described may be verified[4f] and the weight and the number of packages of the goods may be ascertained[4g] by the railway. The Uniform Rules assume that the consignment note will accompany the goods during their carriage.[4h] Upon arrival at the destination, it will be the responsibility of the railway to hand over the consignment note and deliver the goods to the consignee against a receipt and amounts chargeable to the consignee.[4i] Delivery also may be effected by the handing over of the goods to Customs authorities, or the deposit of the goods for storage with the railway, with a forwarding agent or in a public warehouse, provided that such delivery is permitted by the provisions in force at the destination station.[4j]

35–109B   If the carriage of the goods has been prevented by circumstances,[4k] the railway must decide whether it is preferable (presumably in the interests of the consignor) to modify the route or to ask the consignor (or the consignee, if the latter has duly modified the contract[4l]) for instructions.[4m] If it is impossible to continue the carriage or to effect delivery, the consignor shall be asked for his instructions.[4n] The consignor may give his instructions to the forwarding station or the station holding the goods. If the instructions require the changing of the consignee or the destination or are given to the station holding the goods, those instructions must be entered in the duplicate consignment note held by the consignor and given to the railway.[4o] If the consignee refuses delivery, the consignor may give instructions, even if he is unable to produce the duplicate consignment note.[4p] If the consignor fails to give instructions within a reasonable time, the railway may take action in accordance with the provisions in force at the station holding the goods or at the place of delivery, including the sale of the goods, the proceeds of which will be held at the disposal of the consignor, less those amounts chargeable against the goods.[4q] If circumstances alter permitting carriage or delivery, then the railway shall forward the goods to the destination or deliver the goods to the consignee, as the case may be, without waiting for receipt of the consignor's instructions.[4r]

[4a] The handing over of the goods to the railway will be governed by the provisions in force at the forwarding station: Art. 20(1).

[4b] Arts. 11(1) and 12(1).

[4c] Art. 19.

[4d] Art. 20(2).

[4e] Arts. 19(4) and 20(3).

[4f] Art. 21.

^{4g} Art. 22.

^{4h} *cf. infra* CMR, Art. 5(1).

⁴ⁱ CIM, Arts. 28(1) and (4).

^{4j} Art. 28(2).

^{4k} The carrier will not be liable for any loss of or damage to the goods or delay caused by circumstances which are unavoidable by the railway: Art. 36(2).

^{4l} Arts. 33(8) and 34(7).

^{4m} Art. 33(1). *cf. infra* CMR, Art. 14(2).

⁴ⁿ Arts. 33(2) and 34(1).

^{4o} Art. 33(4).

^{4p} Art. 34(3).

^{4q} Arts. 33(6) and 34(6).

^{4r} Arts. 33(7) and 34(2).

Loss, damage and delay

[Insert new reference to "The railway", line 1: page [488]]   **35–110**

NOTE 4a: The concept of "railway" under the CIM Rules will need to be revisited as a result of the recent deregulation of railway services. See *ante*, §35–104A.

[Add to note 5 at end]
The railway's liability may be engaged even before carriage commences, if the railway refuses to accept goods for carriage in accordance with its obligations so to do under Art. 3: Art. 3(6). A failure to comply with the instructions of the person entitled to dispose of the goods during carriage may also render the railway liable for loss or damage caused thereby: Art. 33(5).

[Insert new reference to "(decay, wastage, etc.)", line 12]

NOTE 8a: Where there is wastage in transit of goods which, by reason of their nature, is caused by the sole fact of carriage, the railway will be liable only to the extent that the wastage exceeds specified allowances: Art. 41.

[Add to text at end of second paragraph: page [489]]   **35–111**
In the case of rail-road transport, the carrier's liability is governed by the CMR Convention,^{16a} unless it can be demonstrated that the loss or damage

could only have occurred during the rail (*i.e.* non-road) segment of the carriage, in which case the CIM Uniform Rules will determine the carrier's liability.

[16a] CMR, Art. 2(1).

[*And insert new paragraph at end*]

35–111A   **Ascertainment of loss or damage.** Upon delivery, the consignor or the consignee, as the case may be, may ask the carrier for an opportunity to examine the goods to determine the existence of any loss or damage. Any failure by the railway to permit such an examination will entitle the person entitled to the goods to refuse to accept the goods, even when he has accepted the consignment note and/or paid the outstanding charges.[16b] In the event of the discovery or even an allegation of partial loss of or damage to the goods, the consignor or the consignee, as the case may be, may require the preparation of a report by the railway without delay concerning the condition of the goods and the extent, cause and time of the loss or damage.[16c] If the person entitled to the goods does not accept the report's findings, he can insist upon the circumstances surrounding the loss or damage be investigated by an expert.[16d]

[16b] Art. 28(5).

[16c] Art. 52(1).

[16d] Art. 52(2).

Upper financial limits of liability

35–112   [*Add to text after first sentence*]
The compensation is calculated by reference to the commodity exchange quoted price or other market price of the goods of the same kind and quality at the time and place at which the goods were accepted for the carriage.[18a]

[18a] Art. 40(1).

[*Add to note 19*]
The claimant cannot recover any additional duty or VAT payable in respect of the goods which do not find themselves at their destination: *Anon.*, Cass. Paris, January 28, 1975; *cf. James Buchanan & Co. Ltd v. Babco Forwarding and Shipping (UK) Ltd* [1978] 1 Lloyd's Rep. 119; *contra Anon.*, Supreme Court of Denmark 4.5.87 (1994) 29 E.T.L. 360 (CMR).

[*Delete from text, lines 10–11, "the compensation may . . . carriage charges.[20]" and substitute*]
the compensation may not exceed three times the amount of the carriage charges, although the total compensation for the loss or damage caused by delay and otherwise may not exceed the compensation payable for a total loss.[20]

NOTE 20: Art. 43(5).

[Add to note 23]
as amended by the Protocol adopted by the 2nd General Assembly of OTIF
at Berne in December 1990. "Wilful misconduct" now has been substituted
by a more easily defined concept: limitation of liability may not be invoked
where the loss or damage resulted from an act or omission done with intent
to cause such loss or damage or recklessly with the knowledge that such loss
or damage probably will result. This Protocol has been implemented in the
United Kingdom by the International Transport Conventions Act 1983
(Amendment) Order 1994 (S.I. 1994 No. 1907).

[Add to text at end of paragraph]
The claimant may recover interest on the compensation payable at the
rate of 5 per cent per annum from the time a claim, together with supporting
documents, is submitted in accordance with the CIM Uniform Rules,[23a] or
failing such a claim, from the time of the commencement of legal
proceedings in respect of the claim.[23b]

[23a] Art. 53.

[23b] Art. 47.

Who can claim

[Add to note 30: page [490]]   **35–114**
This includes claims for breach of contract which may be maintained as a
matter of national law. Such claims are embraced by the term "other
actions" in Arts. 54(3) and 55(3): *Anon.*, BGH 14.11.91 (1993) 28 E.T.L. 621.

(c) *Passengers and Luggage by Rail*

(i) *Application and Scope of the Convention*

Application and scope of the Uniform Rules (CIV) under Appendix A to COTIF

[Delete three final sentences of second paragraph]   **35–117**

[Delete note 43 and substitute: page [492]]   **35–118**
Merchant Shipping Act 1995, s.183. The Athens Convention came into
force on April 30, 1987.

[Delete note 44 and substitute]
Carriage of Passengers and their Luggage by Sea (Domestic Carriage)
Order 1987 (S.I. 1987 No. 670), which now takes effect as if made under the
Merchant Shipping Act 1995, s.184. Under s.184(5), the term "contract of

carriage" in the context of the Athens Convention excludes a contract which is not for reward.

(ii) *Passengers and Hand Luggage*

Upper financial limits of liability

35–125   [*Delete final sentence of paragraph with note 64 and substitute: page* [494]]
    The liability of the carrier is, however, not limited at all if the injury results from an act or omission done with intent to cause such injury or recklessly with the knowledge that such injury probably will result or from gross negligence on the part of the railway.[64] In the French text of the Convention "gross negligence" is translated as "*faute lourde*".

    NOTE 64: Art. 42, as amended by the Protocol adopted by the 2nd General Assembly of OTIF at Berne in December 1990. This Protocol has been implemented in the United Kingdom by the International Transport Conventions Act 1983 (Amendment) Order 1994 (S.I. 1994 No. 1907).

(iii) *Registered Luggage*

Upper financial limits of liability

35–134   [*Delete final sentence of paragraph with note 98 and substitute: page* [497]]
    The maximum limits of compensation for loss, damage or delay are doubled if this was due to the gross negligence of the railway, and are removed altogether if it was due to the act or omission of the railway which was done with the intent to cause loss or damage or recklessly with the knowledge that such loss or damage probably will result.[98]

    NOTE 98: Art. 42, as amended by the Protocol adopted by the 2nd General Assembly of OTIF at Berne in December 1990. This Protocol has been implemented in the United Kingdom by the International Transport Conventions Act 1983 (Amendment) Order 1994 (S.I. 1994 No. 1907).

(d) *Goods by Road*

The scope of CMR

35–137   [*Add new reference after* "every contract for the carriage" *in line 1 of text: page* [498]]

    NOTE 13a: CMR will not apply to an existing relationship between the carrier and the purchaser of goods, where the latter is not interested, directly or directly, in the contract of carriage: *Atlanta Companies, Judge & Dolph Ltd v. Pvba Transport Leopold Laureys & Zonen* (1996) 31 E.T.L. 843 (Ghent).

[*Add new reference after* "goods" *in line 2 of text*]

NOTE 13b: For the purposes of CMR, "goods" may include a trailer hauled by the carrier's vehicle if that is what he contracted to carry: *NV Cobelfret v. NV Transport Jaco* (1996) 31 E.T.L. 579 (Antwerp).

[*Add new reference after* "means of transport" *in the penultimate line of text: page* [499]]

NOTE 20a: *PVBA Transport Maes v. NV Centraal Beheer Schadeverzkering* (1996) 31 E.T.L. 558 (Netherlands).

[*Add to note 15*]
It is essential, for the Convention to apply, that the road carriage contemplated by the contract is international. If the contract contemplated, for example, one road leg in one country and one sea leg in another country, the Convention will not apply: *Princes Buitoni Ltd v. Hapag-Lloyd Aktiengesellschaft* [1991] 2 Lloyd's Rep. 383.

[*Insert as new paragraph at end*]
Even if CMR does not apply to the carriage contemplated by the contract, **35–137A** it is still open to the parties to agree to the application of CMR,[21a] presumably in whole or in part. In that event, the fact that the carriage falls outside the scope of application of CMR set out in Article 1 is of no consequence.

[21a] *Princes Buitoni Ltd v. Hapag-Lloyd Aktiengesellschaft* [1991] 2 Lloyd's Rep. 383, 385–386.

[*Add to note 25*] **35–138**
National legislation, however, should not be discriminatory against carriers from other E.U. Member States so as to offend Art. 76 of the EEC Treaty of Rome: *Anon.*, Gerichtshof der Europäischen Gemeinschaften May 19, 1992 (1993) 28 E.T.L. 592.

Interpretation of the Convention

[*Add to note 26*] **35–139**
The House of Lords recently has approved a teleological approach to the interpretation of purely domestic statutes, unfettered by any rule requiring

an exclusive reliance upon the occasionally inadequate words used in the statute itself: *Pepper (Inspector of Taxes) v. Hart* [1993] A.C. 593.

[*Delete from text the fourth sentence, "To construe CMR ... wrong interpretation."*]

[*Add to note 28*]
affirmed on other grounds: [1995] 1 Lloyd's Rep. 297.

35–140   [*Add to note 29 after "Lloyd's Rep. 613": page* [499]]
and *London Tobacco Co. (Overseas) Ltd v. DFDS Transport Ltd* [1994] 1 Lloyd's Rep. 394,

Consignment note

35–141   [*Add to note 35*]
As to the difficulties which may arise when another consignment note is issued during the carriage, see *Harrison & Sons Ltd v. RT Steward Transport Ltd* (1993) 28 ETL 747, where the Court placed more importance on the original consignment note in the context of Art. 34 (*post*, §35–152).

[*Add to text, line 11, after "of the Convention.*[36]*"*]
The consignment note should also include a generally recognised description of the goods, if they are dangerous.[36a] Other particulars which are pertinent to the contemplated carriage should be entered in the consignment note, such as sender's charges, "cash on delivery" charges, insurance requirements, declarations of value,[36b] and any other particulars which the parties deem useful.[36c] The sender will be responsible for any losses, damages and expenses resulting from any deficiency or inadequacy in the particulars furnished in the consignment note.[36d]

[36a] Arts. 6(1)(f) and 22(1). See also the European Agreement concerning the Carriage of Dangerous Goods by Road, Cmnd. 3769 (1968) and E.U. Council Directive 1994/55, November 21, 1994 on the approximation of laws within Member States concerning carriage of dangerous goods by road. As to the meaning of "dangerous", see *Anon.* OLG Düsseldorf January 23, 1992 (1992) TranspR 218; *cf. Giannis NK* [1994] 2 Lloyd's Rep. 171.

[36b] Art. 6(2).

[36c] Art. 6(3). See, for example, *Harrison & Sons Ltd v. RT Steward Transport Ltd* (1993) 28 ETL 747.

[36d] Arts. 7(1) and 22(2).

[*Add to note 39: page* [501]]
Anon., Cass. December 1, 1992 (1993) 28 E.T.L. 745.

[Insert new reference to 41a "prima facie evidence", line 4] **35–142**

[41a] Whilst the signature on the consignment note may be printed or in the form of a stamp (Art. 5(1)), the absence of a signature will render the consignment note of neutral (or at best prima facie) evidential value: *City Vintages Ltd v. SCA.C. Transport International*, unreported, December 1, 1987.

[Insert new reference 41b to "making of the contract of carriage", line 5]

[41b] The Convention does not state when and where the consignment note must be issued, save that Art. 5 requires one copy of the consignment note to accompany the goods, which might suggest that the note should be made out prior to the commencement of the carriage (*cf. M Bardiger Ltd v. Halberg Spedition APS*, unreported, October 26, 1990). Such matters, however, will affect the probative value of the consignment note as evidence of the contract of carriage: *Electronska Industrija Oour TVA v. Transped Oour Kintinentalna* [1986] 1 Lloyd's Rep. 49, 51; *Texas Instruments Ltd v. Nason (Europe) Ltd* [1991] 1 Lloyd's Rep. 146.

[Add to text after note 42]
and of the identity of the parties to the contract[42a];

[42a] *Aqualon (U.K.) Ltd v. Vallana Shipping Corporation* [1994] 1 Lloyd's Rep. 669, 676.

[Delete note 46 and substitute]
Ante, §34–040.

Sender's right of disposal

[Add to text after note 47: page [502]] **35–143**
Article 12(5) of the Convention requires the right of disposal to be exercised by compliance with three conditions: first, the first (the sender's) copy of the consignment note must have the instructions given pursuant to the right of disposal entered upon its face and must be given to the carrier[47a]; secondly, the instructions must be possible to carry out and must not interfere with the carrier's undertaking or prejudice the senders and consignees of the other consignments carried by the carrier[47b]; thirdly, the instructions must not result in a division of the consignment.[47c]

[47a] Art. 12(5)(a). It seems that this condition is not essential: *Anon.* BGH January 27, 1982 (1985) 20 E.T.L. 349. Indeed, under Art. 15(1), where the consignee refuses delivery of the goods, the sender may exercise the right of disposal without producing the first copy of the consignment note. Nevertheless, save for situations covered by Art. 15(1), the carrier will obey the instructions of the sender without the first copy of the consignment note at his risk: Art. 12(7).

[47b] Art. 12(5)(b). The "interference" must be more than merely incidental: Hill & Messent, *CMR: Contracts for the International Carriage of Goods by Road* (2nd ed., 1995), 85; Clarke, *International Carriage of Goods By Road: CMR* (2nd ed. 1991), para. 32a(f). If it is not possible to carry out the instructions, the carrier must notify the person entitled to dispose of the goods "immediately": Art. 12(6).

[47c] Art. 12(5)(c). Whether "consignment" refers to the goods covered by the consignment note or all the goods carried by the carrier is unclear. The former construction is preferable, because the rights of those interested in the other consignments are protected by Art. 12(5)(b). *Contra* Hill & Messent, *CMR: Contracts for the International Carriage of Goods by Road* (2nd ed., 1995), 85.

[Add to the end of paragraph]
or, when the goods having failed to arrive at the contractual destination, the consignee seeks to enforce his rights under the contract of carriage.[50a] When instructions are given to the carrier in accordance with the Convention, the carrier is obliged to obey them.[50b] A failure to comply with valid instructions will render the carrier liable for all resulting loss or damage.[50c] When the right of disposal is exercised, it is exercised without regard to the requirements of contracts other than the contract of carriage.[50d] This right may be exercised in breach of the contract of sale,[50e] although the right of disposal may be instrumental in passing property in the goods being carried.[50f]

[50a] Arts. 12(2) and 13(1). If the consignee exercises the right of disposal by nominating another consignee, that new consignee cannot name yet another consignee (Art. 12(4)), unless it is the original consignee (*Anon.*, Arrond. Amsterdam 16.2.66 S. & S. No. 69). The consignment note may provide that the consignee has the right of disposal from the time the consignment note is drawn up: Art. 12(3). It is only in this last circumstance that the consignee is obliged to produce a copy of the consignment note in exercising the right of disposal: Art. 12(5)(a).

[50b] Arts. 12(1) and (2).

[50c] Art. 12(7).

[50d] *cf. Kala Limited v. International Freight Services (U.K.) Ltd*, unreported, June 7, 1988.

[50e] Benjamin, *Sale of Goods* (4th ed., 1992), para. 21–062.

[50f] *Aqualon (UK) Ltd v. Vallana Shipping Corporation* [1994] 1 Lloyd's Rep. 669, 677. The right of disposal provided for in the CMR Convention must be distinguished from the right of disposal referred to in the Sale of Goods Act 1979, s.19.

[Insert new paragraph at end]

35–143A **Delivery.** The consignment note must specify the destination of the goods and the name and address of the consignee.[50g] With this information, it should be possible for the carrier to deliver the goods in accordance with the contract of carriage.[50h] The consignee has the right to call for delivery of the goods. Under Article 13(1), the consignee is entitled to take delivery of the goods and the second copy of the consignment note upon production by the consignee of a receipt.[50i] Nothing more is required from the consignee.[50j] There is therefore little safeguard for the carrier if faced with a demand for delivery by a plausible, but fraudulent, consignee.[50k] The carrier must not knowingly or recklessly deliver the goods to the wrong person.[50l] Further, if the carrier's suspicions about the credentials of the "consignee" are aroused, the carrier must explore whether these suspicions are justified.[50m] The carrier must exercise a high degree of care that the person to whom he proposes to deliver the goods is the named consignee.[50n] If the carriage or the delivery of the goods is rendered impossible, the carrier must seek instructions from the person entitled to dispose of the goods.[50o] If the goods still are in transit, the carrier may perform the contract taking such steps which seem to the carrier to be in the best interests of the person entitled to dispose of the goods.[50p] If the carriage or delivery remains impossible, the carrier may avail himself of the rights of unloading, storage and sale referred to in Article 16.[50q]

[50g] Arts. 6(1)(d) and (e).

[50h] If the carrier does not have adequate information in this regard, he is obliged (at least as a matter of English law) to make reasonable enquiries and take reasonable steps to locate the place of delivery and the consignee.

[50i] And payment of or security for charges outstanding and shown on the face of the consignment note: Art. 13(2).

[50j] Contrast the use of bills of lading and warehouse warrants.

[50k] Given the liability regime imposed by the Convention: *infra*, §35–144.

[50l] *Sze Hai Tong Bank Co. v. Rambler* [1959] A.C. 576; *Anon.* Court of Cassation, France (1991) 26 ETL 359. See also *Lacey's Footwear (Wholesale) Ltd v. Bowler International Freight Ltd*, *The Times*, May 12, 1997, where the driver delivered the goods to thieves notwithstanding being instructed otherwise; in this case, the carrier was held to be guilty of wilful misconduct because of the act of the driver by virtue of Art. 3.

[50m] *cf. Stephenson v. Hart* (1828) 4 Bing. 475.

[50n] *infra*, §35–146. *cf.* the common law position: *M'Kean v. M'Ivor* (1870) L.R. 6 Ex. 30; Clarke, *International Carriage of Goods By Road: CMR* (2nd ed. 1991), para. 35.

[50o] Arts. 14(1), 15(1) and 15(3).

[50p] Art. 14(2).

[50q] *infra*, §35–158.

Loss, damage and delay

[*Add to note 54*]   **35–144**
affirmed on other grounds: [1995] 1 Lloyd's Rep. 297. See also *Anon.* 14.7.93 (1993) 28 E.T.L. 917, where it was held that a claim based on inaccurate information provided by the carrier as to the location and expected arrival time of his vehicle was a claim under national law and not under the Convention. The Court of Appeal has confirmed that the CMR regime is

inapplicable to personal injury suffered in the course of carriage: *Noble v. RH Group Limited*, unreported, February 5, 1993.

35–145 [*Insert new reference to "agreed time-limit", line 2*]

NOTE 56a: This time limit will be binding, provided that it has been agreed, even if it has not been included in the consignment note: *Anon.* BGH 30.9.93 (1994) 29 E.T.L. 97; *cf.* Art. 6(2)(f). This is not surprising, given Art. 5.

The carrier's exemptions from liability: Article 17(2)

35–146 [*Insert new reference to "neglect of the claimant", line 5*]

NOTE 62a: Whether the word "claimant" in this context refers to the person bringing the claim or those interested in the goods (that is, any person who might bring a claim under the contract) is unclear and subject to debate (Hill & Messent, *op. cit.*, 109). Notwithstanding the unfortunate language used, the purpose of the Convention is to provide a defence to the carrier in circumstances where those interested in the goods or possessed of the right of disposal are responsible for the losses claimed. It is suggested that the latter construction is preferable (*Anon.* App. Paris, December 2, 1981 (1982) BT 73). Otherwise, absurd situations may arise, for example, where the carrier is faced with a claim by both the sender and the consignee. If the former construction were correct, the carrier could not avoid liability (if no other defence were available). If the sender or consignee is prejudiced by the latter construction, he might have a right of action against the other under the relevant contract between them. This broad interpretation is not so broad as to defeat claims against the carrier which clearly are not contemplated by the Convention. See, for example, *Noble v. RH Group Limited*, unreported, February 5, 1993.

[*Add to note 63: page* [503]]
cf. Centrocoop Export-Import SA v. Brit European Transport Ltd [1984] 2 Lloyd's Rep. 618.

[*Add to note 64: page* [504]]
cf. Anon., Hof. Antwerpen, February 23, 1992 (1993) 28 E.T.L. 293.

[*Add to note 65*]
See *Walek & Co. v. Chapman & Ball (International) Ltd* [1980] 2 Lloyd's Rep. 279. In addition, the carrier will not be able to avoid liability if the vehicle is unsuitable for the carriage of the particular goods in the carrier's charge: *Anon.*, Cass., December 22, 1994 (1994) 29 E.T.L. 669.

[*Add to note 66*]
cf. Sidney G Jones Ltd v. Martin Bencher Ltd [1986] 1 Lloyd's Rep. 54.

[*Insert in text, new reference at* "with the utmost care", *line 15*]

NOTE 66a: *J J Silber Ltd v. Islander Trucking Ltd* [1985] 2 Lloyd's Rep. 243, 247.

[Add to note 67]
In *GL Cicatiello SRL v. Anglo European Shipping Services Ltd* [1994] 1 Lloyd's Rep. 678, the Court rejected the claimants' suggestions that the carrier should have had installed a variety of security devices, had a second driver and sought a secure lorry park on the motorway from Rome to Naples, because the loss would have occurred in any event. *cf. M Bardiger Ltd v. Halberg Spedition APS*, unreported, October 26, 1990; *National Semiconductors (U.K.) Ltd v. UPS Ltd* [1996] 2 Lloyd's Rep. 212.

The carrier's exemptions from liability: Article 17(4)

[Add to note 68: page [505]]
cf. Anon. App. Paris 19.10.93 (1993) BT 792. See also *Aquascutum Ltd v. Europa Freight Corporation*, unreported, November 20, 1985.

35–147

[Add to note 69, third paragraph, line 5, after "whole operation"]
even if that carrier is a successive carrier: *Anon.* Hof. Brussel, February 7, 1992 (1993) 28 E.T.L. 286.

[Delete from note 69 fourth paragraph and substitute]
Art. 8 requires the carrier to check the condition of the goods and their packaging. Further, it has been held that Art. 17(4)(c) does not exonerate a carrier from checking the stowage of the goods performed by the sender. If the carrier performs the carriage, notwithstanding obvious inadequacies or defects in the stowage, the carrier will be liable for the resultant damage: *Anon.*, Cass. 1.12.92 (1993) 28 E.T.L. 618; *GIE La Réunion Européene v. SA Warin*, Cass., 31.1.95 (1995) 30 E.T.L. 688. However, it may be that the carrier is under no obligation to check the loading or stowage of the goods, if adequately performed by one who is accustomed to such operations (*i.e.* a specialist): *Anon.* Rechtbank van Koophandel te Antwerpen, May 6, 1993 (1993) 28 E.T.L. 768.

[Add to note 70]
As to the breadth of this defence, see *W Donald & Son (Wholesale Meat Contractors) Ltd v. Continental Freeze Ltd* [1984] S.L.T. 182.

[Add new reference after "carriage of livestock"*]*

NOTE 70a: See art. 18(5) and *Hans Johan Kosta v. Samson Transport Co. A/S* (1997) 32 E.T.L. 230 (Denmark).

[Add to note 71 at end]
contra GIE La Réunion Européene v. SA Warin, Cass., January 31, 1995

(1995) 30 E.T.L. 688. See also *Hans Johan Kosta v. Samson Transport Co.
A/S* (1997) 32 E.T.L. 230 (Denmark).

35–148   *[Insert as new paragraph at end: page* [506]]
35–148A   **Sender's liability.** The Convention identifies specified instances of liability
which may attach to the sender under the contract of carriage. For example,
the sender will be liable for loss, damage and expense caused by any
inaccuracies in or inadequacies of the consignment note,[73a] defective packing
of the goods entrusted to the carrier,[73b] the absence, irregularity or
inadequacy of documents or information required to be given to the carrier
for the purposes of Customs or other formalities[73c] and arising out of the
carriage of dangerous goods, at least where the sender has failed to inform
the carrier, and the carrier is not aware, of the dangerous nature of the
goods.[73d] Any other liability of the sender falls to be determined in
accordance with the contract of carriage and national law.[73e] The sender is
also liable for freight (unless the contract provides otherwise). Such liability
is not, however, one which can form the subject-matter of a set-off against
any liability owed by the carrier to the sender.[73f] Unlike the liability of a
carrier under the CMR regime,[73g] compensation for the sender's liability is
not subject to limitation.[73h]

[73a] Art. 7(1).

[73b] Art. 10.

[73c] Art. 11(2).

[73d] Art. 22(2).

[73e] *cf. Shell Chemicals U.K. Ltd v. P & O Roadtanks Ltd* [1993] 1 Lloyd's Rep. 114;
affirmed on other grounds [1995] 1 Lloyd's Rep. 297.

[73f] *R H & D International Ltd v. I A S Animal Air Services Ltd* [1984] 1 W.L.R. 573;
United Carriers Ltd v. Heritage Food Group (U.K.) Ltd [1995] 2 Lloyd's Rep. 269.

[73g] Arts. 23–26; *infra,* §35–149.

[73h] *cf. Shell Chemicals U.K. Ltd v. P & O Roadtanks Ltd* [1993] 1 Lloyd's Rep. 114;
affirmed on other grounds [1995] 1 Lloyd's Rep. 297. However, the time limitation
provisions of the CMR Convention do apply to claims against the sender: Art.
32(1)(c); for example, see *Anon.* Arrond. Rotterdam June 5, 1992 (1993) S. & S. No.
107.

Upper financial limits of liability and measure of damages

35–149   *[Add to note 75 after "art. 23(2)": page* [506]]
Such exchange, market or normal value is a reference to the standard rate
for the goods and ignores the peculiar situation of the goods in question:
Anon., BGH October 15, 1992 (1993) 28 E.T.L. 740.

[*And add at end of note*]
Contra Anon., Supreme Court of Denmark May 4, 1987 (1994) 29 E.T.L. 360.

[*Add to note 79 at end: page* [507]]
; as do premiums for the insurance of the goods carried: *M Bardiger Ltd v. Halberg Spedition Aps*, unreported, October 26, 1990. The plaintiff will be entitled to a refund under art. 23(4) where the carrier is guilty of wilful misconduct, although the limitation "no further damages shall be payable" will not, in that event, apply: *Lacey's Footwear (Wholesale) Ltd v. Bowler International Freight Ltd*, unreported, March 17, 1995; aff'd *The Times*, May 12, 1997.

[*Add to note 82*]
The compensation which may be awarded pursuant to this provision need not be the carriage charges themselves; the compensation is limited in quantum to the amount of those charges. The provision refers to "damage" resulting from delay. It is suggested that this is a reference to any financial deprivation suffered by the claimant, rather than to physical damage sustained by the goods: *Anon.*, BGH October 15, 1992 (1993) 28 E.T.L. 740. The claimant may recover both damages sustained directly or losses incurred as a result of his liability to another party: *Anon.*, BGH September 30, 1993 (1994) 29 E.T.L. 97.

[*Add to text after note 83*]
The carrier is also liable to the sender for compensation for an amount representing the "cash on delivery" charge,[83a] in the event that the carrier fails to collect that charge.[83b]

[83a] Which should have been entered on the face of the consignment note (Art. 6(2)(c)). Given Art. 4, it is unlikely that the failure to enter the COD charge on the consignment note will deprive any contractual requirement that the charge be collected against delivery to the consignee of its force.

[83b] Art. 21. In *Eastern Kayam Carpets Ltd v. Eastern United Freight Ltd*, unreported, December 6, 1983, the Court held that such a charge was not limited to freight and could extend to the price of the goods. The charge to be collected by the carrier could be in cash or in the form of a draft (*Anon.*, Arrond. Breda 16.2.69 (1970) 5 ETL 670). If the carrier is ordered to deliver the goods against receipt of a certified cheque, this order must be obeyed with all reasonable care to ensure that the carrier receives a certified cheque: *Anon.*, Hof van Cassatie van België 18.2.94 (1994) 29 ETL 464; *cf. Eastern Kayam Carpets Ltd v. Eastern United Freight Ltd, supra*; *Anon.*, BGH October 25, 1995 (1996) 31 E.T.L. 404. The COD charge would not include any document which did not represent payment of the charge (*Eastern Kayam Carpets Ltd v. Eastern United Freight Ltd, supra*).

[*Add new reference after* "excluding or limiting": *line 16*]
NOTE 84a: Art. 29(1); Although the carrier may still continue to rely on those provisions which "fix" his liability such as Art. 23(1), (2) and 27(1), (2): *Lacey's Footwear (Wholesale) Ltd v. Bowler International Freight Ltd, supra; cf.* Art. 28(1).

Where Art. 29 applies to remove any limitation on liability, the plaintiff may recover loss of profits (*Lacey's Footwear (Wholesale) Ltd v. Bowler International Freight Ltd, supra*) or interest in excess of the five per cent limit provided for in Art. 27 (*B Paradise Ltd v. Islander Trucking Ltd*, unreported, January 28, 1985).

[*Add to note 85: page* [508]]
   cf. M Bardiger Ltd v. Halberg Spedition APS, unreported, October 26, 1990; *Anon.*, Rechtbank van Koophandel te Brussel 25.5.92 (1993) 28 ETL 762. See also *National Semiconductors (U.K.) Ltd v. UPS Ltd* [1996] 2 Lloyd's Rep. 212, 214–215; *Lacey's Footwear (Wholesale) Ltd v. Bowler International Freight Ltd, supra*, where the carrier's employee's misconduct was not intentional, but "reckless carelessness"; *The Thomas Cook Group Ltd v. Air Malta Company Ltd*, unreported, May 6, 1997 (Warsaw Convention, Art. 25). *cf. BVBA Transport Nys v. NV Cigna Insurance Company of Europe E.A.* (1996) 31 E.T.L. 840 (Brussels); *Nordland Transportkontor GmbH v. Storebrand Skadeforsikring AS* (1996) 31 E.T.L. 563 (Norway); *Anon.* BGH May 18, 1995 (1996) 31 E.T.L. 703. In *Antwerp United Diamonds BVBA v. Air Europe* [1995] 2 Lloyd's Rep. 224, the Court of Appeal held, in the context of the Carriage By Air Act 1961, that the "misconduct" provision (similar to Art. 29) would permit compensation to be awarded in excess of the limit imposed by virtue of a special declaration of interest (which may be made under CMR pursuant to Arts. 24 and 26).

[*Insert as new paragraphs at end of text*]

35–149A   The CMR provisions relating to the limitation of compensation apply only in the event the carrier is liable for loss of, damage to or delay in the arrival of the goods placed in the carrier's charge.[85a] The CMR provisions are relevant whether the carrier's liability arises under the contract or outside of the contract,[85b] for example in tort or restitution. In respect of any other liability of the carrier[85c] or any liability of any other party to the contract of carriage or at all, the CMR regime concerning compensation is inapplicable.

35–149B   A claimant is entitled to claim interest on the compensation payable. Article 27(1)[85d] sets the interest recoverable at 5 per cent per annum and provides that interest shall accrue from the date on which a claim in writing was sent to the carrier, or in the absence of such a claim, from the date of the institution of legal proceedings. The provision appears expressly to disallow interest accruing before the written claim is made or legal proceedings are commenced.[85e] Such a claim does not have to be quantified; a general intimation of intention to hold the carrier liable is sufficient.[85f] The date on which legal proceedings are commenced, so far as English legal procedure is concerned, is the date on which the writ is issued.[85g]

[85a] Arts. 23–26.

[85b] Art. 28(1).

[85c] For example, the failure by the carrier to perform the contract at all: *Anon.*, Comm. Carpentras 19.2.93 (1994) BT 636; *Anon.*, App. Toulouse 29.3.94 (1994) BT

736; *cf. Anon.*, BGH 3.7.74 (1975) 10 E.T.L. 75. See also *Shell Chemicals U.K. Ltd v. P & O Roadtanks Ltd* [1993] 1 Lloyd's Rep. 114; affirmed on other grounds [1995] 1 Lloyd's Rep. 297; *Anon.*, BGH 14.7.93 (1993) 28 E.T.L. 917; *Noble v. RH Group Limited*, unreported, February 5, 1993, where the Court of Appeal commented upon a late Respondents' Notice, holding that the Convention was not intended to regulate the carrier's liability for personal injury occurring during the carriage. See *Lacey's Footwear (Wholesale) Ltd v. Bowler International Freight Ltd*, *supra*, as to the carrier's failure to comply with his obligation to insure the goods.

[85d] This provision creates an entitlement to interest. The Court has no discretion in the matter: *Elektronska Industrija Oour TVA v. Transped Oour Kintinentalna Spedicna* [1986] 1 Lloyd's Rep. 49, 53.

[85e] It seems also that interest at 5 per cent will run until payment is made (Art. 27(2)). Accordingly, it is unlikely that interest at the Judgments Act 1838 rate will be allowed, although it appears that such interest was awarded at first instance in *James Buchanan & Co. Ltd v. Babco Forwarding and Shipping (U.K.) Ltd* [1978] 1 Lloyd's Rep. 119 (H.L.).

[85f] *William Tatton and Co. Ltd v. Ferrymasters Ltd* [1974] 1 Lloyd's Rep. 203, 207; *Worldwide Carriers Ltd v. Ardtran International Ltd* [1983] 1 Lloyd's Rep. 61, 66; *ICI plc v. MAT Transport Ltd* [1987] 1 Lloyd's Rep. 354, 361.

[85g] *Sidney G Jones Ltd v. Martin Bencher Ltd* [1986] 1 Lloyd's Rep. 54. *cf. Dresser (UK) Ltd v. Falcongate Freight Management Ltd* [1991] 2 Lloyd's Rep. 557, where in the context of the Civil Jurisdiction and Judgments Act 1982, service of the writ was held to be the operative date.

The parties to the contract

[*Add to note 86: page* [508]]   35–150
See *M Bardiger Ltd v. Halberg Spedition Aps*, unreported, October 26, 1990. CMR, however, will not apply to an existing relationship between the carrier and a purchaser of the goods carried, where the latter is not interested in the contract of carriage: *Atlanta Companies, Judge & Dolph Ltd v. Pvba Transport Leopold Laureys & Zonen* (1996) 31 E.T.L. 843 (Ghent).

[*Add to note 87*]
Noble v. RH Group Limited, unreported, February 5, 1993; *Lacey's Footwear (Wholesale) Ltd v. Bowler International Freight Ltd*, unreported, March 17, 1995, aff'd *The Times*, May 12, 1997. See also *Anon.*, Tribunal Supremo (Civil) de España 14.7.87 (1995) 30 E.T.L. 678.

[*Add to note 88*]
which affords to such third parties the benefit of the CMR exclusion or limitation of liability provisions in relation to extra-contractual liability. Although the Convention does not so provide, it would be reasonable to

assume that this protection of the exclusion and limitation provisions would extend to the third parties for whom the carrier is responsible under Art. 3.

[Insert new reference to "the Convention", line 21]

NOTE 90a: See *M Bardiger Ltd v. Halberg Spedition Aps*, unreported, October 26, 1990, where it was held that the CMR Convention does not apply to freight forwarders and any contract which they make, other than a contract of carriage.

[Add to note 91 at beginning]
Infra, §35–004C.

[Add to note 91, line 2, after "on the facts)."]
In *Kala Limited v. International Freight Services (U.K.) Ltd*, unreported, June 7, 1988, the parties accepted that the issuer of a through bill of lading, which provided that the issuer of the bill contracted, not as a carrier, but as a forwarding agent, who was named as the sender on a CMR note with the actual carrier, was not in fact the carrier and that the issuer had not entered into a contract of carriage.

35–151   *[Insert new reference to "claiming under him", line 6: page* [509]]

NOTE 91a: Art. 12(7). It is likely that the sender who has had the right of disposal would retain a title to sue, notwithstanding that the right of disposal has been acquired by the consignee. That is, both the sender and the consignee (and indeed any subrogated insurers) may claim damages on the basis of Art. 12: *Anon.*, Hof. Brussel 7.2.92 (1993) 28 E.T.L. 286. See the discussion in Hill & Messent, *CMR: Contracts for the International Carriage of Goods by Road* (2nd ed., 1995), 89–90.

[Add to note 92]
The consignee also has a right of action where his identity may be deduced from a document attached to the consignment note: *Anon.*, Hof. Antwerpen February 23, 1993 (1993) 28 E.T.L. 934.

Successive carriers

35–152   *[Add to note 93]*
In England, it has been held that a sea carrier, who was sub-contracted by the road carrier who accepted the goods, could be a successive carrier under Art. 34, if the sea carrier became a party to the single contract for the whole of the carriage: *Dresser (U.K.) Ltd v. Falcongate Freight Management Ltd* (1991) 26 E.T.L. 798; *contra. NV Agfa Gevaert v. NV Rhenus Belgium*, App. Anvers. March 15, 1989 (1989) 24 E.T.L. 574.

[*Add to note 96: page* [510]]
cf. NV Travaca v. Roba Ltd (1996) 31 E.T.L. 545 (Belgium).

[*Add to note 97*]
M Bardiger Ltd v. Halberg Spedition APS, unreported, October 26, 1990;
Union des Assurances de Paris v. Planza Transports SA, Tribunal Federal
Suisse 22.11.83 (1995) 30 E.T.L. 675. A successive carrier will be responsible
for the acts of a sub-contractor (Art. 3). The sender has no right of action
against a sub-contractor who is not also a successive carrier, under the
contract of carriage between the sender and the carrier, at least under the
CMR Convention and English law, although there may be a right of action
under another national law. The sender might have an extra-contractual
claim against the sub-contractor, for example a claim arising out of the
bailment of the goods to the sub-contractor, which bailment may be subject
to the terms of the CMR contract of carriage (see, for example, *The Pioneer
Container* [1994] 1 Lloyd's Rep. 593; *The Mahkutai* [1996] 2 Lloyd's Rep. 1);
Spectra International plc v. Hayesoak Ltd [1997] 1 Lloyd's 153; revd. on other
grounds, unreported, April 30, 1997). In the event of an extra-contractual
claim against the sub-contractor, the latter can rely on the Convention's
limitation and exclusion provisions (Art. 28(2)). If the sender has no right of
action against the sub-contractor, he can sue the carrier, who is responsible
for the sub-contractor's acts and omissions.

[*Add to note 98*]   **35–153**
Aqualon (U.K.) Ltd v. Vallana Shipping Corporation [1994] 1 Lloyd's
Rep. 669, 673. It is possible that s.14(2)(d) of the 1965 Act extends the
contract to persons for whom the carrier is responsible under Art. 3: *M
Bardiger Ltd v. Halberg Spedition Aps*, unreported, October 26, 1990;
contra, Aqualon (UK) Ltd v. Vallana Shipping Corporation [1994] 1 Lloyd's
Rep. 669, 673. In *Harrison & Sons Ltd v. RT Steward Transport Ltd* (1993) 28
E.T.L. 747, the Court held, relying on the terms of s.14(2)(c) of the 1965 Act,
that a "carrier" for the purposes of Art. 39 included a carrier who became a
party to the contract of carriage whether by virtue of Art. 34 "or otherwise".

[*Insert new reference to "ordinary meaning", line 8*]

NOTE 98a: In *Harrison & Sons Ltd v. RT Steward Transport Ltd* (1993) 28 E.T.L.
747, the Court held that the "consignment note" referred to in Art. 34 was a reference
to the original consignment note issued by the first carrier, and not a consignment
note issued during an intermediate leg of the contractual journey. *cf. Dresser (U.K.)
Ltd v. Falcongate Freight Management Ltd* (1991) 26 E.T.L. 798.

[*Add to note 1*]
Harrison & Sons Ltd v. RT Steward Transport Ltd (1993) 28 E.T.L. 747;

Dresser (U.K.) Ltd v. Falcongate Freight Management Ltd (1991) 26 E.T.L. 798.

Which carrier may be sued by those interested in the goods

35–154   [*Add to note 3*]
M Bardiger Ltd v. Halberg Spedition APS, unreported, October 26, 1990. The restrictions of Art. 36 do not apply in the event of a counterclaim or the raising of a set-off in proceedings concerning the contract of carriage. As to the difficulties of raising a set-off against a claim for freight, see *United Carriers Ltd v. Heritage Food Group (U.K.) Ltd* [1995] 2 Lloyd's Rep. 269.

[*Add to note 5: page* [511]]
However, the carrier must accept the original consignment note in order to be treated as a successive carrier within the meaning of Chapter VI of the Convention: *Harrison & Sons Ltd v. RT Steward Transport Ltd* (1993) 28 E.T.L. 747; *Dresser (U.K.) Ltd v. Falcongate Freight Management Ltd* (1991) 26 E.T.L. 798. In France, it has been held that where a carrier has been instructed to perform the last leg of the carriage and that carrier does not participate in, but sub-contracts, the actual performance of this last leg, that carrier will not be a last carrier for the purposes of Art. 36: *Skandia Insurance Company Ltd v. Theo Adams Expeditie en Transport*, Cass. 3.5.94 (1995) 30 E.T.L. 685.

35–155   [*Add to note 6*]
In this respect, the allocation of jurisdiction pursuant to rules of the Civil Jurisdiction and Judgments Act 1982 is inappropriate, given the terms of Art. 57 of the Brussels Convention on Jurisdiction and the Enforcement of Judgments in Civil and Commercial Matters, 1968 (implemented by the 1982 Act): *Harrison & Sons Ltd v. RT Steward Transport Ltd* (1993) 28 E.T.L. 747.

Carrier's rights of recovery from other carriers

35–156   [*Add to note 8*]
ITT Schaub-Lorenz Vertriebsgesellschaft mbH v. Birkart Johann Internationale Spedition GmbH & Co. KG [1988] 1 Lloyd's Rep. 487, 494.

35–157   [*Delete from note 17, the third sentence, and substitute: page* [512]]
It is presently open to question whether the jurisdiction provided for in Art. 39(2) is compulsory and exclusive: *Arctic Electronics (U.K.) Ltd v. McGregor Sea and Air Services* [1985] 2 Lloyd's Rep. 510; *contra Harrison & Sons Ltd v. RT Steward Transport Ltd* (1993) 28 E.T.L. 747. Proceedings brought pursuant to Art. 39(2) would not require the leave of the Court under R.S.C. Order 11, rule 1(2): *Harrison & Sons Ltd v. RT Steward*

Transport Ltd, supra. Whilst the carrier from whom a contribution is sought must be a party to the one contract of carriage (*Arctic Electronics (U.K.) Ltd v. McGregor Sea and Air Services* [1985] 2 Lloyd's Rep. 510), it is not necessary that such a carrier is a successive carrier within the meaning of the Convention (*Harrison & Sons Ltd v. RT Steward Transport Ltd, supra*). See *ante*, n. 98.

Extinction of claims

[*Delete whole paragraph with notes 21–25 and substitute*]　　　　　　**35–159**

Reservations at delivery. If, upon taking delivery of the goods, the consignee checks with the carrier the condition of the goods, the result of that check will be conclusive evidence of the condition of the goods at the time of delivery, unless any loss or damage sustained by the goods is not apparent and the consignee has sent to the carrier reservations in writing about the goods within seven days of delivery.[21] Where the consignee takes delivery of the goods without checking their condition with the carrier and without providing reservations to the carrier, the fact that delivery has been accepted shall constitute prima facie evidence that the condition of the goods is that which is represented in the consignment note.[22] Such reservations must be sent to the carrier immediately (in the case of apparent loss or damage[23]) or in writing within seven days (in the case of loss or damage which is not apparent) and provide a general indication of the loss or damage sustained by the goods. Such prima facie evidence may be controverted.[24] The acceptance of delivery in these circumstances does not mean that the consignee loses any right of action because of any failure to make a reservation.[25] Further, the taking of delivery will be evidence of the condition of the goods only so far as the interest of the consignee is concerned. No compensation is payable for delay unless a written reservation is sent to the carrier within 21 days from the time at which the goods were placed at the disposal of the consignee.[25a] A failure to send such a reservation in the case of delay will result in the loss of a right of action.[25b]

Note 21: Art. 30(2).

Note 22: Art. 30(1). The provision is inelegantly drafted by the use of the word "or", rather than "and". Invisible damage, such as contamination of chemicals, can constitute inherent vice and can be the subject of reservations made within seven days of delivery of the goods. Provided that such reservations are made within that period, the absence of any protest in the consignment note at the time of delivery does not give rise to the presumption in the carrier's favour under Art. 30(1): *English and American Insurance Co. Ltd v. Transport Nagels* (1977) 12 E.T.L. 420 (Commercial Court, Antwerp). See also Clarke [1982] L.M.C.L.Q. 533.

Note 23: A verbal reservation is sufficient in the case of apparent damage: *Société Coop UTRA.C. v. SPRL Legrand* (1970) 5 E.T.L. 716 (Court of Appeal, Liège). Reservations are "sent" to the carrier within the meaning of Art. 30(1) if they are noted on the copy of the consignment note in the possession of and to be kept by the carrier: *Anon.* [1978] L.M.C.L.Q. 517 (Court of Cassation, France).

NOTE 24: *Anon.*, Hof. Brussel February 7, 1992 (1993) 28 E.T.L. 286; *Anon.*, App. Douai September 7, 1994 (1994) BT 623.

NOTE 25: *cf. Anon.*, BGH November 14, 1991 (1993) 28 E.T.L. 265.

[25a] Art. 30(3).

[25b] *Anon.*, BGH November 14, 1991 (1993) 28 E.T.L. 265, where the Court also held that the exceptions provided in Art. 29 were inapplicable to situations covered by Art. 30(3).

Limitation of actions

35–160   [*Add to note 29: page* [514]]
ICI plc v. MAT Transport Ltd [1987] 1 Lloyd's Rep. 354, 360.

[*Add to note 30, line 2, after "114, 116"*]
affirmed [1995] 1 Lloyd's Rep. 297, 301.

[*Add to note 31, at end of third paragraph*]
In order to suspend the running of the limitation period, the claim holding the carrier liable must be notified to the carrier in an unambiguous manner by or on behalf of the person entitled to bring the claim and must be accompanied by such supporting documents so as to enable the carrier to define and pronounce his response to the claim, although it is not necessary that the claim describe precisely the level of compensation claimed: *Anon.*, OGH 29.9.94 (1995) 30 E.T.L. 211. *cf. Sprl Transports Cremer v. SA van de Casteele et Cie* (1996) 31 E.T.L. 833 (Brussels).

[*And add to end of note*]
The rejection must be clear and unambiguous so that the claimant must understand that, time having been suspended since the claim was made, there has now come the time when the claimant must decide whether to start proceedings: *Zerowatt SpA v. International Express Company Limited*, unreported, October 6, 1989; *Microfine Minerals and Chemicals Ltd v. Transferry Shipping Co. Ltd* [1991] 2 Lloyd's Rep. 630. The mere non-acceptance or non-admission of the claim is not sufficient. If the rejection is communicated in circumstances attracting privilege (for example, being marked "without prejudice"), the rejection will not restart the running of time within the meaning of Article 32(2): *Zerowatt SpA v. International Express Company Limited, supra*. In order to constitute a valid rejection for the purposes of Article 32(2), the documents which were attached to the claim must be returned to the claimant; this requirement is not limited to such original documents as are provided by the claimant, but includes photocopies: *Microfine Minerals and Chemicals Ltd v. Transferry Shipping Co. Ltd, supra*.

[Add to note 35 at end: page [515]]   **35–161**
See also *United Carriers Ltd v. Heritage Food Group (U.K.) Ltd* [1995] 2
Lloyd's Rep. 269.

[Add to note 38]
Harrison & Sons Ltd v. RT Steward Transport Ltd (1993) 28 E.T.L. 747. *Cf.*
NV Travaca v. Roba Ltd (1996) 31 E.T.L. 545 (Belgium).

Arbitration

[Rename paragraph "Jurisdiction/Arbitration". Add at start]   **35–162**
Article 31(1) prescribes those States in which legal proceedings may be
brought in connection with any contract of carriage to which the CMR
Convention applies, namely the State of the residence of the defendant, the
State where the goods are taken over by the carrier, the place designated for
delivery of the goods or the State which has been agreed by the parties.[39a]
This is intended to provide a self-contained code for the allocation of
jurisdiction,[39b] so that the Brussels Convention on Jurisdiction and the
Enforcement of Judgments in Civil and Commercial Matters, 1968 is
inapplicable.[39c] In the event of more than one set of proceedings being
commenced in more than one State, Article 31(2) provides that the later
action will not be entertained if it concerns the same parties and is brought
on the same grounds.[39d] The plaintiff may bring proceedings against the first
carrier, the last carrier or the carrier who was performing that part of the
carriage where the relevant loss, damage or delay has occurred.[39e] When the
defendant carrier seeks recourse against other carriers concerned in the
carriage, such action is governed by Article 39(2), which is more restrictive
than Article 31(1). Such recourse must (not may, as suggested by the
provision itself) be brought in the State of residence of one of those
carriers.[39f] Once proceedings are instituted against one carrier, the other
carriers may be joined in the same action. It appears not to be open to the
carriers to agree an alternative forum for the determination of the carrier's
recourse claim, except possibly arbitration.[39g]

[39a] Art. 31(1) does not lay down any formal requirements for any jurisdiction
agreement between the parties (*cf.* Art. 17 of the Brussels Convention on
Jurisdiction and the Enforcement of Judgments in Civil and Commercial Matters,
1968 (implemented by the Civil Jurisdiction and Judgments Act, 1982)). Whether the
factual requirement of an "agreement" on jurisdiction will be construed in the
manner adopted by the European Court of Justice in the context of Art. 17 of the
Brussels Convention is unclear. There is much to be said in favour of a consistent
approach, given the difficulties posed by multi-modal transport involving carriage by
road (which in isolation would be governed by CMR) and by sea (which in isolation
would require jurisdiction agreements to comply with Art. 17 of the Brussels
Convention).

[39b] *Arctic Electronics (U.K.) Ltd v. McGregor Sea and Air Services* [1985] 2 Lloyd's
Rep. 510, 514.

[39c] Art. 57 of the Brussels Convention. See *Harrison & Sons Ltd v. RT Steward Transport Ltd* (1993) 28 E.T.L. 747.

[39d] *cf.* the French text of the CMR Convention: "*pour la même cause*". Article 21 of the Brussels Convention would be inapplicable. Similarly, Art. 22 (dealing with "related proceedings") should have no application, given Art. 57. This question was identified but not resolved in *Harrison & Sons Ltd v. RT Steward Transport Ltd* (1993) 28 E.T.L. 747.

[39e] Art. 36.

[39f] *Ante*, §35–157 n. 17. *Harrison & Sons Ltd v. RT Steward Transport Ltd*, unreported, (1993) 28 E.T.L. 747; *Cummins Engine Co. Ltd v. Davis Freight Forwarding (Hull) Ltd* [1981] 2 Lloyd's Rep. 402, 408–409; *contra Arctic Electronics (U.K.) Ltd v. McGregor Sea and Air Services* [1985] 2 Lloyd's Rep. 510, adopting the view of Eveleigh L.J. in *Cummins Engine Co. Ltd v. Davis Freight Forwarding (Hull) Ltd* [1981] 2 Lloyd's Rep. 402, 409. *cf.* Art. 40.

[39g] Art. 33, which gives force to an arbitration clause in the contract of carriage, will bind the parties to the contract of carriage. Such parties are identified in s.14(2)(c) of the 1965 Act.

[*Delete second and third sentence of note 40 and substitute: page* [516]]
By s.7(2) of the 1965 Act as amended, the time at which an arbitration is commenced is determined by the Arbitration Act 1996, s.14(3)–(5).

[*Delete note 42 and substitute: page 516*]
Arbitration Act 1996, s.9; *AB Bofors-UVA v. AB Skandia Transport*, *supra*, at 413.

No contracting out

35–163   [*Add to note 43 after "art. 41(1)."*]
Such provisions are invalidated only to the extent that the subject-matter of such provisions is governed by the CMR regime: *Noble v. RH Group Limited*, unreported, February 5, 1993, where it was held that liability of the carrier for accidents occurring during the unloading of the goods, as opposed to their carriage, and for personal injury was not intended to be regulated by the Convention and therefore any provisions dealing with such liability were not affected by Art. 41. *Quaere* whether unloading of goods may be equated with delivery so as to engage Art. 17; it would depend on whether the carrier is responsible for the unloading of the goods.

CHAPTER 36

CREDIT AND SECURITY

1. – The Consumer Credit Act 1974

Scope of Act

36–002   [*Add to note 1: page* [524]]
Harding, *Consumer Credit and Consumer Hire* (1995).

Regulations, orders etc.

36–006   [*Add to note 18 at end: page* [525]]
S.I. 1994 No. 2420; S.I. 1995 No. 1250; S.I. 1995 No. 2194; S.I. 1996 No. 1445; S.I. 1996 No. 3081; S.I. 1997 No. 211.

(a) *Terminology of the Act*

"Credit"

36–017   In *Legal and General Assurance Society v. Cooper*[a] it was held that an advance of monies against future commission did not constitute the provision of credit. But in *Storlink U.K. v. Thomas*,[b] where a contract for the supply of advertising services provided for payment in full on signing the contract with the alternative of paying by instalments, it was held that the facility of paying by instalments constituted deferment of a debt and the provision of credit.

[a] [1994] C.L.Y. 2656 (Cty.Ct.).

[b] [1996] 10 C.L. 98 (Cty.Ct.).

36–020   "Credit not exceeding £15,000"

[*Add to note 69: page* [529]]
Humberclyde Finance Ltd v. Thompson [1997] 1 C.L. 107 (C.A.).

"Multiple agreement"

36–045   See *National Home Loans Corpn plc v. Hannah* [1997] C.C.L.R. 7 (Cty.Ct.).

(c) *Seeking Business*

Advertising, etc.

36–058   [*Note 89: page* [547]]
The Consumer Credit (Quotations) Regulations 1989 were revoked by the Consumer Credit (Quotations) (Revocation) Regulations 1997 (S.I. 1997 No. 211), as from March 10, 1997.

[*Add to note 90*]
Rover Group Ltd v. Sumner [1995] C.C.L.R. 1.

(d) *Antecedent Negotiations*

"Antecedent negotiations"

[*Note 8: page* [548]]   **36–062**
See also *Williams (J.D.) & Co. v. McCauley Parsons and Jones* [1994]
C.C.L.R. 78 (C.A.); *Woodchester Equipment (Leasing) Ltd v. British
Association of Canned and Preserved Foods Importers and Distributors Ltd*
[1995] C.L.Y. 2459, C.A.; *PB Leasing Ltd v. Patel* [1995] C.C.L.R. 82
(Cty.Ct.).

[*Note 9: page* [549]]
U.D.T. v. Whitfield and First National Securities (now reported in [1987]
C.C.L.R. 60) was not followed in Scotland in *Powell v. Lloyds Bowmaker*
1996 S.L.T. (Sh.Ct.) 117.

(e) *The Agreement*

Failure to comply
See *Smerdon v. Ellis* [1997] 6 C.L. 128 (Cty.Ct.).   **36–070**

[*Note 91: page* [554]]   **36–071**
See *Moorgate Services Ltd v. Kabir*, *The Times*, April 25, 1995; [1995]
C.L.Y. 722, C.A.

(f) *Withdrawal and Cancellation*

Cancellable agreements

[*Note 18: page* [556]]   **36–079**
On the meaning of "representations", see *Moorgate Services Ltd v. Kabir*,
The Times, April 25, 1995; [1995] C.L.Y. 722, C.A.

Timeshare Act 1992

On the relationship between the Timeshare Act 1992 and the Consumer **36–082**
Credit Act 1974, see *Global Marketing Europe v. Berkshire C.C.*[a] The 1992

Act has been amended and extended by the Timeshare Regulations 1997 (S.I. 1997 No. 1081), implementing Council Directive 94/47.

[a] [1994] C.C.L.R. 150, Q.B.D.

(h) *Variation of Agreements*

Unilateral variation under a power in agreement

36–114   But see the Unfair Terms in Consumer Contracts Regulations 1994,[a] in particular Sched. 3, para. 1(j) and (k) and para. 2(b)(c). It is submitted that a term which complies with S.I. 1977 No. 328 (as amended) is not for that reason exempted from the Regulations by Sched. 1, para. (e).[b]

[a] S.I. 1994 No. 3159 (*ante*, §14–099).

[b] See Guest and Lloyd, *Encyclopedia of Consumer Credit Law*, §2–083.

(j) *Restrictions on Enforcement or Termination of Agreement*

Default notice

36–129   A default notice sent to the debtor by post but never received is duly served under s.176(2) of the Act: *Lombard North Central v. Power-Hines*.[a]

[a] [1995] C.C.L.R. 24 (Cty.Ct.).

(k) *Security*

Pledges

36–157   See Macleod, "Pawnbroking: A Regulatory Issue", [1995] J.B.L. 155.

(l) *Judicial Control*

Enforcement orders in case of infringement

36–162   In *PB Leasing Ltd v. Patel*[a] the county court judge refused to make an enforcement order where the hirers under a consumer hire agreement had signed the agreement without the financial details having been filled in and had not been given a copy of the agreement after they had signed it (contrary to sections 61 and 62 of the 1974 Act).

[a] [1995] C.C.L.R. 82 (Cty.Ct.). See also *Smerdon v. Ellis* [1997] 6 C.L. 128 (Cty.Ct.) (no enforcement order in light of multiple breaches of the Act and surrounding circumstances).

Time orders

36–165   [*Note 86: page* [590]]
In *Southern and District Finance Ltd v. Barnes, The Times*, April 19, 1995;

[1995] C.L.Y. 726, C.A., Leggatt L.J. stated that, once the creditor brings possession proceedings, then "as a matter of law as of common sense, he demands payment of the whole sum outstanding under the charge", whether or not the loan has actually been called in, and thus the court can reschedule the whole of the indebtedness.

In *Southern and District Finance Ltd v. Barnes*,[a] Leggatt L.J. stated that, when a time order was made, it would normally be made for a stipulated period on account of temporary financial difficulties. If, despite the giving of time, the debtor was unlikely to be able to resume repayment of the total indebtedness by at least the amount of the contractual instalments, no time order should be made. In such circumstances it would be more equitable to allow the regulated agreement to be enforced.   **36–166**

[a] *The Times*, April 19, 1995; [1995] C.L.Y. 726, C.A.

Power to impose conditions, or suspend operation of order

In *Southern and District Finance Ltd v. Barnes*,[a] Leggatt L.J. stated that, in the case of an agreement secured on land, if justice required the making of a time order, the court should suspend any possession order that it made so long as the terms of the time order were complied with.   **36–169**

[a] *The Times*, April 19, 1995; [1995] C.L.Y. 726, C.A.

Power to vary agreements and securities

[*Note 7: page* [592]]   **36–170**
The dispute referred to in this footnote was settled in *Southern and District Finance Ltd v. Barnes, The Times*, April 19, 1995; [1995] C.L.Y. 726, C.A., where it was held that the court had jurisdiction in consequence of a time order under s.129 to reduce the contractual rate of interest in rescheduling the debt.

(m) *Extortionate Credit Bargains*

Retrospective effect   **36–186**
In *First National Bank Plc v. Ann*[a] it was held that the limitation period in respect of a claim to re-open the credit agreement was, by virtue of section 9 of the Limitation Act 1980, six years and that the period ran from the date of the agreement.

[a] [1997] 2 C.L. 94 (Cty.Ct.).

(n) *Ancillary Credit Businesses*

Credit reference agency

36–194   See Howells, "Data Protection, Confidentiality, Unfair Contract Terms,
Consumer Protection and Credit Reference Agencies", [1995] J.B.L. 343.

2. – LOANS AND INTEREST

(a) Loans of Money

Borrower not personally liable

36–206   See *Levett v. Barclays Bank* [1995] 1 W.L.R. 1260.

[Insert new paragraph after note 25 in text: page [612]]

36–213A   **"No set-off" clauses.** A "no set-off" clause in a loan agreement is not
contrary to public policy or to the Supreme Court Act 1981, s.49(2).[a] But
such a clause might be held to be unenforceable in certain circumstances
under the Unfair Contract Terms Act 1977[b] or the Unfair Terms in
Consumer Contracts Regulations 1994.[c] The statutory set-off in a bankruptcy or winding-up is mandatory.[d]

[a] *Coca-Cola Financial Corpn v. Finsak International Ltd, The Times,* May 1, 1996,
C.A.

[b] See §14–048, note 97, of the Main Work.

[c] S.I. 1994 No. 3159; *ante,* §14–088.

[d] *National Westminster Bank Ltd v. Halesowen Presswork & Assemblies Ltd* [1972]
A.C. 785; *Stein v. Blake* [1996] A.C. 243.

Failure of purposes for which money lent

36–217   *[Add to note 35: page* [613]]
But see *Westdeutsche Landesbank v. Islington L.B.C.* [1996] A.C. 669
(*ultra vires* contract).

Secured loans

36–218   A debt on a bank overdraft remains a simple contract debt even if it is
secured by a mortgage: if the bank seeks to recover the debt, and does not

rely on the mortgage, the action is not a "mortgage action" within R.S.C. Ord. 88, r.1.[a]

[a] *National Westminster Bank Plc v. Kitch* [1996] 1 W.L.R. 1316.

[*Add to note 36: page* [614]]
 Cf. *Re Bank of Credit and Commerce International S.A. (No. 8)* [1996] Ch. 245; *Tam Wing Chuen v. Bank of Credit and Commerce Hong Kong Ltd* [1996] 2 B.C.L.C. 69, P.C.

[*Add to note 39*]
 Levett v. Barclays Bank [1995] 1 W.L.R. 1260. See also *Re Bank of Credit and Commerce International S.A. (No. 8)* [1996] Ch. 245.

[*Add to note 40*]
 M.S. Fashions Ltd v. Bank of Credit and Commerce International S.A. [1993] Ch. 425, 431 (but see the observations on this point in *Re Bank of Credit and Commerce International S.A. (No. 8), supra.*).

See *United Bank of Kuwait plc v. Sahib.*[a]   **36–219**

[a] [1997] Ch. 107 (noted [1995] C.L.J. 249): equitable mortgage by informal deposit of title deeds void for non-compliance with the requirements of s.2(1) of the Law of Property (Miscellaneous Provisions) Act 1989.

(b) *Interest*

General rule at common law

Where a pawnbroker sold articles pawned to him and, after some delay, **36–224** paid to the pawnor the surplus remaining after the sale, it was held that there was no basis for interest to be awarded to the pawnor on the amount paid at common law, but interest was recoverable in equity: *Mathew v. T.M. Sutton Ltd.*[a]

[a] [1994] 1 W.L.R. 1455.

Interest payable in equity

Interest is payable in equity to the pawnor on the surplus remaining after **36–226** the sale of pawned articles by a pawnbroker: *Mathew v. T.M. Sutton Ltd.*[a]

[a] [1994] 1 W.L.R. 1455.

[*Amend note 86: page* [618]]
 Westdeutsche Landesbank v. Islington L.B.C., reversed by the House of Lords: [1996] A.C. 669. See *post*, §36–227.

[*Add to note 87*]
But see *Westdeutsche Landesbank v. Islington L.B.C.*, *supra*.

Compound interest

36–227   [*Amend note 3: page* [619]]
Westdeutsche Landesbank v. Islington L.B.C. was reversed by the House
of Lords: [1996] A.C. 669. In the absence of fraud, equity will not award
compound interest except against a trustee or other person in a fiduciary
position in respect of profits improperly made. See also *President of India v.
La Pintada Compania Navigacion S.A.* [1985] A.C. 104, 116; *Guardian
Ocean Cargoes Ltd v. Banco do Brasil S.A.* [1994] 2 Lloyd's Rep. 152, C.A.

Variation of interest rate

36–230   Council Directive 93/13 has been implemented in the Unfair Terms in
Consumer Contracts Regulations 1994.[a] In particular see Sched. 3, para. 1(j)
and (k) and para. 2(b)(c).
A bank which was in liquidation retained the right under a loan agreement
to fix its own base rate and calculate interest by reference to that rate even
though, following the appointment of a provisional liquidator, market forces
no longer applied to the rate: *Bank of Credit and Commerce International
SA v. Malik.*[b]

[a] S.I. 1994 No. 3159 (*ante*, §14–088).

[b] [1995] C.L.Y. 2853.

Default interest

36–231   A contractual provision the effect of which is to increase the rate of
interest on default will not be struck down as a penalty if the increase can in
the circumstances be explained as commercially justifiable, provided that its
dominant purpose is not to deter the borrower from breach.[a]

[a] *Lonsdale Finance Plc v. Bank of Zambia* [1996] Q.B. 752.

[*Add to note 12: page* [620]]
Lonsdale Finance Plc v. Bank of Zambia, supra (provision for increase of
one per cent on default upheld).

(c) *Effect of the Consumer Credit Act 1974*

Liability of creditor for acts of supplier

In *Jarrett v. Barclays Bank*[a] the Court of Appeal held that claims under
section 75 (or section 56) of the 1974 Act against British banks which had
financed the purchase by debtors of timeshare properties in Spain and

Portugal did not fall within Article 16(1) of the Brussels Convention on Jurisdiction and Enforcement of Judgments in Civil and Commercial Matters (1968) since they did not have as their object rights *in rem* in immovable property or tenancies of immovable property, but were based on the debtor-creditor-supplier agreement. Consequently proceedings to enforce such claims were not excluded from the jurisdiction of the English courts by Article 16(1).

ᵃ *The Times*, November 18, 1996, [1996] N.P.C. 159.

[*Add to note 60 at end: page* [624]]   36–239
See also *Forward Trust v. Hornsby* 1995 S.C.L.R. 574 (Sh.Ct.).

3. – HIRE-PURCHASE AGREEMENTS

(b) *At Common Law*

Consensus ad idem

[*Note 96: page* [628]]   36–248
See also *PB Leasing Ltd v. Patel* [1995] C.C.L.R. 82 (Cty.Ct.).

Title to goods

[*Note 4*]   36–250
s.8 was amended by Sched. 2, para. 4, to the Sale and Supply of Goods Act 1994.

[*Note 5*]
See s.8(3) inserted by Sched. 2, para. 4(1), to the Sale and Supply of Goods Act 1994.

[*Note 8: page* [629]]
See *Barber v. NWS Bank plc.* [1996] 1 W.L.R. 641, C.A. (breach of express term as to title in conditional sale agreement).

[*Note 9*]
See s.8(3) inserted by Sched. 2, para. 4(1), to the Sale and Supply of Goods Act 1994.

s.8(2) was amended by Sched. 2, para. 4(1), to the Sale and Supply of 36–251
Goods Act 1994.

36–252   [*Note 13*]
Supply of Goods (Implied Terms) Act 1973, s.12 was amended by Sched. 2, para. 4(7), of the Sale and Supply of Goods Act 1994.

Payment of rent

36–254   [*Note 18: page* [630]]
See also *Kelly v. Sovereign Leasing* [1995] C.L.Y. 720 (Cty.Ct.).

Termination of agreement by repudiation

36–262   [*Add to note 56 at end: page* [633]]
Kelly v. Sovereign Leasing [1995] C.L.Y. 720 (Cty.Ct.).

[*Note 57*]
cf. Kelly v. Sovereign Leasing [1995] C.L.Y. 720 (Cty.Ct.).

Repossession of the goods

36–269   In *Kelly v. Sovereign Leasing*,[a] the owner wrongfully repossessed a motor car without notice and sold it. It was held that the measure of damages recoverable by the hirer for conversion was that proportion of the market value of the car as the aggregate of the deposit and capital element in the instalments paid bore to the cash price of the car (in this case 67.3 per cent).

[a] [1995] C.L.Y. 720 (Cty.Ct.).

(d) *Defective Goods*

Warranties and representations by dealers

36–306   [*Note 50: page* [651]]
See also *Branwhite v. Worcester Works Finance Ltd* [1969] 1 A.C. 552; *Williams (J.D.) & Co. v. McCauley Parsons and Jones* [1994] C.C.L.R. 78, (C.A.); *Woodchester Equipment (Leasing) Ltd v. British Association of Canned and Preserved Foods Importers and Distributors Ltd* [1995] C.L.Y. 2459, C.A.; *PB Leasing Ltd v. Patel* [1995] C.C.L.R. 82.

Implied terms

36–308   Sections 9 to 11 were amended by Schedule 2, para. 4, to the Sale and Supply of Goods Act 1994.

Letting by description

Section 9 was amended by Schedule 2, para. 4(3), to the Sale and Supply of **36–309**
Goods Act 1994.

Merchantable quality

Section 10 was amended by Schedule 2, para. 4(4), to the Sale and Supply **36–310**
of Goods Act 1994. The amendment substitutes for "merchantable quality"
in subsection (2) the concept of "satisfactory quality". The definition of
"satisfactory quality" is the same as that in section 14 of the Sale of Goods
Act 1979, as amended: see §41–070, *post*.

Fitness for purpose

Section 10(3) was amended by Schedule 2, para. 4(4), to the Sale and **36–311**
Supply of Goods Act 1994.

Sample

Section 11 was amended by Schedule 2, para. 4(5), to the Sale and Supply **36–312**
of Goods Act 1994.

Remedies for breach

A new section 11A was inserted by Schedule 2, para. 4(6), to the Sale and **36–313**
Supply of Goods Act 1994. This provides:

"(1) Where in the case of a hire-purchase agreement
  (a) the person to whom goods are bailed would, apart from this
     subsection, have the right to reject them by reason of a breach on
     the part of the creditor of a term implied by section 9, 10 or 11(a)
     or (c) above, but
  (b) the breach is so slight that it would be unreasonable for him to
     reject them,
then, if the person to whom the goods are bailed does not deal as
consumer, the breach is not to be treated as a breach of condition but
may be treated as a breach of warranty.
  (2) This section applies unless a contrary intention appears in, or is to
be implied from, the agreement.
  (3) It is for the creditor to show—

(a) that a breach fell within subsection 1(b) above, and

(b) that the person to whom the goods were bailed did not deal as consumer."

By section 11A(4) the references in the section to dealing as consumer are to be construed in accordance with Part I of the Unfair Contract Terms Act 1977 (see Main Work, Vol. 1, §14–052).

(e) *Rights and Liabilities of Third Parties*

(i) *Assignment*

36–319 Assignment by owner

Where the owner of goods charged in favour of a bank the rentals payable under hire-purchase agreements but continued to collect them as agent of the bank, it did not hold the rentals in a fiduciary capacity, being free to deal with the money as its own until required by the bank to pay them into a separate account.[a]

[a] *Royal Trust Bank v. National Westminster Bank Plc* [1996] 8 C.L. 66, C.A.

(ii) *Title of Third Parties*

36–322 Buyer in possession

[*Add to note 13: page* [657]]
Contrast *Forthright Finance Ltd v. Carlyle Finance Ltd* [1997] 4 C.L. 143, C.A.

Dispositions of motor-vehicles

36–325 See Davies, "Wrongful Disposition of Motorvehicles—A Legal Quag-mire", [1995] J.B.L. 36.

Extent of protection

36–332 [*Note 43: page* [660]]
Where a seller of goods who has no title to the goods sells them in circumstances in which the buyer acquires a good title to the goods under Part III of the Hire-Purchase Act 1964, he is nevertheless liable to the buyer

for breach of an express undertaking in the contract of sale that he is the owner of the goods: *Barber v. NWS Bank plc.* [1996] 1 W.L.R. 641, C.A.

Sale in market overt

Market overt was abolished with the repeal of section 22(1) of the Sale of **36–333** Goods Act 1979 by the Sale of Goods (Amendment) Act 1994 as from January 3, 1995.

(iii) *Fixtures and Accession*

Fixtures to land

Plant and machinery leased out for installation in local authority premises **36–339** and which had become a fixture to land did not "belong" to the lessor for the purposes of the Finance Acts 1971 and 1985: *Melluish v. B.M.I. (No. 3) Ltd.*[a]
See also Bennett and Davis, "Fixtures, purchase money security interests and dispositions of interests in land".[b]

[a] [1996] A.C. 454, H.L.

[b] (1994) 110 L.Q.R. 448.

7. – MORTGAGES OF PERSONAL PROPERTY

Ships or vessels

[Text to note 8: page [691]] **36–417**
Mortgages of registered ships are now governed by the Merchant Shipping Act 1995, s.16 and Sched. 1.

8. – MORTGAGES OF LAND

Form, etc.

See also *United Bank of Kuwait plc v. Sahib* (equitable mortgage outside **36–425** the 1974 Act made by informal deposit of title deeds void for non-compliance with the requirements of section 2(1) of the Law of Property (Miscellaneous Provisions) Act 1989).[a]

[a] [1997] Ch. 107 (noted [1995] C.L.J. 249).

CHAPTER 37

EMPLOYMENT

EMPLOYMENTS RIGHTS ACT 1996 DESTINATION AND DERIVATION TABLES

Most of the law relating to individual employment rights was consolidated into the Employment Rights Act 1996 (c.18). This contains most of the provisions formerly in the Employment Protection (Consolidation) Act 1978 (c.44) and the Wages Act 1986 (c.48), together with the employment rights provisions of the Sunday Trading Act 1994 (c.20) and the Pensions Act 1995 (c.26). Meanwhile, provisions concerning industrial tribunals and the Employment Appeal Tribunal have been consolidated into the Industrial Tribunals Act 1996 (c.17). Provisions in relation to trade union membership and activities, however, remain in Part III of the Trade Union and Labour Relations (Consolidation) Act 1992 (c.52).

This Annual Supplement, rather than listing the changes in relation to each section or footnote of the Main Work, contains the same information in tabular form. The EMPLOYMENT RIGHTS ACT 1996 DESTINATION TABLE lists all the changes to the paragraphs and corresponding footnotes of the Main Work in page order, showing where the provision or provisions corresponding to that given in the text or note is to be found in the new legislation. The EMPLOYMENT RIGHTS ACT 1996 TABLE OF DERIVATIONS shows the derivation of those sections of the Employment Rights Act, the Industrial Tribunals Act and Part III of the Trade Union and Labour Relations (Consolidation) Act whose antecedents are referred to in the Main Work, with the relevant section, or page and footnote number, of the Main Work.

EMPLOYMENT RIGHTS ACT 1996 DESTINATION TABLE

Bold paragraph numbers refer to the corresponding paragraph number in the Main Work. These are followed by references to footnotes to that section, preceded by the page number in square brackets

PARAGRAPH NUMBER [PAGE] footnote	DERIVATION	DESTINATION
37–005	E.P.C.A. 1978, Part V	E.R.A. 1996, Part X
	E.P.C.A. 1978, Parts II and III	E.R.A. 1966, Parts III, V, VI, VII and VIII
	E.P.A. 1975, Part IV	T.U.L.R.C.A. 1992, Part IV, Ch. II
	s.153(1) E.P.C.A. 1978	s.230(1) E.R.A. 1996
[700]²⁶	E.P.C.A. 1978, Parts I, IV	E.R.A. 1996, Parts I, IX
[700]²⁷	E.P.C.A. 1978, Part VI	E.R.A. 1996, Part XI

PARAGRAPH NUMBER [PAGE] footnote	DERIVATION	DESTINATION
[700]28	s.153(1) E.P.C.A. 1978	s.230(1) ('employee'), s.230(2) ('contract of employment') E.R.A. 1996
[701]30	s.153(1) E.P.C.A. 1978	s.230(1) E.R.A. 1996
[701]31	s.146(2), (3) E.P.C.A. 1978	s.200 E.R.A. 1996
37–007	Part I, W.A. 1986	Part II, s.191(1)–(4), s.192(1), s.201, s.203, s.205(2), s.230(3)–(5), s.231, s.235(1) E.R.A. 1996
[702]46	s.8(2) W.A. 1986	s.230(3) E.R.A. 1996
37–017	E.P.C.A. 1978	E.R.A. 1996
[709]15	s.143(3)(a) E.P.C.A. 178	s.29(2) E.R.A. 1996
[713]52	s.21 Wages Councils Act 1979 (now repealed by Wages Act 1986)	Spent
[715]77	s.153(1) E.P.C.A. 1978	ss.230(1), (2), (4), (5), 235(1) E.R.A. 1996
[715]83	E.P.C.A. 1978, Part VI	E.R.A. 1996, Part XI
[715]84	s.99 and Sched. 5 E.P.C.A. 1978	s.159, 191(6) E.R.A. 1996
[716]85	s.138(1) E.P.C.A. 1978 s.138(3) E.P.C.A. 1978 (unfair dismissal rights do not extend to members of the military services)	s.191(1), (2) E.R.A. 1996 s.192(1) E.R.A. 1996 (unfair dismissal rights **do** extend to members of the military services)
	s.138(5) E.P.C.A. 1978	Repealed by National Health Service and Community Care Act 1990, s.66(2) and Sched. 10
	s.49(1) and Sched. 7, para. 3 T.U.R.E.R.A. 1993	s.193(1), (2) E.R.A. 1996
[718]10	s.3 Sex Discrimination Act 1986	s.109(1) and s.119(4) E.R.A. 1996

PARAGRAPH NUMBER [PAGE] footnote	DERIVATION	DESTINATION
37–033	"s.1 E.P.C.A. 1978 as subsequently amended"	s.1 E.R.A. 1996
[720][32]	s.26 T.U.R.E.A. 1993 provides that ss.1–6 E.P.C.A. 1978 are now as substituted by Sched. 4 to the 1993 Act	ss.1–7 E.R.A. 1996
[720][33]	Sched. 13, E.P.C.A. 1978	ss.210–219 E.R.A. 1996
[720][34]	s.1(2) E.P.C.A. 1978	s.1(4)(d)(iii), s.1(5) E.R.A. 1996
[721][36]	s.3(1)(a) E.P.C.A. 1978	s.3(1)(a) E.R.A. 1996
[721][37]	s.3(2) E.P.C.A. 1978	s.3(2) E.R.A. 1996
[721][38]	s.3(1)(b) and (c) E.P.C.A. 1978	s.3(1)(b), (c) E.R.A. 1996
[721][39]	s.3(1)(d) E.P.C.A. 1978	s.3(5) E.R.A. 1996
[721][40]	s.3(3) E.P.C.A. 1978	s.3(3) E.R.A. 1996
[721][41]	s.2(2) and (3) E.P.C.A. 1978	s.2(2), (3) and s.6 E.R.A. 1996
[721][42]	s.2(4) E.P.C.A. 1978	s.2(4) E.R.A. 1978
[721][43]	s.4(1) E.P.C.A. 1978	s.4(1), (3) E.R.A. 1996
[721][44]	s.4(2), (3) and (4) E.P.C.A. 1978	s.4(2), (4), (5) and s.6 E.R.A. 1996
[721][45]	s.4(5)(a)(i) E.P.C.A. 1978	s.4(6)(a) E.R.A. 1996
[721][46]	s.4(5)(a)(ii) E.P.C.A. 1978	s.4(6)(b) E.R.A. 1996
[721][47]	s.4(6) E.P.C.A. 1978	s.4(8) E.R.A. 1996
[722][51]	s.1 E.P.C.A. 1978	s.1 E.R.A. 1996
[722][52]	s.11(1) E.P.C.A. 1978	s.11(1) E.R.A. 1996
	s.11(2) E.P.C.A. 1978	s.11(2) E.R.A. 1996
	s.11(6) E.P.C.A. 1978	s.12(2) E.R.A. 1996
	s.11(7) E.P.C.A. 1978	Repealed by T.U.R.E.R.A. 1993, s.51 and Sched. 10
[722][53]	s.11(6) E.P.C.A. 1978	s.12(2) E.R.A. 1996
[722][55]	s.11 E.P.C.A. 178	s.11 E.R.A. 1996
[722][57]	s.1 E.P.C.A. 1978	s.1 E.R.A. 1996
[723][58]	s.5(1)(b) E.P.C.A. 1978	Revoked by S.I. 1995 No. 31 BUT S.I. revoked by s.242, Sched. 3, Part II E.R.A. 1996

PARAGRAPH NUMBER [PAGE] footnote	DERIVATION	DESTINATION
[723]⁵⁹	s.144(1) E.P.C.A. 1978	s.199(1) E.R.A. 1996
[723]⁶⁰	s.146(1) E.P.C.A. 1978	Repealed s.21, Sched. 3, Part I, para. 6 E.A. 1982 NOW spent or unnecessary
[723]⁶¹	s.141(1) E.P.C.A. 1978	s.196(1) E.R.A. 1996
[728]⁶	T.U.R.E.R.A. 1993 Sched. 4 substituting new E.P.C.A. 1978, s.2(2) and (3)	s.2(2), (3) and s.6 E.R.A. 1996
[728]⁷	s.1(1)(j) E.P.C.A. 1978	s.1(4)(j) E.R.A. 1996
[728]¹¹	Sched. 2 E.P.A. 1980	Spent
[728]¹²	ss.17–21 E.P.A. 1975	ss.181–185 T.U.L.R.C.A. 1992
[728]¹³	ss.19(1) E.P.A. 1975	s.183(1) T.U.L.R.C.A. 1992
[728]¹⁴	ss.19(1), 20(1) E.P.A. 175	s.183(1), s.184(1) T.U.L.R.C.A. 1992
[728]¹⁵	s.21(1) E.P.A. 1975	s.185(1) T.U.L.R.C.A. 1992
[728]¹⁶	s.21(3) E.P.A. 1975	s.185(3) T.U.L.R.C.A. 1992
[728]¹⁷	s.21(3) and (5) E.P.A. 1975	s.185(3), (4) T.U.L.R.C.A. 1992
[728]¹⁸	s.21(6) E.P.A. 1975	s.185(5) T.U.L.R.C.A. 1992
[728]¹⁹	s.21(3) and (5) E.P.A. 1975	s.185(3), (4) T.U.L.R.C.A. 1992
[730]²⁸	s.140 E.P.C.A. 1978	s.203 E.R.A. 1996
[735]⁸²	s.17 (subject to s.18) E.P.A. 1975	Repealed
[739]³⁴	s.49 E.P.C.A. 1978	s.86 E.R.A. 1996
[739]³⁵	Sched. 13, para. 15 E.P.C.A. 1978	s.216 E.R.A. 1996
[742]⁶⁸	s.1(3) E.P.C.A. 1978	s.1(4) E.R.A. 1996
[742]⁶⁹	ss.8–11 E.P.C.A. 1978	ss.8–12 E.R.A. 1996
[743]⁷⁵	s.1(3)(d)(i) E.P.C.A. 1978 (as substituted by Sched. 4 to T.U.R.E.R.A. 1993)	s.1(4)(d)(i) E.R.A. 1996
[743]⁷⁸	s.1(3)(d)(ii) E.P.C.A. 1978 (as substituted by Sched. 4 to T.U.R.E.R.A. 1993)	s.1(4)(d)(ii) E.R.A. 1996
[743]⁷⁹	Sched. 3, para. 2(1)(b) E.P.C.A. 1978	s.88(1) E.R.A. 1996

PARAGRAPH NUMBER [PAGE] footnote	DERIVATION	DESTINATION
[747]20	s.9 and Sched. 1 E.P.C.A. 1978	s.64 E.R.A. 1978
[747]21	s.19 E.P.C.A. 1978	s.64 E.R.A. 1996
	s.20 E.P.C.A. 1978	s.65 E.R.A. 1996
	s.146(1) E.P.C.A. 1978 (spouse of employer)	Repealed by s.21, Sched. 3, Part I, para. 6 E.A. 1982 NOW spent or unnecessary
	s.144(2) E.P.C.A. 1978 (share fishermen)	s.199(2) E.P.C.A. 1996
	s.141(2) E.P.C.A. 1978 (work outside Great Britain)	s.196(2), (3) E.R.A. 1996
	s.143(3) E.P.C.A. 1978 (contracts for not more than twelve weeks)	s.29(2) E.R.A. 1996
[747]22	s.20(1) E.P.C.A. 1978	s.65(3) E.R.A. 1996
[747]23	s.20(2)(a) E.P.C.A. 1978	s.65(4)(a) E.R.A. 1996
	s.20(2)(b) E.P.C.A. 1978	s.65(4)(b) E.R.A. 1996
[747]24	s.143(2) E.P.C.A. 1978	s.29(1) E.R.A. 1996
[747]25	s.21 and Sched. 14 E.P.C.A. 1978	s.69(1) and ss.220–229 E.R.A. 1996
[747]26	s.21(3) E.P.C.A. 1978	s.69(3) E.R.A. 1996
[747]27	s.22 E.P.C.A. 1978	ss.48, 49 and 70 E.R.A. 1996
37–072	"as re-enacted in the E.P.C.A. 1978"	"as re-enacted in the E.R.A. 1996"
[750]55	"First consolidated into the Contracts of Employment Act 1972 and then into the Employment Protection (Consolidation) Act 1978 …"	"… and then consolidated into the Employment Rights Act 1996."
[750]56	See now Sched. 3 to 1978 Act	s.87(3) and ss.88–91 E.R.A. 1996
[750]57	ss.12–18 E.P.C.A. 1978	ss.28–35 E.R.A. 1996
	s.146(1) E.P.C.A. 1978 (spouse of an employer)	Repealed by s.21, Sched. 3, Part I, para. 6 E.A. 1980 NOW spent or unnecessary

PARAGRAPH NUMBER [PAGE] footnote	DERIVATION	DESTINATION
	s.144 E.P.C.A. 1978 (share fishermen)	s.199 E.R.A. 1996
	s.141 E.P.C.A. 1978 (work outside Great Britain)	s.196 E.R.A. 1996
	s.143(3)–(4) E.P.C.A. 1978 (contract for not more than twelve weeks)	s.29(2) E.R.A. 1996
[750][58]	s.143 E.P.C.A. 1978	s.29 E.R.A. 1996
[750][59]	s.13(1) E.P.C.A. 1978	s.29(3) E.R.A. 1996
[750][60]	s.13(2) E.P.C.A. 1978	s.29(4), (5) E.R.A. 1996
[750][61]	s.14(1) E.P.C.A. 1978	s.30(1) E.R.A. 1996
[750][62]	Sched. 14 E.P.C.A. 1978	ss.221–229 E.R.A. 1996
[750][63]	s.14(2) E.P.C.A. 1978	s.30(2)–(4) E.R.A. 1996
[750][64]	s.15(1) E.P.C.A. 1978 and regulations made from time to time	s.31(1) E.R.A. 1996 and regulations made from time to time
[750][65]	s.15(3) E.P.C.A. 1978 1978	s.31(3)–(5) E.R.A. 1996
[750][66]	s.15(2) E.P.C.A. 1978, as amended by s.14 E.A. 1989	s.31(2) E.R.A. 1996
[750][67]	s.16(2) E.P.C.A. 1978	s.32(2) E.R.A. 1996
[751][68]	s.16(3) E.P.C.A. 1978	s.32(3) E.R.A. 1996
[751][69]	s.17(1) E.P.C.A. 1978 limitation period – s.17(2) E.P.C.A. 1978	s.34(1) E.R.A. 1996 s.34(2) E.R.A. 1996
[751][70]	s.17(3) E.P.C.A. 1978	s.34(3) E.R.A. 1996
[751][71]	s.16(4) E.P.C.A. 1978	s.33 E.R.A. 1996
[751][72]	s.18(1), (2) as amended by Sched. 10 to T.U.R.E.R.A. 1993	s.35(1) and (2) E.R.A. 1996
[751][74]	s.18(4) E.P.C.A. 1978	s.35(4), (5) E.R.A. 1996
37–073	"s.1 of the Wages Act"	"s.14 of the Employment Rights Act 1996"
[751][77]	s.1 E.P.C.A. 1978	s.1 E.R.A. 1996
[752][85]	s.1(1)(a), (3) W.A. 1986	s.13(1), (2) E.R.A. 1996
[752][86]	s.1(5)(e) W.A. 1986	s.14(5) E.R.A. 1996
37–075	"as contained in the E.P.C.A. 1978 and T.U.L.R.C.A. 1992"	"*and* Employment Rights Act 1996"

PARAGRAPH NUMBER [PAGE] footnote	DERIVATION	DESTINATION
[753][98]	s.29 E.P.C.A. 1978	s.50, s.51(1) E.R.A.1996
[753][99]	s.31 E.P.C.A. 1978	ss.52–54 E.R.A. 1996
[753][1]	s.31A E.P.C.A. 1978 (added by s.13 E.A. 1980)	ss.55–57 E.R.A. 1996
[753][4]	s.31 E.P.C.A. 1978	s.53 E.R.A. 1996
[753][10]	s.31(3) E.P.C.A. 1978	s.56(1) E.R.A. 1966
[753][11]	As defined by Sched. 14, Part II E.P.C.A. 1978	ss.221–229 E.R.A. 1996
[754][12]	As defined by Sched. 4, Part I E.P.C.A. 1978	s.234 E.R.A. 1996
[754][13]	s.31(9) E.P.C.A. 1978	ss.53(5), 54(5) E.R.A. 1996
[754][14]	s.31(11) E.P.C.A. 1978	s.53(7) E.R.A. 1996
[754][15]	s.31A(4)–(5) E.P.C.A. 1978	s.56(1)–(4) E.R.A. 1996
[754][16]	s.31A(9)–(10) E.P.C.A. 1978	s.56(5)–(6) E.R.A. 1996
[754][17]	s.31A(6)–(8) E.P.C.A. 1978	s.57(1)–(5) E.R.A. 1996
[754][18]	s.29 E.P.C.A. 1978	s.50 E.R.A. 1996
37–077	Employment Protection (Consolidation) Act 1978	Employment Rights Act 1996
[755][24]	s.8 E.P.C.A. 1978	s.8 E.R.A. 1996
	s.146(1) E.P.C.A. 1978	Repealed by s.21, Sched. 3, Part I, para. 6 E.A. 1982 NOW spent or unnecessary
	s.144 E.P.C.A. 1978	s.199 E.R.A. 1996
	s.141 E.P.C.A. 1978	s.196 E.R.A. 1966
	s.146(5)–(7) E.P.C.A. 1978	Repealed by S.I. 1995 No. 31 BUT in turn repealed by E.R.A. 1996
[755][25]	s.8(a)–(d) E.P.C.A. 1978	s.8(a)–(d) E.R.A. 1996
[755][26]	W.A. 1986	E.R.A. 1996
[755][27]	s.9(1) E.P.C.A. 1978	s.9(1), (2) E.R.A. 1996
[755][28]	s.9(2) E.P.C.A. 1978	s.9(3) E.R.A. 1996
[755][29]	s.9(3) E.P.C.A. 1978	s.9(4) E.R.A. 1996
[755][30]	s.11(1) E.P.C.A. 1978	s.11(1) E.R.A. 1996
[755][31]	s.11(3) E.P.C.A. 1978	Repealed, Sched. 10 T.U.R.E.R.A. 1993

PARAGRAPH NUMBER [PAGE] footnote	DERIVATION	DESTINATION
[755]³²	s.11(8)(a) E.P.C.A. 1978	s.12(3) E.R.A. 1996
[755]³³	s.11(8)(b) E.P.C.A. 1978	s.12(4), (5) E.R.A. 1996
37–078	s.11 E.P.C.A. 1978	ss.11 and 12 E.R.A. 1996
[755]³⁵	s.1 W.A. 1986	ss.13–15 E.R.A. 1996
[756]³⁶	ss.2–4 W.A. 1986	ss.17–22 E.R.A. 1996
[756]³⁷	ss.5–6 W.A. 1986	ss.23–26, s.205(2) and s.203 E.R.A. 1996
[756]³⁸	s.9 W.A. 1986	s.191(1)–(4) and s.192(1) E.R.A. 1996
[756]³⁹	s.10 W.A. 1986	s.201 E.R.A. 1996
[756]⁴⁰	s.6(1) W.A. 1986	s.205(2) E.R.A. 1996
[756]⁴¹	s.6(3) W.A. 1986	s.203(1), (2) E.R.A. 1996
[756]⁴³	s.6(2) W.A. 1986	s.26 E.R.A. 1996
[756]⁴⁴	s.5(1)–(3) W.A. 1986	s.23(1)–(4) E.R.A. 1996
[756]⁴⁵	s.5(4)–(8) E.A. 1986	s.24 and s.25(1)–(5) E.R.A. 1996
37–079	"Under s.1 of the Wages Act 1986"	"Under ss.13–15 E.R.A. 1996"
[756]⁴⁶	s.1(1) W.A. 1986	s.13(1) E.R.A. 1996
[756]⁴⁷	s.1(2) W.A. 1986	s.15(1) E.R.A. 1996
[756]⁴⁸	s.1(1)(a) W.A. 1986	s.13(1)(a) E.R.A. 1996
[756]⁴⁹	s.1(1)(b) W.A. 1986	s.13(1)(b) E.R.A. 1996
[756]⁵⁰	s.1(3)(a) W.A. 1986	s.13(2)(a) and s.15(2)(a) E.R.A. 1996
[756]⁵¹	s.1(3)(b) W.A. 1986	s.13(2)(b) and s. 15(2)(b) E.R.A. 1996
[756]⁵²	s.1(5)(a) W.A. 1986	s.14(1) and s.16(1) E.R.A. 1996
[756]⁵³	s.1(5)(b) W.A. 1986	s.14(2) and s.16(2) E.R.A. 1996
[757]⁵⁴	s.1(5)(c) W.A. 1986	s.14(3) E.R.A. 1996
[757]⁵⁵	s.1(5)(d) W.A. 1986	s.14(4) E.R.A. 1996
[757]⁵⁶	s.1(5)(e) W.A. 1986	s.14(5) and s.16(3) E.R.A. 1996
[757]⁵⁷	s.1(5)(f) W.A. 1986	s.14(6) and s.16(4) E.R.A. 1996
[757]⁵⁸	s.7(1)(a) W.A. 1986	s.27(1)(a) E.R.A. 1996
[757]⁵⁹	s.7(1)(b), (c) W.A. 1986	s.27(1)(g), (h) E.R.A. 1996
[757]⁶⁰	s.7(1)(d)–(f) W.A. 1986	s.27(1)(b)–(f) E.R.A. 1996
[757]⁶¹	s.7(3) W.A. 1986	s.27(3) E.R.A. 1996
[757]⁶²	s.7(2)(a) W.A. 1986	s.27(2)(a) E.R.A. 1996

PARAGRAPH NUMBER [PAGE] footnote	DERIVATION	DESTINATION
[757]63	s.7(2)(b) W.A. 1986	s.27(2)(b) E.R.A. 1996
[757]64	s.7(2)(c), (d) W.A. 1986	s.27(2)(c), (d) E.R.A. 1996
[757]65	s.7(2)(e) W.A. 1986	s.27(2)(e) E.R.A. 1996
[757]66	s.7(4) W.A. 1986	s.27(5) E.R.A. 1996
[757]67	s.8(1), (2) W.A. 1986	s.230(3) E.R.A. 1996
[758]68	s.8(3), (4) W.A. 1986	s.13(3), (4) E.R.A. 1996
37–080	"Part of the Wages Act 1986"	"Part II of the Employment Rights Act 1996"
[758]71	ss.2–4 W.A. 1986	ss.17–22 E.R.A. 1996
[758]72	s.2(1), (2) W.A. 1986	s.18(1), s.17(1)–(3), (6) E.R.A. 1996
	s.2(4), (5) W.A. 1986	s.19(1)–(4) E.R.A. 1996
	s.3(4), (5) W.A. 1986	s.21(1), (2) E.R.A. 1996
	s.4(5), (6) W.A. 1986	s.20(5), s.21(3), s.22(4) E.R.A. 1996
[758]73	s.4(1)–(3) W.A. 1986	s.22(1)–(3) E.R.A. 1996
[758]74	s.3(1)–(3)(a), (6) W.A. 1986	s.20(1)–(3)(a) and s.20(4) E.R.A. 1996
[758]75	s.2(3), s.3(3)(b), s.4(4) W.A. 1986	s.18(2), (3), s.20(3)(b), s.20(5) E.R.A. 1996
[758]76	s.2(2) W.A. 1986	s.17(2), (3) E.R.A. 1996
[759]82	s.8 E.P.C.A. 1978	s.8 E.R.A. 1996
[759]83	s.9 E.P.C.A. 1978	s.9 E.R.A. 1996
37–086	"The Trade Union Reform and Employment Rights Act 1993"	"The Employment Rights Act 1996"
[764]41	s.28 and Sched. 5 T.U.R.E.R.A. 1993	s.44, s.48, s.49, s.98(6), s100, s.105(3), s.108(3), s.109(2), s.117(3), (4), s.118, s.119(1), s.120, s.122(3), s.125, ss.128–132, s.236(3) E.R.A. 1996
[764]42	s.1(3)(c) E.P.C.A. 1978 as substituted by Sched. 4 T.U.R.E.R.A. 1993	s.1(4)(c) E.R.A. 1996

PARAGRAPH NUMBER [PAGE] footnote	DERIVATION	DESTINATION
[764][43]	s.81 E.P.C.A. 1978 (calculation of redundancy payment)	s.162, s.135, s.155, s.139 E.R.A. 1996
	Sched. 3 E.P.C.A. 1978 (rights of employee during period of notice)	ss.87–91 E.R.A. 1996
	s.14 E.P.C.A. 1978 (calculation of guarantee payment)	s.30 E.R.A. 1996
37–091	"The Employment Protection (Consolidation) Act 1978 as amended and The Trade Union and Labour Relations (Consolidation) Act 1992"	"The Trade Union and Labour Relations (Consolidation) Act 1992 and the Employment Rights Act 1996"
[767][71]	ss.29–31 E.P.C.A. 1978	ss.50–63 E.R.A. 1996
	s.146(4) E.P.C.A. 1978	Repealed by S.I. 1995 No. 31 BUT in turn repealed by E.R.A. 1996
	s.141 E.P.C.A. 1978 (work abroad)	s.196 E.R.A. 1996
	s.138 E.P.C.A. 1978	ss.191–193 E.R.A. 1996
[767][72]	ss.27–31 E.P.C.A. 1978	ss.51, 54, 57, 60 E.R.A. 1996
[768][81]	s.29(1), (2), (3) E.P.C.A. 1978	s.50(1)–(3), (5)–(9)
[768][82]	s.29(4) E.P.C.A. 1978	s.50(4) E.R.A. 1996
[768][83]	s.31(1) E.P.C.A. 1978	s.52(1) E.R.A. 1996
[768][84]	s.31(2) E.P.C.A. 1978	s.52(2) E.R.A. 1996
[768][85]	s.31A(1)–(3) E.P.C.A. 1978	s.55(1)–(3) E.R.A. 1996
[768][86]	s.29(6) E.P.C.A. 1978	s.51(1) E.R.A. 1996
	s.31(6) E.P.C.A. 1978	s.54(1) E.R.A. 1996
	s.31A(6) E.P.C.A. 1978	s.57(1) E.R.A. 1996
	s.30(1) E.P.C.A. 1978	s.51(2) E.R.A. 1996
	s.31(7) E.P.C.A. 1978	s.54(2) E.R.A. 1996
	s.31A(7) E.P.C.A. 1978	s.57(2) E.R.A. 1996
[768][87]	s.30(2) E.P.C.A. 1978	s.51(3), (4) E.R.A. 1996 and s.172 T.U.L.R.C.A. 1992

PARAGRAPH NUMBER [PAGE] footnote	DERIVATION	DESTINATION
[768][88]	s.31(8), referring to s.31(5) E.P.C.A. 1978	s.54(3), referring to s.53(4) E.R.A. 1996
[768][89]	s.31(9) E.P.C.A. 1978	s.53(5) and s.54(4) E.R.A. 1996
[769][90]	s.31A(8) E.P.C.A. 1978	s.57(3)–(5) E.R.A. 1996
[773][41]	s.3(1) Sex Discrimination Act 1986	s.109(1) E.R.A. 1996
37–100	"Part III of the Employment Protection (Consolidation) Act 1978"	"Part VIII of the Employment Rights Act 1996"
	"sections 23 and 25 of and Schedules 2 and 3 to the Trade Union Reform and Employment Rights Act 1993"	Unnecessary
	"The new Part III"	"Part VIII"
[775][54]	Part III E.P.C.A. 1978	Part VIII E.R.A. 1996
[775][57]	Part III of the Act	Part VIII of the Act
	s.138(1) E.P.C.A. 1978	s.191(1), (2) E.R.A. 1996
	s.141(2) E.P.C.A. 1978	s.196(2), (3) E.R.A. 1996
	s.144(2) E.P.C.A. 1978	s.199(2) E.R.A. 1996
[775][58]	ss.33–38A E.P.C.A. 1978, as substituted by s.23(2) T.U.R.E.R.A. 1993	ss.71–78 E.R.A. 1996
[775][59]	s.35 E.P.C.A. 1978	s.73 E.R.A. 1996
[775][60]	s.33(1), (2) E.P.C.A. 1978	s.71 E.R.A. 1996
[776][61]	s.34 E.P.C.A. 1978 (commencement of maternity leave period)	s.72 E.R.A. 1996
	s.36 E.P.C.A. 1978 (notice of commencement of leave)	s.74 E.R.A. 1996
	s.37 E.P.C.A. 1978 (requirement to inform employer of pregnancy)	s.75 E.R.A. 1996
[776][62]	s.38 E.P.C.A. 1978	s.77 E.R.A. 1996

PARAGRAPH NUMBER [PAGE] footnote	DERIVATION	DESTINATION
[776][63]	s.38A E.P.C.A. 1978	s.78 E.R.A. 1996
[776][64]	ss.39–44 E.P.C.A. 1978, as substituted by s.23 and Sched. 2 T.U.R.E.R.A. 1993	ss.79–85 E.R.A. 1996
[776][65]	s.39 E.P.C.A. 1978	s.79 E.R.A. 1996
[776][66]	s.40 E.P.C.A. 1978	s.80 E.R.A. 1996
[776][67]	s.42 E.P.C.A. 1978	s.82 E.R.A. 1996
[776][68]	s.41 E.P.C.A. 1978	s.81 E.R.A. 1996
[776][69]	s.44 E.P.C.A. 1978	s.85 E.R.A. 1996
[776][70]	ss.45–47 E.P.C.A. 1978 as substituted by s.25 and Sched. 3 T.U.R.E.R.A 1993	ss.66–70 E.R.A. 1996
[776][71]	s.45 E.P.C.A. 1978	s.66 E.R.A. 1996
[776][72]	s.46 E.P.C.A. 1978	ss.67, 70(4)–(7) E.R.A. 1996
[776][73]	s.47 E.P.C.A. 1978 See for calculation of week's pay E.P.C.A. 1978, Sched. 14, Part II	ss.68–70 E.R.A. 1996 ss.220–229 E.R.A. 1996
[777][74]	ss.45(3)–(6), 47(6)–(8) E.P.C.A. 1978	ss.66(1), (2), 70(1)–(3) E.R.A. 1996
37–106	"Part I of the Employment Protection (Consolidation) Act 1978"	"Part I of the Employment Rights Act"
[779][4]	As substituted by s.26 of and Sched. 4 to T.U.R.E.R.A. 1993	Unnecessary
[779][5]	s.1(3)(e) E.P.C.A. 1978 1978	s.1(4)(e) E.R.A. 1996
[779][6]	s.21(1) E.P.C.A. 1978	s.2(1) E.R.A. 1996
[780][7]	s.1(3)(g) E.P.C.A. 1978	s.1(4)(g) E.R.A. 1996
[788][8]	s.11(1) E.P.C.A. 1978	s.11(1) E.R.A. 1996
[780][9]	s.11(2) E.P.C.A. 1978	s.11(2) E.R.A. 1996
[783][38]	Employment Protection (Consolidation) Act 1978, Part IV	Employment Rights Act 1996, Part IX
[783][40]	s.49 E.P.C.A. 1978 s.144(1) E.P.C.A. 1978 s.141(1) E.P.C.A. 1978	s.38 E.R.A. 1996 s.199(1) E.R.A. 1996 s.196(1) E.R.A. 1996

PARAGRAPH NUMBER [PAGE] footnote	DERIVATION	DESTINATION
[783][41]	s.49(1) E.P.C.A. 1978	s.86(1) E.R.A. 1996
[783][42]	s.49(2) E.P.C.A. 1978	s.86(2) E.R.A. 1996
[783][43]	s.49(3) E.P.C.A. 1978	s.86(3) E.R.A. 1996
[783][44]	s.49(4) E.P.C.A. 1978	s.86(4) E.R.A. 1996
[783][45]	s.143(3)(b) E.P.C.A. 1978	s.86(5) E.R.A. 1996
[783][46]	s.49(5) E.P.C.A. 1978	s.86(6) E.R.A. 1996
[783][47]	s.49 E.P.C.A. 1978	s.86 E.R.A. 1996
[783][48]	s.50; Sched. 3 E.P.C.A. 1978	ss.87–91(4) E.R.A. 1996
[783][49]	s.51 E.P.C.A. 1978	s.91(5) E.R.A. 1996
37–112	"a week counts if the employment was for 16 hours or more … to maintain his continuity of employment"	Spent
[784][50]	Sched. 13 E.P.C.A. 1978	ss.210–219 E.R.A. 1996
[784][51]	s.49 E.P.C.A. 1978	s.86 E.R.A. 1996
[784][52]	Sched. 13, para. 1(1) E.P.C.A. 1978	s.210(3) E.R.A. 1996
[784][53]	Sched. 13, para. 24(1) E.P.C.A. 1978	s.235(1) E.R.A. 1996
[784][54]	Sched. 13, paras. 3, 4 E.P.C.A. 1978	Spent
[784][55]	Sched. 13, para. 5 E.P.C.A. 1978	Repealed by S.I. 1995 No. 31 BUT in turn repealed by E.R.A. 1996
[784][58]	Sched. 13, para. 9(1)(a) E.P.C.A. 1978	s.212(3)(a) E.R.A. 1996
[784][59]	Sched. 13, para. 9(1)(b)	s.212(3)(b) E.R.A. 1996
[784][60]	Sched. 13, para. 9(1)(c) E.P.C.A. 1978	s.212(3)(c) E.R.A. 1996
[784][61]	Sched. 13, para. 9(1)(d) E.P.C.A. 1978	s.212(3)(d) E.R.A. 1996
[785][62]	Sched. 13, para. 10 E.P.C.A. 1978	s.212(2) E.R.A. 1996
[785][63]	Sched. 13, para. 15 as modified by para. 23 E.P.C.A. 1978	s.216 E.R.A. 1996
[785][64]	Sched. 13, para 15 E.P.C.A. 1978	s.216 E.R.A. 1996

PARAGRAPH NUMBER [PAGE] footnote	DERIVATION	DESTINATION
[785][66]	Sched. 13, para 16 E.P.C.A. 1978	s.217 E.R.A. 1996
[785][67]	Sched. 13, para. 18 E.P.C.A. 1978	s.218(6) E.R.A. 1996
[785][68]	Sched. 13, para. 17(2) E.P.C.A. 1978	s.218(2) E.R.A. 1996
	ss.83(2) and 94(2) of 1978 Act	s.136(1)–(3) of 1996 Act
	s.151 of 1978 Act	s.210(5) of 1996 Act
[785][69]	Sched. 13, para. 17(4) E.P.C.A. 1978	s.218(4) E.R.A. 1996
[785][70]	Sched. 13, para. 17(5) E.P.C.A. 1978	s.218(5) E.R.A. 1996
31–113	"1978 Act"	"1996 Act"
[786][74]	s.50, Sched. 3 E.P.C.A. 1978	ss.87–91 E.R.A. 1996
[786][75]	s.49(1) E.R.A. 1978	s.86(1) E.R.A. 1996
[786][76]	s.140 E.P.C.A. 1978	s.203 E.R.A. 1996
[786][77]	s.152 and Sched. 14, Part I E.P.C.A. 1978	s.234 E.R.A. 1996
[786][78]	Sched. 3, para. 2(1) E.P.C.A. 1978	s.88(1) E.R.A. 1996
	Sched. 14, Part II E.P.C.A. 1978	ss.220–229 E.R.A. 1996
[786][79]	Sched. 3, para. 3(1)–(3) E.P.C.A. 1978	s.89(1)–(4) E.R.A. 1996
[786][80]	s.50(3) E.P.C.A. 1978	s.87(4) E.R.A. 1996
[786][81]	Sched. 3, paras 2(2), 3(2) E.P.C.A. 1978	ss.88(2), 89(2) E.R.A. 1996
[786][82]	Sched. 3, para. 4 E.P.C.A. 1978	s.90 E.R.A. 1996
[786][83]	Sched. 3, paras 2(3), 3(4) E.P.C.A 1978	ss.88(3), 89(5) E.R.A. 1996
[787][84]	Sched. 3, para. 5 E.P.C.A. 1978	s.91(1) E.R.A. 1996
[787][85]	Sched. 3, para. 6 E.P.C.A. 1978	s.91(2) E.R.A. 1996
[787][86]	Sched. 3, para. 7(1) E.P.C.A. 1978	s.91(3) E.R.A. 1996
[787][87]	Sched. 3, para. 7(2) E.P.C.A. 1978	s.91(4) E.R.A. 1996

PARAGRAPH NUMBER [PAGE] footnote	DERIVATION	DESTINATION
37–114	"section 49(3) of the 1978 Act"	"section 86(3) of the 1996 Act"
	"section 49(3)"	"section 86(3)"
37–115	"for the purposes of the 1978 Act…"	add now the 1996 Act
	s.140(1) of that Act	add now s.203 of 1996 Act
[790][22]	ss.93(1), 150 of and Sched. 12 to 1978 Act	s.136(5), 206, 207 E.R.A. 1996
[790][23]	Sched. 13, para. 17 E.P.C.A. 1978	s.218(4) E.R.A. 1996
[792][44]	s.2(2) E.P.C.A. 1978	s.2(2), (3) E.R.A. 1996
[793][55]	Sched. 13, para. 17 E.P.C.A. 1978	s.218(5) E.R.A. 1996
[795][77]	s.1(4)(a) E.P.C.A. 1978	Repealed by T.U.R.E.R.A. 1993
[802][45]	s.55(2)(c) E.P.C.A. 1978	s.95(1)(c) E.R.A. 1996
	s.83(2)(c) E.P.C.A. 1978	s.136(1)(c) E.R.A. 1996
37–176	"section 53 of the Employment Protection (Consolidation) Act 1978"	"section 92 of the Employment Rights Act 1996"
	"section 53"	"section 92"
	"completed 26 weeks continuous employment"	"completed 2 years continuous employment"
[803][55]	As amended by T.U.R.E.R.A. 1993, ss.24, 49(2), 51, Sched. 8, para. 11, Sched. 10	Unnecessary
[803][56]	s.145(2) E.P.C.A. 1978 (reg. dock workers)	Repealed by s.7(1), (5), Sched. 1, Part I, Sched. 2, para. 7 Dock Work Act 1989
	s.144(2) E.P.C.A. 1978 (share fishermen)	s.199(2) E.R.A. 1996
	s.141(2) E.P.C.A. 1978 (working outside G.B.)	s.196(2) E.R.A. 1996

PARAGRAPH NUMBER [PAGE] footnote	DERIVATION	DESTINATION
	s.149(1) E.P.C.A. 1978 (other categories as may be specified by order)	s.209(1) E.R.A. 1996
	s.138(1) E.P.C.A. 1978 (section does apply to Crown employment)	s.191(1), (2) E.R.A. 1996
[803]57	s.53(1)(a) and (b) E.P.C.A. 1978	s.92(1)(a) and (b) E.R.A. 1996
[803]59	s.53(1)(c) E.P.C.A. 1978	s.92(1)(c) E.R.A. 1996
[803]60	s.53(1) E.P.C.A. 1978	s.92(2) E.R.A. 1996
[803]62	s.53(2) E.P.C.A. 1978	s.92(3) E.R.A. 1996
	s.151 E.P.C.A. 1978	s.210 E.R.A. 1996
[803]63	s.153(1) E.P.C.A. 1978 referring to Trade Union and Labour Relations Act 1974, Sched. 1, para. 5	s.92(6) E.R.A. 1996
[803]64	s.53(2) E.P.C.A. 1978	s.92(3) E.R.A. 1996
[803]65	s.53(4) E.P.C.A. 1978 limitation period s.53(5) E.P.C.A. 1978	s.93(1) E.R.A. 1996 s.93(3) E.R.A. 1996
[803]66	The "week's pay" is calculated by reference to Sched. 14, especially para. 7(1)(f) and (g) thereof	s.226(2) E.R.A. 1996
[803]67	s.53(4)(b) E.P.C.A. 1978 s.53(4)(a) E.P.C.A. 1978	s.93(2)(b) E.R.A. 1996 s.92(2)(a) E.R.A. 1996
[804]70	s.53(2) E.P.C.A. 1978	s.92(3) E.R.A. 1996
[804]71	s.53(2A) E.P.C.A. 1978	s.92(4) E.R.A. 1996
37–137	"Part I of the Wages Act 1986"	"Part II of the Employment Rights Act 1996"
37–140	"Under section 106 of the Employment Protection (Consolidation) Act 1978"	"Under sections 166 and 167 of the Employment Rights Act 1996"
	"Under section 122 of the E.P.C.A. 1978"	"Under section 184 of the E.R.A. 1996"
	"section 122(3) of the 1978 Act"	"section 184(1) of the 1996 Act"

PARAGRAPH NUMBER [PAGE] footnote	DERIVATION	DESTINATION
[806]⁴	As amended by E.A. 1989, s.29(3) and Sched. 6, para. 21 and E.A. 1990, s.18(1) and Sched. 2, para. 1(4)	Unnecessary
[806]⁵	s.106(5) E.P.C.A. 1978	s.166(6), (7) E.R.A. 1996
[806]⁶	s.106(2) E.P.C.A. 1978	s.167(1) E.R.A. 1996
[806]⁷	s.106(3) E.P.C.A. 1978	s.167(3), (4) E.R.A. 1996
[806]⁸	s.127(1) as in s.106(5) E.P.C.A. 1978	s.183 as in s.166(6), (7) E.R.A. 1996
[806]⁹	s.122(1), (2) E.P.C.A. 1978	ss.182, 185 E.R.A. 1996
[806]¹¹	s.122(3) E.P.C.A. 1978	s.184(1) E.R.A. 1996
[806]¹²	s.122(3) E.P.C.A. 1978	s.184(2) E.R.A. 1996
	s.121(2) E.P.C.A. 1978	Repealed by Insolvency Act 1985, s.235(3), Sched. 10, Part IV
[807]¹⁶	s.122(5) E.P.C.A. 1978	s.186(1) E.R.A. 1996
[807]¹⁷	s.124(1) E.P.C.A. 1978	s.188(1), (2) E.R.A. 1996
[807]¹⁸	s.124(3) E.P.C.A. 1978	s.188(3) E.R.A. 1996
[807]¹⁹	s.125(1), (4) E.P.C.A. 1978	ss.189(1), (5) E.R.A. 1996
[807]²¹	s.125(2) E.P.C.A. 1978	s.189(2) E.R.A. 1996
	s.122(2) E.P.C.A. 1978	s.185 E.R.A. 1996
[807]²²	s.122(2) E.P.C.A. 1978	s.185 E.R.A. 1996
[807]²³	s.65 E.P.C.A. 1978	s.110 E.R.A. 1996
	s.66(2) E.P.C.A. 1978	s.110 E.R.A. 1996
	s.66(3) E.P.C.A. 1978	s.110 E.R.A. 1996
	s.67(3) E.P.C.A. 1978	Repealed by T.U.L.R.C.A. 1992, s.300(1), Sched. 1
	s.67(4) E.P.C.A. 1978	s.111(3), (4) E.R.A. 1996
	s.68 E.P.C.A. 1978	s.112 E.R.A. 1996
37–148	"Under section 131 of the Employment Protection (Consolidation) Act 1978"	"Under s.3 of the Industrial Tribunals Act 1996"
	"section 55(4) of the E.P.C.A. 1978"	"section 97(1) of the E.R.A. 1996"
[814]⁹⁰	As amended by T.U.R.E.R.A. 1993, s.38	Unnecessary

PARAGRAPH NUMBER [PAGE] footnote	DERIVATION	DESTINATION
[814][91]	s.131(8) E.P.C.A. 1978	s.41(2) I.T.A. 1996
[814][92]	s.131(1), (4) E.P.C.A. 1978	s.3(1), s.8(1) I.T.A. 1996
[814][93]	s.131(2)(a) E.P.C.A. 1978	s.3(2)(a) I.T.A. 1996
[814][94]	s.131(3) E.P.C.A. 1978	s.3(3) I.T.A. 1996
[814][95]	s.131(2)(b) E.P.C.A. 1978	s.3(2)(b) I.T.A. 1996
37–150		The unfair dismissal provisions were consolidated into Part X of the E.R.A. 1996
[816][9]	E.P.C.A. 1978, s.54 taken in conjunction with s.153(1) (definition of "employee")	s.94 E.R.A. 1996 taken in conjunction with s.230(1) E.R.A. 1996
37–151	"four weeks"	"one month"
[817][12]	s.138(1) E.P.C.A. 1978	s.191(1) E.R.A. 1996
[817][13]	s.80 E.P.C.A. 1978	s.134 E.R.A. 1996
[817][14]	s.146(2) E.P.C.A. 1978	s.200(1) E.R.A. 1996
[817][15]	s.144(3) E.P.C.A. 1978	s.199(6) E.R.A. 1996
[817][20]	s.146(1) E.P.C.A. 1978	Repealed by s.21, Sched. 3, Part I, para. 6 E.A. 1982 NOW spent or unnecessary
[817][21]	s.141(2) E.P.C.A. 1978	s.196(2), (3) E.R.A. 1996
[817][23]	s.64(1)(b) E.P.C.A. 1978 as substituted by s.3(1) Sex Discrimination Act 1986	s.109(1) E.R.A. 1996
	s.151 E.P.C.A. 1978	ss.210, 211, 212 E.R.A. 1996
	Sched. 13, para. 11 E.P.C.A. 1978	s.213 E.R.A. 1996
[818][24]	s.64(1) E.P.C.A. 1978	s.108(1) E.R.A. 1996
[818][25]	s.64(1)(a) E.P.C.A. 1978 s.151 and Sched. 13, para. 11 E.P.C.A. 1978	s.108(1) E.R.A. 1996 s.213 E.R.A. 1996
[818][26]	s.64(2), s.64A(2) E.P.C.A. 1978	s.108(2) E.R.A. 1996
[818][27]	s.146(1) E.P.C.A. 1996	Repealed by s.21, Sched. 3, Part I, para. 6 E.A. 1982 NOW spent or unnecessary

PARAGRAPH NUMBER [PAGE] footnote	DERIVATION	DESTINATION
	s.141(3) E.P.C.A. 1978	s.199(6) E.R.A. 1996
	s.141(2) E.P.C.A. 1978	s.196(2) E.R.A. 1996
	s.64(1) E.P.C.A. 1978	s.108(1) E.R.A. 1996
	Sched. 15, para. 10(1) E.P.C.A. 1978	Sched. 2, E.R.A. 1996
[818][28]	ss.65–66 E.P.C.A. 1978	s.110 E.R.A. 1996
[818][29]	Sched. 2, para. 2(4) E.P.C.A. 1978	ss.97(6), 108(3), 109(2), 110(2), 119(6), 196(4), 199(3), 226(3), 227(3), (4) E.R.A. 1996
	s.146(2) E.P.C.A. 1978	s.200(1) E.R.A. 1996
[818][31]	s.140(1) E.P.C.A. 1978	s.203(1) E.R.A. 1996
[818][33]	s.142(1) as amended by E.A. 1980, s.8(2)	s.197(1) E.R.A. 1996
[818][34]	s.65(1) and (3) E.P.C.A. 1978	s.110(3) and s.110(1) E.R.A. 1996
[818][35]	s.65(2) E.P.C.A. 1978	s.110(3) E.R.A. 1996
[818][36]	s.66 E.P.C.A. 1978	s.110(4), (5) E.R.A. 1996
[818][37]	s.140(2)(d), (e) E.P.C.A. 1978	s.203(2)(e) E.R.A. 1996
[819][39]	s.55(2) E.P.C.A. 1978	s.95(1) E.R.A. 1996
[819][40]	s.55(2)(a) E.P.C.A. 1978	s.95(1)(a) E.R.A. 1996
[819][42]	s.55(2)(b) E.P.C.A. 1978	s.95(1)(b) E.R.A. 1996
[819][43]	s.55(2)(c) E.P.C.A. 1978	s.95(1)(c) E.R.A. 1996
[819][46]	s.55(3) E.P.C.A. 1978	s.95(2) E.R.A. 1996
[819][48]	ss.56, 56A, 86 E.P.C.A. 1978 (as substituted or amended by T.U.R.E.R.A. 1993, s.49(2) and Sched. 8)	ss.96, 137(1) E.R.A. 1996
[820][49]	Sched. 2 E.P.C.A. 1978	s.96 E.R.A. 1996
[820][51]	ss.56, 86 E.P.C.A. 1978	ss.96, 137(1) E.R.A. 1996
[820][53]	s.93 E.P.C.A. 1978	ss.136(5), 139(4), (5) E.R.A. 1996
[821][60]	s.64(1)(a) E.P.C.A. 1978	s.108(1) E.R.A. 1996
[821][61]	s.64(1)(b) E.P.C.A. 1978	s.109(1) E.R.A. 1996
[821][62]	s.67(2) E.P.C.A. 1978	s.111(2) E.R.A. 1996
[821][63]	s.62(4)(a) E.P.C.A. 1978	s.238(5) T.U.L.R.C.A. 1992
[821][66]	s.73(3) E.P.C.A. 1978	s.119(1) and (2) E.R.A. 1996
[821][68]	Sched. 14, para. 7(1)(h), (i) E.P.C.A. 1978	s.226(6) E.R.A. 1996

[387]

PARAGRAPH NUMBER [PAGE] footnote	DERIVATION	DESTINATION
[821][69]	s.55(4) E.P.C.A. 1978	s.97(1) E.R.A. 1996
[821][70]	s.58(5) E.P.C.A. 1978	Repealed by E.A. 1988, ss.11(b), 33(2), Sched. 4
[822][78]	ss.57–60 E.P.C.A. 1978	ss.98–100, ss.103–105 E.R.A. 1996
[822][79]	s.57(1) E.P.C.A. 1978	s.98(1) E.R.A. 1996
[822][80]	s.57(3) E.P.C.A. 1978 as amended by s.6 E.A. 1980	s.98(4)–(6) E.R.A. 1996
[822][83]	s.5 E.P.C.A. 1978	s.5, s.198 E.R.A. 1996
[822][84]	s.60 E.P.C.A. 1978	s.99 E.R.A. 1996
[822][85]	s.57A E.P.C.A. 1978	s.100 E.R.A. 1996
[822][86]	s.60A E.P.C.A. 1978	s.104 E.R.A. 1996
[822][87]	s.57 E.P.C.A. 1978	s.98 E.R.A. 1996
[823][89]	s.57(1)(a) E.P.C.A. 1978	s.98(1)(a) E.R.A. 1996
[823][90]	s.57(2) E.P.C.A. 1978	s.98(2) E.R.A. 1996
[823][91]	s.57(1)(b) E.P.C.A. 1978	s.98(1)(b) E.R.A. 1996
[823][92]	s.57(4)(a) E.P.C.A. 1978	s.98(3)(a) E.R.A. 1996
[823][93]	s.57(4)(b) E.P.C.A. 1978	s.98(3)(b) E.R.A. 1996
[823][94]	s.57(2)(a) E.P.C.A. 1978	s.98(2)(a) E.R.A. 1996
[823][96]	s.57(2)(b) E.P.C.A. 1978	s.98(2)(b) E.R.A. 1996
[823][98]	s.57(2)(c) E.P.C.A. 1978	s.98(2)(c) E.R.A. 1996
[823][99]	s.153(2) E.P.C.A. 1978	s.235(3) E.R.A. 1996
[823][1]	s.57(2)(d) E.P.C.A. 1978	s.98(2)(d) E.R.A. 1996
[823][2]	s.61(2) E.P.C.A. 1978	s.106(3) E.R.A. 1996
	s.61(1) E.P.C.A. 1978	s.106(2) E.R.A. 1996
[824][3]	s.57(1)(b) E.P.C.A. 1978	s.98(1)(b) E.R.A. 1996
[824][6]	ss.57(1)(a), 61 E.P.C.A. 1978	ss.98(1)(b), 106 E.R.A. 1996
[824][7]	s.57(3) E.P.C.A. 1978	ss.98(4)–(6) E.R.A. 1996
[825][15]	E.P.A. 1975, s.6	s.207 E.R.A. 1996
[825][18]	E.P.C.A. 1978, s.57(3) as amended by E.A. 1980, s.6	s.98(4) E.R.A. 1996
[827][39]	ss.57–60A E.P.C.A. 1978	ss.98, 104, 105 E.R.A. 1996

PARAGRAPH NUMBER [PAGE] footnote	DERIVATION	DESTINATION
[827]⁵¹	s.81(2) E.P.C.A. 1978 s.153(2) E.P.C.A. 1978	s.139(1), (2) E.R.A. 1996 s.235(3) E.R.A. 1996
[827]⁵²	s.57(2) E.P.C.A. 1978	s.98(2) E.R.A. 1996
[827]⁵⁴	s.59 E.P.C.A. 1978	s.105 E.R.A. 1996
[828]⁵⁵	s.59(1)(a), (2) E.P.C.A. 1978 as substituted by T.U.R.E.R.A. 1993, ss.24(2), 29(2), Scheds. 5, 8	s.105(1)–(3), (7) E.R.A. 1996
[828]⁵⁷	s.59(1)(b) E.P.C.A. 1978	Repealed by the Deregulation and Contracting Out Act 1994
[828]⁵⁸	s.57(3) E.P.C.A. 1978	s.98(4)–(6) E.R.A. 1996
[828]⁵⁹	s.91(2) expressly excluded from unfair dismissal issues by Sched. 9, para. 5 E.P.C.A. 1978	s.163(2) E.R.A. 1996 expressly excluded from unfair dismissal issues by s.7(6) I.T.A. 1996
[828]⁶¹	s.73 E.P.C.A. 1978	s.122 E.R.A. 1996
37–161	"s.60 of the Employment Protection (Consolidation) Act 1978 as substituted by s.24 of T.U.R.E.R.A. 1993"	"s.99 of the Employment Rights Act 1996"
[829]⁶⁴	E.P.C.A. 1978, s.64(3)–(5) as inserted by T.U.R.E.R.A. 1993 ss.24(3), 28, 29(3), Sched. 5, para. 5	s.108(3) and s.109(2) E.R.A. 1996
37–162	"Trade Union Reform and Employment Rights Act 1993"	"Employment Rights Act 1996"
37–163	"Employment Protection (Consolidation) Act 1978" "Wages Act 1986"	"Employment Rights Act 1996"
[829]⁶⁵	s.57A as inserted by T.U.R.E.R.A. 1993, s.28 and Sched. 5, para. 3	s.100 E.R.A. 1996

PARAGRAPH NUMBER [PAGE] footnote	DERIVATION	DESTINATION
[829][66]	s.60A as inserted by T.U.R.E.R.A. 1993, s.29(1)	s.104 E.R.A. 1996
37–164	"as re-enacted in the 1978 Act"	"as re-enacted in the 1978 Act and then in the 1996 Act"
[829][70]	ss.68–79 E.P.C.A. 1978	s.112–132 E.R.A. 1996
[830[71]	ss.68–71 E.P.C.A. 1978	ss.112–117 E.R.A. 1996
[830][72]	E.P.C.A. s.72(2), (3) as substituted by T.U.R.E.R.A. 1993, s.28 and Sched. 5, para. 7	s.118(2), (3) E.R.A. 1996
[830][74]	s.68(1) E.P.C.A. 1978	s.112(1), (2) E.R.A. 1996
[830][76]	s.69(1) E.P.C.A. 1978	s.113 E.R.A. 1996
[830][77]	s.69(5) E.P.C.A. 1978	s.116(1) E.R.A. 1996
[830][78]	s.69(5)(a) E.P.C.A. 1978	s.116(1)(a) E.R.A. 1996
[830][79]	s.69(5)(b) E.P.C.A. 1978	s.16(1)(b) E.R.A. 1996
[830][80]	s.69(5)(c) E.P.C.A. 1978	s.116(1)(c) E.R.A. 1996
[830][81]	s.70(1) E.P.C.A. 1978	s.116(5), (6) E.R.A. 1996
[830][82]	s.69(2) E.P.C.A. 1978	s.114(1), (2) E.R.A. 1996
[830][83]	s.69(2)(a) E.P.C.A. 1978 subject to s.70(2) E.P.C.A. 1978	s.114(2)(a) E.R.A. 1996 subject to s.114(4) E.R.A. 1996
[830][84]	s.69(2)(b) E.P.C.A. 1978	s.114(2)(b) E.R.A. 1996
[831][85]	s.69(2)(c) E.P.C.A. 1978	s.114(2)(c) E.R.A. 1996
[831][86]	s.69(3) E.P.C.A. 1978	s.114(3) E.R.A. 1996
[831][87]	s.69(6) E.P.C.A. 1978	ss.116(2)–(4) E.R.A. 1996
[831][88]	s.69(6)(a) E.P.C.A. 1978	s.116(3)(a) E.R.A. 1996
[831][89]	s.69(6)(b) E.P.C.A. 1978 subject to s.70(1) E.P.C.A. 1978	s.116(3)(b) E.R.A. 1996 subject to s.116(5) E.R.A. 1996
[831][90]	s.69(6)(c) E.P.C.A. 1978	s.116(3)(c) E.R.A. 1996
[831][91]	s.69(4) E.P.C.A. 1978	s.115(1), (2) E.R.A. 1996
[831][92]	s.69(1) E.P.C.A. 1978	s.113, s.115(1) E.R.A. 1996
[831][93]	s.69(6) and s.69(6)(c) E.P.C.A. 1978	s.116(4) E.R.A. 1996
[831][94]	s.69(4)(a) E.P.C.A. 1978	s.115(2)(a) E.R.A. 1996
[831][95]	s.69(4)(b), (c) E.P.C.A. 1978	s.115(2)(b), (c) E.R.A. 1996
[831][96]	s.69(4)(d) E.P.C.A. 1978 calculated according to s.70(2) E.P.C.A. 1978	s.115(2)(d) E.R.A. 1996 calculated according to s.115(3) E.R.A. 1996

PARAGRAPH NUMBER [PAGE] footnote	DERIVATION	DESTINATION
[831][97] 37–167	s.69(4)(e) E.P.C.A. 1978 "section 75A of the 1978 Act"	s.115(2)(e) E.R.A. 1996 "section 125 of the 1996 Act"
[831][98]	s.71(1) E.P.C.A. 1978 limited by reference to s.71(1A) as inserted by T.U.R.E.R.A. 1993, s.30(2)	s.117(1) E.R.A. 1996 s.124(3) E.R.A. 1996
[832][99]	s.71(2)(a) E.P.C.A. 1978	s.117(3)(a) E.R.A. 1996
[832][1]	s.71(2)(b) E.P.C.A. 1978	s.117(3)(b), s.117(4)(a) E.R.A. 1996
[832][2]	s.71(2)(b)(ii) E.P.C.A. 1978 Sched. 14 E.P.C.A. 1978 Sched. 14, para. 7(1) E.P.C.A. 1978	s.117(5)(b) E.R.A. 1996 ss.220–229 E.R.A. 1996 s.226 E.R.A. 1996
[832][3]	s.71(2)(b)(i) E.P.C.A. 1978 referring to s.71(3) E.P.C.A. 1978	s.117(5)(a) E.R.A. 1996 referring to s.117(6) E.R.A. 1996
[832][4]	s.71(3)(b), (c) E.P.C.A. 1978	s.117(6)(b) E.R.A. 1996
[832][5]	s.71(2)(b) as qualified by s.71(4) E.P.C.A. 1978	s.117(3)(b) and s.117(4)(a) as qualified by s.117(7) E.R.A. 1996
[832][6]	s.71(5) E.P.C.A. 1978	s.117(8) E.R.A. 1996
[832][8]	E.P.C.A. 1978 s.72(2), (3) as added by T.U.R.E.R.A. 1993, s.28 and Sched. 5, para. 7	s.118(2), (3) E.R.A. 1996
[832][10]	s.75A(2) as added by s.9 of the E.A. 1982 setting a minimum of £18,795 as amended by the Unfair Dismissal (Increase of Limits of Basic and Special Awards) Order 1989 (S.I. 1989 No. 528)	s.125(2) E.R.A. 1996 setting a minimum of £20,600
37–168	"Under the Employment Protection (Consolidation) Act 1978"	"Under the Employment Rights Act 1996"

PARAGRAPH NUMBER [PAGE] footnote	DERIVATION	DESTINATION
[832]¹¹	s.68(2) E.P.C.A. 1978	s.112(4) E.R.A. 1996
[832]¹²	s.72 E.P.C.A. 1978	s.118 E.R.A. 1996
[833]¹⁴	s.73(3) E.P.C.A. 1978	s.119(2) E.R.A. 1996
	s.73(6), (7) E.P.C.A. 1978	s.119(5) E.R.A. 1996
	Sched. 13 E.P.C.A. 1978	ss.210–219 E.R.A. 1996
	s.73(4) E.P.C.A. 1978	s.119(3) E.R.A. 1996
	Sched. 14 E.P.C.A. 1978	ss.220–229 E.R.A. 1996
[833]¹⁵	s.73(4) E.P.C.A. 1978	s.119(3) E.R.A. 1996
[833]¹⁶	Sched. 14, para. 8(1) E.P.C.A. 1978 as amended by statutory instrument from time to time	s.227(1), (2) E.R.A. 1996
[833]¹⁷	s.73(2) E.P.C.A. 1978	s.121 E.R.A. 1996
[833]¹⁸	s.73(7) E.P.C.A. 1978	Repealed by E.A. 1982 ss.4, 21(3), Sched. 4
[833]¹⁹	s.73(7A) E.P.C.A. 1978 as inserted by E.A. 1980, s.9	s.122(1) E.R.A. 1996
[833]²⁰	s.73(7B) E.P.C.A. 1978 as inserted by E.A. 1980, s.9	s.122(2) E.R.A. 1996
37–169	"Under the Employment Protection (Consolidation) Act 1978"	"Under the Employment Rights Act 1996"
[833]²²	s.72 E.P.C.A. 1978 referring to s.74 E.P.C.A. 1978	s.118 E.R.A. 1996 referring to ss.123, 124, 126, 127 E.R.A. 1996
[833]²³	s.74(1) as qualified by s.74(2) E.P.C.A. 1978	s.123(1) as qualified by s.123(2) E.R.A. 1996
[833]²⁴	s.74(1) as qualified by s.74(5) E.P.C.A. 1978	s.123(1) as qualified by s.123(5) E.R.A. 1996
[833]²⁵	s.74(4) E.P.C.A. 1978	s.123(4) E.R.A. 1996
[833]²⁷	s.74(3) E.P.C.A. 1978	s.123(3) E.R.A. 1996
[833]²⁸	s.74(7) E.P.C.A. 1978	s.123(7) E.R.A. 1996
[834]⁴¹	s.74(6) E.P.C.A. 1978	s.123(6) E.R.A. 1996
[834]⁴²	s.73(7) E.P.C.A. 1978	Repealed by E.A. 1982, ss.4, 21(3), Sched. 4
[835]⁴³	ss.74(1), 75(1) E.P.C.A. 1978	ss.123(1), 124(1) E.R.A. 1996

PARAGRAPH NUMBER [PAGE] footnote	DERIVATION	DESTINATION
	proviso to s.74(1) referring (as amended by T.U.R.E.R.A. 1993, s.30(3)(a)) to s.74(8) as inserted by T.U.R.E.R.A. 1993, s.30(3)(b) and to s.76 E.P.C.A. 1978	s.123(1) referring to s.124(1) and to s.126 E.R.A. 1996
[835][44] **37–170**	s.75(3) E.P.C.A. 1978 "Under the Employment Protection (Consolidation) Act 1978"	s.124(5) E.R.A. 1996 "Under the Employment Rights Act 1996"
	"... it shall reduce the amount of both a basic ...")	Repealed
	"except that a basic award may not be so reduced where the dismissal was by reason of redundancy"	Repealed
[835][45]	s.73(7) E.P.C.A. 1978	Repealed (see [834][42])
[835][46]	s.74(6) E.P.C.A. 1978	s.123(6) E.R.A. 1996
[835][47]	s.73(7) E.P.C.A. 1978	Repealed (see [834][42])
[836][54]	s.77(1) E.P.C.A. 1978 1978 as amended by T.U.R.E.R.A. 1993, s.28 and Sched. 5	s.128(1) E.R.A. 1996
[836][55]	s.77(2)(a) E.P.C.A. 1978	s.128(2) E.R.A. 1996
[836][57]	s.77A(4) E.P.C.A. 1978	s.129(5) E.R.A. 1996
[836][58]	s.77A(6) E.P.C.A. 1978	s.129(9) E.R.A. 1996
[836][59]	s.78 E.P.C.A. 1978	s.130 E.R.A. 1996
[836][60]	s.78(2) E.P.C.A. 1978	s.130(2) E.R.A. 1996
[836][61]	s.78A E.P.C.A. 1978	s.131 E.R.A. 1996
[836][62]	s.79 E.P.C.A. 1978	s.132 E.R.A. 1996
37–172	"(and now found in the 1978 Act)"	"(and now found in the 1996 Act)"
[836][63]	Sched. 9 E.P.C.A. 1978	ss.6–15 I.T.A. 1996
[836][64]	s.67(2) E.P.C.A. 1978	s.111(2) E.R.A. 1996
[837][66]	s.67(4) E.P.C.A. 1978	s.111(3), (4) E.R.A. 1996
[837][71]	as extended by s.3 (in the employment field)	as re-enacted by E.R.A. 1996, s.109(1)

PARAGRAPH NUMBER [PAGE] footnote	DERIVATION	DESTINATION
[838][79]	s.76 E.P.C.A. 1978	s.126 E.R.A. 1996
37–177	"Part VI of the Employment Protection (Consolidation) Act 1978"	"Part XI of the Employment Rights Act 1996"
[839][3]	s.140 E.P.C.A. 1978	s.203 E.R.A. 1996
[839][4]	s.81(4) E.P.C.A. 1978	s.155 E.R.A. 1996
[839][5]	ss.88, 89 E.P.C.A. 1978	ss.148–152 E.R.A. 1996
37–178	"Under section 93 of the 1978 Act"	"Under section 136 of the 1996 Act"
[840][8]	s.83(2)(a) E.P.C.A. 1978	s.136(1)(a) E.R.A. 1996
[840][9]	s.83(2)(b) E.P.C.A. 1978	s.136(1)(b) E.R.A. 1996
[840][10]	s.83(2)(c) E.P.C.A. 1978	s.136(1)(c) E.R.A. 1996
[840][11]	s.85 E.P.C.A. 1978	s.142 E.R.A. 1996
[840][12]	s.86 E.P.C.A. 1978	s.137(1) E.R.A. 1996
[840][14]	s.84(1) E.P.C.A. 1978	s.138(1) E.R.A. 1996
[840][15]	s.84(3), (4), (6) E.P.C.A. 1978	s.138(2), (4), (5), s.138(3) E.R.A. 1996
[840][16]	s.84(4), (5) E.P.C.A. 1978	ss.138(3), (6) E.R.A. 1996
[840][17]	s.94(1), (2) E.P.C.A. 1978	Repealed
[841][18]	s.94(2) E.P.C.A. 1978	Repealed
[841][21]	Sched. 13, para. 17(2) E.P.C.A. 1978	Repealed
[841][24]	s.95 E.P.C.A. 1978	Repealed
[841][25]	s.92(4) E.P.C.A. 1978	s.136(2) E.R.A. 1996
[841][26]	s.92(4) E.P.C.A. 1978	s.136(2) E.R.A. 1996
	s.83(2)(c) E.P.C.A. 1978	s.136(1) E.R.A. 1996
[841][27]	Sched. 12, paras 14–16 E.P.C.A. 1978	s.174 E.R.A. 1996
[841][28]	s.93(1) E.P.C.A. 1978	s.136(5) E.R.A. 1996
[841][29]	s.93(2)–(4) E.P.C.A. 1978	s.139(4), (5) E.R.A. 1996
	s.93(4) E.P.C.A. 1978	repealed by T.U.R.E.R.A. 1993, s.51, Sched. 10
37–179	"s.81(2) of the 1978 Act"	"s.139(1) of the 1996 Act"
[842][33]	s.91(2) E.P.C.A. 1978	s.163(2) E.R.A. 1996
[842][38]	s.82(3)–(5) E.P.C.A. 1978	s.141(1)–(3), s.146(2) E.R.A. 1996

CHITTY
PARAGRAPH

PARAGRAPH NUMBER [PAGE] footnote	DERIVATION	DESTINATION
[842]38	s.82(2) E.P.C.A. 1978	s.140(1) E.R.A. 1996
[842]39	s.82(6) E.P.C.A. 1978	s.141(4) E.R.A. 1996
[843]40	s.94(3)–(4) E.P.C.A. 1978	Repealed
[843]45	s.81(1) E.P.C.A. 1978	s.135 E.R.A. 1996
[843]46	s.88(1) E.P.C.A. 1978	s.148 E.R.A. 1996
[843]47	s.87(1) E.P.C.A. 1978	s.147(1) E.R.A. 1996
[843]48	s.87(2) E.P.C.A. 1978	s.147(2) E.R.A. 1996
[843]49	s.88(1) E.P.C.A. 1978	s.148(1) E.R.A. 1996
[843]50	s.88(3), (4) E.P.C.A. 1978	s.151(2) E.R.A. 1996
[843]51	s.88(2) E.P.C.A. 1978	s.150(1), (2) E.R.A. 1996
[843]52	s.81(1) E.P.C.A. 1978	s.162(1) E.R.A. 1996
[843]53	s.81(4) E.P.C.A. 1978	s.155 E.R.A. 1996
[844]54	Sched. 4, para. 2 E.P.C.A. 1978	s.162(1), (2) E.R.A. 1996
[844]55	Sched. 4, para. 3 E.P.C.A. 1978	s.162(3) E.R.A. 1996
[844]56	Sched. 4, para. 4 E.P.C.A. 1978	s.162(4), (5) E.R.A. 1996
[844]57	Sched. 4, para. 1 E.P.C.A. 1978	s.162 E.R.A. 1996
[844]59	Sched. 13, para. 14(1)–(4) E.P.C.A. 1978	s.215(2)–(5) E.R.A. 1996
[844]60	Sched. 13, para. 12 E.P.C.A. 1978	s.214 E.R.A. 1996
37–182	"Schedule 14 to the 1978 Act"	"ss.220–229 of the 1996 Act"
	"Under that Schedule"	"Under those provisions"
[844]63	s.152 subject to Sched. 14, para. 7	Unnecessary
[845]65	Sched. 14, para. 3(2) E.P.C.A. 1978	s.221(2) E.R.A. 1996
[845]66	Sched. 14, para. 3(4) E.P.C.A. 1978	s.221(4) E.R.A. 1996

PARAGRAPH NUMBER [PAGE] footnote	DERIVATION	DESTINATION
[845][68]	Sched. 14, para. 3(3) E.P.C.A. 1978	s.221(3) E.R.A. 1996
[845][71]	Sched. 14, para. 8(1)(c), (2) E.P.C.A. 1978	s.227(1)(c), (2) E.R.A. 1996
	s.148 E.P.C.A. 1978	s.208 E.R.A. 1996
37–183	"Part I of Schedule 14 to the Employment Protection (Consolidation) Act 1978"	"section 234 of the Employment Rights Act 1996"
[845][74]	s.152 E.P.C.A. 1978	Unnecessary
[845][75]	Sched. 14, para. 1 E.P.C.A. 1978	s.234(1), (2) E.R.A. 1996
37–184	"1978 Act"	"1996 Act"
[846][80]	s.100(2) E.P.C.A. 1978	s.161(1) E.R.A. 1996
[846][82]	s.82(1) E.P.C.A. 1978 as substituted by s.16(1) of the Employment Act 1989	s.156(1) E.R.A. 1996
[846][83]	s.144(3) E.P.C.A. 1978	s.199(6) E.R.A. 1996
[846][85]	s.142(2) E.P.C.A. 1978	s.197(3) E.R.A. 1996
[846][87]	Sched. 15, para. 12 E.P.C.A. 1978	Sched. 2, para. 12(1) E.R.A. 1978
[846][88]	s.82(2) E.P.C.A. 1978	s.140(1) E.R.A. 1996
[846][89]	s.141(3)–(4) E.P.C.A. 1978	s.196(6) E.R.A. 1996
	s.144(3) E.P.C.A. 1978	s.199(6) E.R.A. 1996
[846][90]	s.96 E.P.C.A. 1978	s.157 E.R.A. 1996
[846][91]	Sched. 5 E.P.C.A. 1978	Repealed 1990
[846][92]	s.145(3)–(4) E.P.C.A. 1978	Repealed by the Dock Work Act 1989, s.7(1), (5), Sched. 1, Part I, Sched. 2, para. 7
[846][93]	s.144(2) E.P.C.A. 1978	s.199(2) E.R.A. 1996
[846][94]	s.99(1) E.P.C.A. 1978	s.159 E.R.A. 1996
[846][95]	s.146(1) E.P.C.A. 1978	Repealed by s.21, Sched. 3, Part I, para. 6 E.A.—NOW SPENT
[846][96]	s.91 E.P.C.A. 1978	s.163 E.R.A. 1996
[847][97]	By virtue of Sched. 9 E.P.C.A. 1978	s.7 of the I.T.A. 1996
	s.136 of the 1978 Act	s.21 of the I.T.A. 1996
	s.135 E.P.C.A. 1978	s.22 I.T.A. 1996

PARAGRAPH NUMBER [PAGE] footnote	DERIVATION	DESTINATION
[847]⁹⁸	s.101(1) E.P.C.A. 1978	s.164(1) E.R.A. 1996
	s.153(1) E.P.C.A. 1978	s.235(1) E.R.A. 1996
	s.90 E.P.C.A. 1978	ss.145, 153 E.R.A. 1996
[847]⁹⁹	s.101(1) E.P.C.A. 1978	s.164(1) E.R.A. 1996
[847]¹	s.101(2) E.P.C.A. 1978	s.164(2), (3) E.R.A. 1996

EMPLOYMENT RIGHTS ACT 1996 DERIVATIONS TABLE

This table lists those sections of the Employment Rights Act 1996, Industrial Tribunals Act 1996 and Trade Union and Labour Relations (Consolidation) Act 1992 (Part III) whose antecedents are discussed in the Main Work in this Chapter and shows the section, or page and note number, where the discussion may be found.

Bold paragraph numbers refer to the corresponding paragraph number in the Main Work. These are followed by references to footnotes to that section, preceded by the page number in square brackets.

NEW LEGISLATION	DERIVATION	PARAGRAPH NUMBER [PAGE] footnote
Part I of E.R.A. 1996	"Part I of the Employment Protection (Consolidation) Act 1978"	**37–106**
Parts I, IX of E.R.A. 1996	E.P.C.A. 1978, Parts I, IV	[700]²⁶
Part II of E.R.A. 1996	"Part I of the Wages Act 1986"	**37–080**
Part II of E.R.A. 1996	"Part I of the Wages Act 1986"	**37–137**
Part II, s.191(1)–(4), s.192(1), s.201, s.203, s.205(2), s.230(3)–(5), s.231, s.235(1) E.R.A. 1996	Part I, WA 1986	**37–007**
Parts III, V, VI, VII and VIII of E.R.A. 1996	E.P.C.A. 1978, Parts II and III	**37–005**
Part VIII E.R.A. 1996	"The new Part III"	**37–100**
Part VIII of E.R.A. 1996	"Part III of the Employment Protection (Consolidation) Act 1978"	**37–100**
Part XI of E.R.A. 1996	E.P.C.A. 1978, Part VI	[700]²⁷
Part XI of E.R.A. 1996	E.P.C.A. 1978, Part VI	[715]⁸³
Part XI of E.R.A. 1996	"Part VI of the Employment Protection (Consolidation) Act 1978"	**37–177**

NEW LEGISLATION	DERIVATION	PARAGRAPH NUMBER [PAGE] footnote
Part X of E.R.A. 1996	E.P.C.A. 1978, Part V	**37–005**
Part IX of E.R.A. 1996	Employment Protection (Consolidation) Act 1978, Part IV	[783][38]
Part VIII of E.R.A. 1996	Part III E.P.C.A. 1978	[775][54]
Part VIII of E.R.A. 1996	Part III of the Act	[775][57]
ss.1–7 E.R.A. 1996	s.26 T.U.R.E.R.A. 1993 provides that ss.1–6 E.P.C.A. 1978 are now as substituted by Sched. 4 to the 1993 Act	[720][32]
s.1 E.R.A. 1996	"s.1 E.P.C.A. 1978 as subsequently amended"	**37–033**
s.1 E.R.A. 1996	s.1 E.P.C.A. 1978	[722][51]
s.1 E.R.A. 1996	s.1 E.P.C.A. 1978	[722][57]
s.1 E.R.A. 1996	s.1 E.P.C.A. 1978	[751][77]
s.1(4) E.R.A. 1996	s.1(3) E.P.C.A. 1978	[742][68]
s.1(4)(c) E.R.A. 1996	s.1(3)(c) E.P.C.A. 1978 as substituted by Sched. 4 T.U.R.E.R.A. 1993	[764][42]
s.1(4)(d)(i) E.R.A. 1996	s.1(3)(d)(i) E.P.C.A. 1978 (as substituted by Sched. 4 to T.U.R.E.R.A. 1993)	[743][75]
s.1(4)(d)(ii) E.R.A. 1996	s.1(3)(d)(ii) E.P.C.A. 1978 (as substituted by Sched. 4 to T.U.R.E.R.A. 1993)	[743][78]
s.1(4)(d)(iii), s.1(5) E.R.A. 1996	s.1(2) E.P.C.A. 1978	[720][34]
s.1(4)(e) E.R.A. 1996	s.1(3)(e) E.P.C.A. 1978	[779][5]
s.1(4)(g) E.R.A. 1996	s.1(3)(g) E.P.C.A. 1978	[780][7]
s.1(4)(j) E.R.A. 1996	s.1(1)(j) E.P.C.A. 1978	[728][7]
s.2(1) E.R.A. 1996	s.2(1) E.P.C.A. 1978	[779][6]
s.2(2), (3) E.R.A. 1996	s.2(2) and (3) E.P.C.A. 1978	[721][41]
s.2(2), (3) E.R.A. 1996	T.U.R.E.R.A. 1993 Sched. 4 substituting new E.P.C.A. 1978, s.2(2) and (3)	[728][6]

NEW LEGISLATION	DERIVATION	PARAGRAPH NUMBER [PAGE] footnote
s.2(2), (3) E.R.A. 1996	s.2(2) E.P.C.A. 1978	[792][44]
s.2(4) E.R.A. 1978	s.2(4) E.P.C.A. 1978	[721][42]
s.3(1)(a) E.R.A. 1996	s.3(1)(a) E.P.C.A. 1978	[721][36]
s.3(1)(b), (c) E.R.A. 1996	s.3(1)(b) and (c) E.P.C.A. 1978	[721][38]
s.3(2) E.R.A. 1996	s.3(2) E.P.C.A. 1978	[721][37]
s.3(3) E.R.A. 1996	s.3(3) E.P.C.A. 1978	[721][40]
s.3(5) E.R.A. 1996	s.3(1)(d) E.P.C.A. 1978	[721][39]
s.4(1), (3) E.R.A. 1996	s.4(1) E.P.C.A. 1978	[721][43]
s.4(2), (4), (5) E.R.A. 1996	s.4(2), (3) and (4) E.P.C.A. 1978	[721][44]
s.4(6)(a) E.R.A. 1996	s.4(5)(a)(i) E.P.C.A. 1978	[721][45]
s.4(6)(b) E.R.A. 1996	s.4(5)(a)(ii) E.P.C.A. 1978	[721][46]
s.4(8) E.R.A. 1996	s.4(6) E.P.C.A. 1978	[721][47]
s.5 E.R.A. 1996	s.5 E.P.C.A. 1978	[822][83]
s.6 E.R.A. 1996	s.2(2) and (3) E.P.C.A. 1978	[721][41]
s.6 E.R.A. 1996	T.U.R.E.R.A. 1993 Sched. 4 substituting new E.P.C.A. 1978, s.2(2) and (3)	[728][6]
s.6 E.R.A. 1996	s.4(2), (3) and (4) E.P.C.A. 1978	[721][44]
s.8 E.R.A. 1996	ss.8–11 E.P.C.A. 1978	[742][69]
s.8 E.R.A. 1996	s.8 E.P.C.A. 1978	[755][24]
s.8 E.R.A. 1996	s.8 E.P.C.A. 1978	[759][82]
s.8(a)–(d) E.R.A. 1996	s.8(a)–(d) E.P.C.A. 1978	[755][25]
s.9 E.R.A. 1996	ss.8–11 E.P.C.A. 1978	[742][69]
s.9 E.R.A. 1996	s.9 E.P.C.A. 1978	[759][83]
s.9(1), (2) E.R.A. 1996	s.9(1) E.P.C.A. 1978	[755][27]
s.9(3) E.R.A. 1996	s.9(2) E.P.C.A. 1978	[755][28]
s.9(4) E.R.A. 1996	s.9(3) E.P.C.A. 1978	[755][29]
s.10 E.R.A. 1996	ss.8–11 E.P.C.A. 1978	[742][69]
s.11 E.R.A. 1996	ss.8–11 E.P.C.A. 1978	[742][69]
s.11 1996	s.11 E.P.C.A. 1978	**37–078**
s.12 E.R.A. 1996	ss.8–11 E.P.C.A. 1978	[742][69]
s.12 E.R.A. 1996	s.11 E.P.C.A. 1978	**37–078**
s.11 E.R.A. 1996	s.11 E.P.C.A. 1978	[722][55]
s.11(1) E.R.A. 1996	s.11(1) E.P.C.A. 1978	[722][52]

NEW LEGISLATION	DERIVATION	PARAGRAPH NUMBER [PAGE] footnote
s.11(1) E.R.A. 1996	s.11(1) E.P.C.A. 1978	[755]³⁰
s.11(1) E.R.A. 1996	s.11(1) E.P.C.A. 1978	[788]⁸
s.11(2) E.R.A. 1996	s.11(2) E.P.C.A. 1978	[722]⁵²
s.11(2) E.R.A. 1996	s.11(2) E.P.C.A. 1978	[780]⁹
s.12(2) E.R.A. 1996	s.11(6) E.P.C.A. 1978	[722]⁵²
s.12(2) E.R.A. 1996	s.11(6) E.P.C.A. 1978	[722]⁵³
s.12(3) E.R.A. 1996	s.11(8)(a) E.P.C.A. 1978	[755]³²
s.12(4), (5) E.R.A. 1996	s.11(8)(b) E.P.C.A. 1978	[755]³³
ss.13–15 E.R.A. 1996	s.1 W.A. 1986	[755]³⁵
s.13–15 E.R.A. 1996	"Under s.1 of the Wages Act 1986"	**37–079**
s.13(1) E.R.A. 1996	s.1(1) W.A. 1986	[756]⁴⁶
s.13(1)(a) E.R.A. 1996	s.1(1)(a) W.A. 1986	[756]⁴⁸
s.13(1)(b) E.R.A. 1996	s.1(1)(b) W.A. 1986	[756]⁴⁹
s.13(1), (2) E.R.A. 1996	s.1(1)(a), (3) W.A. 1986	[752]⁸⁵
s.13(2)(a) E.R.A. 1996	s.1(3)(a) W.A. 1986	[756]⁵⁰
s.13(2)(b) E.R.A. 1996	s.1(3)(b) W.A. 1986	[756]⁵¹
s.13(3), (4) E.R.A. 1996	s.8(3), (4) W.A. 1986	[758]⁶⁸
s.14 E.R.A. 1996	"s.1 of the Wages Act"	**37–073**
s.14(1) E.R.A. 1996	s.1(5)(a) W.A. 1986	[756]⁵²
s.14(2) E.R.A. 1996	s.1(5)(b) W.A. 1986	[756]⁵³
s.14(3) E.R.A. 1996	s.1(5)(c) W.A. 1986	[757]⁵⁴
s.14(4) E.R.A. 1996	s.1(5)(d) W.A. 1986	[757]⁵⁵
s.14(5) E.R.A. 1996	s.1(5)(e) W.A. 1986	[752]⁸⁶
s.14(5) E.R.A. 1996	s.1(5)(e) W.A. 1986	[757]⁵⁶
s.14(6) E.R.A. 1996	s.1(5)(f) W.A. 1986	[757]⁵⁷
s.15(1) E.R.A. 1996	s.1(2) W.A. 1986	[756]⁴⁷
s.15(2)(a) E.R.A. 1996	s.1(3)(a) W.A. 1986	[756]⁵⁰
s.15(2)(b) E.R.A. 1996	s.1(3)(b) W.A. 1986	[756]⁵¹
s.16(1) E.R.A. 1996	s.1(5)(a) W.A. 1986	[756]⁵²
s.16(2) E.R.A. 1996	s.1(5)(b) W.A. 1986	[756]⁵³
s.16(3) E.R.A. 1996	s.1(5)(e) W.A. 1986	[757]⁵⁶
s.16(4) E.R.A. 1996	s.1(5)(f) W.A. 1986	[757]⁵⁷
ss.17–22 E.R.A. 1996	ss.2–4 W.A. 1986	[756]³⁶
ss.17–22 E.R.A. 1996	ss.2–4 W.A. 1986	[758]⁷¹
s.17(1)–(3), (6) E.R.A. 1996	s.2(1), (2) W.A. 1986	[758]⁷²
s.17(2), (3) E.R.A. 1996	s.2(2) W.A. 1986	[758]⁷⁶
s.18(1) E.R.A. 1996	s.2(1), (2) W.A. 1986	[758]⁷²
s.18(2), (3) E.R.A. 1996	s.2(3), s.3(3)(b), s.4(4) W.A. 1986	[758]⁷⁵

NEW LEGISLATION	DERIVATION	PARAGRAPH NUMBER [PAGE] footnote
s.19(1)–(4) E.R.A. 1996	s.2(4), (5) W.A. 1986	[758][72]
s.20(1)–(3)(a) E.R.A. 1996	s.3(1)–(3)(a), (6) W.A. 1986	[758][74]
s.20(3)(b) E.R.A. 1996	s.2(3), s.3(3)(b), s.4(4) W.A. 1986	[758][75]
s.20(4) E.R.A. 1996	s.3(1)–(3)(a), (6) W.A. 1986	[758][74]
s.20(5) E.R.A. 1996	s.2(3), s.3(3)(b), s.4(4) W.A. 1986	[758][75]
s.20(5) E.R.A. 1996	s.4(5), (6) W.A. 1986	[758][72]
s.21(1), (2) E.R.A. 1996	s.3(4), (5) W.A. 1986	[758][72]
s.21(3) E.R.A. 1996	s.4(5), (6) W.A. 1986	[758][72]
s.22(1)–(3) E.R.A. 1996	s.4(1)–(3) W.A. 1986	[758][73]
s.22(4) E.R.A. 1996	s.4(5), (6) W.A. 1986	[758][72]
ss.23–26 E.R.A. 1996	ss.5–6 W.A. 1986	[756][37]
s.23(1)–(4) E.R.A. 1996	s.5(1)–(3) W.A. 1986	[756][44]
s.24 E.R.A. 1996	s.5(4)–(8) E.A. 1986	[756][45]
s.25(1)–(5) E.R.A. 1996	s.5(4)–(8) E.A. 1986	[756][45]
s.26 E.R.A. 1996	s.6(2) W.A. 1986	[756][43]
s.27(1)(a) E.R.A. 1996	s.7(1)(a) W.A. 1986	[757][58]
s.27(1)(b)–(f) E.R.A. 1996	s.7(1)(d)–(f) W.A. 1986	[757][60]
s.27(1)(g), (h) E.R.A. 1996	s.7(1)(b), (c) W.A. 1986	[757][59]
s.27(2)(a) E.R.A. 1996	s.7(2)(a) W.A. 1986	[757][62]
s.27(2)(b) E.R.A. 1996	s.7(2)(b) W.A. 1986	[757][63]
s.27(2)(c), (d) E.R.A. 1996	s.7(2)(c), (d) W.A. 1986	[757][64]
s.27(2)(e) E.R.A. 1996	s.7(2)(e) W.A. 1986	[757][65]
s.27(3) E.R.A. 1996	s.7(3) W.A. 1986	[757][61]
s.27(5) E.R.A. 1996	s.7(4) W.A. 1986	[757][66]
ss.28–35 E.R.A. 1996	ss.12–18 E.P.C.A. 1978	[750][57]
s.29 E.R.A. 1996	s.143 E.P.C.A. 1978	[750][58]
s.29(1) E.R.A. 1996	s.143(2) E.P.C.A. 1978	[747][24]
s.29(2) E.R.A. 1996	s.143(3)(a) E.P.C.A. 1978	[709][15]

NEW LEGISLATION	DERIVATION	PARAGRAPH NUMBER [PAGE] footnote
s.29(2) E.R.A. 1996	s.143(3)–(4) E.P.C.A. 1978 (contract for not more than twelve weeks)	[747][21]
s.29(2) E.R.A. 1996	s.143(3) E.P.C.A. 1978 (contracts for not more than twelve weeks)	[750][57]
s.29(3) E.R.A. 1996	s.13(1) E.P.C.A. 1978	[750][59]
s.29(4), (5) E.R.A. 1996	s.13(2) E.P.C.A. 1978	[750][60]
s.30(1) E.R.A. 1996	s.14(1) E.P.C.A. 1978	[750][61]
s.30 E.R.A. 1996	s.14 E.P.C.A. 1978 (calculation of guarantee payment)	[764][43]
s.30(2)–(4) E.R.A. 1996	s.14(2) E.P.C.A. 1978	[750][63]
s.31(1) E.R.A. 1996 and regulations made from time to time	s.15(1) E.P.C.A. 1978 and regulations made from time to time	[750][64]
s.31(2) E.R.A. 1996	s.15(2) E.P.C.A. 1978, as amended by s.14 E.A. 1989	[750][66]
s.31(3)–(5) E.R.A. 1996	s.15(3) E.P.C.A. 1978	[750][65]
s.32(2) E.R.A. 1996	s.16(2) E.P.C.A. 1978	[750][67]
s.32(3) E.R.A. 1996	s.16(3) E.P.C.A. 1978	[751][68]
s.33 E.R.A. 1996	s.16(4) E.P.C.A. 1978	[751][71]
s.34(1) E.R.A. 1996	s.17(1) E.P.C.A. 1978	[751][69]
s.34(2) E.R.A. 1996	limitation period— s.17(2) E.P.C.A. 1978	[751][69]
s.34(3) E.R.A. 1996	s.17(3) E.P.C.A. 1978	[751][70]
s.35(1), (2) E.R.A. 1996	s.18(1), (2) as amended by Sched. 10 to T.U.R.E.R.A. 1993	[751][72]
s.35(4), (5) E.R.A. 1996	s.18(4) E.P.C.A. 1978	[751][74]
s.41(2) I.T.A. 1996	s.131(8) E.P.C.A. 1978	[814][91]
s.44 E.R.A. 1996	s.28 and Sched. 5 T.U.R.E.R.A. 1993	[764][41]
s.48 E.R.A. 1996	s.28 and Sched. 5 T.U.R.E.R.A. 1993	[764][41]
s.48 1996	s.22 E.P.C.A. 1978	[747][27]
s.49 E.R.A. 1996	s.28 and Sched. 5 T.U.R.E.R.A. 1993	[764][41]
s.49 E.R.A. 1996	s.22 E.P.C.A. 1978	[747][27]

NEW LEGISLATION	DERIVATION	PARAGRAPH NUMBER [PAGE] footnote
s.50 E.R.A. 1996	s.29 E.P.C.A. 1978	[753][98]
s.50 E.R.A. 1996	s.29 E.P.C.A. 1978	[754][18]
ss.50–63 E.R.A. 1996	ss.29–31 E.P.C.A. 1978	[767][71]
s.50(1)–(3), (5)–(9)	s.29(1), (2), (3) E.P.C.A. 1978	[768][81]
s.50(4) E.R.A. 1996	s.29(4) E.P.C.A. 1978	[768][82]
ss.51, 54, 57, 60 E.R.A. 1996	ss.27–31 E.P.C.A. 1978	[767][72]
s.51(1) E.R.A. 1996	s.29 E.P.C.A. 1978	[753][98]
s.51(1) E.R.A. 1996	s.29(6) E.P.C.A. 1978	[768][86]
s.51(2) E.R.A. 1996	s.30(1) E.P.C.A. 1978	[768][86]
s.51(3), (4) E.R.A. 1996 and s.172 T.U.L.R.C.A. 1992	s.30(2) E.P.C.A. 1978	[768][87]
ss.52–54 E.R.A. 1996	s.31 E.P.C.A. 1978	[753][99]
s.52(1) E.R.A. 1996	s.31(1) E.P.C.A. 1978	[768][83]
s.52(2) E.R.A. 1996	s.31(2) E.P.C.A. 1978	[768][84]
s.53 E.R.A. 1996	s.31 E.P.C.A. 1978	[753][4]
s.53(5) and s.54(4) E.R.A. 1996	s.31(9) E.P.C.A. 1978	[768][89]
ss.53(5), 54(5) E.R.A. 1996	s.31(9) E.P.C.A. 1978	[754][13]
s.53(7) E.R.A. 1996	s.31(11) E.P.C.A. 1978	[754][14]
s.54(1) E.R.A. 1996	s.31(6) E.P.C.A. 1978	[768][86]
s.54(2) E.R.A. 1996	s.31(7) E.P.C.A. 1978	[768][86]
s.54(3), referring to s.53(4) E.R.A. 1996	s.31(8), referring to s.31(5) E.P.C.A. 1978	[768][88]
ss.55–57 E.R.A. 1996	s.31A E.P.C.A. 1978 (added by s.13 E.A. 1980)	[753][1]
s.55(1)–(3) E.R.A. 1996	s.31A(1)–(3) E.P.C.A. 1978	[768][85]
s.56(1) E.R.A. 1996	s.31(3) E.P.C.A. 1978	[753][10]
s.56(1)–(4) E.R.A. 1996	s.31A(4)–(5) E.P.C.A. 1978	[754][15]
s.56(5)–(6) E.R.A. 1996	s.31A(9)–(10) E.P.C.A. 1978	[754][16]
s.57(1) E.R.A. 1996	s.31A(6) E.P.C.A. 1978	[768][86]
s.57(1)–(5) E.R.A. 1996	s.31A(6)–(8) E.P.C.A. 1978	[754][17]
s.57(2) E.R.A. 1996	s.31A(7) E.P.C.A. 1978	[768][86]

NEW LEGISLATION	DERIVATION	PARAGRAPH NUMBER [PAGE] footnote
s.57(3)–(5) E.R.A. 1996	s.31A(8) E.P.C.A. 1978	[769][90]
s.64 E.R.A. 1978	s.19 and Sched. 1 E.P.C.A. 1978	[747][20]
s.64 E.R.A. 1996	s.19 E.P.C.A. 1978	[747][21]
s.65 E.R.A. 1996	s.20 E.P.C.A. 1978	[747][21]
s.65(3) E.R.A. 1996	s.20(1) E.P.C.A. 1978	[747][22]
s.65(4)(a) E.R.A. 1996	s.20(2)(a) E.P.C.A. 1978	[747][23]
s.65(4)(b) E.R.A. 1996	s.20(2)(b) E.P.C.A. 1978	[747][23]
s.66 E.R.A. 1996	s.45 E.P.C.A. 1978	[776][71]
ss.66–70 E.R.A. 1996	ss.45–47 E.P.C.A. 1978 as substituted by s.25 and Sched. 3 T.U.R.E.R.A. 1993	[776][70]
ss.66(1), (2), 70(1)–(3) E.R.A. 1996	ss.45(3)–(6), 47(6)–(8) E.P.C.A. 1978	[777][74]
ss.67, 70(4)–(7) E.R.A. 1996	s.46 E.P.C.A. 1978	[776][72]
ss.68–70 E.R.A. 1996	s.47 E.P.C.A. 1978	[776][73]
s.69(1) and ss.220–229 E.R.A. 1996	s.21 and Sched. 14 E.P.C.A. 1978	[747][25]
s.69(3) E.R.A. 1996	s.21(3) E.P.C.A. 1978	[747][26]
s.70 E.R.A. 1996	s.22 E.P.C.A. 1978	[747][27]
s.71 E.R.A. 1996	s.33(1), (2) E.P.C.A. 1978	[775][60]
ss.71–78 E.R.A. 1996	ss.33–38A E.P.C.A. 1978, as substituted by s.23(2) T.U.R.E.R.A. 1993	[775][58]
s.72 E.R.A. 1996	s.34 E.P.C.A. 1978 (commencement of maternity leave period)	[776][61]
s.73 E.R.A. 1996	s.35 E.P.C.A. 1978	[775][59]
s.74 E.R.A. 1996	s.36 E.P.C.A. 1978 (notice of commencement of leave)	[776][61]
s.75 E.R.A. 1996	s.37 E.P.C.A. 1978 (requirement to inform employer of pregnancy)	[776][61]
s.77 E.R.A. 1996	s.38 E.P.C.A. 1978	[776][62]
s.78 E.R.A. 1996	s.38A E.P.C.A. 1978	[776][63]
s.79 E.R.A. 1996	s.39 E.P.C.A. 1978	[776][65]

NEW LEGISLATION	DERIVATION	PARAGRAPH NUMBER [PAGE] footnote
ss.79–85 E.R.A. 1996	ss.39–44 E.P.C.A. 1978, as substituted by s.23 and Sched. 2 T.U.R.E.R.A. 1993	[776][64]
s.80 E.R.A. 1996	s.40 E.P.C.A. 1978	[776][66]
s.81 E.R.A. 1996	s.41 E.P.C.A. 1978	[776][68]
s.82 E.R.A. 1996	s.42 E.P.C.A. 1978	[776][67]
s.85 E.R.A. 1996	s.44 E.P.C.A. 1978	[776][69]
s.86 E.R.A. 1996	s.49 E.P.C.A. 1978	[739][34]
s.86 E.R.A. 1996	s.49 E.P.C.A. 1978	[783][40]
s.86 E.R.A. 1996	s.49 E.P.C.A. 1978	[783][47]
s.86 E.R.A. 1996	s.49 E.P.C.A. 1978	[784][51]
s.86(1) E.R.A. 1996	s.49(1) E.P.C.A. 1978	[783][41]
s.86(1) E.R.A. 1996	s.49(1) E.R.A. 1978	[786][75]
s.86(2) E.R.A. 1996	s.49(2) E.P.C.A. 1978	[783][42]
s.86(3) E.R.A. 1996	s.49(3) E.P.C.A. 1978	[783][43]
s.86(3) E.R.A. 1996	"section 49(3)"	[783][43]
s.86(3) E.R.A. 1996	"section 49(3) of the 1978 Act"	**37–114**
s.86(4) E.R.A. 1996	s.49(4) E.P.C.A. 1978	[783][44]
s.86(5) E.R.A. 1996	s.143(3)(b) E.P.C.A. 1978	[783][45]
s.86(6) E.R.A. 1996	s.49(5) E.P.C.A. 1978	[783][46]
s.87(3) and ss.88–91 E.R.A. 1996	See now Sched. 3 to 1978 Act	[750][56]
s.87(4) E.R.A. 1996	s.50(3) E.P.C.A. 1978	[786][80]
s.88(1) E.R.A. 1996	Sched. 3, para. 2(1)(b) E.P.C.A. 1978	[743][79]
s.88(1) E.R.A. 1996	Sched. 3, para. 2(1) E.P.C.A. 1978	[786][78]
s.89(1)–(4) E.R.A. 1996	Sched. 3, para. 3(1)–(3) E.P.C.A. 1978	[786][79]
ss.87–91 E.R.A. 1996	Sched. 3 E.P.C.A. 1978 (rights of employee during period of notice)	[764][43]
ss.87–91 E.R.A. 1996	s.50, Sched. 3, E.P.C.A. 1978	[786][74]
ss.87–91(4) E.R.A. 1996	s.50; Sched. 3 E.P.C.A. 1978	[783][48]
ss.88(2), 89(2) E.R.A. 1996	Sched. 3, paras. 2(2), 3(2) E.P.C.A. 1978	[786][81]

NEW LEGISLATION	DERIVATION	PARAGRAPH NUMBER [PAGE] footnote
ss.88(3), 89(5) E.R.A. 1996	Sched. 3, paras. 2(3), 3(4) E.P.C.A. 1978	[786][83]
s.90 E.R.A. 1996	Sched. 3, para. 4 E.P.C.A. 1978	[786][82]
s.91(1) E.R.A. 1996	Sched. 3, para. 5 E.P.C.A. 1978	[787][84]
s.91(2) E.R.A. 1996	Sched. 3, para. 6 E.P.C.A. 1978	[787][85]
s.91(3) E.R.A. 1996	Sched. 3, para. 7(1) E.P.C.A. 1978	[787][86]
s.91(4) E.R.A. 1996	Sched. 3, para. 7(2) E.P.C.A. 1978	[787][87]
s.91(5) E.R.A. 1996	s.51 E.P.C.A. 1978	[783][49]
s.92 E.R.A. 1996	"section 53 of the Employment Protection (Consolidation) Act 1978"	**37–176**
s.92(1)(a) and (b) E.R.A. 1996	s.53(1)(a) and (b) E.P.C.A. 1978	[803][57]
s.92(1)(c) E.R.A. 1996	s.53(1)(c) E.P.C.A. 1978	[803][59]
s.92(2) E.R.A. 1996 s.92(2)(a) E.R.A. 1996	s.53(1) E.P.C.A. 1978 s.53(4)(a) E.P.C.A. 1978	[803][60]
s.92(3) E.R.A. 1996	s.53(2) E.P.C.A. 1978	[803][62]
s.92(3) E.R.A. 1996	s.53(2) E.P.C.A. 1978	[803][64]
s.92(3) E.R.A. 1996	s.53(2) E.P.C.A. 1978	[804][70]
s.92(4) E.R.A. 1996	s.53(2A) E.P.C.A. 1978	[804][71]
s.92(6) E.R.A. 1996	s.153(1) E.P.C.A. 1978 referring to Trade Union and Labour Relations Act 1974, Sched. 1, para. 5	[803][63]
s.93(1) E.R.A. 1996	s.53(4) E.P.C.A. 1978	[803][65]
s.93(2)(b) E.R.A. 1996	s.53(4)(b) E.P.C.A. 1978	[803][67]
s.93(3) E.R.A. 1996	limitation period, s.53(5) E.P.C.A. 1978	[816][65]
s.94 E.R.A. 1996 taken in conjunction with s.230(1) E.R.A. 1996	E.P.C.A. 1978, s.54 taken in conjunction with s.153(1) (definition of "employee")	[816][9]
s.95(1) E.R.A. 1996	s.55(2) E.P.C.A. 1978	[819][39]
s.95(1)(a) E.R.A. 1996	s.55(2)(a) E.P.C.A. 1978	[819][40]

NEW LEGISLATION	DERIVATION	PARAGRAPH NUMBER [PAGE] footnote
s.95(1)(b) E.R.A. 1996	s.55(2)(b) E.P.C.A. 1978	[819][42]
s.95(1)(c) E.R.A. 1996	s.55(2)(c) E.P.C.A. 1978	[802][45]
s.95(1)(c) E.R.A. 1996	s.55(2)(c) E.P.C.A. 1978	[819][43]
s.95(2) E.R.A. 1996	s.55(3) E.P.C.A. 1978	[819][46]
s.96 E.R.A. 1996	Sched. 2 E.P.C.A. 1978	[820][49]
ss.96, 137(1) E.R.A. 1996	ss.56, 56A, 86 E.P.C.A. 1978 (as substituted or amended by T.U.R.E.R.A. 1993, s.49(2) and Sched. 8)	[819][48]
ss.96, 137(1) E.R.A. 1996	ss.56, 86 E.P.C.A. 1978	[820][51]
s.97(1) E.R.A. 1996	"section 55(4) of the E.P.C.A. 1978"	
ss.97(6), 108(3), 109(2), 110(2), 119(6), 196(4), 199(3), 226(3), 227(3), (4) E.R.A. 1996	Sched. 2, para. 2(4) E.P.C.A. 1978	[818][29]
ss.98(1)(b), 106 E.R.A. 1996	ss.57(1)(a), 61 E.P.C.A. 1978	[824][6]
ss.98(4)–(6) E.R.A. 1996	s.57(3) E.P.C.A. 1978	[824][7]
ss.98, 104, 105 E.R.A. 1996	ss.57–60A E.P.C.A. 1978	[827][39]
ss.98–100, ss.103–105 E.R.A. 1996	ss.57–60 E.P.C.A. 1978	[822][78]
s.97(1) E.R.A. 1996	s.55(4) E.P.C.A. 1978	[821][69]
s.98 E.R.A. 1996	s.57 E.P.C.A. 1978	[822][87]
s.98(1) E.R.A. 1996	s.57(1) E.P.C.A. 1978	[822][79]
s.98(1)(a) E.R.A. 1996	s.57(1)(a) E.P.C.A. 1978	[823][89]
s.98(1)(b) E.R.A. 1996	s.57(1)(b) E.P.C.A. 1978	[823][91]
s.98(1)(b) E.R.A. 1996	s.57(1)(b) E.P.C.A. 1978	[824][3]
s.98(2) E.R.A. 1996	s.57(2) E.P.C.A. 1978	[823][90]
s.98(2) E.R.A. 1996	s.57(2) E.P.C.A. 1978	[827][52]
s.98(2)(a) E.R.A. 1996	s.57(2)(a) E.P.C.A. 1978	[823][94]
s.98(2)(b) E.R.A. 1996	s.57(2)(b) E.P.C.A. 1978	[823][96]
s.98(2)(c) E.R.A. 1996	s.57(2)(c) E.P.C.A. 1978	[823][98]
s.98(2)(d) E.R.A. 1996	s.57(2)(d) E.P.C.A. 1978	[823][1]
s.98(3)(a) E.R.A. 1996	s.57(4)(a) E.P.C.A. 1978	[823][92]
s.98(3)(b) E.R.A. 1996	s.57(4)(b) E.P.C.A. 1978	[823][93]
s.98(4) E.R.A. 1996	E.P.C.A. 1978, s.57(3) as amended by E.A. 1980, s.6	[825][18]

NEW LEGISLATION	DERIVATION	PARAGRAPH NUMBER [PAGE] footnote
s.98(4)–(6) E.R.A. 1996	s.57(3) E.P.C.A. 1978 as amended by s.6 E.A. 1980	[822]^{80}
s.98(4)–(6) E.R.A. 1996	s.57(3) E.P.C.A. 1978	[828]^{58}
s.98(6) E.R.A. 1996	s.28 and Sched. 5 T.U.R.E.R.A. 1993	[764]^{41}
s.99 E.R.A. 1996	"s.60 of the Employment Protection (Consolidation) Act 1978 as substituted by s.24 of T.U.R.E.R.A. 1993	**37–161**
s.99 E.R.A. 1996	s.60 E.P.C.A. 1978	[822]^{84}
s.100 E.R.A. 1996	s.28 and Sched. 5 T.U.R.E.R.A. 1993	[764]^{41}
s.100 E.R.A. 1996	s.57A E.P.C.A. 1978	[822]^{85}
s.100 E.R.A. 1996	s.57A as inserted by T.U.R.E.R.A. 1993, s.28 and Sched. 5, para. 3	[829]^{65}
s.104 E.R.A. 1996	s.60A E.P.C.A. 1978	[822]^{86}
s.104 E.R.A. 1996	s.60A as inserted by T.U.R.E.R.A. 1993, s.29(1)	[829]^{66}
s.105 E.R.A. 1996	s.59 E.P.C.A. 1978	[827]^{54}
s.105(1)–(3), (7) E.R.A. 1996	s.59(1)(a), (2) E.P.C.A. 1978 as substituted by T.U.R.E.R.A. 1993, ss.24(2), 29(2), Scheds. 5, 8	[828]^{55}
s.105(3) E.R.A. 1996	s.28 and Sched. 5 T.U.R.E.R.A. 1993	[764]^{41}
s.106(2) E.R.A. 1996	s.61(1) E.P.C.A. 1978	
s.106(3) E.R.A. 1996	s.61(2) E.P.C.A. 1978	[823]^{2}
s.108(1) E.R.A. 1996	s.64(1)(a) E.P.C.A. 1978	[818]^{25}
s.108(1) E.R.A. 1996	s.64(1) E.P.C.A. 1978	
s.108(1) E.R.A. 1996	s.64(1)(a) E.P.C.A. 1978	[821]^{60}
s.108(1) E.R.A. 1996	s.64(1) E.P.C.A. 1978	[818]^{24}
s.108(2) E.R.A. 1996	s.64(2), s.64A(2) E.P.C.A. 1978	[818]^{26}
s.108(3) E.R.A. 1996	s.28 and Sched. 5 T.U.R.E.R.A. 1993	[764]^{41}

NEW LEGISLATION	DERIVATION	PARAGRAPH NUMBER [PAGE] footnote
s.108(3) E.R.A. 1996	E.P.C.A. 1978, ss.64(3)–(5) as inserted by T.U.R.E.R.A. 1993 ss.24(3), 28, 29(3), Sched. 5, para. 5	[829][64]
s.109(1) E.R.A. 1996	s.3 Sex Discrimination Act 1986	[718][10]
s.109(1) E.R.A. 1996	as extended by s.3 (in the employment field)	[837][71]
s.109(1) E.R.A. 1996	s.3(1) Sex Discrimination Act 1986	[773][41]
s.109(1) E.R.A. 1996	s.64(1)(b) E.P.C.A. 1978 as substituted by s.3(1) Sex Discrimination Act 1986	[817][23]
s.109(1) E.R.A. 1996	s.64(1)(b) E.P.C.A. 1978	[821][61]
s.109(2) E.R.A. 1996	E.P.C.A. 1978, s.64(3)–(5) as inserted by T.U.R.E.R.A. 1993 ss.24(3), 28, 29(3), Sched. 5, para. 5	[829][64]
s.109(2) E.R.A. 1996	s.28 and Sched. 5 T.U.R.E.R.A. 1993	[764][41]
s.110 E.R.A. 1996	s.65 E.P.C.A. 1978	[807][23]
s.110 E.R.A. 1996	s.66(2) E.P.C.A. 1978	[807][23]
s.110 E.R.A. 1996	s.66(3) E.P.C.A. 1978	[807][23]
s.110 E.R.A. 1996	ss.65–66 E.P.C.A. 1978	[818][28]
s.110(3) and s.110(1) E.R.A. 1996	s.65(1) and (3) E.P.C.A. 1978	[818][34]
s.110(3) E.R.A. 1996	s.65(2) E.P.C.A. 1978	[818][35]
s.110(4), (5) E.R.A. 1996	s.66 E.P.C.A. 1978	[818][36]
s.111(2) E.R.A. 1996	s.67(2) E.P.C.A. 1978	[821][62]
s.111(2) E.R.A. 1996	s.67(2) E.P.C.A. 1978	[836][64]
s.111(3), (4) E.R.A. 1996	s.67(4) E.P.C.A. 1978	
s.111(3), (4) E.R.A. 1996	s.67(4) E.P.C.A. 1978	[837][66]
ss.112–117 E.R.A. 1996	ss.68–71 E.P.C.A. 1978	[830][71]
s.112 E.R.A. 1996	s.68 E.P.C.A. 1978	
s.112(1), (2) E.R.A. 1996	s.68(1) E.P.C.A. 1978	[830][74]

NEW LEGISLATION	DERIVATION	PARAGRAPH NUMBER [PAGE] footnote
s.112(4) E.R.A. 1996	s.68(2) E.P.C.A. 1978	[832][11]
s.112–132 E.R.A. 1996	ss.68–79 E.P.C.A. 1978	[829][70]
s.113 E.R.A. 1996	s.69(1) E.P.C.A. 1978	[830][76]
s.113 E.R.A. 1996	s.69(1) E.P.C.A. 1978	[831][92]
s.114(1), (2) E.R.A. 1996	s.69(2) E.P.C.A. 1978	[830][82]
s.114(2)(a) E.R.A. 1996 subject to s.114(4) E.R.A. 1996	s.69(2)(a) E.P.C.A. 1978 subject to s.70(2) E.P.C.A. 1978	[830][83]
s.114(2)(b) E.R.A. 1996	s.69(2)(b) E.P.C.A. 1978	[830][84]
s.114(2)(c) E.R.A. 1996	s.69(2)(c) E.P.C.A. 1978	[831][85]
s.114(3) E.R.A. 1996	s.69(3) E.P.C.A. 1978	[831][86]
s.115(1) E.R.A. 1996	s.69(1) E.P.C.A. 1978	[831][92]
s.115(1), (2) E.R.A. 1996	s.69(4) E.P.C.A. 1978	[831][91]
s.115(2)(a) E.R.A. 1996	s.69(4)(a) E.P.C.A. 1978	[831][94]
s.115(2)(b), (c) E.R.A. 1996	s.69(4)(b), (c) E.P.C.A. 1978	[831][95]
s.115(2)(d) E.R.A. 1996 calculated according to s.115(3) E.R.A. 1996	s.69(4)(d) E.P.C.A. 1978 calculated according to s.70(2) E.P.C.A. 1978	[831][96]
s.115(2)(e) E.R.A. 1996	s.69(4)(e) E.P.C.A. 1978	[831][97]
s.116(1) E.R.A. 1996	s.69(5) E.P.C.A. 1978	[830][77]
s.116(1)(a) E.R.A. 1996	s.69(5)(a) E.P.C.A. 1978	[830][78]
s.116(1)(b) E.R.A. 1996	s.69(5)(b) E.P.C.A. 1978	[830][79]
s.116(1)(c) E.R.A. 1996	s.69(5)(c) E.P.C.A. 1978	[830][80]
s.116(2)–(4) E.R.A. 1996	s.69(6) E.P.C.A. 1978	[831][87]
s.116(3)(a) E.R.A. 1996	s.69(6)(a) E.P.C.A. 1978	[831][88]
s.116(3)(b) E.R.A. 1996 subject to s.116(5) E.R.A. 1996	s.69(6)(b) E.P.C.A. 1978 subject to s.70(1) E.P.C.A. 1978	[831][89]
s.116(3)(c) E.R.A. 1996	s.69(6)(c) E.P.C.A. 1978	[831][90]
s.116(4) E.R.A. 1996	s.69(6) and s.69(6)(c) E.P.C.A. 1978	[831][93]
s.116(5), (6) E.R.A. 1996	s.70(1) E.P.C.A. 1978	[830][81]
s.117(1) E.R.A. 1996	s.71(1) E.P.C.A. 1978	[831][98]
s.117(3) E.R.A. 1996	s.28 and Sched. 5, T.U.R.E.R.A. 1993	[764][41]
s.117(3)(a) E.R.A. 1996	s.71(2)(a) E.P.C.A. 1978	[832][99]

NEW LEGISLATION	DERIVATION	PARAGRAPH NUMBER [PAGE] footnote
s.117(3)(b) and s.117(4)(a) as qualified by s.117(7) E.R.A. 1996	s.71(2)(b) as qualified by s.71(4) E.P.C.A. 1978	[832][5]
s.117(3)(b), s.117(4)(a) E.R.A. 1996	s.71(2)(b) E.P.C.A. 1978	[832][1]
s.117(5)(a) E.R.A. 1996 referring to s.117(6) E.R.A. 1996	s.71(2)(b)(i) E.P.C.A. 1978 referring to s.71(3) E.P.C.A. 1978	[832][3]
s.117(5)(b) E.R.A. 1996	s.71(2)(b)(ii) E.P.C.A. 1978	[832][2]
s.117(6)(b) E.R.A. 1996	s.71(3)(b), (c) E.P.C.A. 1978	[832][4]
s.117(8) E.R.A. 1996	s.71(5) E.P.C.A. 1978	[832][6]
s.118 E.R.A. 1996	s.28 and Sched. 5 T.U.R.E.R.A. 1993	[764][41]
s.118 E.R.A. 1996	s.72 E.P.C.A. 1978	[832][12]
s.118 E.R.A. 1996 referring to ss.123, 124, 126, 127 E.R.A. 1996	s.72 E.P.C.A. 1978 referring to s.74 E.P.C.A. 1978	[833][22]
s.118(2), (3) E.R.A. 1996	E.P.C.A. s.72(2), (3) as substituted by T.U.R.E.R.A. 1993, s.28 and Sched. 5, para. 7	[830][72]
s.118(2), (3) E.R.A. 1996	E.P.C.A. 1978 s.72(2), (3) as added by T.U.R.E.R.A. 1993, s.28 and Sched. 5, para. 7	[832][8]
s.119(1), E.R.A. 1996	s.28 and Sched. 5 T.U.R.E.R.A. 1993	[764][41]
s.119(1) and (2) E.R.A. 1996	s.73(3) E.P.C.A. 1978	[821][66]
s.119(2) E.R.A. 1996	s.73(3) E.P.C.A. 1978	[833][14]
s.119(3) E.R.A. 1996	s.73(4) E.P.C.A. 1978	[833][14]
s.119(3) E.R.A. 1996	s.73(4) E.P.C.A. 1978	[833][15]
s.119(4) E.R.A. 1996	s.3 Sex Discrimination Act 1986	[718][10]
s.119(5) E.R.A. 1996	s.73(6), (7) E.P.C.A. 1978	[833][14]
s.120 E.R.A. 1996	s.28 and Sched. 5 T.U.R.E.R.A. 1993	[764][41]
s.121 E.R.A. 1996	s.73(2) E.P.C.A. 1978	[833][17]

NEW LEGISLATION	DERIVATION	PARAGRAPH NUMBER [PAGE] footnote
s.122 E.R.A. 1996	s.73 E.P.C.A. 1978	[828][61]
s.122(1) E.R.A. 1996	s.73(7A) E.P.C.A. 1978 as inserted by E.A. 1980, s.9	[833][19]
s.122(2) E.R.A. 1996	s.73(7B) E.P.C.A. 1978 as inserted by E.A. 1980, s.9	[833][20]
s.122(3) E.R.A. 1996	s.28 and Sched. 5 T.U.R.E.R.A. 1993	[764][41]
s.123(1) E.R.A. 1996	ss.74(1), 75(1) E.P.C.A. 1978	[835][43]
s.123(1) as qualified by s.123(2) E.R.A. 1996	s.74(1) as qualified by s.74(2) E.P.C.A. 1978	[833][23]
s.123(1) as qualified by s.123(5) E.R.A. 1996	s.74(1) as qualified by s.74(5) E.P.C.A. 1978	[833][24]
s.123(1) referring to s.124(1) and to s.126 E.R.A. 1996	proviso to s.74(1) referring (as amended by T.U.R.E.R.A. 1993, s.30(3)(a)) to s.74(8) as inserted by T.U.R.E.R.A. 1993, s.30(3)(b) and to s.76 E.P.C.A. 1978	[835][43]
s.123(3) E.R.A. 1996	s.74(3) E.P.C.A. 1978	[833][27]
s.123(4) E.R.A. 1996	s.74(4) E.P.C.A. 1978	[833][25]
s.123(6) E.R.A. 1996	s.74(6) E.P.C.A. 1978	[834][41]
s.123(6) E.R.A. 1996	s.74(6) E.P.C.A. 1978	[835][46]
s.123(7) E.R.A. 1996	s.74(7) E.P.C.A. 1978	[833][28]
s.124(1) E.R.A. 1996	ss.74(1), 75(1) E.P.C.A. 1978	[835][43]
s.124(3) E.R.A. 1996	limited by reference to s.71(1A) as inserted by T.U.R.E.R.A. 1993, s.30(2)	[931][98]
s.124(5) E.R.A. 1996	s.75(3) E.P.C.A. 1978	[835][44]

NEW LEGISLATION	DERIVATION	PARAGRAPH NUMBER [PAGE] footnote
s.125 E.R.A. 1996	"section 75A of the 1978 Act"	**37–167** [835][43]
s.125(2) E.R.A. 1996 setting a minimum of £20,600	s.75A(2) as added by s.9 of the E.A. 1982 setting a minimum of £18,795 as amended by the Unfair Dismissal (Increase of Limits of Basic and Special Awards) Order 1989 (S.I. 1989 No. 528)	[832][10]
s.126 E.R.A. 1996	s.76 E.P.C.A. 1978	[838][79]
ss.128–132 E.R.A. 1996	s.28 and Sched. 5 T.U.R.E.R.A. 1993	[764][41]
s.128(1) E.R.A. 1996	s.77(1) E.P.C.A. 1978 as amended by T.U.R.E.R.A. 1993, s.28 and Sched. 5	[836][54]
s.128(2) E.R.A. 1996	s.77(2)(a) E.P.C.A. 1978	[836][55]
s.129(5) E.R.A. 1996	s.77A(4) E.P.C.A. 1978	[836][57]
s.129(9) E.R.A. 1996	s.77A(6) E.P.C.A. 1978	[836][58]
s.130 E.R.A. 1996	s.78 E.P.C.A. 1978	[836][59]
s.130(2) E.R.A. 1996	s.78(2) E.P.C.A. 1978	[836][60]
s.131 E.R.A. 1996	s.78A E.P.C.A. 1978	[836][61]
s.132 E.R.A. 1996	s.79 E.P.C.A. 1978	[836][62]
s.134 E.R.A. 1996	s.80 E.P.C.A. 1978	[817][13]
s.135 E.R.A. 1996	s.81(1) E.P.C.A. 1978	[843][45]
s.135 E.R.A. 1996	s.81 E.P.C.A. 1978 (calculation of redundancy payment)	[764][43]
s.136 E.R.A. 1996	"Under section 93 of the 1978 Act"	**37–178**
s.136(1) E.R.A. 1996	s.83(2)(c) E.P.C.A. 1978	[841][26]
s.136(1)(a) E.R.A. 1996	s.83(2)(a) E.P.C.A. 1978	[840][8]
s.136(1)(b) E.R.A. 1996	s.83(2)(b) E.P.C.A. 1978	[840][9]
s.136(1)(c) E.R.A. 1996	s.83(2)(c) E.P.C.A. 1978	[840][10]
s.136(1)(c) E.R.A. 1996	s.83(2)(c) E.P.C.A. 1978	[840][10]
s.136(1)–(3) of 1996 Act	ss.83(2) and 94(2) of 1978 Act	[785][68]
s.136(2) E.R.A. 1996	s.92(4) E.P.C.A. 1978	[841][25]
s.136(2) E.R.A. 1996	s.92(4) E.P.C.A. 1978	[841][26]
s.136(5), E.R.A. 1996	s.93 E.P.C.A. 1978	[820][53]
s.136(5) E.R.A. 1996	s.93(1) E.P.C.A. 1978	[841][28]

NEW LEGISLATION	DERIVATION	PARAGRAPH NUMBER [PAGE] footnote
s.136(5) E.R.A. 1996	ss.93(1), 150 of and Sched. 12 to 1978 Act	[790]²²
s.137(1) E.R.A. 1996	s.86 E.P.C.A. 1978	[840]¹²
s.138(1) E.R.A. 1996	s.84(1) E.P.C.A. 1978	[840]¹⁴
s.138(2), (4), (5) E.R.A. 1996	s.84(3), (4), (6) E.P.C.A. 1978	[840]¹⁵
s.138(3) E.R.A. 1996	s.84(3), (4), (6) E.P.C.A. 1978	[840]¹⁵
s.138(3), (6) E.R.A. 1996	s.84(4), (5) E.P.C.A. 1978	[840]¹⁶
s.139 E.R.A. 1996	s.81 E.P.C.A. 1978 (calculation of redundancy payment)	[764]⁴³
s.139(1) E.R.A. 1996	"s.81(2) of the 1978 Act"	**37–179**
s.139(1), (2) E.R.A. 1996	s.81(2) E.P.C.A. 1978	[827]⁵¹
s.139(4), (5) E.R.A. 1996	s.93(2)–(4) E.P.C.A. 1978	[841]²⁹
s.139(4), (5) E.R.A. 1996	s.93 E.P.C.A. 1978	[820]⁵³
s.140(1) E.R.A. 1996	s.82(2) E.P.C.A. 1978	[842]³⁸
s.140(1) E.R.A. 1996	s.82(2) E.P.C.A. 1978	[846]⁸⁸
s.141(1)–(3) E.R.A. 1996	s.82(3)–(5) E.P.C.A. 1978	[842]³⁸
s.141(4) E.R.A. 1996	s.82(6) E.P.C.A. 1978	[842]³⁹
s.142 E.R.A. 1996	s.85 E.P.C.A. 1978	[840]¹¹
s.145 E.R.A. 1996	s.90 E.P.C.A. 1978	
s.146(2) E.R.A. 1996	s.82(3)–(5) E.P.C.A. 1978	[842]³⁸
s.147(1) E.R.A. 1996	s.87(1) E.P.C.A. 1978	[843]⁴⁷
s.147(2) E.R.A. 1996	s.87(2) E.P.C.A. 1978	[843]⁴⁸
ss.148–152 E.R.A. 1996	ss.88, 89 E.P.C.A. 1978	[839]⁵
s.148 E.R.A. 1996	s.88(1) E.P.C.A. 1978	[843]⁴⁶
s.148(1) E.R.A. 1996	s.88(1) E.P.C.A. 1978	[843]⁴⁹
s.150(1), (2) E.R.A. 1996	s.88(2) E.P.C.A. 1978	[843]⁵¹
s.152(1) E.R.A. 1996	s.88(3), (4) E.P.C.A. 1978	[843]⁵⁰
s.153 E.R.A. 1996	s.90 E.P.C.A. 1978	[847]⁹⁸
s.155 E.R.A. 1996	s.81(4) E.P.C.A. 1978	[839]⁴

NEW LEGISLATION	DERIVATION	PARAGRAPH NUMBER [PAGE] footnote
s.155 E.R.A. 1996	s.81(4) E.P.C.A. 1978	[843]^{53}
s.155 E.R.A. 1996	s.81 E.P.C.A. 1978 (calculation of redundancy payment)	[764]^{43}
s.156(1) E.R.A. 1996	s.82(1) E.P.C.A. 1978 as substituted by s.16(1) of the Employment Act 1989	[846]^{82}
s.157 E.R.A. 1996	s.96 E.P.C.A. 1978	[846]^{90}
s.159 E.R.A. 1996	s.99(1) E.P.C.A. 1978	[846]^{94}
s.159 E.R.A. 1996	s.99 and Sched. 5 E.P.C.A. 1978	[715]^{84}
s.161(1) E.R.A. 1996	s.100(2) E.P.C.A. 1978	[846]^{80}
s.162 E.R.A. 1996	Sched. 4, para. 1 E.P.C.A. 1978	[844]^{57}
s.162 E.R.A. 1996	s.81 E.P.C.A. 1978 (calculation of redundancy payment)	[764]^{43}
s.162(1) E.R.A. 1996	s.81(1) E.P.C.A. 1978	[843]^{52}
s.162(1), (2) E.R.A. 1996	Sched. 4, para. 2 E.P.C.A. 1978	[844]^{54}
s.162(3) E.R.A. 1996	Sched. 4, para. 3 E.P.C.A. 1978	[844]^{55}
s.162(4), (5) E.R.A. 1996	Sched. 4, para. 4 E.P.C.A. 1978	[844]^{56}
s.163 E.R.A. 1996	s.91 E.P.C.A. 1978	[846]^{96}
s.163(2) E.R.A. 1996	s.91(2) E.P.C.A. 1978	[842]^{33}
s.163(2) E.R.A. 1996 expressly excluded from unfair dismissal issues by s.7(6) I.T.A. 1996	s.91(2) expressly excluded from unfair dismissal issues by Sched. 9, para. 5 E.P.C.A. 1978	[828]^{59}
s.164(1) E.R.A. 1996	s.101(1) E.P.C.A. 1978	[847]^{98}
s.164(1) E.R.A. 1996	s.101(1) E.P.C.A. 1978	[847]^{99}
s.164(2), (3) E.R.A. 1996	s.101(2) E.P.C.A. 1978	[847]^{1}
s.166 and s.167 E.R.A. 1996	"Under section 106 of the Employment Protection (Consolidation) Act 1978"	**37–140**
s.166(6), (7) E.R.A. 1996	s.106(5) E.P.C.A. 1978	[806]^{5}

NEW LEGISLATION	DERIVATION	PARAGRAPH NUMBER [PAGE] footnote
s.167(1) E.R.A. 1996	s.106(2) E.P.C.A. 1978	[806]⁶
s.167(3), (4) E.R.A. 1996	s.106(3) E.P.C.A. 1978	[806]⁷
s.174 E.R.A. 1996	Sched. 12, paras 14–16 E.P.C.A. 1978	[841]²⁷
ss.182, 185 E.R.A. 1996	ss.122(1), (2) E.P.C.A. 1978	[806]⁹
s.183 as in s.166(6), (7) E.R.A. 1996	s.127(1) as in s.106(5) E.P.C.A. 1978	[806]⁸
s.184 E.R.A. 1996	"Under section 122 of the E.P.C.A. 1978"	[140]³⁷
s.184(1) E.R.A. 1996	"section 122(3) of the 1978 Act"	**37–140**
s.184(1) E.R.A. 1996	s.122(3) E.P.C.A. 1978	[806]¹¹
s.184(2) E.R.A. 1996	s.122(3) E.P.C.A. 1978	[806]¹²
s.185 E.R.A. 1996	s.122(2) E.P.C.A. 1978	[807]²²
s.186(1) E.R.A. 1996	s.122(5) E.P.C.A. 1978	[807]¹⁶
s.188(1), (2) E.R.A. 1996	s.124(1) E.P.C.A. 1978	[807]¹⁷
s.188(3) E.R.A. 1996	s.124(3) E.P.C.A. 1978	[807]¹⁸
s.189(1), (5) E.R.A. 1996	s.125(1), (4) E.P.C.A. 1978	[807]¹⁹
s.189(2) E.R.A. 1996	s.125(2) E.P.C.A. 1978	[807]²¹
ss.191–193 E.R.A. 1996	s.138 E.P.C.A. 1978	[767]⁷¹
s.191(1) E.R.A. 1996	s.138(1) E.P.C.A. 1978	[817]¹²
s.191(1), (2) E.R.A. 1996	s.138(1) E.P.C.A. 1978	[716]⁸⁵
s.191(1), (2) E.R.A. 1996	s.138(1) E.P.C.A. 1978 (section does apply to Crown employment)	[803]⁵⁶
s.191(1), (2) E.R.A. 1996	s.138(1) E.P.C.A. 1978	[803]⁵⁶
s.191(1)–(4) and s.192(1) E.R.A. 1996	s.9 W.A. 1986	[756]³⁸
s.191(6) E.R.A. 1996	s.99 and Sched. 5 E.P.C.A. 1978	[715]⁸⁴
s.192(1) E.R.A. 1996 (unfair dismissal rights **do** extend to members of the military services)	s.138(3) E.P.C.A. 1978 (unfair dismissal rights do not extend to members of the military services)	[716]⁸⁵

NEW LEGISLATION	DERIVATION	PARAGRAPH NUMBER [PAGE] footnote
s.193(1), (2) E.R.A. 1996	s.49(1) and Sched. 7, para. 3 T.U.R.E.R.A. 1993	[716][85]
s.196 E.R.A. 1996	s.141 E.P.C.A. 1978 (work outside Great Britain)	[750][57]
s.196 E.R.A. 1996	s.141 E.P.C.A. 1978	[755][24]
s.196 E.R.A. 1996	s.141 E.P.C.A. 1978 (work abroad)	[767][71]
s.196 E.R.A. 1996	s.141(1) E.P.C.A. 1978	[723][61]
s.196(1) E.R.A. 1996	s.141(1) E.P.C.A. 1978	[783][40]
s.196(2) E.R.A. 1996	s.141(2) E.P.C.A. 1978 (working outside G.B.)	[803][56]
s.196(2) E.R.A. 1996	s.141(2) E.P.C.A. 1978	
s.196(2), (3) E.R.A. 1996	s.141(2) E.P.C.A. 1978 (work outside Great Britain)	[747][21]
s.196(2), (3) E.R.A. 1996	s.141(2) E.P.C.A. 1978	[817][21]
s.196(2), (3) E.R.A. 1996	s.141(2) E.P.C.A. 1978	[818][27]
s.196(6) E.R.A. 1996	s.141(3)–(4) E.P.C.A. 1978	[846][89]
s.197(1) E.R.A. 1996	s.142(1) as amended by E.A. 1980, s.8(2)	[818][33]
s.197(3) E.R.A. 1996	s.142(2) E.P.C.A. 1978	[846][85]
s.198 E.R.A. 1996	s.5 E.P.C.A. 1978	[822][83]
s.198 E.R.A. 1996	s.5 E.P.C.A. 1978	[822][83]
s.199 E.R.A. 1996	s.144 E.P.C.A. 1978 (share fishermen)	[747][21]
s.199 E.R.A. 1996	s.144 E.P.C.A. 1978	[755][24]
s.199(1) E.R.A. 1996	s.144(1) E.P.C.A. 1978	[723][59]
s.199(1) E.R.A. 1996	s.144(1) E.P.C.A. 1978	[783][40]
s.199(2) E.R.A. 1996	s.144(2) E.P.C.A. 1978 (share fishermen)	[803][56]
s.199(2) E.R.A. 1996	s.144(2) E.P.C.A. 1978 (share fishermen)	[747][21]
s.199(2) E.R.A. 1996	s.144(2) E.P.C.A. 1978	[775][57]
s.199(2) E.R.A. 1996	s.144(2) E.P.C.A. 1978	[846][93]
s.199(6) E.R.A. 1996	s.144(3) E.P.C.A. 1978	[817][15]
s.199(6) E.R.A. 1996	s.141(3) E.P.C.A. 1978	[818][27]

NEW LEGISLATION	DERIVATION	PARAGRAPH NUMBER [PAGE] footnote
s.199(6) E.R.A. 1996	s.144(3) E.P.C.A. 1978	[846][83]
s.199(6) E.R.A. 1996	s.144(3) E.P.C.A. 1978	[846][89]
s.200 E.R.A. 1996	s.146(2), (3) E.P.C.A. 1978	[701][31]
s.200(1) E.R.A. 1996	s.146(2) E.P.C.A. 1978	[817][14]
s.200(1) E.R.A. 1996	s.146(2) E.P.C.A. 1978	[818][29]
s.201 E.R.A. 1996	s.10 W.A. 1986	[756][39]
s.203 E.R.A. 1996	ss.5–6 W.A. 1986	[756][37]
s.203 E.R.A. 1996	s.140 E.P.C.A. 1978	[730][28]
s.203 E.R.A. 1996	s.140 E.P.C.A. 1978	[786][76]
s.203 E.R.A. 1996	s.140 E.P.C.A. 1978	[839][3]
s.203(1) E.R.A. 1996	s.140(1) E.P.C.A. 1978	[818][31]
s.203(1), (2) E.R.A. 1996	s.6(3) W.A. 1986	[756][41]
s.203(2)(e) E.R.A. 1996	s.140(2)(d), (e) E.P.C.A. 1978	[818][37]
s.205(2) E.R.A. 1996	s.6(1) W.A. 1986	[756][40]
s.205(2) E.R.A. 1996	ss.5–6 W.A. 1986	[756][37]
s.206 E.R.A. 1996	ss.93(1), 150 of and Sched. 12 to 1978 Act	[790][22]
s.207 E.R.A. 1996	ss.93(1), 150 of and Sched. 12 to 1978 Act	[790][22]
s.207 E.R.A. 1996	E.P.A. 1975, s.6	[825][15]
s.208 E.R.A. 1996	s.148 E.P.C.A. 1978	[845][71]
s.209(1) E.R.A. 1996	s.149(1) E.P.C.A. 1978 (other categories as may be specified by order)	[803][56]
s.210 E.R.A. 1996	s.151 E.P.C.A. 1978	[803][62]
ss.210, 211, 212 E.R.A. 1996	s.51 E.P.C.A. 1978	[817][23]
ss.210–219 E.R.A. 1996	Sched. 13 E.P.C.A. 1978	[720][33]
ss.210–219 E.R.A. 1996	Sched. 13 E.P.C.A. 1978	[784][50]
ss.210–219 E.R.A. 1996	Sched. 13 E.P.C.A. 1978	[833][14]
s.210(3) E.R.A. 1996	Sched. 13, para. 1(1) E.P.C.A. 1978	[784][52]
s.210(5) of 1996 Act	s.151 of 1978 Act	[785][68]
s.212(2) E.R.A. 1996	Sched. 13, para. 10 E.P.C.A. 1978	[785][62]
s.212(3)(a) E.R.A. 1996	Sched. 13, para. 9(1)(a) E.P.C.A. 1978	[784][58]
s.212(3)(b) E.R.A. 1996	Sched. 13, para. 9(1)(b) E.P.C.A. 1978	[784][59]

NEW LEGISLATION	DERIVATION	PARAGRAPH NUMBER [PAGE] footnote
s.212(3)(c) E.R.A. 1996	Sched. 13, para. 9(1)(c) E.P.C.A. 1978	[784][60]
s.212(3)(d) E.R.A. 1996	Sched. 13, para. 9(1)(d) E.P.C.A. 1978	[784][61]
s.213 E.R.A. 1996	Sched. 13, para. 11 E.P.C.A. 1978	[817][23]
s.213 E.R.A. 1996	s.151 and Sched. 13, para. 11 E.P.C.A. 1978	[818][25]
s.214 E.R.A. 1996	Sched. 13, para. 12 E.P.C.A. 1978	[844][60]
s.215(2)–(5) E.R.A. 1996	Sched. 13, para. 14(1)–(4) E.P.C.A. 1978	[844][59]
s.216 E.R.A. 1996	Sched. 13, para. 15 E.P.C.A. 1978	[739][35]
s.216 E.R.A. 1996	Sched. 13, para. 15 as modified by para. 23 E.P.C.A. 1978	[785][63]
s.216 E.R.A. 1996	Sched. 13, para. 15 E.P.C.A. 1978	[785][64]
s.217 E.R.A. 1996	Sched. 13, para. 16 E.P.C.A. 1978	[785][66]
s.218(2) E.R.A. 1996	Sched. 13, para. 17(2) E.P.C.A. 1978	[785][68]
s.218(4) E.R.A. 1996	Sched. 13, para. 17(4) E.P.C.A. 1978	[785][69]
s.218(4) E.R.A. 1996	Sched. 13, para. 17 E.P.C.A. 1978	[790][23]
s.218(5) E.R.A. 1996	Sched. 13, para. 17(5) E.P.C.A. 1978	[785][70]
s.218(5) E.R.A. 1996	Sched. 13, para. 17 E.P.C.A. 1978	[793][55]
s.218(6) E.R.A. 1996	Sched. 13, para. 18 E.P.C.A. 1978	[785][67]
ss.220–229 E.R.A. 1996	See for calculation of weeks pay E.P.C.A. 1978, Sched. 14, Part II	[776][73]
ss.220–229 E.R.A. 1996	Sched. 14, Part II E.P.C.A. 1978	[786][78]
ss.220–229 E.R.A. 1996	Sched. 14 E.P.C.A. 1978	[832][2]
ss.220–229 E.R.A. 1996	Sched. 14 E.P.C.A. 1978	[833][14]

NEW LEGISLATION	DERIVATION	PARAGRAPH NUMBER [PAGE] footnote
ss.220–229 E.R.A. 1996	"Schedule 14 to the 1978 Act"	**37–182**
ss.221–229 E.R.A. 1996	Sched. 14 E.P.C.A. 1978	[750][62]
ss.221–229 E.R.A. 1996	As defined by Sched. 14, Part II E.P.C.A. 1978	[753][11]
s.221(2) E.R.A. 1996	Sched. 14, para. 3(2) E.P.C.A. 1978	[845][65]
s.221(3) E.R.A. 1996	Sched. 14, para. 3(3) E.P.C.A. 1978	[845][68]
s.221(4) E.R.A. 1996	Sched. 14, para. 3(4) E.P.C.A. 1978	[845][66]
s.226 E.R.A. 1996	Sched. 14, para. 7(1) E.P.C.A. 1978	
s.226(2) E.R.A. 1996	The "week's pay" is calculated by reference to Sched. 14, especially para. 7(1)(f) and (g) thereof	[803][66]
s.226(6) E.R.A. 1996	Sched. 14, para. 7(1)(h), (i) E.P.C.A. 1978	[821][68]
s.227(1)(c), (2) E.R.A. 1996	Sched. 14, para. 8(1)(c), (2) E.P.C.A. 1978	[845][71]
s.227(1), (2) E.R.A. 1996	Sched. 14, para. 8(1) E.P.C.A. 1978 as amended by statutory instrument from time to time	[833][16]
s.230(1) E.R.A. 1996	s.153(1) E.P.C.A. 1978	**37–005**
s.230(1) E.R.A. 1996	s.153(1) E.P.C.A. 1978	[701][30]
s.230(1) ("employee"), s.230(2) ("contract of employment") E.R.A. 1996	s.153(1) E.P.C.A. 1978	[700][28]
s.230(3) E.R.A. 1996	s.8(2) W.A. 1986	[702][46]
s.230(3) E.R.A. 1996	s.8(1), (2) W.A. 1986	[757][67]
ss.230(1), (2), (4), (5), 235(1) E.R.A. 1996	s.153(1) E.P.C.A. 1978	[715][77]
s.234 E.R.A. 1996	"Part I of Schedule 14 to the Employment Protection (Consolidation) Act 1978"	**37–183**
s.234 E.R.A. 1996	As defined by Sched. 4, Part I E.P.C.A. 1978	[754][12]

NEW LEGISLATION	DERIVATION	PARAGRAPH NUMBER [PAGE] footnote
s.234 E.R.A. 1996	s.152 and Sched. 14, Part I E.P.C.A. 1978	[786][77]
s.234(1), (2) E.R.A. 1996	Sched. 14, para. 1 E.P.C.A. 1978	[845][75]
s.235(1) E.R.A. 1996	Sched. 13, para. 24(1) E.P.C.A. 1978	[784][53]
s.235(1) E.R.A. 1996	s.153(1) E.P.C.A. 1978	[847][98]
s.235(3) E.R.A. 1996	s.153(2) E.P.C.A. 1978	[823][99]
s.235(3) E.R.A. 1996	s.153(2) E.P.C.A. 1978	[827][51]
s.236(3) E.R.A. 1996	s.28 and Sched. 5 T.U.R.E.R.A. 1993	[764][41]

SCHEDULES

Sched. 2 E.R.A. 1996	Sched. 15, para. 10(1) E.P.C.A. 1978	[818][27]
Sched. 2, para. 12(1) E.R.A. 1978	Sched. 15, para. 12 E.P.C.A. 1978	[846][87]

ITA

s.3 I.T.A. 1996	"Under section 131 of the Employment Protection (Consolidation) Act 1978"	**37–148**
s.3(1), s.8(1) I.T.A. 1996	s.131(1), (4) E.P.C.A. 1978	[814][92]
s.3(2)(a) I.T.A. 1996	s.131(2)(a) E.P.C.A. 1978	[814][93]
s.3(2)(b) I.T.A. 1996	s.131(2)(b) E.P.C.A. 1978	[814][95]
s.3(3) I.T.A. 1996	s.131(3) E.P.C.A. 1978	[814][94]
s.7 I.T.A. 1996	By virtue of Sched. 9 E.P.C.A. 1978	[847][97]
s.21 I.T.A. 1996	s.136 of the 1978 Act	[847][97]
s.22 I.T.A. 1996	s.135 E.P.C.A. 1978	[847][97]

T.U.L.R.C.A. 1992

T.U.L.R.C.A. 1992, Part IV, Ch. II	E.P.A. 1975, Part IV	**37–005**

NEW LEGISLATION	DERIVATION	PARAGRAPH NUMBER [PAGE] footnote
ss.181–185 T.U.L.R.C.A. 1992	ss.17–21 E.P.A. 1975	[728][12]
s.183(1) T.U.L.R.C.A. 1992	s.19(1) E.P.A. 1975	[728][13]
s.183(1), s.184(1) T.U.L.R.C.A. 1992	ss.19(1), 20(1) E.P.A. 1975	[728][14]
s.185(1) T.U.L.R.C.A. 1992	s.21(1) E.P.A. 1975	[728][15]
s.185(3) T.U.L.R.C.A. 1992	s.21(3) E.P.A. 1975	[728][16]
s.185(3), (4) T.U.L.R.C.A. 1992	s.21(3) and (5) E.P.A. 1975	[728][17]
s.185(3), (4) T.U.L.R.C.A. 1992	s.21(3) and (5) E.P.A. 1975	[728][19]
s.185(5) T.U.L.R.C.A. 1992	s.21(6) E.P.A. 1975	[728][18]
s.238(5) T.U.L.R.C.A. 1992	s.62(4)(a) E.P.C.A. 1978	[821][63]

1. – Introduction

Introduction

37–001   [*Note 1: page* [697]]
Add the following abbreviations: Employment Rights Act 1996 (E.R.A.) and Industrial Tribunals Act 1996 (I.T.A.).

The modern approach to definition of the contract of employment

37–003   [*Notes 12–14: page* [699]]
For evidence of an increasing tendency, at least in the case of skilled workers, to prefer a business test—here in the form of "whose business is it?"—see the decision of the Court of Appeal in *Lane v. Shire Roofing Company (Oxford) Ltd* [1995] I.R.L.R. 593.

Classification for particular purposes

37–006   For possible emergence of a greater willingness to engage in a different approach to classification in the safety at work field, see the decision of the Court of Appeal in *Lane v. Shire Roofing Company (Oxford) Ltd.*[a]

   [a] [1995] I.R.L.R. 593.

2. – The Factors Identifying a Contract of Employment

Control and the corporate employer

37–012   [*Note 79: page* [706]]
In *Buchan v. Secretary of State for Employment* [1997] I.R.L.R. 80 the EAT held, however, that an individual such as managing director with a controlling beneficial interest in the shares of a company might be regarded as not being an employee of the company for the purposes of employment protection legislation.

Special cases: (2) agency workers

37–025   For further discussion of the question whether and when an agency worker has a contract of employment either with the agency or with its client business to which the agency sends the worker, and for the assertion that

[424]

there is no rule of law against there being a contract of employment either with the agency or with the client business, see now *McMeechan v. Secretary of State for Employment*.[a]

[a] [1997] I.C.R. 549, C.A.

Special cases: (3) office-holders

[*Note 62: page* [714]]   **37–026**
See also *Diocese of Southwark v. Coker, The Times*, July 17, 1997 (EAT).

3. – FORMATION OF THE CONTRACT

Public policy, restraint of trade and illegality

[*Notes 96, 97: page* [717]]   **37–030**
Compare the decision of the Employment Appeal Tribunal in *Leighton v. Michael* [1995] I.C.R. 1091 that an employee whose wages were paid without deduction of tax could nevertheless complain of unlawful sex discrimination in employment without enforcing, relying on or founding a claim on the contract of employment.

Selection for employment and the terms on which employment may be offered

[(1) Disabled persons]   **37–031**
The Disability Discrimination Act 1995 (c. 50) confers new rights on disabled persons in respect of access to employment and the terms on which employment may be offered.

4. – COLLECTIVE AGREEMENTS AND STATUTORY AWARDS OF TERMS

(b) *Incorporation of collective agreements into individual contracts of employment*

Express incorporation

As to the latitude of construction which is allowed (or denied) in relation **37–040** to changed industrial relations circumstances, see *Adams v. British Airways plc*.[a]

[a] [1996] I.R.L.R. 574, C.A.

[*Add to note 88: page* [726]]
See also now *Whent v. T. Cartledge Ltd* [1997] I.R.L.R. 153.

5. – RIGHTS AND DUTIES UNDER AND ASSOCIATED WITH A CONTRACT OF EMPLOYMENT

(a) *Duties of the Employee*

Duty of fidelity

[*Notes 49–50: page* [732]]
The proposition in the text has been the subject of an important re-affirmation, in the context of a contract of employment between a solicitor-employee and the firm by which he was employed, in *Wallace Bogan & Co. v. Cove* [1997] I.R.L.R. 453, C.A.

37–051 [*Note 54*]
The cross-reference should be to §37–146. Compare also *GFI Group Ltd v. Eaglestone.*[a]

[a] [1997] I.C.R. 25.

(b) *Duties of the employer*

(i) *Remuneration*

No express or fixed provision for remuneration

37–064 See, as to the situation where an annual hours contract is silent as to payment for overtime working, *Ali v. Christian Salvesen Food Services Ltd.*[a]

[a] [1996] I.C.R. 1.

Holidays and holiday pay

37–065 [*Note 76: page* [743]]
The Court of Appeal decided in *Morley v. Heritage Ltd* [1993] I.R.L.R. 400 that neither this provision nor general considerations of business efficacy required the implication of an entitlement upon termination of employment to payment in lieu of accrued holiday not previously taken.

Payment during the absence due to sickness: the position at common law

37–066 [*Add to text after note 89: page* [744]]
(6) It should be noted that the existence of an express sick pay scheme may

result in an implied term restricting the employer's power to terminate the contract during the absence of the employee due to sickness.[89a]

[89a] Compare *Aspden v. Webbs Poultry & Meat Groups (Holdings) Ltd* [1996] I.R.L.R. 521. (As to the effect on such a scheme of the termination of the insurance policy which supports it, compare *Bainbridge v. Circuit Foil (U.K.) Ltd* [1997] I.C.R. 541, C.A.)

Statutory Sick Pay

[*Note 11: page* [746]]   **37–068**
The Statutory Sick Pay Act 1994 (c. 2) removed the right of employers, other than small employers, to recover sums paid by them by way of statutory sick pay.

Statutory Maternity Pay

[*Note 43: page* [748]]   **37–070**
See now also the Statutory Maternity Pay (Compensation of Employers and Miscellaneous) Amendment Regulations 1994 (S.I. 1994 No. 1882).

General restrictions on deductions

[*Note 68: page* [758]]   **37–079**
It was held in *Bruce v. Wiggins Teape (Stationery) Ltd* [1994] I.R.L.R. 536 that unilateral reduction of wages by the employer might amount to unauthorised deduction within the meaning of the Act. Compare also *post*, §37–137.

(ii) *Other Duties*

Employer's liability to provide for safety of employee

[*Note 8: page* [761]]   **37–084**
It was held in *Walker v. Northumberland County Council* [1995] I.C.R. 702 that the employer was liable in respect of psychiatric illness suffered by the employee as the result of stress associated with his workload, and which the employer had been, in the particular circumstances of the case, negligent in failing to prevent.

Compulsory employers' liability insurance

[*Notes 20, 22: page* [762]]   **37–085**
The Employers' Liability (Compulsory Insurance) General Regulations have been amended in various respects by the Employers' Liability (Compulsory Insurance) General (Amendment) Regulations 1994 (S.I. 1994 No. 3301) with effect from January 1, 1995.

The rights of the employee in relation to trade union membership and activities

37–090   *[Note 61: page* [766]]
See also now *Department of Transport v. Gallacher* [1994] I.C.R. 967.

[Note 69: page [767]]
See now *Associated Newspapers Ltd v. Wilson, Associated British Ports v. Palmer* [1995] I.C.R. 406, in which the House of Lords reversed the decision of the Court of Appeal; the proposition in the text is not, however, affected.

Statutory rights of employees to time off

37–091   [(3) Public Duties: *page* [768]]
Rights extended to members of police authorities by the Time Off for Public Duties Order 1995 (S.I. 1995 No. 694) with effect from April 1, 1995.

Equality clauses in contracts of employment

37–093   *[Note 4: page* [770]]
See *British Coal Corporation v. Smith* [1996] I.C.R. 515, H.L.

37–093   *[Note 6]*
The decision of the House of Lords in *North Yorkshire County Council v. Ratcliffe* [1995] I.C.R. 833 places some restriction upon the scope for treating market forces as a material factor other than the difference of sex. See also *British Coal Corporation v. Smith* [1996] I.C.R. 515, H.L.

[Notes 14–16: page [771]]
The procedure for such claims was altered, so that industrial tribunals considering such claims are no longer obliged to refer the question of equal value to an independent expert, by the Sex Discrimination and Equal Pay (Miscellaneous Amendments) Regulations 1996 (S.I. 1996 No. 438), in force, in this respect, from July 31, 1996.

Sex Discrimination during the period of employment

37–094   *[Note 21]*
The approach taken to employers' dress codes in *Schmidt v. Austick's Bookshops Ltd, supra,* was followed in *Smith v. Safeway plc* [1996] I.C.R. 808.

[*Notes 33–36; page* [772]]
The remedies available for sex discrimination during the period of employment were extended in certain respects by the Sex Discrimination and Equal Pay (Miscellaneous Amendments) Regulations 1996 (S.I. 1996 No. 438), in force, in this respect, from March 25, 1996.

Racial Discrimination during the period of employment

[*Note 46: page* [774]]   **37–097**
It having become clear that the protection which these provisions confer upon employees extends to racial harassment in the workplace, and given that under s.32(1) of the Act the employer is liable for acts done by an employee "in the course of his employment", it was held in *Jones v. Tower Boot Co. Ltd* [1997] I.C.R. 254, C.A. that this phrase bore a wider meaning than under the common law principles of vicarious liability.

(1) The general right to maternity leave

[*Note 58: page* [775]]   **37–101**
See now the Maternity (Compulsory Leave) Regulations 1994 (S.I. 1994 No. 2479), which implement with effect from October 19, 1994 the requirement of Council Directive 92/85 that maternity leave must include compulsory maternity leave of at least two weeks both before and after confinement.

[*Note 61: page* [776]]
For the question whether the contract of employment remains in being during maternity absence where the statutory and any contractual notification requirements have not been fulfilled, see *Crouch v. Kidsons Impey Ltd* [1996] I.R.L.R. 79.

(3) Rights in connection with suspension from work on maternity grounds

[*Note 70*]   **37–103**
See now the Suspension from Work on Maternity Grounds Order 1994 (S.I. 1994 No. 2930) which gives effect, from December 1, 1994, to relevant requirements of Council Directive 92/85.

Implied duties and constructive dismissal

See, for authority for the view that the employer has an implied duty to **37–105**
provide an effective grievance procedure, *W.A. Goold (Pearmak) Ltd v.*

McConnell.[a] Another important development consisted in the recognition, in *Malik v. Bank of Commerce and Credit International SA*[b] that there might be a breach of the implied term of trust and confidence, giving rise to "stigma damages", where the conduct of the employer's business was so disreputable as the damage the employee's prospects of obtaining other employment—a conclusion which the House of Lords ruled was not precluded by their older decision in *Addis v. Gramophone Co. Ltd*[c].

[a] [1995] I.R.L.R. 516.

[b] [1997] I.C.R. 606.

[c] [1909] A.C. 488; see §37–142, *post*.

6. – TERMINATION OF THE CONTRACT

(a) *Termination by notice*

"Continuous employment"

[*Note 50: page* [784]]
The legislation is now to be read subject to the Employment Protection (Continuity of Employmnet) Regulations 1996 (S.I. 1996 No. 3417), in force from January 13, 1997, which provide for the preservation of continuity of employment in certain special circumstances relating to the remedy of reinstatement or re-engagement of the employee.

37–112   [*Notes 54–57 and associated text: page* [784]]
The provisions here referred to, by defining "continuous employment" so as to exclude part-time employment below the stated thresholds of weekly hours, excluded part-time employment as thus defined from the scope of various statutory employment protection rights, most significantly rights to protection against unfair dismissal and to redundancy payments. It was clear from the decision of the House of Lords in *R. v. Secretary of State for Employment, ex parte Equal Opportunities Commission* [1995] 1 A.C. 1 that some or all of these exclusionary provisions in relation to part-time employment violated E.C. requirements of equal pay and treatment as between men and women (that is to say, they unlawfully discriminated against women). The exclusionary provisions were accordingly removed by the Employment Protection (Part-time Employees) Regulations 1995 (S.I. 1995 No. 31) with effect from February 6, 1995.

(b) *Termination by Payment in Lieu of Notice*

Payment in lieu of notice

37–114   The approach to the employee's claim to payment in lieu of notice as typically a claim to a contractual entitlement and as such not subject to a duty on the part of the employee to mitigate his or her loss, which was taken in *Delaney v. Staples*, is further supported by the decision of the Court of Appeal in *Abrahams v. Performing Rights Society Ltd.*[a]

[a] [1995] I.C.R. 1028.

Termination by agreement

[*Note 7: page* [789]]   **37–115**
A further example of this vigilance is provided by the decision of the Court of Appeal in *Hellyer Bros. v. Atkinson* [1994] I.R.L.R. 88.

(e) *Assignment, winding up and changes in the employing enterprise*

Transfer of employment: (2) the effect of the Transfer Regulations

[*Add to Note 50: page* [793]]   **37–120**
Compare, as to the effectiveness of variations in transferred contracts, *Wilson v. St. Helen's B.C.* [1997] I.R.L.R., C.A.

Appointment of a receiver

[*Note 71a: page* [795]]   **37–123**
The House of Lords has now, in its decision on a set of consolidated appeals in *Powdrill v. Watson* [1995] I.C.R. 1100, pronounced upon the circumstances in which a receiver or administrator will be regarded as having adopted the contracts of employment of those in the employment of the company at the date of the receiver or administrator's appointment, and upon the consequences of such adoptions occurring before March 15, 1994. See §9–049 *ante*.

(g) *Wrongful Dismissal or Repudiation*

Termination by wrongful dismissal or repudiation

[*Notes 31–40: page* [800]]   **37–134**
The Court of Appeal in its decision in *Boyo v. Lambeth London Borough Council* [1994] I.C.R. 727 has taken the elective view of wrongful repudiation by the employer. In the case where the employer wrongfully purported

to treat the contract of employment as frustrated, the contract was treated, for the purpose of assessing contractual compensation, as not validly terminated until the time that notice to terminate would have expired if given after a disciplinary process had been provided and had been completed within a reasonable period of time.

(h) *Constructive Dismissal*

Termination as the result of constructive dismissal

37–135   [*Add to Note 47: page* [802]]
Compare now, on the question of breach of the implied term of trust and confidence arising out of the transfer of an undertaking, *Sita (G.B.) Ltd v. Burton, The Times*, December 5, 1996 (EAT).

[*Notes 49 and 50*]
For attempted imposition of a variation in terms, coupled with the threat of dismissal if variation rejected, as constructive dismissal, see *Greenaway Harrison Ltd v. Wiles* [1994] I.R.L.R. 380.

7. – REMEDIES, AND RIGHTS INCIDENTAL TO THE TERMINATION OF EMPLOYMENT

(b) *Recovery of remuneration*

Payment for services actually rendered

37–137   [*Note 77: page* [804]]
The employee's claim in respect of "unlawful deduction" may extend to the withholding of part of the employee's remuneration following a purported but wrongful demotion of the employee—see *Morgan v. West Glamorgan County Council* [1995] I.R.L.R. 68.

Apportionment of wages or salary

37–138   [*Add to text after Note 84: page* [805]]
It was held in *Thames Water Utilities plc v. Reynolds*[84a] that accrual "day by day" is to be calculated by reference to calendar days rather than working days.

[84a] [1996] I.R.L.R. 186.

(d) *Damages for Wrongful Dismissal*

Damages for loss of earnings following wrongful dismissal

It was decided by the Court of Appeal in *Hopkins v. Norcross*[a] that the **37–141**
employee did not have to give credit for retirement pension payments
received following wrongful dismissal, these being exempt collateral benefits within the principle of *Parry v. Cleaver*.

[a] [1994] I.C.R. 11.

[*Note 24: page* [807]]
For the working out of the details of this measure of damages in relation to
the wrongful dismissal of the chief executive of a large public company, see
Clark v. BET plc [1997] I.R.L.R. 348.

[*Note 30: page* [808]]
Compare also now *Fosca Services (U.K.) Ltd. v. Birkett* [1996] I.R.L.R.
325.

[*Note 32*]
Compare also now *Boyo v. Lambeth London Borough Council* [1994]
I.C.R. 727; see *ante* §37–134.

Damages for other lost benefits

[*Notes 43–45: page* [809]]   **37–142**
The proposition that damages for wrongful dismissal do not include
damages for loss of reputation, or for stigma associated with the employment or the manner of its ending, must now be read as subject to the decision
of the House of Lords in *Malik v. Bank of Credit and Commerce
International SA* [1997] I.C.R. 606. (See §37–105 of this supplement).

(f) *Industrial Tribunal Jurisdiction*

Jurisdiction of industrial tribunals in relation to contracts of employment

[*Note 97b: page* [814]]   **37–148**
It was held in *Sarker v South Tees Acute Hospitals NHS Trust* [1997]
I.R.L.R. 328 that this extended to the case of the employer's wrongfully
resiling from a contract of employment before employment had
commenced.

8. – Unfair and Discriminatory Dismissal

(a) Unfair Dismissal

(i) General Considerations

Employments covered and employments specifically excluded

37–151 [*Note 23: page* [817]]
As to "normal retiring age" see also *O'Brien v. Barclays Bank plc* [1995] 1 All E.R. 438, *Bratko v. Beloit Walmsley Ltd* [1996] I.C.R. 76; as to the effect on "normal retiring age" of the employer's attempt unilaterally to impose a new contractual retiring age, see *Patel v. Nagesan* [1995] I.C.R. 988.

[*Note 24: page* [818]]
It is no longer necessary to distinguish between full-time and part-time employees, by reason of the Employment Protection (Part-time Employees) Regulations 1995 (S.I. 1995 No. 31)—see *ante* §37–112.

[*Note 25: page* [818]]
The question whether the two-year qualifying period is indirectly discriminatory against women so as to violate the requirements of the E.C. Equal Treatment Directive, has been the subject of a request by the House of Lords to the ECJ for a preliminary ruling in *R. v. Secretary of State for Employment ex p. Seymour-Smith* [1997] I.C.R. 371.

(iii) Unfairness

Substantial reasons for dismissal

37–156 [*Note 5: page* [824]]
See, for further amendments, the Collective Redundancies and Transfer of Undertakings (Protection of Employment) (Amendment) Regulations 1995 (S.I. 1995 No. 2587).

Reasonableness of dismissal

37–157 [*Note 22: page* [826]]
In *Duffy v. Yeomans & Partners Ltd* [1995] I.C.R. 1, the Court of Appeal treated it as permissible for the employer to argue that consultation would

[434]

have been pointless although the employer had not at or before the time of dismissal taken a decision about the utility of consultation.

Fairness in redundancy cases

[Add to text at note 57 and add to note 57: page [828]]   **37–160**
The statutory provision relating to selection contravening a customary arrangement or agreed procedure relating to redundancy was repealed without replacement by the Deregulation and Contracting Out Act 1994.

Dismissal in health and safety cases, or on the ground of assertion of statutory right

(2) Assertion of statutory right   **37–163**

[Note 66: page [829]]
See, for the scope of this provision, *Menell v. Newell and Wright Transport Contractors Ltd*, *The Times*, May 2, 1996.

(iv) *Remedies*

Compensation for unfair dismissal: the basic award

[Note 16: page [833]]   **37–169**
The latest statutory instrument amending the stated limit is the Employment Protection (Increase of Limits) Order 1995 (S.I. 1995 No. 1953), operative from September 27, 1995.

Procedure

[Note 63 at end: page [836]]   **37–172**
As now amended by the Industrial Tribunals (Constitution and Rules of Procedure) (Amendment) Regulations 1994 (S.I. 1994 No. 1623) with effect from July 12, 1994.

(b) *Discriminatory Dismissals*

Dismissals unlawful under the Race Relations Act 1976

[Notes 91–93: page [838]]   **37–175**
This right of complaint has been held not to extend to complaint in respect of the conduct of (and presumably also the withholding of) an internal appeal against a dismissal which has already taken effect, on the ground that the complainant is no longer an "employee" within the meaning of the Act: *Post Office v. Adekeye* [1997] I.C.R. 110, C.A.

9. – REDUNDANCY PAYMENTS AND PROCEDURE

(a) *Redundancy Payments*

Introduction

37–177   [*Note 4: page* [839]]
The requirement of "continuous employment" formerly excluded part-time employment but no longer does so by reason of S.I. 1995 No. 31: see *ante*, §37–112.

Redundancy

37–179   [*Note 36: page* [842]]
Compare now *Safeway Stores plc v. Burrell* [1997] I.C.R. 523.

Redundancy payments

37–181   [*Notes 52, 58: pages* [843], [844]]
The rules relating to the computation of "continuous employment" formerly excluded part-time employment but no longer do so by reason of S.I. 1995 No. 31: see *ante*, §37–112.

(b) *Redundancy Procedure*

Consultation with the representatives or recognised trade unions

37–187   Very important changes to these consultation requirements were made by the Collective Redundancies and Transfer of Undertakings (Protection of Employment) (Amendment) Regulations 1995[a] with effect from October 26, 1995. Requirements to consult in relation to proposed redundancies and proposed transfers of undertakings are no longer confined to consultation with the representatives of recognised trade unions; they are now requirements to consult, at the choice of the employer, either with the representatives of recognised trade unions or with elected representatives of the employees who are affected by the proposed redundancies or the proposed transfer. The requirement to consult in relation to proposed redundancies now attaches only where it is proposed to make 20 or more employees redundant.

[a] S.I. 1995 No. 2587.

CHAPTER 38

GAMING AND WAGERING

1. – DEFINITIONS

(a) *Wagering Contracts*

One to lose, other to win

[*Add to note 8: page* [852]]   **38–003**
Contrast the treatment of football pools in Scots law: *Ferguson v. Littlewoods Pools Ltd* 1997 S.L.T. 309.

Contracts for differences

[*Add to note 44: page* [856]]   **38–009**
Morgan Grenfell & Co. Ltd v. Welwyn Hatfield D.C. [1995] 1 All E.R. 1, 12–14 (interest rate swaps).

(b) *Gaming Contracts*

Common law definitions

38–011   [*Add to line 4 of text after* "fall within the definition": *page* [852]]

A "game" connotes some form of contest between the parties. Consequently, a "snowball" or "pyramid" scheme is not a "game" or "gaming" for the purposes of the Gaming Acts of 1845 and 1968.[47a] It follows that the rule that money paid under such a contract (which is an unlawful lottery) is not governed by the rule that money paid by the loser of a bet is irrecoverable (see Main Work §§38–024, 38–025).

[47a] *One Life Ltd v. Roy, The Times*, July 12, 1996.

CHAPTER 39

INSURANCE

1. – THE NATURE OF INSURANCE

Definition

[*Add to note 2: page* [885]]   **39–001**
  See also *Re Sentinel Securities Plc.* [1996] 1 W.L.R. 316, where it was held
that a guarantee protection scheme (under which a company undertook to
the customers of suppliers that, in the event of a supplier ceasing to trade
because of financial failure, it would honour the supplier's guarantee of the
goods supplied and installed) constituted insurance business.

[*Add to note 5*]
  See also *Fuji Finance Inc. v. Aetna Life Insurance Co. Ltd* [1996] L.R.L.R.

365, 372–373, 378–379, where it was held that the benefit payable must be contingent on the event uncertain; it is not necessary for the insurer to be exposed to a risk of loss.

[*Add to note 6 after the first sentence: page* [886]]
Fuji Finance Inc. v. Aetna Life Insurance Co. Ltd, supra, 378.

Indemnity

39–002   [*Add to note 11*]
The indemnity essentially is an undertaking by the insurer that the assured will not suffer loss caused by specified events or perils so that if such loss occurs, the insurer is in breach of his contract and is liable to the assured in unliquidated damages: *Irving v. Manning* (1847) 1 H.L. Cas. 287; *Firma C-Trade SA v. Newcastle Protection and Indemnity Association* [1991] 2 A.C. 1; *Ventouris v. Mountain, The Italia Express* [1992] 2 Lloyd's Rep. 281; *Sprung v. Royal Insurance (U.K.) Ltd* [1997] CLC 70; *cf. Callaghan v. Dominion Insurance Company Ltd, The Times*, July 14, 1997.

[*Add to note 12*]
Fuji Finance v. Aetna Life Insurance Co. Ltd [1996] L.R.L.R. 365.

2. – INSURABLE INTEREST

Definition of insurable interest

39–004   [*Add to note 23: page* [887]]
and *Mark Rowlands Ltd v. Berni Inns Ltd* [1985] 2 Q.B. 211, 228. For a consideration of the different senses in which "insurable interest" can be used, see *Glengate-KG Properties Ltd v. Norwich Union Fire Insurance Society Ltd* [1996] 2 All E.R. 487; [1996] 1 Lloyd's Rep. 614, 621–624.

[*Add to text after note 25*]
The nature of the interest required for the purposes of the insurance will depend on the nature of the cover provided and the loss against which the insurance has been obtained.[25a]

[25a] *Glengate-KG Properties Ltd v. Norwich Union Fire Insurance Society Ltd, supra*, 621–624; see *post* §39–005.

Types of insurable interest

39–005   [*Add to note 40: page* [888]]
In order to insure against loss of profits or other consequential loss suffered by virtue of damage to the property, the assured need not have an interest *in* the property, but only in the event insured against: *Glengate-KG*

Properties Ltd v. Norwich Union Fire Insurance Society Ltd [1996] 1 Lloyd's Rep. 614, 622, 624, *cf.* Marine Insurance Act 1906, s.5.

[*Add to the beginning of note 42*]
The policy may dictate that the liability of the assured may arise by virtue of his particular interest, in which case there must be a sufficient connection between the liability and the interest: see *C.F. Turner v. Manx Line Ltd* [1990] 1 Lloyd's Rep. 137, 143; *Chrismas v. Taylor Woodrow Civil Engineering Ltd* [1997] 1 Lloyd's Rep. 407, 410–411.

Insurance of another's interest

[*Add to note 72 after* Petrofina (U.K.) Ltd v. Magnaload Ltd: *page* [890]]   **39–007**
National Oil Well (U.K.) Ltd v. Davy Offshore Ltd [1993] 2 Lloyd's Rep. 582, 608–612.

[*Add to note 75*]
See, for example, *Newcastle Protection and Indemnity Association v. V Ships (USA) Inc.* [1996] 2 Lloyd's Rep. 515.

[*Add new paragraph after note 82 in text: page* [891]]   **39–007A**
If the interests of all the assureds are such that in the event of an insured loss occurring, their loss is the same because their interests in the subject matter insured is the same, the insurance may be characterised as "joint". The insurance is described as "composite" if the loss affects each of the assureds in different ways, which is often, but not always, manifested in the differing quantum of their losses.[82a] The classic example of a composite insurance is that which covers the interests of the landlord and tenant of property.[82b] Even if any or all of the assureds (such as a bailor and bailee of property) may recover under the policy in respect of the whole loss sustained by the subject-matter insured, because their interest relates to the whole of the subject matter insured, their interests, whilst "pervasive", may differ so as to characterise the insurance as composite.[82c] The classification of the insurance as joint or composite is necessary to gauge the effect of a breach of duty or misconduct by one assured as regards his co-assured.[82d]

[82a] *Samuel & Company Ltd v. Dumas* [1924] A.C. 431; *General Accident Fire & Life Assurance Corp. Ltd v. Midland Bank Ltd* [1940] 2 K.B. 388, 404–406; *New Hampshire Insurance Company v. MGN Ltd* [1997] L.R.L.R. 24; *The State of the Netherlands v. Youell* [1997] CLC 938.

[82b] *General Accident Fire & Life Assurance Corp. Ltd v. Midland Bank Ltd, supra.*

[82c] *The State of the Netherlands v. Youell, supra.* See also *Tomlinson (Hauliers) Ltd*

v. Hepburn [1966] A.C. 451; *Petrofina (U.K.) Ltd v. Magnaload Ltd* [1983] 2 Lloyd's Rep. 91, 95–96.

[82d] See, *post* §39–018 and §39–030.

Life Assurance Act 1774

39–010   *[Add to note 88: page* [892]*]*
The view of the Court of Appeal in the *Mark Rowlands* case to the effect that the Act was not intended to apply to indemnity insurance was expressly approved by the Privy Council in *Siu v. Eastern Insurance Co. Ltd* [1994] 2 A.C. 199, despite the doubts expressed in *MacGillivray and Parkington* (8th ed., 1988) at para. 154.

[Add to text after note 88]
A capital investment bond paying out a benefit on the death of a person has been held to be an insurance on the life of that person, even though the same benefit was also payable on early surrender.[88a]

[88a] *Fuji Finance Inc. v. Aetna Life Insurance Co. Ltd* [1996] L.R.L.R. 365, C.A., holding that it was enough that a benefit was payable on an event which was sufficiently life or death related (as was the case here, since the policy came to an end on the death of the person, and the right to surrender was related to the continuance of life). Furthermore, even *were* it necessary for the benefit payable upon surrender to be different from the benefit payable upon death, the Court of Appeal saw no reason why the difference had to arise from the description or formula adopted for the purpose of fixing the benefit payable. It was sufficient that, given market fluctuations, in practice it was almost inevitable that the benefit payable on death would be different from the value payable on surrender (which would, itself, vary according to when surrender occurred).

[Add new reference, line 10 of page, after "assured's own interest"]
NOTE 93a: *Fuji Finance Inc. v. Aetna Life Insurance Co. Ltd* [1996] L.R.L.R. 365.

Marine Insurance Act 1906

39–012   *[Add to text at end of paragraph]*
Section 5 requires the assured to have an insurable interest in the marine adventure insured, in particular by standing in a "legal or equitable relation to the adventure" or any property within the adventure of a nature such as to allow him to benefit by the safety of the subject matter insured or be prejudiced by its adversity.

3. – THE EVENT INSURED AGAINST

Event insured against

39–014   *[Add new reference, line 2, after "happening of the event": page* [893]*]*
NOTE 9a: The word "event" here refers to the "peril" insured against. In many

policies, the word "event" (and "occurrence") is used to identify the factual bedrock from which the relevant perils may spring, often in contradistinction to the peril insured against: *Kuwait Airways Corporation v. Kuwait Insurance Co. SAK* [1996] 1 Lloyd's Rep. 664, 686; app. on other grounds, unreported, May 21, 1997. As to the meanings given to the terms "event", "occurrence" and "claim", see *Caudle v. Sharp* [1995] L.R.L.R. 80, 433; [1995] L.R.L.R. 433; *Cox v. Bankside Members Agency Ltd* [1995] 2 Lloyd's Rep. 437; [1996] 1 Lloyd's Rep. 26; *Municipal Mutual Insurance Ltd v. Sea Insurance Co. Ltd* [1996] L.R.L.R. 265; *Axa Reinsurance (U.K.) plc v. Field* [1996] 2 Lloyd's Rep. 233, 239; *American Centennial Insurance Co. v. Insco Ltd* [1996] L.R.L.R. 407, 413; *Haydon v. Lo & Lo* [1997] 1 Lloyd's Rep. 336.

(a) *The Nature of the Event*

Uncertainty

[*Add to note 11: page* [894]]   **39–016**
See also *Promet Engineering (Singapore) Pte Ltd v. Sturge*; *The Nukila* [1997] 2 Lloyd's Rep. 146.

Wilful misconduct

[*Add to note 17*]   **39–018**
Cf. *Compania Maritima San Basilio S.A. v. Oceanus Mutual Underwriting Association (Bermuda) Ltd: The Eurysthenes* [1977] 1 Q.B. 49; *Manifest Shipping Co. Ltd v. Uni-Polaris Insurance Co. Ltd*; *The Star Sea* [1997] 1 Lloyd's Rep. 360 concerning the assured's "privity" under Marine Insurance Act 1906, s.39(5).

[*Add to note 18*]
Marine Insurance Act 1906, s.55(2)(a) does not permit the policy to allow an assured to recover in respect of his own wilful misconduct: *The State of the Netherlands v. Youell* [1997] CLC 938.

[*Add to note 21 after* "[1969] 1 Lloyd's Rep. 575"]
See also *The State of the Netherlands v. Youell, supra.* See *ante*, § 39–007A.

[*Add to the text after note 23 and add new reference*]
Except in the case of marine insurance,[23a]

NOTE 23a: Section 55(2)(a) of the Marine Insurance Act 1906; *The State of the Netherlands v. Youell, supra.*

[*Add to note 27: page* [895]]
See also *Dhak v. Insurance Company of North America (UK) Ltd* [1996] 1 W.L.R. 936 where it was held, in the context of a personal accident policy which covered bodily injury "caused by accidental means", that bodily injury which was the natural and direct consequence of a course of conduct embarked upon by an assured taking a calculated risk (in this case, excessive alcohol consumption) was not covered by the policy.

[*Add to note 27*]
Cf. Lacey's Footwear (Wholesale) Ltd v. Bowler International Freight Ltd, The Times, May 12, 1997 as to the meaning of "wilful misconduct" under the CMR Convention: §35–149.

Public policy

39–019   [*Add to the beginning of note 29: page* [895]
As to illegality and public policy in the context of a marine war risks policy and the payment of ransom to recover detained property, see *Royal Boskalis Westminster NV v. Mountain,* unreported, December 18, 1995; rev'd [1997] 2 All E.R. 929.

[*Add to note 31*]
Unless perhaps the insurance is compulsorily required: *Lancashire County Council v. Municipal Mutual Insurance Ltd* [1996] 3 All E.R. 545, 554.

39–019   [*Add to text after note 32*]
It is not contrary to public policy for an insured to recover under a contract of insurance in respect of a liability to pay exemplary damages awarded because of oppressive, arbitrary or unconstitutional acts by government servants.[32a]

[32a] *Lancashire County Council v. Municipal Mutual Insurance Ltd* [1996] 3 All E.R. 545, holding that there was nothing contrary to public policy *per se* in an insurance which, amongst other things, covered the vicarious liability of a chief constable to pay exemplary damages for wrongful arrest, malicious prosecution, and false imprisonment.

[*Add to the end of note 34*]
See also *Total Graphics Ltd v. AGF Insurance Ltd* [1997] 1 Lloyd's Rep. 599, 606.

[*Add to text after note 34 and add new reference*]
There are certain types of insurance policy which are positively encouraged by public policy considerations.[34a]

NOTE 34a: Such as legal expenses insurance: see *Murphy v. Young & Co.'s Brewery plc* [1996] LRLR 60, 65–66; [1997] 1 Lloyd's Rep. 236, 244.

(b) *The Time of the Event*

The period of cover

39–020   [*Delete "of" in the 3rd line of text and replace with "or"*]

Event and loss during period of cover

[*Add to the beginning of text: page* [897]]   **39–021**
"Subject to the terms of the policy,"

[*Add to note 44*]
Promet Engineering (Singapore) Pte Ltd v. Sturge; *The Nukila* [1997] 2
Lloyd's Rep. 146.

[*Add to note 45*]
and *Kuwait Airways Corporation v. Kuwait Insurance Co. SAK* [1996] 1
Lloyd's Rep. 664, 690; app. on other grounds, unreported, May 21, 1997.

[*Add to the text in the penultimate line before* "discharge"]
"ascertainment or"

[*Add to note 47*]
Municipal Mutual Insurance Ltd v. Sea Insurance Co. Ltd [1996] LRLR
265, 270.

(c) *The Place of the Event*

Place of event

[*Add to note 51*]   **39–022**
Kuwait Airways Corporation v. Kuwait Insurance Co. SAK [1996] 1
Lloyd's Rep 664, 689, 692–693; app. on other grounds, unreported, May 21,
1997 (definition of "any one location" in policy limit).

(d) *The Nature of the Loss*

Nature of loss

[*Add new reference after* "extend only to loss" *in second line: page* [898]] **39–023**

NOTE 51a The loss must be a real loss and not a notional loss (*Royal Boskalis
Westminster NV v. Mountain* [1997] 2 All E.R. 929, where the waiver of a contractual
claim unenforceable because of illegality or duress did not constitute a damnifiable
loss) nor a negligible loss (*Glengate-KG Properties Ltd v. Norwich Union Fire
Insurance Society Ltd* [1996] 1 Lloyd's Rep. 614, 620). See also *McMahon v. AGF
Holdings (U.K.) Ltd* [1997] LRLR 159.

[*Add to note 59*]
As to the distinction between actual and constructive total loss in marine

insurance law, see *Fraser Shipping Ltd v. Colton; The Shakir III* [1997] 1 Lloyd's Rep. 586.

[Add new paragraph after note 60 in text]

39–023A   **Expenses incurred to prevent loss.** If an assured incurs expense, sacrifices property or waives valuable rights [60a] in order to avert or minimise loss, in the absence of a contractual provision to the contrary the assured may not be able to recover such expense, even though the insurer benefits as a result.[60b] Such expenses may be recovered if they may be said to be a loss caused by the event insured against.[60c] It is commonplace, particularly in marine policies, to include a provision[60d] allowing the assured to recover from the insurer such expenses.

[60a] *Royal Boskalis Westminster NV v. Mountain* [1997] 2 All E.R. 929, 940, 951, 973.

[60b] *Yorkshire Water Services Ltd v. Sun Alliance and London Insurance plc* [1997] 2 Lloyd's Rep. 21. *Cf. Clarke, The Law of Insurance Contracts* (2nd ed. 1994), pp.742–743, para 28–8G

[60c] See, for example, *Berens v. Rucker* (1760) 1 Wm Bl 313, 315; *Dent v. Smith* (1869) LR 4 Q.B. 414.

[60d] Known as a "sue and labour" clause in marine policies: see *Aitchison v. Lohre* (1879) 4 App.Cas. 755; *Royal Boskalis Westminster NV v. Mountain* [1997] 2 All E.R. 929.

4. – UBERRIMA FIDES

Utmost good faith

39–024   *[Add to note 61: page* [898]*]*
See, however, *GMA v. Storebrand and Kansa* [1995] LRLR 333, 348–349, where scepticism was expressed as to whether contracts closely analogous to those of insurance could attract the duty of disclosure attached to contracts *uberrimae fidei.*

[Delete note 63 and substitute: page [899]*]*
Black King Shipping Corporation v. Massie; The Litsion Pride [1985] 1 Lloyd's Rep. 437; *Bank of Nova Scotia v. Helenic Mutual War Risks Association (Bermuda) Ltd, The Good Luck* [1990] 1 Q.B. 818, 888 (revd. on other grounds by the House of Lords [1992] 1 A.C. 233); *Royal Boskalis Westminster NV v Mountain* [1997] LRLR 523 (revd. on other grounds by the Court of Appeal: [1997] 2 All E.R. 929); *Manifest Shipping & Co. Ltd v. Uni-Polaris Insurance Co. Ltd; The Star Sea* [1997] 1 Lloyd's Rep. 360. See also Clarke, *The Law of Insurance Contracts* (2nd ed. 1994), pp.708, para. 27–1A.

[*Add new reference, line 8 of page, after* "duty not to make fraudulent claims"]

NOTE 64a: It is now established that there is no general duty of disclosure in respect of claims: *Royal Boskalis Westminster NV v. Mountain, supra; Manifest Shipping Co. Ltd v. Uni-Polaris Insurance Co. Ltd; The Star Sea, supra.*

[*Delete from line 12/13 of the text* "arising out of equity's jurisdiction to prevent imposition": [899]]

The duty to disclose material facts

[*Add to note 70: page* [899]]   **39–025**
Pan Atlantic Insurance Co. Ltd v. Pine Top Insurance Co. Ltd [1995] 1 A.C. 501.

[*Delete from text third sentence with notes 71–73, and substitute*]
The test of materiality, therefore, is not what the assured considers material,[71] nor what a reasonable assured would consider material,[72] but whether the circumstance would be taken into account by a prudent insurer when assessing the risk (even if it would not, of itself, have had a decisive effect on his decision whether to accept the risk and, if so, at what premium).[73]

NOTE 71: *Bates v. Hewitt* (1867) L.R. 2 Q.B. 595, 607; *Joel v. Law Union and Crown Insurance Co.* [1908] 2 K.B. 863, 884; *Godfrey v. Britannic Insurance* [1963] 2 Lloyd's Rep. 515, 529; *Roselodge v. Castle* [1966] 2 Lloyd's Rep. 113.

NOTE 72: *Lambert v. Co-Operative Insurance Society Ltd* [1975] 2 Lloyd's Rep. 485.

NOTE 73: *Pan Atlantic Insurance Co. Ltd v. Pine Top Insurance Co. Ltd, supra* (rejecting the "decisive influence" test of materiality, but holding that an insurer cannot rely upon a material non-disclosure (or misrepresentation) as a ground for avoiding the contract if the non-disclosure (or misrepresentation) did not actually *induce* the making of the contract), as interpreted by the Court of Appeal in *St Paul Fire & Marine Insurance Co. (UK) Ltd v. McConnell Dowell Constructors Ltd* [1996] 1 All E.R. 96. On this basis, a circumstance can be "material" even if it actually *decreases* the risk, but this does not mean that such a circumstance would have to be disclosed because, in the absence of inquiry, Marine Insurance Act 1906, s.18(3)(a) specifically exempts the assured from having to disclose any circumstance which diminishes the risk: see *St Paul Fire & Marine Insurance Co. (U.K.) Ltd v. McConnell Dowell Constructors Ltd, supra,* at 107.

[*Add to note 76*]
Roberts v. Plaisted [1989] 2 Lloyd's Rep. 341, 347–348.

Scope of duty of disclosure

[*Delete from text second sentence and substitute*]   **39–026**
In marine insurance, an assured is deemed to know every circumstance

which in the ordinary course of business ought to be known to him[82] so that the assured may be liable to disclose facts known to someone acting on his behalf of which he is unaware. The kinds of situation in which the knowledge of an agent will so affect the position of the assured have been summarised[82a] as being: (i) where the agent, although not effecting the insurance on behalf of the assured, is relied upon by the assured for information concerning the subject-matter of the insurance (sometimes referred to as an "agent to know")[82b]; (ii) where the agent is in such a predominant position in relation to the assured that his knowledge can be regarded as the knowledge of the assured[82c]; and (iii) where the agent is used to effect the insurance (in which case the agent is required to disclose not just all material circumstances which the assured is bound to disclose, but also every material circumstance which ought to be known by the agent, or communicated to him, in the ordinary course of business).[82d] However, the assured will not be adversely affected by the knowledge of his agent where the information concerns the agent's own fraud on his principal.[82e] Although it has never been authoritatively determined that similar principles apply in cases of non-marine insurance, in principle there can be little reason for distinguishing between marine and non-marine insurance in this respect, and cases frequently proceed upon the assumption that there is no material difference.[83]

[*Add to note 82*]
Marine Insurance Act 1906, s.18(1).

[82a] See *Simner v. New India Assurance Co. Ltd* [1995] L.R.L.R. 240.

[82b] See, in particular, *Fitzherbert v. Mather* (1785) 1 T.R. 12; *Gladstone v. King* (1813) 1 M. & S. 35; *Proudfoot v. Montefiore* (1867) L.R. 2 Q.B. 511; *Blackburn Low & Co. v. Vigors* (1887) 12 App.Cas. 531.

[82c] As to when an agent will be treated as being in such a position that his knowledge is attributed to his principal, see *Simmer v. New India Assurance Co. Ltd*, *supra*; *PCW Syndicates v. PCW Reinsurers* [1996] 1 All E.R. 774; *Deutsche Ruckversicherung AG v. Walbrook Insurance Co. Ltd* [1996] 1 All E.R. 791; and, more generally, *Meridian Global Funds Management Asia Ltd v. Securities Commission* [1995] 2 A.C. 500.

[82d] See Marine Insurance Act 1906, s.19. The section does not operate by imputing the knowledge of the agent to the assured, but by requiring the agent to disclose the material circumstances, and enabling the insurer to avoid the policy if he does not: *Société Anonyme D'Intermédiaires Luxembourgeois v. Farrex Gie.* [1995] L.R.L.R. 116; *PCW Syndicates v. PCW Reinsurers*, *supra*. However, the section applies only to an agent who actually deals with the insurer, and makes the contract in question, and not to "intermediate" agents: *PCW Syndicates v. PCW Reinsurers, supra.* nor to an agent who earlier had been instructed to effect the insurance, but did not in fact place the insurance: *Blackburn Low & Co. v. Vigors* (1887) 12 App.Cas. 531.

[82e] *PCW Syndicates v. PCW Reinsurers, supra*; *Deutsche Ruckversicherung AG v. Walbrook Insurance Co. Ltd, supra.* Further, the agent's knowledge of any "irregularity" in the performance of his duty, short of fraud, will not be imputed to

the assured, if it cannot be inferred that the agent would have informed the assured of that irregularity in the ordinary course of business: *Kingscroft Insurance Company Ltd v. Nissan Fire and Marine Insurance Company Ltd*, unreported, March 4, 1996; November 7, 1996.

[*Substitute for note 83*]
See, *e.g. Société Anonyme D'Intermédiaires Luxembourgeois v. Farrex Gie.*, *supra*. See, also, *March Cabaret Club v. London Assurance* [1975] 1 Lloyd's Rep. 169, 174.

[*Add to text after note 83: page* [901]]
Where, however, the assured is a private individual, or effects insurance otherwise than "in the course of business",[83a] it is his duty to disclose those facts which are known to him, not those which ought to be known to him.[83b]

[83a] Marine Insurance Act 1906, s.18(1).

[83b] *Economides v. Commercial Union Assurance Co. plc* [1997] 3 All E.R. 636; *cf. Group Josi Reinsurance Co. Ltd v. Walbrook Insurance Co. Ltd* [1996] 1 W.L.R. 1152, 1159. However, if a material fact is known to a private assured, but he does not appreciate its materiality, even though a reasonable man would be aware that the fact is material, the failure to disclose the fact to the insurer will constitute a breach of the duty: *Joel v. Law Union and Crown Insurance Company* [1908] 2 K.B. 863, 883–884.

[*Add to note 84*]
See also *Aldridge Estates Investments Co. Ltd v. McCarthy* [1996] E.G.C.S. 167; *Marc Rich & Co. A.G. v. Portman* [1997] 1 Lloyd's Rep. 225, 231–232.

[*Add to note 86*]
Marc Rich & Co. A.G. v. Portman, *supra*, 234.

[*Add to note 88*]
See *Power v. Provincial Insurance plc, The Times*, February 27, 1997; *cf. Reynolds v. Phoenix Assurance Co. Ltd* [1978] 2 Lloyd's Rep. 440.

Time of disclosure

[*Add new reference after* "undecided": *page* [902]]   39–027
NOTE 93a: The Court of Appeal has expressed the opinion (*obiter*) that it is only the alteration which is affected: *Manifest Shipping & Co. Ltd v. Uni-Polaris Insurance Co. Ltd; The Star Sea* [1997] 1 Lloyd's Rep. 360, 370.

[*Add to note 97*]
In *New Hampshire Insurance Company v. MGN Ltd* [1997] LRLR 24, it was held that the insurer's contractual right of cancellation does not impose on the assured a continuing duty of disclosure. However, if there is a "held covered" provision whereby the insurer is required to extend cover on

agreement of an additional premium, the assured will be subject to a duty of disclosure: *Overseas Commodities Ltd v. Style* [1958] 1 Lloyd's Rep. 546, 559; *Liberian Insurance Agency Inc. v. Mosse* [1977] 2 Lloyd's Rep. 560, 568; *Black King Shipping Corporation v. Massie; The Litsion Pride* [1985] 1 Lloyd's Rep. 437, 511–2; *New Hampshire Insurance Co. v. MGN Ltd, supra.*

[*Add to note 98*]
As to the effect of such provisions, see *Hussain v. Brown* [1996] 1 Lloyd's Rep. 627, 631 and *Kausar v. Eagle Star Insurance Co. Ltd* [1997] C.L.C. 129.

Misrepresentation

39–028   [*Add to text after note 4*]
So long as the assured honestly entertains his opinion or belief, there need be no reasonable grounds for the opinion or belief: *Economides v. Commercial Union Assurance Co. plc* [1997] 3 All E.R. 636; see Marine Insurance Act 1906, s.20(5); *contra, Highlands Insurance Co. v. Continental Insurance Co.* [1987] 1 Lloyd's Rep. 109.

[*Add to note 9: page* [903]]
See Marine Insurance Act 1906, s.20(4); *cf. Svenska Handelsbanken v. Sun Alliance and London Insurance plc* [1996] 1 Lloyd's Rep. 519, 561–562.

Honesty

39–029   [*Add to note 10*]
Cf. Economides v. Commercial Union Assurance Co. plc [1997] 3 All E.R. 636.

Effect of non-disclosure or misrepresentation

39–030   [*Add to note 13: page* [903]]
The decision of the House of Lords in *Pan Atlantic Insurance Co. Ltd v. Pine Top Insurance Co. Ltd* [1995] 1 A.C. 501 has now established, however, that an insurer cannot rely upon the misrepresentation or non-disclosure of a material fact to avoid the insurance if that misrepresentation or non-disclosure did not in fact induce the making of the contract on the terms accepted (in the sense in which "inducement" is used in the general law of misrepresentation).

Whether the insurer has been induced is a question of fact, not one of degree; therefore, if the non-disclosure or misrepresentation had only a slight or trivial effect on the decision of the insurer (for example, if he would have insisted on only slightly different terms), he will have been induced: *Aldridge Estates Investments Co. Ltd v. McCarthy*, [1996] E.G.C.S. 167; however, if the non-disclosed or misrepresented fact is deemed trivial by a prudent underwriter, the fact may not be material. There is said to be a presumption of inducement: *Pan Atlantic Insurance Co. Ltd v. Pine Top Insurance Co. Ltd* [1994] 2 Lloyd's Rep. 427, 453; *St Paul Fire & Marine Insurance Co. (U.K.) Ltd v. McConnell Dowell Contractors Ltd* [1995] 2 Lloyd's Rep. 116, 127; *Svenska Handelsbanken v. Sun Alliance and London Insurance plc* [1996] 1 Lloyd's Rep. 519, 564; *Gunns v. Par Insurance Brokers* [1997] 1 Lloyd's Rep. 173, 176. In *Marc Rich & Co. A.G. v. Portman* [1996] 1 Lloyd's Rep. 430, 441–442, the court suggested that the presumption should be relied upon where the underwriter cannot be called for good reason to give evidence and no reasonable supposition can be made that he acted imprudently (affd. [1997] 1 Lloyd's Rep. 225).

[*Add to note 16: page* [904]]
Similarly, it may be that the settlement may be avoided if the settlement was procured by a material non-disclosure or misrepresentation: *Royal Boskalis Westminster NV v. Mountain* [1997] LRLR 523 (*obiter*); rev'd on other grounds [1997] 2 All E.R. 929; *cf. Diggens v. Sun Alliance and London Insurance plc*, unreported, July 29, 1994.

[*Add to text note 22*]
However, if one co-assured under a composite, as opposed to a joint, insurance fails to disclose or misrepresents a material fact, the insurance contract with each innocent co-assured may not be avoided, unless he is implicated in a breach of the duty of the upmost good faith.[22a]

[22a] *New Hampshire Insurance Company v. MGN Ltd* [1997] LRLR 24.

Affirmation

[*Add to note 24*]   **39–031**
Svenska Handelsbanken v. Sun Alliance and London Insurance plc [1996] 1 Lloyd's Rep. 519, 569.

[*Add to note 27*]
As to whether the issuance of a policy may constitute an affirmation, see *Morrison v. The Universal Marine Insurance Company* (1872) L.R. 8 Ex. 40; (1873) L.R. 8 Ex. 197; *cf. Svenska Handelsbanken v. Sun Alliance and London Insurance plc* [1996] 1 Lloyd's Rep. 519, 569.

[*Add to note 28: page* [905]]
As to when an insurer will be treated as knowing all the relevant facts by reason of the knowledge of an agent being imputed to it, compare *Evans v. Employers' Mutual Insurance Association Ltd* [1936] 1 K.B. 505, and *Malhi v. Abbey Life Assurance Co. Ltd* [1996] LRLR 237. If the affirming conduct was that of an agent, rather than the aggrieved party himself, that agent himself must have the authority and capacity to affirm the contract: *Tate &*

Sons v. Hyslop (1885) 15 Q.B.D. 368, 374; *Aldridge Estates Investments Co. Ltd v. McCarthy* [1996] E.G.C.S. 167.

[*Add to note 29*]
and *Insurance Corporation of the Channel Islands Ltd v. McHugh* [1997] LRLR 94.

Modification of the duty by contract

39–032   [*Add to note 31 after* "[1970] 2 Lloyd's Rep. 314"]
Svenska Handelsbanken v. Sun Alliance and London Insurance plc, [1996] 1 Lloyd's Rep. 519, 551–553. Such terms are to be interpreted in accordance with established rules of construction and, unless the parties so intended, will not be interpreted as a continuing warranty: *Hussain v. Brown* [1996] 1 Lloyd's Rep. 627, 629.

[*Add to note 32*]
Toomey v. Eagle Star (No. 2) [1995] 2 Lloyd's Rep. 88, where it was held that it is possible in principle to include a provision excluding the right to rescind for material misrepresentation or non-disclosure, but that the clause in that case (which provided that the policy was "neither cancellable nor voidable by either party") did not, on its proper construction, preclude rescission for a misrepresentation or non-disclosure made negligently *Cf. Highlands Insurance Co. v. Continental Insurance Co.* [1987] 1 Lloyd's Rep. 109, 116–117; *Pan Atlantic Insurance Co. Ltd v. Pine Top Insurance Co. Ltd* [1992] 1 Lloyd's Rep. 101, 108–109; [1993] 1 Lloyd's Rep. 496, 502–503 (both cases concerned an "errors and omissions" clause which purported to excuse inadvertent misrepresentations and non-disclosures). Regard should also be had to section 3 of the Misrepresentation Act 1967, which treats contractual provisions relieving a misrepresentor from liability as invalid, unless reasonable; it is unlikely that such clauses will be struck down, at least from the assured's perspective, given the harshness of the remedy of avoidance as perceived by the court. See, *ante*, §6–082 *et seq.*

[*Add to the text after note 32*]
or by defining the extent of disclosure required from the assured.[32a]

[32a] *Sumitomo Bank Ltd v. Banque Bruxelles Lambert S.A.* [1997] 1 Lloyd's Rep. 487, 495.

Statements of Insurance Practice

39–033   [*Add to note 36 after* "General Insurance Practice Statement"]
"revised in 1995,"

[*Add to note 37*]
This provision does not apply to marine and aviation policies.

[*Add to note 39: page* [906]]
See *Economides v. Commercial Union Assurance Co. plc* [1997] 3 All E.R.
636.

5. – THE PARTIES

The assured

[*Add to note 42*]   **39–034**
See *New Hampshire Insurance Company v. MGN Ltd* [1997] LRLR 24,
56; *Sumitomo Bank Ltd v. Banque Bruxelles Lambert S.A.* [1997] 1 Lloyd's
Rep. 487, 495. As to the insurance for the benefit of more than one assured,
see *ante*, §39–007A.

The insurer

[*Delete from note 45 final sentence and substitute: page* [906]]   **39–035**
See now the Insurance Companies (Third Insurance Directives) Regu-
lations 1994 (S.I. 1994 No. 1696), which came into force on July 1, 1994,
giving effect to the Third Non-Life Insurance Directive (92/49) and the
Third Life Assurance Directive (92/96); and also the Insurance Companies
Regulations 1994 (S.I. 1994 No. 1516) which also came into force on July 1,
1994, and provides for the amendment of the Insurance Companies Act 1982
in a substantial number of respects. Section 95 of the Act defines "insurance
business" to include the "effecting and carrying out ... of contracts [of
insurance]". This definition includes reinsurance business: *Re NRG Victory
Reinsurance Ltd* [1995] 1 All E.R. 533; *New Hampshire Insurance Co. v.
Grand Union Insurance Co. Ltd* [1996] LRLR 102, 104 (H.K. Court of
Appeal). This inclusive definition covers the making and performance of
insurance contracts (*Bedford Insurance Co. Ltd v. Institutio de Resseguros
do Brasil* [1985] 1 Q.B. 966, 981–982; *Bates v. Barrow Ltd* [1995] 1 Lloyd's
Rep. 680, 689; *Group Josi Reinsurance Co. Ltd v. Walbrook Insurance Co.
Ltd* [1996] 1 Lloyd's Rep. 345, 369) and the negotiation which begin not later
than the invitation to treat (*R. v. Wilson* [1997] 1 All E.R. 119, 126; see *ante*
§§2–004—2–005).

[*Add to note 52: page* [907]]
The effect of the Insurance Companies Act 1982 is to make the contract

unlawful at common law even if English law is not the proper law of the contract: *DR Insurance Co. v. Central National Insurance Co.* [1996] 1 Lloyd's Rep. 74.

[*Add to note 53*]
New Hampshire Insurance Co. v. Grand Union Insurance Co. Ltd, supra.

[*Delete from note 53 final sentence and substitute*]
Section 132 operates retrospectively to permit enforcement of contracts entered into before s.132 came into force (January 12, 1987): *Bates v. Barrow Ltd* [1995] 1 Lloyd's Rep. 680, and *Deutsche Ruckversicherung A.G. v. Walbrook Insurance Co. Ltd* [1996] 1 All E.R. 791. It would seem, however, that as a result of the wording of s.132(1), the statutory right of the assured to recover money paid under the contract if he elects not to enforce it, and the discretionary remedy available to the insurer under s.132(3), are available only in respect of contracts entered into *after* s.2 of Insurance Companies Act 1982 came into force (January 28, 1983); but that the assured is nevertheless entitled to *enforce* the carrying out of a contract, even if it was entered into before that date: *Bates v. Barrow Ltd* [1995] 1 Lloyd's Rep. 680, 689.

Agents of the insurer

39–036   [*Add to note 60*]
Evans v. Employers' Mutual Insurance Association Ltd [1936] 1 K.B. 505; *Malhi v. Abbey Life Assurance Co. Ltd* [1996] L.R.L.R. 237, 242–243.

Broker

39–037   [*Add to note 62: page* [908]]
See also *Roberts v. Plaisted* [1989] 2 Lloyd's Rep. 341, 343; *Pryke v. Gibbs Hartley Cooper Ltd* [1991] 1 Lloyd's Rep. 602, 614–615; *Searle v. A. R. Hales & Co. Ltd* [1996] L.R.L.R. 68, 71. As to the authority of the broker, when the assured is placed into provisional liquidation, see *Pacific and General Insurance Company Ltd v. Hazell* [1997] L.R.L.R. 65.

[*Add before the last sentence in note 65*]
Bates v. Barrow Ltd [1995] 1 Lloyd's Rep. 680, 689–691.

[*Add to note 65*]
and by a sub-broker, see *Tudor Jones v. Crowley Colosso Ltd* [1996] 2 Lloyd's Rep. 619.

[*Delete from note 68 reference to the* Insurance Brokers Registration Council (Code of Conduct) Approval Order 1978, *and substitute: page* [908]]
Insurance Brokers Registration Council (Code of Conduct) Approval Order 1994 (S.I. 1994 No. 2569), which came into force on November 21, 1994.

[*Delete from note 69 reference to the* Brokers Registration Council (Code of Conduct) Approval Order 1978.]

Lloyd's

[*Add to note 73: page* [909]]   **39–038**
This is a formal or evidential requirement; the contract of marine insurance is concluded when the proposal is accepted by the insurer, by the signing of his line of the slip: s.21; *General Accident Fire & Life Assurance Corp v. Tanter*; The *Zephyr* [1984] 1 Lloyd's Rep. 58, 69.

[*Add to note 74*]
Punjab National Bank v. De Boinville [1992] 1 W.L.R. 1138. The slip evidences the contract of insurance. If the policy is issued in terms which contradict the terms recorded on the slip, the policy will be conclusive evidence of the contract, unless and until the policy is rectified, provided that the policy's terms have been agreed by the parties. If the policy's terms have not been agreed, the slip may be considered as evidence of the contract. See *New Hampshire Insurance Company v. MGN Ltd* [1997] L.R.L.R. 24, 32–34, 53–54.

[*Add to text after note 76: page* [909]]
Furthermore, where the underwriters of one or more lead syndicates are permitted under a "leading underwriter's clause" contained in the slip to make amendments to cover, they have (subject to the particular terms of the clause) actual authority to bind the members of other syndicates on the same slip, and act as their agents in doing so.[76a]

[76a] *Roadworks (1952) Ltd v. J.R. Charman* [1994] 2 Lloyd's Rep. 99 (where it was held that the particular leading underwriter's clause under consideration even gave the leading underwriter authority to waive a contingent condition to which the entire cover had been subject).

[*Add to note 77*]
In *Aneco Reinsurance Underwriting Ltd (in liq.) v. Johnson & Higgins*, unreported, August 1, 1997, it was held that each of the following underwriters could avoid their contract of insurance if the reassured failed to disclose the fact that a material misrepresentation had been made to the leading underwriter.

[*Add to text at end of paragraph*]
It is also the practice at Lloyd's for Lloyd's brokers to collect claims on

behalf of underwriters when called upon to do so, and a Lloyd's broker is under a continuing duty to exercise reasonable care and skill to retain the information enabling him to advance the claim for as long as a reasonable broker would regard a claim as possible.[78a]

[78a] *Johnstone v. Leslie & Godwin* [1995] L.R.L.R. 472, holding also that the broker is under a duty not to destroy a policy held on behalf of his principal (which is the principal's property) or, where there is no policy, the slip (which belongs to the broker) without the consent of the principal.

6. – THE CONTRACT OF INSURANCE

Formation of the contract

39-039   [*Add to note 80: page* [910]]
For the application of agency principles of undisclosed principal and ratification where a named insured takes out insurance cover on behalf of another as well as himself, see *National Oil Well (UK) Ltd v. Davy Offshore Ltd* [1993] 2 Lloyd's Rep. 582, 592–602. See, also, *Siu v. Eastern Insurance Co. Ltd* [1994] 2 A.C. 199 (P.C.), holding that the personal nature of an insurance contract does not, of itself, preclude the application of the doctrine of undisclosed principal to contracts of indemnity insurance.

[*Add to note 82*]
See also *Yona International Ltd v. La Réunion Française Société Anonyme d'Assurances et de Réassurances* [1996] 2 Lloyd's Rep. 84, 109–111; *New Hampshire Insurance Company v. MGN Ltd* [1997] L.R.L.R. 24, 32–34, 54.

[*Add to note 86 between* "include a" *and* "statement"]
"prominent"

[*Add to text at end of paragraph*]
When insurance cover is taken out pursuant to a covenant to insure contained in a mortgage, the interest of the mortgagee in the policy is by way of charge to secure the mortgage debt (whether the policy is effected in the name of the mortgagor or mortgagee), the charge taking effect as a partial equitable assignment.[86a]

[86a] *Colonial Mutual Insurance Co. Ltd v. ANZ Banking Group (New Zealand) Ltd* [1995] 1 W.L.R. 1140 (P.C.)

Repayment

39-045   [*Add to note 29: page* [914]]
In the case of marine insurance, the premium will not be returnable in the event of fraud: Marine Insurance Act 1906, s.84(3)(a).

7. – Conditions and Warranties

Classification of terms

[Add to text after note 43: page [915]]   **39–046**
Furthermore, conditions will be construed in the context of the commercial purpose of the policy, so that, for example, a condition requiring the assured to take reasonable precautions to prevent an accident, or to take all reasonable steps to safeguard any property insured, will usually be construed as requiring more than mere negligence upon the part of the assured before the condition is breached.[43a]

[43a] *Fraser v. B.N. Furman (Productions) Ltd* [1967] 1 W.L.R. 898 (where a condition in an employers' liability policy requiring the assured to take reasonable precautions to prevent an accident was construed as applying only where inadequate measures are taken by the assured in the face of a recognised danger, without caring whether or not it was averted); *Sofi v. Prudential Insurance Com Ltd* [1993] 2 Lloyd's Rep. 559 (applying a similar approach to a property insurance, where the policy required all reasonable steps to be taken to safeguard the property). In *Gunns v. Par Insurance Brokers* [1997] 1 Lloyd's Rep. 173, 177, it was suggested that this approach should apply to all types of insurance policy. In *Devco Holder Ltd v. Legal & General Assurance Society Ltd* [1993] 2 Lloyd's Rep. 567, a similar approach was applied in the context of a motor policy, but the Court of Appeal left open whether ordinary negligence might have sufficed in such a context. It has now been held in *Amey Properties Ltd v. Cornhill Insurance plc* [1996] LRLR 259 that, in the case of motor policies, a condition requiring a vehicle to be kept in good repair will not have been satisfied if the insurer proves the assured simply to have been negligent in the upkeep of his vehicle.

Warranties and their effect

[Add to text at end of paragraph page [916]]   **39–048**
When construing whether a statement in a proposal form gives rise to a promissory warranty or a warranty as to past or existing fact, there is no special principle of insurance law requiring answers to be read as importing promises as to the future.[51a]

[51a] *Hussain v. Brown* [1996] 1 Lloyd's Rep. 627, where the answer yes to a question "Are the premises fitted with any system of intruder alarm?" was held not to constitute a continuing warranty that the premises would be fitted with such an alarm.

Waiver

[Add to note 62: page [917]]   **39–050**
Svenska Handelsbanken v. Sun Alliance and London Insurance plc [1996] 1 Lloyd's Rep. 519, 569.

8. – ASSIGNMENT

Assignment of the policy

39–053   [*Add new reference after* "will have ceased to be in force": *page* [919]]

NOTE 80a: See Marine Insurance Act 1906, s.51.

[*Add to text at end of paragraph: page* [919]]
A partial equitable assignment of an insurance policy occurs when it is taken out pursuant to a covenant to insure contained in a mortgage. If the policy is effected in the name of the mortgagor, the mortgagee has a charge to secure repayment of the mortgage debt, which takes effect by way of assignment; if it is effected in the name of the mortgagee, the mortgagees' interest remains by way of charge, and he is accountable to subsequent mortgagees or the mortgagor for any surplus.[80b]

[80b] *Colonial Mutual Insurance Co. Ltd v. ANZ Banking Group (New Zealand) Ltd* [1995] 1 W.L.R. 1140 (P.C.).

Position of assignees

39–054   [*Add to note 81 after first sentence*]
See Marine Insurance Act 1906, s.50(2).

[*Delete last sentence of paragraph (but retain notes) and substitute*]
After the policy is assigned, the assignor will cease to be interested in the policy so that any breach of the duty of the upmost good faith by the assignor after the assignment cannot be relied upon by the insurer to avoid the policy, because the assignor no longer owes such a duty to the insurer.

[*Add to the beginning of note 83*]
Bank of Nova Scotia v. Hellenic Mutual War Risks Association (Bermuda) Ltd; Good Luck [1988] 1 Lloyd's Rep. 514, 546–547; [1989] 2 Lloyd's Rep. 238, 264; *cf.*

Assignment of the proceeds of the policy

39–055   [*Add to note 89; page* [920]]
Bank of Nova Scotia v. Hellenic Mutual War Risks Association (Bermuda)

Ltd; Good Luck [1988] 1 Lloyd's Rep. 514, 546–547; [1989] 2 Lloyd's Rep. 238, 264.

9. – Claims

Contractual provision

[*Add to note 94: page* [920]]   39–056
Hamptons Residential Ltd v. Field [1997] 1 Lloyd's Rep. 302.

[*Add to note 96*]
Municipal Mutual Insurance Ltd v. Sea Insurance Co. Ltd [1996] L.R.L.R. 265, 274–275; *Callaghan v. Dominion Insurance Company Ltd, The Times*, July 14, 1997.

Notice of loss

[*Add new reference at the end of the first sentence: page* [921]]   39–057

NOTE 96a: *Hamptons Residential Ltd v. Field, supra; Layher Ltd v. Lowe, The Times*, January 8, 1997, where it was held that an assured was not obliged, under a clause requiring the assured to notify the insurer of an occurrence "likely" to give rise to a claim, to notify the insurer of the mere possibility of a claim.

[*Add to note 98: page* [921]]
The reasoning in the *Pioneer Container* case was expressly approved by the Privy Council in *Motor and General Insurance Co. Ltd v. Pavy* [1994] 1 W.L.R. 462, 469 as fully and correctly stating the law. See also *Total Graphics Ltd v. AGF Insurance Ltd* [1997] 1 Lloyd's Rep. 599, 608.

Arbitration

[*Delete from note 7* "See Arbitration Act 1950, s.27." *and substitute*]   39–059
Cf. Callaghan v. Dominion Insurance Company Ltd, The Times, July 14, 1997.

[*Add to text after note 7*]
The arbitration clause in the policy is treated as separable from the insurance contract[7a] so that if the contract is void or avoided *ab initio*, the arbitration clause will survive and bind the parties to resolve their dispute by arbitration, unless the arbitration agreement may be avoided.[7b] There is implied into an arbitration agreement a term that the parties will keep confidential the resulting arbitration award, unless it is necessary to disclose the award to a third party in order to enforce or protect the legal rights of one of the parties.[7c]

[7a] Arbitration Act 1996, s.7.

[7b] *Harbour Assurance Co. (U.K.) Ltd v. Kansa General International Insurance Co. Ltd* [1993] 1 Lloyd's Rep. 455.

[7c] *Insurance Co. v. Lloyd's Syndicate* [1995] 1 Lloyd's Rep. 272. See also *Hassneh Insurance Co. v. Mew* [1993] 2 Lloyd's Rep. 243.

[Delete final sentence of paragraph and substitute]
Arbitration, if commenced after January 30, 1997, is governed by the Arbitration Act 1996.[8a]

[8a] Arbitrations commenced before January 30, 1997 are governed by the Arbitration Acts 1950, 1975 and 1979. By the 1996 Act, international insurance arbitration agreements now may exclude the court's jurisdiction in respect of any appeal on a point of law, whereas previously such agreements were ineffective (Arbitration Act 1979, ss.3 and 4). Such exclusion agreements relating to "domestic" arbitrations are effective if agreed after the commencement of proceedings (Arbitration Act, 1996, s.87(1)).

Fraudulent Claims

39–060   *[Add to note 10: page [922]]*
Orakpo v. Barclays Insurance Services [1995] L.R.L.R. 443; *Royal Boskalis Westminister NV v. Mountain* [1997] LRLR 523; rev'd on other grounds [1997] 2 All E.R. 929; *Manifest Shipping & Co. Ltd v. Uni-Polaris Insurance Co. Ltd; The Star Sea* [1995] 1 Lloyd's Rep. 651; [1997] 1 Lloyd's Rep. 360. The duty not to make a fraudulent claim persists even after the insurer wrongfully repudiates the policy: *Transthene Packaging Co. Ltd v. Royal Insurance (U.K.) Ltd* [1996] L.R.L.R. 32, 43.

[Delete the second sentence and note 12 and substitute]
Furthermore, it is an implied term of the contract of insurance that the making of a fraudulent claim will result in the assured forfeiting all benefit under the policy[11a] and not just the benefit which attaches to the fraudulent claim or fraudulent part of the claim.[11b]

[11a] *Diggens v. Sun Alliance and London Assurance plc*, unreported, July 29, 1994; *Orakpo v. Barclays Insurance Services, supra,* 451–452; *Royal Boskalis Westminster NV v. Mountain* [1997] LRLR 523; rev'd on other grounds [1997] 2 All E.R. 929. As to forfeiture clauses, see *Insurance Corporation of the Channel Islands Ltd v. McHugh* [1997] L.R.L.R. 94; *cf. Fargnoli v. GA Bonus plc* [1997] CLC 653.

[11b] *Orakpo v. Barclays Insurance Services, supra,* 451–452; *Royal Boskalis Westminster NV v. Mountain, supra.* It has been said that the insurer has the right simply to defend the fraudulent claim and keep the remainder of the policy intact (*Black King Shipping Corporation v. Massie; The Litsion Pride* [1985] 1 Lloyd's Rep. 437, 514–516; *Continental Illinois National Bank & Trust Co. of Chicago v. Alliance*

Insurance Co. Ltd; The Captain Panagos D.P. [1986] 2 Lloyd's Rep. 470, 511–512; *Roadworks (1952) Ltd v. J. R. Charman* [1994] 2 Lloyd's Rep. 99, 107). However, it is perhaps more accurate to say that the insurer may waive the assured's forfeiture of all benefit under the policy other than the fraudulent claim.

[*Add to note 13*]
Orakpo v. Barclays Insurance Services, supra, 451.

[Delete from line 11 "mortgage" and substitute]
"assignee"

[*Add to note 18*]
New Hampshire Insurance Company v. MGN Ltd [1997] L.R.L.R. 24.

[*Add to text after note 18*]
The duty of good faith does not impose any duty to disclose or not to misrepresent material facts in connection with a claim wider than the duty not to present a fraudulent claim.[18a]

[18a] *Royal Boskalis Westminster NV v. Mountain* [1997] LRLR 523; rev'd on other grounds [1997] 2 All E.R. 929; *Manifest Shipping Co. Ltd v. Uni-Polaris Insurance Co. Ltd; The Star Sea* [1997] 1 Lloyd's Rep. 360.

The burden of proof

[*Add to note 26: page* [923]]   39–061
Where the insurer alleges fraud or wilful misconduct, the standard of proof remains the civil standard, although the difficulty in satisfying the court will be greater in proportion to the seriousness of the insurer's charge. *Hornal v. Neuberger Products Ltd* [1957] 1 Q.B. 247, 258; *The Zinova* [1984] 2 Lloyd's Rep. 264; *Black King Shipping Corporation v. Massie; The Litsion Pride* [1985] 1 Lloyd's Rep. 437, 479; *The Ikarian Reefer* [1995] 1 Lloyd's Rep. 455, 459; *Royal Boskalis Westminster NV v. Mountain* [1997] LRLR 523; rev'd on other grounds [1997] 2 All E.R. 929; *Transthene Packaging Co. Ltd v. Royal Insurance (U.K.) Ltd* [1996] L.R.L.R. 32, 37.

Causation

[*Add to note 40: page* [924]]   39–062
Yorkshire Water v. Sun Alliance & London Insurance [1997] 2 Lloyd's Rep. 21 (where the assured unsuccessfully sued for the recovery of expenses

incurred to prevent the incurring of insured liabilities on the alternative grounds that the event which would result in the insured liability had already occurred, although the insured peril had not yet operated, and that it was an implied term of the policy that such expenses would be indemnified).

[*Add to note 41*]
Indeed, a failure reasonably to attempt to minimise such loss may interfere with the chain of causation and deprive the assured of an indemnity for some or all of his loss: *National Oilwell (U.K.) Ltd v. Davy Offshore Ltd* [1993] 2 Lloyd's Rep. 582, 618–619; *The State of The Netherlands v. Youell* [1997] CLC 938.

[*Add to note 46*]
Cf. *Kuwait Airways Corporation v. Kuwait Insurance Co. SAK* [1996] 1 Lloyd's Rep. 664; unreported, May 21, 1997, C.A.

The amount recoverable

39–063 [*First line on page* [925] *delete* "eems" *and substitute:* "seems"]

[*Add to note 48: page* [925]]
Accordingly, the assured may not recover as damages any losses occasioned as a result of the insurer's failure to pay other than that which was to be indemnified under the policy: *Ventouris v. Mountain; The Italia Express* [1992] 2 Lloyd's Rep. 281; *Sprung v. Royal Insurance (U.K.) Ltd* [1997] CLC 70; *Callaghan v. Dominion Insurance Company Ltd, The Times,* July 14, 1997; *contra Grant v. Co-operative Insurance Society Ltd* (1983) 134 NLJ 81; *Transthene Packaging Co. Ltd v. Royal Insurance (U.K.) Ltd, supra,* 41. The assured's entitlement to damages may be different if the insurer is in breach of other obligations under the insurance contract: *Transthene Packaging Co. Ltd v. Royal Insurance (U.K.) Ltd, supra; cf. Sprung v. Royal Insurance (U.K.) Ltd, supra.*

[*Add new reference after* "case of valued contracts"]
NOTE 48a: The policy may be in part a valued policy and in part an unvalued policy: *Grimaldi Ltd v. Sullivan* [1997] CLC 64.

[*Add to the end of note 53*]
Cf. *Anderson v. Commercial Union,* unreported, May 23, 1996 (Scottish Court of Session), where it was held that whilst the insurer was bound to indemnify the assured against the costs of repair, he was not obliged (absent a clause) to indemnify the assured *as and when* such costs were incurred.

[*Add to note 55*]
As to claims for partial losses under the Marine Insurance Act 1906, ss.69

and 77, see *Manifest Shipping Co. Ltd v. Uni-Polaris Insurance Co. Ltd; The Star Sea* [1995] 1 Lloyd's Rep. 651, 664–666; *Kusel v. Atkin* [1997] CLC 554.

[*Add to text after note 56*]
Where the assured has a number of claims to be presented under the policy, the assured, not the insurer, has the right to determine the sequence in which the claims are presented against the insurer.[56a] Where two or more assureds, or third parties deriving title to sue, present claims under the one policy and there is insufficient cover to indemnify all the claimants, the available cover shall respond to each claim in the order it is established under the policy[56b] and if each of the claims are established at the same time, the claims must be satisfied on a *pro rata* basis.[56c]

[56a] *Cox v. Deeny* [1996] L.R.L.R. 288, 298–299.

[56b] *Cox v. Bankside Members' Agency Ltd* [1995] 2 Lloyd's Rep. 437.

[56c] *Cox v. Deeny* [1996] L.R.L.R. 288, 299.

Indemnification aliunde

[*Add to the end of note 57*]   **39–064**
Cf. Royal Boskalis Westminster NV v. Mountain [1997] 2 All E.R. 929, where the Court of Appeal held that the fact that the waiver of contractual claims was ineffective as a matter of law meant that no damnifiable loss was suffered.

[*Add to the end of note 63*]
See also *Colonia Versicherung AG v. Amoco Oil Co.* [1997] 1 Lloyd's Rep. 261, 270–271.

10. – THE RIGHTS OF THE INSURER UPON PAYMENT

Salvage

[*Add to note 89: page* [928]]   **39–071**
See Marine Insurance Act 1906, s.79(1).

[*Add to note 91*]
In *Fraser Shipping Ltd v. Colton; The Shakir III* [1997] 1 Lloyd's Rep. 586, 591–593, it was held that if the insured vessel was salvageable even at exorbitant cost, the vessel was constructively, not actually, lost.

Subrogation

[*Add to note 3: page* [929]]   **39–072**
This is occasionally referred to as the "top-down" principle, namely that

any recoveries from third parties are applied to the uppermost layer of the loss first and the bottom-most last. See also *Kuwait Airways Corporation v. Kuwait Insurance Co. SAK* [1996] 1 Lloyd's Rep. 664, 694–695; app. on other grounds, unreported, May 21, 1997.

[*Add to note 5*]
See also *Royal Boskalis Westminster NV v. Mountain*, unreported, December 18, 1995; rev'd on other grounds [1997] 2 All E.R. 929 and *Colonia Versicherung AG v. Amoco Oil Co.* [1997] 1 Lloyd's Rep. 261. In the last case, the Court of Appeal confirmed that the assured need not account for the voluntary payment only if the donor intended to benefit the assured to the exclusion of the insurer and rejected the suggestion that the donor had to intend to benefit the insurer.

[*Add to note 7*]
See also Marine Insurance Act 1906, s.79.

[*Add to note 10 at the end of the first sentence.*]
Brown v. Albany Construction Co. [1995] NPC 100; *Europe Mortgage Company v. Halifax Estate Agencies, The Times,* May 23, 1996.

[*Add to note 11*]
The State of the Netherlands v. Youell [1997] CLC 938.

[*Add to note 12: page* [930]]
cf. Woolwich Building Society v. Brown, The Independent, January 22, 1996, where it was held that an insurer who had paid the assured building society under a mortgage indemnity insurance was entitled, by way of subrogation, to sue the defaulting mortgagor in the name of the building society, since the insurance against the mortgagor's non-payment was not for the joint benefit of mortgagee and mortgagor in the relevant sense contemplated in the *Rowlands* case.

[*Add to the end of the text: page* [930]]
Where the insurer recovers funds which are in excess of the amount to which the insurer is entitled pursuant to his right of subrogation, the insurer will hold that excess on "trust" for the assured so that the assured will have an equitable proprietorial interest in that excess.[19a]

[19a] *Lonrho Exports Ltd v. Export Credit Guarantee Department* [1996] 2 Lloyd's Rep. 649, 661–663; *cf. Lord Napier and Ettrick v. Kershaw* [1993] 1 Lloyd's Rep. 197.

Duty of assured

39–073   [*Add to note 21*]
cf. Marc Rich & Co. AG v. Portman [1996] 1 Lloyd's Rep. 430, 440; aff'd [1997] 1 Lloyd's Rep. 225.

Contribution

[*Add to note 22*]   **39–074**
See also Marine Insurance Act 1906, s.32.

[*Delete "29–010" from note 24 and substitute*]
39–010

11. – SPECIFIC TYPES OF INSURANCE CONTRACT

(a) *Liability Insurance*

Duty to insure

[*Add to text at end of paragraph: page* [933]]   **39–077**
The Act does not impose any civil liability upon an employing company,
or its directors, for the consequences of a failure to insure.[42a]

[42a] *Richardson v. Pitt-Stanley* [1995] Q.B. 123.

Statutory subrogation

[*Add to text after note 44: page* [933]]   **39–078**
If two or more third party claimants obtain judgments against an insolvent
assured, their respective statutory rights to claim directly from his insurer
take effect in the order in which the extent of the assured's liability to the
third parties was ascertained: there is no mechanism, either under the
general law or under the Act, to enable rateable division of the proceeds of
the insurance policy between the third party claimants, except where their
judgments are simultaneous.[44a]

[44a] *Cox v. Bankside Members' Agency Ltd* [1995] 2 Lloyd's Rep. 437; *Cox v. Deeny*
[1996] L.R.L.R. 288, 299.

[*Add to note 45: page* [933]]
and defences based on public policy, see *ante* § 39–019.

(b) *Motor Insurance*

[*Add to note 52; page* [934]]   **39–079**
Stinton v. Stinton [1995] RTR 167; *Hatton v. Hall, The Times*, May 15,
1996.

[*Add to the end of note 53*]
See also *O'Connor v. Royal Insurance*, unreported, September 30, 1996
(public car park); *Cutter v. Eagle Star Insurance Co. Ltd, The Times*,
December 3, 1996 (public car park).

[*Add new reference after* "out of such use" *in fourth line*]

NOTE 54a: In *Dunthorne v. Bentley* [1996] RTR 428, the Court of Appeal held that the plaintiff's injuries were caused by the defendant who, having run out of petrol had left her car to seek assistance, ran in front of the plaintiff's car, and that the injuries arose out of the defendant's use of her vehicle.

Rights of third parties

39–080   [*Add to the beginning of note 76: page* [936]]
Cambridge v. Callaghan, The Times, March 21, 1997; *Silverton v. Goodall*, unreported, March 26, 1997.

[*Add to the text after note 77*]
European Council Directives[77a] require Member States to ensure that insurance coverage exists for civil liability for personal injuries and property damage arising as a result of the use of motor vehicles. The intention of the Directives is to ensure that the victims of motor accidents are able to prosecute and establish their claims in comparable ways in each Member State.[77b]

[77a] Directives 72/166, 84/5 and 90/232.

[77b] *Criminal Proceedings against Ruiz Bernáldez*, Case C–129/94 [1996] All E.R. (EC) 741. The Directives are presently under review by the European Commission with a view to the victim being permitted to proceed directly against the insurer without the necessity of obtaining judgment against the user of the vehicle.

(c) *Reinsurance*

General characteristics

39–081   [*Add to note 82: page* [937]]
See also *Excess Insurance Co. Ltd v. Mander* [1997] 2 Lloyd's Rep. 119; *cf. Municipal Mutual Insurance Ltd v. Sea Insurance Co. Ltd* [1996] L.R.L.R. 265, 275.

[*Add to note 87: page* [938]]
Re NRG Victory Reinsurance Ltd [1995] All E.R. 533 (holding, also, that retrocessions are "insurance" business for the purposes of the 1982 Act). See also *New Hampshire Insurance Co. v. Grand Union Insurance Co. Ltd* [1996] L.R.L.R. 102.

Liability of the reinsurer

39–082   [*Delete* "reinsurance" *from the third line and substitute*]
insurance

[*Add to note 88*]

In an excess of loss reinsurance, the contract may provide for reimbursement of losses in excess of an ultimate net loss which is to be determined by reference to the sum actually *paid* in settlement of losses. In *Charter Reinsurance Co. Ltd v. Fagan* [1996] 3 All E.R. 46, H.L., however, it was held that, on a proper construction of the policies before the Court, this did not mean that payment of the relevant losses by the reassured was a condition precedent to the liability of the reinsurer to reimburse him.

[*Add to note 91*]

The clause does not require the reinsurer to indemnify the reinsured in respect of his costs of investigating, settling and defending claims under the underlying insurance nor will a term be implied to such effect: *Baker v. Black Sea & Baltic General Insurance Co. Ltd* [1996] L.R.L.R. 353. As to the reinsurer's right of inspection of the reinsured's records of his settlement of the underlying claim, see the recent decisions in *Pacific & General Insurance Co. Ltd (in liq.) v. Baltica Insurance Co. (U.K.) Ltd* [1996] L.R.L.R. 8; *Commercial Union Assurance Co. v. Mander* [1996] 2 Lloyd's Rep. 540.

[*Add to text after note 93: page* [938]]

In *Hill v. Mercantile & General Reinsurance Co. Plc*,[93a] a "follow settlements" clause which provided for all loss settlements by the reinsured to be binding on its reinsurers "providing such settlements are within the terms and conditions of the original policies and/or contracts ... and within the terms and conditions of this reinsurance" was held by the House of Lords to contemplate a distinction between the facts generating a particular claim, and the legal extent of the respective covers. Although the reinsurers could be bound by the reassured's honest conclusions as to the former, it would not be bound by its determination of the latter, since this would enable the reinsured to bind its reinsurers to a definition of cover different from that which they had contracted to accept.

[93a] [1996] 1 W.L.R. 1239.

(f) *Life Insurance*

[Add new reference after "securities": page [940]]   **39–085**

NOTE 8a: *Cf. Fuji Finance Inc. v. Aetna Life Insurance Co. Ltd* [1996] L.R.L.R. 365.

CHAPTER 40

RESTRICTIVE AGREEMENTS AND COMPETITION

[468]

1. – INTRODUCTION

Scope and plan of the chapter

[*Add to text after note 2: page* [942]]　　　　　　　　　　　　　　**40–001**
A useful introductory guide to domestic competition law has been
published by the Office of Fair Trading, *An Outline of United Kingdom
Competition Policy* (OFT, April 1995).

[*Insert as new paragraph at end: page* [945]]　　　　　　　　　　**40–011**
Deregulation and Contracting Out Act 1994. The Deregulation and **40–011A**
Contracting Out Act 1994 effected changes to both the monopoly and the
merger provisions of the Fair Trading Act 1973, to the Restrictive Trade
Practices Act 1976 and to the Competition Act 1980. Where relevant, these
changes will be noted below.

1988 Green Paper and 1989 White Paper

[*Delete text from "However, despite the Government's commitment" to*　**40–012**
the end of the paragraph and substitute: page [946]]
These Papers have now been superseded by the DTI's Consultation
Document *Tackling Cartels and the Abuse of Market Power: Implementing
the Government's Policy for Competition Law Reform* (March 1996), as to
which see §40–013A, *post*.

1992 Green Paper

[*Delete from text, final sentence, and substitute*]　　　　　　　　**40–013**
Minor amendments to the legislation dealing with the abuse of market
power are suggested in the DTI's Consultation Document *Tackling Cartels
and the Abuse of Market Power: Implementing the Government's Policy for
Competition Law Reform* (March 1996), as to which see *post*, §40–013A.

[*Insert new paragraph at end*]
The DTI has published a Consultation Document *Tackling Cartels and the* **40–013A**
*Abuse of Market Power: Implementing the Government's Policy for Compe-
tition Law Reform* (March 1996) in which detailed proposals for the reform
of the restrictive trade practices legislation are set out, together with some
procedural alterations in relation to the abuse of market power.

As to restrictive trade practices, the Consultation Document suggests the
adoption of legislation based on Article 85 of the E.C. Treaty. However, the
possibility that "vertical" agreements (between undertakings operating at
different levels of the market) might be excluded from the legislation is

mooted. The new legislation would confer wide-ranging powers on the Director General of Fair Trading, for example to request information and to conduct on-the-spot investigations. Fines would be introduced for infringements of the new legislation, which would be imposed by a newly-constituted Restrictive Practices Tribunal; above a certain level the fines would be imposed by the High Court.

As to the abuse of market power, the Director General of Fair Trading would be given greater investigative powers, and the possibility that interim measures might be made available pending the outcome of an investigation into a particular matter is considered.

It is understood that legislative time may be available in the Autumn of 1996 for the Government to introduce a Bill to implement these proposals. A draft Bill was published by the DTI in August 1996.

2. – SUMMARY OF CURRENT LEGISLATION AND INSTITUTIONS

The Secretary of State

40–018   [*Delete from text and notes, "Minister for Corporate and Consumer Affairs" and substitute "Minister for Competition and Consumer Affairs"*]

The Director General of Fair Trading

40–019   The Director General of Fair Trading no longer publishes reports under the Competition Act: see section 12 of the Deregulation and Contracting Out Act 1994 and the amendments effected thereby to the relevant provisions of the Act of 1980.

[*Add to text at end: page* [950]]
The Director General of Fair Trading has published a *Code of Practice on Enforcement* (January 1994) in which, *inter alia*, time-limits are established within which the OFT will endeavour to deal with various matters arising under the domestic competition legislation.

3. – RESTRICTIVE TRADE PRACTICES ACT 1976

(a) *Restrictive Agreements Relating to Goods: Registrability*

(i) *General Scheme of the Act*

General Scheme of the Act

40–025   [*Add to note 82: page* [954]]
The Office of Fair Trading has published four booklets explaining aspects of the Restrictive Trade Practices Act 1976: *Restrictive Agreements: a Basic*

Guide (January 1995); *Restrictive Trade Practices: a Detailed Guide* (December 1995); *Restrictive Trade Practices Act in the Bus Industry* (March 1995); and *Cartels: Detection and Remedies—a Guide for Purchasers* (March 1995).

(ii) *Agreements and Arrangements*

[Insert as new paragraphs at end: page [958]]   **40–030**
The Aberdeen Solicitors Case. In *Aberdeen Solicitors' Property Centre* **40–030A**
Ltd and Another v. Director General of Fair Trading[20a] the Restrictive
Practices Court (Scotland) considered the *Fisher* and *RICS* cases in relation
to the use by Scottish firms of solicitors of the services of companies
established to provide property advertising services. The Court, following
the *RICS* case, concluded that there were horizontal arrangements between
the solicitors' firms. However, it proceeded to hold that the arrangements
were not registrable, since they did not relate to designated services, as to
which see *post*, §40–124.
In *Re Supply of Ready-mixed Concrete: Director General of Fair Trading* **40–030B**
v. Pioneer Concrete (UK) Ltd and another[20b] the House of Lords held that
companies which had expressly prohibited their employees to enter into
registrable agreements were nevertheless parties to the agreements actually
entered into by those employees.

[20a] Scots Law Report, *The Times*, February 20, 1996.

[20b] [1995] 1 All E.R. 135.

(vi) *Disregarded Restrictions and Excepted Requirements*

[Insert as new paragraph at end]   **40–068**
In *Associated Dairies Ltd v. Baines*[58a] the Court of Appeal gave further **40–068A**
consideration to section 9(3). Clause 4.3 of the agreement between the
parties required Baines "not to sell milk by way of retail to any customers of
the company". This clause gave rise to two restrictions, (i) not to resell the
milk acquired from Associated Dairies to its customers and (ii) not to sell
milk acquired from third parties to Associated Dairies' customers. The
question arose of the application of section 9(3). Section 9(3) provides that
"no account shall be taken of any term which relates to the goods supplied
...". The Court of Appeal considered that the word "term" should bear its
normal meaning: since clause 4.3 did not relate only to milk supplied by
Associated Dairies, it followed that it could not be disregarded. The
agreement was therefore registrable. The Court of Appeal rejected any
suggestion that the word "term" in section 9(3) should be regarded as
synonymous with "restriction". On appeal, the House of Lords reversed the
judgment of the Court of Appeal[58b] and concluded that the agreement was
not registrable. Part (i) of clause 4.3 could be disregarded under section 9(3)

of the Act, while part (ii) related to milk obtained elsewhere, and fell within Schedule 3(2)(b) of the Act.

[58a] Court of Appeal [1996] I.C.R. 183: the case at first instance is reported at [1995] I.C.R. 296.

[58b] *M.D. Foods plc (formerly Associated Dairies) v. Baines* [1997] 2 WLR 364.

Section 9(5): British Standards Institution, etc.

40–070   [*Add to note 65 at end: page* [978]]
Restrictive Trade Practices Act (Standards and Arrangements) (Goods) Order (S.I. 1993 No. 2473); Restrictive Trade Practices (Standards and Arrangements) Order 1995 (S.I. 1995 No. 3129) (both as to Electricity Association Services Ltd).

40–091   [*Add to text as new paragraph: page* [985]]
40–091A   **Variation of exempt agreements under sections 29 and 30**. The Deregulation (Restrictive Trade Practices Act 1976) (Amendment) (Variation of Exempt Agreements) Order 1996[16a] amends the Restrictive Trade Practices Act to change and simplify the procedure for dealing with variations to agreements that are exempted under these provisions.

[16a] S.I. 1996 No. 346.

Exemption of certain undertakings

40–096   Schedule 11, paragraph 4, Deregulation and Contracting Out Act, 1994 adds to the list of exempt agreements undertakings accepted pursuant to a proposal under section 56A, Fair Trading Act (undertakings in lieu of a monopoly reference, introduced by section 7 of the 1994 Act).

Other exemptions

40–097   [*Add to note 35: page* [998]]
S.I. 1996 No. 1327

[*Add to text at end of paragraph*]
The Broadcasting (Restrictive Trade Practices Act 1976) (Exemption for Networking Arrangements) Order 1994[35a] exempts various agreements between Channel 3 licensees and the Independent Television Association Limited. The Restrictive Trade Practices (Gas Conveyance and Storage) Order 1996[35b] exempts from the Act certain agreements made on or after March 2, 1995 containing provisions relating to or to activities connected with gas pipe-line systems or storage facilities operated by a public gas transporter.

[35a] S.I. 1994 No. 2540.

[35b] S.I. 1996 No. 385.

(c) *Restrictive Agreements Relating to Services: Registrability*

(i) *General Scheme of the Act*

Services

[*Add to note 89 after reference to the Director General of Fair Trading's*   **40–110**
Annual Report for 1976: page [995]]
The OFT's *Restrictive Trade Practices: a Detailed Guide* (December 1995)
repeats the point at page 17.

(v) *Acceptance of Relevant Restrictions by Two or More Parties*

Matters in respect of which restrictions must be accepted

[*Add to text at end of paragraph: page* [999]]   **40–123**
In *Racecourse Association Ltd and Satellite Information Services Ltd*[a] a
restriction "not to offer or make available to third parties any of the
designated services ... on terms which are in any respect more favourable
than the terms on which they are offered or made available to Satellite
Information Services" was found to be a restriction covered by Article 3(2)
of the Order.

[a] Order of the Restrictive Practices Court, January 11, 1994.

Designated services

[*Add to end of paragraph*]   **40–124**
In *Aberdeen Solicitors' Property Centre Ltd and Another v. Director
General of Fair Trading*[32a] the Restrictive Practices Court (Scotland) held
that a restriction on a company that advertised property on behalf of
solicitors, preventing that company from advertising properties being
marketed jointly by a solicitor's firm and an estate agency, related to the
provision of estate agency services which, in the Scottish context, were to be
regarded as legal services. It followed that the restriction related to
non-designated services and that therefore the Act was not applicable.

[32a] Scots Law Report, *The Times*, February 20, 1996.

(vi) *Disregarded Restrictions and Excepted Agreements*

Section 18(5): British Standards Institution, etc.

[*Add to note 41: page* [1000]]   **40–128**
Restrictive Trade Practices Act (Standards and Arrangements) (Services)

Order (S.I. 1993 No. 2453); Restrictive Trade Practices (Standards and Arrangements) (Services) Order 1995 (S.I. 1995 No. 3130) (both as to Electricity Association Services Ltd).

(e) *The Duty to Furnish Particulars*

40–146   [*Add to text as new paragraph: page* [1006]]
40–146A   **Non-notifiable agreements**. Section 10 of the Deregulation and Contracting Out Act 1994 inserted section 27A of the Restrictive Trade Practices Act 1976, which enables the Secretary of State by order to provide that certain descriptions of agreement, other than price-fixing agreements, shall be non-notifiable. As a consequence, restrictions in such agreements will not be void for want of notification.

Two orders have been made under this provision. The Restrictive Trade Practices (Non-notifiable Agreements) (Turnover Threshold) Order 1996[91a] provides that an agreement to which the parties are persons whose aggregate annual turnover in the United Kingdom does not exceed £20 million on the date on which the agreement is made is a non-notifiable agreement. The Order applies to agreements made on or after March 19, 1996.

The Restrictive Trade Practices (Non-notifiable Agreements) (E.C. Block Exemptions) Order 1996[91b] provides that an agreement which is exempt from Article 85(1) E.C. Treaty by virtue of a block exemption under Article 85(3) (as to which see *post*, §40–307) is a non-notifiable agreement. The same is true of an agreement which, if it were to be caught by Article 85(1), would benefit from a block exemption. The Order applies to agreements made on or after March 19, 1996.

[91a] S.I. 1996 No. 348.

[91b] S.I. 1996 No. 349.

Inspection of the Register

40–149   [*Amend note 1: page* [1007]]
As from March 27, 1995, the Register has been moved to The Office of Fair Trading, Room 05, Field House, 15–25 Bream's Buildings, London EC4A 1PR.

[*Add to text at end of paragraph: page* [1008]]
It should be noted that section 11 of the Deregulation and Contracting Out Act 1994 amends section 23(3) of the Restrictive Trade Practices Act 1976 by replacing sub-paragraph (b) in such a way as slightly to expand the range of matters that might be entered in the special section of the register.

Time within which particulars must be furnished

[*Add to text at end of paragraph*]   **40–151**
The position has however now been changed in relation to agreements
made on or after March 19, 1996 by the Deregulation (Restrictive Trade
Practices Act 1976) (Amendment) (Time Limits) Order 1996.[10a] This Order,
made under section 1 of the Deregulation and Contracting Out Act 1994,
provides that it is no longer necessary to furnish particulars before the
restrictions in an agreement take effect: it now suffices that particulars of the
agreement are furnished within three months from the date of the
agreement.

[10a] S.I. 1996 No. 347.

Consequences of failure to furnish particulars

[*Add to text at end of paragraph: page* [1009]]   **40–153**
The OFT announced early in 1995 a campaign to identify secret price
fixing and market sharing cartels: *OFT Launches New Drive Against
Cartels*,[19a] and has proceeded in a number of cases since then. Examples of
action on the part of the OFT, apart from cases dealt with elsewhere in the
text, are *Grounds maintenance price-fixing*[19b] and *Pre-stressed and reinforced
concrete flooring in Northern Ireland.*[19c]

[19a] OFT Press Release 5/95, February 2, 1995.

[19b] OFT Press Release 28/95, May 25, 1995.

[19c] OFT Press Release 8/96, March 21, 1996.

(f) *Consequences of Registration*

Community provisions: effect on jurisdiction of court

[*Add to text at end of paragraph: page* [1023]]   **40–180**
However the Court will not stay an action simply because the same
agreement is the subject of investigation by the European Commission: see
DGFT v. The Publishers Association[44a] and *British Sugar v. DGFT.*[44b]

[44a] Unreported, judgment of August 9, 1995.

[44b] Unreported, judgment of August 9, 1995.

Contempt of court

[*Note 46*]   **40–181**
In *Re Supply of Ready-mixed Concrete: Director General of Fair Trading
v. Pioneer Concrete (UK) Ltd and another* [1995] 1 All E.R. 135 the House of
Lords reversed the judgment of the Court of Appeal, which had held that a
company could not be liable for contempt where it had expressly forbidden

its employees to enter into registrable agreements and, in disobedience of those orders, the employees nevertheless concluded agreements allocating markets. The employees had been acting in the course of their employment and were carrying on the business of the companies in question. The fact that they had been instructed to refrain from making registrable agreements would be relevant in mitigation of penalties, but not in establishing whether that had been contempt.

[Add to text at end of paragraph: page [1024]]
In August 1995 the Restrictive Practices Court imposed record fines of £8.375 million on 17 ready-mixed concrete companies involved in secret price-fixing and market-sharing agreements.[52a] This is by far the largest fine ever imposed in a competition law case in the U.K., and demonstrates a new determination on the part of the Court to punish serious cases of cartelisation that continues after a court order or the giving of undertakings.

[52a] OFT Press Release 38/95, August 4, 1995.

4. – MONOPOLIES, MERGERS AND ANTI-COMPETITIVE PRACTICES

(a) *References under the Fair Trading Act 1973*

Introduction

40–188   *[Add to note 88: page* [1030]]
The OFT has published two booklets summarising the relevant provisions on these matters: *Monopolies and Anti-competitive Practices* (OFT, March 1995) and *Mergers* (October 1995).

40–200   *[Add to text as new paragraph at end: page* [1035]]
40–200A   **Undertakings in lieu of a reference.** Section 7 of the Deregulation and Contracting Out Act inserts sections 56A–56G into the Fair Trading Act 1973 to enable undertakings to be given in lieu of a monopoly reference.

Mergers

40–201   *[Add to text at end of paragraph: page* [1036]]
As a result of section 147 of the Companies Act 1989 and section 9 of the Deregulation and Contracting Out Act 1994, section 75 of the Fair Trading Act 1973 has been amended so that undertakings as to divestiture or future behaviour may be given in lieu of a merger reference.

[Note 66]
The two publications referred to have been updated: see *Mergers* (OFT, October 1995); *Mergers: the Content of Submissions* (OFT, November 1995).

Procedure to the Commission

[*Add to note 81: page* [1037]]   **40–204**
R. v Monopolies and Mergers Commission, ex p. Stagecoach Holdings plc,
The Times, July 23, 1996.

Actions on reports of Commission

[*Add to note 89: page* [1038]]   **40–205**
The Electrical Contracting (London Exhibition Halls) Order 1995 (S.I.
1995 No. 3299).

[*Add to text at end of paragraph*]
The Director General of Fair Trading has published a *Register of
Undertakings and Orders* (June 1995), which contains details of all extant
undertakings under the Fair Trading Act 1973 and the Competition Act
1980.

[*Add to text after note 92*]   **40–205**
Sections 93 and 93A of the Fair Trading Act do not confer a right of action
upon private persons for breaches of orders or undertakings given under the
Act.[92a]

[92a] *Mid Kent Holdings plc v. General Utilities plc* [1996] 3 All E.R. 132.

(b) *References under the Competition Act 1980*

Scheme of the Act

[*Note 95*]   **40–206**
s.12 Deregulation and Contracting Out Act 1994 has eliminated the
requirement for the Director General of Fair Trading to publish a report
setting out his findings before the matter can be referred to the Monopolies
and Mergers Commission.

Preliminary investigation by the Director

[*Add to text at end of paragraph: page* [1041]]   **40–211**
Section 12 of the Deregulation and Contracting Out Act 1994 has
eliminated the requirement for the Director General of Fair Trading to
publish a report setting out his findings before the matter can be referred to
the Monopolies and Mergers Commission.

5. – RESALE PRICE MAINTENANCE

(a) *Goods Not Enjoying Exemption under 1976 Act*

(i) *Avoidance of Conditions for Maintaining Resale Prices*

Exempt Goods

40–224   [Add at the end of the paragraph]
The exemption for books was revoked by the Restrictive Practices Court on March 13, 1997.[58a]

[58a] *Net Book Agreement 1957, The Times*, March 20, 1997.

6. – COMPETITION RULES UNDER THE E.C. TREATY

(a) *In General*

Purpose of this section

40–278   [*Amend note 81: page* [1068]]
Kerse is now in its 3rd edition (1995).

Principal sources of law

40–282   [*Amend note 92: page* [1069]]
Hartley is now in its 3rd edition (1994).

[*Amend note 93*]
The *Butterworths Competition Law Handbook* is now in its 4th edition (1995).

European Economic Area

40–284   Several of the countries formerly in the EEA have now become full members of the European Union. Austria, Finland and Sweden joined the European Union on January 1, 1995 and are now subject to the provisions of the E.C. Treaty rather than the agreement on the EEA.
Liechtenstein became a member of the EEA as from May 1, 1995: see Decision of EEA Council No. 1/95 [1995] O.J. L86/58 and L140/30.

(b) *Article 85(1)*

Undertaking

40–287   [*Note 5: page* [1071]]
In *Re COAPI*, [1995] O.J. L122/37, [1995] 5 C.M.L.R. 468, the Com-

mission held that professional intellectual property agents are undertakings and the rules of their professional association constitute an agreement between undertakings.

[*Note 9*]
See now Case C–364/92, *SAT Eurocontrol v. Commission* [1994] I E.C.R. 43, [1994] 5 C.M.L.R. 208 (body set up under international law to levy air transport charges not an undertaking); Case C–159/91, *Pourcet v. Commission* [1993] I E.C.R. 637 (body administering state sickness benefit not an undertaking); Case C–244/94, *Fédération Française des Sociétés d'Assurance v. Ministère de l'Agriculture et de la Pêche* [1995] I E.C.R. 4013 (organisation managing an optional supplementary social security scheme is an undertaking). In Case C–343/95, *Diego Calì & Figli v. Servizi ecologici Porto di Genova*, judgment of March 18, 1997, the ECJ stated in an Article 86 case that a distinction must be drawn between the situation where the State acts in the exercise of official authority and where it carries on economic activities of an industrial or commercial nature.

Parents and subsidiaries

A striking recent example of the application of this concept was Case **40–288** T–102/92, *Viho Europe BV v. Commission.*[a] There it was alleged that Parker Pen operated a policy whereby its subsidiaries in the different Member States were instructed not to sell Parker products outside their particular territories. The Court of First Instance upheld the Commission's analysis that since the subsidiaries did not have autonomous decision making powers, the policy did not fall within Article 85. Clearly had this policy been imposed on independent distributors it would have been a serious breach of the Treaty.

[a] [1995] II E.C.R. 17 (Decision upheld by ECJ: [1997] I E.C.R. 5457, [1997] 4 C.M.L.R. 419).

Agreements

[*Note 20: page* [1072]]   **40–290**
The C.A.'s judgment in *Re Supply of Ready Mixed Concrete* was overturned by the H.L.: [1994] 3 W.L.R. 1249.

The test to be applied

[*Note 37: page* [1074]]   **40–295**
See also Case C–250/92, *Gøttrup-Klim* [1994] I E.C.R. 5641, [1996] 4

C.M.L.R. 191 where the ECJ, examining the rules of an agricultural purchasing co-operative, applied a "reasonableness" test when deciding whether a rule preventing members from belonging to a competing co-operative fell within Art. 85(1).

Requirement of appreciable effect

40–298 The Court of First Instance applied the *Delimitis* test when examining exclusive purchasing agreements in the retail ice cream market: Case T–7/93, *Langnese-Iglo v. Commission.*[a]

[a] [1995] 5 C.M.L.R. 602.

Notice concerning agreements of minor importance

40–299 The turnover threshold in this Notice has been raised to 300 million ECU.[a] The Court has confirmed that the fact than an agreement exceeds the thresholds in the Notice does not automatically mean that it has an appreciable effect.[b]

[a] [1994] O.J. C368/20. For the Commission's proposal to revise this Notice see [1997] 4 C.M.L.R. 500.

[b] Case T–77/94, *VGB & Others v. Commission,* judgment of May 14, 1997.

Effect on trade between Member States

40–301 For a recent case confirming the broad construction given to this requirement see Case T–77/92, *Parker Pen v. Commission.*[a]

[a] [1994] II E.C.R. 549.

[Note 61: page [1077]]
In Case T–77/94, *VGB & Others v. Commission*, judgment of May 14, 1997, the CFI annulled a Commission finding that an agreement with an agricultural cooperative had no effect on trade, holding that it had to be judged in the context of the rules laid down by the agricultural cooperative as a whole and not in isolation.

(c) *Article 85(3): Individual and Block Exemption*

Block exemptions

40–306 Note now that if the agreement falls within a block exemption it does not need to be notified under the Restrictive Trade Practices Act 1976: Restrictive Trade Practices (Non-notifiable Agreements) (E.C. Block Exemptions) Order 1996.[a]

[a] S.I. 1996 No. 349.

Block exemptions currently in force

Regulations 2349/84 (patent licences) and 556/89 (know-how agreements) **40–307** have been replaced by Regulation 240/96[a] which applies, from April 1, 1996, to technology transfer agreements.

Regulation 123/85 which exempted certain selective distribution agreements for motor vehicles expired on September 30, 1995 and has been replaced by Regulation 1475/95 which came into force on July 1, 1995.[b] Regulations 1983/83 and 1984/83 were due to expire at the end of 1997 but the Commission has extended them to the end of 1999.[c]

[a] [1996] O.J. L31/2: see *post*, §40–330.

[b] [1995] O.J. L145/25: see *post*, §40–334.

[c] [1997] O.J. L214/27.

(d) *Application of Article 85 to specific agreements*

Typical horizontal agreements

[*(i) Price fixing: page* [1079]]
For two recent price fixing decisions see *P&O European Ferries*,[a] where the Commission fined channel ferry operators for colluding to impose a uniform currency surcharge on freight following a devaluation of sterling, and *Fenex*.[b]

[a] [1997] 4 C.M.L.R. 798.

[b] [1996] O.J. L181/28.

[*(iii) Exchange of information: page* [1080]]   **40–308**
For two recent cases discussing the conditions in which exchange of commercial information between competitors is incompatible with Article 85(1) see Case T–34/92, *Fiatagri UK Ltd and New Holland Ford v. Commission*[a] and Case T–35/92, *John Deere Ltd v. Commission*.[b]

[a] [1994] II E.C.R. 905.

[b] [1994] II E.C.R. 957.

[*Note 96: page* [1080]]
The decision in *Soda Ash—Solvay, ICI* [1994] 4 C.M.L.R. 454, 482 was annulled because of procedural irregularities in the conduct of the investigation: see Cases T–30/91 and T–36/91 [1995] II E.C.R. 1775 & 1847. For

more recent examples of major market sharing cartels see *European Cement Producers* [1994] O.J. L343/1, [1995] 4 C.M.L.R. 327; *Cartonboard* [1994] O.J. L243/1, [1994] 5 C.M.L.R. 547; *Steel beam manufacturers* [1994] O.J. L116/1, [1994] 5 C.M.L.R. 353.

Restrictions on imports or exports

40–313   A clause impeding exports "unless such an obligation is prohibited by law in the contract territory" is still illegal and liable to fine.[a]

[a] See *Novalliance/Systemform* [1997] O.J. L47/11. This case is a good recent illustration of the Commission's approach to territorial exclusivity.

[*Note 19: page* [1083]]
The decision in *Newitt/Dunlop Slazenger and others* [1993] 5 C.M.L.R. 352 was partly overturned on appeal: see Case T–38/92, *All Weather Sports BV v. Commission* [1994] II E.C.R. 211 (decision and fine against AWS annulled on procedural grounds) and Case T–43/92, *Dunlop Slazenger v. Commission* [1994] II E.C.R. 447 (duration of infringement and hence fine reduced). The Commission has since fined another tennis ball manufacturer for adopting similar measures to impede parallel imports: *Tretorn and others* [1994] O.J. L378/45 (appeal dismissed: Case T–49/95, judgment of December 11, 1996).

Other measures impeding parallel imports

40–315   In *Zera/Montedison, Hinkens/Stähler*,[a] the Commission held that the parties had impeded exports by product differentiation, *i.e.* by distributing a slightly different formulation of their herbicide product in some Member States from that distributed in Germany in order to prevent parallel imports into Germany where the prices were higher.

[a] [1993] O.J. L272/28.

Resale price maintenance

40–316   A clause requiring the joint setting of prices by supplier and reseller is illegal even if it is never enforced.[a]

[a] *Novalliance/Systemform* [1997] L47/11.

Application of the block exemption

40–318   [*Note 28: page* 1084]]
For a recent case where additional restrictions deprived an agreement of the benefit of Reg. 1983/93 see *Novalliance/Systemform* [1997] O.J. L47/11.

[482]

Patents and know-how block exemptions

Regulations 2349/84 (patent licences) and 556/89 (know-how agreements) **40–330**
have been replaced by Regulation 240/96ᵃ which applies, from April 1, 1996,
to technology transfer agreements. This new regulation covers patent
licensing agreements, know-how licensing agreements and mixed patent and
know-how agreements, including agreements containing ancillary provisions relating to intellectual property rights other than patents. The block
exemption sets out the extent to which the licensee can be granted the
exclusive right to exploit the technology and to manufacture and sell
goods incorporating the technology in different Member States. Various
other restrictions are exempted but there is a list of terms which will
deprive the agreement of the benefit of the exemption. There is an
"opposition procedure" similar to that in the former patent and know-how
regulations.

ᵃ [1996] O.J. L31/2.

Franchise agreements

Note that car dealerships are to be considered under the motor vehicle **40–331**
block exemption Regulation 1475/95 and not under the franchise block
exemption: see Article 12 of Regulation 1475/95, *post*, §40–334 note 74.

Selective distribution systems

There was a spate of judgments of the Court of Justice in relation to motor **40–334**
vehicle distribution networks prior to the new Regulation coming into force:
see Case C–70/93, *Bayerische Motorenwerke v. ALD Auto-Leasing*, [1995] I
E.C.R. 3439; Case C–266/93, *Bundeskartellamt v. Volkswagen and VAG
Leasing* [1995] I E.C.R. 3477; Case C–226/94, *Grand garage albigeois v.
Garage Massol* [1996] I E.C.R. 651; Case C–309/94, *Nissan France v.
Jean-Luc Dupasquier du Garage Sport Auto* [1996] I E.C.R. 677.

[Note 74: page [1091]]
Reg. 123/85 has been replaced by Reg. 1475/95, [1995] O.J. L145/25, [1996]
4 C.M.L.R. 69 and the explanatory notice has been replaced by a booklet
published by the Commission which can be obtained from the Commission's
London offices: fax 0171 973 1900 (marked "publications"). The *Yves Saint
Laurent* decision was annulled in part in Case T–19/92, *Groupement D'achat
Edouard Leclerc v. Commission* [1997] 4 C.M.L.R. 995.

(e) *Article 86*

Examples of abusive contractual provisions

40–337 [*Note 81: page* [1092]]
The *Tetra Pak II* decision has been upheld by the ECJ: [1997] 4 C.M.L.R. 662.

[*Note 82*]
The decision in *BPB Industries/British Gypsum* was upheld on appeal to the CFI: Case T–65/89, [1993] II E.C.R. 389 and to the ECJ: Case C–310/93P, [1995] I E.C.R. 865.

Refusal to contract as abusive conduct

40–338 For an interesting analysis of developing obligations of undertakings which own "essential facilities" to make those facilities available to competitors see Furse "*The 'Essential Facilities' Doctrine in Community Law*" [1995] 8 E.C.L.R. 469.

[*Note 86*]
The CFI's judgment in *Radio Telefis Eireann* was upheld by the ECJ: see Cases C–241 & 242/91P, [1995] 4 C.M.L.R. 718.

(f) *Enforcement in the national courts*

Severance of void terms

40–340 [*Note 89*]
The decision in *Inntrepreneur v. Mason* has been upheld by the Court of Appeal: *Inntrepreneur Estates (G.L.) Ltd v. Boyes* [1995] E.C.C. 16.

Role of the national courts

40–341 For an important application of this principle see *Iberian UK Ltd v. BPB Industries plc*,[a] where Laddie J. held that it was an abuse of process for a party which had been found by the E.C. Commission to have infringed Article 86 then to dispute that finding when subsequently sued for damages in the national court. There is now a similar Antitrust Enforcement (Co-operation) Notice 1995 concerning co-operation between national courts and the EFTA Surveillance Authority.[b]
For cases in which the grant of a stay of English court proceedings pending the completion of a Commission investigation into the same conduct was considered see *MTV Europe v. BMG Records (UK) Ltd*,[c] and the cases cited therein.
But this duty to cooperate cannot undermine the Commission's duty to

[484]

protect confidential documents: in *Postbank NV v. Commission*,[d] the CFI condemned the Commission for purporting to authorise a third party to disclose in proceedings in the national court confidential documents arising from the Commission's investigation into Postbank's business.

[a] [1997] I.C.R. 164, [1996] 2 C.M.L.R. 601.

[b] [1995] O.J. C112/7, [1995] 5 C.M.L.R. 358.

[c] [1995] 1 C.M.L.R. 437.

[d] [1997] II E.C.R. 921, [1997] 4 C.M.L.R. 44.

[*Add to Note 90*]
See now Case C–39/96 *KVB v. Free Record Shop*, judgment of April 24, 1997, where the ECJ confirmed that provisional validity is not time limited and expires only when the Commission reaches a positive or negative decision on the agreement. The validity extends to any amendments of the agreement, provided they only mitigate the restrictive effect of the agreement.

Breaches of Articles 85 and 86 as a cause of action

A challenge under Article 85 to the validity of exclusivity clauses in the **40–343** recording contract of the pop star George Michael was rejected in *Panayiotou v. Sony Music Entertainment*.[a]

[a] [1994] E.C.C. 395.

[*Note 97*]
The issue of whether there is a Community right to damages for breach of a Treaty *by a Member State* is the subject of rapidly developing jurisprudence: see most recently the third *Factortame* judgment of the ECJ; Cases C–46 & 48/93, [1996] I E.C.R. 1029, and Case C-392/93 *R. v. H.M. Treasury ex p. British Telecom* [1996] I E.C.R. 1631, [1996] 2 C.M.L.R. 217.

(g) *Notification and enforcement at the Community level*

Commission procedure relating to notified agreements

The content of Form A/B was in fact set out in the Annex to Regulation 27 **40–349** not Regulation 17 as stated in the text. Regulation 27 has now been replaced by the Antitrust Procedure (Applications and Notifications) Regulation No. 3385/94[a] which sets out the procedures for notification including a new Form A/B.

[a] [1995] O.J. L377/28, [1995] 5 C.M.L.R. 507.

Commission investigations and adverse decisions

40–351 [*Note 18: page* [1096]]
For further developments of the procedure for dealing with complaints see Case T–114/92, *BEMIM v. Commission* [1995] II E.C.R. 147; Case T–5/93, *Roger Tremblay v. SELL* [1995] II E.C.R. 185 and Case T–74/92, *Ladbroke Racing (Deutschland) v. Commission* [1995] II E.C.R. 118.

Fines and other remedies

40–353 [*Note 23: page* [1097]]
The Commission will reduce the fine imposed on a company which "blows the whistle" on a cartel of which it is a member: see Commission Notice [1996] O.J. C207/4.

CHAPTER 41

SALE OF GOODS

1. – IN GENERAL

(b) *Definitions*

Definitions

41–005   Section 61(1) of the 1979 Act was amended by s.2 of the Sale of Goods (Amendment) Act 1995 in the following respects—

(1) after the definition of "action" there was inserted: " 'bulk' means a mass or collection of goods of the same kind which—
    (a) is contained in a defined space or area; and
    (b) is such that any goods in the bulk are interchangeable with any other goods therein of the same number or quality;"

(2) at the end of the definition of "delivery" there was added the words "except that in relation to sections 20A and 20B above it includes such appropriation of goods to the contract as results in property in the goods being transferred to the buyer;"

(3) at the end of the definition of goods there was added the words "and includes an undivided share in goods;"

(4) at the end of the definition of "specific goods" there was added "and includes an undivided share, specified as a fraction or percentage, of goods identified and agreed on as aforesaid".

The definition of "quality" was repealed by Sched. 3 of the Sale and Supply of Goods Act 1994.

A computer disk encoded with a program is within the definition of "goods": *St. Alban's City and District Council v. International Computers Ltd.*[a]

[a] [1996] 4 All E.R. 481, C.A. But see *Beta Computers (Europe) Ltd v. Adobe Systems (Europe) Ltd* 1996 S.L.T. 604 (O.H.) and Hedley [1997] C.L.J. 21, 23.

2. – FORMATION OF THE CONTRACT

(d) *Subject-matter*

Specific, ascertained and unascertained goods

But by an amendment effected by s.2 of the Sale of Goods (Amendment) **41–028**
Act 1995, there was added to the definition of "specific goods" in s.61(1) "an
undivided share, specified as a fraction or percentage, of goods identified
and agreed upon as aforesaid".

3. – TERMS OF THE CONTRACT

(a) *Conditions, warranties, misrepresentations and puffs*

Effect of breach of condition

A new s.15A was inserted by s.5 of the Sale and Supply of Goods Act 1994. **41–045**
This provides:

"(1) Where in the case of a contract of sale—
(a) the buyer would, apart from this subsection, have the right to
    reject goods by reason of a breach on the part of the seller of a
    term implied by section 13, 14 or 15 above, but
(b) the breach is so slight that it would be unreasonable for him to
    reject them,
then, if buyer does not deal as consumer, the breach is not to be treated
as a breach of condition but may be treated as a breach of warranty.
(2) This section applies unless a contrary intention appears in, or is to
be implied from, the agreement.
(3) It is for the seller to show that a breach fell within subsection 1(b)
above."

By s.61(5A) the references in the section to dealing as consumer are to be
construed in accordance with Part I of the Unfair Contract Terms Act 1977
(see Main Work, Vol. 1, §14–052), and for the purposes of the 1979 Act, it is
for a seller claiming that the buyer does not deal as consumer to show that he
does not.

Loss of right to reject

Section 2(1) of the Sale and Supply of Goods Act 1994 set out new **41–047**
provisions defining acceptance in s.35 of the 1979 Act.[a] By s.3 of the 1994
Act, s.11(4) of the 1979 Act was made subject to a new s.35(A) which
provides that acceptance of part of the goods does not cause the buyer to lose
his right to reject the rest. But see section 35(7),[b] where the contract is for the
sale of goods making one or more commercial units.

[489]

^a See §§41–215 to 41–219, *post.*

^b §41–218, *post.*

(b) *Implied Conditions and Warranties*

[Add at end of paragraph: page [1125]]
41–051   By section 55(2) of the Act, an express term does not negate a term implied by the Act unless inconsistent with it.^a

^a See *Central Regional Council v. Uponor* 1996 S.L.T. 645 (O.H.) (express term that pipes should conform to a British standard did not necessarily negative the terms as to quality and fitness implied by ss.14(2)(3) of the 1979 Act).

(i) *Implied Undertakings as to Title*

Implied undertakings as to title

41–052   Section 12 was amended by Schedule 2, para. 5, to the Sale of Goods (Amendment) Act 1994.

41–054   *[Add to note 41 at end: page* [1126]]
And where a seller of goods who has no title to the goods sells them in circumstances in which the buyer acquires a good title to the goods under Part III of the Hire-Purchase Act 1964, he is nevertheless liable to the buyer for breach of an express undertaking in the contract of sale that he is the owner of the goods: *Barber v. NWS Bank plc.* [1996] 1 W.L.R. 641, C.A.

(ii) *Implied Condition as to Description*

Sale by description

41–062   Section 13 was amended by Sched. 2, para. 5, of the Sale of Goods (Amendment) Act 1994.

Correspondence with description

41–066   *[Add to note 2: page* [1133]]
Total International Ltd v. Addax B.V. [1996] 2 Lloyd's Rep. 333 ("usual Dakar refinery quality" not part of description).

(iii) *Implied Conditions as to Quality or Fitness for Purpose*

Implied condition as to merchantable quality

41–070   By section 1 of the Sale and Supply of Goods Act 1994, for section 14(2) there was substituted—

"(2) Where the seller sells goods in the course of a business, there is an implied term that the goods supplied under the contract are of satisfactory quality.

(2A) For the purposes of this Act, goods are of satisfactory quality if they meet the standard that a reasonable person would regard as satisfactory, taking account of any description of the goods, the price (if relevant) and all the other relevant circumstances.

(2B) For the purposes of this Act, the quality of goods includes their state and condition and the following (among others) are in appropriate cases aspects of the quality of the goods—

  (a) fitness for all the purposes for which goods of the kind in question are commonly supplied,

  (b) appearance and finish,

  (c) freedom from minor defects,

  (d) safety, and

  (e) durability.

(2C) The term implied by subsection (2) above does not extend to any matter making the quality of goods unsatisfactory—

  (a) which is specifically drawn to the buyer's attention before the contract is made,

  (b) where the buyer examines the goods before the contract is made, which that examination ought to reveal, or

  (c) in the case of a contract for sale by sample, which would have been apparent on a reasonable examination of the sample".

Sale through an agent

Section 14(5) applies to any sale by an agent whether the principal is **41–072** disclosed or undisclosed. Thus where a sale was effected by an agent in the course of a business when acting on behalf of an undisclosed principal who did not sell in the course of a business, and no steps were taken to bring this latter fact to the notice of the buyer, the principal was liable to the buyer for breach of the conditions implied by s.14 of the Act: *Boyter v. Thomson*.[a]

  [a] [1995] 2 A.C. 628 (noted (1996) 112 L.Q.R. 225).

Time for compliance

In *Burnley Engineering Products Ltd v. Cambridge Vacuum Engineering* **41–076** *Ltd*,[a] it was held, in respect of a contract for the sale of a welding machine, that the relevant time was at the end of a reasonable time for the bedding down and commissioning of the machine.

  [a] (1996) 50 Const. L.R. 10

Reliance may be rebutted

41–080   See *Central Regional Council v. Uponor*[a] (burden of rebutting reliance on seller).

   [a] 1996 S.L.T. 645 (O.H.)

[*Add to note 58: page* [1140]]
Cf. Central Regional Council v. Uponor, supra.

Reasonably fit for purpose

41–081   In *Slater v. Finning Ltd*[a] the defenders agreed to supply and fit a replacement camshaft in the engine of a particular fishing vessel owned by the pursuers. The replacement was not a success, nor were subsequent replacements any more successful. This was found to be due to the fact that the engine of the vessel suffered from a particular abnormality or idiosyncrasy, namely, a tendency to create excessive torsional resonance in camshafts, a fact of which the defenders were not made aware. The House of Lords held that, in the circumstances, the condition set out in section 14(3) of the 1979 Act had not been breached. Lord Keith said;[b] "As a matter of principle ... where a buyer purchases goods from a seller who deals in goods of that description there is no breach of the implied condition of fitness where the failure of the goods to meet the intended purpose arises from an abnormal feature or idiosyncrasy, not made known to the seller by the buyer, in the buyer or in the circumstances of the use of the goods by the buyer. That is the case whether or not the buyer is himself aware of the abnormal feature or idiosyncrasy."

   [a] [1997] A.C. 473.

   [b] At p. 483.

(iv) *Sale by Sample*

Sale by sample

41–085   Section 15 was amended by s.1(2) and Sched. 2, para. 5, of the Sale of Goods (Amendment) Act 1994. Section 15(2)(b) was repealed by Sched. 3 of the 1994 Act. See also s.14(2C)(c), substituted by s.1 of the 1994 Act (*ante*, §41–070).

   By s.34 (as amended by s.2(2) of the 1994 Act) the seller is bound, in the case of a contract for sale by sample, to afford the buyer a reasonable opportunity of comparing the bulk with the sample, and by s.35(2)(b) (as substituted by s.2(1) of the 1994 Act) the buyer is not deemed to have accepted the goods under s.35(1) until he has had a reasonable opportunity of examining them for the purpose of comparing the bulk with the sample.

(v) *Exclusion of Terms Implied by Sections 13, 14 and 15*

Reasonableness

In *St. Alban's City and District Council v. International Computers Ltd*[a] a **41–092** term in a computer software contract made with a local authority limited the liability of the supplier to £100,000. It was held that this limitation was unreasonable, having regard to the fact that the supplier had ample resources to meet any liability and was insured for £50 million worldwide, that very few companies could meet the authority's requirements and all of those companies dealt on similar standard terms, that the supplier was in a strong bargaining position and that no evidence was adduced to show why the limit of £100,000 was justified.

In *AEG (U.K.) Ltd v. Logic Resource Ltd*[b] a term in a contract for the sale of radar equipment provided that all warranties and conditions implied by the Sale of Goods Act 1979 were excluded, save for a warranty that the equipment was free of defects caused by faulty materials or bad workmanship. This was held in the circumstances to be unreasonable.

[a] [1995] F.S.R. 686, affd. [1996] 4 All E.R. 481, C.A.

[b] [1996] C.L.G. 265 (noted [1996] L.M.C.L.Q. 334).

[*Amend note 16: page* [1147]]
Edmund Murray Ltd v. BSP International Foundations Ltd is reported in (1994) 33 Con.L.R. 1, C.A.

E.C. Directive on unfair terms in consumer contracts

Council Directive 93/13 has been implemented, as of July 1, 1995, by the **41–094** Unfair Terms in Consumer Contracts Regulations 1994.[a]
See Harrison, *Good Faith in Sales* (1996), Chap. 19.

[a] S.I. 1994 No. 3159, *ante*, §14–088.

4. – CONSUMER SAFETY

(b) *Consumer Protection Act 1987*

Consumer safety

See also the General Product Safety Regulations 1994.[a] These implement **41–108** Council Directive 92/59 which imposes general safety requirements on products intended for, or likely to be used by, consumers.

[a] S.I. 1994 No. 2328, noted [1995] J.B.L. 268.

5. – Effects of the Contract

(a) *Transfer of Property as Between Buyer and Seller*

Unascertained goods

41–114   By an amendment effected by s.1(1) of the Sale of Goods (Amendment) Act 1995, s.16 of the 1979 Act was made subject to the newly introduced ss.20A and 20B, *post*, §41–126.

By s.2 of the 1995 Act there was added to the definition of "specific goods" in s.61(1) "an undivided share, specified as a fraction or percentage, of goods identified and agreed on [at the time a contract of sale is made]". Such an undivided share is therefore no longer unascertained goods.

[*Note 40: page* [1159]]
But see *Re Stapylton Fletcher Ltd* [1994] 1 W.L.R. 1181, *post*, §41–126.

Specific goods in a deliverable state

41–120   But by an amendment effected by section 2 of the Sale of Goods (Amendment) Act 1995, the definition of "specific goods" in s.61(1) was expanded to include "an undivided share, specified as a fraction or percentage, of goods identified and agreed on as aforesaid".

Sale or return

41–124   [*Add to note 61: page* [1162]]
Atari Corpn. (U.K.) v. The Electronic Boutique Stores (U.K.) Ltd, *The Times*, July 25, 1997, C.A.

Unascertained or future goods

41–125   By section 1(2) of the Sale of Goods (Amendment) Act 1995, there was added at the end of rule 5 the following—

"(3) Where there is a contract for the sale of a specified quantity of unascertained goods in a deliverable state forming part of a bulk which is identified either in the contract or by subsequent agreement between the parties and the bulk is reduced to (or to less than) that quantity, then, if the buyer under that contract is the only buyer to whom goods are then due out of the bulk—
(a) the remaining goods are to be taken as appropriated to that contract at the time when the bulk is so reduced; and
(b) the property in those goods then passes to that buyer.

(4) Paragraph (3) above applies also (with the necessary modifications) where a bulk is reduced to (or to less than) the aggregate of the quantities due to a single buyer under separate contracts relating to that bulk and he is the only buyer to whom goods are then due out of that bulk."

"Bulk" is defined in s.61(1), *ante*, §41–005.

Separation from bulk

Where a seller sold to a number of buyers certain cases and bottles of **41–126** identified wine which were stored separately, or segregated, from the seller's trading stock, property in the wine passed to the buyers as tenants in common even though none of the cases or bottles were separated from the bulk of the wine in the store or appropriated to any individual buyer's contract: *Re Stapylton Fletcher Ltd*.[a] But it is otherwise if the bulk is itself (even in breach of contract) unascertained, in which case no property or interest passes to the buyers either at law or in equity: *Re Goldcorp Exchange Ltd* (property in bullion did not pass to non-allocated claimants).[b]

Subsequent to these cases, however, s.1(3) of the Sale of Goods (Amendment) Act 1995 introduced two new sections 20A and 20B into the 1979 Act to deal with the sale of goods forming part of a bulk. These new sections were introduced to give effect to the recommendation of the Law Commission and Scottish Law Commission in their report *Sale of Goods Forming Part of a Bulk*.[c] They are as follows—

> "*Undivided shares in goods forming part of a bulk*
> 20A.—(1) This section applies to a contract for the sale of a specified quantity of unascertained goods if the following conditions are met—
>   (a) the goods or some of them form part of a bulk which is identified either in the contract or by subsequent agreement between the parties; and
>   (b) the buyer has paid the price for some or all of the goods which are the subject of the contract and form part of the bulk.
> (2) Where this section applies, then (unless the parties agree otherwise), as soon as the conditions specified in paragraphs (a) and (b) of subsection (1) above are met or at such later time as the parties may agree—
>   (a) property in an undivided share in the bulk is transferred to the buyer, and
>   (b) the buyer becomes an owner in common of the bulk.
> (3) Subject to subsection (4) below, for the purposes of this section the undivided share of a buyer in a bulk at any time shall be such share as the quantity of goods paid for and due to the buyer out of the bulk bears to the quantity of goods in the bulk at that time.
> (4) Where the aggregate of the undivided shares of buyers in a bulk

determined under subsection (3) above would at any time exceed the whole of that bulk at that time, the undivided share in the bulk of each buyer shall be reduced proportionately so that the aggregate of the undivided shares is equal to the whole bulk.

(5) Where a buyer has paid the price for only some of the goods due to him out of a bulk, any delivery to the buyer out of the bulk shall, for the purposes of this section, be ascribed in the first place to the goods in respect of which payment has been made.

(6) For the purposes of this section payment of part of the price for any goods shall be treated as payment for a corresponding part of the goods.

Deemed consent by co-owner to dealings in bulk goods

20B.—(1) A person who has become an owner in common of a bulk by virtue of section 20A above shall be deemed to have consented to—

(a) any delivery of goods out of the bulk to any other owner in common of the bulk, being goods which are due to him under the contract;

(b) any dealing with or removal, delivery or disposal of goods in the bulk by any other person who is an owner in common of the bulk in so far as the goods fall within that co-owner's undivided share in the bulk at the time of the dealing, removal, delivery or disposal.

(2) No cause of action shall accrue to anyone against a person by reason of that person having acted in accordance with paragraphs (a) or (b) of subsection (1) above in reliance on any consent deemed to have been given under that subsection.

(3) Nothing in this section or section 20A above shall—

(a) impose an obligation on a buyer of goods out of a bulk to compensate any other buyer of goods out of that bulk for any shortfall in the goods received by that other buyer;

(b) affect any contractual arrangement between buyers of goods out of a bulk for adjustments between themselves; or

(c) affect the rights of any buyer under his contract."

"Bulk" is defined in s.61(1).[d]

[a] [1994] 1 W.L.R. 1181.

[b] [1995] 1 A.C. 74 (P.C.) (noted [1994] C.L.J. 443).

[c] Law Com. No. 215 and Scot. Law Com. No. 145.

[d] *ante*, §41–005. See Burns [1996] 59 M.L.R. 260; Ulph [1996] L.M.C.L.Q. 93.

[*Note 75: page* [1164]]

See s.18, rule 5, paragraphs (3) and (4), inserted by s.1(2) of the Sale of Goods (Amendment) Act 1995, *ante*, §14–125.

[*Add to note 76 at end*]
Re Stapylton Fletcher Ltd [1994] 1 W.L.R. 1181, 1203; *Re Goldcorp Exchange Ltd* [1995] 1 A.C. 74 (P.C.) (noted [1994] C.L.J. 443).

[*Note 77*]
But such an estoppel creates no interest binding upon a third party who holds a fixed charge, or a floating charge which has crystallised, over the goods: *Re London Wine Shippers Ltd* [1986] P.C.C. 121; *Re Stapylton Fletcher Ltd* [1994] 1 W.L.R. 1181, 1203.

Appropriation of goods to be manufactured by seller

[*Add to note 96: page* [1167]]   **41–131**
Cf., *Re Cosslett Contractors Ltd* [1997] Ch. 23 (provision that all plant, goods and material owned by contractor was to be deemed to be the property of the employer held to create a specific charge) (noted [1997] C.L.J. 257).

"Romalpa" clauses: retention of title

See also *Mercer v. Craven Grain Storage Ltd*[a] (proprietary rights in a   **41–135**
floating mass of fungible goods).

[a] [1994] C.L.C. 328 H.L. (noted (1995) 111 L.Q.R. 10).

[*Note 13: page* [1169]]
See also *Stroud Architectural Systems v. John Laing Construction* [1994] B.C.C. 18.

[*Note 15*]
Contrast Cowan, Clark and Goldberg, "Will English Romalpa Clauses becomes Registrable Securities?" [1995] C.L.J. 43.

Products

[*Note 32: page* [1171]]   **41–136**
See also *Highway Foods International* (*In Administrative Receivership*), *The Times*, November 1, 1994; [1995] BCLC 209 (noted [1996] C.L.J. 26 (processed meat)).

[*Add to note 33 after* Modelboard Ltd v. Outer Box Ltd]
Ian Chisholm Textiles v. Griffiths [1994] B.C.C. 96 (cloth cut and worked

on with a view to being made into garments); *Chaigley Farms Ltd v. Crawford, Kaye & Grayshire Ltd* [1996] B.C.C. 957 (noted [1997] C.L.J. 28) (slaughtered cattle).

[*Add to note 39 after* Modelboard Ltd v. OuterBox Ltd]
Ian Chisholm Textiles v. Griffiths [1994] B.C.C. 96; *Chaigley Farms Ltd v. Crawford, Kaye & Grayshire Ltd* [1996] B.C.C. 957.

Claims against sub-purchasers

41–139   A seller of goods may nevertheless claim title to the goods in the hands of a sub-purchaser if the sale and sub-sale are both made subject to retention of title clauses: *Highway Foods International (In Administrative Receivership)*.[a]

[a] *The Times*, November 1, 1994; [1995] BCLC 209 (noted [1996] C.L.J. 26).

Building contracts

41–140   In *Stroud Architectural Systems v. John Laing Construction*[a] the plaintiffs supplied glazing units to a building sub-contractor subject to a retention of title clause. The sub-contractor went into receivership and the plaintiffs brought an action against the employer claiming damages for conversion of the units. It was held that the retention of title clause, on its true construction, created a floating charge over the assets of the sub-contractor. Since the charge had not been registered it was void against the receiver, though not against the employer. However, since it was a floating and not a fixed charge, the plaintiffs could not claim against the employer until the charge had ceased to float.

In *Aircool Installations v. British Telecommunications*[b] air conditioning equipment which was supplied to a building sub-contractor by the plaintiffs subject to a retention of title clause, and which was installed by the sub-contractor in the employer's premises as a fixture, could not be recovered by the plaintiffs from the employer.

[a] [1994] B.C.C. 18.

[b] [1995] C.L.Y. 821 (Cty.Ct.).

Fixtures

41–141   [*At end of paragraph add new note 73a: page* [1175]]

[73a] See *Melluish v. B.M.I. (No. 3) Ltd* [1996] A.C. 454; *Aircool Installations v. British Telecommunications* [1995] C.L.Y. 821 (Cty.Ct.); Bennett and Davis "Fixtures, purchase money security interests and dispositions of interests in land" (1994) 110 L.Q.R. 448.

(b) *When the Risk Passes*

Goods to which risk relates

Section 20A of the 1979 Act, introduced by section 1(3) of the Sale of **41–147**
Goods (Amendment) Act 1995, *ante*, §41–126, now provides that, in certain
circumstances, property in an undivided share in an identified bulk will be
transferred to the buyer. It is arguable that section 20B(3)(c), which provides
that nothing in sections 20A or 20B is to "affect the rights of any buyer under
his contract", requires the transfer of property in an undivided share under
section 20A to be disregarded in relation to the passing of risk. But it is
submitted that the risk will prima facie pass to the buyer together with the
transfer of such property (especially since the definition of "goods" in
section 61(1) of the Act, as amended, now includes an undivided share in
goods).

(c) *Transfer of Title*

(i) *Sale by person not the Owner*

Sales under special powers or court orders

A purchaser acquiring an abandoned vehicle from a local authority selling **41–158**
it under powers conferred by the Road Traffic Regulation Act 1984 and the
Removal and Disposal of Vehicles Regulations 1986 acquires title to the
vehicle even if the vehicle has been stolen before coming into the hands of
the local authority: *Bubruin Ltd v. Romanyszyn*.[a]

[a] [1994] R.T.R. 273.

Market overt

Market overt was abolished with the repeal of section 22(1) of the Sale of **41–159**
Goods Act 1979 by the Sale of Goods (Amendment) Act 1994 as from
January 3, 1995.

The meaning of avoidance

[*Note 79: page* [1186]] **41–163**
In Scotland, rescission must be communicated: *Young v. D.S. Dalgleish &
Son (Hawick)* 1994 S.C.L.R. 696 (Sh.Ct.), following *Macleod v. Kerr* cited in
this footnote.

"Having bought or agreed to buy"

41–172   [*Add to note 20: page* [1190]]
Contrast *Forthright Finance Ltd v. Carlyle Finance Ltd* [1997] 4 C.L. 143,
C.A.

Delivery or transfer

41–176   Where a seller of goods delivers possession of the goods to a buyer under a
contract of sale in which the seller retains title to the goods sold, no title will
be acquired by a bona fide purchaser to whom the buyer has re-sold the
goods subject to a similar retention of title provision: *Highway Foods
International (In Administrative Receivership).*[a]

    [a] *The Times*, November 1, 1994; [1995] BCLC 209 (noted [1996] C.L.J. 26).

6. – PERFORMANCE OF THE CONTRACT

(b) *Rules Governing Delivery*

Delivery

41–185   By section 2 of the Sale of Goods (Amendment) Act 1995 at the end of the
definition of "delivery" there was added the words "except that in relation to
sections 20A and 20B above it includes such appropriation of goods to the
contract as results in property in the goods being transferred to the buyer;".
For ss.20A, 20B, see *ante*, §41–126.

(v) *Defective Delivery*

Defective delivery

41–196   By section 4(2) of the Sale and Supply of Goods Act 1994, after subsection
(2) of the 1979 Act there was inserted—

> "(2A) A buyer who does not deal as consumer may not—
>   (a) where the seller delivers a quantity of goods less than he
>   contracted to sell, reject the goods under subsection (1) above, or
>   (b) where the seller delivers a quantity of goods larger than he
>   contracted to sell, reject the whole under subsection (2) above,
> if the shortfall or, as the case may be, excess is so slight that it would be
> unreasonable for him to do so.
>   (2B) It is for the seller to show that a shortfall or excess fell within
> subsection 2(A) above."

By section 61(5A) the references in the section to dealing as consumer are
to be construed in accordance with Part I of the Unfair Contract Terms Act

1977 (see Main Work, Vol. 1, §14–052), and for the purposes of the 1979 Act, it is for a seller claiming that the buyer does not deal as consumer to show that he does not.

[*Note 34: page* [1202]]
See Apps [1994] L.M.C.L.Q. 525.

Delivery of mixed goods

Section 30(4) was repealed by section 3(3) and Schedule 3 of the Sale and **41–200** Supply of Goods Act 1994. Where the buyer has the right to reject goods by reason of a breach affecting some of them, he may accept some of them, including all goods unaffected by the breach, without losing the right to reject the rest: section 35A(1), *post*, §41–215.

(c) *Acceptance*

Examination of goods

By section 2(2) of the Sale and Supply of Goods Act 1994, in section 34 of **41–213** the 1979 Act the words from the beginning to "(2)" were repealed (*cf.* 41–216, *post.*) At the end of the section there was inserted "and, in the case of a contract for sale by sample, of comparing the bulk with the sample".

Waiver

By section 35(3) of the 1979 Act (inserted by section 2(1) of the Sale and **41–214** Supply of Goods Act 1994) where the buyer deals as consumer, he cannot by agreement waiver or otherwise lose his right to claim that he has not accepted the goods under section 35(1) until he has had a reasonable opportunity to examine them. By section 61(5A) the reference in this subsection to dealing as consumer is to be construed in accordance with Part I of the Unfair Contract Terms Act 1977 (see Main Work, Vol. 1, §14–052), and it is for a seller claiming that the buyer does not deal as consumer to show that he does not.

Acceptance

By section 2(1) of the Sale and Supply of Goods Act 1994, section 35(1) of **41–215** the 1979 Act was replaced by new provisions (section 35(1)–(8)).

Section 35(7) provides that, where the contract is for the sale of goods making one or more commercial units, a buyer accepting any goods included in a unit is deemed to have accepted all the goods making the unit, and in this subsection "commercial unit" means a unit division of which would materially impair the value of the goods or the character of the unit.

Otherwise, by virtue of section 35(A), inserted by section 3 of the 1994 Act, acceptance of part of the goods does not cause the buyer to lose his right to reject the rest.

Intimation of acceptance

41–216   See now section 35(1)(a) of the 1979 Act (as substituted by section 2(1) of the Sale and Supply of Goods Act 1994). Section 35(2) makes it clear that an intimation of acceptance by the buyer is subject to his having had a reasonable opportunity of examining the goods. By section 35(6)(a) the buyer is not deemed to have accepted the goods merely because he asks for, or agrees to, their repair by or under an arrangement with the seller.

See also section 35(3) (*ante*, §41–214) (buyer who deals as consumer cannot lose his right to rely on subsection (2) by agreement waiver or otherwise).

Act inconsistent with ownership of seller

41–217   See now section 35(1)(b) (as substituted by section 2(1) of the Sale and Supply of Goods Act 1994).

41–218   Section 35(2) of the 1979 Act (as substituted by section 2(1) of the Sale and Supply of Goods Act 1994) provides that acceptance by an act inconsistent with the ownership of the seller is subject to the buyer having had a reasonable opportunity of examining the goods. By section 35(6)(b) the buyer is not deemed to have accepted the goods merely because they are delivered to another under a sub-sale or other disposition.

See also section 35(3) (*ante*, §41–214) (buyer who deals as consumer cannot lose his right to rely on subsection (2) by agreement waiver or otherwise).

Reasonable time

41–219   See now section 35(4) (as substituted by section 2(1) of the Sale and Supply of Goods Act 1994). By section 35(5) the questions that are material in determining for the purposes of subsection (4) whether a reasonable time has elapsed include whether the buyer has had a reasonable opportunity of examining the goods.

Acceptance of part

41–221   Under section 35(A) of the 1979 Act, inserted by section 3 of the Sale and Supply of Goods Act 1994, acceptance of part of the goods does not cause the buyer to lose his right to reject the rest. But see section 35(7), *ante*, §41–215.

7. – REMEDIES OF THE SELLER

(a) *Rights of Unpaid Seller against the Goods*

(iii) *Sub-sales and Other Subsequent Transactions*

Sub-sale by buyer

[*Add to note 46: page* [1239]]   **41–253**
See now the Sale of Goods (Amendment) Act 1995 (*ante* §41–125).

(iv) *Resale by the Seller*

Forfeiture of deposits

[*Add to note 57: page* [1248]]   **41–267**
The Unfair Terms in Consumer Contract Regulations 1994 may also
apply: see *ante* §§14–088 *et seq.*

(c) *Action for Damages*

Damages for non-acceptance

[*Add to note 23: page* [1255]]   **41–274**
The Court of Appeal may now be more willing to depart from "prima
facie" rules in the Act: see *Bence's* case, §§41–305 and 41–307, *post.*

An available market

[*Add to note 32: page* [1256]]   **41–275**
The existence or absence of an available market need not be specifically
contemplated by the parties: *Coastal (Bermuda) Petroleum Ltd v. V.T.T.
Vulcan Petroleum S.A. (No. 2) ("The Marine Star")* [1994] 2 Lloyd's Rep.
629.

[*Add to note 46: page* [1257]]
In the case of the sale of 10,000 tonnes of gasoline it was held that there
could be an available market where the seller could have disposed of the
gasoline in smaller cargo loads of 1,000 to 3,000 tonnes over a period of about

two weeks from the buyer's breach: *Petrotrade Inc. v. Stinnes Handel GmbH* [1995] 1 Lloyd's Rep. 142.

(d) *Other Remedies of the Seller*

Declarations

41–284   [*Add to note 49: page* [1266]]
Cf. Deeny v. Gooda Walker Ltd (No. 3) [1995] 4 All E.R. 289 (not a sale of goods case).

8. – Remedies of the Buyer

(a) *Damages for Non-delivery*

The market price

41–291   [*Add to notes 19 and 24: page* [1273]]
Cf. Bence's case: §§41–305 and 41–307, *post.*

Loss of profits under sub-sale

41–295   [*Add to note 48: page* [1276]]
But *cf. Bence's* case: §§41–305 and 41–307, *post.*

41–296   [*Add to note 65 at end: page* [1277]].
But *cf. Bence's* case: §§41–305 and 41–307, *post.*

Loss of profits on resale: no available market

41–297   [*Add to note 72: page* [1278]]
Coastal (Bermuda) Petroleum Ltd v. V.T.T. Vulcan Petroleum S.A. (No. 2) (The "Marine Star") [1994] 2 Lloyd's Rep. 629.

Damages payable by the buyer to the sub-buyer

41–298   [*Add to note 81: page* [1279]]
Cf. Deeny v. Gooda Walker Ltd (No. 3) [1995] 4 All E.R. 289.

(b) *Damages for Delay in Delivery*

Resale prices are irrelevant

41–300   [*Add to note 91: after references to* Slater's *case and* Wertheim's *case: page* [1280]]
But *cf. Bence's* case, §§41–305 and 41–307, *post.*

(c) *Damages for Defective Quality*

(i) *Diminution in Value*

Breach of warranty

[*Add to note 8: page* [1283]]   **41–303**
Cf. also *Connaught Restaurants Ltd v. Indoor Leisure Ltd* [1994] 4 All
E.R. 834 (not a sale of goods case).

Damages for diminution in market value

[*Add to note 20 after* Slater's *case: page* [1284]]   **41–304**
But *cf.* Bence's *case* §§41–305 and 41–307, *post.*

[*Add to text at the end of the paragraph after note* 27]   **41–305**
In *Bence Graphics International Ltd v. Fasson U.K. Ltd*[27a] the Court of
Appeal held that section 53(3) provided only a "prima facie" rule, which
should not be applied if it would give the buyer "more than his true loss".[27b]
Section 53(2) should be "the starting point".[27c]

[27a] [1997] 3 W.L.R. 205 (see §41–307, *post*)

[27b] *ibid.* at p.217.

[27c] *ibid.*

Damages for the cost of adaptations, or of substitute goods

[*Add to note 30: page* [1285]]   **41–306**
But *cf.* Bence's *case, ante* §41–305 and *post* §41–307.

Buyer performing sub-contract despite seller's breach

[*Add to note 34: page* [1286]].   **41–307**
In *Bence's case, supra,* at pp. 218–220, Auld L.J. approved the decision in
Wertheim's case.

Add to the text at the end of paragraph after note 34]
The authority of *Slater v. Hoyle and Smith Ltd* (cited in note 34 to this
paragraph) has been severely undermined by a decision of the Court of

Appeal in *Bence Graphics International Ltd v. Fasson U.K. Ltd*[34a]: the seller knew that the buyer would sell on to others (after manufacturing the goods into another product); the Court of Appeal held that the parties contemplated that the measure of damages for defects in the goods should be the extent of the buyer's liability (if any) to those others resulting from the defect. In *Bence's* case the decision in *Slater's* case was doubted, on the ground that section 53(3) laid down only a prima facie rule, which should not be applied if it would give the buyer "more than his true loss".[34b]

[34a] [1997] 3 W.L.R. 205.

[34b] *ibid.* at p. 217 (see §§41–305, *ante*).

(ii) *Losses other than Diminution in Value*

Compensation paid to a stranger (other than a sub-buyer)

41–318   [*Add to note 94: page* [1293]]
See §§41–320, note 7, *infra*.

Compensation paid by the buyer to a sub-buyer

41–320   [*Add to note 7: page* [1294]]
The standard basis of taxation is now the proper basis for the recovery of the plaintiff's costs incurred in litigation with a third party: *British Racing Drivers' Club Ltd v. Hextall Erskine & Co.* [1996] 3 All E.R. 667 (not a sale of goods case). This basis replaces the previous rule laid down in *Sidney Bennett Ltd v. Kreeger, supra*; *Biggin & Co. Ltd v. Permanite Ltd, supra.*

Compensation paid to sub-buyers in a series of "string contracts"

41–321   [*Add to note 26: page* [1296]]
This principle was followed in *Bence's* case: see §§41–305 and 41–307, *ante*.

(d) *Other Remedies of the Buyer*

Restitution: recovery of money paid to the seller

41–324   [*Add to note 36 after* Rowland v. Divall *page* [1297]]
Barber v. NWS Bank plc [1996] 1 W.L.R. 641.

Specific performance

41–325   The Sale of Goods (Amendment) Act 1995 changes the law on the sale of unascertained goods forming part of an identified bulk: see *supra*, §41–114.

Section 2(d) of the 1995 Act adds to the definition of "specific goods" found in section 61(1) of the 1979 Act by adding the words "and includes an undivided share, specified as a fraction or percentage, of goods identified and agreed on as aforesaid". For the effect of these changes on the availability of specific performance, see *ante*, §27–011.

SURETYSHIP

1. – IN GENERAL

General nature of the contract

42–001 [*Add to note 2: page* [1305]]
Cf. Trafalgar House Construction (Regions) Ltd v. General Surety & Guarantee Co. Ltd [1996] 1 A.C. 199.

Assignment by creditor of benefit of contract guaranteed

42–005 [*Note 19: page* [1307]]
The Landlord and Tenant Act 1995, ss.17–19, restrict the liability of former tenants and their guarantors in various respects, these provisions applying to tenancies made before as well as after this Act: *ibid.* s.1(2) and see *post*, §42–005A.

[*Add to text at end of paragraph: page* [1308]]

However, by section 3(1) of the Landlord and Tenant (Covenants) Act 1995:

the benefit and burden of all landlord and tenant covenants of a tenancy—

(a) shall be annexed and incident to the whole, and to each and every part, of the premises demised by the tenancy and of the reversion in them, and

(b) shall in accordance with this section pass on an assignment of the whole or any part of those premises or of the reversion in them.

Thus, with the qualifications which appear in section 3(3) of the Act, the benefit of a covenant by a surety guaranteeing the tenant's covenants will pass on assignment by the landlord whether or not it "touches and concerns the land". This provision of the 1995 Act applies only to "new tenancies" as defined by s.1 of the same Act, which include notably those arising after January 1, 1996.[23c]

[23c] S.I. 1995 No. 2963, C. 66.

[*And insert as new paragraph at end*]

Guarantees of tenancy covenants on assignment. At common law, a **42–005A** tenant remains liable on assignment of his interest under the lease for the payment of rent and due performance of other tenants' covenants, this being the result of privity of contract remaining between the landlord and original tenant, even though assignment creates privity of estate between the landlord and tenant's assignee: *City of London Corpn. v. Fell.*[23d] Furthermore, any guarantee of a tenant's covenants in principle also remains enforceable by the landlord (and, as we have seen, often by the landlord's assignees[23e]) notwithstanding assignment by the tenant. However, this position has been radically altered by the provisions of the Landlord and Tenant (Covenants) Act 1995. First, the key purposes of this Act were to "break privity of contract" after assignment by the tenant and, on the fulfillment of certain conditions, by the landlord, terminating their contractual obligations *inter se*, but to preserve and extend the effectiveness of tenancy obligations for those within privity of estate.[23f] However, this "breaking of privity" does not rule out the creation of liability in a former tenant for the performance of the tenant's covenants by his assignee as section 16(1) of the 1995 Act provides that "where on an assignment a tenant is to any extent released from a tenant covenant of a tenancy by virtue of this Act ... nothing in this Act ... shall preclude him from entering into an authorised guarantee agreement with respect to the performance of that covenant by the assignee", section 16(8) expressly declaring that "the rules of law relating to guarantees (and in particular those relating to the release of sureties) are, subject to its terms, applicable in relation to any authorised guarantee agreement as in relation to any other guarantee agreement." It is clearly important to note that section 16 applies only to "*new* tenancies" as defined by section 1 of the Act, which include, notably, those made after January 1, 1996[23g] and is carefully restricted by subsections 3 and 4 of section 16, to which further reference should be made.

Secondly, section 17 of the Landlord and Tenant (Covenants) Act 1995, which applies to *all tenancies* whether new or otherwise,[23h] subjects the liability of a former tenant *or his guarantor* for rent, service charge or liquidated damages for breach of covenant to a condition of service by the landlord within six months of the charge becoming due of a notice informing either the tenant, or the guarantor as the case may be, "that the charge is now due; and that in respect of the charge the landlord intends to recover from the former tenant [or guarantor] such amount as is specified in the notice and (where payable) interest calculated on such basis as is so specified".[23i] Where such a notice has been served, the former tenant or guarantor's liability is in principle restricted to the amount specified in it.[23j] Moreover, section 19(1) of the Act provides that where any person makes full payment as he has been duly required to under section 17, then he "shall be entitled ... to have the landlord under that tenancy grant him an overriding lease of the premises demised by the tenancy". The purpose of such a legally imposed lease is to give the claimant some control over the defaulting tenant and in this respect section 19(8)(a) provides that where two or more requests for such an overriding lease are made on the same day, then a request by a former tenant shall be treated as made before a request made by a guarantor.

Thirdly, section 18(1) & (2) provide that a former tenant "shall not be liable ... to pay any amount in respect of the covenant to the extent that the amount is referable to any relevant variation of the tenant covenants of the tenancy effected after the assignment", "relevant variation" being defined by s.18(4). Similarly, section 18(3) provides that a *guarantor* of a former tenant's covenants "(where his liability ... is not wholly discharged by any such variation of the tenant covenants of the tenancy) shall not be liable under the agreement to pay any amount in respect of the covenant to the extent that the amount is referable to any such variation". It is to be noted that section 18 applies to *all tenancies* whether new or otherwise,[23k] but *only to new variations* of tenant covenants (*i.e.* those effected on or after January 1, 1996).[23l]

[23d] [1994] 1 A.C. 458, 465.

[23e] Main Work, §42–005.

[23f] See especially, *ibid.* ss.3–8. For analysis of these and other provisions of the Landlord and Tenant (Covenants) Act 1995, see Bridge (1996) 55 C.L.J. 313.

[23g] 1995 Act, s.1(1), S.I. 1995 No. 2963, C. 66.

[23h] s.1(2).

[23i] See s.17(2), (3).

[23j] s.17(4).

[23k] s.1(2).

[23l] s.18(6), S.I. 1995 No. 2963, C. 66.

Guarantees and indemnities distinguished

[*In second paragraph, add new reference to text at end of first sentence: page* [1309]]   **42–007**

NOTE 29a: However, the mere fact that a guarantor's liability arises upon default of the principal debtor does not mean that damage caused by a third party's negligent advice to enter the contract of guarantee arises only on that default. The issue of when such damage arises is a question of fact: *Tabarrok v. E.D.C. Lord & Co. (a Firm) The Times*, February 4, 1997.

[*Add to note 30*]
See also, by way of example, the decision of the Court of Appeal in *Clement v. Clement* (1996) 3 C.L. 64.

Performance guarantees

[*Add to note 34: page* [1310]]   **42–008**
Attaleia Marine Co. Ltd v. Bimeh Iran (Iran Insurance Co.) ("The Zeus") [1993] 2 Lloyd's Rep. 497. *Cf. Trafalgar House Construction (Regions) Ltd v. General Surety & Guarantee Co. Ltd* [1996] 1 A.C. 199.

[*Amend note 39*]
United Trading Corp. SA v. Allied Bank Ltd (Note) is reported at [1985] 2 Lloyd's Rep. 554. Add: *Cf. Themehelp Ltd v. West* [1995] 3 W.L.R. 751 which concerned a claim by the principal debtor for an injunction to restrain the beneficiary of the bond from serving notice under the guarantee.

[*Add new reference to "guarantee is granted", line 26*]
NOTE 39a: *cf. Wahda Bank v. Arab Bank plc, The Times*, February 26, 1996 in which the Court of Appeal held that such a counter-guarantee was intimately connected with such a performance bond with the result that, in the absence of any express choice, it felt entitled to find that the parties intended the counter-guarantee to be governed by the same law as governed the guarantees.

[*Add to text after note 40: page* [1311]]
Such a counter-indemnity by a customer in favour of a guaranteeing bank takes effect according to its terms. For example, where the customer agrees to indemnify the bank in respect of claims made "under or *in connection with* the issue of the guarantee" and the guarantee obligations are expressed not to be "in any way discharged or diminished" by the guarantee's total or partial invalidity, then the bank may claim on the indemnity in respect of payments made by it under or in connection with the guarantee even if the latter was at no time legally valid: *Gulf Bank K.S.C. v. Mitsubishi Heavy Industries (No. 2).*[40a]

[40a] [1994] 2 Lloyd's Rep. 145. And see further (on a different point of construction) *Mitsubishi Heavy Industries Ltd v. Gulf Bank K.S.C.* [1997] 1 Lloyd's Rep. 343, C.A.

[*Add new paragraph to text after note 41: page* [1311]].

Finally, it has been held in *Cargill International SA v. Bangladesh Sugar and Food Industries Corpn*[41a] that any money paid under a performance bond to a party who has suffered no damage in consequence of the other's breach of contract may recover that money from that other party. According to Morrison J.,

> it seems to me implicit in the nature of a bond, and in the approach of the court to injunction applications, that, in the absence of some clear words to a different effect, when the bond is called, there will, at some stage in the future, be an 'accounting' between the parties in the sense that their rights and obligations will be finally determined at some future date.[41b]

He later added that "under no circumstances is the performance bond to provide to the buyer a windfall payment".[41c] Morrison J's approach was adopted by Potter L.J. in *Comdel Commodities Ltd v. Siporex Trade S.A.*[41d]

[41a] [1996] 4 All E.R. 563.

[41b] *ibid.* at p. 558.

[41c] *ibid.* at p. 573.

[41d] [1997] 1 Lloyd's Rep. 424, 431.

[*Add new paragraph: page* [1311]]

41–008A **"Charge-back transactions".** In *Tam Wing Chuen & Anor v. Bank of Credit & Commerce Hong Kong Ltd*[41e] the Privy Council considered the legal effect of a deposit of funds by A to B to be used to secure a loan by B to C, a transaction known as a "charge-back". It held that the question whether A (the depositor) should be considered *personally liable* to B in respect of the loan (and therefore a guarantor) is a question of construction of the contract under which he made the deposit. In this respect, Lord Mustill observed that the mere "[c]onsistency with [such a personal] liability [in the depositor] which could have been expressed is no ground for imposing a liability which was not expressed.[41f]

[41e] [1996] B.C.C. 388.

[41f] *ibid.* at p. 393.

2. – FORMATION OF THE CONTRACT

(c) *Grounds of vitiation of the contract*

Mistake and non est factum

42–015 [*Add to note 83: page* [1316]]
Cf. *Barclays Bank plc v. Schwartz, The Times*, August 2, 1995.

Fraud, misrepresentation or undue influence by a third party

For discussion of the many cases which have interpreted and applied the **42–017—** decisions of the House of Lords in *Barclays Bank plc v. O'Brien* [1994] 1 **42–018** A.C. 180 and *C.I.B.C. Mortgages plc v. Pitt* [1994] 1 A.C. 200, see *ante*, §6–016.

Non-disclosure

[*Add to text after note 33: page* [1323]] **42–020**
A somewhat different approach has been taken at first instance by the courts in *Levett v. Barclays Bank plc*[33a] and *Crédit Lyonnaise Bank Nederland v. Export Credit Guarantee Department.*[33b] In *Levett*[33c] Michael Burton, Q.C. considered that "the cases appear to establish that the nature of the duty to disclose differs depending upon the kind of guarantee in question, whether it be a guarantee of a cash obligation, a fidelity guarantee or a guarantee of performance of a particular transaction". He stated that "the principle appears to be that there is imposed upon the creditor a duty to disclose what in general terms may be described as unusual features, unknown to the surety", relying on a passage from Phillips and O'Donovan's *The Modern Law of Guarantee*, pp. 110–112 which quotes dicta of Gibbs C.J. in *Commercial Bank of Australia Ltd v. Amadio*[33d] and on dicta in *Hamilton v. Watson.*[33e] On the facts of *Levett*, the nature of the transaction entered with the debtor did possess such unusual features as demanded disclosure (namely, use of the proceeds of Treasury stock given as security to satisfy the debt on its maturity date rather than being returned to the guarantors unencumbered before such date).
On the other hand, while in the somewhat later case of *Crédit Lyonnaise Bank Nederland v. Export Credit Guarantee Department*, Longmore J. also accepted the existence of a duty of disclosure, he limited it to cases of unusual features in the *transaction* and held that it did not extend to unusual features of the risk. The learned judge considered that in a case such as this of a guarantee of a bank's customer's debts by the Export Credit Guarantee Department, the concept of "implied representation" found in *London General Omnibus Co. v. Holloway*[33f] (which is discussed *ante*) could not apply as easily as to a guarantee of a servant's fidelity and he preferred instead the approach found in a dictum of Gibbs C.J. in *Commercial Bank of Australia Ltd v. Amadio*[33g]:

> It would be commercially unreal to suggest that a bank has a duty to reveal to a surety all the facts within its knowledge which relate to the transactions and financial position of a customer in any case where those transactions are out of the ordinary. The obligation is to reveal anything in the transaction between the banker and the customer which

has the effect that the position of the customer is different from that which the surety would naturally expect, particularly if it affects the nature or degree of the surety's responsibility.

On the facts of the case before him, Longmore J. concluded that all but one of the non-disclosures complained of did not relate to the *transaction* and in the case of the one which could be said to do so the bank did not know of the matter but merely suspected it.[33h]

Such an overt duty of disclosure, even if restricted to cases of unexpected aspects of the *transaction* rather than other facts material to the guarantor's risk, goes beyond the position at least as recently recognised by English courts. Moreover, it should be noted that *Commercial Bank of Australia Ltd v. Amadio* concerned a significantly different situation from the *Crédit Lyonnaise* case and that while Gibbs C.J.'s decision agreed with the majority of the High Court of Australia, his grounds for coming to it differed from the majority's. *Amadio* was a case where the bank was aware of the fact that the prospective guarantors (who had limited knowledge of written English and were the parents of the director of the principal debtor company) had been mis-informed as to the extent of the liability which was to be undertaken by the guarantee in respect of its temporal limits (though the true position was then explained) and therefore could be seen as a classic case for the application of the doctrine of constructive notice recently approved by the House of Lords in *Barclays Bank plc v. O'Brien*.[33i] Moreover, while the bank in *Amadio* had *conceded* that it had a duty to disclose matters between it and the customer which a prospective guarantor might not expect to have taken place in relation to the customer's affairs, Gibbs C.J. explained that "the reason why a creditor is bound to reveal to an intending surety anything in the transaction between himself and the debtor which the surety would expect not to exist is that a failure to make disclosure in those circumstances would amount to an implied representation that the thing does not exist"[33j] and he ultimately founded his decision on the existence of such an implied misrepresentation.[33k] Finally, it is to be noted that the majority of the High Court preferred to hold the contract of guarantee unenforceable on the ground of "unconscionable conduct" in the bank rather than non-disclosure or misrepresentation.

Notwithstanding these possible distinguishing features of *Amadio*, it is submitted, with respect, that the approach of the courts in *Levett v. Barclays Bank plc.* and *Crédit Lyonnaise Bank Nederland v. Export Credit Guarantee Department* is to be welcomed. It is certainly consonant with the *general effect* of the application of the doctrine of constructive notice in *Barclays Bank plc v. O'Brien, ante*; but it is to be noted that it goes further in one respect, in that it applies even in relation to a commercial or otherwise well-informed prospective guarantor (as in the case of the Export Credit Guarantee Department). Certainly, if such a limited duty of disclosure of the

[514]

nature of the transaction between the creditor and the principal debtor is to be imposed on creditors, it is welcome that it should be done candidly and without resort to the unhelpful and easily fictitious notion of implied misrepresentation.

33a [1995] 1 W.L.R. 1260.

33b [1996] 1 Lloyd's Rep. 200.

33c *ante* at p. 1273.

33d (1983) 151 C.L.R. 447, 457.

33e (1845) XII Cl. & Fin. 108, 118–119.

33f [1912] 2 K.B. 72.

33g [1996] 1 Lloyd's Rep. 200, 227, citing (1983) 151 C.L.R. 447, 457.

33h [1996] 1 Lloyd's Rep. 200, 227.

33h [1994] 1 A.C. 180.

33j (1983) 151 C.L.R. 447, 455, citing *London General Omnibus Co. Ltd*, *ante*.

33k *ibid.* at p. 458.

Liability in damages for misrepresentation and non-disclosure

[*Text at notes 37 & 38*]   42–021
For discussion of the recent interpretation of *Hedley Byrne & Co. Ltd v. Heller & Partners Ltd* [1964] A.C. 465 by the House of Lords in *Henderson v. Merrett Syndicates Ltd* [1995] 2 A.C. 145 and *White v. Jones* [1995] 2 A.C. 207, see *ante*, §§1–048—1–071.

(d) *Effect on Surety of Vitiation of the Transaction Guaranteed*

Other invalidating cause

[*Add to note 51: page* [1324]]   42–023
Gulf Bank K.S.C. v. Mitsubishi Heavy Industries (No. 2) [1994] 2 Lloyd's Rep. 145.

3. – FORMALITIES

"Debt, default or miscarriage"

[*Add to text after note 53: page* [1324]]   42–025
It has been said that "since a contract of guarantee is a contract to answer for the debt, default or miscarriage of another who is primarily liable to the creditor, it follows that if, or at any rate in so far as, a contract covers loss to the creditor which does not involve a liability of the other to him, that contract cannot be a contract of guarantee".53a Thus, a contract under which

a person stands "surety" for a building contractor's due *performance* of a contract and which is subject to a condition of automatic termination on that contractor's voluntary liquidation is not a contract of guarantee since it imposes responsibility on the "surety" on the mere *non-performance* of the contractor's obligations and not only on their breach, there being no breach on operation of the condition.[53b]

[53a] *Northwood Development Co. Ltd v. Aegon Insurance Co. (U.K.) Ltd* [1994] 10 Const.L.J. 157, 163, *per* H.H. Judge Harvey, Q.C.

[53b] *ibid.*

[*Add at end of paragraph*]
However, any subsequent agreement between the guarantor and the lender which creates a *new contract* must comply with these formal requirements.[54a]

[54a] *Samuels Finance Group plc v. Beechmanor Ltd* (1994) 67 P. & C.R. 282, 284–285.

Requirements of the section

42–028 [*Add to note 76: page* [1327]]
State Bank of India v. Kaur, The Times, April 22, 1995 and *M.P. Services Ltd v. Lawyer* (1996) 72 P. & C.R. D49.

4. – CONSTRUCTION OF THE CONTRACT

General

42–032 [*Add to note 94: page* [1330]]
West Horndon Industrial Park Ltd v. Phoenix Timber Group plc [1995] 1 EGLR 77.

[*Add to text after note 95*]
However, the strict approach applies also to attempts to exclude rules of common law or equity incidental to the contract of suretyship. As Lord Jauncey of Tullichettle recently observed, "there is no doubt that in a modern contract of guarantee parties may, if so minded, exclude any one or more of the normal incidents of suretyship. However if they choose to do so clear and unambiguous language must be used."[95a]

[95a] *Trafalgar House Construction (Regions) Ltd v. General Surety & Guarantee Co. Ltd* [1996] 1 A.C. 199, 208.

[*Add to text at end of paragraph*]
Finally, where a contract of guarantee of a tenant's covenants provided both for the release of the guarantors on notice by the tenants and for the provision by them of substitute guarantors, it was held that the release did

not take effect *ipso facto* by notice, but was conditional on the provision of substitutes: *Grovewood (L.E.) v. Lundy Properties.*[99a] Quite apart from arguments from the surrounding terms of the contracts, according to Parker J. "it does not seem . . . to accord with business common sense . . . that a lease which on the one hand requires the presence of sureties for the tenants' obligations . . . should at the same time allow, as a matter of drafting, for a situation where the lease may continue on foot without any sureties at all".[99b]

[99a] (1995) 69 P. & C.R. 507.

[99b] *ibid.* at p. 515.

Co-extensiveness principle

[*Add to note 1*]   **42–033**
For an example of the use of the co-extensiveness principle in the interpretation of a guarantor's liability to pay interest, see *M.P. Services Ltd v. Lawyer* (1996) 72 P. & .C.R. D49. In this case, Millett L.J. considered that the surety before him had not agreed to pay interest as a primary liability, but rather that his liability to do was only secondary. In his opinion, "[t]hat can only . . . mean that he guaranteed to pay interest on the loan at the contractual rate payable by the principal debtor" (*ibid.* at p. D50).

Estoppel by convention

[*Insert new section 4A and paragraphs*]   **42–041**

4A. – Discharge of Debtor

General. No special rules apply to the discharge of a debtor whose debt is   **42–041A**
guaranteed where this results either from payment of the debt or release by deed. As to the effect of part payment of the debt by the debtor or an agreement to accept part payment of a debt, reference should be made to the relevant passages of Volume I of the Main Work.[40a]

Discharge of debtor by payment by surety. In *Milverton Group Ltd v.*   **42–041B**
Warner World Ltd,[40b] the Court of Appeal held that part payment of a debt by a surety would discharge the principal debtor by the amount of the payment. That case concerned the liabilities of an original tenant under a lease whose assignees' sureties had paid monies to the landlord's assignee in consideration of their release by deed. The landlord's assignee argued that these payments did not affect the original tenant's liability to pay rent under the lease: but the Court of Appeal rejected this argument. According to Hoffmann L.J., "for the purpose of deciding whether money owed by more than one person has been paid, I do not think that it is possible for the creditor and one of the debtors to characterise a payment in return for a release as anything other than a part performance of the obligation. If this

[517]

were possible, a creditor could pick off his debtors one by one and recover in total more than the whole debt. For the payment to count as part discharge of the common obligation, it is sufficient for the payment to be referable to the guarantee".[40c] (For changes in the law regarding the liability of former tenants and their guarantors, see *ante*, §42–005A).

[40a] See §§3–085 *et seq.*

[40b] [1995] 2 EGLR 28.

[40c] *ibid.* at p. 31.

5. – DISCHARGE OF SURETY

(a) *Discharge of Surety by Payment or Set-off*

General

42–042   [*Insert new reference to "pro tanto", line 3: page* [1335]]

NOTE 40a: As to the discharge of the debtor, see *ante*, new section 4A.

(b) *Discharge of Surety through Discharge of Principal Debtor*

Discharge of debtor by bankruptcy

42–047   [*Add to text after note 74: page* [1339]]
The view expressed in the text as to the effect on a surety's liability of "voluntary arrangements" as to the principal's debtor's liability made under Part 8 of the Insolvency Act 1986 was disapproved by Jacobs J. in *R.A. Securities Ltd v. Mercantile Credit Co. Ltd* [1995] 3 All E.R. 581, confirmed in *Johnson v. Davies* [1997] 1 All E.R. 921.

[*Delete text from note 74 to end of paragraph ending with note 80 and substitute:*]
Although earlier authority on the effect of "composition arrangements" made under the Bankruptcy Act 1869 on a surety's liability conflicted,[75] it has recently been held that "voluntary arrangements" made under Part 8 of the Insolvency Act 1986, which include both compositions in satisfaction of a debtor's debts and schemes of arrangements made under the 1986 Act, do not discharge the surety.[76] "Voluntary arrangements" made under the 1986 Act are not "voluntary acts" of a creditor so as to attract the operation of the rule that a debtor's discharge by agreement with the creditor discharges the surety.[77-80]

[75] *cf. Megrath v. Gray, Gray v. Megrath* (1874) L.R. 9 C.P. 216, *ex parte Jacobs* (1875) L.R. 10 Ch. App. 211 and *Ellis v. Wilmot* (1874) 10 Ex. 10, esp. at 14.

[76] *R.A. Securities Ltd v. Mercantile Credit Co. Ltd* [1995] 3 All E.R. 581, confirmed in *Johnson v. Davies* [1997] 1 All E.R. 921, preferring the approach of the court in *ex parte Jacobs* (1875) L.R. 10 Ch. App. 211.

[77-80] See ante, §42–044.

Discharge of debtor through creditor's breach of contract

[*Add to note 87 after first case: page* [1340]]   **42–048**
cf. *Trafalgar House Construction (Regions) Ltd v. General Surety & Guarantee Co. Ltd* [1996] 1 A.C. 199.

[*Insert new reference at end of paragraph*]

NOTE 90a: *Trafalgar House Construction (Regions) Ltd v. General Surety & Guarantee Co. Ltd, supra.*

Discharge of debtor by operation of law

[*Delete from text second sentence and the first word of the third sentence,*   **42–051**
with notes 2–4: page [1342]]
(The Court of Appeal's decision in *Stacey v. Hill* [1901] 1 K.B. 426 as to the effect of disclaimer by a tenant debtor's trustee in bankruptcy was overruled in *Hindcastle Ltd v. Barbara Attenborough Associates Ltd* [1996] 1 All E.R. 737.)

[*Add to text after note 6*]
On the other hand, the House of Lords has recently held that a disclaimer of a lease by a corporate tenant debtor's liquidator does not discharge the liability of a guarantor of the tenant's liabilities: *Hindcastle Ltd v. Barbara Attenborough Associates Ltd, ante,* applying the decision of the House in *Hill v. East and West India Dock Co.*[6a] and overruling the decision of the Court of Appeal in *Stacey v. Hill, ante.* The reason for this failure to discharge the tenant's guarantors is to be found in section 178(4) of the Insolvency Act 1986, which provides that such a disclaimer "does not, except so far as is necessary for the purpose of releasing the company from any liability, affect the rights or liabilities of any other person".

[6a] (1884) 9 App.Cas. 448.

(c) *Discharge of Surety through Variation of Contract between Debtor and Creditor*

Variation of the contract between creditor and debtor

[*Add to note 9*]   **42–052**
West Horndon Industrial Park Ltd v. Phoenix Timber Group plc [1995] 1 EGLR 77; *Howard de Walden Estates Ltd v. Pasta Place Ltd* [1995] 1 EGLR

79. For the effect of the Landlord and Tenant (Covenants) Act 1995, section 18 on the effectiveness of some variations of a tenant's covenants on guarantees by either a former tenant or his guarantor, see *ante*, new §42–005A.

[*Add to note 12*]
Howard de Walden Estates Ltd v. Pasta Place Ltd; supra. And see *De Montfort Insurance Co. plc v. Lafferty* (1997) G.W.D. 4–140, [1997] 4 C.L. 818 (Outer House of Court of Session), where a novation of the contract between A and B which did not change the liability of B, alter the scope of its obligations nor amend the provision for determining its remuneration did not discharge C, who had guaranteed due performance of B's obligations under the contract.

Agreement to allow variation or giving of time

42–057   [*Add to text after note 39: page* [1346]]
   In *West Horndon Industrial Park Ltd v. Phoenix Timber Group plc*,[39a] it was accepted that the court should construe any clause allegedly permitting variation according to ordinary canons of construction, but in cases of doubt or uncertainty in favour of the surety. In that case, the court had held that a contract of guarantee of a tenant's covenants in general was restricted to the tenant's obligations under the original lease and did not extend to additional burdens such as could be imposed under a subsequent license to assign. This being the case, the court held that a provision by which the guarantor's obligations were expressed to exist "notwithstanding ... any other act or thing whereby but for this provision the Guarantor would have been released" did not cover a variation in the lease on assignment which could be prejudicial to both tenant and guarantor: such a "complete *carte blanche* to entitle the landlord to extract every and any additional burden from the surety" had to be provided for expressly or by clearer implication.[39b] The court instead found other situations which could and were intended to be covered by the clause in question, but which did not include prejudicial variations of the type before it. On the other hand, where a clause provided that "any other variation of the provisions of this charge or other dealing between the Borrower and Lender shall not affect the liability of the Surety" Lloyd L.J. rejected the guarantor's argument that it should bear a restricted meaning as clauses are often drafted in such a way as to refer specifically to various grounds on which sureties may be released, as he "would not wish to encourage unnecessary verbosity, providing the meaning is clear": *Samuels Finance Group plc v. Beechmanor Ltd*.[39c]

[39a] [1995] 1 EGLR 77.

[39b] *ibid.* at p. 79, *per* Mr Roger Kaye, Q.C.

[39c] (1994) 67 P. & C.R. 282, 285.

[*Add to note 41*]

The E.C. Directive on Unfair Terms in Consumer Contracts 1993 was implemented in English law by the Unfair Terms in Consumer Contracts Regulations 1994 (S.I. 1994 No. 3159), *ante*, §14–088.

(d) *Discharge of Surety on Other Grounds*

Altering the terms of guarantee

[*Add to note 47: page* [1347]]   **42–059**
cf. Goss v. Chilcott, The Times, June 6, 1996, P.C. (discharge of mortgagor on ground of alteration of mortgage deed).

[*Add to text after note 48*]

Furthermore, it has been held that where a guarantee document consists otherwise of print, type and ink writing, the most natural inference to draw of an amendment to that document *in pencil* is that it is not, and is not intended to be, an operative and final alteration with the result that it does not count as an alteration of the document so as to discharge the guarantor.[48a] This decision was explained on the basis that the rule as to alteration of a guarantee leading to discharge rests on a policy of deterrence or punishment of attempted fraud, a policy which cannot apply where, as with a pencilled alteration to a document of this kind, there is no chance of committing a fraud.[48b]

[48a] *Co-operative Bank v. Tipper* [1996] 4 All E.R. 366, 372, *per* Roger Cooke, J.

[48b] *ibid.*

Release of co-surety

[*Add to text after note 57: page* [1348]]   **42–061**
It has been held that an appropriately drafted clause in a contract of guarantee may oust the normal rule by which the release of one jointly and severally liable surety discharges the others, even as to the release of guarantors after judgment.[57a]

[57a] *Bank of Montreal v. Dobbin and Dobbin* [1996] 5 Bank. L.R. 190 (Court of Queen's Bench of New Brunswick).

Other conduct of creditor prejudicial to surety

[*Add to note 88: page* [1351]]   **42–064**
Socomex Ltd v. Banque Bruxelles Lambert S.A. [1996] 1 Lloyd's Rep. 156, 197–199.

7. – Legislative Protection of Sureties

Introduction

42–075 [*Note 77: page* [1360]]
The E.C. Directive on Unfair Terms in Consumer Contracts 1993 was implemented in English law by the Unfair Terms in Consumer Contracts Regulations 1994 (S.I. 1994 No. 3159); *ante*, §14–088.

(b) *E.C. Directive on Unfair Terms in Consumer Contracts*

[*Note 99: page* [1362]]
The E.C. Directive on Unfair Terms in Consumer Contracts 1993 (the "1993 Directive") was implemented in English law by the Unfair Terms in Consumer Contracts Regulations 1994 (S.I. 1994 No. 3159) (the "1994 Regulations"). Subsequent references in this supplement will indicate where appropriate the corresponding provisions of the 1994 Regulations to the 1993 Directive.

The ambit of the Directive

[*Note 5*]
And see 1994 Regulations, s.2(1) "seller", "supplier".

[*Note 9*]
And see 1994 Regulations, s.3(1).

[*Note 11*]
And see 1994 Regulations, see s.3(2), 4 and Schedule 2.

[*Note 12: page* [1363]]
And see 1994 Regulations s.4(4). The Annex to the 1993 Directive is found in Schedule 3 of the 1994 Regulations.

[*Note 13*]
And see 1994 Regulations, s.5.

Application of the Directive to contracts of suretyship

42–078 Arts. 1(1) and 2 of the 1993 Directive, discussed in the text, find their corresponding provisions in the 1994 Regulations ss.3(1) and 2(1) "seller", "supplier" and "consumer" respectively.

[522]

Vulnerable types of clause

[*Note 22: page* [1364]]
And see 1994 Regulations s.4(1).

[*Note 28: page* [1365]]
And see 1994 Regulations s.4(1).

[*Note 29*]
And see 1994 Regulations s.4(4). The Annex to the 1993 Directive
appears as Schedule 3 of the 1994 Regulations.

[*Note 37*]
And see 1994 Regulations s.4(1).